BERMUDA

ROSEMARY JONES

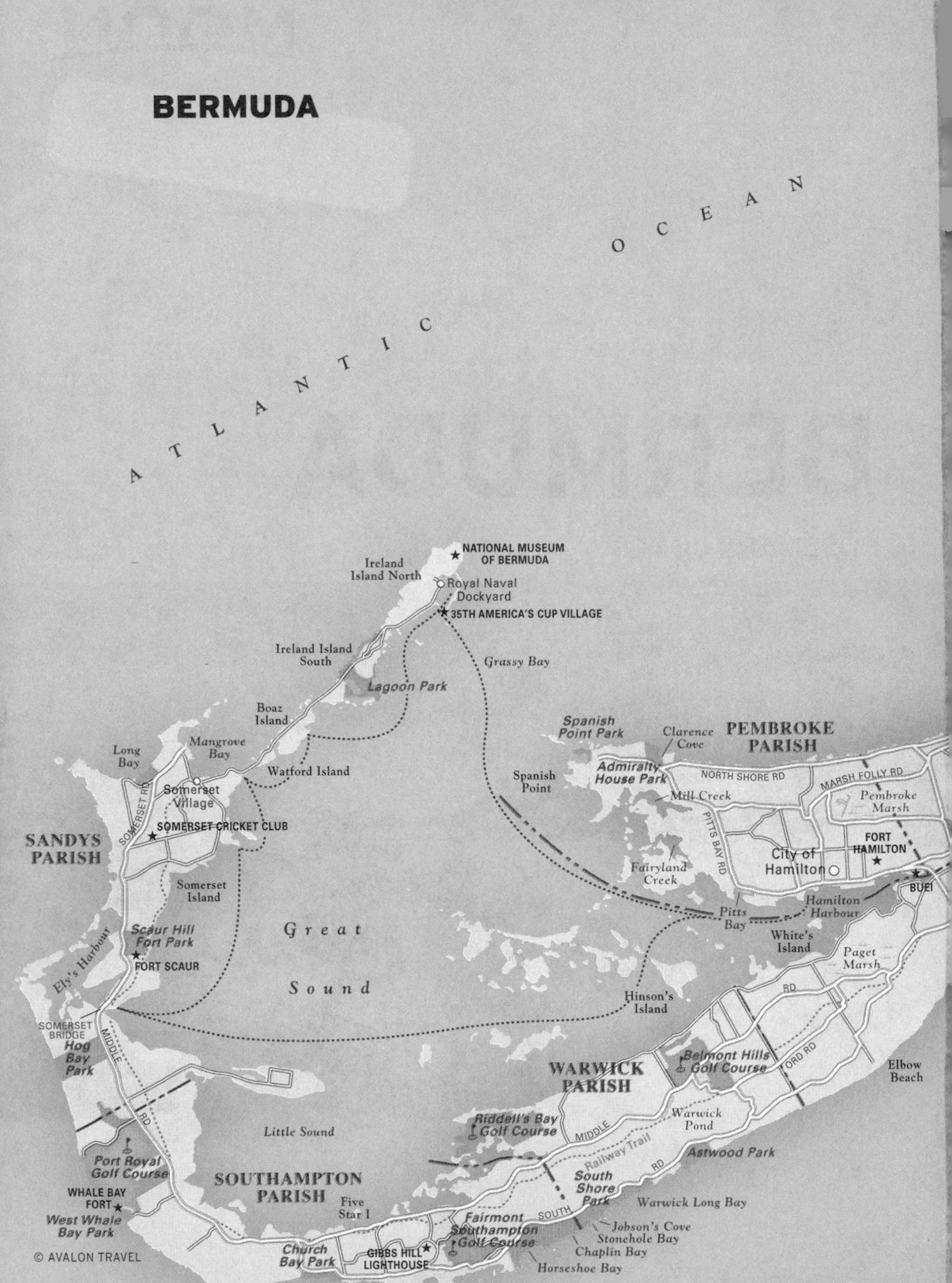

BERMUDA

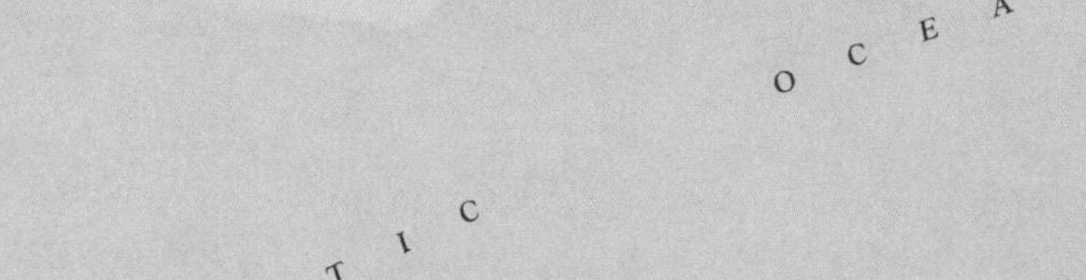

ATLANTIC OCEAN
NATIONAL MUSEUM OF BERMUDA
Ireland Island North
Royal Naval Dockyard
35TH AMERICA'S CUP VILLAGE
Ireland Island South
Grassy Bay
Lagoon Park
Boaz Island
Spanish Point Park
Clarence Cove
PEMBROKE PARISH
Long Bay
Mangrove Bay
Watford Island
Admiralty House Park
NORTH SHORE RD
MARSH FOLLY RD
Spanish Point
Somerset Village
Mill Creek
Pembroke Marsh
SOMERSET RD
PITTS BAY RD
SOMERSET CRICKET CLUB
SANDYS PARISH
FORT HAMILTON
Fairyland Creek
City of Hamilton
Somerset Island
BUEI
Hamilton Harbour
Pitts Bay
Great Sound
Scaur Hill Fort Park
White's Island
FORT SCAUR
Paget Marsh
Ely's Harbour
Hinson's Island
RD
SOMERSET BRIDGE
Hog Bay Park
MIDDLE
Belmont Hills Golf Course
ORD RD
Elbow Beach
WARWICK PARISH
Riddell's Bay Golf Course
Warwick Pond
RD
Little Sound
MIDDLE
Railway Trail
Port Royal Golf Course
Astwood Park
RD
SOUTHAMPTON PARISH
South Shore Park
WHALE BAY FORT
Five Star I
Warwick Long Bay
West Whale Bay Park
Fairmont Southampton Golf Course
SOUTH
Jobson's Cove
Stonehole Bay
Church Bay Park
GIBBS HILL LIGHTHOUSE
Chaplin Bay
Horseshoe Bay

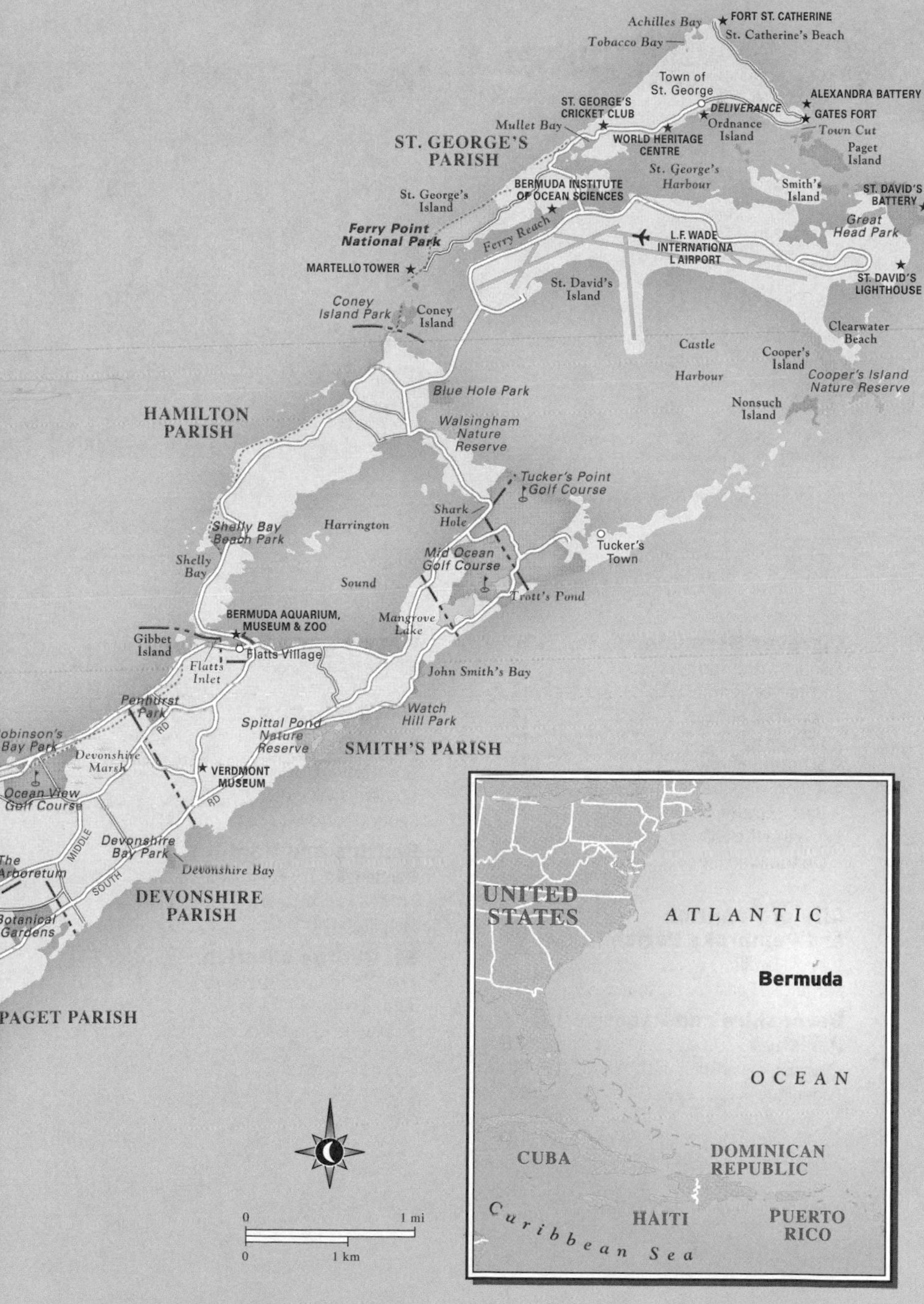

Achilles Bay
FORT ST. CATHERINE
St. Catherine's Beach
Tobacco Bay
Town of St. George
ST. GEORGE'S CRICKET CLUB
DELIVERANCE
ALEXANDRA BATTERY
GATES FORT
Mullet Bay
Ordnance Island
Town Cut
WORLD HERITAGE CENTRE
Paget Island
ST. GEORGE'S PARISH
St. George's Harbour
Smith's Island
ST. DAVID'S BATTERY
BERMUDA INSTITUTE OF OCEAN SCIENCES
St. George's Island
Great Head Park
Ferry Point National Park
Ferry Reach
L.F. WADE INTERNATIONAL AIRPORT
MARTELLO TOWER
ST. DAVID'S LIGHTHOUSE
St. David's Island
Coney Island Park
Coney Island
Clearwater Beach
Castle Harbour
Cooper's Island
Cooper's Island Nature Reserve
Blue Hole Park
Nonsuch Island
HAMILTON PARISH
Walsingham Nature Reserve
Tucker's Point Golf Course
Shark Hole
Harrington Sound
Shelly Bay Beach Park
Shelly Bay
Tucker's Town
Mid Ocean Golf Course
Trott's Pond
BERMUDA AQUARIUM, MUSEUM & ZOO
Mangrove Lake
Gibbet Island
Flatts Village
Flatts Inlet
John Smith's Bay
Penhurst Park
Watch Hill Park
Spittal Pond Nature Reserve
Robinson's Bay Park
SMITH'S PARISH
Devonshire Marsh
VERDMONT MUSEUM
Ocean View Golf Course
RD
MIDDLE
SOUTH
Devonshire Bay Park
The Arboretum
Devonshire Bay
DEVONSHIRE PARISH
Botanical Gardens
PAGET PARISH
UNITED STATES
ATLANTIC OCEAN
Bermuda
CUBA
DOMINICAN REPUBLIC
HAITI
PUERTO RICO
Caribbean Sea
0
1 mi
1 km

Contents

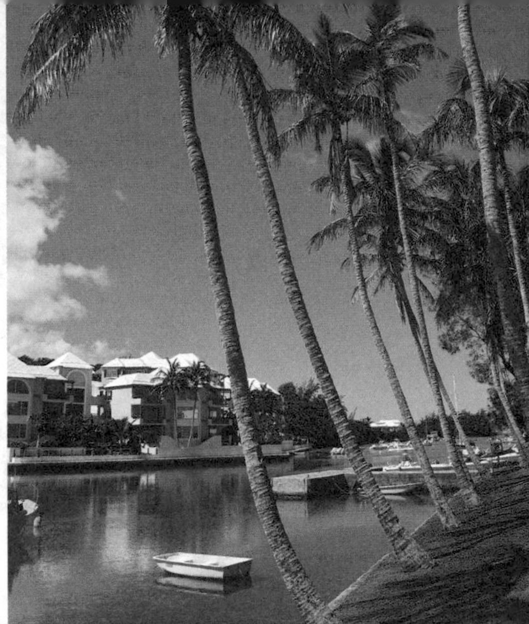

DISCOVER

Bermuda

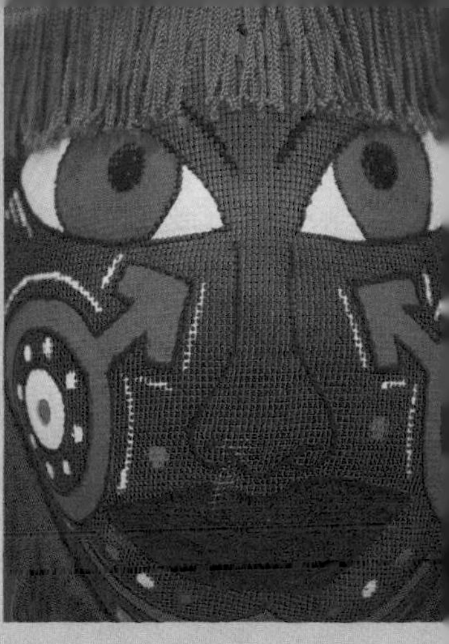

Bermudians often refer to the "Real World" as if theirs isn't. Perhaps it's truer to say the island is "Another World," as local crooner Hubert Smith and his 1960s band the Coral Islanders sang in what is accepted as Bermuda's unofficial national anthem. He was right, of course—there is definitely an ephemeral, cotton candy element to the 21-square-mile island with its hallmark hue of confectionery pink that brands buses, hibiscus, cottages, and those legendary linen shorts.

That element of pure fantasy has attracted visitors here for centuries, and this British Overseas Territory's charms cast just as strong a spell today. Arriving over impossibly turquoise bays, so translucent you can almost spot the parrotfish frolicking beneath the silky surface, is to experience a suspension of disbelief normally reserved for Hollywood make-believe. The trilling tree frogs, wobbly scooter rides, perfumed breezes, and laid-back lifestyle probably won't do much to shatter the illusion.

For Bermuda's 64,000 residents, this little piece of paradise is home—a quirky combo of British, North American, West Indian, and Portuguese influences that feels alternately sophisticated and small-town. Petty politics shares daily

Clockwise from top left: children at play, Cooper's Island; Flatts Inlet; Gombey tribal mask; the Great Sound; lizard; church on Church Street, Hamilton.

mind space with world-stage triumphs, all wrapped up in the scope of nine tiny, stunning parishes. But it's the people who will win you over most of all. With their heritage of pioneers and pirates, islanders embody a pragmatic stoicism, jaunty pride, and wicked humor wrapped in an easy friendliness that relaxes you faster than your first rum swizzle.

Bermudians go with the flow literally: the Gulf Stream—the warm current, not the private jet, though there are plenty of those here too—has shaped their destiny. The Atlantic island's balmy temperatures, its storm patterns, and much of its flora and fauna, including the Sargasso Sea and the most northerly coral reef in the world, owe their subtropical nature to the swift gyre that ties Cape Hatteras to Newfoundland.

Bermuda's allure is truly unforgettable. Mark Twain likened Bermuda to heaven. John Lennon discovered *Double Fantasy* here. And when you head back to that Real World you live in, you might just wonder if it's all been a brilliant figment of your own imagination.

Clockwise from top left: a harvest of loquats; Warwick Long Bay; typical island architecture; hibiscus.

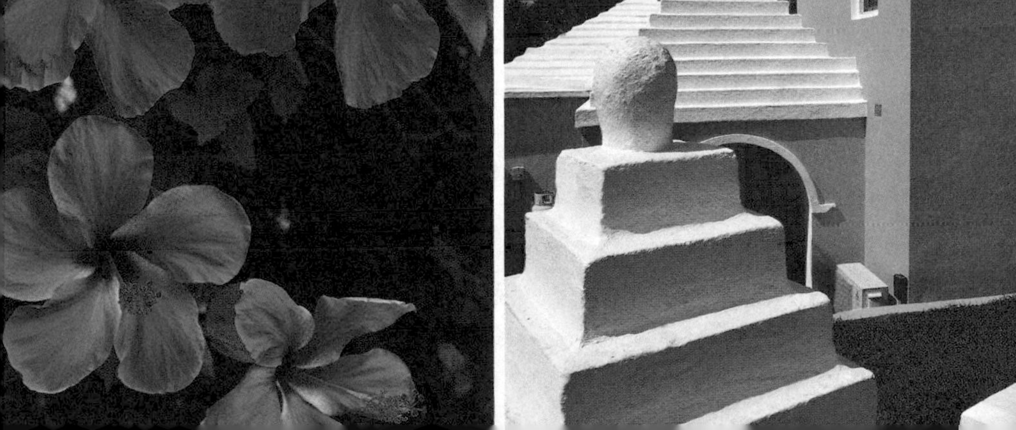

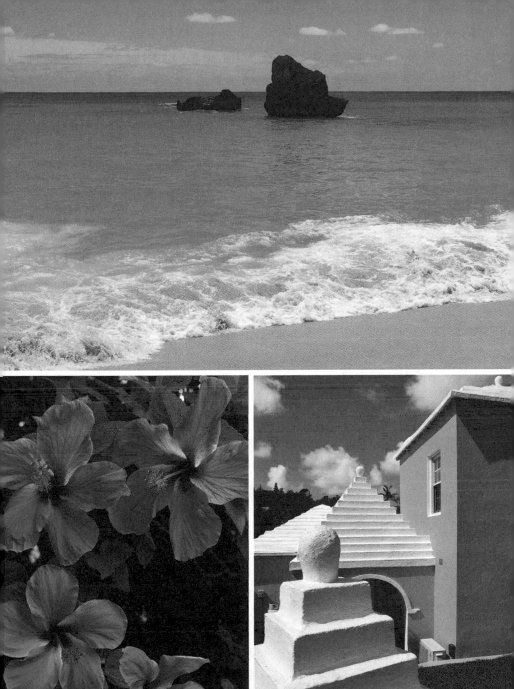

Planning Your Trip

Where to Go

City of Hamilton and Pembroke Parish

Whether you foray into "Town" for **shopping, restaurants,** or **nightclubs,** or use the capital (since 1815) as a base from which to explore the rest of the island, the city and its environs are a logical place to start a tour of the parishes. Hamilton currently has no hotels, but Pembroke has several excellent options offering access to the city and bus and ferry terminals. Attractions include **art galleries, parks, cathedrals,** and an **1870s fort. Harbor cruises** leave from the waterfront, and the tour center can help you book adventures islandwide and year-round.

Devonshire and Paget Parishes

Deep country is found in Devonshire, with **old estates, farmland,** and **seaside communities.** Paget offers suburban attractions such as **golf, tennis,** and **top-notch restaurants.** Resorts and guesthouses abound in Paget, while colorful local eateries, **churches,** and **nature reserves** enhance Devonshire's allure. Key attractions include the **Arboretum, Bermuda Botanical Gardens, Masterworks Museum of Bermuda Art,** and **Elbow Beach.**

Warwick and Southampton Parishes

Beach bums beware: You might never leave the pink-sand confines of these western parishes. This is the realm of **scuba, water sports, horseback riding,** and **snorkeling,** not to mention **tennis, golf,** and pampering **spas** at several major resorts. Jocks and sun-worshippers will find nirvana here. There are a few historic sites, including **Gibbs Hill**

a scarlet ibis at the Bermuda Aquarium, Museum & Zoo's free-flight Caribbean exhibit

Lighthouse—which provides the island's best view. Both parishes offer a plethora of gourmet and comfort food, and accommodations to suit various budgets.

Sandys Parish

The historic military gems of the fortified **Royal Naval Dockyard,** including the **National Museum of Bermuda,** are the biggest collective magnet drawing visitors to the West End. This outer parish has a quaint, countrified character that invites gentle exploration. **Somerset Village** and its surroundings provide rural lanes to meander, plus shops, restaurants, and water sports. **Deep-sea fishing** boats are also based in this parish. One major resort and several guesthouses provide accommodations, but fast ferries from Hamilton can get you (and your scooter) here in 20 minutes.

Smith's and Hamilton Parishes

Packed with attractions, Smith's Parish and Hamilton Parish—the latter not to be confused with the capital city—offer plenty to see, plus pretty pathways to the East End. Explore history and nature at **Verdmont Museum,** a historic home, before taking a hike at the 34-acre oceanfront bird sanctuary **Spittal Pond Nature Reserve,** both in Smith's. **Bermuda Aquarium, Museum & Zoo** in Hamilton Parish is a favorite island attraction. The cave-honeycombed Harrington Sound provides a scenic route east, and several beautiful beaches—**Shelly Bay Beach, John Smith's Bay**—are inviting distractions.

St. George's Parish

A UNESCO World Heritage Site, the 400-year-old Town of St. George and its related forts in the East End appeal to **history** lovers. The parish incorporates the island's first capital, along with the airport, the island of **St. David's,** and outlying regions like **Ferry Point National Park.** Built by English settlers, St. George's boasts **winding streets,** many landmarks, **a public square,** and a **yacht-laden waterfront.**

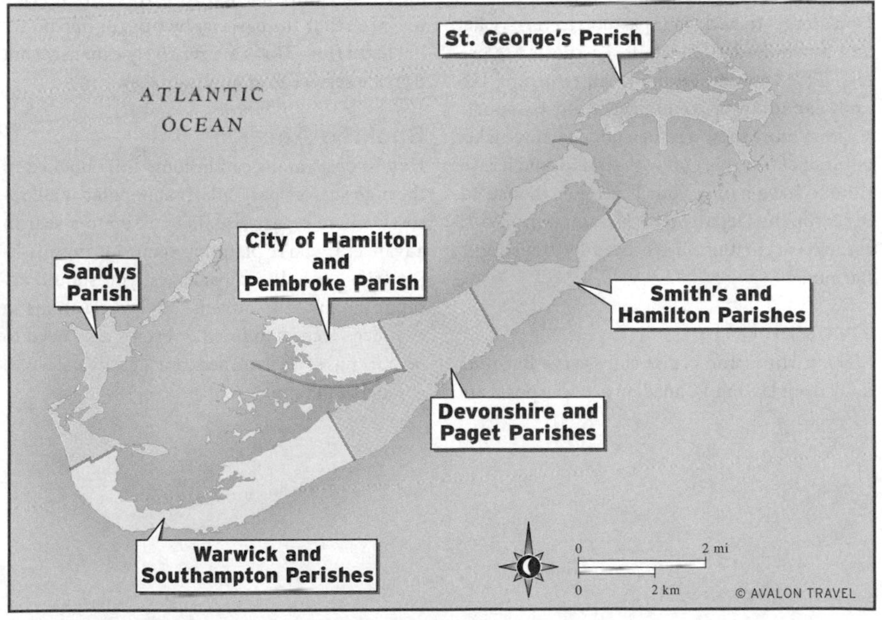

The surrounding **forts** are a tribute to the island's British military heritage, while former U.S. baselands boast an expanse of now-public beaches. Parish accommodations range from backstreet bed-and-breakfasts to a boutique Rosewood hotel.

When to Go

Bermuda is farther north than the Caribbean hot spots, so don't expect perfect weather all year round. The **winter off-season** (November-March) has average 68°F temperatures, compared to the high 80s of **midsummer. Spring** (April-May) and **fall** (September-November) are perhaps the most pleasant periods, especially October, as summer's humidity falls away.

You may want to time your visit around **cultural and sports events.** Local favorites include Cup Match (a two-day cricket holiday in late July/early August) and Bermuda Day (May 24). Easter brings kites and Christmas boasts a boat parade and festival of lights. International events include the Bermuda Festival of the Performing Arts (dance, opera, theater) in January and February; October's Argo Group Gold Cup (for match-race sailing); and November's World Rugby Classic.

Before You Go

Passports, Visas, and Vaccinations

Don't forget to pack your passport, return ticket, and accommodation details. Passports are preferred for entering Bermuda; all returning U.S. and Canadian citizens need valid passports. Visitors must show a return or departure ticket, or proof of transport off of the island, and it saves time to have handy your hotel/guesthouse address for the Department of Immigration officer. No vaccinations are needed for traveling to Bermuda.

Transportation

Major airlines and cruise ships serve Bermuda daily from U.S. and Canadian gateway ports and cities, as well as the United Kingdom. On the island, you can rent a **scooter** (there are no cars for hire), tour the parishes by **bus,** or hop on reliable **ferries. Taxis** are relatively expensive but provide service to all nine parishes.

Booking Ahead

Hotels' best rooms can become fully booked in the high season, particularly at popular small resorts, where repeat visitors book up to a year in advance. If you're planning scuba outings, fishing trips, or golf/spa packages, you should arrange tee times, treatments, and reservations in advance. Tickets to premier events also need to be purchased early. Check for details on www.gotobermuda.com.

The Best of Bermuda

With its short distances and efficient public transport, Bermuda reveals much of itself to energetic travelers during a weeklong stay. Look below the surface of this reef-fringed paradox and you'll discover a melting pot of culture, history, and outdoor adventure encompassing all nine parishes.

Day 1

Touch down at L. F. Wade International Airport and grab a cab to your hotel. Ask the driver where to find the island's best fish sandwich, a Bermudian staple. Shake off your mainland cobwebs with an afternoon at **Elbow Beach,** strolling the soft sand and testing the turquoise waters. Later, choose a waterfront terrace, such as the trendy **Seabreeze Lounge** on Paget's South Shore, **The Dock** in Southampton, or sunset-soaked **1609 Bar & Restaurant** on Hamilton Harbour, for an alfresco dinner.

Day 2

Head into "Town" (aka **Hamilton**) for down-home breakfast with Bermudians at **The Spot.** Try traditional codfish and potatoes, if it's on the menu. Spend the morning exploring Front, Reid, and Church Streets' boutiques, art galleries, and churches. Climb **Holy Trinity Cathedral**'s landmark tower to overlook the city. Try lunch at sushi hot spot **Beluga Seafood Bar** or tapas at **Ten.** In the afternoon, rent a scooter or hop on a bus and cruise the North Shore to visit **Crystal Cave and Fantasy Cave.** Watch the sun go down over Harrington Sound with mussel pie and cassava fries at Rosewood's **Tucker's Bar.**

Day 3

Cool out on the beach today. Go to pristine **Warwick Long Bay** for bodysurfing, sandcastles, and snorkeling. Pack a picnic and follow the trail west through protected, dune-cradled South Shore National Park to sample **Jobson's Cove,** which is followed by **Chaplin, Stonehole, and**

Warwick Long Bay

Horseshoe Bays. Take a dip at each. In the late afternoon, escape the sun and indulge in a spa treatment at a resort (book your treatment days in advance if possible).

Day 4

Take the ferry from Hamilton across the Great Sound to the **Royal Naval Dockyard,** scooter optional. Book a half-day scuba outing, rent a kayak, or take a snorkeling or paragliding tour of the West End. Celebrate the neighborhood's British heritage with a pub lunch, then learn stories of soldiers, slaves, immigrants, and war vets at the **National Museum of Bermuda.** Grab a rum cake, a piece of blown glass, or a painting from the **Bermuda Arts Centre** to take home.

Day 5

Take the ferry along the North Shore to **St. George's.** Explore the museums and backstreets of the old town, a UNESCO World Heritage Site. Visit area forts (also UNESCO gems), including **Gates Fort, Alexandra Battery,** the **Martello Tower** at Ferry Reach, and **Fort St. Catherine,** with its commanding views of the bay where the first settlers landed. Climb **St. David's Lighthouse** and then share a feast of lobster and tuna—and dark 'n' stormies—at quirky **Black Horse Tavern Bar and Restaurant**.

Day 6

Walk in John Lennon's footsteps at the **Bermuda Botanical Gardens** in Paget, where *Double Fantasy* was born, and pay a visit to the **Masterworks Museum of Bermuda Art.** Head to North Hamilton for a Caribbean-style lunch at one of the many cafés, such as **Jamaican Grill, Rotis,** or **Fish & Tings.** Climb up to nearby **Fort Hamilton** for moat gardens and panoramic views. Return to the city for an evening of avant-garde poetry, rap, rock or spoken-word performances at **Chewstick Neo-Griot Lounge and Café** on Front Street.

Day 7

Grab an early-morning beach run or walk along the South Shore and cool off with a dip in the balmy water before your flight out.

A Romantic Retreat

Moongates, hidden beaches, star-speckled skies, and blossom-scented breezes—Bermuda's charms, like the setting of an over-the-top pulp romance, soon put lovebirds in the mood. The island is a popular destination for couples planning a romantic long weekend, not least because of the easy flight from North American East Coast cities (flight times range from 90 minutes to 2.5 hours). Long a honeymoon destination, Bermuda's natural beauty and languorous pace are seductive to anyone hoping to celebrate a new romance or fall in love all over again.

Day 1

Most flights from North America arrive in Bermuda at midday or early afternoon, leaving lots of time to begin unwinding. Check into the gorgeously renovated "Pink Palace," aka the historic **Fairmont Hamilton Princess,** where you can sip swizzles or mango lemonade beside the infinity pool overlooking the motoryachts and passing spinnakers. Stretch your legs along Front Street, where you and your honey can compare the scents of "Coral" and "Pink" at **The Bermuda Perfumery**'s boutique, or buy a pair of bona fide Bermuda shorts. In the evening, book into **Marcus',** celebrity chef Marcus Samuelsson's latest restaurant that puts his award-winning spin on island cuisine.

Day 2

Share a scooter (perfect for two) and enjoy exploring the postcard-pretty West End. Explore **Somerset**'s pastel lanes on foot, then pick up a takeout lunch from the **Village Café, Woody's Drive-in Two Bar and Restaurant,** or **Gloria's**

Best Beaches

MOST BEAUTIFUL BEACHES

- **Horseshoe Bay** (South Shore—Southampton): A sweeping pink stretch hemmed by emerald foliage and sparkling turquoise—plus showers, washrooms, a café, lifeguards, and beach gear rentals.
- **Warwick Long Bay** (South Shore—Warwick): A serene antidote to neighboring beach crowds, with deep white sand and crashing surf.
- **Elbow Beach** (South Shore—Paget): Offers pillow-soft sand and frolicking parrotfish, along with volleyball and kitesurfing.
- **John Smith's Bay** (South Shore—Smith's): Framed by coconut palms, this picturesque bay has shady caves, lifeguards, and nearby reefs for snorkeling.

MOST SECLUDED BEACHES

- **Astwood Cove** (South Shore—Warwick): Hard to access, except by a steep cliffside path, but the privacy and crystal-clear water are worth the trouble.
- **Jobson's Cove** (South Shore—Warwick): A favorite of romantics and families with children due to its cliff-sheltered swimming hole.
- **West Whale Bay** (West End—Southampton): Hidden below Whale Bay Fort with a string of coves and caves connected by pristine sand at low tide.
- **Turtle Bay, Long Bay,** and **Soldier Bay** (East End—Cooper's Island Nature Reserve, St. George's): This 44-acre peninsula offers a plethora of gorgeous, off-the-beaten-track beaches, facing both Castle Harbour and South Shore and bordered by bird sanctuaries.

BEST SNORKELING BEACHES

- **Church Bay** (South Shore—Southampton): Easy-to-reach boiler reefs make it a perennial top pick among devoted snorkelers.
- **Clarence Cove** (North Shore—Pembroke): A sheltered, reef-fringed bay inside a national park. Popular with scuba divers, snorkelers, and children.

Horseshoe Bay

- **Snorkel Park Beach** (West End—Royal Naval Dockyard): At the foot of towering ramparts, shallow waters and reef-speckled coastline prove a hit with locals and visitors alike.
- **Tobacco Bay** (East End): A snorkeler's heaven (when not crowded with cruise ship passengers), thanks to its natural underwater columns and reef life.

WHERE LOCALS GO

- **Horseshoe Bay** (South Shore—Southampton): Local teens and twentysomethings lend a beach-party atmosphere to summer weekend afternoons here.
- **Somerset Long Bay** (West End—Somerset Island): Turtles can be seen grazing in the shallows, alongside a public park and nature reserve.
- **Clearwater Beach** (East End—Southside, St. George's): With its accessible water and nearby playground, parkland, and fast-food restaurants, this aptly named swimming venue is a summer hot spot with locals.
- **St. Catherine's Beach** (East End): A sandy arc on the island's easternmost tip where shipwrecked English colonists struggled ashore.

Scouting Shipwrecks

Bermuda is known as the shipwreck capital of the Atlantic, with 500 years of human history snared on its 280-square-mile reef platform. Most of these unfortunate vessels, from treasure-laden galleons to U.S. Civil War-era steamers, lie less than 60 feet deep, making accessibility a breeze. Here are a few of the best dive sites:

- ***Sea Venture***: the most recent artificial dive site, this decommissioned 75-foot ferry is named for the shipwreck that accidentally brought the first English settlers in 1609. It was sunk off Bermuda's northwest corner in 2007.
- ***Constellation***: a 192-foot, four-masted, wooden American schooner that served as a cargo ship in World War II before it sank off the West End in 1943. It inspired Peter Benchley's novel *The Deep.*
- ***L'Herminie***: an impressive warship wreck, this three-masted French wooden frigate crashed in 1838, scattering dozens of cannons over the ocean floor on the island's western side.
- ***Cristobal Colon***: the biggest of Bermuda's shipwrecks, a 499-foot Spanish luxury liner that went down off the island's northeast corner in 1936.

Bermuda water temperatures vary from an average 65°F in the winter months (though water clarity is better then) to average highs of 85°F in the summer. Check out **www.gotobermuda.com** for details on wrecks, dive operators, rates, and seasonal schedules, plus photo galleries of the most intriguing caverns, swim-throughs, and reef life.

Kitchen for a private picnic and paddle at Black Bay. Relax with a couples massage at Cambridge Beaches' **Ocean Spa** before heading back to **Hamilton** to watch the sunset—or moonrise—from the porch of **Red Steakhouse & Bar** or **Harry's Bar.**

Day 3

Start the day with breakfast coffee at **Muse**—coupled with a crepe or chocolate lava cake savored with two spoons. Meander your way east to **Cooper's Island Nature Reserve,** a 44-acre peninsula bordered by secluded beaches; their azure privacy mimics scenes from romantic flicks like *The Sandpiper* or *The Blue Lagoon.* Visit historic **St. George's** for island-crafted treasures for him and her from **Davidrose Jewelry** before an intimate soiree at **Tempest Bistro,** off a cobblestoned lane on the waterfront.

Day 4

Make sure you book an afternoon flight out if possible, to make the most of the morning. Have another swim, or tour the harbor and Great Sound by ferry before you leave.

Vacation with the Kids

Being a kid in Bermuda is like stepping into *Fantasia* or *Alice in Wonderland.* There are plenty of weird animals—lizards, trilling tree frogs, manta rays gliding like UFOs under Flatts Bridge. Roadsides are polka-dotted with trails of Technicolor blossoms, perfect for pretend princesses. And sunshine-packed days spill over with sandcastles, real-life forts, and bubblegum-colored buses. For a calendar of kid-friendly activities, check www.nothingtodoinbermuda.com and www.bermudafamilyactivities.com. Tickets for movies and events can be purchased online at www.bdatix.com or www.premierticketsglobal.com.

Sights and Recreation

ROYAL NAVAL DOCKYARD

The ferry ride to the West End alone is entertainment enough, but little ones will adore up-close encounters with dolphins inside the National

Museum grounds, plus the adjacent playground with its mini-lighthouse entwined by a 70-foot moray eel. Outside in the Dockyard, don't miss the games room in the Frog and Onion Pub, or the frozen yogurt and ice cream vendors at Dockyard Terrace and the Clocktower Mall.

WORLD HERITAGE CENTRE

Make a beeline for the East End, where kids can be immersed in history they will actually enjoy. The World Heritage Centre in St. George's lets youngsters dress up and experience the sights and sounds of times gone by. Children can also imagine long-gone life at sea by clambering aboard *Deliverance*, the replica 17th-century vessel on the old town's waterfront. Head up to Fort St. Catherine to hide out in tunnels or climb atop cannons with panoramic views. Who can't be a pirate with those kind of props?

BERMUDA AQUARIUM, MUSEUM & ZOO

Ring-tailed lemurs, harbor seals, and a black grouper dubbed Darth Vader keep youngsters, and their adult companions, entertained for hours at the island's favorite attraction. There's also a playground on-site with a conveniently situated café for lunch—or a glass of grownup vino while the kids try out the slides.

Beaches

JOBSON'S COVE AND BABY BEACH

Bodysurfers may love the sweeping, wave-crashed strands of Warwick Long Bay or Southampton's Horseshoe, but less experienced beach bums may feel more confident in the adjoining coves, protected and shaded by tall limestone cliffs. Kids can entertain themselves for hours here playing in rock pools, collecting shells, or spying on reef life with a mask and snorkel. Make sure to bring hats, shades, and plenty of sunblock.

CLARENCE COVE

This gentle, picture-perfect bay within Pembroke's Admiralty House Park is on bus routes and accessible from all central parishes. A soft, sandy beach, a dock, and coastal reefs provide all the ingredients for hours of fun whether you're traveling with toddlers or teens. They'll likely meet some local counterparts to play with, too.

Tiny Jobson's Cove is a perfect little swimming hole encircled by cliffs.

Best Extreme Sports in Bermuda

While many Bermuda residents spend weekends and downtime testing their limits against the island's physical challenges, visitor activities were often somewhat, well, sedate. That's all changed in the last few years with the arrival of numerous vendors offering outsiders a feel of the "real"—read extreme—Bermuda. Sign on for epic adventures that demonstrate Bermuda truly does have it all, from cliff jumping to kayak trips and offshore snorkeling. Book and pay in advance via vendors directly, or through the Island Tour Centre at www.islandtourcentre.bm:

- Get airborne with **Coconut Rockets/Bermuda Flyboard** (441/504-7197, www.coconutrockets.com). Attached via boots and bindings to a pressurized flyboard, the "pilot" is propelled by the water jet pack up to 35 feet above the ocean surface. Experience stuntman-style antics in and over the water.
- If you balk at riding the killer wakes of his awesome speedboat, John Martin will simply tell you he's already taught his five-year-old twins to do it. His company, **AXIS Adrenaline Projects** (441/537-1114, www.axisadrenaline.com), picks up islandwide and will zoom you past eye-popping scenery to Castle Harbour or other turquoise expanses where you can get your balance and learn mastery of such extreme arts from a true maestro.
- Hawaii Ironman and multisport athlete Kent Richardson is the real deal when it comes to conquering the outdoors. At **Bermuda Waterski & Wakeboard Centre** (441/234-3354 or 441/335-1012, www.islandwindsbermuda.com), he'll test your mettle with thrills like jumping off Diving Board Island or full-throttle waterskiing along the North Shore. If you're up for tamer stuff, just say so—he's happy to show off Bermuda with slower-paced snorkeling or sightseeing too.

Wakeboarding is one of scores of popular water sports in Bermuda.

- The wow factor of **North Rock**'s barrier reef has even bona fide Bermudians catching their breath. If you have a spare afternoon, book a truly unforgettable trip to the landmark beacon nine miles off the North Shore. Outfitters like **ÜberVida** (441/236-2222, www.ubervida.net) or the **Bermuda Zoological Society** (441/293-2727, www.bamz.org) run four-hour snorkel trips to the spectacular underwater world that's like diving into a scene from *Finding Nemo*.

Entertainment and Events

HARBOUR NIGHTS

Kids can ride the toylike train or dance to the rhythms of gombeys at the high season's stay-up-late Wednesday night street festival, where loads of local food and craft vendors shut down Front and Queen Streets to allow pedestrian-only traffic.

BERMUDA KITE FESTIVAL

Easter weekend is a riot of colorful attractions as traditional local kites take to the skies, many with long, homemade tails that buzz loudly over every parish neighborhood. At Horseshoe Bay, kites miniscule and gargantuan compete for attention—and prizes. Armed with the day's mandatory fish cake sandwich, who wouldn't be captivated?

CHRISTMAS BOAT PARADE
The sight of motoryachts, sailboats, and even pint-sized dinghies decked out in themed lights provides no-holds-barred magic for kids. Watch contestants encircle Hamilton Harbour, choose your favorite, and then top off the night with the shower of fireworks that wraps up the festivities.

Exploring the Railway Trail

Stretching the length of the island, the Railway Trail provides a serene 20-mile artery through Bermuda's parishes, safely away from trafficked thoroughfares. Abandoned as a train route when the island's railway fell into disrepair after a brief run in the 1930s and '40s, the trail today belongs to the National Parks System. Well maintained and signposted with interpretive historical information, as well as historic limestone parish markers, the trail is popular with runners, walkers, horseback riders, and nature-lovers. Try two of the best sections on foot or bicycle:

Paget-Southampton

The trail provides a green getaway in these busy central commuter parishes, making a perfect nature-filled expedition through residential neighborhoods. Enter at **Rural Hill, Paget,** on South Road just west of the Trimingham Hill roundabout. You can park a scooter here at the entrance gates or **rent a mountain bike** from nearby **Oleander Cycles** for an out-and-back of your desired distance (the huge limestone quarry at Khyber Pass, near St. Mary's Church, and back is about 5 miles, out and back to Gibbs Hill Lighthouse is closer to 9 miles). Proceed westwards, through a limestone-walled tunnel, past **Paget Marsh** and **Elbow Beach**—accessible via tribe roads—and onwards past the historic **Cobbs Hill Methodist Church,** scenic **Belmont Hills Golf Club,** and through thick **spice tree woodlands** populated with cardinals, lizards, and wild fruits like loquats and cherries. Various main roads will intersect your journey; be extremely careful when crossing, as there are no speed bumps, stoplights, or crosswalks as yet. You'll also have to step, or lift your bike, over the metal trail gates meant to prevent motorized traffic. At Tribe Road 2, scoot up to **Gibbs Hill** for lunch at the onsite **Dining Room** restaurant, or just ogle the stunning 360-degree views, before retracing your steps.

Somerset Island

The beauty of the Railway Trail is that it offers a fairly flat, as-the-crow-flies route for taking in most of Bermuda. The Somerset section is a perfect example, including tarmacadam sections that make it the smoothest stretch for riding a pedal bike. If you're on a scooter, park at **Somerset Bridge,** the world's smallest drawbridge, and watch occasional boats making their way between the **Great Sound** and **Ely's Harbour** in **Sandys.** Walk westwards through fascinating deep limestone cuts in the cliffsides, now covered in rubber tree roots and other exotic foliage. The trail hugs the coastline for long stretches here, giving marvelous views of the Great Sound. You can venture down to the shore edge, where several spots offer good swimming points to cool off. Continuing on, it's worth climbing up to historic **Fort Scaur** to check out the cannons and eagle-eye views. At **Mangrove Bay,** where the final Somerset Station stood, you can explore **Somerset Village** before heading back (out-and-back distance is about 3.5 miles). If you start at **Dockyard** instead, you can do the route in reverse, bringing a scooter or pedal bike on the ferry from **Hamilton,** or renting them at Dockyard's Oleander Cycles outlet.

On the Wild Side

a family of ducks at Spittal Pond Nature Reserve

Bermuda may seem like a manicured garden, but its somewhat limited open spaces nevertheless give an intriguing glimpse of the island's wildlife. Well-managed government national parks in many parishes, as well as nature reserves owned by the Bermuda National Trust and Bermuda Audubon Society, account for 850 acres of green space and boast spectacular scenery.

PEMBROKE PARISH

Bermuda Underwater Exploration Institute (BUEI)

Part museum (with exhibits on Bermuda shells, geology, wildlife, and shipwrecks), part conference center, and hub for ocean-based activities around the island, BUEI attracts the ecologically inclined. Sign up for monthly lectures, spring whale-watching tours, or moonlit cruises to watch phosphorescent glowworms.

DEVONSHIRE PARISH

Arboretum

Devonshire's largest open space is a beautifully unkempt 19-acre spread of rolling meadows, upland forest, and bluebird and cardinal sanctuaries. Cedars, avocado trees, giant rubber trees, and fiddlewood groves abound.

SANDYS PARISH

Hog Bay Park

This is a rugged, 38-acre reserve in Sandys Parish where hikers can walk undulating trails through farmland, forest, and coastline, stopping to spot turtles and take a dip.

SMITH'S PARISH

Spittal Pond Nature Reserve

A magnet for migratory birds, this 34-acre park hugs the South Shore in Smith's Parish. Trails, brackish ponds, and phenomenal ocean outlooks draw birders, cross-country runners, and local families, but like all the parks, it is quiet and underused.

HAMILTON PARISH

Bermuda Aquarium, Museum & Zoo

Tour this historic Flatts facility, home to more than 200 local fish and invertebrate species, a 140,000-gallon reef tank, and a Natural History Museum that tells the story of Bermuda's origins. Zoo exhibits reflect links with island environments around the globe. Its support charity runs snorkeling and turtle-spotting marine excursions.

ST. GEORGE'S PARISH

Bermuda Institute of Ocean Sciences

Visitors are welcome at this world-renowned institution at Ferry Reach in the East End. Take a free morning tour of the station, where scientists come to study global warming, natural disasters, genomes, marine science technology, and potential medicines from the sea.

City of Hamilton and Pembroke Parish

Look for ★ to find recommended sights, activities, dining, and lodging.

Highlights

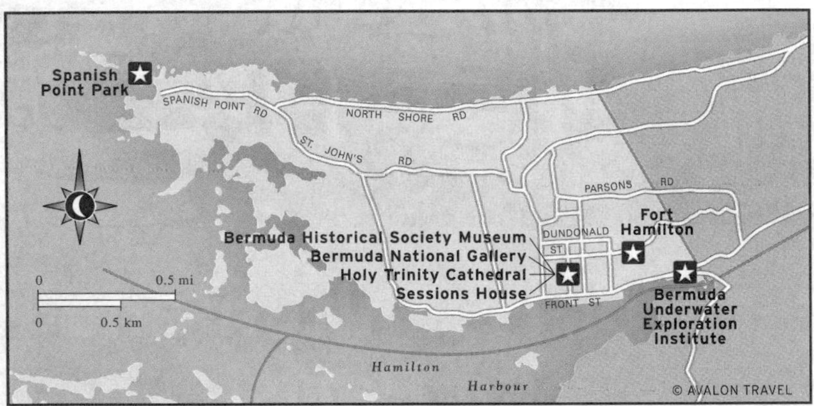

★ **Bermuda Historical Society Museum:** Three rooms of antiquities, explained by attendant historians, tell the history of Bermuda in this tiny museum inside the parkside Bermuda National Library (page 28).

★ **Bermuda National Gallery:** Lunchtime lectures, high-profile shows, a respected biennial exhibition, and an internationally renowned collection of artwork make this museum the perfect artistic milieu of island culture (page 30).

★ **Holy Trinity Cathedral:** Climb up the 155 winding stairs to the top platform of this church tower for dramatic views of Hamilton on all sides. The historic Anglican landmark's interior is breathtaking, too (page 30).

★ **Sessions House:** Bermuda's Italianate Parliament building holds the boisterous Friday afternoon House of Assembly meetings upstairs, and staid, bewigged Supreme Court sessions below. All are open to the public (page 32).

★ **Spanish Point Park:** A grassy promontory stretching into the main sea channel into Hamilton, this oft-forgotten park is a neighborhood favorite. Stretch out on a bench, take a dip in one of its North Shore coves, or watch the locals enjoy cards and Cockspur rum (page 62).

★ **Fort Hamilton:** With a stunning panorama that stretches from Paget across the city and up the Great Sound, this well-preserved fort of the 1870s boasts historic ramparts, underground passages, a cannon, and an exotic moat garden. Bagpipers play here in the winter months (page 64).

★ **Bermuda Underwater Exploration Institute:** Make like explorers William Beebe and Jacques Cousteau at this showcase of Bermuda's surrounding deep ocean, which includes a simulated 12,000-foot descent to the seafloor—plus encounters with giant squid. Kids will love the shipwreck treasure, shell collection, and pretend shark cage (page 65).

At the center of Bermuda, the city of Hamilton—and Pembroke, the parish in which it lies—form the crux of island life on many levels. Home to the seat of government, including the House of Assembly and the Senate, the city is also the island's main port and its major headquarters for local and international business, the justice system (Supreme and Magistrates Courts and legal offices), civil service, commerce, employment, restaurants, and nightclubs. The island's central ferry and bus terminals, which feed service throughout the parishes, are located here. And because it is where most Bermudians work, shop, and eat, Hamilton and, by physical association, Pembroke are also the barometers of national mood: Here is where you'll find the political issues of the day hotly discussed, the latest gossip relayed, the merriment of an imminent public holiday bursting forth, or the staid pomp and ceremony of events such as Budget Day or the Throne Speech celebrated. It is where you may rub shoulders with both the country's richest—the old-money merchants or insurance CEOs—and its least privileged, as it is probably the only place on the island where you'll see a few homeless panhandlers.

The city, named for its first mayor, Henry Hamilton, had its genesis in the need for a central port midway between St. George's and Dockyard. It was an issue both of convenience, so that Bermudian merchants didn't have to travel the length of the island to get their trading done, and control, so that authorities could clamp down on Bermudian vessels, which were increasingly offloading cargoes in western parishes in order to avoid paying heavy duties at the East End. Hamilton's location made these mischievous tactics far more difficult, and eventually the practice died out.

Over two centuries, the city has morphed from a sleepy port for sailing ships into a global corporate powerhouse that now rivals New York and London markets in insurance industry capital. Hamilton's exponential growth in international business since the 1980s has changed the city and its social dynamics more than anything in its history.

Previous: Front Street's Heyl's Corner; North Hamilton. **Above:** Spanish Point Park.

Today, while quaint china and linen stores do their business as timelessly as ever behind pastel waterfront facades, multibillion-dollar deals are being struck in the buildings along the block. While those directly employed in the number-one industry are the ones with the Boss suits, Ferragamo bags, and restaurant charge accounts, everyone benefits from the trickle-down. Meantime, gaggles of brokers and actuaries shuttle between the airport and city boardrooms, pulling their luggage to powwows that ultimately protect nations around the world from financial disasters caused by tornadoes, tsunamis, or terrorism.

Pembroke, once the countrified outskirts of the city, is now—with a few neighborhood exceptions—a heavily trafficked suburban parish, catching Hamilton's commercial overflow, providing vital housing and schools, and playing noisy hub for public and private transport to other points on the island.

Together, Hamilton and Pembroke offer numerous attractions and sights, world-class restaurants, and shops that form an integral part of a visit to the island. Pembroke's accommodations cater to a variety of budgets, though most are geared to higher-end business travelers not seeking beaches or water sports. Theatrical events, art show openings, the annual film festival, national parades, and big sporting events are also rooted in Hamilton and Pembroke, allowing you to experience the different features and offerings of the city and its environs.

PLANNING YOUR TIME

Unless you're staying in the Town of St. George or the West End, each with its own culinary and retail offerings, Hamilton will likely be your first point of reference as you explore Bermuda. If you are a business visitor, you would be wise to stay in outlying Pembroke, namely in the cluster of Pitts Bay hotels and guesthouses, which offer quick access to city meetings and also cater to corporate needs and schedules.

Both the East End (St. George's) and the West End (Sandys, including the Royal Naval Dockyard) are a 30- to 40-minute drive from the city (quicker if you hop on the westbound fast ferry, longer if you board a leisurely pink bus). Hamilton makes a perfect starting place to visit either by public transport or rental scooter, as its main routes run through Pembroke and launch you on your way to all the other parishes.

Sightseeing in Hamilton could take a few hours or several days, depending on your itinerary. Make sure to spend time poking around its boutiques and art galleries, visiting a few sights, and walking its busy streets, because drifting amid the daily hustle and bustle is a great way to get a feel for Bermudians and the way they live. You may choose to break up your Hamilton experiences by, for example, spending a morning shopping and sightseeing, then going to the beach or another parish before returning for happy hour and dinner in one of the city's many clubs or restaurants.

Hop on a ferry—around Paget and Warwick, or to Dockyard and back—and see the juxtaposition of insurance industry towers and age-old landmarks; nowhere is the city's skyline as dramatic as from the waterfront. In the early 2000s, contemporary glass and marble buildings popped up around the city, as business-sector demand for office space boomed. Ferry rides are also a good place to mix with locals and see the smaller islands of Hamilton Harbour and the Pembroke shore.

The city's size means it is entirely walkable if you are able, and, though there are a few steep hills, Hamilton is easy to cover over the course of a day. If you have a scooter here, parking may be your biggest frustration; spaces are few and far between, given the city's swelling working population. Bike theft is also a substantial problem, though rentals are not coveted like other scooter types.

A scooter tour of Pembroke Parish takes just a few hours, depending on the sights you stop to visit—and there are a few fascinating things to see, including Fort Hamilton, the Bermuda Underwater Exploration

Institute, and Admiralty House Park. Outside Hamilton, Pembroke has no ferry service, but buses serve various parts of the parish.

Hamilton and Pembroke are generally safe places to walk. Take a little more caution after dark, as bag-snatchers have been a problem in quieter regions and tourist-heavy areas around Pitts Bay and western Hamilton. North Hamilton's retail and residential areas are as safe as any in the daytime; at night, avoid the area's remote streets, because visitors and locals have been accosted or robbed here. Closed-circuit cameras have been installed at numerous points for security.

City of Hamilton

Bermuda's capital since incorporation in 1793, Hamilton, or "Town" in islanders' vernacular, borders the north shore of a long natural harbor at Bermuda's middle, making it the main port for cargo vessels that cross the Atlantic every week delivering the vital imports of food, clothing, and other goods the island survives on. Until 2008, it was also the main port for cruise ships through the high summer season, but now most ships, including all the large ones, berth at the West End's Dockyard. The city's central location makes it the natural launchpad for explorations east and west through the parishes; no matter where you're staying, you will probably want to take a good look around Hamilton first.

Strict building codes throughout Hamilton's history retained many of the old-time facades, though the late 1990s and early 2000s brought a plethora of contemporary office architecture and, for the first time, urban residential units. Global players in the island's international business industry are all based in Hamilton. Indeed, towers belonging to insurance companies have reshaped the city's profile from east to west, and while Hamilton's official borders have not expanded, many of its businesses have spilled over in recent years to Pembroke—west along Pitts Bay, and east toward Crow Lane. By 2008, the global economic downturn had brought an end to Hamilton's building boom, driving down corporate rents, but as Bermuda's economy recovers, that could change in the future if yet another flight of corporate capital to the island drives demand skyward once again.

The previously novel concept (for Bermuda) of city living has taken root, though it's popular mostly with the unmarried and downsizing empty-nesters. Urban-style condominiums have pushed Hamilton north, providing apartment suites for Bermudians and expatriate city workers, as well as investment properties. No tourist accommodations fall within the strict city limits, although there are numerous lodgings in Pembroke, within a 15-minute walk from Hamilton's retail center.

The city is not difficult to navigate, with a straightforward grid system of streets running east-west (Front, Reid, Church, Victoria, Dundonald) and north-south (King, Court, Parliament, Burnaby, Queen, Par-la-Ville, Bermudiana). Several are one-way streets; look carefully at signs before entering on a scooter. The main flow of traffic comes back and forth via Front Street, or down Reid's one-way lanes up Queen and back out of the city via Church Street (also a one-way passage). The actual city borders are defined by King Street to the east, Parson's Lane in the north, Bermudiana Road in the west, and Front Street, along the harborfront, to the south. Within that space are two beautiful and well-used parks—Queen Elizabeth and Victoria—and numerous sights, restaurants, cafés, museums, galleries, and shopping attractions.

Indeed, aside from the nine-to-five weekday, shopping is what brings most people to Hamilton, whether they're locals or visitors.

City of Hamilton

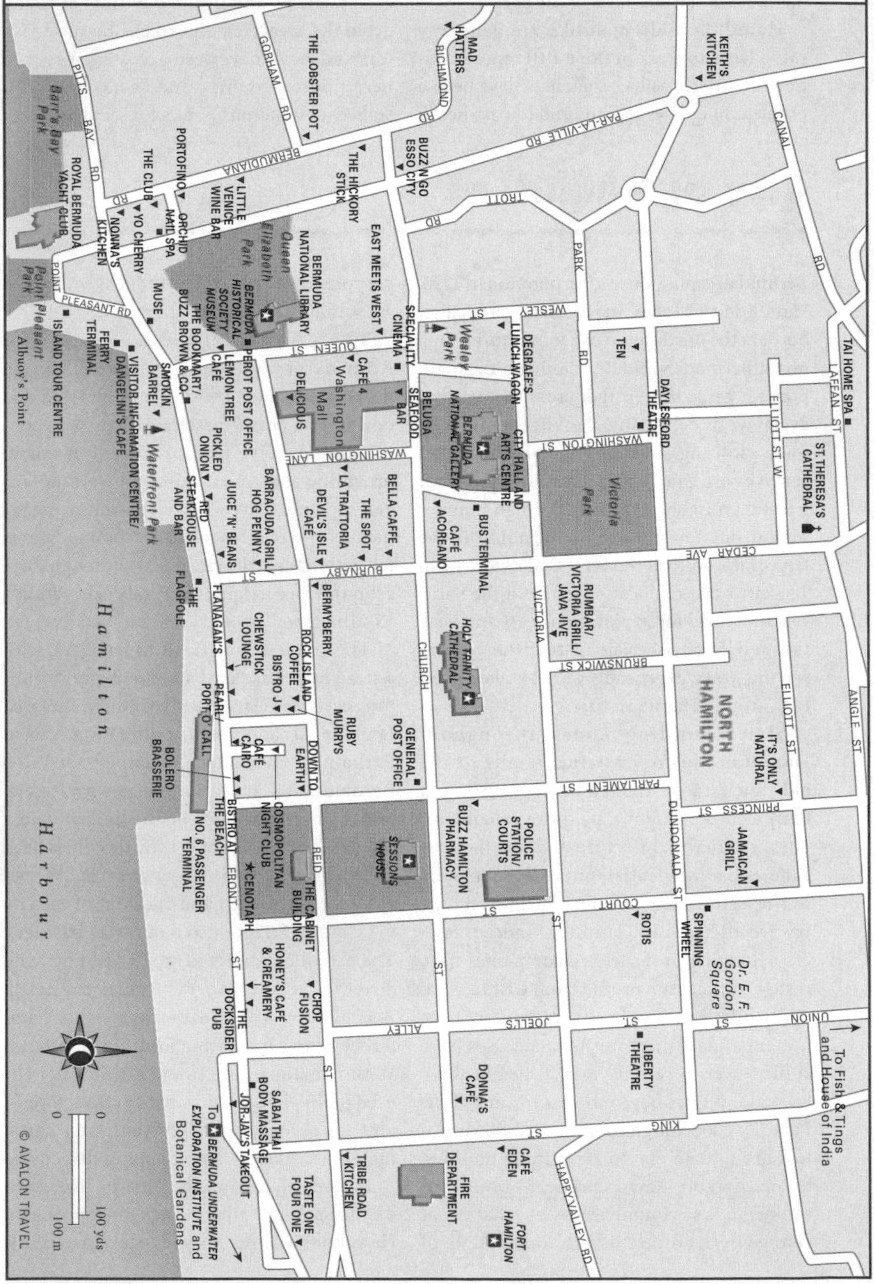

Hamilton Harbour
NORTH HAMILTON
Barr's Bay Park
Point Pleasant Park
Albuoy's Point
Queen Elizabeth Park
Washington Mall
Wesley Park
Victoria Park
Waterfront Park
Dr. E. F. Gordon Square
PITTS BAY RD
BERMUDIANA RD
GORHAM RD
RICHMOND RD
PAR-LA-VILLE RD
TROTT RD
PARK RD
CANAL RD
POINT PLEASANT RD
QUEEN ST
WESLEY ST
WASHINGTON LANE
WASHINGTON ST
BURNABY ST
CEDAR AVE
ELLIOTT ST W
ELLIOTT ST
LAFFAN ST
ANGLE ST
VICTORIA ST
CHURCH ST
BRUNSWICK ST
PARLIAMENT ST
PRINCESS ST
DUNDONALD ST
REID ST
FRONT ST
COURT ST
JOELL'S ALLEY
UNION ST
KING ST
HAPPY VALLEY RD
KEITH'S KITCHEN
MAD HATTERS
THE LOBSTER POT
THE HICKORY STICK
BUZZ N GO ESSO CITY
EAST MEETS WEST
BERMUDA NATIONAL LIBRARY
BERMUDA HISTORICAL SOCIETY MUSEUM
THE BOOKMART/ BUZZ BROWN & CO.
PEROT POST OFFICE
LEMON TREE CAFÉ
SPECIALITY CINEMA
CAFÉ 4 DELICIOUS
SEAFOOD BAR
BELUGA
DEGRAFF'S LUNCH WAGON
BERMUDA NATIONAL GALLERY
CITY HALL AND ARTS CENTRE
TEN
DAYLESFORD THEATRE
TAI HOME SPA
ST. THERESA'S CATHEDRAL
LITTLE VENICE WINE BAR
PORTOFINO
THE CLUB
ORCHID NAIL SPA
YO CHERRY
NONNA'S KITCHEN
ROYAL BERMUDA YACHT CLUB
MUSE
SMOKIN BARREL
VISITOR INFORMATION CENTRE/ DANGELINI'S CAFE
FERRY TERMINAL
ISLAND TOUR CENTRE
PICKLED ONION
JUICE 'N' BEANS
BARRACUDA GRILL/ HOG PENNY
LA TRATTORIA
DEVIL'S ISLE CAFÉ
BELLA CAFFE
THE SPOT
RED STEAKHOUSE AND BAR
CAFÉ ACOREANO
BUS TERMINAL
THE FLAGPOLE
FLANAGAN'S
CHEWSTICK LOUNGE
BERMYBERRY
ROCK ISLAND COFFEE
BISTRO J
RUBY MURRYS
HOLY TRINITY CATHEDRAL
RUMBAR/ VICTORIA GRILL/ JAVA JIVE
IT'S ONLY NATURAL
PEARL/ PORT O' CALL
BOLERO BRASSERIE
CAFÉ CAIRO
DOWN TO EARTH
GENERAL POST OFFICE
BISTRO AT THE BEACH
NO. 6 PASSENGER TERMINAL
COSMOPOLITAN NIGHT CLUB
CENOTAPH
THE CABINET BUILDING
SESSIONS HOUSE
BUZZ HAMILTON PHARMACY
POLICE STATION/ COURTS
JAMAICAN GRILL
ROTIS
SPINNING WHEEL
HONEY'S CAFÉ & CREAMERY
CHOP FUSION
THE DOCKSIDER PUB
LIBERTY THEATRE
DONNA'S CAFÉ
SABAI THAI BODY MASSAGE
JOR-JAY'S TAKEOUT
TASTE ONE FOUR ONE
TRIBE ROAD KITCHEN
FIRE DEPARTMENT
CAFÉ EDEN
FORT HAMILTON
To Fish & Tings and House of India
To BERMUDA UNDERWATER EXPLORATION INSTITUTE and Botanical Gardens
0 100 yds
0 100 m

Front Street—once the domain of Bermuda's white power bloc, whose key merchants were nicknamed the "Forty Thieves"—has today become a far more pluralistic thoroughfare. Gone are all but one of Front Street's old-money department stores; only A. S. Cooper & Sons remains. Smaller boutiques like Atelerie, Max Mara, and Lusso draw shoppers, while events like Harbour Nights, the Front Street Mile race, the Bermuda Day Half-Marathon, and the Christmas Boat Parade bring out Bermuda residents from every parish and background to celebrate annual traditions along the waterfront. Many Front Street retailers are geared to tourists, while Reid, Queen, and Church Streets remain major shopping destinations, connected by the rambling Washington Mall, which underwent a major expansion in recent years.

Don't restrict your visit to the city's most trafficked regions. Long denigrated as "back o' town," culturally vibrant North Hamilton has plenty to offer. Strolling around the region's streets, you can enjoy the West Indian architecture, with wooden verandas, brightly hued cottages, and walled gardens harking back to a quieter time in old Bermuda. Don't miss the neighborhood's retail bargains or popular eateries, either.

SIGHTS

Hamilton's small size means there are no vastly different "neighborhoods" to explore. Sights and attractions are scattered throughout the city blocks. North Hamilton is the only really distinct section, mainly because it has not been privy to major development to date and has therefore retained more of its quaint original architecture than other areas.

Albuoy's Point

Busy Albuoy's Point is the wedge of parkland behind the ferry terminal off Front Street. Mature baygrape trees shade the little patch of grass and benches surround the harborfront dockside—the city's main boat pickup spot for day and evening charters, including snorkeling and glass-bottomed boat excursions, sailing trips, and festive cruises. Public toilets are located on Point Pleasant Road, the lane linking the park to Front Street, which also has a few souvenir shops and charter tour company offices. On the park's western side sits the salmon-colored **Royal Bermuda Yacht Club,** its members-only clubhouse and marina the headquarters of the Argo Group Gold Cup match-racing competition and the biennial **Newport Bermuda Race,** now over 100 years old. Across the harbor is

Barr's Bay Park on the Hamilton waterfront is a staging point for concerts.

The Birdcage

Front Street's odd-looking blue-and-white "Birdcage" at Heyl's Corner, the junction with Queen Street, has become a beloved island symbol, thanks to traffic police who, over the years, have posed for thousands of holiday snapshots from the kiosk in their Bermuda shorts.

While the platform, which acts as a traffic island, *does* look like Tweety Bird's hangout, it actually got its name from a former City of Hamilton official, the late Geoffrey Bird, who in the 1950s devised its design to keep "bobbies" safe while directing traffic. Though it's become nothing more than a tourist-pleasing gimmick in the 21st century, the Birdcage remains a Hamilton icon, even celebrated in the form of gold charm jewelry.

government-owned White's Island, once a U.S. Coast Guard base in World War II and today the fireworks venue for public celebrations such as the Christmas Boat Parade.

Barr's Bay Park

From Albuoy's Point, a thin stretch of land on the north side of the Yacht Club links to Pembroke's Barr's Bay Park, another shady lawn for watching yachts come and go up the harbor. You can also access this park from Pitts Bay Road. Musical and other events are staged here throughout the year. A plaque and a sculpture by Bermudian Chesley Trott commemorate the 1835 landing site of the American slave ship *Enterprise*, whose human cargo won freedom through the courts in an emancipated Bermuda. Like Albuoy's, Barr's Bay is also a common pickup area for rental boat companies.

★ Bermuda Historical Society Museum

On the edge of Queen Elizabeth Park in a trio of rooms inside the Bermuda National Library is the charming little **Bermuda Historical Society Museum** (13 Queen St., tel. 441/295-2487 or 441/236-4193, apbermingham@logic.bm, 10am-2pm Mon.-Fri. May-Oct., 10:30am-1pm Mon.-Wed. and Fri. Oct.-Apr., admission free). The museum is run by knowledgeable volunteers, including some published historians, on behalf of the Bermuda Historical Society, a nonprofit group dating back to 1895 that promotes interest in the island's past. Par-la-Ville, the 1814 building that now houses the library, was once a gracious Georgian homestead, like many that lined Hamilton's streets in the 19th century. It has remained intact, its wooden veranda today overlooking the crush of traffic on Reid Street. Outside, the landmark giant rubber tree also survives; it was planted in 1847 by the merchant William Perot, who built and lived in the house. The museum's prize artifacts include original Hogge money; 18th-century cedar furniture including a cradle and prayer chair; silver flatware made in Bermuda; oil portraits of key figures, such as the island's founder, Admiral Sir George Somers; and ceramics and glassware that once belonged to local sea captains. Be sure to take a look at the exquisite etched-glass hurricane shades in the dining room and the carved palmetto seats of the Queen Anne cedar chairs.

Queen Elizabeth Park

Formerly known as "Par-la-Ville," but renamed to mark Queen Elizabeth II's Diamond Jubilee in 2012, this beautifully landscaped park (8am-sunset daily, admission free) is the city's most-used green space, popular with office workers for outdoor lunches in the spring and fall (summer's torpid heat and humidity tend to discourage anyone wearing a suit from leaving the comfort of air-conditioning for more than a few minutes). Mosaic pathways lead through the oasis, connecting Queen Street with Par-la-Ville Road, which lies parallel to the west (there's a delightful moongate entrance on this side). A third entrance/exit runs through the Par-la-Ville parking lot from

Church Street to the north. Rock gardens, flower beds, trellises, pergolas, and shady mature trees can be found throughout, as well as wooden benches. The park was once the private garden of the Perot family. The merchant William Perot's son, William Bennet Perot, served as the island's postmaster from 1818 to 1862. He designed Bermuda's first stamp, the circular Perot stamp, of which there are only 11 in the world today. Visit the quaint **Perot Post Office** (11 Queen St., tel. 441/292-9052, 9am-5pm Mon.-Fri.), still a working post office, on the park's eastern border.

Wesley Park

At the corner of Wesley and Church Streets, on the southwest corner of the City Hall parking lot, is a pocket-sized park that pays tribute to one of the milestone civil-rights episodes in Bermuda history. The Theatre Boycott by peaceful black activists in June 1959 protested segregation in the island's cinemas. But the 10-day boycott was so successful, it also brought racial barriers in churches, hotels, and other institutions tumbling down. The park features a tall bronze sculpture by Bermudian artist Chesley Trott called *When Voices Rise,* depicting figures with their raised arms holding protest placards. The park is a shady little stopping place with benches, brick pavers, palms, and a tamarind tree.

City Hall and Arts Centre

Hamilton's central landmark and public gathering spot, the **City Hall and Arts Centre** (Church St., tel. 441/292-1234, www.cityhall.bm, 9am-5pm Mon.-Fri., admission free) is the masterpiece of legendary Bermudian architect Wil Onions, who was renowned for adapting cottage aesthetics to almost every project he undertook. Completed in 1960, the building, whose design is basically an oversized cottage with a slate roof and tower, was inspired by Stockholm's city hall. Though Onions died before its completion, the whitewashed structure embodies his aim of simple lines and traditional features. Its 90-foot tower supports a distinctive weathervane sporting a bronze rendition of the shipwrecked *Sea Venture.* Bronze statues by Bermudian sculptor Desmond Fountain depict children playing in fountains set in a water lily pond.

City Hall serves many functions. It is home to the offices of the Corporation of Hamilton on the ground floor, where portraits of mayors and Queen Elizabeth II hang in the stairwell. The main theater on the building's west side hosts performing arts, including

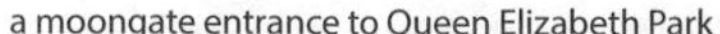
a moongate entrance to Queen Elizabeth Park

dance recitals, theatrical presentations, and Christmas pantomimes. The **Bermuda National Gallery** and the **Bermuda Society of Arts** are up the grand cedar stairs. Outside, public performances like choir recitals, Christmas marching band concerts, and occasional government press conferences are held on City Hall's steps.

★ Bermuda National Gallery

Home to a fine permanent collection of artwork, and host of regularly changing shows of work by contemporary local artists, **Bermuda National Gallery** (upstairs in the City Hall and Arts Centre, Church St., tel. 441/295-9428, fax 441/295-2055, www.bermudanationalgallery.com, 10am-4pm Mon.-Fri., 10am-2pm Sat., closed holidays, admission free) was created in 1992 to promote public education and art appreciation through its national collection, exhibitions, and outreach programs. The original core collection comprised works of European masters—Gainsborough, Murillo, Reynolds—gifted by Bermudian Hereward T. Watlington. The Watlington Collection has since been joined by African art, a provocative collection of black-and-white photographs by Bermudian Richard Saunders, and Hale Woodruff linocuts. The gallery hosts seasonal exhibitions featuring artwork by international and local artists, including the popular summer-long Bacardi Limited Biennial every two years. You may join a free tour of the gallery Thursday mornings at 10:30am. The BNG also hosts a regular program of films, seminars, cocktail parties, and evening lectures by visiting curators and art historians, and free lunchtime lectures on Wednesdays (12:30pm-1:30pm) by Bermudian historians and artists.

★ Holy Trinity Cathedral

I was an adult before I climbed the 155 stairs to the top of "The Cathedral," as **Holy Trinity Cathedral** (Church St., tel. 441/292-4033, fax 441/292-5421, 8am-5pm daily, admission free) is called by Bermudians, but as soon as I'd reached the tower's eye-popping view over Hamilton, I wished I hadn't waited so long. It's one of the best ways to really get a sense of the city and its surrounding parishes—like looking at Manhattan from the bird's-eye view of the Empire State Building. To the north lie Government House, Pembroke Marsh, and the North Shore shipping channel; to the east the House of Assembly, King Edward VII Memorial Hospital, and the freight docks; to the west, City Hall, Hamilton's city grid,

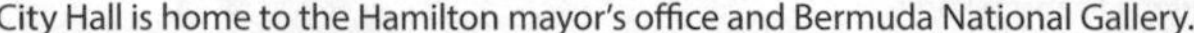

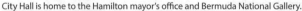

City Hall is home to the Hamilton mayor's office and Bermuda National Gallery.

"Guilty—With an Explanation"

There can't be a more authentic slice of island life than a morning spent hearing the convoluted excuses, remonstrations, and final verdicts of Plea Court. The special session of **Magistrates Court** (Dame Lois Browne Evans Building, 58 Court St., tel. 441/295-5151, ext. 1230) is held at 10am every weekday. Open to the public, it brings out every segment of the population to answer to accused crimes, both trivial and serious. Intoxication, shoplifting, handbag-snatching, assault, swearing in public—the litany of "summary-only" offenses can rarely be tried in Supreme Court and must be dealt with by a magistrate.

One by one, defendants are called to enter a plea to their respective charges. If they choose "not guilty," the court adjourns the case for reviews, social reports, or to fix a trial date. But it is the "guilty" pleas to trivial offenses that are most entertaining, when defendants of all social standings let their creative juices flow as they try to win a lighter sentence or fine before the magistrate's bench. "Guilty—with an explanation" is almost always the prelude to a hilarious yarn; it's met by anticipatory sniggers all around. If he's had a coffee break or it's Friday, the presiding magistrate may join in the fun with snappy comebacks or personal anecdotes that delight the press box, lawyers, prosecutor, public, even the other defendants awaiting their turns. Of course, a crotchety magistrate can put a damper on the jovial proceedings just as easily.

The whole proceedings used to evoke an almost Dickensian aura amid the old-time, wood-paneled courtrooms of its former location on Parliament Street; now ensconced in contemporary headquarters, Plea Court has evolved somewhat—but the entertainment value remains.

the Great Sound, and Dockyard; and to the south, Front Street, White's Island, and the harbor. The neo-Gothic Anglican church, whose interior has stunning stained glass windows, flying arches, lady and warrior chapels, and a carved altar screen, was originally called Trinity Church. Its first cornerstone was laid in 1844, though construction suffered numerous setbacks over subsequent decades, including an arson fire in 1884 that forced authorities to tear down the whole structure and start again. Work began again in 1886, with imported stone from Nova Scotia, Scotland, and Indiana used in conjunction with Bermuda's own limestone. Plans by Scottish architect William Hay called for a spire to rise above the 144-foot tower, but these were scrapped after various delays. The **cathedral's tower** was finally completed in 1905 and is now open to the public (10am-4pm Mon.-Fri., $3 adults, $2 seniors and students, children under five free). The climb—up a slightly claustrophobic spiral, followed by regular stairs to the terrace—is not for the completely unfit, but you can take breaks along the way on two spacious landings. Watch out for the piles of pigeon dung toward the end.

Victoria Park

Anyone interested in Bermuda botany should take a stroll through **Victoria Park** (8am-sunset daily, admission free), where shaded winding paths move between beds of decorative flora and mature trees and shrubs. Scented gardenia bushes, golden acacia trees, even towering Norfolk pines thrive here in this small but pretty park in Hamilton's northern section. On its main lawn there is a historic, cast-iron Victorian bandstand, which underwent a complete restoration in the United Kingdom in 2008 before being shipped back and reconstructed. The park is bordered by Victoria Street, Dundonald Street, Cedar Avenue, and Washington Street. There are public washrooms located here also.

St. Theresa's Cathedral

An ornate contrast to its Anglican counterpart across town, Bermuda's Roman Catholic

St. Theresa's Cathedral (13 Elliott St., tel. 441/292-0607 or 441/292-8486, sttheresas@northrock.bm, 6:30am-7pm daily, admission free) was built in 1932 and named for St. Theresa of Lisieux, "The Little Flower." The church's tower was not finished until 1947, and 20 years later, St. Theresa's became a cathedral when Bermuda was officially named a diocese. St. Theresa's boasts the largest weekly attendance of worshippers on the island, with numerous masses and evening services. The Portuguese Bermudian community's religious *festas,* which honor certain saints, use the cathedral as a base for the colorful spectacles. One of the best known is the procession of Santo Cristo, when hundreds gather at St. Theresa's on the fifth Sunday after Easter seeking miracles for the sick and poor during a march through the city. The cathedral's **gift shop** (tel. 441/292-0416, 10am-2pm Mon.-Sat.) sells rosaries, bibles, cards, candles, and English and Portuguese books.

★ Sessions House

From the harbor, the **Sessions House** (21 Parliament St., tel. 441/292-7408, fax 441/292-2006, office hours 8:45am-5pm Mon.-Fri., parliamentary sessions 10am-12:30pm and 2pm onwards Fri. only Nov.-July, admission free) is the landmark Italianate-style building that defines Hamilton; like Toronto's CN Tower or Chicago's Willis Tower, the impressive structure identifies the city's skyline. The Sessions House was built in 1819, and the tower was added decades later to celebrate Queen Victoria's golden jubilee. Today, sitting atop Parliament Street, the Sessions House contains Bermuda's Supreme Court on its ground floor and the House of Assembly—one of the oldest parliaments in the world—upstairs. Parliament sits every Friday throughout the winter and spring, breaking for the summer and reconvening after November's ceremonious Throne Speech—when the governor reads the government's to-do list to members of Parliament (MPs), dressed in their formal finest.

As in the British House of Commons, members of Parliament are seated according to political party, with opponents facing each other across the floor. A speaker, sporting a traditional black robe and a wig, oversees the proceedings, which count at least a couple of all-nighters every year—probably due to the fact there is no strict cutoff for debates, nor time limits on speeches. Heckling opponents while they are speaking is termed "interpolating" and is allowed within reason,

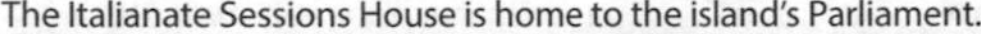
The Italianate Sessions House is home to the island's Parliament.

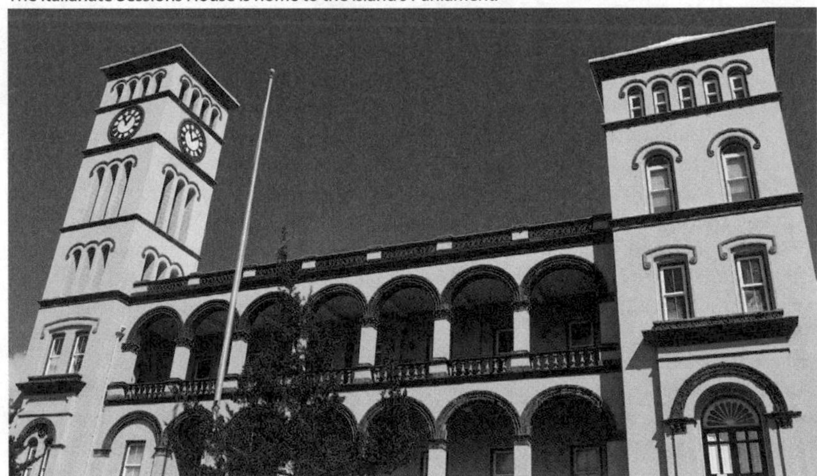

provided hecklers do it from their appointed seat. Famous debates have covered everything from whether to allow motorcars onto the island back in the 1940s (the "yes" vote finally held sway in 1946) to the Golden Arches in 1995 (a move to bring in McDonald's and other fast-food franchises was voted down). Feel free to watch the frivolity from the public gallery during parliamentary sessions (10am Fri. Nov.-June). You can also visit the empty gallery to inspect its cedarwood, portraits and the speaker's silver mace on weekdays, when Sergeant-at-Arms Albert Fox is happy to talk about the House of Assembly and show visitors around.

The Cabinet Building and the Cenotaph

South of the Sessions House sits the **Cabinet Building** (105 Front St., tel. 441/292-5501, fax 441/292-8397, 9am-5pm Mon.-Fri., admission free), where the "Upper House," or Senate, meets every Wednesday morning at 10am (Nov.-July). The imposing two-story building, completed in 1833, is home to the premier's office and headquarters of his cabinet of government ministers, whose navy sedans are usually parked outside.

The Cabinet Building lawn is the venue of the annual November Throne Speech, which the governor delivers before a packed crowd of dignitaries and MPs in hats, topcoats, and tails; Bermuda Regiment soldiers, Band Company, and Corps of Drums; as well hundreds of public onlookers and curious tourists. Here also stands an imposing bronze statue depicting Sally Bassett, a legendary heroine of Bermuda's slavery days. According to folklore, Bassett, a slave, was implicated in the poisoning of her master and his wife, and was publicly burned to death.

Along the lawn's south perimeter stands the 1920 Cenotaph, a limestone monument honoring Bermudian soldiers killed in the two World Wars and other international conflicts. Next to it, on the southeast side of the Cabinet lawn, a polished black granite memorial lists more than 3,000 local war veterans. A solemn Remembrance Day ceremony is held here each November 11, when surviving vets parade down Front Street; the occasion sees wreaths of symbolic poppies laid down and a gun salute fired by the Bermuda Regiment. The day is a public holiday on the island, and hundreds attend the event.

ENTERTAINMENT AND EVENTS

Hamilton is the staging point for numerous big local and international events throughout the year. The city also has a busy nightlife, particularly in the summer, when visitors swell the bars and clubs. Winter can be very quiet during the week, but you can usually count on Bermudians to party on Friday and Saturday nights. Tickets for all major events, as well as movies, can be purchased online at www.ptix.bm and www.bdatix.bm. Check out www.nothingtodoinbermuda.com for the most complete weekly and monthly listings. Highlight events are usually billboarded with lamppost banners throughout the city.

Bars

An urban vibe rocks **Beluga Seafood Bar** (Washington Mall III, 18 Church St. opposite City Hall, tel. 441/542-2859, 11:30am-2:45pm and 6pm-10pm Mon.-Sat.) where owner-manager Matteo Gilardoni and his team welcome newbies as if they were regulars. Located in the mall's basement, its décor is Miami hip—glowing neon, nightclub chandeliers, and white lacquer complement the shots of Beluga Noble Russian vodka, fine champagne, and caviar hors d'oeuvres.

Hamilton newcomer **Red Steakhouse & Bar** (55 Front St., wheelchair-accessible entrance via Reid St., 441/292-7331, www.redbermuda.com, noon-2am Tues.-Fri., 6pm-2am Sat. and Sun.) serves up a sophisticated atmosphere, signature cocktails, an impressive wine list (with more than a dozen wines by the glass) and VIP balcony seating overlooking Hamilton Harbour. Regular live entertainment ranges from stand-up to chill, Ibiza-style tunes care of DJ Felix Tod.

North Hamilton's Revival

"Back o' town," as North Hamilton is known, was long castigated as a drug-ridden, crime-plagued neighborhood with nothing of value to Bermuda travelers. But that reputation is changing as the culturally vibrant neighborhood stakes its future on celebrating the island's black culture and its residents' own architectural, musical, and political achievements.

Court Street was the oft-troubled artery running up from the harborfront—and rival Front Street—through the heart of North Hamilton. Like New York's Harlem, its name became something far greater than a simple geographical locator in the public imagination, a moniker that, for black Bermudians especially, is symbolic of a society ignored during decades of white political and economic control. For many white residents, by contrast, the area is a complete enigma. Long linked to drug-selling, robberies, and dangerous elements (though the truth is that those problems affect every parish), Court Street and North Hamilton were often avoided as a result.

In recent years, grassroots groups have worked to change those perceptions, reinvigorating North Hamilton with cultural centers, public events, and new businesses, plus initiatives to encourage residents to preserve some of the most historic and beautiful architecture on the island. Indeed, the area has been likened to New Orleans's French Quarter. Between King Street to the east, Parson's Road to the north, Cedar Avenue to the west, and Victoria Street to the south, North Hamilton boasts both a vibrant business center and quaint residential lanes, where gingerbread architecture, pastel homes, and quiet walled gardens have been largely undisturbed by the rampant development of the rest of Hamilton. The region counts scores of clothing stores, salons, bakeries, nightclubs, and popular restaurants, which attract patrons from across the island for fresh fish and Caribbean cuisine.

"My roots are here—my grandfather built the First Church of God on Angle Street, so I do have a heritage that binds me to North Hamilton," says Elmore Warren, a neighborhood native who heads up a Court Street-based television station, Fresh TV, and runs an entrepreneurial company called Fresh Creations. "I grew up here and now I work here, so I have a self-interest in figuring out ways to bring value to this area."

Court Street's stigma in recent history stems back to 1977, when televised race riots included a showdown between crowds of fire-bombing black youth and armed police. But residents say they are tired of disparaging attitudes toward their neighborhood, and they feel North Hamilton's time for rejuvenation has come.

"This is the place where cultural tourism should begin," says Warren. "This is the place where revolutionaries were born—the black heroes of Bermuda, the ones who fought for equal rights and desegregation." A plaza at Union and Dundonald Streets is dedicated to the legendary E. F. Gordon, a firebrand lawyer and black-rights pioneer of the 1950s, who rallied black Bermudians and sowed the seeds for the breakthrough Theatre Boycott in 1959, which saw segregation's barriers fall in hotels, restaurants, churches, and other public institutions. North Hamilton's **Pembroke Youth Centre** nurtured Bermuda's only Olympic medalist, boxer Clarence Hill. American social activist Marcus Garvey had an office on Angle Street. And the first black press, the historic **Bermuda Recorder,** was also based here.

Since the government declared North Hamilton an "Empowerment Zone" in 2005, North Ham-

Toast a sunset with the cool crowd at Hamilton's loftiest drinks perch, the rooftop "skybar" of **Muse** (17 Front St. opposite the ferry terminal, tel. 441/296-8788, www.muse.bm, happy hours 5pm-7pm Mon.-Sat., 10am-midnight Mon. Sun..). Themed weekdays include "Taco Tuesdays," "Wine Down Wednesdays," and a DJ plus $5 drinks on Fridays. Among the inspired cocktails: the Ritz Fizz (champagne, amaretto, blue curaçao, lime cordial), Victoria's Secret (vodka, strawberry, Midori, cranberry, Sprite), and Petite Fleur (white rum, Cointreau, grapefruit).

Lunch spot by day, **Lemon Tree Cafe** (7 Queen St., tel. 441/292-0235) is a party place to be on Friday nights, when its happy hour

A North Hamilton mural pays tribute to Bermudian soccer stars.

ilton entrepreneurs have benefited from a concerted effort to bolster the neighborhood via financial advice, financing arrangements, and business and management expertise—elements that for many years were sorely unavailable to black businesspeople in Bermuda. One of the most innovative additions of the 2000s was the opening of **Chewstick,** a foundation launched by artist-musician Gavin Smith to heal racial divisions and inspire youth through the arts. The organization spent its formative years at the corner of Elliot and Courts Streets, attracting audiences to its Friday live bands or Sunday night open-mic sessions at its fire engine-red corner headquarters. Chewstick moved to 81 Front Street in 2015, where it continues to showcase everything from rap and ballet to bagpipes and spoken word.

A visit to North Hamilton should include a tour of the architectural history of Angle Street, Elliott Street, Ewing Street, and Princess Street, where Victorian row housing, wooden verandas, and cute-as-a-button cottages can be found around every corner. Court Street between Victoria and Dundonald Streets is home to a wonderful array of fashion boutiques, music and shoe stores, and several food outlets. Visit the **Caribbean Food Market** (47 Court St., tel. 441/293-9260), where specialty items like cassava, coconut milk, yams, and green seasoning are available.

Indeed, North Hamilton's culinary offerings alone are enough to tempt visitors. **Rotis** (55 Court St., tel. 441/293-7684, rotisbermuda@gmail.com) is famous for its West Indian wraps. **Fish & Tings** (45 Angle St., tel. 441/292-7389) satisfies anyone craving curried fish, barbecued chicken leg, or a side of plantain. Crowds jam **Jamaican Grill** (32 Court St., tel. 441/296-6577) for jerk chicken, oxtail, and brown stew. Don't miss vibrant street markets and family fun days here, when live music, arts and crafts vendors, and food stalls bring flocks of locals and visitors to the area.

(5pm-midnight Fri.) takes flight. A DJ spins for a mixed-age crowd that packs the back parkside patio for sangria, free gourmet nibbles, or mulled wine when the weather turns.

Little Venice Wine Bar (32 Bermudiana Rd., tel. 441/295-3503, noon-1am Mon.-Fri., 6:30pm-1am Sat.) is an offshoot of the popular adjoining restaurant, attracting a more mature crowd than other venues' twenty-somethings; fans of Little Venice come for fine wines, cosmopolitans, and other cocktails, plus tapas ranging from mini-burgers to dumplings, meat and veggie skewers, and a sampling of cheeses. Patrons can sit at tables indoors or out on the patio.

An intimate ambience can be found at the

pocket-sized bar inside **Barracuda Grill** (5 Burnaby Hill, 441/292-1609, www.barracuda-grill.com, 5:30pm-11:30pm daily), where bartender Ryan Gibbons mixes masterly martinis and other classics amid the snug but stylish interior. Downstairs, landmark sister venue **Hog Penny** (5 Burnaby Hill, tel. 441/292-2534, www.hogpennypub.com, 11:30am-1am daily) is a well-loved, British-style pub with draft pints, ciders, rum swizzles, and local craft brews, along with comfort staples like bangers and mash and Cornish pasties. During most of the year, live music is on tap, too.

With its liquid tiles, South Beach vibe, and more than 100 rums on offer, **Rumbar** (29 Victoria St., tel. 441/296-5050, www.irg.bm, noon-11pm Mon.-Fri., 5pm-1am Sat.) has been a hip addition to the local nightlife scene. It's located downstairs from **Victoria Grill.** Couches, an outdoor patio, and a raw bar serving ceviche (and no sushi for a change) attract happy-hour crowds.

Corporate happy hour crowds pour off the streetside patios Friday evenings at the chic **Port O' Call** (87 Front St., tel. 441/295-5373, www.portocall.bm, 4pm-7pm). Mix with software engineers and private bankers over specials on wines, beers, and custom cocktails.

Like its moniker, **Ten** (10 Dundonald St., tel. 441/295-0857, www.ten.bm, happy hour 4pm-7pm Mon.-Fri., 7am-9pm Mon.-Fri., 8am-2:30pm Sat.) is Euro-cool, with floor-to-ceiling artwork, couch-and-cube seating, and an alfresco patio that has made it one of the city's favorite café-bars. Tucked away on a block few tourists usually make it to, the venue sits on the street level of a condominium building that blazed a residential trail into the city's northwest. A well-stocked wine cellar, elegant tapas, and award-winning cocktails attract a full house for weekday happy hours.

Friday night happy hour brings regulars to **Coconut Rock** (Williams House, 20 Reid St., tel. 441/292-1043, 11:30am-3am Mon.-Sat., 6pm-1am Sun.), where a DJ or karaoke provide entertainment. Clientele can partake of bleu cheese burgers and other main menu items or visit the Yashi Sushi Bar in the back.

The Docksider Pub & Restaurant (121 Front St., tel. 441/296-3333, www.dockies.com, 11am-2am Mon.-Fri., 10am-3am Sat.-Sun.) is one of the hot spots among Bermuda's youth, who are attracted by reasonable drink prices, pizza, and pub grub. The popular sports bar opens for live games shown on its big-screen TVs weekend mornings, when the crowd consists largely of bleary-eyed expats eager to catch a British soccer showdown.

Lively happy hours, reasonable prices, and televised sports bring a full house to **Bermuda Bistro at The Beach** (103 Front St. at Parliament St., tel. 441/292-0219, www.thebeachbermuda.com, 10am-3am daily).

On either side of Burnaby Hill, Front Street's **Flanagan's Irish Pub** (Emporium Building, 69 Front St., tel. 441/295-8299, www.flanagans.bm, 10:30am-1am Mon.-Fri., 9am-1am Sat. and Sun) and **Pickled Onion** (53 Front St., tel. 441/295-2263, www.thepickledonion.com, 11am-1am daily) are popular among both locals and visitors for nighttime carousing, and both have panoramic terraces overlooking the harbor. Flanagan's is an especially good venue for viewing the finish line of January's Front Street Mile race. Flanagan's has an adjoining sports bar, **Outback** (opens at 5pm Mon.-Thurs., 11am Fri., Sat., and Sun.), with 22 high-definition TV screens, including a 63-inch giant and individual screens with remote controls at each booth.

The Captain's Sports Bar & Grill (Reid St. at Washington Ln., tel. 441/293-9546) and **Casey's Cocktail Lounge** (25 Queen St., tel. 441/292-9994, 10am-10pm Mon-Sat.) both attract a very Bermudian crowd, especially on Friday afternoons before public holiday weekends.

Clubs

The Club (12 Bermudiana Rd., tel. 441/747-7777, www.theclub.bm, 9:30pm-1am Wed.-Thurs., 9:30pm-3am Fri.-Sat., 10:30pm-3am Sun.) sets the bar for upscale nightclubbing,

A New-Look Harborfront?

Hamilton's waterfront has been the focus of much debate over the past 20 years, with assorted architects, city planners, and creative members of the public proposing plans on how to make the area more people-friendly.

Former premier and millionaire developer Sir John Swan hired architects to draw up a full blueprint of his vision for the harborfront area—one that would do away with the noisy cargo docks and replace them with marinas, boardwalks, and a casino.

While locals like the sound of a harborside promenade, reaction was mixed to the casino and the container port relocation; the main problem with the latter is that parts of the island's coastline would have to be destroyed to accommodate the docks elsewhere.

The public brainstorming also prompted the Corporation of Hamilton to devise its own development plan that included land reclamation, a new cruise ship jetty, an open-air amphitheater, a park, and restaurants, but a political row over the tendering process in late 2013 put it on hold.

with a mature crowd and three DJs playing house sounds of London, Ibiza, and Miami. Harking back to the company's popular 1980s venue of the same name just down the block, MEF Ltd. reopened The Club in the summer of 2014 with an ultracool, neon-lit interior and a smart-casual dress code. ID is required.

Cosmopolitan Night Club (95 Front St, tel. 441/705-2582, info@thecellar.bm, 9pm-3am Mon.-Sat.) draws dancing crowds of late-night partiers year-round to its indoor/outdoor venue at Bermuda House Lane linking Front and Reid Streets. Themed evenings like "2 for 1 Fridays" and "Happy Hour Saturdays," as well as popular DJs, make it a lively and busy place.

Perenially voted the island's "best pick-up bar," **Café Cairo** (93 Front St., tel. 441/295-5155, cafecairo@northrock.bm, 5pm-3am Tues.-Sat.), has long been popular for after-hours schmoozing. While the venue has won raves for its Middle Eastern restaurant, it morphs into a club after 10pm, when the DJ arrives and devoted night owls hit the dance floor.

North Hamilton's **Spinning Wheel** (33 Court St., tel. 441/292-7799, 3pm-3am Sun. Thurs., 1pm-3am Fri.-Sat.) and **Place's Place** (43 Dundonald St. at E. F. Gordon Square, tel. 441/293-9268) are busy weekend hangouts.

For authentically grassroots entertainment with your beer or vino, there's nowhere in Bermuda quite like the **Chewstick Neo-Griot Lounge & Café** (81 Front St.., tel. 441/292-2439, www.chewstick.org, 6pm-9pm Tues.-Sat., 8pm-1am Sun., closed Mon.) where a diverse crowd enjoys a cozy setting, full bar, and free Wifi.

Cinemas

Hamilton has two cinemas, both of which show major box-office releases, including 3D blockbusters and the occasional Oscar-nominated indie. Twice-nightly showings, plus weekend matinees, keep movies around for a week or two. Tickets can be purchased at the door or online via the cinemas' websites or www.ptix.bm.

The Speciality Cinema and Grill (12 Church St., tel. 441/292-2135, www.specialitycinema.bm, 11am-9pm Mon.-Wed., 11am-10pm Thurs.-Fri., 9am-10pm Sat., 12pm-8pm Sun.) has two cinemas within its complex, both with comfortable seating and surround sound, plus a café and deli where moviegoers buy tickets and popcorn and other snacks. You can also sit down for a cold drink or hot meal (roast beef, grilled chicken, fish sandwiches) before the show.

The Liberty Theatre (49 Union Square, between Victoria St. and Dundonald St., tel. 441/292-7296, www.libertytheatre.bm) is a larger venue with a regular-sized screen, though the surroundings are not quite up to par with the average North American multiplex. After a good run at The Liberty, films usually head west to Dockyard for a second run at The Liberty's sister cinema, The Neptune.

Theater, Music, and Dance

Plays, musicals, dance recitals, and other live performances are held in Hamilton throughout the year. Check www.nothingtodoinbermuda.com or *The Royal Gazette* to see what's going on. Schedules and online tickets are available at www.bdatix.bm and www.ptix.bm.

Daylesford Theatre (Washington St. opposite Victoria Park, tel. 441/292-0848, bar tel. 441/295-5584, bar hours from 5pm Mon.-Fri., www.bmds.bm) is headquarters of the Bermuda Musical and Dramatic Society (BMDS), which stages regular plays throughout the year, as well as the popular Christmas pantomime at City Hall.

The **City Hall and Arts Centre** (17 Church St.) is the island's major venue for theatricals and performing arts such as dance, theater, and orchestral performances, including many of the international acts that visit for the Bermuda Festival of the Performing Arts (Jan.-Mar.).

Bermudian singers, poets, rappers, musicians, dancers, and spoken-word performers display their talents at **Chewstick** (81 Front St., tel. 441/292-2439, www.chewstick.org, office 9am-5pm Mon.-Fri.). The organization offers a diverse and thoroughly inclusive window into Bermuda's avant-garde arts scene, hosting Sunday night open-mic jam sessions and showcases of everything from bagpipes to hip-hop at its Front Street lounge. Founded in 2002, Chewstick has won kudos in recent years for creative programs and events aimed at using the arts to heal social problems in the Bermudian community. Check out Chewstick's website for performance dates and schedules.

Festivals and Events

BERMUDA FESTIVAL OF THE PERFORMING ARTS

The New Year brings the **Bermuda Festival of the Performing Arts** (tel. 441/295-1291, www.bermudafestival.org), a two-month cultural showcase of top international acts, from contemporary dance troupes and circuses to ballet and orchestral performances. Several venues are used, but most performances take place in the evenings at Hamilton City Hall and Arts Centre.

BERMUDA INTERNATIONAL FILM FESTIVAL

The March **Bermuda International Film Festival** (tel. 441/293-3456, fax 441/293-7769, www.biff.bm) adds an unusual touch of bohemia to Hamilton's normally conservative ambience, as black-garbed twentysomethings from the West Village and Hollywood wander around incongruously between screenings. The showcase has made a name for itself on the world's celluloid circuit and draws not only award-winning indie directors from the United States, Africa, and Eastern Europe, but international film financiers intrigued by Bermuda's offshore benefits. BIFF has also drawn a few celebrity visitors, with appearances by Michael Douglas, Jim Sheridan, Carrie Fisher, Willem Dafoe, and the late Michael Clarke Duncan.

HARBOUR NIGHTS

Held on Wednesday evenings 7pm-9pm throughout the high season, this crowded street festival includes arts and crafts stalls, bouncy castles and train rides for kids, alfresco food, and live performances by Bermuda bands and gombey troupes. The fun takes place on Front Street, which is closed to traffic between Parliament and Par-la-Ville Streets. Reid Street is also shut down for the evening.

BERMUDA DAY PARADE

The Bermuda Day Parade on May 24 is the island's version of Caribbean Carnival.

Following a half-marathon, which travels on alternate years from either the West or East Ends through Front Street's cheering crowds to a Pembroke finish, an hours-long parade of majorettes, gombeys, decorated floats, dance troupes, and other community performers winds through the city. Families stake out their seats the night before to get a good viewing spot, and then camp out on sidewalks most of the day.

OTHER EVENTS

The **Queen's Birthday Parade** in June brings colonial pomp and ceremony to Front Street to mark the British monarch's special day. A gun salute is followed by a marching parade featuring the Bermuda Regiment Band Company and Corps of Drums.

In December, kids and parents pack Front and Church Streets for the festive **Santa Claus Parade,** which features colorful illuminated floats, parish majorettes, gombeys, and Santa riding on a vintage fire engine. "Elves" toss bags of candy to onlookers. The **Christmas Boat Parade** that traverses Hamilton Harbour is also a holiday must-see—it's a magical parade of yachts, barges, charter boats, and pleasure craft decked out in cleverly themed light displays. The best viewing is from Front Street docks or restaurant terraces and along Harbour Road.

SHOPPING

The bulk of Hamilton's retail stores are found along the length of Reid, Front, Queen, Burnaby, and Church Streets, as well as Court Street in North Hamilton. There are also several malls, which link these major thoroughfares and are packed with boutiques and shops of all kinds. These include the **Walker Arcade** (between Front and lower Reid), which also connects to the **Old Cellar** (off Front St.); **Butterfield Walkway** (Front St., alongside Butterfield Bank); the **Emporium** (69 Front St., east of Butterfield Walkway); the **Bermudiana Arcade** (west off Queen St.); **Windsor Place** (east off Queen St.), and the **Washington Mall** (with several floors of shops extending between Reid St. and Church St.).

Most Hamilton stores open at 10am, though a few open as early as 8:30am., and operate until 5pm or 5:30pm. Special Christmas season (Fri. night) and summerlong Harbour Nights (Wed. only) hours mean some Front Street, Queen Street, and Reid Street stores stay open later. Sunday afternoon shopping also happens occasionally in busy seasons.

Reid Street is Hamilton's busiest shopping area.

Virtually all retail stores, save a few smaller, homespun outlets, accept major credit cards. Many carry store details and post special offers and promotional events on Facebook, and a few are also on Twitter.

Books

Bermuda Book Store (3 Queen St., near Heyl's Cor. at Front St. junction, tel. 441/295-3698, www.bermudabookstore.com, 10am-6pm Mon.-Sat.) embodies the best elements of a successful, independent book shop, from its wooden floors and rambling rows of carefully curated titles to owner-manager Hannah Willmott's precociously well-read staff. The store is housed in a historic building it has inhabited for decades. Bookworms will enjoy browsing through new fiction, bestsellers, beach reads, and a comprehensive selection of Bermuda editions. There's also a well-stocked section for kids and teens.

Brown & Co.'s **The Bookmart** (35 Front St., tel. 441/279-5443, www.phoenixstores.com, 8:30am-6pm Mon.-Sat., 1pm-5pm Sun.) is a good place to find the latest best seller, as well as Bermuda publications, international magazines, coffee-table books, cookbooks, and popular kids' series, like the United Kingdom's Mr. Men collection. Its well-stocked children's section is one of the island's best. Alongside it on the top level of the department store is a **Buzz Café** outlet serving java, smoothies, wraps, sandwiches, and cool drinks. Take your snack out on the veranda, which has sweeping views of Front Street and the harbor. It's also a convenient place to wait for your ferry, as it's located just across the street from the main terminal.

Clothes and Shoes

While many Bermudians beef up their wardrobes on overseas shopping sprees every year, there's still plenty to please fashionistas in Hamilton's stores. Some of Front Street's old-money department stores are now gone, but smaller city boutiques like Atelerie, Max Mara, and Lusso now draw shoppers.

Atelerie (9 Reid St., tel. 441/296-0280, www.atelerie.com) moved into Hamilton's center in 2013 after building a loyal trendsetter following with less-accessible outlets in Paget and the city's outskirts. The current multibrand boutique is small but well stocked, with designer labels such as DVF, Rag and Bone, Paige Denim, Rebecca Taylor, Joie, Helmut Lang, and Velvet. Artist-photographer Heather Macdonald has her finger on the pulse of what women really want and the fast evolution of her brainchild proves her instincts have been faultless. Cozy PJs, seamless lingerie, silk scarves, scented candles, and jewelery galore make it a trove of endless treasures.

For that Pucci scarf, Prada clutch, or pair of Jimmy Choos, join high-end mavens at **Lusso** (51 Front St., tel. 441/295-6734, lusso@tess.bm), purveyor of the latest catwalk designs, including evening and corporate suits, slacks, and swimsuits, plus luxury labels such as Rebecca Minkoff and L. K. Bennett. Ask to be shown the sale products, including top designer shoes and bags, as discounts sometimes are unmarked. Its sister store, **Boutique C.C.** (1 Front St. W., tel. 441/295-3935), is where locals shop for floral cocktail dresses, eveningwear, and career suits—at reasonable prices.

Owned by the same group, **Sisley** (7 Front St. at Par-la-Ville Rd., tel. 441/295-2112, ext. 121), **Benetton** (24 Reid St., tel. 441/295-2112, ext. 105, www.calypsobermuda.com), **Max Mara** (57 Front St., tel. 441/295-2112, ext. 130), and **French Connection** (15 Reid St. at Washington Ln., tel. 441/295-2112, www.calypsobermuda.com) all carry style-savvy urban selections, as does Italian knitwear and fashion brand **Stefanel** (12 Walker Arcade at Reid St., tel. 441/295-5698). **A. S. Cooper & Sons** (59 Front St., tel. 441/295-3961, www.ascoopers.bm) and British bastion **Marks & Spencer** (28 Reid St., tel. 441/295-5516) have more mainstream fashion offerings, including corporate and evening wear, shoes, nightwear, and accessories.

Go-to men's stores are few, but include **A. S. Cooper Man** (29 Front St., tel. 441/295-3961, www.ascooper.bm), **Gibbons Company** (21

Reid St., tel. 441/295-0022, www.gibbons.bm), and **French Connection** (15 Reid St., tel. 441/295-0022, www.calypsobermuda.com). Genuine Bermuda linen-blend shorts (pink, yellow, red, $59.95) can be found at **English Sports Shop** (49 Front St., tel. 441/295-2672, 9:30am-5:30pm Mon.-Sat.), along with linen and wool blazers ($250-275), Bermuda silk ties (sporting longtails, horse and carriage, and Hamilton's pastel skyline), a Nautica boutique, and conservative women's fashions.

Bermudians head to **Calypso** (45 Front St., tel. 441/295-2112, www.calypsobermuda.com) every spring for their new bathing suits—everything from string bikinis to racing backs. Head upstairs for discounts on Eileen Fisher, Max Mara, and evening wear. Beach bums and surfer dudes also love **Makin' Waves** (Chevron Building, 11 Church St., tel. 441/292-4609, www.makinwaves.bm), a 3,000-square-foot store stocked with flip-flops and swimwear; Maui Jim, VonZipper, and Oakley shades; standup paddleboards (SUP); scuba and snorkeling equipment; and accessories from Mares, US Divers, Sherwood, O'Neill, and Body Glove, plus casual wear by Billabong, Rip Curl, Roxy, Quiksilver, Patagonia, North Face, and Columbia.

For shoes and handbags, **Perry Collections** (2 Reid St., tel. 441/296-0014) has the most coveted selection, with designer names like Badgley Mischka, Kate Spade, and Stuart Weitzman. For upscale European styles, visit **Voilà** (Butterfield Walkway, 67 Front St., tel. 441/295-2112, ext. 120, www.calypsobermuda.com). **Colosseum** (80 Reid St, tel. 441/297-2012, colosseumltd@yahoo.com) carries trendsetting shoes and bags from Italy, as well as Louis Vuitton bags on consignment. The Walkway **Nine West** (23 Reid St., tel. 441/295-0022) and **Trends** (22 Reid St., tel. 441/295-6420) stock a full range of shoes and bags. **W. J. Boyle & Son** (31 Queen St., tel. 441/295-1887) is the island's leading footwear chain, carrying a wide range of men's, women's, and children's styles; one of its Hamilton sister shops, **Sports Locker** (Windsor Pl., 18 Queen St., tel. 441/292-3300), stocks Merrell hiking boots, Teva sandals, Sperry boat shoes, and running and fashion sneakers. **Casual Footware** (14 Parson's Rd., North Hamilton, tel. 441/295-9968, 10am-5pm Mon.-Fri., 1pm-3pm Sun.) sells comfortable Birkenstock, Mephisto, and Hogan footwear for men, women, and kids.

Jeans purists, male and female, will love the racks of True Religion and Diesel styles at **Mambo** (Old Cellar Ln., Front St., tel. 441/295-3003), while teens and club-hoppers gravitate to the more affordable **Zig-Zag Boutique** (31 Dundonald St., tel. 441/295-0785).

For lingerie, **Women's Secret** (14 Reid St., tel. 441/295-2112, ext. 150, www.womensecret.com) and **Gibbons Company** (21 Reid St., tel. 441/295-0022, www.gibbons.bm) are the island's primary purveyors.

Perfume and Cosmetics

Long an East End landmark, **The Bermuda Perfumery** opened an elegant little Hamilton boutique in 2014 (Butterfield Walkway, 67 Front St., 441/296-2885, www.lilibermuda.com) to offer more clientele its island-inspired fragrances for men and women. Several other stores sell designer perfumes and cosmetics. **MAC Boutique** (53 Front St., tel. 441/295-8843) is staffed by enthusiastic young makeup artists. The large department store **Gibbons Company** (21 Reid St., tel. 441/295-0022, www.gibbons.bm) carries most of the major cosmetics lines, at U.S.-competitive prices. **A. S. Cooper & Sons** department store (59 Front St., tel. 441/295-3961, www.ascooper.bm) also has a large, well-stocked floor of major brands, including Clarins, Dior, Bobbi Brown, Shu Uemura, Clinique, Estée Lauder, and La Prairie. **Strands** (31 Reid St., tel. 441/295-0935, www.strands.bm, 8:45am-6pm Mon.-Sat.) carries Clarins exclusively and its knowledgeable staff is able to offer product advice, as well as on-site skin spa treatments. **Brown & Co.** (35 Front St., tel. 441/279-5524, www.brown.bm) stocks a full range of most designer perfumes on its convenient Front Street level.

Bargain Buys

Bargain-hunters scouting for great buys on designer labels, shoes, or cutting-edge fashions will usually be disappointed in Bermuda. The island carries such a limited and expensive range of clothing and footwear that even average Bermudians travel abroad frequently to load up their wardrobes in U.S. and Canadian malls—a longtime trend the Bermuda Chamber of Commerce tries to combat with its "Buy Bermuda" campaign.

Of course, if you're simply in the mood for fashion shopping, and not too worried about comparing price tags, you will find plenty to spend on. The good news is that Hamilton's once-stuffy, though beloved, department stores are being forced to compete—both by Bermudians' foreign retail therapy and the advent of designer boutiques, which have sprung up around town.

Truly good buys, however, are to be had in perfumes, European cosmetics, jewelry (mostly conservatively designed gold and silver), and fine china and crystal. Wedgwood, Kosta Boda, Orrefors, Hermès, Royal Doulton, and Limoges can be found at several Front Street retailers, at prices competitive with, or better than, those in the United States. Scottish woolens and hand-embroidered Irish linens, which are hard to find in North America or very expensive, are also worth stocking up on.

Although they used to be sold in Hamilton, duty-free items are now only available at **Bermuda Duty Free** (Departures Hall, tel. 441/293-2870), the retail outlet at L. F. Wade International Airport. Popular merchandise includes the island's hallmark Gosling's Black Seal Rum, rum cakes, Outerbridge's sherry peppers, and perfumes.

Gifts and Souvenirs

Pulp & Circumstance (4 Washington Ln., tel. 441/542-9586) is a mecca for soaps and bath products, bags, stuffed toys, novelty items, baby shower gifts, and beautiful wrapping paper and greeting cards.

The Island Shop (3 Queen St., tel. 441/292-5292, www.islandexports.com) carries artist Barbara Finsness's hand-designed tablecloths, ceramics, pillowcases, handbags, linens, and Christmas ornaments, as well as gorgeous Venetian glass jewelry.

A Front Street landmark, the quaint little **Irish Linen Shop** (31 Front St., tel. 441/295-4089, www.theirishlinenshop.com) sells Madeira hand embroideries, table and bed linens, children's clothes, and handkerchiefs by Souleiado, Le Jacquard Français, and Yves Delorme. You can also find one-of-a-kind gifts here, including soaps, candles, toys, exquisite Bermuda cedar trays, doorstops, and goblets made by craftsman Jeremy Johnson.

Proceeds from **Trustworthy Gift Shop** (Old Cellar Ln., 47 Front St., tel. 441/296-4164, www.bnt.bm), which stocks Bermuda books, Christmas ornaments, and local arts and crafts, help support Bermuda National Trust's historic homes and nature reserves.

Sporting Goods

Sportseller (Washington Mall, lower level, 9 Reid St., tel. 441/295-2692, sales@sportseller.bm, 10am-5pm Mon.-Sat.) is the island's premier running and triathlon store, with shoes and apparel by Nike, Asics, Saucony, BOA, New Balance, and Under Armour for women and men; Danskin yoga gear; racing suits and goggles by Nike, Speedo, and Tyr; and CamelBak hiking packs, stopwatches, backpacks, reflector vests, hydration belts, and heart-rate monitors. You can register for local road race events at the shop.

Pro Shop (17 Reid St., at the corner of Washington Ln., tel. 441/292-7487, proshop@ibl.bm) stocks soccer, tennis, and running gear, including Adidas, Reebok, and Umbro brands.

International Sports Shop (Washington Mall, upper floor—new phase, tel. 441/295-4183, www.issl.bm) carries soccer and other sporting gear and clothing, fitness equipment, and trophies and awards.

Cuban Cigars

Cuban cigars are highly popular Bermuda souvenirs—even though they're no longer illicit.

Americans don't have to risk confiscation, mega fines, or criminal prosecution anymore—until late 2014, though, taking them back into the United States was an offense under economic sanctions enforced against Cuba since 1963.

After President Obama normalized U.S. diplomacy with Cuba in late 2014, ending 50 years of frozen relations, retailers say Americans are still their best customers, either taking the opportunity to enjoy their Romeo y Julietas and Cohibas during their vacation, or taking home stockpiles in their luggage.

Cigar retailers include **Chatham House** (Front St., at the corner of Burnaby Hill, tel. 441/292-8422, 8am-6pm Mon.-Thurs., 8am-5pm Fri,-Sat.), a specialty tobacco shop that stocks Punch, Partagas, Romeo y Julieta, H. Upmann, Montecristo, Cohiba, and Bolivar. **Churchill's** (Duke of York St., St. George, tel. 441/297-1650, 8am-9pm Mon.-Sat.) carries a full range of Cuban, Dominican, Costa Rican, Nicaraguan, and Jamaican cigars. **Cuarenta Bucaneros** (Continental Building, corner of Cedar Ave. and Church St., 2nd floor, tel. 441/295-4523, 9am-5pm Mon.-Fri.) sells boxes of 25 cigars ($175-340) in top Cuban brands, including Cohiba, Montecristo, and Romeo y Julieta.

The **Upstairs Golf and Tennis Shop** (26 Church St., tel. 441/295-5161, alan@upstairsgolf.bm) stocks big-name brands like Ping, Callaway, and Titleist, including clubs, rackets, and accessories for both sports.

Downstairs in the same building, **Flybridge Tackle** (26 Church St., tel. 441/295-1845, rrego@knickknack.com) is the local representative for Penn reels and rods, and sportfishing products by Mustad, Yo-Zuri, Rupp, and Victorinox.

Sports R Us (61 Church St., tel. 441/292-1891, 8:30am-6pm Mon.-Sat.) is the island's largest sports store, with everything from weightlifting equipment to running, golf, soccer, tennis, and competitive swim gear. There's also a large range of shoes, beach slippers, and waterproof slides.

Winners' Edge Bike Shop (73 Front St., tel. 441/295-6012, www.winnersedge.bm) stocks Trek, Gary Fisher, Lemond, Scott USA, and Cannondale bicycles, as well as gear, clothing, and accessories. An on-site shop does repairs.

Bicycle Works (13 Tumkins Ln., tel. 441/297-8356, www.bicycleworks.bm) is the island's authorized dealer of Specialized brand cycles, and also carries accessories, clothing, and shoes for all ages. Repairs can also be done on-site.

CB Dive Shop (15 Burnaby Street, tel. 441/292-3839, cbwholesaleanddive@logic.bm) stocks top-brand masks, fins, snorkels, wetsuits, and water shoes.

China and Crystal

Historic **Bluck's** (4 Front St., tel. 441/295-5367) is the island's oldest vendor of fine china and crystal. Opened in 1844, the forest-green cottage-style building wedged between Front Street's financial and insurance blocks is famous for both classic and contemporary designs by Kosta Boda, Baccarat, Herend, Royal Doulton, and Spode.

Department store **A. S. Cooper & Sons** (59 Front St., tel. 441/295-3961) is a wedding registry go-to, thanks to major lines of china and crystal from Europe and around the world.

Jewelry, Watches, and Sunglasses

Treasures inside **Alexandra Mosher Studio Jewellery** (Washington Mall West, lower level, 7 Reid St., tel. 441/236-9009, alexandramosher.com, 9:30am-5:30pm Mon.-Sat.) are handcrafted by the Best of Bermuda Award-winning artist in sterling silver and gold, her designs inspired by island flora and fauna—and many incorporating Bermuda's hallmark pink sand.

Another contemporary addition to Bermuda's jewelry scene, **Atlantic Jewellery Studio** (Washington Mall, lower level, 9 Reid St., tel. 441/542-1554, www.atlanticjewellery.com) features the work of gemologist and metalsmith Jacquie Lohan, who also blends island motifs and materials (beach sand) into her award-winning creations for men and women. The island's two largest retailers for jewelry and watches are **Crisson** (55 Front St. and 16 Queen St., tel. 441/295-2351, www.crisson.com) and **Astwood Dickinson** (83-85 Front St., opposite No. 6 Shed, tel. 441/292-5805, www.astwooddickinson.com). Bermuda-themed gold pieces featuring the local onion, kites, and the Bermudiana flower can be found at the latter, while both carry major brand names, including Rolex, Tag Heuer, Paloma Picasso, Tiffany & Co., Cartier, Omega, David Yurman, Pandora, Marco Bicego, Roberto Coin, and Mont Blanc.

Walker Christopher (9 Front St., tel. 441/295-1466, walkerchris@cwbda.bm) is known for its own designs in fine jewelry, especially a beautiful collection of sterling silver Christmas ornaments featuring Bermuda icons like gombeys and angelfish. A new edition is created each year.

Swiss Timing (95 Front St., tel. 441/295-1376) specializes in European watch brands, including Zenith, Concord, and Certina.

Gem Cellar (Old Cellar Ln., 47 Front St., tel. 441/292-3042, www.gemcellar.bm) makes Bermuda charms and custom-designed pieces, and also does valuations and repairs.

E. R. Aubrey Jewellers (101 Front St., tel. 441/296-3171, and 19 Queen St., tel. 441/295-3506, www.bermudaluckystone.com) manufactures and imports sterling silver and titanium, diamond rings, pendants, earrings, gemstones, and pearl and create-your-own designs.

Style mavens seeking eyewear will find good choices at several Hamilton locations. Opened by actor Michael Douglas and reggae artist Collie Buddz (both Bermudians) in 2014, **The Sunglass and Watch Shop** (13 Reid St., tel. 441/292-7933) stocks designer brands such as Gucci, Ray-Ban, Tom Ford, Dior, Michael Kors, and Maui Jim. **Eyes On Sail On** (Washington Mall West, lower level, 7 Reid St., tel. 441/295-0808, 9:30am-5pm Mon.-Fri., 9am-5pm Sat.) stocks Ray-Ban, Tory Burch, Maui Jim, Gucci, and other major brands, along with Helly Hansen and Patagonia rain jackets and outdoor wear. **Makin' Waves** (31 Queen St., at Church

Alexandra Mosher sells award-winning jewelry at her Washington Mall boutique.

St., tel. 441/292-4609, www.makinwaves.bm) has Maui Jim, VonZipper, and Oakley shades. **Argus Sunwear** (Melbourne House, 11 Parliament St. at Victoria St., tel. 441/295-7861), a 2013 spinoff of a nearby optometry business, offers Oliver Peoples, Dolce & Gabbana, Coach and Prada shades at its corner boutique.

Technology

All things technological cost substantially more in Bermuda than on the mainland, but for any techie needs you may have while in Bermuda, there are ample retailers to keep you connected. For Apple products and accessories, visit authorized reseller **iClick** (Williams House, 20 Reid St, tel. 441/542-5425, www.iclickbermuda.bm), whose gurus can help you with iTunes gift cards, iPhones, iPods, iPads, and MacBooks, as well as gadget cases, laptop backpacks, and Beats and Bose headphones. Its parent store, **The Complete Office** (Kenwood Building, 17 Reid St., tel. 441/292-4333, www.tco.bm), sits directly opposite and, along with Apple inventory, also deals in Sony, Compaq, Hewlett-Packard, and other brands. **P-tech** (3 Reid St., tel. 441/295-5496, www.ptech.bm) is a general electronics store, offering cameras, MP3 players, cell phone accessories, and photo frames and albums, with brands including Nokia, Nikon, Motorola, Samsung, and Sony. An online prints and photo cards service is also located inside. **Computer Solutions** (7 Victoria St., tel. 441/297-3331, www.computersolutions.bm) stocks Toshiba laptops, HP desktop computers, Blu-ray disc players, cables, surge protectors, speakers, and software.

Leisure Time (28 Queen St., tel. 441/296-4386, www.leisure.bm, 10am-10pm Mon.-Sat., 1pm-6pm Sun.) has a full range of movies on DVD and Blu-ray disc for rent or sale, plus games for PlayStation 3 and 4, Xbox 360, and Wii, along with a bounty of movie munchies.

Alongside Hamilton's bus terminal, **Audio-Visual Electronics** (4 Washington St., tel. 441/292-1354, 10am-6pm Mon.-Sat.) deals in televisions, DVDs, Blu-ray players, and mobile phones and cellular accessories, including Apple and Samsung brands.

For Kids

Several stores will interest kids and their parents. Favorites include: **Treats of Bermuda** (Washington Mall, 7 Reid St., tel. 441/296-1123) for candy, Klutz games kits, Lego, and Thomas the Tank Engine; **The Annex** (upstairs in the Phoenix Centre, 3 Reid St., tel. 441/279-5410), where Lego, Barbie, candy, and toys can also be found; **Pulp & Circumstance** (4 Washington Ln., tel. 441/292-9586), a treasure trove of stuffed animals, nursery lamps, and upscale baby gifts; **Otto Wurz** (3-5 Front St., tel. 441/295-1247), at the corner of Front Street and Bermudiana Road, home of beautiful wooden handmade toys, silver spoons, dollhouses, piggybanks, puppets, and dress-up hats to suit any occasion or costume; and **Daisy & Mac** (27 Queen St., tel. 441/295-7477, www.daisyandmac.com), with brands including Lego, Playmobil, Air Fix, Hot Wheels, Barbie, and Mattel, plus shoes and clothes for young children. **People's Pharmacy** (62 Victoria St., tel. 441/292-7527, www.peoplespharmacy.bm) has one of the best children's toy sections, with Lego, Playmobil, board games, arts and crafts, and baby gear, as well as candy and chocolate.

Gibbons Company (21 Reid St., tel. 441/295-0022, www.gibbons.bm, 9:30am-6pm Mon.-Sat., 1pm-5pm Sun.) has a large clothing and toys department for children and babies near its Church Street entrance, opposite the main bus terminal—including a Gap boutique that opened in 2014 and a wide selection of toys and accessories.

For stylish European clothes for kids, don't miss **Benetton** (24 Reid St., upstairs, tel. 441/295-2112), which stocks fashionable shoes and well-made boys' and girls' cotton and wool outfits. **The Irish Linen Shop** (31 Front St., tel. 441/295-4089), a fixture of Front Street for over a century, sells hand-stitched babies' layette sets, embroidered dresses, booties, and other precious gift items. **English Sports Shop** (49 Front St., tel. 441/295-2672) also has a children's department, with preppy woolens, golf shirts, and turtlenecks, while its sister store **Marks & Spencer** (28 Reid St., tel. 441/295-0031) has a great selection of the UK brand's kids' clothes, including bathrobes, slippers, socks, and undergarments. The **W. J. Boyle & Son** outlet in eastern Hamilton (70 Church St. East, tel. 441/295-1887) is kid-focused, with socks, leather and outdoor sandals, boots, school shoes, and running sneakers.

SPORTS AND RECREATION

The **Island Tour Centre** (Albuoy's Point, 5 Point Pleasant Park, tel. 441/236-1300, fax 441/296-4661, www.islandtourcentre.com, 8am-6pm daily summer, 9am-4pm daily winter) acts as a centralized booking agent for all kinds of water-based and landlubber activities islandwide, including scuba dives, private sailing charters, kayak and Jet Ski tours, flyboarding, powerboating, eco-expeditions, horseback riding, booze cruises, parasailing, and glass-bottomed boat tours. The center represents more than 20 vendors. Check out the wide assortment of brochures and flyers inside to choose your adventure, or view options online via the Island Tour Centre website. Payment is required at reservation, whether booked by phone, email, or online.

Popular land-based activities include walking tours that allow you to explore Hamilton streets on foot. Or you can rent bicycles to get a workout while you're on holiday (though high humidity and heat may deter all but the hardy in summertime). If you're more in the mood for relaxing, the city has several spas where you can enjoy a treatment and chill out.

Scuba and Water Sports

No scuba operators depart from Hamilton and most water sports outfits are run out of Dockyard. But several sail and boat tours depart from Albuoy's Point or alongside the ferry terminal on Front Street and can be booked and paid either directly or through the adjacent Island Tour Centre. Albuoy's pickups can usually be arranged with private charters, even if their vessels are kept elsewhere. Some of the best are: catamaran cruises aboard ***Chelonia*** (tel. 441/334-9771, www.chelonia-bermuda.com), ***Restless Native*** (tel. 441/531-8149, restless@logic.bm), and ***Sally Bum Bum*** (tel. 441/335-3099, www.sallybumbum.com); sail charters on a 51-foot ketch run by **Sail Bermuda** (tel. 441/737-2993, www.sailbermuda.com); and glass-bottomed boat tours aboard ***Reef Explorer*** (tel. 441/535-7333, www.bermudareefexplorer.com).

Crewed motoryacht charters, offering full catering and watersports, are run from Hamilton Harbour aboard the three "lady boats" of **Tam-Marina** (tel. 441/236-0127, www.ladyboats.com)—motoryachts ***Lady Tamara*** and ***Lady Charlotte*** and sportfisherman ***Boss Lady;*** Captain Dean DaCosta's 75-foot motoryacht ***Spellbound*** (tel. 441/236-6556 or 441/505-2628, www.spellbound.bm); and the sumptuous, 100-foot ***Venetian*** (tel. 441/704-3000, www.diningbermuda.com), owned and run by the MEF Enterprises restaurant group. Multiple Best of Bermuda Award-winner ***ÜberVida*** (tel. 441/236-2222, www.ubervida.net, pickup from No. 1 Dock, Front St., east of the ferry terminal) is a 70-foot, multideck converted catamaran that has become a big favorite among Bermudians and visitors alike for its 90-minute Friday sunset cruises (with DJ and cocktails), all-day excursions to Bermuda's northern barrier reef, and themed special events (reggae, Cup Match, and Oktoberfest cruises). With capacity for 150 guests, it's also a top choice for private corporate parties, weddings, and charters for other celebrations.

Prefer to do your own thing? Popular (self-drive) rental boat company **Aquatic Bermuda** (tel. 441/236-2200 or 441/747-9443, www.aquaticbermuda.com) lets you be the captain, renting Beachcat pontoon boats with storage for picnics, snorkeling gear, and water toys—perfect for a whole day or half day of exploration. Hamilton Harbour, the Great Sound and its "Paradise Lakes" (tranquil bays between numerous islands), and the Sandys shoreline are perfect for this and all are accessible from a Hamilton starting point.

Tours

Walking is a great way to explore Hamilton's relatively small grid, peppered with historic and interesting sights like museums, churches, and Parliament buildings. Hamilton Town Crier **Ed Christopher** (tel. 441/777-9738 or 441/292-1234, eschrist@logic.bm) impresses with his official uniform and feathered hat, as well as his local knowledge, in free weekday walkabouts starting at the City Hall steps on Church Street (10:30am Mon.-Fri. Apr.-Oct., by private booking Nov.-Mar.). His two-hour mosey explores much of North Hamilton's quaint streets and architecture. If you'd like to rest your legs, book a tour with the mini-train via **Bermuda Train Company** (441/236-5972, www.bermudatrain.com, bermudatrain@logic.bm, pickup and dropoff at Front Street's flagpole), which offers a one-hour tour ($25) of the city center's main sights plus a trip to Paget's Botanical Gardens, and a 2.5-hour tour ($45) of Hamilton with a visit to the **Bermuda Underwater Exploration Institute** (museum entrance fee included).

Spas

Smartly positioned in the heart of the business district, **Orchid Nail Spa** (Vallis Bldg., 54 Par-la-Ville Rd., tel. 441/296-8696, www.orchidspabda.com, 9am-6pm Mon.-Sat., noon-5pm Sun.) is a Best of Bermuda Award winner for its mani-pedis for men and women (one-hour mini treatment, $90). Other services include shellac, acrylic, Gelish, and gel nail treatments.

Polished (1 Reid St. at Queen St., tel. 441/232-6245, info@polishedbermuda.com, 9am-7pm Mon.-Sat., 9am-5pm Sun.) is stocked with London's Butter brand of polishes and offers manicures, pedicures, nail art and extensions, waxing, eyelash and eyebrow tinting, and party lashes.

Upstairs in the Washington Mall, **Lush Makeup**'s **Lash & Brow Bar** (1 Washington Mall, Level B, tel. 441/295-5874, 9:30am-5pm Mon.-Sat.) specializes in makeup, eyelash extensions, eyebrow shaping, tinting and threading, and underarm waxing.

La Serena Express Spa (A. S. Cooper & Sons, 3rd floor, tel. 441/239-0184, laserenaspa@thereefs.bm) is the Hamilton offshoot of The Reefs Resort's award-winning spa in Southampton, offering 30- to 45-minute sessions, including "fast and fabulous" facials ($79), "brief bikini" waxes ($40), and a "manicure in minutes" ($35).

Siam Thai Massage and Herbal Spa (Williams House, 1st floor, 20 Reid St., tel. 441/295-3999, siamspa.bda@gmail.com, 10am-8pm daily), located in the middle of Hamilton, offers massages with and without oil, herbal body treatments, and beauty services including facials, waxes, and mani-pedis. Favorites are the herbal compress massage (one hour, $105) and traditional Thai massage (30 minutes $55, 120 minutes $195).

Just up the street, Hamilton hallmark **Strands** (31 Reid St., tel. 441/295-0353, www.strands.bm, 8:45am-6pm Mon.-Fri, 8:45am-5pm Sat.) has a day spa with a full menu of Clarins skin treatments for men and women (75-minute facials $150, body treatments $165, body wraps $155).

Sabai Thai Body Balancing Massage & Spa (131 Front St., tel. 441/292-6456, www.thaimassagebermuda.com, 10am-7:30pm Mon.-Sat.) offers traditional Thai body massage starting at $110 per hour for a light session and ranging up to $220 for a two-hour "Thai Boxing" or sports massage. Online bookings should be made 36 hours in advance.

Further from central Hamilton's bustle is **Tai Home Spa** (14 Laffan St. off Cedar Ave., tel. 441/297-2347, www.taihomespa.bm, 9am-7pm daily), whose menu includes Thai, Balinese, Swedish, hot stone, and deep tissue massage, along with other treatments ranging from facials, waxing, and threading to pedicures (one-hour massage $89, 75-minute full-body mud wrap $119). The spa's calm rooms sit inside the gingerbread architecture of a traditional Bermuda cottage, located on a residential street behind St. Theresa's Cathedral.

ACCOMMODATIONS

There are presently no hotels or guesthouses located within Hamilton's boundaries (though many are nearby in Pembroke). Negotiations have been ongoing for several years between the Bermuda government and developers in a bid to build a five-star hotel and condos on the site of the Par-la-Ville parking lot.

FOOD

Hamilton's culinary scene is emerging from the recessionary pinch with exciting additions, including gluten-free cafés, ice cream and frozen yogurt bars, contemporary small-plates lounges, new ethnic and vegetarian offerings, and a trend towards more sidewalk dining. Could the arrival of *Top Chef* star Marcus Samuelsson at Pembroke's Fairmont Hamilton Princess be raising the bar? Maybe. Restaurateurs are displaying a new competitive energy, reaching out to foodies with digital come-ons, updated restaurant interiors, and more innovative menus that tap into locavore trends and put creative spins on Bermudian traditions. Look for fresh local produce and seafood—the catch-of-the-day ranges from Bermuda wahoo and tuna to rockfish, yellowtail, or grouper. Sushi is ubiquitous, either eat-in or take-out. All restaurants are nonsmoking by law. Most accept credit cards and have free WiFi, and many promote daily specials on their Facebook pages. Restaurant dress code is generally smart-casual—so avoid wearing sneakers or T-shirts to dinner.

Ice Cream and Yogurt Bars

Meltdown Ice Cream (Old Cellar Ln., off Front St., tel. 441/538-0065, 11:30am-5:30pm Mon.-Sat.) opened its pocket-sized eatery in 2014, offering the popular Bermuda Artisan Ice Cream brand in flavors such as rum swizzle and black rum and ginger. Owned and run by husband and wife Bruce and Sheree Lines, the little outlet calls to overheated passersby with its cool subway tiles, shady tables, and cheery flowerpots.

Yo Cherry (8 Bermudiana Rd., tel. 441/292-2020, www.yocherry.com, 11am-10pm Mon.-Thurs., 11am-12:30am Fri., 10:30am-12:30am Sat., 10am-10pm Sun.) is another newcomer launched by a Bermudian couple, Carlos and Regina Francis. It quickly nabbed a Best of Bermuda Award for its daily flavors of self-serve "fro-yo" such as chocolate custard, caramel sea salt, and red velvet, offered alongside sorbet, gelato, and ice cream, plus a sea of more than 50 toppings. Its location on Bermuda's "Restaurant Alley" and generous opening hours also make it a cure for after-dinner munchies.

BermyBerry (31 Reid St. at Burnaby St., tel. 441/533-2233, 9am-7pm Mon.-Sat.) opened a second Bermuda outlet in Hamilton after its fat-free frozen yogurt went down well with cruise ship crowds at Dockyard. Along with funky flavors like chocolate-orange and gingersnap, the city version offers extras such as breakfast Greek yogurt parfaits, specialty coffees, and pastries, and you can enjoy your snack while sitting outside on the sidewalk terrace. There's free WiFi too.

La Trattoria Shop (22 Washington Ln., tel. 441/295-9499, 9am-4pm Mon.-Sat.) sells decadent homemade gelato from a little outlet opposite La Trattoria restaurant.

Opening in 2015 is **Honey's Café & Creamery** (Brunswick Mall, 119 Front St.), featuring 16 flavors, including dairy-free, sugar-free, sorbet, and soft-serve varieties. The venue will incorporate local Bermuda honey in its toppings and smoothies, hence the name.

Lunch Wagons

Jovial husband-and-wife team Keith and Elaine DeSilva do a rip-roaring weekday lunchtime trade at their Best of Bermuda Award-winning **Keith's Kitchen** (48 Woodlands Rd. at BAA parking lot, tel. 441/295-1310, $5-6.50). Join the line of locals for the latest gossip, served up with hefty tuna sandwiches, BLTs, and straight-off-the-grill burgers at the landmark blue truck, which has spread out on this site over the years and now has attached shaded waiting areas and nearby picnic tables. Tucked inside the gates of the BAA soccer stadium, the truck is a five-minute walk north from Front Street up Par-la-Ville Road and across a small roundabout at the Serpentine Road junction.

Office workers line up weekdays at lunchtime for burgers, sandwiches, and friendly chitchat at **DeGraff's Lunch Wagon** (City Hall parking lot, tel. 441/799-3904, 9am-3pm Mon.-Fri., $4.75-5.50).

Jor-Jay's Takeout (Front St., in the parking lot opposite The Supermart, tel. 441/296-3114, 8am-3pm Mon.-Thurs., 8am-4am Fri., 11:30am-4am Sat., $3-6) is very popular with hungry late-night revelers on their way out of town. The lunch wagon makes scrumptious homemade burgers, sandwiches, fries, and fish cakes, and although the wait is sometimes a good half hour, it's worth it.

You can't miss Kemar Maybury's fire truck-red **Smokin' Barrel** (1 Waterfront Park, Front St., directly outside the ferry terminal, tel. 441/337-0211, 7am-11pm Mon.-Thurs., 7am-3am Fri. and Sat.). The hugely successful barbecue joint cooks up plates of Momma Slappin' wings ($10), jerk shrimp ($18), burgers and ribs ($10-12), curry chicken, and lemon-pepper fish. Maybury, son of a well-known Bermudian drummer, hopes to parlay his hit into a permanent Reid Street restaurant called the Smokin' Barrel Tropical Café.

Cafés, Diners, and Delis

Cafés, diners, and delis are located all over Hamilton, though a few catering to the corporate crowd are closed Saturdays. An increasing number of licensed lounges have given Hamilton a hipper edge, and more are on the way; an example is **Juno,** set to open on Reid Street at the Walker Arcade in 2015 with a stylin' Miami décor, sidewalk terrace, open kitchen, upstairs party room, and a small-plates menu for lunch and dinner. There are plenty of places to drop in for a takeaway bite too; a food court is slated for the Washington Mall's Church Street section, and good delis are located in the larger supermarkets such the MarketPlace (Church Street), The Supermart (Front Street), and Miles Market (Pitts Bay Road).

One of the island's longtime "local" joints, ★ **The Spot** (6 Burnaby St., tel. 441/292-6293, 6:30am-10pm Mon.-Sat. summer, 6:30am-7pm Mon.-Sat. winter) is a Bermudian melting pot, remarkable for the way it attracts customers of all races, ages, and backgrounds, who come for great homemade dishes and the convivial atmosphere. The place is a landmark

A popular city diner for more than 60 years, The Spot is known for homestyle dishes and a cheery staff.

in Hamilton, having been at its present location for more than 60 years. The diner's longtime owner, businessman Ted Powell, sits down for a welcoming chat with visitors if he is on the premises. Try the soups (red bean, barley, split pea, $5.75), hot sandwiches with gravy ($14.95), thick shakes ($6.50), and pancakes-with-bacon breakfasts ($11.75). Takeout is fast, and the service is ultra-friendly (and kid-friendly). Don't leave without a hand of sweet Bermuda bananas, regularly sold from the checkout counter.

Bella Caffè (Thistle House, 4 Burnaby St., tel. 441/295-9857, 7:30am-5pm Mon.-Fri., 9am-4pm Sat., $2.50-9.50), alongside The Spot, serves up gourmet coffee, biscotti, smoothies, pastries, sandwiches, fish cakes, Bermuda banana bread, and more from its pocket-sized space, and owner-manager Michael Tessitore treats all his customers like regulars.

Perfectly placed for passing passengers, **Dangelini's Café** (8 Front St., next to the ferry terminal, tel. 441/295-5272, 7:30am-5pm Mon.-Fri., 7:30am-4pm Sat., $2-8.50) wins fans for its fresh-baked goodies, including gluten-free creations, as well as sandwiches, wraps, paninis, frappes, and gourmet coffee.

Drop into **Rock Island Coffee** (48 Reid St., tel. 441/296-5241, www.rockisland.bm, 7am-6pm Mon.-Fri., 8am-1pm Sat.) for great java and one of the city's more interestingly mixed crowd of patrons. Dreadlocked "trust-afarians"—trust-funded bohemians—linger over lattes, while lawyers and actuaries rush in for espresso and a chocolate chip cookie. The staff roasts, grinds, and brews beans from Colombia, Kenya, Jamaica, and elsewhere. The artsy surroundings—a wood-floored cottage decorated in ever-changing local paintings and photography—add to the ambience of pure Bermudian bohemia. There's a garden out front with tables, umbrellas, and views of the cruise ships in the summer.

Newcomer **Nonna's Kitchen** (4 Bermudiana Rd., tel. 441/295-7687, 7am-3pm Mon.-Fri.) has quickly won accolades for its healthy fare, including energy shakes, breakfast burritos ($7), warm, dairy-free oatmeal ($3.95), salad bar with roasted turkey, quinoa and fresh vegetables ($11.95 per pound), lentil soup ($5.50), fair-trade coffee, cold drinks, and gluten-free cornbread, pumpkin bread, and banana bread. WiFi is available.

★ **Tribe Road Kitchen** (87 Reid St. at King St., tel. 441/734-1637, www.trk.bm, lunch 10am-2:30pm Tues.-Sun., dinner 6pm-10pm Wed.-Sat.) showcases the talents of Culinary Institute of America graduate chef Karsten Krivenko, aka "The Barefoot Baker," who has wowed customers and garnered awards—plus loads of Facebook "likes"—with her decadent baked goods and stomach-purring creations. Breakfast, lunch, and dinner customers can't get enough of her bacon-crusted pumpkin pancakes, smoked spareribs, quinoa power bowls, or jauntily named signature specials such as "Fowl Play" sandwiches ($13), "Pig Floyd" pizza ($20), and the "Holy Cow" burger (half-pound $12). The eclectic café, located in a former art gallery space, has hardwood floors with tables inside, or outdoors in the tiny garden next to a lily pond.

You can get an authentic taste of Portuguese cuisine at **Café Açoreano** (Russell Eve Building, 2 Washington St., tel. 441/296-0402, 6am-8:30pm daily), where deep-fried *malasada* (Portuguese donuts, $1.25 each) are a Bermudian breakfast favorite, among other sweet treats. Great coffee and a convenient location alongside the central bus terminal also make this tiny, 20-year-old café worth a visit, along with its extended hours and hot deli items ($11 per pound) such as *frango a canarinho* (chicken leg), *feijao vermelho com chourico* (red beans and chourico), and *bacalhau dourado* (codfish casserole).

Mingle with a mixture of Miu Miu heels, iPads, and Crossfit spandex at ★ **Ten** (10 Dundonald St., tel. 441/295-0857, www.ten.bm, 7am-10:30pm Mon.-Fri., 8am-3pm Sat.), where corporate coffee-breakers share space with hydrating gym rats and coffee klatches. The delicious, light fare (falafel and salsa verde sandwiches $12, Asian noodle salad $8, evening tapas $10-15) is as good as the Euro-cool décor and snappy service by ShayJuan, Carrie, and the team. Enjoy your quiche, pizza, or panini alfresco while people-watching from the patio in the warmer seasons.

Java Jive (29 Victoria St., tel. 441/296-5050, www.irg.bm, 7am-5pm Mon.-Fri., $2.95-11.50), a tiny offshoot of Victoria Grill at the same address, sells hot and cold coffees, breakfast wraps, fresh-baked muffins, croissants, salads, and daily panini specials. The friendly manager Glynis will make you feel at home. Take it out, or watch the corporate world go by from the patio.

Lemon Tree Cafe (7 Queen St., tel. 441/292-0235, 7:30am-3pm Mon.-Fri., 11am-3pm Sat., happy hour 5pm-midnight Fri.) tempts lunchgoers with gourmet offerings, from hot dishes like parmesan-dusted mahimahi ($15) and spiced pumpkin soup to ciabatta sandwiches-of-the-day ($13.95), salads ($15), healthy wraps ($10), and melt-in-your-mouth chicken pies ($9.95). Take out, or sit on the terrace next to the cool, green expanse of Queen Elizabeth Park.

Owned by the Flanagan's Irish Pub group, **The Snug** (Emporium Building, 69 Front St., tel. 441/295-8299, 7am-4pm Mon.-Sat.) is a tucked-away café in the ground floor of the same building, offering breakfast sandwiches ($4.75) and bacon-and-egg platters ($11) and lunch soups, chili, sandwiches, buffalo wings, and burgers ($6-10).

A favorite deli is ★ **The Hickory Stick** (Clarendon Building, 2 Church St., tel. 441/292-1781, 6:30am-3pm Mon.-Fri.), whose Dagwood-esque sandwiches are legendary. Construction workers, bankers, journalists, and tourists traipse in for footlong subs stuffed with deli meats and smothered in melted cheese. Deli sandwiches range from $4 (for basic tuna) to $10 (for multi-item creations, or daily specials such as the Cajun chicken and grilled vegetable wrap). Salads, from coleslaw to Hawaiian, are $5-10.95. Cornish pasties, pies, and quiche ($7.50) and home fries ($3) are also served up daily. Cold drinks, chips, pastries, baked goods, tea, and coffee are also sold. Staff set up a sandwich-making assembly line to efficiently serve long lines of customers snaking through the little eatery noon-2pm. Go early or late to avoid a wait.

Sitting on the steep stairway between Front and Reid Streets, **Dorothy's Coffee Shop** (3 Chancery Ln., tel. 441/292-4130, 7:15am-3:30pm Mon.-Fri., $5) is best known for its award-winning homemade burgers—juicy

Tribe Road Kitchen wows with award-winning sandwiches, salads, and pizzas.

creations made on the little diner's grill while you watch. Sit at barstools to watch the proceedings, or at one of the few tables. Takeout is available.

A fabulous people-watching perch is a window seat at **Paradiso Café** (7 Reid St., tel. 441/295-3263, 7am-5pm Mon.-Sat.). Enjoy pastries ($2.95), sandwiches ($7.50), paninis ($10.95), and unending cups of tea or coffee while you watch passersby.

Further inside the Washington Mall's ground-floor level, **Delicious** (tel. 441/295-5890, 8am-5pm Mon.-Sat.) is a fast-service sandwich and snack outlet. **China Grill** (tel. 441/295-5890, 8am-5pm Mon.-Sat.) offers up Asian noodles and other hot Chinese deli items for takeout, or for enjoying at its several tables.

Mall shoppers take a break at **Café 4** (Windsor Building, 18 Queen St., tel. 441/295-8444, www.cafe4.bm, 7:30am-5pm Mon.-Thurs., 7:30am-7am Fri., 8am-4pm Sat., $2.50-12.50), whose umbrella-shaded patio is perfect for late breakfasts, lunch, or drinks and dinner. A sushi bar, barbecue grill, hot buffet, made-to-order gourmet sandwiches, salads, wraps, bento boxes, and desserts cater to all appetites; sit indoors or out. Best of all, you can order online and skip the queues.

L'Oriental Express West (1 Church St. at Par-la-Ville Rd., tel. 441/296-7475, www.lorientalexpress.bm, 8am-7pm Mon.-Fri., $5-14) and its sidekick **L'Oriental Express East** (47 Victoria St. at Parliament St., tel. 441/296-5378, $5-14) are extremely popular with area office workers, thanks to eat-in or take-out menus of sushi, sandwiches, wraps, paninis, build-your-own salads, and breakfast specials.

Hidden away in the hallway of a retail building, **Donna's Café** (Shopper's Fair Building, 61 Church St., next to Sports R Us, tel. 441/292-2009, 7:30am-3pm Mon.-Fri., $3-6) is a throwback to the 1950s, with fluorescent lights, a smiley face collection, and revolving stools pushed up to the yellow linoleum bar. Breakfast sandwiches, burgers, and shakes are the menu favorites. Service is a no-fuss affair in the friendly hands of owner/manager Donna Warwick.

Family-run **Jamaican Grill** (32 Court St., tel. 441/296-6577, 6:30am-9pm Mon.-Thurs., 24 hours Fri. and Sat., $7-18) attracts aficionados of Caribbean cuisine with a scrumptious menu of oxtail, jerk chicken and pork, brown stew, stuffed whole fish, coco bread, ackee and saltfish, and West Indian curries. Fast service and delicious meals keep crowds coming back—and lining up at 5pm every Friday and Saturday for the outdoor jerk chicken barbeque. Order your meal as takeout or enjoy it in the atmospheric little diner, which has a cluster of tables downstairs and a few overlooking the jovial gathering from on high.

More Caribbean-inspired food can be found a block away at North Hamilton's **Rotis** (55 Court St., 293-7684, rotisbermuda@gmail.com, 7am-4pm Wed.-Fri, 10am-6pm Sat.), which is gaining a loyal following for its people-pleasing goat and chicken wraps ($15), as well as chicken patties, Johnny bread, and fish sandwiches.

An efficient franchise of four **Buzz** cafés (www.buzzcafe.bm) around Hamilton serve clientele on the go with gourmet coffee, smoothies ($6.75-9.75), wraps and paninis ($9.95), quesadillas ($12.75), milk shakes ($6.25-9.25), and more. They are: **Buzz Washington Mall** (upper level, Washington Mall, Church St., tel. 441/295-1979, 7:30am-5pm Mon.-Fri., 9am-5pm Sat.); **Buzz Hamilton Pharmacy** (17 Parliament St., tel. 441/292-5160, 8am-4:30pm Mon.-Sat.); **Buzz Brown & Co.** (inside the Brown & Co. store, between Front St. and Reid St., tel. 441/279-546, 8:30am-5pm Mon.-Sat.); and **Buzz N Go Esso City** (37 Richmond Rd., at Par-la-Ville Rd. junction, tel. 441/296-2390, 6am-4:30am daily).

★ **Devil's Isle Kitchen & Bar** (16 Burnaby St., tel. 441/296-1129, www.devilsislecoffee.bm, 8am-midnight Mon.-Fri., 9am-midnight Sat.) opened in the heart of Hamilton in late 2014, with both a restaurant-bar and a takeout deli area. Breakfast, lunch, and dinner menus are very locavore-friendly, with a farm-to-table mission driving everything that comes out of the kitchen. Dishes include home-brewed coffees and vegan muesli ($10) for breakfast, sandwiches and salads for lunch ($10-16), and a creative dinnertime array of small or large plates (roasted duck pasta $13, lamb lollies $14). Eat in the coffee house-inspired restaurant or outside on the sidewalk patio.

Vegetarian and Vegan

It's the popular smoothie bar that brings folks all day long into **Down to Earth** (56 Reid St., tel. 441/292-5639, 9am-5:30pm Mon.-Sat.), but as you wait for your spinach-raspberry-almond butter-chia seed creation, many other healthful goodies will catch your eye. A little grocery store of vegan-friendly products—granola cereals, green teas, gluten-free pizza, nuts galore—it also stocks a full selection of vitamins and natural supplements.

Mother-daughter team Anjula and Ashley Bean cater to a phalanx of regulars with their vegan-friendly menu at **Juice 'n' Beans** (61 Front St., tel. 441/292-6454, 7:30am-8pm Mon.-Sat., 12pm-6pm Sun., deli items $13.99 per pound). Hot deli offerings include breakfast (a tofu-and-black bean variation on sausages and scrambled eggs), Indian curries, and changing daily specials. Nonvegans come in for the delicious baked goodies, gourmet coffee, smoothies, and window seats that offer prime Front Street people-watching.

Vegans, vegetarians, and health nuts in general make a beeline to **Café Eden** (9am-4pm Mon.-Thurs, 9am-noon Fri.) inside **ABC Natural Foods** (41 King St. at the Hamilton Seventh-Day Adventist Church, tel. 441/292-4111, 9am-5:45pm Mon., Tues, Thurs., 9am-6:15pm Wed., 9am-1:15pm Fri., closed Sat., 10am-1:45pm Sun.) for smoothies, veggie hot dogs and burgers, dried fruits, cereals and nuts, soy and dairy-free products, dairy-free ice cream, and organic juices.

★ **It's Only Natural** (8 Princess St., tel. 441/292-6617, itsonlynatural@onelove.bm) puts on a noontime vegan hot lunch deli every Friday, serving up tasty lentil or chickpea burgers, Asian tofu, split pea soup, and vegetable lasagna—until it runs out. Accountants line up with Rastafarians and veggie-seeking tourists for a take-out or stay-put meal (at a couple of tables inside the health store).

My Sereni-Tea (Chancery Hall, 52 Reid St., tel. 441/296-2114, www.myserenitea.com, 8:30am-4:30pm) has a large selection of holistic teas (hot and iced), plus vegan-friendly soups and snacks, along with a selection of essential oils, health books, and crystals, as well as massage, acupuncture, and yoga treatments.

Pub Fare

Technically it's a bar, but the **Pickled Onion** (53 Front St., tel. 441/295-2263, www.thepickledonion.com, lunch 11:30am-5pm, dinner 5:30pm-10pm daily, $8-20) has a restaurant-caliber menu, with a variety of nicely presented appetizers, pastas, fresh fish, salads, steaks, and desserts. The live music and drinks are just a bonus.

You couldn't find a more British-looking establishment than **Hog Penny** (5 Burnaby Hill, tel. 441/292-2534, www.hogpennypub.com, lunch 11:30am-4:30pm, dinner 5:30pm-10pm daily, $11-22), where home-cooked and typically ill-named staples like shepherd's pie and toad-in-the-hole are comfortable favorites. Its "crusted dinners" (beef Wellington, scaloppini veal chop) are well liked, too.

Flanagan's Irish Pub (Emporium Building, 69 Front St., tel. 441/295-8299, www.flanagans.bm, 11am-1am Mon.-Fri, 9am-1am Sat. and Sun., $12-29) has a crowd-pleasingly extensive menu of steaks, burgers, mussels, fresh fish, daily pasta specials, soups, salads, and desserts. Don't miss the authentic codfish and potato breakfast on weekend mornings.

Bermuda Bistro at The Beach (103 Front St. at Parliament St., tel. 441/292-0219, www.thebeachbermuda.com, 10am-3am daily, $12-25) gets a full house for its paninis, burgers, pizza, seafood, and bar snacks.

All-day breakfasts, super sandwiches, pizza, and build-your-own burgers get top billing at **The Docksider Pub & Restaurant** (121 Front St., tel. 441/296-3333, www.dockies.com, 11am-2am Mon.-Fri., 10am-3am Sat.-Sun., $11-14), a crowded hangout all year round. Earlier opening hours accommodate soccer and rugby fans who come to watch live televised games.

Asian

L'Oriental (32 Bermudiana Rd., above Little Venice, tel. 441/296-4477, www.diningbermuda.com, lunch noon-3pm Mon.-Fri., dinner 6pm-11pm daily) has sushi and sashimi ($7.50-10.50), dim sum ($18.75), *teppanyaki* ($32-39), and main courses like beef Szechuan ($28.75) and crispy duck ($33.75).

Busy Chinese and Thai takeout **Chop Fusion** (88 Reid St., tel. 441/292-0791, www.bermudarestaurants.com, lunch 11:30am-2:30pm Mon.-Fri., dinner 5pm-11pm daily) is popular for eating in as well. The dramatically designed dining room allows for large parties or dinner for two, and service is efficient and friendly. Staples include fried rice ($11-15), pad thai ($17), and vegetable or meat chow mein ($13-16).

Indian

Outstanding Indian fare, equal to the caliber found in London, Toronto, or New York, is the strength of ★ **House of India** (Park View Plaza, 57 North St., tel. 441/295-6450, lunch 11am-2:30pm Mon.-Fri., dinner 5pm-10pm daily), where a dedicated team of Indian chefs turns out lunch buffets and nightly feasts of tandoori, biryani, and balti specialties. The award-winning chicken *passanda* ($15.50), chicken and beef kormas ($14.75), and chicken and lamb tikka masalas ($12.95) are particularly well done. The warm fluffy naan breads in garlic or plain flavors, as well as stuffed *kulcha* varieties, are to die for. There is also a wide selection of vegetarian dishes. Appetizers include *bhajiyas, pakoras,* and samosas. With ultrafriendly and professional service, the restaurant's popularity prompted its 2011 expansion into a second dining room on the premises.

Opened in 2014 by the Port O' Call restaurant group, **Ruby Murrys** (2 Chancery Ln., tel. 441/295-5058, www.portocall.bm, lunch noon-2:30pm Mon.-Fri., dinner 5:30pm-11pm Mon.-Sun.) was a hit straight out of the blocks. Named for Cockney rhyming slang for "curry" (after a popular 1950s singer from south Belfast), the restaurant mixes traditional and modern Indian cuisine such as tandoori-roasted salmon ($15), Goan coconut fish ($22), or beef madras ($17.50), plus a wide choice of naans and *kulchas.* Vegetarians will appreciate the mushroom *pulao, dal makhani, chana masala, baigan bharta,* and umpteen other nonmeat choices.

Like its Southampton outlet, Hamilton's **East Meets West** (27 Bermudiana Arcade off Queen St., 2nd floor, tel. 441/295-8580, 7:30am-10pm Mon.-Sat.) cooks up a diverse ethnic menu that merges burgers, sandwiches, wraps, pizza, and Asian noodles with a full slate of delicious and reasonably priced Indian specialties.

Italian

Little Venice (32 Bermudiana Rd., tel. 441/295-3503, www.diningbermuda.com, lunch noon-2:15pm Mon.-Fri., dinner 6:30pm-10pm daily) was the vanguard of Bermuda's lovefest with Italian cuisine back in the 1960s. Today, it's still going strong, and the restaurant's owners, Capri natives, have succeeded beyond their wildest dreams, with a dozen popular restaurants and a catering service that feeds the island's social scene. Little Venice was always the power-lunch venue, and it still attracts insurance-industry movers and shakers, as well as occasional celebrities (Michael Douglas has dined here). Efficient, entertaining staff members keep the dining room buzzing. Appetizers like roasted octopus ($18.75), homemade pastas (gnocchi $20.75, spaghetti with clams $29.75), meat dishes (pork tenderloin with porcini mushrooms $27.75), and lovingly crafted desserts (tiramisu $10) make up the menu.

Just down the street, **Portofino** (20 Bermudiana Rd., tel. 441/292-2375, www.portofino.bm, lunch 11:30am-3pm Mon.-Fri., dinner 6pm-10:45pm Mon.-Thurs. and Sun., 6pm-11:45pm Fri. and Sat.), one of the island's few Italian restaurants not owned by the Little Venice Group, has been wildly popular for more than 30 years. Speedy waiters, daily pasta specials ($14-28), tasty salads ($7-8) and meats ($26-34), and a cozy, red-checkered interior make Portofino a hit. Dinner reservations (for groups of more than two) are recommended to avoid lining up down the street on summer weekend evenings. A fast, wide-ranging takeout service is offered alongside the main restaurant.

★ **La Trattoria** (Washington Mall, 22 Washington Ln., tel. 441/295-1877, lunch 11am-3pm Mon.-Sat., dinner 5pm-10pm daily) makes diners feel they've stepped into the terra-cotta courtyard of an eatery in Naples or Rome. The menu, which has always been a crowd-pleaser, remains excellent, with homemade pastas (orecchiette with sausage $20.25), award-winning pizzas ($17-20) baked in the dining room's wood-fired oven, and great appetizers (*trio del mare* $16.85), breads, and desserts, including homemade gelato. La Trattoria's Caesar salad ($8.75) and cappuccino are arguably the best on the island. Topping even the food is the eatery's stellar service; nothing is perceived as a problem, least of all wailing children or order-off-the-menu clientele. The professional team smoothly fulfills everyone's wishes, and fast. Kids are well accommodated with crayons, balls of dough to play with, cost-effective smaller platters, and even "white" pizzas (should they turn their noses up at tomato sauce). As a result, the place is full of families but somehow manages to attract couples and adult dinner parties, too.

Seafood and Sushi

Multi-award-winning ★ **Beluga Seafood Bar** (Washington Mall III, 18 Church St. opposite City Hall, tel. 441/542-2859, lunch 11:30am-2:45pm, dinner 6pm-10pm Mon.-Sat., $7-25) earns its kudos with what many aficionados swear is Bermuda's best sushi, created by maestro Sammy Wong, a Malaysia native who trained in Japan. The sleek little venue, on the mall's lower level, is a perfect drop-in spot for lunch, or before heading out to the cinema in the evening. The whole menu is melt-in-your-mouth delicious, but don't miss the Japanese pizza (a vegetable tempura, $12), the coconut shrimp ($9.25), the diamond dragon sushi roll, or the number-one request, the Sammy roll (named for its buoyant creator, $16.75). Regulars sometimes just let Sammy

La Trattoria serves up delicious Italian cuisine.

have free rein—ask him to make something special for you using the day's fresh fish arrivals, then watch him get creative.

Located upstairs at Port O' Call Restaurant, **Pearl** (87 Front St., 441/295-9150, www.portocall.bm/pearl.php, lunch noon-2:30pm and dinner 5pm-10pm Mon.-Fri., dinner only 6pm-10pm Sat., $8-18) tops the wish lists of many serious sushi-lovers with its fresh ingredients and creative spins on classic dishes.

The Lobster Pot (6 Bermudiana Rd., tel. 441/292-6898, lobsterpot@ibl.bm, 11:30am-10pm Mon.-Fri., 5:30pm-10pm Sat., 6pm-10pm Sun., $27-46) has been a beloved fixture of this corner of Hamilton for decades, and it still has one of the island's most enjoyable bars, as well as an atmospheric dining room where you might as well be below deck on a sumptuous ocean liner. Fresh Bermuda or Maine lobsters and pan-fried rockfish, snapper, and grouper—and an award-winning version of Bermuda's traditional fish chowder—make this one of the island's best seafood venues.

North Hamilton's **Fish & Tings** (45 Angle St., tel. 441/292-7389, fish&tings@hotmail.com, 10am-10pm Mon.-Thurs., 10am-11pm Fri. and Sat., $12-14) specializes in Jamaican dishes, like fish curries, stews, and jerk everything.

International

Winner of a Wine Spectator Award of Excellence, foodie favorite ★ **Barracuda Grill** (5 Burnaby Hill, tel. 441/292-1609, www.barracuda-grill.com, lunch noon-2:30pm Mon.-Fri., dinner 5:30pm-10pm daily) pleases with both a cutting-edge interior and outstanding seafood, steaks, and chops. Grilled artichoke hearts or figs ($15), bone-in ribeye ($42), grilled Bermuda rockfish ($35), lobster gnocchi ($33), and salted caramel pot de crème ($10) are among the favorites.

Red Steakhouse & Bar (55 Front St., wheelchair-accessible entrance via Reid St., 441/292-7331, www.redbermuda.com, noon-2am Tues.-Fri., 6pm-2am Sat. and Sun.) brings cosmopolitan flair to a prime Front Street location. Its dinner menu offers faves like oysters on the half shell ($18), sea bass in citrus ($34), rosemary rack of lamb ($42), and grilled vegetable Napoleon with quinoa. But beef is king here; all cuts of the filet mignon, T-bone, striploin, rib-eye and cowboy are certified Angus beef and can be accompanied by decadent sides such as truffle mac'n'cheese ($9) or gorgonzola and crispy onions ($4). Enjoy sunset from the balcony and stay for the DJ after dessert.

Contemporary hip is the mood at **Muse** (17 Front St. opposite the ferry terminal, tel. 441/296-8788, www.muse.bm, breakfast 8am-11am, lunch noon-3pm, dinner 6pm-10pm Mon.-Sat.), which in 2014 added an alfresco dining room balcony to its bird's-eye location across from the ferry terminal. The menu is French-Asian fusion made from fresh local produce. Creations include Thai scallops in a green curry sauce ($13), Bermuda codfish cake on raisin toast with gombey tartar sauce ($13), blackened Atlantic salmon on a bed of artisanal greens ($29), and sticky-finger black-rum barbecue beef short ribs ($33). A good selection of French and American wines complement the fare. Early birds can enjoy breakfasts of frittatas, omelets, crepes, and steak and eggs (8am-11am); evening visitors will prefer the top-floor Skybar's happy hour (4pm-7pm).

Southern-style bistro **Victoria Grill** (29 Victoria St., tel. 441/296-5050, www.victoria-grill.com, lunch noon-2:30pm Mon.-Fri., dinner 5:30pm-10pm Mon.-Thurs. and Sat., 5:30pm-11pm Fri.) serves up comfort dishes in a sleek-but-cozy interior appropriate for both a power lunch and a family meal. Rave reviews pour in for the made-at-your-table guacamole appetizer ($10). The mains menu ($29) boasts chicken and waffles and shrimp 'n' grits, while the popular small-plates selection ($17) offers mac 'n' cheese, pulled pork sliders, and veggie treats like buffalo carpaccio (with hearts of palm and smoked aioli). The beetroot salad with goat cheese is also a hit. Finish it off with a pile of churros with caramel dip ($9). Outdoor seating on a terrace is also available in summer.

Run by the culinary talents behind the former Splendido restaurant at Paget's Horizons resort, **Angelo's Bistro** (Walker Arcade, 15 Reid St., tel. 441/232-1000, bistroangeleo@logic.bm, 9:30am-9:30pm Mon.-Sat.) occupies the arcade space between Reid and Front Streets, including a Mediterranean-style courtyard with a bubbling fountain. The menu also makes you feel as if you might have landed in Capri for the day: Thin-crust pizzas ($17), caprese salad ($12), chicken piccata ($26), and truffled mushroom risotto ($15) highlight lunch and dinner, and there are breakfasts of sweet rolls, omelets, and eggs Benedict. Takeout is available.

"World fusion" is the menu's ambition at **Café Cairo** (93 Front St., tel. 441/295-5155, cafecairo@northrock.bm, 5pm-3am Mon.-Sat., happy hour 5pm-7pm, ID required and patrons must be 18 or older after 10pm), where diners can sit on floor cushions in a tented room or on the harborfront terrace. A favored hangout for its hipster bar scene, exotic decor, and Middle Eastern fare, the restaurant boasts Egyptian-inspired wood, clay, and copper interiors, and a menu to suit all tastes. Specialties include a Middle Eastern "feast," featuring a four-course sampling of typical dishes accompanied by Moroccan mint tea ($49 per person). Regular appetizers include grilled *kofta* ($12) and red pepper hummus ($9), while entrées include moussaka ($18), Moroccan almond-crusted fish ($38), and vegetarian, meat, and fish tagines ($22-38).

Sophistication, in both ambience and menu, distinguishes **Port O' Call** (87 Front St., tel. 441/295-5373, www.portocall.bm, lunch noon-2:30pm Mon.-Fri., dinner 6pm-10pm daily), where you can dine inside or on the streetside terrace. Dishes such as roasted pumpkin puree soup, tempura-fried oysters, spice-crusted pork chop, and grilled Bermuda lobster won't disappoint. A private dining room can accommodate special parties. Owned by the same restaurant group, tiny **Bistro J** (102 Chancery Ln., tel. 441/296-8546, lunch noon-2:30pm Mon.-Fri., dinner 6pm-10pm Mon.-Sat.) has a more relaxed charm, with blackboard menus offering a limited but tasty assortment of daily specials.

With a European-themed cuisine, ★ **Bolero Brasserie** (95 Front St., entrance off Bermuda House Ln., tel. 441/292-4570, www.bolerobrasserie.com, lunch 11:30am-2:30pm, tapas 2:30pm-6pm, dinner 6pm-10:30pm Mon.-Sat.) not only has a prime Front Street dining porch, but a consistently award-winning menu featuring an extensive wine list as well as vegetarian choices. Classic brasserie dishes have a contemporary twist: trout with bacon and Brussels sprouts ($32), poutine with foie gras and truffles ($39), deep-fried calf's brains ($16), cassoulet of pork cheek and trotter ($33), and avocado fries ($9).

Grocery Stores

One of the island's best-stocked grocery stores, **The Supermart** (125 Front St., tel. 441/292-2064, www.supermart.bm, 7am-10pm Mon.-Sat., 11am-6pm Sun.) carries the British line of Waitrose products, along with other UK lines. Its meat department, cheese boutique, and fresh Bermuda produce section are also excellent. There's a broad wine and liquor range, as well as an expansive hot and cold deli. Parking is on the street or opposite in the small parking lot.

Flagship of the islandwide chain, the **Hamilton MarketPlace** (42 Church St., tel. 441/295-6066, 7am-10pm Mon.-Sat., 9am-7pm Sun.) is a massive food emporium, offering a full liquor store, meat department, enormous bakery, full-scale deli with hot and cold dishes and salad bars daily, and all manner of foodstuffs. Kids will enjoy the special carlike trolleys for family use and the remote-control train that runs on a circuit overhead tooting its horn. Parking is available outside and in a dedicated parking lot beneath the store.

The **Shopping Centre** (35 Victoria St., tel. 441/292-4545, 7am-10pm Mon.-Sat., 9am-7pm Sun.) is a MarketPlace branch and carries a much smaller selection of goods.

Arnold's Express (135 Front St. East, tel. 441/292-4301, 6:30am-midnight daily), belonging the successful islandwide grocery store chain, stocks essential sundries, plus wine, beer, and liquor.

INFORMATION AND SERVICES

Hamilton's **Visitor Information Centre** (tel. 441/295-1480, 9am-4pm Mon.-Sat.) is located alongside the ferry terminal building on Front Street. Knowledgeable staff offers advice, information, and brochures on the island's tours, activities, attractions, and events, as well as bus and ferry tickets, tokens, and passes.

The **Hamilton Police Station** (52 Victoria St. at Court St., tel. 441/295-0011 or 441/242-1704, fax 441/299-4589, www.police.bm) is located in a large, modern building that also houses courtrooms and government offices. A reception desk handles walk-in queries or problems.

The **Government Administration Building** (30 Parliament St., tel. 441/295-5151) houses numerous government departments, including the Department of Immigration, which deals with work permits and vacation extension requests.

Opposite the General Post Office is Bermuda's biggest travel agency, **Worldview Travel** (35 Church St., tel. 441/292-3033, fax 441/292-3205, www.worldviewtravel.bm, 8am-5pm Mon.-Fri.), offering expertise in cruises, seat sales, and flight queries. **Watlington & Conyers Travel** (The Armoury Bldg., 1st floor, 37 Reid St., tel. 441/295-3815, watlingtonandconyers.com, 9am-5pm Mon.-Fri.) is also an IATA-accredited agency.

Public toilets are located at the General Post Office; Point Pleasant Road at Albuoy's Point; at Waterfront Park opposite HSBC on Front Street; in Queen Elizabeth Park; and at banks and department stores.

Quickie Lickie Laundromat (74 Serpentine Rd., tel. 441/295-6097) is a longtime fixture of the city. Located amid corporate office blocks, **Just Shirts Launderers & Drycleaners** (20 Bermudiana Rd., tel. 441/292-3063) caters to a lot of business clientele.

ATMs are at all banking centers, inside A. S. Cooper & Sons and the Brown & Co. stores on Front Street, in the General Post Office (universal swipe card access after 6pm—swipe any credit card at the door to enter), at the BIU gas station on Dundonald Street, inside the Windsor Place Mall on Queen Street, on the ground floor of the Washington Mall, and inside two grocery stores: The Supermart (Front Street) and Hamilton MarketPlace (Church Street).

Banks

HSBC (Harbourview Centre, 37 Front St.; Church St. branch, 64 Church St.; Compass Point, 9 Bermudiana Rd.; main switchboard tel. 441/295-4000, www.hsbc.bm, 9am-4:30pm Mon.-Fri.) also has branches in Somerset and St. George's.

Butterfield Bank (head office 65 Front St. at Burnaby Hill; Rosebank Centre, 11 Bermudiana Rd. at Richmond Rd.; Reid St.; main switchboard tel. 441/295-1111, www.butterfieldbank.com, 9am-4pm Mon.-Fri., 10am-3pm Sat. at Rosebank Centre) has ATMs islandwide and branches on Pitts Bay Road and in Pembroke, Somerset, and St. George's.

Clarien Bank (19 Reid St., tel. 441/296-6969, www.clarienbank.com, 8:30am-4pm Mon.-Fri., 9:30am-1:30pm Sat.) offers financial, investment, and insurance services.

Pharmacies

Phoenix Centre (3 Reid St., tel. 441/279-5451, www.phoenixstores.bm, 8am-6pm Mon.-Sat., noon-6pm Sun. and holidays) is the island's largest general drugstore and flagship of an islandwide chain of pharmacies. The Hamilton location also has a big toy store and carries international magazines and newspapers.

Clarendon Pharmacy (31 Victoria St., ground floor, tel. 441/295-9137, clarendon_dispensary@psl.bm, 8am-6pm Mon.-Sat.)

carries chocolates, greeting cards, baby products, and other drugstore items.

Hamilton Pharmacy (Parliament St., tel. 441/295-7004, 8am-9pm Mon.-Sat.) is a busy but friendly little store, complete with dispensary, Buzz Café outlet, toys, books, magazines, and stationery. It is conveniently located just a stone's throw from Parliament, the law courts, and the General Post Office.

People's Pharmacy (62 Victoria St., tel. 441/292-7527, prescriptions tel. 441/292-9261, fax 441/295-0639, www.peoples.bm, 8am-8:30pm Mon.-Sat., 10am-6pm Sun.) is efficient and very well stocked, with friendly staff and easy parking. The large, modern store carries loads of drugstore products, but it also has magazines, a children's toy store and book section, greeting cards, gifts, candy, and household supplies.

Post Offices

The **General Post Office** (56 Church St. at Parliament St., tel. 441/297-7893, www.bermudapostoffice.com, 8am-5pm Mon.-Fri., 8am-noon Sat.) sells stamps (including first-day covers and collectors' issues), has a mail drop, offers parcel and express post, has ATMs, and offers kiosks allowing free Internet access.

Historic **Perot Post Office** (11 Queen St., tel. 441/292-9052, 8am-5pm Mon.-Fri.) is the only sub-post office in Hamilton.

Internet Access

Hamilton has numerous wireless Internet hot spots, including most of its cafés and restaurants, which offer free WiFi. There are also a few dedicated outlets that offer use of broadband-enabled PCs or wireless Internet. All post offices also offer free public Internet access.

The **Bermuda National Library** (13 Queen St., tel. 441/295-3104 or 441/295-2905, www.bnl.bm, 8:30am-6pm Mon.-Thurs., 10am-5pm Fri., 9am-5pm Sat.) offers free WiFi and free Internet access (30-minute limit) on its five PCs. Printing costs $0.25 a page.

TeleBermuda International (Victoria Pl., 31 Victoria St., Hamilton, tel. 441/296-9000, www.telebermuda.com, 9am-4:30pm Mon.-Fri.) has a customer-care center in Hamilton offering Internet access via WiFi and two broadband-enabled PCs.

Gas Stations

Bermuda Industrial Union Gas Station (22 Dundonald St., tel. 441/292-2726, 7am-midnight daily) has helpful staff and a convenience store selling hot dogs, cold drinks, snacks, newspapers, and candy.

Esso City Tigermarket (37 Richmond Rd., tel. 441/295-3776, 24 hours daily) is the island's only 24-hour service station. Its busy convenience store stocks hot and cold snacks, including hot dogs, pies, coffee, and cold drinks.

Liquor Stores

You can buy beer, wine, and spirits in most grocery stores, which were finally allowed Sunday liquor sales at the end of 2013, but there are also dedicated liquor merchants in Hamilton.

Historic **Gosling Brothers** (33 Front St. at Queen St., tel. 441/298-7337, www.goslingsrum.com, 9:30am-6:30pm Mon.-Sat.) is famous for its Black Seal Rum and dark 'n' stormies but also supplies much of the island's fine wines, ports, and other liquors. Gosling's has a dedicated **Wine Shop** (9 Dundonald St., tel. 441/298-7368 or 441/298-7377, info@goslingsstore.com, 10am-5pm Mon.-Fri., 9am-5pm Sat.), a retail outlet that attracts serious wine-lovers from Bermuda and overseas. With more than 1,000 bottles on sale from California, France, Italy, Germany, New Zealand, Argentina, and Australia, it has no equal in Bermuda. The store also stocks champagnes, liquors, and Riedel crystal glasses.

Front Street Liquors (57 Front St., just west of Burnaby St., tel. 441/292-6620, 9:30am-7pm Mon.-Sat.) sits opposite the Flagpole.

Burrows Lightbourn (127 Front St., tel. 441/295-1554, 9am-6pm Sat.-Thurs, 9am-9pm

Fri.) has an outlet alongside popular grocery store The Supermart.

Carousel Liquors (137 Front St. East, tel. 441/292-2559, 8am-9pm Mon.-Sat.), next to Arnold's Express, sells wine, beer, and spirits.

Court Street Liquors (29 Court St., tel. 441/295-7457, 9am-9pm Mon.-Sat.) is located in North Hamilton.

GETTING THERE AND AROUND

Buses

The central bus terminal—the **Hubert W. "Sparky" Lightbourne Central Terminal** (Washington St. at Church St., tel. 441/292-3854)—is named for a longtime driver. It is the central hub for all bus routes running throughout the parishes. Tickets, tokens, and passes can be purchased here also.

Ferries

Hamilton Ferry Terminal (6:30am-8pm Mon.-Fri., 7:30am-6pm Sat., 8:30am-6pm Sun. and holidays), serving Paget, Warwick, Southampton, the West End, and the East End, is on Front Street, alongside Albuoy's Point. A ferry ride to Dockyard is a mere 20 minutes (scooters allowed), to the Town of St. George a scenic 45. Fares on the Blue (West End/Dockyard), Orange (St. George's), and Green (Rockaway Southampton) Routes are $4.50 adults, $2.50 children 5-16, and on the Pink (Hamilton/Paget) Route $3 adult, $2.50 children 5-16. Children under five are free on all routes. No cash or change accepted; tickets or tokens only. For information, call **Sea Express** (tel. 441/295-4506 or 441/295-6575, www.seaexpress.bm).

Scooters and Bicycles

There are no scooter liveries located within the city limits, but there are two in neighboring Pembroke. One of the island's top bicycle stores rents road bikes to visitors out of its North Hamilton location: **Bicycle Works** (13 Tumkins Ln., off Woodlands Rd., tel. 441/297-8356, www.bicycleworks.bm) offers a variety of brands ($70-95 per day, discounts for longer periods).

Taxis

There are taxi stands along Front Street outside Brown & Co. near the ferry terminal and just west of City Hall on Church Street, alongside the city parking lot. Otherwise, contact the island's three main cab companies to arrange pickup: **Bermuda Industrial Union Co-op** (tel. 441/292-4476, cooptaxi@fkbnet.bm), **Bermuda Island Taxi** (tel. 441/295-4141, www.bermudaislandtaxi.com), or **BTA Dispatching Ltd.** (tel. 441/296-2121, www.taxibermuda.bm). Typical average taxi rates from Hamilton to the airport are $35, to St. George's $45, to the Southampton beaches $23, and to Dockyard $50.

Pembroke Parish

From back o' town to Fairylands and everything in between, Pembroke encompasses a diverse world of Bermudian culture on the city coattails of Hamilton, which sits within the parish. Encompassing the insurance towers of Pitts Bay, the grandiose, old-money mansions of the harborfront, the salt-sprayed charm of Spanish Point, and the vibrantly scrappy chutzpah of the Marsh Folly community, Pembroke might be the best microcosm of Bermuda as a whole—the best, worst, richest, and least fortunate distilled into its coasts and valleys. Once the rural environs of Hamilton, where the distant clip-clop of horse hooves or the splash of oars from a skiff rowing past were the only disturbances, Pembroke now is completely suburban, even 100 percent urban in parts, because the borders shared

Pembroke Parish

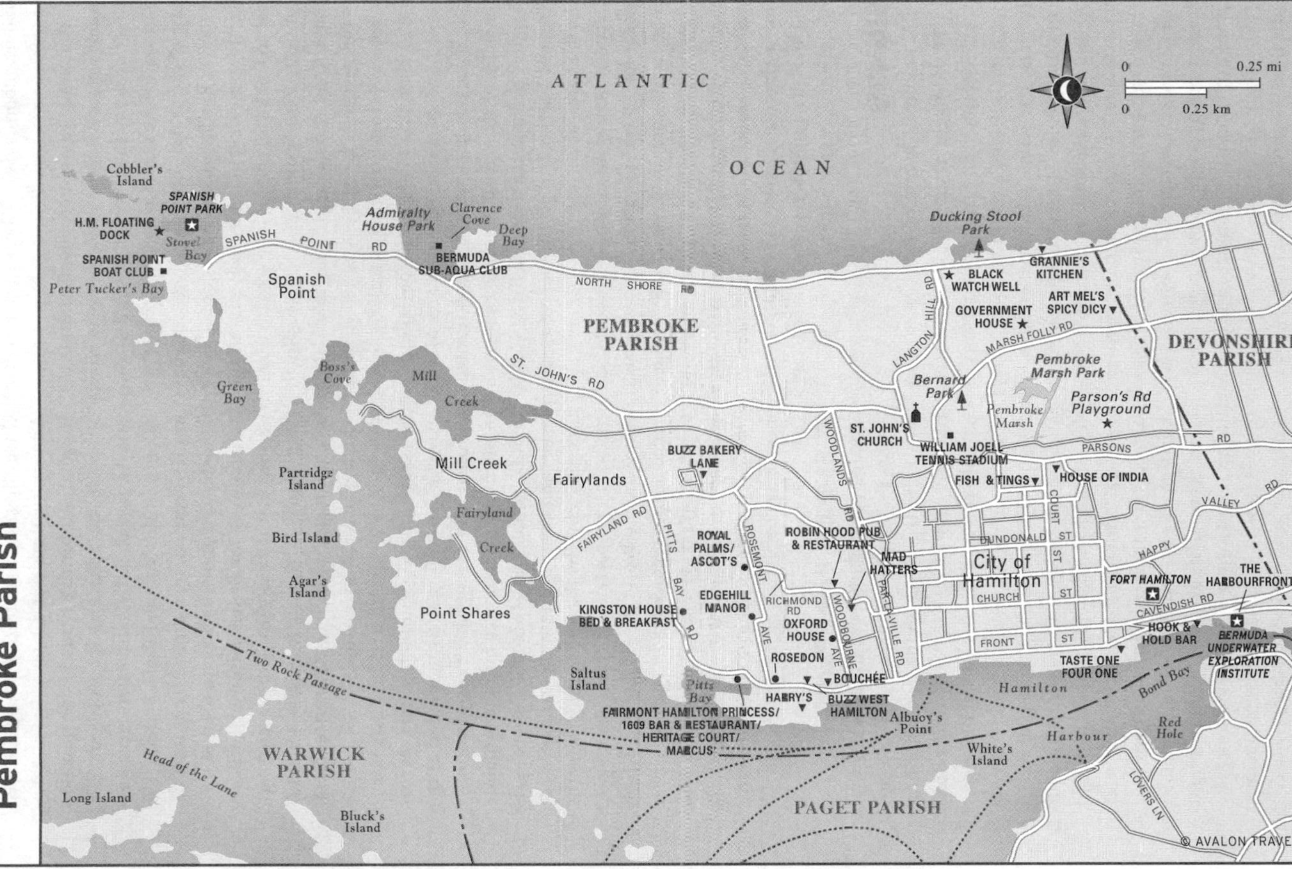

with Hamilton have blurred. Its once-tranquil neighborhoods now bear the aural scar of roaring traffic.

Pembroke begins where Hamilton ends: all points west of Bermudiana Road, east of King Street as far as the Devonshire border, and north of Parson's Lane to the North Shore are part of the parish. The main routes include Pitts Bay Road, which winds out of the city into tony residential neighborhoods, all the way to Cox's Hill and St. John's Road, which connects with Spanish Point Road. North Shore Road runs along the northern edge of the parish as far as Mission Lane, when it enters Devonshire. East Broadway leads out of Hamilton along the harbor's edge to Crow Lane. Parson's, Palmetto, and Marsh Folly Roads are major thoroughfares through the belly of the parish north of Hamilton. Langton Hill and the dramatic Black Watch Pass cut north through the parish to the North Shore.

The variety of interesting neighborhoods makes for great explorations, from Spanish Point, a self-contained community steeped in maritime history, to Fairylands and Point Shares, where high pastel walls hide centuries-old waterfront spreads, and areas of North Hamilton, where West Indian cafés and local playgrounds reveal a totally different facet of Bermudian life.

SIGHTS

Pitts Bay Road is one of Bermuda's most scenic thoroughfares; lined by guesthouses, pastel mansions, and sprawling gardens, it is one of the island's wealthiest old-money districts. The serene residential enclaves of Fairylands, Point Shares, and Mill's Point contain centuries-old waterfront homes of Bermudian merchant families, many of whose descendants still live here. These are private property, of course, but a stroll down the network of neighborhood lanes is nevertheless peacefully revealing. In the early spring, many homes have gardens carpeted with freesias, and the sound of traffic is nonexistent.

Admiralty House Park

Once the site of an 1816 residence named Admiralty House and later a Royal Navy Hospital, **Admiralty House Park** (junction of North Shore Rd. and Spanish Point Rd., sunrise-sunset daily, admission free) now belongs to the National Parks System. The former mansion, torn down except for a dilapidated, off-limits ballroom, used to provide housing for British admiralty officers who worked at Dockyard. The graceful park has gorgeous old trees, nature trails, and small beaches, including shallow **Clarence Cove,** which, sheltered by a sturdy dock (which kids love to jump and dive off), is a popular neighborhood swimming venue. Across the cove, **Deep Bay** is also well used in the summer, with young daredevils performing in-air stunts on their way into the turquoise depths. Notable also are the tunnels, galleries, and caves dug into the park's seaside limestone cliffs by the British military in the 1850s. The property was a Royal Navy signal center during World War II, but the British pulled out of Bermuda in 1951, turning it over to the island's government. The park tends to be packed when school is out and is especially crowded during Cup Match and other summer weekends.

★ Spanish Point Park

Situated on a picturesque promontory that defines the channel entrance for all ships approaching the Great Sound and Hamilton Harbour, **Spanish Point Park** (sunrise-sunset daily, admission free) is a delightful excursion—either for a quick visit and photos or a whole day's relaxation. Utterly peaceful, it sits at the tip of Spanish Point, a historic little community whose charming cottages and rambling tributaries evoke a long and direct connection with the sea. Spanish Point Road twists down past the offshoots of Doubloon Lane, Stormalong Lane, and Ocean Bright to the shorefront park at the bottom. The route is fringed by gingerbread architecture, candy-pink walls, and even a few rare wooden homes. One resident has labeled his property,

"The Home that Jack Built, 1924." Beside a parking lot, a beach edges Stovell Bay, a tiny harbor where pint-sized fishing boats, dinghies, and ruby sailboats like the kind in kids' storybooks sit at a collection of moorings.

At the bay's mouth lies a rusty hulk and pontoons, the remains of **H. M. Floating Dock,** once a magnificent example of Victorian maritime engineering. Launched in Woolwich on the Thames in 1869, the 47,000-cubic-foot dry dock was towed across the Atlantic by three Royal Navy steam frigates, HMS *Black Prince, Warrior,* and *Terrible,* arriving in Bermuda 39 days later. The largest dry dock in the world at the time, the structure was able to heave 10,000 tons and was used by the Royal Navy at Dockyard. By the early 1900s, however, it was outdated, unable to accommodate new, larger vessels, and was sold and towed to Spanish Point to be dismantled. But World Wars I and II intervened, and the effort was finally abandoned. Although it's an eyesore, the hulk today provides a sheltered harbor for local boats.

The park itself lies inside a tiny gate, its shady lawns, whispering pines, and baygrapes stretching along the finger of land bordered by the North Shore and Great Sound. There are picnic tables and benches, and a sprinkling of reefs and islets just a few yards off the North Shore side has created calm, shallow coves perfect for snorkeling. Walk to the end of the park that looks out over the shipping channel toward Dockyard—a good vantage point to watch the comings and goings of ocean liners and cargo ships. The park attracts a local crowd who wash cars or play cards near the beach. There are public toilets near the parking lot.

Black Watch Well

Ignored by passing Bermudian motorists, Black Watch Well sits at a sometimes chaotic three-way intersection between North Shore Road, Langton Hill, and Black Watch Pass. It is marked by a sign that explains the little structure's history. The well takes its name from the heroic Scottish soldiers of the 1st Battalion of the 42nd Regiment of Loyal Highlanders, who are forever remembered here as having come to the aid of the area's "poor and their cattle in the long drought of 1849." The limestone well they dug down to an underwater lens still bears its wooden roof, though its interior has been capped for safety reasons. Park at nearby C-Mart's parking lot, or across the road at the **Ducking Stool Park,** whose name refers to its history as a site like St. George's, where 17th-century

Just a few minutes from the city center, Spanish Point Park offers tranquil bays for swimming and snorkeling.

public punishments, using a seat on a log to dunk sinners, were frequently staged. These days, it is a popular Cup Match campsite, with deep swimming holes off its scenic cliffs. The dramatic Black Watch Pass is also worth driving or walking through; its towering limestone walls, which were carved by hand in the 1930s, demonstrate a magnificent feat of engineering and also show the crumbling geological strata of local limestone. The pass links North Shore Road with Marsh Folly and Palmetto Roads.

Government House

From the junction of Black Watch Pass and North Shore Road, you can also see the impressive lawns of Government House, whose Victorian towers overlook North Hamilton and the North Shore. While open days for public visits are held occasionally, the property is home to Bermuda's resident British governor who holds numerous official functions here. Built in the late 1800s, the 30-room house sits on 33 acres of manicured lawns and gardens, tennis courts, an Olympic-length swimming pool, forests of cedar and spice trees, and mature plantings made over the years by previous British governors or royal visitors. The grounds are cared for by the Bermuda government's Parks Department. Queen Elizabeth II and Prince Philip have stayed here, as have Prince Charles, Sir Winston Churchill, and President John F. Kennedy. The property, which flies the British governor's own flag when he's on the island, was tainted with a horrific crime in 1973, when then-governor Sir Richard Sharples was shot dead while walking his dog at night, as was his aide-de-camp, Captain Hugh Sayers. Two Bermudian men were convicted of the crime and hanged, and ensuing race riots marked the most bitter, turbulent episode in the island's modern history. The property is used for national and ceremonial functions such as the Queen's Birthday cocktail party in June, held to honor Bermudians receiving lifetime achievement awards bestowed by Buckingham Palace on Commonwealth citizens.

St. John's Church

Built in 1621, the original **St. John's Church** (127 St. John's Rd., tel. 441/292-5308, fax 441/296-9173, admission free) was one of the island's first churches, with a wooden structure and thatched palmetto roof. It was destroyed less than a century later by a hurricane-fed fire and replaced by a stone church, which was demolished in 1821 and rebuilt to meet the needs of a larger congregation. Numerous additions and renovations have been done since then, but the Anglican church remains a historic and popular community landmark ministering to the parish's varied demographics. The church's beautiful interior is notable for its stained glass, bell tower, and 2,418-pipe organ, rebuilt in 1989. The crowded graveyard contains historic family plots—stacked to make more room—interspersed with ancient cedars and other shady trees and shrubs. Funerals are held many weekday afternoons here; there have even been graveside performances by colorfully garbed gombey troupes.

Pembroke Marsh Park

Used as the island's trash dump for the latter part of the 20th century, **Pembroke Marsh Park** (bordered by Marsh Folly Rd. and Parson's Rd., sunrise-sunset daily, admission free) bears the scars of longtime pollution that could take decades to erase. The good news is, that process has already begun, with trash now disposed of at the North Shore incinerator and the marsh today the focus of government plans to return it to public parkland. While scientists say pollution levels in the water are high, the area remains a popular birding site; egrets and herons are seen in the vicinity, along with endemic plantlife. Access is difficult and dirty, however. A public playground, alongside the park on Parson's Road, is a popular attraction for children of all ages.

★ Fort Hamilton

Built in the 1870s, **Fort Hamilton** (Happy Valley Rd. off King St., tel. 441/292-1234, sunrise-sunset daily, admission free), like

Fort St. Catherine in St. George's, remains one of the best-kept examples of the island's historic fortifications. It's equally interesting to historians, gardeners, and sightseers, thanks to its awesome panorama of Hamilton and Pembroke, as well as the Paget shoreline. The fort served as the southern end of the Royal Navy's Prospect defensive line—intended to halt an enemy attack on Spanish Point and thereby protect the Royal Naval Dockyard and fleet anchored at Grassy Bay.

Managed by the Corporation of Hamilton, the fort is used today as a plant nursery, the reason for its meticulously landscaped gardens. Mosaic pathways lead among vibrant flower gardens, and benches are positioned on lower lawns and atop the ramparts, where cannons point out over Hamilton's corporate streets below.

A wooden drawbridge leads into the fort, where a guardroom sits at the entrance. Inside, steps near the entrance lead down into the circular moat garden, planted with gorgeous varieties of ferns, waxy elephant ears, orchids, bromeliads, and other shade-loving species. A skinny dirt path follows the moat completely around; despite the occasional mosquito, it is one of my favorite walks. Along the way, doorways lead into the fort's dungeons, which are worth exploring if you have time. The smell of thick, damp limestone permeates this network of subterranean galleries, which kids especially will find fascinating, though perhaps a little frightening if they're very young. The catacomb is usually well lit, and there are various entrances and exits, including one set of stairs that must number in the hundreds.

A caretaker's cottage is situated on the main lawn, and there are well-maintained restrooms here. Every Monday at noontime throughout the November-March season, kilted dancers and drummers perform a bagpipe "skirling" ceremony at the fort (tel. 441/292-1681 to confirm schedule).

★ Bermuda Underwater Exploration Institute

The world's last frontier—the ocean—is the domain of the **Bermuda Underwater Exploration Institute** (BUEI, 40 Crow Ln., East Broadway, tel. 441/292-7219, ticket desk tel. 441/297-7314, fax 441/236-6141, www.buei.org, 9am-5pm Mon.-Fri., 10am-5pm Sat.-Sun., last ride at 4pm, $12.50 adults, $10 seniors, $6 children 6-17, kids under 5 free). Opened in 1997, the facility's mission to advance understanding and appreciation of the world's oceans is carried out through a small

Fort Hamilton is one of the island's best-preserved examples of British military history.

but interesting array of hands-on exhibits and eye-popping artifacts. The notable collection of early diving apparatus includes a diving bell, exosuit, and a bathysphere replica of the famous metal pod in which William Beebe and Otis Barton descended a half mile down off Bermuda in the 1930s. The adventure starts with a simulated (and rather hokey) submersible dive to the 12,000-foot bottom of Bermuda's seamount.

The institute is a tribute to the career of the late Teddy Tucker, a world-renowned Bermudian diver who retrieved artifacts and dived on most of the island's 150 or more known shipwrecks. The **Tucker Shipwreck Gallery** features a map of known wrecks and exhibits of their contents, including cannons, bottles, and clay jars. The **Treasure Room** displays Spanish gold and pirates' booty collected from local dive sites, as well as a replica of the infamous "Tucker Cross," which mysteriously disappeared from the Bermuda Maritime Museum (now the National Museum of Bermuda) just before Queen Elizabeth II's visit in 1975.

Science at Sea uses interactive exhibits to teach visitors about the body's reaction to the pressures of the deep, and a wall of bioluminescent creatures down a darkened tunnel mimics the feel of the deep ocean. Kids and ichthyologists will especially like the video-simulated shark cage that allows you to experience the charge of a great white. Upstairs, don't miss the **Jack Lightbourn Shell Collection,** showcasing some 1,200 of the Bermudian diver's own shells, including 1,000 different species, of which 110 are Bermudian.

Oceans Gift Shop sells marine-inspired books, games, and toys, including pirate gear and Christmas ornaments. A gourmet restaurant, **The Harbourfront,** is located on the site's waterfront.

BEACHES

Clarence Cove at Admiralty House Park off North Shore Road is a delightful little beach, tucked at the foot of the park and shallow enough for young children. Shady baygrape trees provide welcome cool. Nearby **Deep Bay** is best accessed farther down the North Shore (via unmarked steep, stone steps cut into the hillside off North Shore Road near a bus stop). At low tide, there's a beach here, but it is most popular for diving and jumping into its deep swimming hole.

The coves and bays off **Spanish Point Park**'s North Shore edge are perfect for snorkeling or bathing when the wind's from the

Bermuda Underwater Exploration Institute and the Harbourfront restaurant

south (most of the summer). Shallow reefs here can be seen through clear water even from the shoreline. The route 4 bus comes by here from Hamilton, or you can come by scooter and leave vehicles in the small parking lot.

ENTERTAINMENT AND EVENTS

Weekly **skirling ceremonies** featuring the Bermuda Islands Pipe Band are held at Fort Hamilton (noon on Mon., Nov.-Mar. only). Dancers and drummers in kilts perform for the crowd atop the fort's panoramic ramparts. A weekend film series called **"Bermuda Docs"** (tel. 441/236-3870, www.bermudadocs.com) attracts aficionados on Sunday afternoons throughout the year to the Tradewinds Auditorium at the Bermuda Underwater Exploration Institute (BUEI). Tickets can be purchased from the **BUEI's Oceans Gift Shop** (tel. 441/294-0204) or online via www.bdatix.bm.

Nightlife

"Marina Nights" bring happy-hour crowds on Fridays to the **Fairmont Hamilton Princess**'s harborside terrace (76 Pitts Bay Rd., tel. 441/295-3000, fax 441/295-1914, www.fairmont.com/hamilton-bermuda, 5pm-9pm Fri., Apr.-Oct. only). The big attraction is the elegant hotel's lobby bar and its alfresco terrace, perfect for schmoozing at sunset on the water's edge. Happy-hour drink specials ($5 for beers and rum cocktails) are offered. Rain or shine, there's a live band, DJ, barbecue grill, and cash bar. The Heritage Court bar is open year-round (10am-1am daily). It is, perhaps, Bermuda's most elegant bar, projecting an old-world feel that makes for enjoyable evenings—the $12 martinis notwithstanding.

Many start the weekend early at nearby **Harry's** (The Waterfront, 96 Pitts Bay Rd., tel. 441/292-5533, www.harrys.bm, noon-10pm Mon.-Sat.), where customers can enjoy special prices on martinis or sample the award-winning wines and champagnes in the popular spot's clublike atmosphere or on its waterside patio.

Located on the ground floor of Bermuda's tallest corporate glass tower, **Taste One Four One** (141 Front Street East, tel. 441/292-0777, 5pm-9pm Mon.-Thurs., 5pm-midnight Fri.) is a contemporary watering hole with Friday night happy-hour tapas (tempura wahoo nuggets $7) and a live DJ or band on tap.

Get local with a visit to the **Spanish Point Boat Club** (Spanish Point Rd., tel. 441/295-1030, fax 441/292-8024, 11:30am-midnight Mon.-Thurs. and Sun., 11:30am-1am Fri. and Sat.), whose bar has a nightly gathering of neighborhood residents, local fishers, and other regulars who like the $3 highballs and beer. Like its sign says, the facility is a members' club, but tourists are welcome.

Another waterfront drinking spot with authentically Bermudian ambience is the Blue Water Anglers Club's **Hook & Hold Bar** (28 East Broadway, tel. 441/292-5529, www.bwac.bm, 5pm-midnight Fri.), where Friday nights see a reunion of regulars who come for waterside sunset cocktails and DJ entertainment.

The Robin Hood Pub & Restaurant (25 Richmond Rd., tel. 441/295-3314, fax 441/292-9338, www.robinhood.bm, 11:30am-1am daily) has a lively sports-bar scene, including quiz nights and live soccer and NHL showdowns on big-screen TVs. It's a favorite stomping ground for British and Canadian expat residents.

SHOPPING

Jeremy Johnson's Village Carpentry (127 North Shore, tel. 441/292-2088 or 441/295-5370, villagecraft@northrock.bm, 8am-4pm Mon.-Fri.) has been a roadside institution since the 1960s. Today Johnson's aromatic workshop, spreading the scent of cedar along this stretch of North Shore, is worth a visit to get a glimpse of cedar craftspeople at work. He sells cedar trinkets, animals, bowls, trays, bookends, and other sweet-smelling mementos from the roadside building.

SPORTS AND RECREATION

Tennis

Anyone can play at the government-owned **William Joell Tennis Stadium** (2 Marsh Folly Rd. at Cedar Ave., tel. 441/292-0105, fax 441/292-4802, 8am-10pm Mon.-Fri., 8am-7pm Sat.-Sun., $10 an hour). The busy facility, named for the Bermudian recognized for knocking down racial barriers in the sport, has eight courts (three clay, five hard courts), three of which are lit for night play and can be rented for an additional $8 fee. Traditional tennis attire is required, and advance bookings are recommended. Peak times are after 5pm and on Saturday mornings. Tennis pro **Terry Smith** (tel. 441/335-2468, itptennis@ibl.bm) gives private lessons (adults $70 an hour, juniors $60). The shop sells cold drinks and tennis balls and also rents rackets.

Scuba and Water Sports

The **Bermuda Sub-Aqua Club** (Admiralty House Park, tel. 441/292-9656 or 441/291-5640, www.bsac.bm) is a NAUI-registered training and diving organization. It arranges regular expeditions for its 150 members throughout the year. Club nights are held on Wednesday evenings after 7:30pm at the clubhouse, a pink building on the right as you enter the park. Visitors are welcome.

Fishing

Spanish Point Boat Club (Spanish Point Rd., tel. 441/295-1030, fax 441/292-8024) is one of the island's main sportfishing hubs, with docks and hauling equipment outside where boats land their record catches. A members' club, it nevertheless welcomes tourists.

Veteran sportfishing king Allen DeSilva runs **Mako Charters** (11 Abri Ln., Spanish Point, tel. 441/295-0835, fax 441/295-3620, www.fishbermuda.com) aboard his 56-foot air-conditioned Carolina sportfisher, *Mako*, the island's largest charter fishing vessel. DeSilva holds the current blue marlin record at 1,352-pounds, and boasts one-day hauls such as 44 yellowfin tuna. Full-day (nine hours) charters for four people, beverages included, cost $2,000 ($100 per extra person), six hours $1,700; a $500 deposit is required. Charters carry a maximum of eight people.

Tuna specialist Captain Kevin Winter operates **Playmate Charters** (4 Mill Point Ln., tel. 441/292-7131, boat cell 441/335-5172 or 441/799-8862, fax 441/292-9598, www.playmatefishing.bm), offering full-day ($1,350), three-quarter day ($1,200), and half-day

William Joell Tennis Stadium

With its lush display of mature flora, Fort Hamilton's moat is a botanical treasure.

($900) charters aboard the 43-foot *Playmate,* a Torres Sports Fisherman outfitted with tournament tackle, a fighting chair, two fishing chairs, outriggers, downriggers, kites, and other accessories for modern game-fishing. Maximum 10 people for all charters.

Soccer

Evening and weekend soccer games are held at the clubhouse field of the **Bermuda Athletic Association** (BAA, 24 Woodlands Rd., tel. 441/292-3161), an organization that has promoted a wide gamut of sports on the island—football (soccer), badminton, rugby, swimming, track and field—for over a century. Admission is usually free.

Spas

Inner Sanctum Spa & Salon (Outerbridge Bldg., 85 Pitts Bay Rd., spa tel. 441/296-9009, salon tel. 441/295-4808, www.bermudaspasandsalons.com, 9am-6pm Mon., Tues., Sat., and Sun., 9am-8pm Wed., Thurs., and Fri.) offers massage (25 minutes $80), facials, body treatments, waxing, manicures (45 minutes $52), and pedicures, as well as hairdressing, for men and women.

For Kids

The government-run **Parson's Road Playground** is a popular attraction for children from all over the island. Parents bring their kids after school at 3:30pm, and holidays find the swings, slides, tunnels, fort, and pirate ship crowded with happy youngsters. There's also plenty of parking.

Spanish Point Park's tiny coves and quiet, shallow bays are just what children love, and kids can spend hours here exploring rock pools, snorkeling, and swimming. The park's North Shore edge, dotted with coves, is best when the wind is blowing from the south; in the winter the water gets choppy. Shady trees, lawns for playing, and picnic tables make this a perfect family spot.

Don't miss **Fort Hamilton's moat garden and dungeons** (Happy Valley Rd. off King St., tel. 441/292-1234, 8am-sunset daily, admission free), one of the Hamilton area's best kid-pleasing attractions, or **Admiralty House Park**'s forested trails and rocky tunnels (junction of North Shore Rd. and Spanish Point Rd., sunrise-sunset daily, admission free).

ACCOMMODATIONS

Under $200

Tucked into a residential lane off Pitts Bay, **Kingston House Bed & Breakfast** (5 Turnstile Ln. off Pitts Bay Rd., tel. 441/295-6597, www.bbbermuda.com, $145-180 s, $170-220 d) has won glowing reviews for Bermudian hosts Harry and Marlie Powell, who converted their 1921 two-story homestead into a B&B in 1999. The house, which boasts an Endless-brand pool and is surrounded by mature gardens, has three rentals. The elegant Palmetto Suite is the largest, with a queen bed, en suite bathroom, and sitting room with fireplace and balcony. The Bird of Paradise Room has twin beds that can be converted into a king, an en suite bathroom,

Made in Bermuda

There's always a T-shirt or paperweight to take home, but if you look around, you'll find far more interesting souvenirs of your trip to Bermuda.

Established in 1928, the **Bermuda Perfumery** (Stewart Hall, 5 Queen St., St. George's, tel. 441/293-0627, toll-free U.S. tel. 800/527-8213, www.bermuda-perfumery.com or www.lilibermuda.com) used to operate out of the rambling gardens of a historic estate in Hamilton Parish. When the land was sold in the late 1990s, the business moved to the Town of St. George, and today, the popular Lili line of fragrances, including perfume (0.5 oz./15 ml $95), soaps, body lotions, and bath and shower gel, is sold in stores islandwide. In 2014, a Lili boutique opened in Hamilton (Butterfield Walkway, 67 Front St., 441/296-2885). The scents appear to have a fervent fan base overseas, including Bermudians' friends and relatives who get hooked on the scent of Frangipani, or who *must* have a bottle of Pink to wear at their wedding. Other scents include Easter lily, jasmine, oleander, and passion flower. You can learn all about their production by visiting the Bermuda Perfumery and its pretty little garden, now housed at a historic Bermuda National Trust property.

There's nothing more Bermudian than cedar—the *Juniperus bermudiana* variety, of course. Cedar trinkets are sold in various stores around the island, but you can watch the maestro in person at the **Bermuda Arts Centre** (tel. 441/234-2809, www.artbermuda.bm) at Dockyard. Cedar craftsman Chesley Trott is often there, working wonders out of a pile of gnarled silver twigs or tree trunks. Pull-toys and public-art sculptures are his specialty; all of Trott's works demand top prices. **Jeremy Johnson's Village Carpentry** (127 North Shore, Pembroke, tel. 441/292-2088) is also worth dropping into. The aromatic roadside workshop sells cedar animals and other hand-carved mementos. In Paget, high-polish cedar trays and goblets made by prison inmates and sold at the **Masterworks Museum of Bermuda Art** (in Bermuda Botanical Gardens,183 South Rd., www.bermudamasterworks.com) make gorgeous gifts.

Gosling's Black Seal Rum will ensure your enjoyment of black 'n' cokes and dark 'n' stormies long after you leave Bermuda. Bottles of rum (one-liter $13), as well as Gosling's and Horton's rum cakes, can be found at **Bermuda Duty Free** (Departures Hall, tel. 441/293-2870), the retail outlet at L. F. Wade International Airport.

and a balcony, while the Jacaranda Room has a queen bed and en suite bathroom. A light breakfast is served in the dining room or on the outside patio. The property's convenient location on the edge of Hamilton allows easy access to ferries, bus stops, shopping, and city dining.

$200-300

The **Oxford House** (20 Woodbourne Ave., tel. 441/295-0503, fax 441/295-0250, www.oxfordhouse.bm, $246 s, $270 d including breakfast) has seen its cityside neighborhood drastically change over the past few decades: The Bermudiana Hotel once stood opposite until its site was transformed into insurance towers for the ACE and XL companies in the 1990s. But this quaint, British-style, two-story guesthouse has proudly stood its ground against the corporate invasion—and benefited hugely, thanks to the influx of business travelers. Oxford's small, elegant rooms offer exactly what's demanded by anyone attending meetings within a few blocks, or visitors who plan to spend most of their time in Hamilton or want a central location that's not on a beach. Twelve guest rooms are furnished like private residences, almost dollhouse-like with dressers and curtains and floral bedspreads. Each has a private bath, coffeemaker, air-conditioning, and cable TV. Free WiFi throughout. Continental breakfast is served in the lounge every morning.

Edgehill Manor (36 Rosemont Ave., tel. 441/295-7124, fax 441/295-3850, www.edgehillmanorguesthouse.bm, $250 s, $280 d) is a refurbished Colonial-style mansion turned bed-and-breakfast. Seven large rooms—four

Island artworks are some of the highest quality and nicest products visitors can buy to take Bermuda home with them. **The Bermuda Society of Arts** (City Hall and Arts Centre, tel. 441/292-3824) holds regular shows, and its office stocks members' oils, acrylics, watercolors, sculpture, and other media for sale. Artist Barbara Finsness's popular **Island Shop** (3 Queen St., tel. 441/292-5292, or 49 Front St., Old Cellar Ln., tel. 441/292-6307) carries her designs on linen tablecloths and place settings, handbags, Christmas ornaments, and ceramics. Gift shop **Pulp & Circumstance** (4 Washington Ln., tel. 441/292-9586) has greeting cards by Bermudian artists and photographers.

Bermuda stamps and coins make good souvenirs. The General Post Office's **Philatelic Bureau** (corner of Church St. and Parliament St., tel. 441/297-7807) sells collections of commemorative stamps, featuring themes of cultural and historical significance to the island. Numismatists seek out the **Bermuda Monetary Authority** (43 Victoria St., tel. 441/295-5278, www.bma.bm) for boxed gift sets of Bermuda coins, including commemoratives such as 2005's gold and silver quincentennial issue and the island's distinctive new set of vertical notes, released in 2009.

Support internationally recognized Bermudian writers and musicians. **Nadia Aguiar**'s books, *The Lost Island of Tamarind* and *Secrets of Tamarind* (Macmillan/Feiwel & Friends, 2008 and 2011)—two volumes of an upcoming trilogy for the youth market that was heavily inspired by Bermuda—have won glowing reviews and can be found in bookstores on both sides of the Atlantic. Buy a CD by Bermudian **Heather Nova** (www.heathernova.com), an ethereal singer-songwriter with Lilith Fair and movie-soundtrack credits to her name. Her ninth studio album, recorded in Charleston, South Carolina, but inspired by Bermuda's nature and ocean, was to be released in 2015. Find her music at **The Music Box** (58 Reid St., tel. 441/295-4839), on the racks in North America and Europe, or online. Reggae and dancehall star **Collie Buddz** (www.colliebuddz.com) also has Bermuda roots; he grew up on the island, married a Bermudian, and spends time here when he is not selling out tour venues in the United States and Canada. Both his albums, *Collie Buddz* (2007) and *Playback* (2011) were critically acclaimed, and in 2014, he teamed up with Riff Raff and Snoop Dogg for a reggae-inspired hit called "Yesterday."

upstairs with private balconies and splendid views—have air-conditioning, ceiling fans, private bathrooms, cable TV, WiFi, small refrigerators, microwaves, safes, and clock radios. The property also has a large freshwater pool in the quiet garden. It's located in a pretty neighborhood just a seven-minute walk from central Hamilton.

Winner of TripAdvisor's 2014 Traveler's Choice Award for best hotel in the Caribbean, ★ **Royal Palms** (24 Rosemont Ave., tel. 441/292-1854, U.S. toll-free tel. 800/678-0783, Canada toll-free tel. 800/799-0824, fax 441/292-1946, www.royalpalms.bm, $375-472 d, including breakfast) is a former manor house on the edge of Hamilton, set in a gorgeous English-style garden overflowing with birdsong, bougainvillea, and citrus trees. The sophisticated little hotel offers impeccable rooms, professional service, and relaxing surroundings that make you wish you were permanently on holiday. With its hallmark white shutters and wraparound veranda, the turn-of-the-20th-century property's other big draw is its standout restaurant, **Ascot's.** A total of 32 rooms and suites are decorated in European florals with high ceilings, classic moldings, and window seats overlooking the lawns. All have cable TV, air-conditioning, and high-speed Internet access. There's also a small but very private pool. Not surprisingly, Royal Palms is usually fully booked by business visitors on weekdays, but it makes a perfect weekend escape for couples. A few minisuites have kitchenettes. Owned and operated by the Bermudian Smith family, it is one of the island's best small hotels.

Elegant **Rosedon** (61 Pitts Bay Rd., tel.

441/295-1640, fax 441/295-5904, www.rosedon.com, $310-484 d) stands opposite the Fairmont Hamilton Princess and is one of Pitts Bay's grand old mansions, built in 1906. Decorated like an English manor home, with rooms boasting oak, mahogany, cherry, and redwood, the small bed-and-breakfast hotel is popular with business travelers, given its amenities and short walk from Hamilton. Rosedon's 44 rooms—some in the main house, but most in an adjacent building next to the pool—have cable TV, air-conditioning, private baths, phones, refrigerators, coffeemakers, and WiFi. "Royal Rooms" are a step up, with CD players and whirlpool tubs. Same-day laundry service is available. Guests have a choice of picnic lunches or poolside à la carte service, and at 4pm every day, staff members serve a grand afternoon tea. The hotel also offers wedding and honeymoon packages.

Over $300

Fondly known locally as "The Princess" and often dubbed the "Pink Palace," the ★ **Fairmont Hamilton Princess** (76 Pitts Bay Rd., tel. 441/295-3000, toll-free 800/330-8272, fax 441/295-1914, www.fairmont.com/hamilton-bermuda, 410 rooms, $480-3,200 in high season) has been a fixture of the Pitts Bay waterfront since Victorian times. The candy-pink hotel was built in honor of Queen Victoria's daughter, Princess Louise, who visited Bermuda in 1883, launching a tourism industry in her wake. The historic landmark property is currently enjoying an exciting renaissance, thanks to its 2012 purchase by the Bermuda-based billionaire Green family who launched a $90-million refurbishment. The massive makeover has brought substantial upgrades to the lobby and **Heritage Court** area as well as to 69 guestrooms and suites, along with construction of a state-of-the-art, 60-berth marina, large infinity pool with hot tub, private cabanas with bar/food service, and two new restaurants with eye-popping views—the open-air **1609** on the marina, and **Marcus',** a 3,000 square-foot eatery in the former Gazebo Room scheduled for opening in 2015 by celebrity chef Marcus Samuelsson.

The Princess, famous during World War II as an intelligence center where mail and radio communications were analyzed by more than 1,000 British "censorettes," is just a scenic 15-minute walk from Hamilton's center. Guest rooms and suites offer either harbor views or a garden/pool outlook such as the redone, poolside Poinciana Wing. Some have private balconies with views stretching up the Great Sound. The property is a favorite with Hamilton's corporate visitors, offering high-speed Internet, dataports, spacious work desks, telephones with voicemail, and cable TV. "Fairmont Gold" suites offer even more business amenities. Guests are able to use facilities at the Fairmont Southampton Resort, including a golf course, beach, scuba center, tennis courts, and large world-class spa. A bespoke oceanfront club for The Princess is also on the horizon: the Green family purchased the sweeping former Sonesta Beach Resort site on Southampton's South Shore in 2013, and plans were forging ahead to open the **Princess Beach Club** on Sinky Beach in 2015. The complex would have amenities such as an open-air pavilion, six cabanas, and waiter service via an on-site restaurant.

FOOD

Cafés, Pubs, and Takeout

One of Bermuda's best and most gargantuan fish sandwiches can be found at ★ **Art Mel's Spicy Dicy** (9 St. Monica's Rd., north off Marsh Folly Rd., tel. 441/295-3965, noon-10pm Mon.-Fri., noon-8pm Sat.), which, though tucked away in Pembroke's backstreets since the 1960s, is searched out by fish-lovers, from uniformed school students and construction workers to suited actuaries, thanks to its word-of-mouth praise. Run by the jovial Art Smith, his eldest son Rockking, and other family members, the simple eatery cooks up its multi-award-winning stacked sandwich ($16.50) with your choice of plain or toasted white, wheat, or raisin bread and coleslaw, cheese, or onions, along with melt-in-your mouth fries, crispy fish cakes on buns ($5), burgers ($5.25), and other fast food. Follow your nose—and the lines of people.

Grannie's Kitchen (113 North Shore Rd., opposite First Church of God, tel. 441/292-2914, 7am-5:30pm Mon.-Fri., 8am-5:30pm Sat., 8am-2:30pm Sun.) is another badly kept local secret—the go-to café for fish sandwiches and fish cakes, in particular, along with burgers and sandwiches. In-the-know tour guides make pit stops here to show off true "Bermy" cuisine.

Chill to a contemporary vibe at **Taste One Four One** (141 Front St. East, tel. 441/292-0777, breakfast 8am-11am, lunch 11am-3pm, tapas 5pm-9pm Mon.-Fri.), where corporate types pull in en route to nearby offices for morning bacon-and-egg wraps. The seasonally inspired lunch menu ranges from salads ($10), fish sandwiches ($16.50), veggie and bacon burgers ($15), and "B.Y.O.S." (Build Your Own Sandwiches, $14.50) to entrées such as curry pumpkin and couscous ($15.50) and Cajun salmon ($18.50). Try a deep-fried Snickers bar for dessert. Small plates in the evening offer up truffle fries, fish tacos, flatbreads, and sliders.

Buzz West Hamilton (69 Pitts Bay Rd., tel. 441/295-1723, www.buzzcafe.bm, 6:30am-5pm Mon.-Fri., 8am-4pm Sat., 8am-3pm Sun.) is one of two Pembroke outlets of the busy coffee-and-snacks franchise, along with the more hidden **Buzz Bakery Lane** (19 Bakery Ln. off Serpentine Rd., tel. 441/292-2311, 7am-6pm Mon.-Fri., 8am-4:30pm Sat.).

Tasty pizzas ($13-25, including take-out service) and loads of beer and pub grub get crowds to **The Robin Hood Pub & Restaurant** (25 Richmond Rd., tel. 441/295-3314, fax 441/292-9338, www.robinhood.bm, lunch 11am-4pm daily, dinner 4pm-10pm, bar open until 1am), where British soccer and Tuesday quiz nights entertain regulars. Breakfast sandwiches ($7.50), steak platters ($27), pastas ($16), nachos ($9.75), UK staples like bangers and mash ($16.25), and Indian curries ($16) keep customers satisfied with big helpings and reasonable prices. Opening hours depend on scheduled live sports events, which are carried via satellite TV.

International

Foodies were abuzz with anticipation for the provisionally named ★ **Marcus',** the new 180-seat restaurant to be launched in May 2015 by celebrity chef, author, and TV personality Marcus Samuelsson at the Fairmont Hamilton Princess (76 Pitts Bay Rd., tel. 441/295-3000, fax 441/295-1914, www.fairmont.com/hamilton-bermuda). The dapper Ethiopian Swedish star of TV's *Chopped* and *Iron Chef* series, who owns several award-winning restaurants in the United States and Sweden including Harlem's Red Rooster, made a well-received Bermuda foray in 2014 with a two-month "pop-up" taster of things to come. Included on the menu were small-plate dishes fusing fresh Bermuda fish and produce and the island's own culinary hits with Southern, West Indian, and Portuguese influences (fish chowder croquettes, dark 'n' stormy sorbet, jerk pork belly, cornbread madeleines). The new permanent, open-floor plan rendition, inhabiting 3,000 square feet in the former Gazebo Room plus a 1,500 square-foot veranda above the harbor, will be one of Bermuda's largest eateries.

Location, location, location has brought swooning lunch, dinner, and happy-hour crowds to **1609 Bar & Restaurant** (Fairmont Hamilton Princess, 76 Pitts Bay Rd., tel. 441/295-3000, fax 441/295-1914, www.bermuda1609.com, 11am-10pm daily, early spring to late fall) since it opened at the hotel in the summer of 2014. The 2,500-square-foot open-space bar and grill—named for the date Bermuda's first 150 colonists made landfall after their ship wrecked—stretches along the landmark property's new state-of-the-art, 60-berth marina, serving up breathtaking views of the harbor and Great Sound along with a casual comfort-food menu. The seasonal venue, part of the hotel's $90-million renovation, has 125 seats, of which 25 are along the expansive bar. Dishes include salads, pizzas ($20), burgers, pulled pork and grilled local wahoo sandwiches ($20), roasted red snapper ($32), and steak frites ($38). With its contemporary glass walls and push-out shutters, there's perhaps no other local venue that quite screams "island life" so thrillingly. Savor a grapefruit cosmo in the balmy breeze while you watch spinnakers sail home and the sun melt over the West End.

Ask a local foodie their go-to choice, and chances are **Mad Hatters** (22 Richmond Rd., tel. 441/297-6231, www.madhatters.bm, lunch noon-2pm Mon.-Fri., dinner 6pm-9pm Mon.-Sat.) will trip off their tongue. Despite its rather humble, though intimate, appearance, tucked into a dining room and outdoor patio of the Mariners Club sailors' home, the restaurant never fails to impress with stellar service and outstanding dishes that showcase the talents of British chef Ben Jewett. Fresh seafood, including flown-in mussels and oysters, highlights a menu that includes creations like scallops and shrimp in Thai green curry sauce ($34), banana-nut-crusted Bermuda rockfish in dark'n'stormy sauce ($36), a shrimp and gravlax tower ($18), mussels in garlic cream sauce ($17), and rack of lamb ($38). Vegetarians can also enjoy innovative culinary treatment daily—just make your request to the chef. Inside, a collection of wacky hats speaks to the venue's Alice-in-Wonderland inspiration; in the spirit of British bonhomie that pervades the restaurant, diners can try these on or don a favorite bonnet for the night.

Multi-award-winning restaurant **Harbourfront** (at Bermuda Underwater Exploration Institute, 40 Crow Ln., East Broadway, tel. 441/295-4207, www.diningbermuda.com/harbourfront, lunch 11:45am-3pm Mon.-Sat., dinner 6pm-10pm daily, happy hour 5pm-6:30pm Mon.-Fri.) is one of the island's best-patronized establishments; everyone from Bermuda's politicos to local athletes to international CEOs dines here. That's no surprise, given the venue's winning combination of fine service, a delicious menu—including a full sushi and tempura selection—indoor or dockside dining, and water views all the way up the harbor. Whether you order an oyster tempura appetizer ($22), venison ravioli ($34), pan-seared yellowfin tuna ($35), dry-aged boneless striploin steak ($49), or a tray of sashimi and *temaki*, you won't be disappointed by the food or ambience. Maître d' Pierangelo Lanfranchi, a Lake Como native, makes all his customers feel like VIPs.

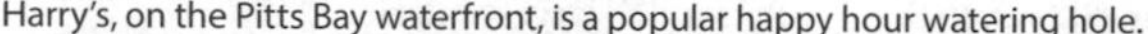
Harry's, on the Pitts Bay waterfront, is a popular happy hour watering hole.

Onion Nation

If you call someone on the island "a real onion," there can be no stronger endorsement of their genuine Bermudian-ness. "Onion" is a popular term of endearment among locals, and numerous businesses also use onion in their names, though none have anything to do with selling the aromatic vegetable.

Bermuda's fascination with onions dates back to the late 1800s, when crates of the pungent bulb grown by island farmers were shipped off to winter markets in New York, Philadelphia, and other East Coast urban centers, along with potatoes, tomatoes, lilies, and arrowroot. Hamilton's docks were the major shipment hub for thousands of barrels and crates of produce. Red or white Bermuda onions—known for their mild, sweet taste—remained a major island export until cheaper produce from California and Florida, coupled with higher U.S. import tariffs, put an end to the handsome profits in the early 1900s.

Bermuda still harvests onions, but not for export. Seek them out at farmer's markets or roadside stands—their legendary taste will not disappoint. You'll also find onion tarts, jams, chutneys and other dishes on many local restaurant menus.

Named for bon vivant Harry Cox, the 20th-century patriarch of Bermuda's veritable Cox family, ★ **Harry's** (The Waterfront, 96 Pitts Bay Road, tel. 441/292-5533, www.harrys.bm, lunch noon-2:30pm, dinner 6pm-10pm, tapas at the bar noon-10pm Mon.-Sat.) is a gourmand's heaven. Tucked down at the Cox-owned corporate complex on the harborside, across the lane from that other foodie mecca, Miles Market, the elegantly designed steakhouse boasts a 300-strong wine list, granite and dark wood finishes, and a menu that can't help but impress. Menu highlights include appetizers like steamed clams, tempura lobster, and beef tartare ($10-21); entrées include honey-glazed pork chops ($39), braised beef shortrib risotto ($39), a sea bass bowl ($36), and rack of lamb with truffle bread pudding ($40), with must-have sides such as creamed spinach and house-cut fries with truffle oil. A private dining room can be booked for special group occasions. Don't miss the extraordinary urinal in the men's bathroom—designed like a giant lily.

Comfort meets cosmopolitan at **Bouchée** (75 Pitts Bay Rd., tel. 441/295-5759, fax 441/296-0166, www.bouchee.bm, breakfast 7:30am-11:30am Mon.-Fri., lunch 11:30am-2:30pm Mon.-Fri., dinner 6pm-10pm Mon.-Sat., breakfast/brunch 7:30am-2:30pm Sat. and Sun.), where you will be made to feel at home with local regulars. The French-inspired menu includes breakfast fare such as omelets, crepes, pancakes, and eggs Benedict ($10-15), along with a weekend-only codfish and potatoes tradition ($16.50). For lunch, tuck into croques and crevettes, quiches, moules frites (full portion $32), and croissant sandwiches. Dinner dishes include foie gras ($15.50), pan-seared duck breast ($28), butternut squash gnocchi ($17), organic salads, and Bermuda fish chowder ($8).

Ascot's (Royal Palms Hotel, 24 Rosemont Ave., tel. 441/295-9644, 441/296-0831, or 441/292-0980, fax 441/292-4986, www.ascotsrestaurant.bm, lunch noon-2:30pm Mon.-Fri., dinner 6:30pm-10pm Mon.-Sat.) is where Northern Ireland's Edmund Smith cut his chef's teeth before winning international awards with his fresh take on Bermudian cuisine. Entrées include pasta and vegetarian dishes, as well as grilled salmon with mangoes and roasted almonds ($42.50), roasted veal tenderloin ($45), and sautéed tiger shrimp with Thai laksa sauce ($45). Lunch at **Just 24,** on the veranda of this 19th-century manor house, offers more casual dining with salads, burgers, and open-faced sandwiches

($8-25)—plus views of the gardens spilling with bougainvillea, shady poincianas, and citrus.

Tearooms

An over-the-top afternoon tea is served daily in the expanded ★ **Heritage Court** (Fairmont Hamilton Princess, 76 Pitts Bay Rd., tel. 441/295-3000, fax 441/295-1914, www.fairmont.com/hamilton-bermuda). A Best of Bermuda Award winner, and repeatedly recognized as one of the top 10 afternoon teas in the world, the feast includes finger sandwiches, scones with jam and clotted cream, pastries, sorbets—and 14 teas, including several loose-leaf black varieties, as well as green, herbal, and fruit teas. The tea (starting at $17.95) is served 2pm-5pm daily in the lobby-area court, which got an update in 2014 with outdoor terrace seating, fire pits, and pergolas where the koi ponds used to be.

Groceries

To describe **Miles Market** (The Waterfront, Pitts Bay, tel. 441/295-1234, customer-service fax 441/296-4537, www.miles.bm, 7:30am-7pm Mon.-Sat., noon-5pm Sun.) as a mere grocery store is a bit of an understatement. The specialty food store—owned by the Cox family, to whom the entire surrounding waterfront complex belongs—Miles has been a fixture of the gourmet scene since 1862. Today, in a modern headquarters, it boasts highly professional staff and pretty much any foodstuff an epicurean could desire. Of course, you need a trust fund to shop here: It's hard to escape without spending at least $100 just on sundries. Miles's meat department is the island's best, with melt-in-your-mouth cuts and both wet-aged and dry-aged beef selections. Treats include cheeses from around the world; fresh croissants, muffins, and *pains du chocolat*; a menu of olive oils and marmalades; ethnic sections; wines from France, Napa, and Lebanon; and organic everything. Dinner-party hostesses live here. Miles also has a coffee bar, Café Godiva, so you can sip a latte or cappuccino while you shop. The store's Miles To Go deli offers takeout feasts (salads, fish cakes, polenta, grilled vegetables), and staff pack up lunch boxes or gourmet picnics to order (smoked salmon, grilled chicken, fresh fruit platter, strawberry tartlet). Picnic menus start at $19.95; to order call 441/295-1234, ext. 255.

Garden Market (13 Serpentine Rd., tel. 441/292-7000, fax 441/295-1260, 7am-7pm Mon.-Thurs., 7am-8pm Fri. and Sat.) is a family business with friendly staff, vegetables from local farmers, flowers, wine, and liquor.

Arnold's Family Market (113 St. John's Rd., tel. 441/292-3310, 6:30am-midnight daily) is a bustling neighborhood hub that has morphed over recent years from a tiny, cramped grocery to a modern expanse. There's a large liquor section, meats, produce, baked goods, magazines, and pharmaceuticals. The place is a zoo on Friday and Saturday nights.

With ample parking on the stretch of North Shore leading east from Hamilton, **C-Mart** (96 North Shore Rd., at the corner of Black Watch Pass and Langton Hill, tel. 441/292-5332, fax 441/292-4245, 7am-6pm Mon-Thurs., 7am-7pm Fri. and Sat., 8am-12:30pm Sun.) makes a convenient stop for snacks, drinks, newspapers, or liquor. The tiny outlet, a favorite with Cup Match campers who set up in the seafront park opposite, also sells fresh baked goods, hot pies, sodas, and dry and frozen goods.

Point Mart (Cox's Hill, tel. 441/292-0342, 8am-9pm Mon.-Sat.) is tiny but well stocked.

Manuel Soares & Son (Old House Ln., Spanish Point, tel. 441/292-1426, 7am-8pm Mon.-Sat.) is the only grocery store down in the heart of Spanish Point.

Liquor Stores

Serpentine Liquors (15 Serpentine Rd., tel.441/292-7842, 8am-8pm Mon.-Sat.) touts "the coldest beer around" along with a full wines and spirits selection.

INFORMATION AND SERVICES

Woodbourne Chemist (Woodbourne Ave., tel. 441/295-2663, 8am-6pm Mon.-Sat.) is Pembroke's only pharmacy, conveniently located near several hotels and guesthouses.

Gas stations around the parish include: Rubis East Broadway Service Station (25 Crow Ln., tel. 441/296-7225, 7am-midnight Mon.-Sat., 8am-10pm Sun.); Rubis St. John's Road Station (61 St. John's Rd., tel. 441/297-5111, 7am-7pm Mon.-Sat., 10am-6pm Sun.); and Rubis Waterfront (2 Waterloo Ln. at The Waterfront, tel. 441/295-3185, 8am-6pm Mon.-Sat. Apr.-Oct., 8am-5pm Mon.-Sat. Nov.-Apr.).

Public toilets are in Spanish Point Park, Admiralty House Park, Fort Hamilton, hotels, and restaurants.

ATMs are located at the Butterfield Bank Waterfront branch (90 Pitts Bay Rd., tel. 441/294-2070).

GETTING THERE AND AROUND

The beauty of staying in Pembroke is that all points in Hamilton are walkable. Pembroke has no ferry stops, but the Front Street terminal is close by.

Buses

Numerous bus routes serve Pembroke, all departing from the **central bus terminal** in Hamilton (Washington St. between Church St. and Victoria St., tel. 441/292-3854). To visit Spanish Point, take route 4 (buses run every 20 minutes). Routes 10 and 11 (every 15 minutes) head north through Pembroke on their way to St. George's; route 10 takes North Shore Road (Black Watch Pass) and route 11 goes via Palmetto Road. Route 5 (hourly, or every half hour at peak commuter times) travels to Pond Hill via Glebe Road. Route 9 (hourly) runs between Hamilton and Prospect, Devonshire. Bus routes 2 (hourly) and 3 (every half hour) head east out of Hamilton, the route 2 along East Broadway (Bermuda Underwater Exploration Institute) and route 3 along Cavendish Road into Devonshire (Fort Hamilton). Fares to Hamilton Parish and St. George's are $4.50, to all other areas on these routes $3 (exact change or tokens, tickets, or passes required). Children under age 5 ride free; the charge for all zones for kids 5 to 15 is $2.50.

Scooters and Bicycles

Oleander Cycles (15 Gorham Rd., tel. 441/295-0919, 441/236-5235 for after-hours assistance, www.oleandercycles.bm, 8:30am-5:30pm Mon.-Sat.) rents standard single or double scooters. Rates ($55 standard/$65 double for one day, $225 standard/$266 double per week, $17/$21 per day after seven days) include scooter delivery and pickup (or hotel pickup), first tank of gas, helmet, lock, basket, $30 third-party insurance, and islandwide roadside service for breakdowns. Prefer to pedal? Mountain bikes are $40 a day, $175 per week, $10 a day after seven days.

Smatt's Cycle Livery (74 Pitts Bay Rd., tel. 441/295-1180, fax 441/295-2539, www.smattscyclelivery.com, 8am-5pm daily) is directly outside the Fairmont Hamilton Princess. The outlet rents single-seat ($50 per day) and dual-seat ($55) scooters ($225/$267 per week). Islandwide roadside assistance is part of the deal. Pedal bikes are also available, for $55 per day, $160 per week.

Taxis

There are taxi stands outside the Fairmont Hamilton Princess. To order a cab, call the island's three main cab companies: **Bermuda Industrial Union Co-op** (tel. 441/292-4476, cooptaxi@fkbnet.bm), **Bermuda Island Taxi** (tel. 441/295-4141, www.bermudaislandtaxi.com), or **BTA Dispatching Ltd.** (tel. 441/296-2121, www.taxibermuda.bm).

Devonshire and Paget Parishes

Like sisters who may look alike but behave entirely differently, Devonshire and Paget share common traits but occupy divergent places in the collective imagination. With their verdant valleys, rolling farmland, old estates, centuries-old churches, and nature reserves, the regions are fairly similar in appearance and incorporate a variety of geography, from coastal regions to inland farms. Both are heavily residential, and steeped in history—Paget's of the seafaring variety, Devonshire more military-minded. Unfortunately, both parishes have also borne the brunt of modern-day progress, serving as conduits for ever-increasing streams of traffic moving between the city and the rest of the Bermuda.

Yet the parishes' differences become more apparent by spending time in each. Devonshire is deep country in the most laid-back sense, with deserted coast-view trails, quiet cedar-fringed farms, stables, and tucked-away family estates where, amid walled meadows and wooded drives, you might imagine you were in the heart of the English countryside. Its shoreline communities are just as relaxed, with fishers' stalls and dry goods stores that belong to another century. Noisier, more developed Paget has its quiet spots, certainly, but overall, it proffers a more suburban edge—no surprise, since it gazes across the narrow foot of the harbor at the city, and its coveted Harbour Road properties were earned long ago by merchants and traders, yesterday's movers and shakers. Together, both parishes encompass central Bermuda and, along with Pembroke, are generally considered the most desirable areas in real estate. They boast a massing of old money and a convenient proximity to Hamilton (5-10 minutes, with fewer traffic jams than other areas en route to the city).

Devonshire's bucolic borders begin northeast of Hamilton, touching Pembroke at the junction of Spruce Lane and North Shore Road, and continuing south along Glebe Road to Paget's edge at Foot of the Lane. Devonshire's contents then spill east, spreading between South and North Shores as far as Collector's Hill and Cable Hill. Undulating

Previous: elegant Camden House in the Bermuda Botanical Gardens; Coral Beach & Tennis Club's pink strand. **Above:** Freesias welcomes visitors to Palm Grove Gardens.

Look for ★ to find recommended sights, activities, dining, and lodging.

Highlights

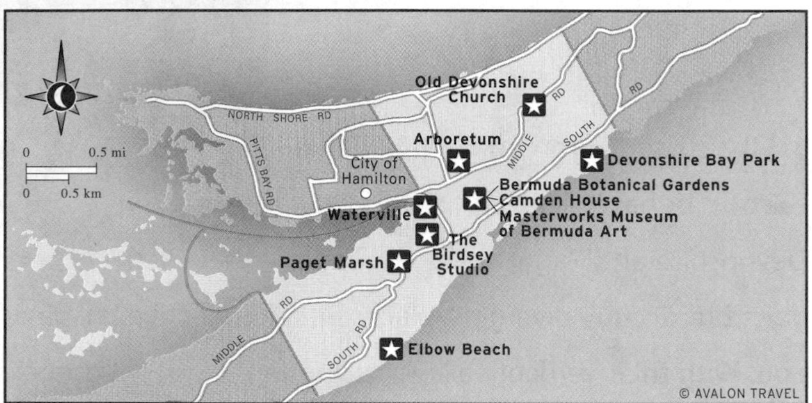

★ **Arboretum:** Quiet trails wind through fiddlewood forests and meadows alive with bluebirds and cardinals. Don't miss the limestone quarry gardens, palm collections, or ornamental bridges (page 84).

★ **Old Devonshire Church:** Centuries old, this whitewashed, pocket-sized church is notable for its traditional architecture, cedar-fused interior, and quaint gardens (page 85).

★ **Devonshire Bay Park:** This bay encompasses a tiny beach that's great for kids and nonswimmers, a small national park with a spectacular outlook on the South Shore, and the ruin of an early coastal fort (page 88).

★ **Bermuda Botanical Gardens:** Bermuda's favorite park has rolling lawns, storybook trees, gardens boasting roses, herbs, and medicinal plants, and a visitors center offering tea, sandwiches, and souvenirs (page 95).

★ **Camden House:** The premier's official residence is open for public tours twice a week (page 96).

★ **Masterworks Museum of Bermuda Art:** This groundbreaking institution is the work of a nonprofit agency that has spent a quarter-century repatriating Bermuda artworks by Winslow Homer, Georgia O'Keeffe, and other luminaries. Local artists' work is also on display in a former arrowroot factory (page 97).

★ **Waterville:** Antiques and oils adorn the interior of this gracious waterfront homestead, headquarters of the Bermuda National Trust, but the roses, mangroves, and gardens outside are even more spectacular. Watch ducks and boaters in the tranquil Foot of the Lane, or picnic in the quaint gazebo (page 99).

★ **The Birdsey Studio:** From her studio, watercolorist Jo Birdsey-Linberg dispenses practical advice, witty anecdotes, and local knowledge—along with landscapes and beautifully whimsical portraits, just like her famous father, Alfred Birdsey, did (page 101).

★ **Paget Marsh:** Teeming with birdlife, this former peat marsh can easily be explored via a quaint boardwalk (page 101).

★ **Elbow Beach:** One of Bermuda's most famous pink stretches, this beach links several private South Shore resorts, but you're still free to walk from end to end and swim in the clear turquoise rollers (page 102).

Middle Road rambles through the parish center, while North Shore and South Shore Roads hem its edges on both sides. Devonshire includes large tracts of farmland, including the lovely Orange Valley and Locust Hall Nature Reserve, owned and managed by the National Trust, where acres of lilies and snapdragons spring from the earth during Easter season.

Paget, meanwhile, moves west from the quirkily named Happy Talk Drive, continuing past the Bermuda Botanical Gardens. Trimingham Hill, a highway hub from Hamilton, channels traffic westward through Paget via pretty, winding Harbour Road, central Middle Road, or South Shore Road, all of which connect with and continue through Warwick Parish after the north-south boundary of Cobb's Hill. Paget's north boundary includes several islands in Hamilton Harbour, namely: White's, where youth groups enjoy summer camps; large residential Hinson's, which has a ferry stop on the Paget-Warwick run; and smaller outcrops such as Doctor's and Burnt Islands.

PLANNING YOUR TIME

Unless you're ensconced in a resort, it's likely you will pass through the central parishes of Devonshire and Paget many times on your way into or out of Hamilton, or moving between the East and West Ends. Both parishes provide a highly scenic passageway, but both also offer sights, restaurants, bars, and beautiful outdoor spaces in their own right and are certainly worth dedicated visits. Buses run several regular routes through Devonshire and Paget, and ferries are a scenic way to explore Paget's harborside and beyond. The old tribe roads in both parishes also make for interesting tangents; east-west main roads are linked via these skinny north-south divisions that travel past red fields of newly sown soil, schoolyards, or Bermudian back gardens.

Devonshire, the more rural of the two, with few shopping and no hotel options, is an oasis of historic family estates, tracts of farmland and forest, a marsh protected as a nature reserve, a popular little spa, and a golf course, with the majority of land composed of residential property. While Paget also lays claim to important natural spaces, the parish houses the island's major hospital, King Edward VII Memorial, with its expanding medical environs; two major hotels, beaches, bars, and restaurants also lie within the parish. Wrapped around the bottom of Hamilton Harbour, it is closely connected to the city physically and philosophically.

Outdoor and sports enthusiasts will find plenty to do in both Devonshire and Paget, thanks to numerous resorts' tennis facilities, a nine-hole golf course (at Ocean View Golf Club), and walking, riding, and running trails, not to mention two of the island's most expansive public parks, the Arboretum and Bermuda Botanical Gardens. Stretches of the Railway Trail in both parishes are great for exploring the countryside. Either parish is good for simply sampling Bermuda's gardenlike atmosphere. Buy sunflowers or fresh honey from a farm stand on Saturday morning. Stop for a Foot of the Lane picnic along Pomander Road's harborside, or walk the Railway Trail from Barker's Hill, the glistening North Shore panorama laid out before you like a movie backdrop.

Devonshire Parish

As a born-and-bred Devonshire resident, I must admit the bucolic, valley-dotted parish, infused as it is with childhood memories, is my favorite parish in all of Bermuda. Spend time here, and you will find yourself not only in the physical crux of Bermuda, thanks to its central position, but also in the heart of the island's "country" roots. Devonshire conjures old gardens on rambling estates that tumble down gentle hills and fenced meadows, North Shore cottages clustered in salt-sprayed pastels, the echo of surf on South Shore verandas, and lily fields and footpaths through fiddlewood forests. Historically, Devonshire (pronounced "DEV-on-sure," not "shire" as North Americans are tempted to say) is named for the southwest corner of England, birthplace of William Cavendish, the first Earl of Devonshire and one of the prominent London investors behind Bermuda's early development.

Sparsely populated until the 20th century due to its lack of natural harbors (and therefore disconnected from the boom in maritime industry), Devonshire prospered primarily through farming. Military history runs deep here, too. It was the British Army that had the greatest impact on the parish starting in the mid-1800s, after appropriating a quarter of the land and establishing forts, a military hospital, and a garrison at Prospect. Montpelier (long the home of the deputy governor) and the neighboring Arboretum became part of a huge military complex that covered Fort Hill—a vantage point chosen for its commanding view of land and sea stretching as far as the Royal Naval Dockyard. When the army pulled out of Bermuda in 1951, the area became headquarters for the Bermuda Police Service. Today it is also home to one of the island's largest public high schools (CedarBridge Academy) and a well-used cultural center, the Ruth Seaton James Centre for the Performing Arts.

Centuries-old families such as the Cox, Watlington, and Dill clans have managed to preserve from destruction or development their impressive historic mansions and large landholdings. Today, these, along with government lands held as open space, contribute to the sense of natural beauty in the parish and help offset eyesores such as the Tynes Bay Incinerator, an ugly tower rising off former North Shore farmland, where the island's garbage is trucked and burned.

With just one hotel property (the Dills' Ariel Sands Resort, which is currently undergoing an \$85-million redevelopment), few dedicated attractions, and no village or commercial center for shopping or dining out, Devonshire can be considered the least tourist-focused parish. The exception is November, when crowds pour in for the annual World Rugby Classic at the Bermuda National Sports Centre. The rest of the time, residents live and work and enjoy outdoor pursuits here, but despite the lack of advertised sights, visitors will find many corners worth spending time in. Lying on the western outskirts of Hamilton, Devonshire is wedged snugly between Pembroke and Smith's. Its western border, with Pembroke, runs from Cavendish Heights to the North Shore; southward, it connects with Paget at the foot of Hamilton Harbour and follows Middle Road nearly to Tee Street, then continues east, spanning both shorelines. Navigate its hilly terrain via a few main roads: sea-swept North Shore Road and Palmetto Road to the north, Middle Road through the center, and South Shore Road (aka South Road) as far as the Smith's Parish border.

It might be true to say Devonshire is a state of mind rather than a destination. It demands slowing down, kicking back, and soaking in a different time when rhythms of life were connected to the earth rather than the minute or the dollar.

Devonshire Parish

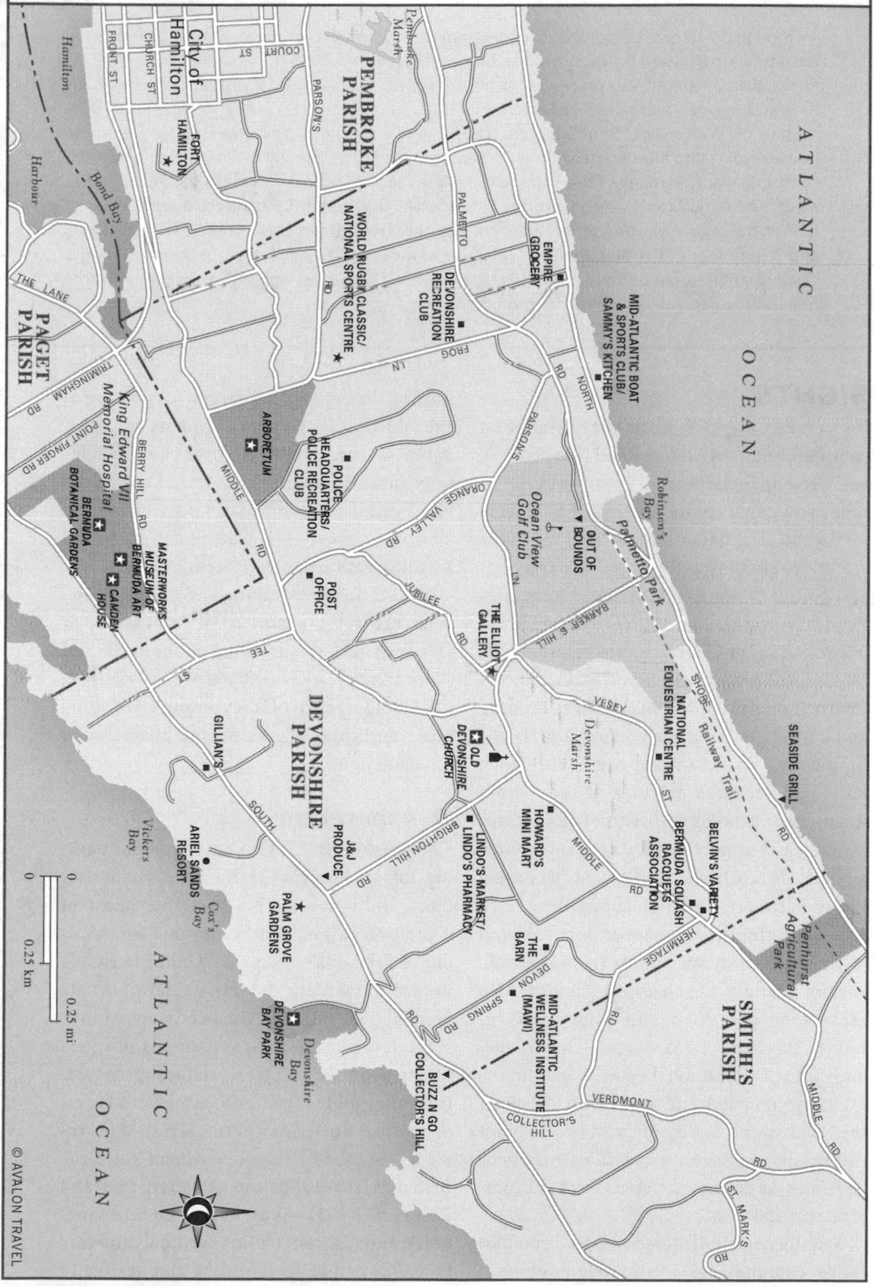

House Names

If a foreign postal carrier had been dropped into Bermuda not so long ago, he or she might have been totally perplexed by the island's archaic address system. Until the 1980s, Bermudians generally relied on identifying properties by house names, because private residences throughout the parishes rarely had numbers. Letters, therefore, simply went to "Anstey," Middle Road, Devonshire; or "Windswept," Southampton. When giving a guest directions, you might refer to the house color—"the blue house with white shutters, second on the right." Making matters more confusing was that many of the more remote lanes and neighborhood roads had no names at all, at least not officially. The government changed all that in the 1990s, methodically giving all roads a title—though sometimes rather curious ones (Happy Talk Drive, Frolic Lane, Pain Lane, and Stepmother's Drive among the oddities)—and numbering every house. Today everything is clearly identified, but Bermudians still like to name their houses (as well as their boats), and most homes have decorative nameplates prominently displayed.

SIGHTS

If you take Cavendish Road out of Hamilton continuing east via Middle Road (bus route 3), you'll end up in the heart of Devonshire. From here, you can explore the parish's diverse nooks and crannies, where many of the sights are not posted attractions, but the comings and goings of regular daily life. Montpelier Road and Frog Lane lead to North Shore Road, passing circuitous Happy Valley before climbing past the grand Bermuda National Sports Centre (home to an Olympic-sized swimming and diving pool, hockey pitches, and a running track). Frog Lane connects with Dock Hill, a short, steep exit onto North Shore Road. Take time to hang out at the former military cargo port Devonshire Dock, now a public dock where dreadlocked fishermen gather in the afternoons to cut up their catch and sell fresh fillets of snapper, rockfish, and other sweet-meat specialties from roadside coolers. Many of the ancestral homes in this area—some garnished with gingerbread verandas, gazebos, even a crenellated tower—belong to the Dill family; they were built in the 1700s by privateers and merchants. All along the North Shore, far less affluent homes boast rich traditional features, including front-door fanlights, keystones, parapets, and welcoming-arms stairways.

Staying on Middle Road will lead you past farms, churches, and inland neighborhoods. Rolling Orange Valley, largely consisting of age-old family estates, connects to major Palmetto Road or switches back along delightfully rural Parson's Lane toward Devonshire Marsh and Jubilee Road, Old Devonshire Church, Locust Hall Nature Reserve, and Vesey Street's equestrian areas.

If you head east along the South Shore, you can stroll the gardens of Palm Grove or Devonshire Bay—another public park and swimming area where some of the best fresh fish is sold straight off the commercial fishing boats on Fridays. Look for the hand-drawn roadside sign.

★ Arboretum

The **Arboretum** (main entrance and parking lot on Montpelier Rd., sunrise-sunset daily, admission free), a 19-acre expanse of meadows, palms, and fiddlewood forests, is one of Bermuda's best parks. Unlike Bermuda Botanical Gardens, it consists not of ornate planted beds but wild tracts of wooded hillsides, large soft lawns, and stands of interesting plants and trees, including cedars, flowering golden acacias, avocados, and acres of mature Surinam cherry forest. The reserve—owned by the government since the British Army pulled out of Montpelier and Fort Hill in 1951—is an important bird sanctuary, and flocks of trilling cardinals and rare bluebirds can be seen feeding and nesting in meadows off Middle Road. A giant olive tree at the roadside spreads its dark foliage over the sidewalk, and gargantuan rubber trees with endless root systems and hanging tendrils bear testimony to the centuries-old age of the park. Also off Middle Road, an ornamental bridge crafted with rustic cedar planks and railings leads into the park, and two quarry gardens inside, one with tiny pools, are planted with interesting ferns and other shade-loving flora. Children will enjoy the mature grove near Fort Hill, Prospect, with poincianas that drop red carpets of petals every summer and giant rubber trees, their tendrils providing natural swings. There's also an exquisitely planted butterfly garden, attracting monarchs and other species all year round. Don't miss the nearby limestone buttery topped by exotic night-blooming cereus flowers in summer. A do-it-yourself exercise trail erected in a half-mile loop includes sit-up benches and balancing bars. Running clubs use the park for afternoon workouts, and joggers, birders, families, and dog-walkers come for the tranquil trails, grassy spaces, and birdsong.

★ Old Devonshire Church

Cute as a button, **Old Devonshire Church** (106 Middle Rd., tel. 441/236-3671, 10am-3pm daily except Tues., admission free), a pint-sized, whitewashed example of pure Bermudian architecture, dates back to 1624, when the original structure was built. The first was thatched in palmetto and destroyed by the hurricane of 1715; the current version was rebuilt of limestone the following year. Interestingly, the church's construction demonstrates the same techniques employed by those who crafted ships of the era. Various enlargements were made over the years, but the plain style beloved by early parishioners was kept. Centuries later, the old church suffered severe damage in a 1970 fire, but reconstruction was faithful to its original and very simple design—a marked contrast to the Gothic revival of the nearby Christ Church, built by the parish in 1851 when the old church was too small to hold the growing congregation. Notable in the historic building's interior is a Bermuda cedar screen decorated with quaint hearts and fleurs-de-lis. The pulpit and pews are also of cedar. Outside, the graveyard holds the tombs of parish residents and an 1817 hearse house built in the style of the church. Surrounded by climbing roses, flaming poinsettia plants, and old cedars, the church is popular for candlelit weddings, and carol services are an annual holiday staple.

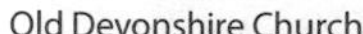
Old Devonshire Church

The Elliot Gallery

The Elliot Gallery (27 Jubilee Rd., tel. 441/542-9000, www.kaleidoscopeartsfoundation.com, 10am-4pm Tues.-Fri., 10am-2pm Sat., and by appointment, free) is tucked away within the Kaleidoscope Arts Foundation building, in a rural corner just off Devonshire's main thoroughfare. Exhibitions by local and visiting artists are held throughout the year. The facility is sometimes used by studio artists, and by children who attend popular after-school and holiday camps.

Devonshire Marsh

Botanists and bug-lovers will want to visit **Devonshire Marsh** (sunrise-sunset daily, admission free), a protected wetland cradled in the Middle Road valley and once dubbed "Brackish Pond"—which became a popular nickname for the whole parish in centuries past. The **Firefly Nature Reserve** and the **Freer Cox Nature Reserve** comprise the Bermuda National Trust's 10-acre marsh and have been set aside as a special sanctuary for birds and endangered island fauna. Waterways meander through the marshland, leading past natural orchids and a wealth of insects and birdlife. Unlike Paget Marsh, it remains largely the realm of scientists or birders, as the ground is deep and boggy; to date, no boardwalks or educational signage have been erected to guide public visits. The grassy borders of the marsh are harvested for fodder for the island's dairy cows.

Palm Grove Gardens

Owned by the Gibbons family, the **Palm Grove Gardens** (38 South Shore Rd., tel. 441/295-0022, 9am-5pm Mon.-Thurs., admission free) is a beautifully landscaped 18-acre estate that stretches from the main road to the sea. Private property, it is open to the public during daytime hours most of the week. The property is very popular for staging wedding photos, thanks to its well-planted gardens complete with statues, water lily ponds designed in the shape of a miniature map of the island, stunning night-blooming cereus, sago, coconut, and Canary Island palms, ivy-coated limestone huts (called butteries), and a traditional Bermuda moongate—said to bestow good luck upon newlyweds. There is also a tropical bird aviary with a collection of parrots. At the foot of sweeping lawns, rock pools sit before a reef-strewn shoreline.

a statue of the Greek god Pan, Palm Grove Gardens

Butterfly Garden at Brighton Nurseries

Budding naturalists will love a visit to the **Butterfly Garden at Brighton Nurseries** (2 Brighton Lane, Brighton Hill, tel. 441/236-5862), where monarchs, red admirals, buckeyes, and other varieties depending on the season, flutter among flowering plants in a specially created greenhouse. Lady, the resident dog, will greet you upon arrival.

Historic Military Buildings

A scattering of historic military buildings once used by the British Army can still be seen around the Fort Hill-North Shore area. At **Prospect,** former military barracks today

Shakespeare and *The Tempest*

There's a certain theme to Bermuda nomenclature, one that will gradually become apparent as you explore Hamilton and the parishes. In the city, one of the large reinsurance companies goes by the name of Ariel Re. In the old town of St. George's, there's a popular new restaurant called Tempest Bistro. Over in Devonshire, the Dill family's resort, Ariel Sands (currently closed), sports a bronze statue of its namesake sprite leaping from the South Shore rollers. At least one home—Ross Perot's three-acre spread in Tucker's Town—is named Caliban. And various businesses carry stormy appellations (Tempest Employment Agency, ACE Tempest Re). If you're starting to feel the slightest bit Elizabethan, you're on the right track. Historians believe William Shakespeare's play *The Tempest* has Bermuda to thank for its creation.

The violent 1609 shipwreck of the *Sea Venture* and its lucky castaways was chronicled in two contemporary accounts, one by crewman Silvanus Jourdan and one by passenger William Strachey, both of which circulated in London in 1610. *The Tempest* was first performed in 1611. It is known that descriptions of the disaster and enchanting island whetted English enthusiasm for New World discoveries. Shakespeare undoubtedly would have been privy to the writings; among other connections, one of his major patrons was the Earl of Southampton, Henry Wriothesley, an investor in both the Virginia and Bermuda Companies. So experts believe it's no coincidence that his verse depicts a fanciful island, supposedly in the Mediterranean, but described in historically accurate terms for Bermuda as having "hogges of force and bignesse," "a pleasant drinke" made of cedar berries, and raucous seabirds whose tongues could "walke as fast as any Englishwomen's."

"The greatest writer of the English language was a bit of a literary pickpocket," notes Hobson Woodward, author of the 2009 book *A Brave Vessel: The True Tale of the Castaways Who Rescued Jamestown and Inspired Shakespeare's The Tempest.*

Shakespeare's allegorical romance featuring characters Prospero, his daughter Miranda, the elf Ariel, and savage Caliban happens to be launched by a monstrous storm whose "dreadful thunderclaps and sulphurous roaring" mirror the *Sea Venture*'s nemesis. "Enter Mariners, wet," the first act begins. Certainly the work's main themes—the roles of destiny and chance—also tie in appropriately to Bermuda's own story and its eventual Latin motto, *Quo Fata Ferunt* (Whither the Fates Carry Us).

belong to **Police Headquarters,** where the complex of buildings is used for executive offices, cadet training, media relations, and traffic squad police offices. An Edwardian officers' mess with views of Hamilton and the Great Sound is now the Police Recreation Club. On Fort Hill, the **Prospect Cemetery** contains the graves of soldiers posted on the island through the 19th and 20th centuries. Farther north, where Orange Valley meets Palmetto Road, an old military hospital, like the barracks displaying hallmark iron verandas, is now a government office building overlooking the North Shore.

BEACHES

Robinson's Bay

Below hilly Palmetto Park on North Shore Road (just west of the Palmetto Road roundabout), Robinson's Bay is a perfect place for a quick dip in the heat of summer, when parish children dive from the high rocky ledges into an azure natural swimming hole. With its rocky formations and reefy edges, there are several areas to swim here, and snorkeling in and out of the tiny bays amid yellowtail, butterfly fish, and striped sergeants major is a great way to while away a morning or afternoon. As a child, I enjoyed many waterlogged birthday parties here, and my brother and I considered an after-school dip here the ultimate treat. The property, now public and rather run-down, bears the telltale signs of British military use in years past: steps carved into the water at various points, natural stone bridges between rocky outcrops, and old changing huts made of thick limestone. Locals can often be found line-fishing off the rocks.

★ Devonshire Bay Park

Tucked away at the end of a narrow South Shore lane, Devonshire Bay Park is easy to miss. But don't—because this scenic little corner of Bermuda offers a perfect place to relax, swim, picnic, explore, and meet Bermudians who frequent a decidedly non-touristy venue. There's a clean beach fringed by baygrapes and palmettos, and the quiet bay is good for swimming, except on very windy days when surf rolls through the channel into the natural harbor. Nearby residents keep small boats here, as do fishers, who return to clean and sell their catch on weekday afternoons. Friday is usually a sure bet to find them chopping up fillets for a loyal crowd of customers. A hand-drawn sign is usually posted at the main road to advertise the catch.

One of Bermuda's many coastal fortifications, **Devonshire Bay Battery,** a rebuilt version of "Brackish Pond Fort," as it was once known, is located here, on a promontory in the adjacent park. The original was built in the 1750s, a square-shaped redoubt with a parapet and a central magazine—what's left are now archaeological remains. Around the shoreline of the national park, bordered by boiler reefs, you can see the whole south coast and wade in pools where trapped crabs, shrimp, and tiny jewel-like fish dart until high tide returns them to the ocean.

To get there, turn off South Road toward the sea on Devonshire Bay Road. Follow this hedge-lined residential lane a couple hundred yards as it veers to a sharp right, then hugs the bay as it swings left again into a small parking area. From here, you can walk into the park.

ENTERTAINMENT AND EVENTS

Parish events are mostly of the sporting nature, including regular soccer and cricket matches at Devonshire Recreation Club, squash tournaments at the Bermuda Squash Racquets Association, and track and field and other events at the Bermuda National Sports Centre. Check *The Royal Gazette*, wwww.nothingtodoinbermuda.com, or www.gotobermuda.com for details of scheduled events.

Nightlife

Despite Devonshire's tranquility, there are a few parish bars, and all deliver very different nightlife experiences.

The bar at **Ocean View Golf Club** (2

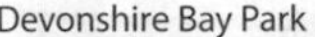
Devonshire Bay Park

Barkers Hill, tel. 441/295-4916, 11am-1am daily) is a friendly place to stop in, if only to inhale the gorgeous North Shore view. Visitors are welcome at **Police Recreation Club** (Headquarters Hill, Prospect, bar tel. 441/299-4261, noon-11pm Mon., noon-1am Tues.-Sun.), where members of the Bermuda police service socialize after hours. Somewhat rowdier are **Mid-Atlantic Boat & Sports Club** (37 North Shore Rd., tel. 441/295-0172, 4pm-8pm Fri. happy hour) and the bar at **Devonshire Recreation Club** (20 Frog Ln., tel. 441/292-5539, 4pm-1am daily), with festivities peaking on Friday and Saturday nights.

World Rugby Classic

Launched in 1988, the popular **World Rugby Classic** (tel. 441/295-6574 or 441/278-1446, fax 441/296-7318, www.worldrugby.bm) attracts thousands to the Bermuda National Sports Centre at Prospect to watch a week-long showdown of former top international players. Teams from Canada, Australia, New Zealand, Scotland, Wales, England, South Africa, Argentina, Spain, and the United States face off in what has grown into a veritable Seniors World Cup of Rugby. Stars including Willie McBride, Matt Dawson, Olivier Roumat, and Joost van der Westhuizen have entertained crowds over the years; when she was living in Bermuda, Welsh-born actress Catherine Zeta-Jones used to turn up to support the Welsh team. Daily admission is $25 (five-day pass $100). VIP passes with access to hospitality tents where visiting players hang out and nonstop cocktail parties are hosted by corporate entities cost $650 per person, or $1,100 per couple, for the five match days ($150 for day pass).

SHOPPING

With no central community or village, Devonshire is not a shopper's paradise. One quirky exception is **The Barn** (53 Devon Spring Rd., tel. 441/236-3155, 9am-2pm Tues., Thurs., and Sat.), a bargain hunter's treasure trove, spilling over with secondhand toys, collectibles, and an impressive stock of books, from vintage and just-released fiction to kids' mystery series from the 1970s and 1980s. Items often cost just a quarter or two, and nothing is more than a few dollars. The nonprofit facility raises funds for several island charities. Opposite The Barn stands Bermuda's other hospital, the Mid-Atlantic Wellness Institute, a psychiatric treatment facility.

SPORTS AND RECREATION

Devonshire has plenty to offer the active traveler, including a golf course, a spa that's become a not-too-well-kept secret among locals, and several dedicated sports centers—the Bermuda National Sports Centre, the National Equestrian Centre, the Bermuda Squash Racquets Association—but the parish is also full of outdoor spaces in which you can exercise while enjoying nature.

Swimming, Diving, and Athletics

Site of the former National Stadium, the government's **Bermuda National Sports Centre** (50 Frog Ln., tel. 441/295-8085, fax 441/295-5573, www.bermudasportscentre.bm, entrance via Roberts Ave. off Parson's Rd., pool open 6:30am-7pm Mon.-Fri., 1pm-5pm Sat., 9am-1pm Sun.) is the island's premier athletics and sporting venue, and has hosted numerous international events, including the 2012 CARIFTA Games and the NatWest Island Games in 2013. The South Field contains an internationally sanctioned 400-meter track, all-weather field hockey turf, a soccer pitch, and a 2,000-seat grandstand (Usain Bolt secured his junior world record title in the 200 meters—19.93 seconds—in the 2004 CARIFTA Games here). Fees are charged for public use of the main competition track (adults $8 per day, $25 per month). The North Field hosts cricket, soccer, and rugby events. An aquatics facility with an Olympic-sized (50-meter) eight-lane pool, 10-meter dive tower and springboards, and lockers and changing rooms opened in 2013; drop-in rates (adults $16), 10-visit multi-pack ($140), and monthly passes ($110) are available. The nearby **Arboretum** provides perfect cross-country running terrain in a relaxing natural setting; you can make a workout out of a track warmup followed by a few hilly loops of the park.

Railway Trail (Devonshire)

The Devonshire portion of the **Railway Trail** is one of the most panoramic stretches of this national park, with elevated, 180-degree views of the main shipping channel into the Great Sound and Hamilton Harbour. Much of the North Shore is visible, from Dockyard to Shelly Bay. It is a particularly good spot to watch cruise ships and tankers moving through the channel into port or back out to the open ocean. Starting at Barker's Hill (leave scooters in the roadside Ocean View Golf Club parking lot), you can trek a good mile along the shady tarmacadam path, past Loyal Hill Playground and historic Bermudian cottages such as Firefly Hall and through busy pastel-colored communities peppered with children, dogs, and clotheslines. The trail continues through Smith's, past more lush vegetation, all the way to Gibbet Beach and Flatts Inlet—an out-and-back run of about four miles to and from Barker's Hill, offering a refreshing swim mid-route.

Golf

With a spectacular view of the North Shore channel, **Ocean View Golf Club** (2 Barker's Hill Rd., tel. 441/295-9092, pro shop tel. 441/295-9093 or 441/295-9077, tee times tel. 441/295-9092, fax 441/295-9097, www.oceanviewgolfbermuda.bm) is one of two government-owned courses currently operating on the island, along with Port Royal. Well maintained, the nine-hole, par-35 course (with 18 tee positions for a double round) offers a leisurely though not challenging outing and is best suited to mid-handicappers. With a putting green, well-stocked pro shop, and a comfortable clubhouse with well-run bar and restaurant, plus a panoramic terrace, the club has benefited from many improvements over recent years. Pro shop hours are 7:30am-6:30pm daily April-October and 7:30am-5:30pm daily November-March. The daily greens fee is $77 (18 holes with a cart) or $50 (9 holes with a cart), and club rentals (Nike, Callaway) are $30 (18 holes) or $15 (9 holes). The club offers reduced "sunset" fees after 3pm. The dress code calls for collared shirts, Bermuda shorts or long trousers, and soft spikes.

Horseback Riding

With its relaxed country atmosphere, Devonshire is the perfect parish in which to go horseback riding, and it has a long equestrian history. The parish's wooded hills, paths, and valleys, as well as its scenic stretch of Railway Trail, provide rare peaceful paths for riding in Bermuda's overdeveloped environment.

Competitive harness pony racing is a popular event held most weekends September-May at the new **National Equestrian Centre** (48 Vesey St., Bermuda Equestrian Federation president Michael Cherry tel. 441/234-0485, www.bef.bm). Formerly called the Vesey Street Racetrack, the center has an egg-shaped track, a few bleachers, washrooms, and a canteen that's open during races, which are held evenings (under lights) or Sunday afternoons and are usually advertised. Admission is $6 for ages 12 and over, $4 for seniors, children under 12 free. Horse shows are also held at the center, where local riders vie for honors in dressage, equitation, jumping, and show jumping.

Squash

Visitors can play on any of four courts at the **Bermuda Squash Racquets Association** (111 Middle Rd., tel. 441/292-6881, fax 441/295-8718, www.bermudasquash.com, 10am-10pm Mon.-Fri., 10am-5pm Sat. and Sun.) for a guest fee of $15. Contact the club if you need a partner. Lessons ($51 for 40 minutes) are available from club pros, including club director **Patrick Foster** (patrickf@bermudasquash.com), formerly on the pro squash tour. As well as showers, changing rooms, and a licensed bar, the club has a small, well-equipped gym, with Cybex bikes and equipment, dumbbells, and Stairmasters; use is included in guest fees.

Soccer and Cricket

Crowds flock to **Devonshire Recreation Club** (20 Frog Ln., tel. 441/292-5539), dubbed "Devonshire Rec," for evening and weekend soccer games (the resident team is the green-and-gold Cougars) throughout the fall and winter, and cricket showdowns all summer long. Few of the sports fans who party here may appreciate it, but the building that houses the club, with its billiards hall, bar, and canteen, is actually a historic Georgian structure, built in 1760 as one of the Dill family's ancestral homes.

Spas

It looks like a roadside cottage, but in-the-know spagoers choose **Gillian's** (14 South Shore Rd., tel. 441/232-0496, www.gilliansbermuda.com, 8:45am-9pm Mon.-Fri., 8:45am-5pm Sat.-Sun.) for its luxurious but low-key appeal. Inside, the ambience invites immediate relaxation: candles, soothing music, antique furniture, and heated neck collars upon arrival. Experienced therapists offer everything from hot stone massages (one hour, $140) and detoxifying mud treatments (120 minutes, $190), Thai facials (one hour, $125), French manicures ($58), tanning, even teeth whitening. Pamper packages include a six-hour "Pure Day of Heaven" ($460) that might leave you never wanting to return to the real world.

ACCOMMODATIONS

After a six-year closure, in late 2014 groundbreaking finally took place on an $85-million redevelopment of **Ariel Sands Resort** (34 South Shore Rd., www.arielsands.com). Owned by one of the island's oldest clans, the Dills (relatives of actor Michael Douglas), the historic property, slated to re-open as a contemporary cottage colony, is Devonshire's only hotel, though several holiday units or apartments in private homes can be found via sites such as www.bermudarentals.com, www.airbnb.com, and www.vrbo.com.

FOOD

Delis and Takeout

Esso Collector's Hill Tigermarket (65 South Shore Rd. next to Collector's Hill, tel. 441/236-6574, 6am-11pm daily) might qualify as the island's friendliest petrol stop. Cheery staff and a well-stocked convenience store make the facility a popular way station for motorists and neighborhood regulars. Along with corner-store-style sundries (milk, crackers, cereal, soda, chips, chocolate, candy, and car supplies), the store is also home to **Buzz N Go Collector's Hill,** serving up a full menu of hot and cold deli items, including omelets, wraps, paninis, sandwiches, pizza, salads, smoothies, and specialty coffees. You can enjoy your refreshment on-site; grab a stool at the people-watching window counter.

If you want a taste of true Bermuda, don't miss the Saturday farm stand run by **J&J Produce** (foot of Brighton Hill at South Rd., tel. 441/236-8616, 7:30am-4:30pm Sat. only). Husband and wife Junior and Patty Hill's cornucopia of seasonal fruits and vegetables includes hands of sweet Bermuda onions, bananas, strawberries, pumpkins, tomatoes, kale, fresh-picked corn, fellow farmers' quail eggs and goat, plus sunflowers, lilies, and snapdragons in the spring. Better than anything imported into the grocery aisles.

Winner of a coveted 2014 Best of Bermuda Award for "Best Fish Sandwich," **Seaside Grill** (81 North Shore Rd., tel. 441/292-1241, noon-10pm Mon.-Fri., 8am-1pm Sun., $5.50-16) is making a name for its wahoo-stuffed creations cooked up inside a bright turquoise roadside takeout. Customers can choose wheat, white, or rye and select their choice of toppings—tomato, cheese, bacon, coleslaw, and onions raw or fried. Everyone has a favorite version—but the taste is universally thumbs-up.

Cafés

Sammy's Kitchen (Mid-Atlantic Boat & Sports Club, 34 North Shore Rd., office tel. 441/295-0172, kitchen tel. 441/296-2697, 11am-11pm Mon.-Sat., 8am-midnight Sun., $7.50-18) serves up chicken, burgers, and island comfort food like peas 'n' rice and macaroni 'n' cheese during the week and draws a loud, jovial bar crowd on Friday nights. But the roadside club is best known for its authentic Sunday-morning codfish and potatoes breakfasts, appreciated by club members and other regulars who gather here for a laid-back café-style spread at the popular social and boating club, which sits a few feet from the water's edge. Be warned: Breakfast starts early and only lasts "until it's all gone," says a club staffer.

Take in a bird's-eye view of the North Shore seascape at **Out of Bounds** (Ocean View Golf Club, 2 Barker's Hill Rd., tel. 441/295-4916, fax 441/295-3692, 9:30am-4:30pm Mon.-Fri., 7am-5pm Sat. and Sun.). The licensed club bar and restaurant has a full breakfast menu (eggs, pancakes, meats) and a lunchtime offering of soups, salads, burgers, codfish cakes, fish tacos, shrimp po' boys, and vegetarian wraps (dishes $7-16). Golfers, caddies, locals, and visitors also drop in for tasty nibbles such as popcorn shrimp, codfish balls, and conch fritters. The restaurant has an inside dining area, but the best tables are on the terrace overlooking the greens and the azure swath of ocean beyond. Locals swarm here for an out-of-town Friday happy hour (5pm-7pm) and for the popular Sunday brunch of codfish and potatoes, dished out with the staple accompaniments: bananas, avocado, tomato sauce, eggs, bacon, and toast.

Grocery Stores

Belvin's Variety (1 Vesey St., tel. 441/236-6644, 6am-midnight daily) stocks beer, liquor, dry goods, and frozen goods, and also sells fresh-baked hot beef, chicken, and mussel pies.

Empire Grocery (12 North Shore Rd., tel. 441/292-0277 or 441/295-2625, 8am-6pm Mon.-Thurs., 8am-8pm Fri. and Sat.) has been part of the North Shore community since 1927 when the DeSilva family first opened its doors. Relatives still run the friendly, efficient convenience store, packed with "as much as we can fit," says an employee. That includes liquor, beer, grocery products, and deli meats.

Howard's Mini Mart (99 Middle Rd., tel. 441/236-7037, fax 441/236-7000, 6am-8pm Mon.-Sat., 6am-1pm Sun.) is a family-owned roadside grocery offering all the basics, including some straight-from-the-farm fruits and vegetables.

Lindo's Market (4 Watlington Rd. East, tel. 441/236-5623, www.lindos.bm, 8am-7pm Mon., Tues., Thurs.; 8am-8pm Wed., Fri., and Sat.) is the only major supermarket in Devonshire, and one of the island's biggest and best stocked. Owned by the Italian Bermudian Zanol family, the modern floor space includes a harvest of organic foods and Bermuda-grown produce, cheeses from around the world, a carefully stocked wine section, magazines, children's books, thermoses and outdoor party goods, and a good fish and meat department offering fresh-caught Bermuda wahoo and tuna, traditional Bermuda codfish cakes, and a wide selection of imports. There is also a large hot and cold deli counter, serving up fish cakes, mac 'n' cheese, sandwiches, and other goodies Monday through Saturday.

INFORMATION AND SERVICES

Bermuda's second-largest hospital, the **Mid-Atlantic Wellness Institute** (formerly St. Brendan's Hospital, 44 Devon Springs Rd., tel. 441/236-3770, www.bermudahospitals.bm) is a psychiatric treatment facility with 130 in-patient beds.

Lindo's Pharmacy (inside Lindo's Market, 4 Watlington Rd. East, tel. 441/236-7732, pharmacy@lindos.bm, 8am-7pm Mon., Tues., Thurs.; 8am-8pm Wed., Fri., and Sat.) is a handy stop-in located inside the main grocery store, just left of the main entrance area.

Devonshire Post Office (2 Orange Valley Rd., tel. 441/236-0281, 8am-5pm Mon.-Fri.) is another parish outlet with helpful staff. There is plenty of parking outside and free public Internet access within.

ATMs are located at Lindo's Market, on Watlington Road, and Esso Collector's Hill Tigermarket.

Public toilets are located at the Bermuda National Sports Centre, Robinson's Bay, and area restaurants.

GETTING THERE AND AROUND

Buses

Regular bus service runs every half hour through Devonshire between Hamilton and Grotto Bay (route 3) in Hamilton Parish via Middle Road, Devil's Hole, and the caves, making for convenient sightseeing transport. Other Devonshire bus routes include South Shore Road (route 1) between Hamilton and St. George's every half hour via Spittal Pond and the Tucker's Town golf courses, and North Shore Road (routes 10 and 11) to and from St. George's every 15 minutes via the aquarium and Bailey's Bay. Bus fare to Devonshire falls into the three-zone tariff, which is $3 adults, $2 children 5-16, kids under 5 free (exact change or tokens, tickets, or passes required). Transfers are free.

Ferries

There is no ferry service to or from Devonshire.

Taxis

With no taxi stands, hailing a cab in Devonshire is hard work. A better strategy is to call one of the cab companies to arrange a pickup: **Bermuda Industrial Union Co-op** (tel. 441/292-4476, cooptaxi@fkbnet.bm), **Bermuda Island Taxi** (tel. 441/295-4141, www.bermudaislandtaxi.com), or **BTA Dispatching Ltd.** (tel. 441/296-2121, www.taxibermuda.bm).

Scooters and Bicycles

There are no livery services based in Devonshire, but all the scooter rental companies provide a free shuttle service to their nearest outlets (in Hamilton or Paget).

Paget Parish

Hemmed by the South Shore on one side and Hamilton Harbour on the other, most of Paget is contained within what on a map looks like a trouser leg on a pair of sideways pants (matched across the harbor by the spread of Pembroke and the city). As the outskirts of Hamilton, Paget is a bustling, thriving community passed through every morning by thousands of city-bound commuters from the western parishes, and every night by the same residents heading home. The river of traffic has brought noise and congestion to what once were peaceful country lanes leading horses and carriages, bicycles, and pedestrians into a very different Bermuda. But beyond the main thoroughfares, Paget's charm endures, and the beauty of its historic places, family estates, nature reserves, beaches, and meandering harborfront make it a treasure trove of discoveries around every hairpin turn.

Off the South Shore Road, for example, take a tangent down neighborhood lanes and feel man-made turbulence evaporate into the sound of blue surf instead. Tool down Middle Road, bordered by elegant old homes and their impossibly green gardens; dawdle down narrow lanes that roll into valleys or over hills where silence is, finally, golden. Of course, there's plenty to occupy a visitor who wants to be busy in Paget—restaurants, bars, top-quality sports facilities, and events to go with them.

Named for William Paget, the fourth Lord of Paget, the parish has seen modern amenities built or improved in the last decade,

Paget Parish

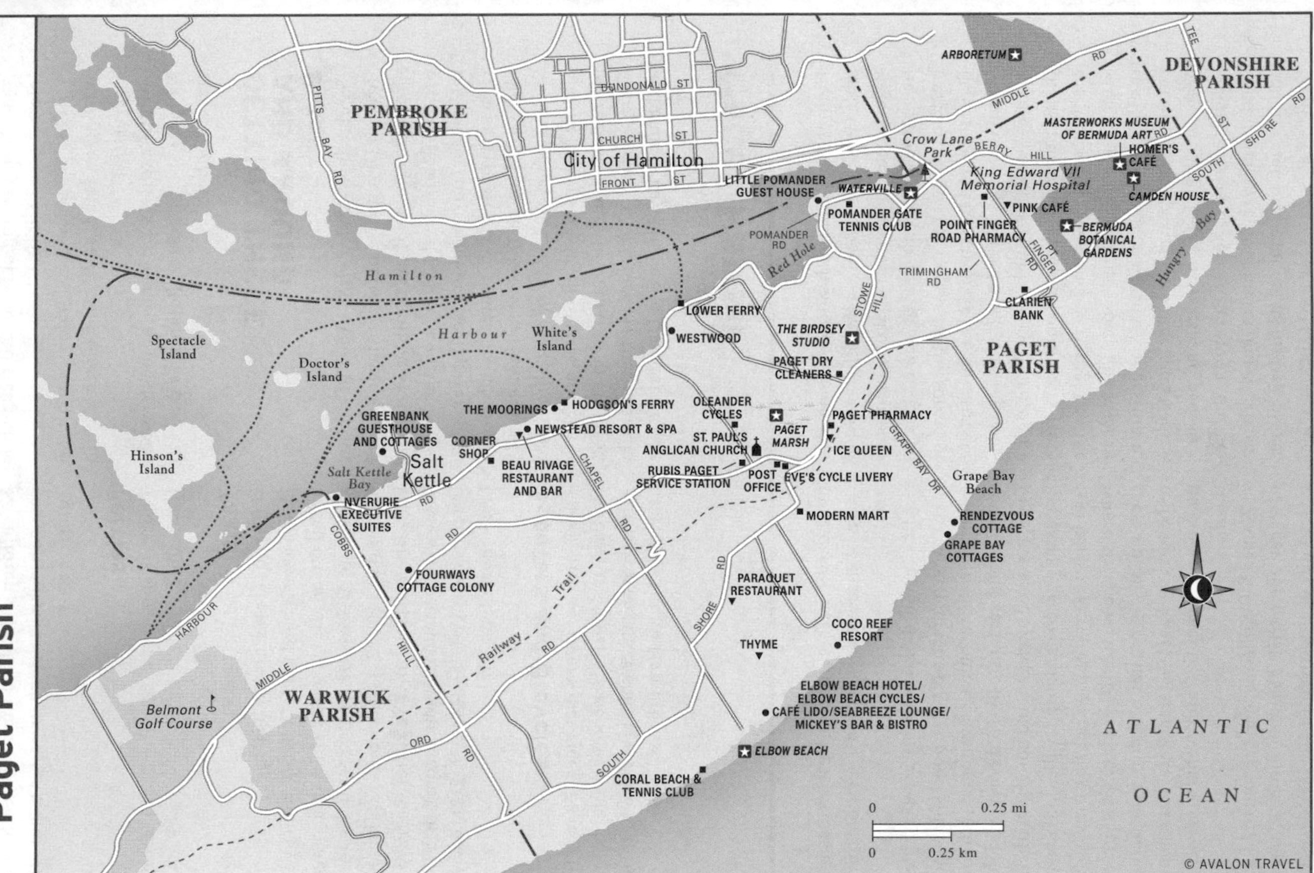

and today it has three hotels (Elbow Beach Hotel, Newstead Resort & Spa, and Coco Reef Resort), acclaimed restaurants, high-end spas, tennis courts, and an 18-hole golf course.

And then there is the Paget that never seems to change—the quaint limestone walls of seafaring Salt Kettle, Foot of the Lane ducks, the Elbow Beach breakers, the herb gardens of Camden, and, of course, the smile of Johnny Barnes—the beloved, self-appointed greeter of morning motorists, who waves and wishes "I love you!" from his perch at the Crow Lane roundabout.

SIGHTS

★ Bermuda Botanical Gardens

Bermuda's most visited and historic park, the **Bermuda Botanical Gardens** (183 South Rd., tel. 441/236-5902, sunrise-sunset daily, admission free, bus routes 1, 2, and 7) encompass 36 acres of rolling lawns, horticultural halls boasting orchids and cacti, and myriad outdoor gardens planted with exotica (ficus, rubber, and cotton trees) and down-home varieties (medicinal herbs). One-hour guided tours depart from the visitors center parking lot at 10:30am Tuesday, Wednesday, and Friday, weather permitting.

Opened in 1898, the original "Public Gardens" totaled just 10 acres. They were renamed and expanded to their current size in 1965, when the government bought the Camden estate to the east from the Tucker family. Since then, specimens from around the world have been gathered and planted here, making the property the biggest and best natural showcase of both endemic and nonnative flora on the island.

The gardens are maintained by the government's Department of Parks. There are four entrances: North Gate on Berry Hill Road, South Gate at 183 South Road, Peace Lutheran Gate (opposite that church), and West Gate (for pedestrians only) on Point Finger Road next to the King Edward VII Memorial Hospital's modern Acute Care Wing. The **visitors center** (tel. 441/236-5291, 9am-5pm Mon.-Fri.) has washrooms—and a new café planned for 2015—and is staffed by volunteers from the Bermuda Botanical Society; it's near North Gate, but can be accessed from any entrance. All proceeds are used for park projects or student scholarships.

Highlights of the gardens in the North Gate area include a cacti hillside, with alien-looking aloes, agaves, and other succulents that occasionally sprout spectacular blossoms; a

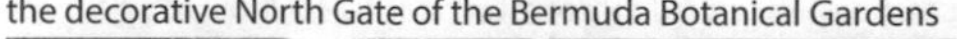

the decorative North Gate of the Bermuda Botanical Gardens

collection of subtropical native conifers, including Bermuda's own cedar; and a "blue garden" featuring plants with blue fruit, flowers, or foliage. Behind Camden House, a display developed in 2006 showcases a kitchen garden, with edibles and cut flowers; an economic garden, with tobacco, arrowroot, cotton, and indigo, which early settlers cultivated for trade; and medicinal herbs used in old-time Bermuda. This area also has aviaries with peacocks, ducks, parrots, doves, and budgies, and a delightful walled rose garden, one of Bermuda's best.

Hilly lawns spill down from Camden to South Road, peppered with mature trees such as acacias and cedars. Bordering the top lawns are wide beds planted with bulbs that flower at different times with colorful lilies, freesias, dahlias, and others. This was the famous site where John Lennon saw a freesia named "Double Fantasy" during a 1980 visit to the island—inspiring Lennon's album of that name and leaving a lasting legacy.

The western section of the gardens contains a wealth of miniature environments, from butterfly and maze gardens to subtropical fruit and palm collections to mammoth rubber and ficus trees that send down aerial roots to support their huge overhanging branches. There is also a lovely walled "sensory garden" planted with rosemary, jasmine, and other sweet-scented flora, with a gurgling fountain in the center, and several slat houses containing orchids, bromeliads, ferns, and cacti. Another interesting feature nearby is a tiny, whitewashed Bermuda cottage, built for the 2001 Smithsonian Folklife Festival to showcase island architecture. Thousands of Bermudians come to the gardens every April for the three-day **Bermuda Annual Exhibition,** a cultural and agricultural fair that's one of the island's biggest events.

★ Camden House

An elegant landmark visible from South Road atop the Bermuda Botanical Gardens' rolling lawns, **Camden House** (183 South Rd., tel. 441/236-5732, public tours noon-2pm

Elegant Camden House in the Botanical Gardens is open for tours.

Tues. and Fri., free) is definitely worth a visit. The 18th-century mansion has an imposing wooden facade comprising a two-story veranda offering sweeping views of the distant seascape. The government-owned Camden House is sometimes described as Bermuda's counterpart to 10 Downing Street or the White House (and yes, it is white), but the head of state doesn't actually live here. Instead, the building is used for occasional public events and VIP receptions; foreign dignitaries including Princess Margaret, former U.S. secretary of state General Colin Powell, ex-U.K. prime minister Margaret Thatcher, and civil rights leader Reverend Jesse Jackson have all dined in the house.

Camden House is an example of Georgian architecture; while it is not known exactly when it was constructed, the main structure and some additions were completed between 1714 and 1830. The first owner of the house, Francis Jones, died of yellow fever in 1795. The home was passed to the Tucker family, and Hamilton mayor Henry James Tucker

Painters in Paradise

Bermuda is a place "to hide and hush," wrote American painter Marsden Hartley after a 1917 visit—a sentiment that would have found favor with other art-world luminaries, including Winslow Homer, Georgia O'Keeffe, and Charles Demuth, who all found the island a calm and creative inspiration.

Scores of artists made their way to Bermuda in the 18th, 19th, and 20th centuries, finding respite from "real world" challenges in the island's sea, sun, tropical colors, unusual light, flora and fauna, and human personalities. In the process, many found fresh energy to paint and draw, reviving stalled careers or launching new artistic avenues that would win them further celebrity back in their home environments.

O'Keeffe recovered from a nervous breakdown during her 1933-1934 sojourns in Somerset, where she eschewed her typical explosive colors for charcoal sketches of banana flowers and banyan trees. Fauvist E. Ambrose Webster (1869-1935) was struck by the island's palette of purples, blues, and oranges, which he used to capture evocative landscapes as well as bold portraits of native Bermudians. And Homer, one of the most influential American painters of the 20th century, enjoyed exploring the coastline by horse and buggy, by foot, and by ferry when he visited Bermuda in 1899 and 1900, recording his sightseeing in 21 known watercolors of the island, which he proclaimed "as good an example as I have ever done."

Today the works of Bermuda by these and other internationally renowned artists from North America and Europe are being brought back to the island, thanks to the efforts of the Masterworks Foundation. The nonprofit group opened a dedicated $9 million museum—the Masterworks Museum of Bermuda Art—in Paget's Bermuda Botanical Gardens in 2008 to showcase the collection. Masterworks has gathered nearly 1,000 artworks, photos, and artifacts, among them: two O'Keeffe charcoals; two of Homer's seascapes, *Inland Water* and *Bermuda (The S.S. Trinidad)*; an Andrew Wyeth street scene of St. George's (*Royal Palms*); Ross Sterling Turner's impressionist views of gardens and neighborhood cottages; and photographer Karl Struss's three-dimensional color record of a postwar island in the 1950s. These and other works are featured *Masterworks at 25*, a 2012 coffee-table book celebrating the group's 25th anniversary.

lived here until his death in 1870. It was during this time that an arrowroot factory was opened in buildings behind the main house (now the headquarters of the Masterworks Foundation). In 1966, Camden House was sold to the government as part of the Bermuda Botanical Gardens and has been a public treasure ever since; the huge facing property on South Road is still owned by Tucker descendants.

Camden's interior received a designer makeover in 2003, when much of its plumbing, upholstery, and woodwork—including mountains of cedar—was refurbished. In the dining room, which features carved paneling that reportedly took a mid-1800s cabinetmaker 30 years to finish, ornate walls set off a stunning hand-carved Bermuda cedar table and chairs (to seat 22); boîte-like powder rooms recall a gentler age of tea parties and parasols; and expansive drawing rooms and studies, accented by historic antiques, artwork, books, crystal chandeliers, and gilded mirrors, make this one of the finest restored homes open to the public. One special feature on carved panels is the bird's-eye cedar, prized for its eye-catching grain. The William and Mary cushion-molded mirror over the dining-room fireplace is also worth a close look.

★ Masterworks Museum of Bermuda Art

Opened in 2008, the **Masterworks Museum of Bermuda Art** (MMBA, Arrowroot Building, Bermuda Botanical Gardens, 183 South Rd., tel. 441/299-4000, fax 441/236-4402, www.bermudamasterworks.com, 10am-4pm Mon.-Sat., 11am-4:30pm Sun., admission

$5, children under 12 free) is the brainchild of the Masterworks Foundation, an indefatigable nonprofit whose mission since 1987 has been the repatriation of Bermuda artwork by famous artists including Winslow Homer, Georgia O'Keeffe, and Charles Demuth. The group's Tom Butterfield and Elise Outerbridge have gathered an impressive collection of more than 1,000 paintings, drawings, photographs, maps, and memorabilia, much of which is now showcased in the $9 million museum. Housed in a former arrowroot-processing factory, the complex comprises three gallery spaces, a gallery mezzanine, members' lounge and book collection, classroom, art conservation room, art storage facility, and the aptly named **Homer's Café.** Next to it, the **Arrowroot Gift Shop** is one of the best places to find Bermuda cedar artifacts, such as goblets, trays, and bookends, and other authentic Bermuda gifts. The museum features outdoor sculptures—including a life-sized moose and, at the entrance, a stylized steel tribute to John Lennon's 1980 Bermuda visit and his resulting album, *Double Fantasy*, named for a freesia in the park. Masterworks has become a showcase for contemporary Bermuda artists as well as foreign luminaries past and present. The foundation runs an annual artist-in-residence program and has an active calendar of outreach and educational programs, including art camps for kids, painters' picnics, Art in the Park festivals, workshops, and biweekly openings of temporary shows. Check the schedule on the website.

Crow Lane

Crow Lane Park (sunrise-sunset daily, admission free), at the foot of Corkscrew Hill near the parish boundary with Devonshire, has a small lawn tucked along the water side of Foot of the Lane, the bottom of Hamilton Harbour. It's a good place for picnics or watching the sun set. A multitude of small pleasure craft are moored here next to the mangroves. Despite the sunny surroundings, the park has a sordid history. In 1730, slave Sally Bassett was publicly executed by burning here after being accused of poisoning a slave-owning Sandys couple (her bronze statue now stands in the grounds of the Cabinet Building on Front Street). Her case was the most notorious of many so-called poison plots used as a form of rebellion by slaves who practiced the religious art of Obeah. Bassett has been remembered in island folklore, and the park is now one of the sights on the African Diaspora Trail through the island.

A statue commemorating John Lennon's last summer in Bermuda sits outside the Masterworks Museum of Bermuda Art.

John Lennon in Bermuda

Bermuda has reestablished a fascinating connection with John Lennon's legacy. The former Beatle spent the final summer of his life on the island—a two-month sojourn in June and July 1980 that's been credited as a creative reawakening of the star who had stepped away from his career in 1975 to spend time raising his son Sean with Yoko Ono in New York. Lennon sailed to Bermuda from Newport, Rhode Island, on a storm-wracked sailboat, landing in St. George's before he rented a home in Fairylands, Pembroke. Ending a creative dry spell, he began to write again and during a visit to the Botanical Gardens, he was inspired by a flower bed sign bearing the fanciful name of a freesia—"Double Fantasy." The moniker would become the title of his comeback album, recorded in New York just three weeks before he was fatally shot on December 8, 1980, on the sidewalk outside his Upper West Side apartment.

"I thought, 'Double Fantasy—that's a great title!' because it's got so many meanings that you couldn't begin to think what it meant. It means everything you can think of," Lennon said in an RKO radio interview recorded the day he died.

Bermuda-based journalist Scott Neil, author of a 2012 book, Bermuda Fantasy: John Lennon's Island Journey, said Lennon benefited from the laid-back ambiance of the island. "Here, he was to reignite his songwriting talent, finding inspiration in his new surroundings," says Neil. "He worked on and refined the last songs he would ever write." Sounds from Bermuda can be heard in a number of the songs on both of Lennon's posthumous albums with Yoko, Double Fantasy and Milk & Honey, including the lapping of waves on a beach in the track "Beautiful Boy," which also features steel drums.

In 2012, musician/entrepreneur Tony Brannon (www.doublefantasybermuda.com)—who saw Lennon when the rock star visited his nightclub, Front Street's 40 Thieves & Disco 40, during the singer's 1980 visit—staged a concert tribute in the Botanical Gardens' show ring on Peace Day, September 21, and produced a double-CD box set featuring Lennon covers by local and overseas artists, including U.K. reggae star Maxi Priest. The "Peace Concert" has since become an annual event. LennonNYC filmmaker Michael Epstein directed "John Lennon: The Bermuda Tapes," an interactive album app chronicling the 1980 visit that was released through iTunes in 2013 to benefit a global antihunger campaign. The Masterworks Museum gave its own kudos in the form of a commemorative steel sculpture created by Bermudian artist Graham Foster that incorporates mirror images of doves, blossoms, and Lennon's distinctive profile. The circular, 4,000-pound structure now welcomes visitors into the museum at the gardens—just yards away from where Lennon spied the fateful freesia's name.

His bronze statue stands just 50 yards away, but you can see **Johnny Barnes** in person every morning, rain or shine, at the Crow Lane roundabout. With his white beard, straw hat, and a smile to stop traffic, the nonagenarian Bermudian waves rigorously to motorists on their way to work, shouting out loudly, "I love you!" While many thought Johnny was plain nuts when he first began his morning ritual in the 1980s, commuters now have come to expect and even look forward to his beaming face. Indeed, when Johnny misses a rare day, hundreds of calls flood local media to find out if he's okay. A group of area citizens decided to honor his goodwill with the statue, erected in 1996 along the garden verge at the start of East Broadway. A documentary short titled *Mr. Happy Man* was made by American Matt Morris about "the Johnny phenomenon" in 2012; it went on to win numerous accolades at several film festivals.

★ Waterville

A rambling 1725 homestead set on parkland that curls around the foot of the harbor, **Waterville** (corner of The Lane and Pomander Rd., tel. 441/236-6483, www.bnt.bm, 9am-5pm Mon.-Fri., admission free) is the headquarters of the Bermuda National Trust (BNT). Its elegant Georgian proportions ensure the building's status as a listed property, and stepping inside makes for instant time travel back to the 18th century. Somber oil portraits grace the walls in the lounge and dining room near the trellised entrance, and antiques, china, and a grandfather clock carry visitors back to early Bermuda. Originally a private home, Waterville belonged to the Trimingham family and later was the site of the first Trimingham's (the legendary but now defunct Front Street department store).

Waterville's gardens and surrounding park are even more stunning. A landmark tamarind tree blew down in 2003's Hurricane Fabian, but the **Heritage Rose Garden,** established in 1988 by the Bermuda Rose Society and showcasing many old Bermuda varieties, lights up the front lawn with color. Waterville Park includes a Victorian-style, wooden gazebo—perfect for a picnic—and Duck Island, a low, mangrove-covered islet where herons and waterfowl nest and ducks alight on the boats moored at Foot of the Lane. Neighborhood boaters access their vessels via this park, making it a hive of activity on summer weekends. A dirt path winds through thick cherry hedges along the waterfront and past an old horse-watering station to the main-road sidewalk.

Pomander Road

Meander by scooter or foot along the quaint harborside edging Pomander Road, a one-way, largely residential lane that slips off the bustle of The Lane into yesteryear. Ducks paddle past the mangroves and moored pleasure boats, wooden dinghies sit on the shoreline, and grassy nooks invite roadside picnics.

Despite its tranquility, there are a few enterprises along the loop back to Harbour Road. **Aberfeldy Nurseries** (3 Pomander Rd., at the junction with The Lane, tel. 441/236-2927), one of the oldest and largest plant retailers, is a good place to look at hundreds of the island's endemic and ornamental garden plants. Farther west along The Lane is Little Pomander Guest House, which has a waterfront property. Opposite it sits **Pomander Gate Tennis Club** (Pomander Ln., tel. 441/236-5400, www.pgtc.bm).

At the junction of Pomander and Harbour Roads is the **Royal Hamilton Amateur Dinghy Club** (tel. 441/236-2250, www.rhadc.bm), cosponsor of the biennial Marion Bermuda Race and home to hundreds of motorboats and fine yachts that have docking rights and moorings. Hugged by the serpentine main road, **Red Hole** is the name for the sheltered bay here, home to a working

Waterville, the historic Bermuda National Trust headquarters

boatyard and a tiny beach, where dinghies used to ferry boat-owners to their yachts are pulled up on the sand at low tide.

★ The Birdsey Studio

Bermuda travelers who met Alfred Birdsey (1912-1996) would not easily forget him. The unassuming but prolific painter welcomed thousands of visitors over the years to his Paget studio, where he often treated them to tea and a chat, no matter whether any art changed hands. Renowned outside of Bermuda, his Impressionistic, even Asian-influenced, brushstrokes of island landscapes, yachts, harbors, and backstreets revolutionized the way Bermuda was captured in art and caught the imagination of collectors worldwide. Today his daughter, Jo Birdsey-Linberg, carries on the family tradition at **The Birdsey Studio** (Rosecote, 5 Stowe Hill, tel. 441/236-6658, linberg@northrock.bm, 10:30am-1pm Mon.-Fri., appointments recommended). Like her father, she breaks artistic conventions—and makes guests feel entirely at home. Birdsey-Linberg's breezy watercolor landscapes and whimsical animal portraits—popular children's gifts—range in price from $80 to $450; oils are priced $400 and up. The studio also sells note cards of Alfred Birdsey's work, which Birdsey-Linberg is in the process of memorializing in a book. Park your scooter in front of the house and follow the path on the left to the back garden, where the studio is located amid roses, lilies, cacti, and paw-paw trees. Birdsey-Linberg, a Latin scholar, musician, and mother, can be found here most weekday mornings, with her "assistant managers"—two miniature dachshunds, Mango and Pickle.

★ Paget Marsh

A 25-acre natural wetland lying in the ample valley between the South Shore and Hamilton Harbour, **Paget Marsh** (Lovers Ln. off South Rd., sunrise-sunset daily, admission free) is jointly owned and managed by the Bermuda National Trust and Bermuda Audubon Society. Today a highlight on any island ecotour, the marsh was long neglected and inaccessible until 1998, when the two agencies launched an innovative conservation project that re-created the pond, rid the area of much non-endemic plantlife, and encouraged the return of native and migratory birds. The entrance is on Lovers Lane opposite the mailbox/dry cleaners building; head down the steep hill and park at the bottom, where banana groves and adjacent agricultural lands form a barrier against the nearby intersection. Renovated signage on birdlife and plantlife leads the way to a charming wooden boardwalk that winds through the mangroves into the marsh. Benches have been built into the walkway at intervals, allowing for peaceful communing with nature.

Paget Marsh is special among Bermuda's nature reserves because it is essentially a remnant from a previous era, much of its interior virtually untouched by man. As a result, it is home to centuries-old stands of cedar and palmetto forest, ancient mangrove forests, native wax myrtles, and Bermuda sedge, which is unique to the island and found only in this reserve. All are sustained by a primordial anchor of peat, which also serves to keep down mosquito populations. The marsh supports varied birdlife, including green and night herons, great egrets, kingfishers, moorhens, and yellow-throated warblers, which feed on the abundance of insects and larvae. The wetland is also a breeding ground for the giant toad, which was introduced to Bermuda in 1885.

The marsh consists of several interesting microhabitats. Ancient red mangroves overhang the first section, their distinctive boughs and prop roots creating a tunnel-like effect over the walkway. With the water glistening around their silver root tangle, they represent relics from an era when the marsh was a tidal saltwater pond. This first section of the marsh is flooded, and ducks and other waterfowl can be seen here gathering food. Moving forward, huge vine-covered cedars, rustling palmettos, giant ferns, and bulrushes create a thick forest wall on both sides, but as the creaky boardwalk turns a corner, there emerges an open area of sawgrass savannah, similar to vegetation in the Florida Everglades. Serrated leaves poke through the boardwalk like green swords, the grassland stretching like a sea on either side. This is a seasonally flooded area, where heavy rains drastically raise water levels in the winter. The boardwalk's end, reaching into the belly of the marsh, brings you to forests of original cedars and palmettos—a scene not unlike what the first settlers would have encountered in 1612. In the shade of these trees grow cinnamon, royal, and sword ferns, along with southern bracken and rare sedge. Environmentalists constantly cull invasive species such as the guava, Brazilian pepper, and Chinese fan palm to preserve the reserve's important endemic populations.

Visible from Paget Marsh is the silver spire of **St. Paul's Anglican Church** (Middle Rd. at Valley Rd. junction, tel. 441/236-5880), an area landmark. Inside the church are beautiful stained glass windows, old wooden pews, and cedar accents; outside, a historic graveyard with cedars and bougainvillea vines contains the whitewashed tombs of parishioners.

Salt Kettle

The spirits of pirates and privateers inhabit the tidy pastel lanes of Salt Kettle, home to Bermudian mariners and merchants over hundreds of years. Turn off Harbour Road onto Salt Kettle Road and follow it down into the intriguing promontory, which is now laden with historic homesteads, waterside gardens, and picturesque bays, all invested with the island's maritime history. A guest property is located here, Greenbank Guest House & Cottages. The Paget-Warwick ferry stops regularly at the public dock at the farthest point.

BEACHES

★ Elbow Beach

Originally called Elba Beach, before the Elbow Beach Hotel opened its doors in 1908, this prime stretch of South Shore strand curves a good half mile, incorporates two other private beachfront properties (Coco Reef Resort and Coral Beach & Tennis Club) as well as a public section, accessible by Tribe Road 48. Signs point to the beach from the main South Shore Road. Since all Bermuda beaches are public below the high-tide mark, locals enjoy this one just as much as resort guests—joggers, swimmers, and snorkelers can feel free to make use of the entire length of the beach. Elbow is a popular site for kitesurfers when the wind swings around to the south, and beach tennis

Elbow Beach, Paget

Homes and Gardens

Sotheby's antiques. Mystery roses by the dozen. Art by Warhol, Rembrandt, and El Greco. These are the treasures to be found at the ancestral homes that welcome visitors every spring in the popular **Open Houses and Gardens.** The program, organized by **The Garden Club of Bermuda** (tel. 441/232-5515, www.gardenclubbermuda.org), every year showcases a different parish whose elegant—sometimes unbelievably extravagant—properties provide a revealing behind-the-scenes look at privileged Bermuda. A half dozen or so homes throw open their doors to the public one day a year (usually a Wednesday) to raise money for club scholarships given to Bermudians studying horticulture or the environment. The homes and gardens selected are usually in the same neighborhood, so visitors can walk easily between the featured properties. While centuries-old homes and no-holds-barred interior design make for eye-popping walkabouts, visitors will usually find the featured gardens no less spectacular, works of art in themselves. Feel free to photograph the flora and outdoor areas; no photography is allowed inside homes for security reasons. Check the club's tour brochures, distributed annually to hotels, guesthouses, and www.gotobermuda.com, for details of dates, times, and locations.

and volleyball tournaments are held on the sand near the public steps. Elbow's clean, soft sand, cerulean breakers, and mostly gentle surf (hurricane season notwithstanding) make it a perfect beach for all swimming abilities, but note that there are no lifeguards at the public section. Even if you're not a guest at the Elbow Beach Hotel, you can purchase a day pass ($60), which provides two deck chairs, towels, umbrella, and waiter service from the beachside bar and bistro, Mickey's. There are also washrooms and an outdoor shower for guests at the hotel's beachfront, so you don't have to take the sand home.

Private **Grape Bay** is restricted to guests of area guest properties and homeowners in the tony neighborhood nearby. While the water is legally public, access is difficult, with no direct main roads leading to this quiet bit of coastline.

ENTERTAINMENT AND EVENTS

Social butterflies will feel at home in Paget, home to numerous restaurants, bars, and popular cultural events.

Nightlife

An Ibiza-style party draws see-and-be-seen crowds to **"The Big Chill"** (www.the-bigchill.com) Friday nights at ★ **Seabreeze Lounge** (Elbow Beach Hotel, 60 South Shore Rd., tel. 441/232-3999 or 441/236-9884, 5pm-midnight daily May through Sept.), where a panoramic terrace off the Café Lido complex offers views of Elbow Beach edged by coconut palms. DJ Felix Tod (husband-producer of songstress Heather Nova) joins Joy T. Barnum and guitarist TonyB at this tapas night-turned-dance party that has become the biggest happy hour for kicking off a summer weekend. Make a reservation days in advance—or you won't get a seat.

On the beach below, **Mickey's Bar & Bistro** (Elbow Beach Hotel, 60 South Shore Rd., tel. 441/236-9107, 10am-1am daily May-Oct., 10am-6pm Sat. and Sun. only Nov.-April) is a popular venue for a romantic glass of wine or a beachside hangout with friends.

Beau Rivage Restaurant & Bar (Newstead Resort & Spa, 27 Harbour Rd., tel. 441/232-8686, beaurivagebda.com, 1pm-9pm daily) offers one of the best alfresco sunset-spying spots, with sweeping views of Hamilton Harbour beyond the resort's infinity pool.

The **Peg Leg Bar** (Fourways Inn, 1 Middle Rd., tel. 441/236-6517, fax 441/236-5528, www.fourwaysinn.com, 6pm-midnight daily) is as irresistible as its name, with an authentically historic and snug British pub-like interior. It is often booked for private parties, so call ahead.

Lennon Bermuda Peace Concert

Launched in 2012 under a full moon at the Botanical Gardens, the **Lennon Bermuda Peace Concert** (tel. 441/334-8669, tonyb@transact.bm, www.doublefantasybermuda.com) commemorates former Beatle John Lennon's artistic connections to the island, where he spent the last summer of his life in 1980. The event, Bermuda's only real grassroots rock concert, has become a much-anticipated end to summer, normally scheduled around the United Nations International Day of Peace (Sept. 21). Local and foreign artists take to the stage in a professionally orchestrated night of good music and revelry (complete with food, t-shirts, CDs, and other takeaways) to raise money for island charities. Yoko Ono gave her blessing at the first event via video greeting.

Bermuda Annual Exhibition

If you're planning a trip to the island from mid- to late April, don't miss the **Bermuda Annual Exhibition** (Bermuda Botanical Gardens, 169 South Shore Rd., tel. 441/239-2351, fax 441/236-4812, www.bdaexhibition.bm, 8am-6pm Thurs.-Sat., $10 adults, $5 seniors and children 5-15, kids under 5 free), a truly local event that is one of the highlights on Bermudians' social calendars.

For decades it was purely an agricultural competition, but the beloved "Ag Show" got a new name and makeover in the 2000s, evolving into a broader cultural celebration showcasing island traditions like kite-making and cedar craftsmanship, as well as horticulture, culinary arts, and sports. Entrants compete for prizes for the best artwork, cakes, roses, healthy lunch boxes, and recyclable critters, to name a few. Real animals—farmyard pigs, cattle, harness ponies, pet rabbits—are highlights for children, and a foreign troupe of dancers, clowns, or acrobats is usually invited to perform.

The three-day fair also offers a sampling of food stalls selling cotton candy, fish sandwiches, fruit kabobs, and other favorites. Everyone from politicians and the governor to buses of grandmothers and society rose-growers comes out to support what has become a true island institution. For the fair at its best, go on Thursday (Friday brings schoolchildren who get a special day off classes to attend, and Saturday is a complete zoo).

SHOPPING

Arrowroot Gift Shop (tel. 441/236-2950, www.bermudamasterworks.com, 10am-4pm Mon.-Sat., 11am-4:30pm Sun.) at the Masterworks Museum of Bermuda Art in the Bermuda Botanical Gardens sells postcards, quality cedar souvenirs (many made by prison inmates), china from the Masterworks Bermudiana Collection, vintage travel posters, and other Bermuda mementos you won't find anywhere else on the island. Its location used to be part of an arrowroot factory.

SPORTS AND RECREATION

Paget is one of the sportiest parishes, packed with running trails, tennis galore, volleyball, water sports like kayaking and kitesurfing, and a scuba and snorkeling outlet.

Tennis

Paget resort properties have tennis courts that can be rented by nonguests at an hourly rate. There are five Plexi-pave hard courts at **Elbow Beach Hotel** (30 South Shore Rd., tel. 441/236-3535, tennis shop tel. 441/236-8737, www.elbowtennisbda.com, 8am-7pm daily spring/summer, 8am-5:30pm daily fall/winter); two of these have floodlights for night play. Resident pros include David Lambert—Bermuda's Davis Cup team coach and past president of the Bermuda Lawn Tennis Association—his wife, Barbara, and champion daughters Tara and Jackie, who all give lessons (one hour $75). The pro shop has a restroom and stocks balls, outfits, cold drinks, ice cream, and other snacks. Racquets can be rented or strung here. Court fees are $12 (one hour) or $18 with lights. For competitive play, call David Lambert at the shop to set up a

Coral Beach & Tennis Club's pink strand connects with Elbow Beach.

game or hit-up session with available top local players (only court fees apply).

Coral Beach & Tennis Club (34 South Shore Rd., tennis shop tel. 441/239-7223, www.coralbeachclub.com) is a private members' club with eight Har-Tru courts monitored to ATP standards. Three courts have lights. Visitors who are not club members can book lessons here ($100 per hour) or games with club members. The tennis shop stocks clothing emblazoned with the club's insignia, plus balls. Racquets can be rented. Note that all-white tennis attire is required. Several club pros, led by James Collieson, give private or group coaching.

Tiny **Pomander Gate Tennis Club** (Pomander Lane, tel. 441/236-5400, www.pgtc.bm) is nestled in a quiet harborfront neighborhood, with its clubhouse and five hard courts the headquarters for several annual local tournaments. Court fees are $100 per hour for nonmembers; an overseas membership package ($35) is also offered to visitors, allowing weeklong use of courts during non-peak hours.

Railway Trail (Paget)

It's hard to get away from traffic in Bermuda, and Paget's busy, hilly, narrow roads—major thoroughfares to and from Hamilton—often lack sidewalks and are far from ideal for running and walking. The Railway Trail is the perfect escape from the hubbub, a flat, shady path cutting through scenic neighborhoods. The Paget portion of the trail starts at the top of Trimingham Hill on South Road, where signs and a crosswalk lead to the entrance. Passing through a short tunnel and between thick limestone cuts in the hillside, the trail runs past Grape Bay, with wide-open views of Paget Marsh and the city of Hamilton's skyline beyond. Although the trail occasionally hits tarmacadam sections and has to cross a couple of main roads—be extremely careful of the blind-corner crossing just west of the Paget traffic lights near Modern Mart—it soon enters a long, wide, tranquil stretch that passes through thick cherry woods and past farmers' fields and spice forests, leading to Warwick and beyond. If you keep going, you can actually make it all the way to Mangrove Bay in Sandys—this I know from many a marathon-training session!

Spas

The Spa at Elbow Beach (Elbow Beach Hotel, 60 South Shore Rd., tel. 441/239-8900, fax 441/239-8906, www.elbowbeachbermuda.com, 9am-6pm daily), which celebrated its 10th anniversary in 2014, is one of Bermuda's most luxurious resort spas. If you feel like treating yourself, this is the place to go. Six private treatment suites (four single and two couples) offer daybeds, granite soaking tubs, pebble-lined showers, bamboo floors, and glittering ocean views from private balconies. Thai, Balinese, and Tibetan influences permeate the facility, located off the hotel pool area. Treatments include the Rum Swizzle Ritual—yes, the cocktail comes with it, along with a full body scrub, bath, and body/scalp massage (three hours, $435); the Ocean Body Wrap (80 minutes, $125); and the Holistic Facial (120 minutes, $229). The spa also has ESPA products and treatments for teens. Forty-eight-hour advance bookings are highly recommended.

With an elegant setting at the Newstead Resort & Spa on the Paget shore of Hamilton Harbour, **Newstead Spa & Salon** (27 Harbour Rd., tel. 441/249-7119, www.newsteadbelmonthills.com, 9am-6pm daily) has four treatment rooms, a couples suite, a wet room, lounge, and hair salon. Treatments including a deep-tissue massage (60 minutes, $140); four hands massage (60 minutes, $198, carried out by two therapists); energizing foot treatment (30 minutes, $55); Yon-Ka face and body treatments; and waxing, eyelash and eyebrow tints, and mani-pedis—for adults and kids. Men's spa rituals include a hot basalt stone massage (30 minutes, $75) and a Thai massage (1 hour, $130). Half-day (2.5 hours, $470) and evening packages are also offered, with use of the pool, gym, and steam rooms included.

ACCOMMODATIONS

Under $200

For 50 years, Bermuda's Ashton family has run **Greenbank Guest House & Cottages** (17 Salt Kettle Rd., tel. 441/236-3615, fax 441/236-2427, www.greenbankbermuda.com, $190-275 d), a historic and picturesque property located on the water's edge at Salt Kettle, conveniently just a minute or so from the ferry dock. Basically furnished cottages and apartments all have kitchenettes, private entrances, and free WiFi. Most can sleep up to three people; larger units with two bathrooms can sleep up to four. A pretty garden, serene neighborhood, access to public transport, and a prime vantage point for soaking up sunsets make it a favorite with repeat visitors.

$200-300

High on a hill in Paget's historic Highwood neighborhood, Beth and Tom Miller's home ★ **Westwood** (8 Westwood Lane, Paget, tel. 441-232-2447, elizabethgmiller8@gmail.com, $200 d, plus $100 cleaning fee, three-night minimum stay) might be the quintessential poster property for elegant island living. The adjoining self-catering apartment lets you experience that, if only temporarily. The impeccably renovated two-story rental used to be part of the main family home, but now has a separate entrance and pure cottage privacy in a lush garden setting—along with use of a large infinity pool with Bermuda cedar gates and panoramic views of Hamilton Harbour. The air-conditioned apartment's downstairs has a modern full kitchen with stainless appliances, a fireplace, and a beautifully upholstered living room with a twin-sized sofa bed. Climb the spiral staircase to a charming wood-floored bedroom outfitted with a queen bed, desk, fireplace, island artworks, a large closet, and contemporary en suite bathroom. Hostess Beth, whose family traces its roots back centuries, handles all details adeptly—right down to the current activities brochures and ironed cotton sheets. The lofty view extends over neighborhood gardens.

Fourways Cottage Colony (1 Middle Rd., tel. 441/236-6517, www.fourways.bm, starting at $245 d including continental breakfast) has 11 cottages situated on a beautiful estate better known for its historic restaurant, Fourways Inn. Each unit is simple but comfortable, with king-sized beds, air-conditioning, flat-screen TVs, free WiFi, and separate showers and bathrooms. Suites have living rooms and private terraces. With the famous dining room on-site, a gourmet dinner plan can be booked at a reduced price.

Set to open in 2015, **Inverurie Executive Suites** (1 Harbour Rd., tel. 441/232-5700) should appeal to upmarket business travelers housed by Hamilton's global corporations for extended stays. While rates and online booking mechanisms were still being worked out at press time, the property—which was completely gutted and renovated in 2014—offers ultramodern comforts and a breathtaking view of the harbor's blue expanse from every room's king-sized bed. The adjacent ferry dock, Darrell's Wharf, allows easy access to Hamilton via a seven-minute ride. Five suites boast full kitchens, bedrooms, and lounges, while 10 single rooms have galley kitchens and bathrooms. Top-tier amenities include WiFi, flat-screen TVs, and bathroom iPod docks. A concierge service will also be provided. Wooden decks front each of the rooms over the water.

Over $300

The 60-room ★ **Newstead Resort & Spa** (27 Harbour Rd., tel. 441/236-6060, www.newsteadbelmonthills.com, starting at $450 d) offers harborfront serenity in an ultra-contemporary setting. Basic 450-square-foot "Deluxe" suites, calmly inviting with their oatmeal decor, have double beds, Bose sound systems, flat-screen TVs, wireless Internet access, IP phone service, and views of the harbor, which sits just feet away. "Studio Deluxe" rooms include king beds, small kitchens, more space, and a waterfront balcony. One-, two- and three-bedroom suites have Jacuzzi tubs. The property's amenities include a spa, gourmet Beau Rivage restaurant, two tennis courts, and a stunning infinity pool overlooking the harbor. Room and concierge service are also available, and a dedicated water taxi ferries guests back and forth to Hamilton regularly in the mornings and evenings. Under a special arrangement, Newstead guests are also able to use the Coco Reef Resort's private beach, accessible via a complimentary shuttle that can also deliver you to Newstead's sister property in Warwick, the 84-acre Belmont Hills Golf Club. In 2014, both properties got a new owner, New York tycoon Larry Doyle, after four years in receivership.

For anyone seeking a little more solitude than a hotel or guesthouse can offer, ★ **Grape Bay Cottages** (Grape Bay Dr. off South Shore Rd., tel. 441/236-2515, fax 441/236-1194, www.gbcbermuda.com, 1-4 adults, with up to two children, $355 Apr.-Nov., $270 Nov.-Mar., minimum stay five nights) may offer the perfect solution. Two cottages, Beach Crest and the beachfront Beach Home, each with two bedrooms, a kitchen, a living/dining area, and one bathroom, sit on ultraexclusive, absolutely tranquil Grape Bay Drive (address of millionaires and bigwigs, including the former premier of Bermuda). Especially popular in summertime, the cottages afford easy access to private Grape Bay Beach, and each has its own small garden and barbecue for self-catering. Other amenities include cable TV, wireless Internet, phones, and air-conditioning. Owners Doug and Maria Frith make all their guests feel welcome, which must be why they get so many repeat visitors year after year.

Another good choice on this same beachfront is **Rendezvous Cottage** (Grape Bay Dr. off South Shore Rd., tel. 441/234-0693, www.bermudagetaway.com, $415 Apr.-Oct., $325 Nov.-Mar.), with two bedrooms (one with a king, one with twin beds), a full bathroom, living room, and fully equipped, renovated kitchen. Cable TV and wireless internet access are also provided, as well as an outdoor barbecue area and a washer-dryer. The nonsmoking cottage, which also comes with maid service, can accommodate four adults, or two adults and three young children.

Fancy living like a bona fide Bermudian? Artist Charles Zuill's ancestral waterfront property, ★ **The Moorings** (31 Harbour Rd., tel. 441/293-5918, cvzuill@gmail.com, $5,500 per week May-Oct., $3,000 Nov.-April), belonged to his great-great-grandfather, William Smith Hutchings, the last captain of a sailing barque named *Pearl* who in 1855 went to sea "and never came back." Such maritime legend inhabits every nook and cranny of the renovated two-story 17th-century house, which is cradled by quarry walls and hidden on the waterfront between Hodgson's ferry stop and the next-door Newstead Resort. Utter privacy in a comfortable home setting is the result. The air-conditioned three-bedroom house has wood floors throughout, open-beamed ceilings, kitchens on both levels, sitting rooms and patios for entertaining or relaxation, a dock for swimming—and to-die-for views of the Hamilton cityscape and the ocean a few feet away. Barbecues and a washer and dryer make it a home away from home. Ideal maximum occupancy is six adults.

Owned by the Saudi Arabian royal family, **Elbow Beach Hotel** (60 South Shore Rd., tel. 441/236-3535, toll-free tel. 800/223-7434, starting at $700 d) reopened as an independent resort advised by the Burns Group after the Mandarin Oriental Group's contract expired in 2014, but the 50-acre seafront resort remains one of Bermuda's premier properties. While only the lobby and conference rooms are operating in the landmark main building that awaits renovation, 98 boutique cottages and suites are located within the gardens of the sprawling property. All have private sundecks, high ceilings with exposed beams, marbled bathrooms with glass showers, goose-down bedding, LCD TVs, iPod docking, high-definition cable service, air-conditioning, WiFi, and broadband access. The resort has a deluxe spa, five top-rate tennis courts, a climate-controlled pool, fitness center, putting green, and a trio of beachfront restaurants. Three stand-alone cottages can also be booked. The beach is the property's crown jewel, stretching outside the hotel in a pristine, half-mile arc linking to next-door Coral Beach. Between them, a public-access section makes this a popular spot in the summer, but the hotel's beach facilities (deck chairs, umbrellas, showers, and changing rooms) are reserved for paying guests.

Coco Reef Resort (3 Stonington Circle, South Shore Rd., tel. 441/236-5416, fax 441/236-0371, www.cocoreefbermuda.com, $350-499 d) is an oceanfront resort with 63 units (32 with ocean views, 31 beachfront). All are nonsmoking, each with a balcony or patio, cable TV, and wicker and floral furniture. The property includes a lobby with a 50-foot atrium and crystal skylight, a bar and restaurant, a gift shop, a library, and an outdoor dining area. With far fewer facilities or high-end amenities, the property isn't in the same league as neighboring Elbow Beach Hotel, but rates are slightly lower and the beach outside is shared with the Elbow Beach Hotel. Coco Reef Resort has two free-use tennis courts and a heated swimming pool overlooking the ocean.

FOOD

Paget enjoys a thriving restaurant scene, thanks to the plethora of hotels and guesthouses and its location on the outskirts of Hamilton. From burgers and comfort food to beachside Mediterranean menus, cutting-edge Bermudian cuisine, and à la carte silver service, foodies of all tastes will find plenty to sample.

Cafés and Takeout

With a quaint walled rose garden on one side of the French doors, and a cobblestone patio with shaded tables on the other, **Homer's Café** (inside the Masterworks Museum of Fine Art, Bermuda Botanical Gardens, 183 South Rd., tel. 441/299-4001, 10am-4pm Mon.-Sat., 11am-4:30pm Sun.) is a delightful spot to grab a light lunch bite—with a glass of Sauvignon blanc. The café serves up baked goods, quiches, sandwiches, paninis, soups and other snacks, along with coffees, cold drinks, beer, and a selection of fine wines. Relax outdoors in the courtyard or in Dobbie's Hideaway, the downstairs lounge furnished with couches and kids' activities. Wheelchair-accessible via an elevator and ramps.

The Pink Café (King Edward VII Memorial Hospital, 7 Point Finger Rd., ground floor, tel. 441/239-2057, 9am-3:30pm Mon.-Fri., closed weekends) is partly run by the facility's ubiquitous "Pink Ladies" and teenage "Candy Stripers"—volunteers from the charitable Women's Hospital Auxiliary, who, identifiable in their hallmark rosy uniforms, work in virtually every department of the hospital aiding nurses with patient care. Their much-loved little coffee shop serves up local favorites like fish cakes, black-eyed pea soup, gingerbread, and chicken pies to a constant crowd of medical staff, hospital visitors, and drop-in passersby. Hot lunch specials range $8.50-12.

The hospital's **cafeteria** (first floor, tel. 441/236-2345, breakfast 7:30am-9:30am Mon.-Fri., lunch noon-2pm Mon.-Fri., $4.50-12) is also open to the public and offers a truly local experience, complete with loads of well-priced comfort food (burgers, chicken legs, macaroni 'n' cheese).

Like its after-hours Hamilton counterpart of the same name, **The Ice Queen** (Rural Hill Plaza, South Rd., tel. 441/236-3136, 10am-5am daily, $3-15) sees lines out the door for its takeout cheeseburgers, chicken, and skinny fries when Hamilton bars close on Friday and Saturday evenings. Lunch brings a calmer clientele—construction workers, school kids, and seniors. The menu highlights are the delicious fish tenders (Bermuda wahoo) and fish sandwich. Prices are reasonable and the offerings hearty.

★ **The Paraquet Restaurant** (68 South Shore Rd., tel. 441/236-9742, 8am-midnight daily) is more public forum than restaurant, a welcome roadside drop-in for taxi drivers, police patrols on coffee breaks, flip-flopped beachgoers, senior citizens, and families with children. The eatery, owned by Portuguese Bermudians, has been around for as long as most locals can remember. Today, it keeps on serving favorites like the delectably crusted fish cake on a bun ($6.40; fish cakes can also be purchased by the half dozen), hearty soups ($6.25), breakfast specials ($10.95), wraps, toasted subs, hot and cold sandwiches ($5-14), meatloaf, fish and chicken dinners, chicken wings, cakes, pies, thick milk shakes—and several dishes featuring black rum. Special holiday menus are popular during the Easter, Christmas, and Thanksgiving seasons. The Paraquet's bakery offerings are also worth sampling: banana bread, gingerbread, rolls, and hot-cross buns (at Easter) are stacked daily on shelves near the entrance. Bermudians also bulk-order their Christmas cassava pies and Easter fish cakes (arguably the best on the island) from here. Opt for a stool at the foyer bars to get the full experience: Cabbies and other regulars hold debates on the political issues of the day here most afternoons.

International

For a casual setting and fare, step onto the terrace overlooking Elbow Beach, where the **Seabreeze Lounge** (Elbow Beach Hotel, 60 South Shore Rd., tel. 441/232-3999 or 441/236-9884, snacks 2:30pm daily, tapas 5:30pm daily) serves tasty small plates, sushi, cocktails, and wine. Tapas ($5-16) include burger sliders, chicken satay, coconut shrimp, oysters, Cajun pork ribs, lamb kofta, olive tapenade, manchego, and a full sushi menu. A custom gazebo allows all-weather outings; in winter, heat lamps, fire pits, and comfort dishes make it a cozy retreat. The popular "Big Chill" event on Friday nights through the high season turns up the energy level with a DJ, live music, and a dance floor.

Just below, ★ **Mickey's Bar & Bistro** (on the beach, Elbow Beach Hotel, 60 South Shore Rd., tel. 441/236-9107, May-Oct. only, lunch noon-3pm, snacks 3pm-5pm, dinner 6:30pm-9:30pm, bar service 10am-1am daily) sits on a deck under an elegant custom canopy on the sand within a few yards of the thunderous surf. The casual-chic eatery offers a modern, Euro vibe and a delicious menu—salads, pastas, steaks, and seafood, including many vegetarian options (main courses $16-34). Service is stellar, the dishes beautifully concocted, and the alfresco surroundings utterly relaxing, even by Bermuda standards. Parents love it, because kids can go build a sandcastle while they sit and chat between courses.

Hidden away in the clubhouse of a residential condominium complex, **Thyme** (1 Cataract Hill, tel. 441/236-1379, www.thyme.bm, lunch 11:30am-2:30pm Tues.-Sat., dinner 6pm-9pm Wed.-Sat., bar opens at 5:30pm) is something of a local secret. But it's worth a scouting mission. Bermudian chef Joe Gibbons's eatery serves up food with flair in a relaxing and off-the-beaten path local neighborhood. After scaling the precipitous hill off South Road, you'll see the restaurant sitting alongside the pool on the other side. Menu highlights include daily soup, sandwich, or fish specials like lemon-lime-marinated tuna steak ($28), lobster-avocado sandwich ($24), grilled rib-eye ($36), burgers ($19), thin-crust pizzas ($16-22), and satisfying desserts like bread-and-butter pudding ($9). Evening happy hours serve up rum punch ($10), martinis ($12), and a selection of wine and beer.

Fine Dining

Café Lido (at the beachfront, Elbow Beach Hotel, 60 South Shore Rd., tel. 441/236-9884, fax 441/236-8496, www.lido.bm, 6:30pm-9pm daily) is an elegant and sophisticated ocean-front dining room adjoining the outdoor Seabreeze Lounge. With picture windows looking out to Elbow Beach's blue horizons and the surf just a staircase away, the restaurant oozes modern ambience with its terra-cotta and wood decor and very professional service from manager Ennio Lucarini and his attentive staff. The award-winning menu is outstanding, loaded with fresh fish and vegetarian options. Appetizers include roasted octopus ($16.75), crispy foie gras ($16), and tuna tartare ($17.75). Entrées offer a wide choice of seafood (sea bass, tuna, bouillabaisse), meat (filet mignon $38.75), pastas (lobster risotto, chickpeas tagliatelle), and daily-changing desserts (Bermuda honey crème brûlée).

★ **Beau Rivage Restaurant & Bar** (Newstead Resort & Spa, 27 Harbour Rd., tel. 441/232-8686, www.beaurivagebda.com, breakfast 7am-10:30am, lunch 11:30am-2:30pm, dinner 6:30pm-9:30pm Mon.-Sat.; Sunday brunch 11:30am-2pm) has both a commanding vantage point and impressive menu. Award-winning French chef Jean-Claude Garzia chose the perfect venue to impress his diners—a harborfront terrace with views of the city skyline and an infinity pool—but his tantalizing dishes would do that anyway. Lunch features refreshingly Continental fare like niçoise salad ($24), a south of France *pan bagnat* ($15.50), and croques monsieur ($15.50), as well as tempura fish 'n' chips ($22.50), burgers ($24), pizza ($16), and a little kids' menu. As you enjoy one of the best views of an island sunset, you can savor an equally satisfying dinner menu with items like tuna tataki ($18.50), rockfish fillet ($38), steak au poivre ($38), and chicken piccata ($33). Vegetarians will be pleased to find custom creations including green herb risotto ($25) or grilled garden vegetable cake. Happy hour on the infinity pool terrace is also dreamy.

Boasting a fabled, 300-year-old reputation, **Fourways Inn** (1 Middle Rd., tel. 441/236-6517, fax 441/236-5528, www.fourwaysinn.com, dinner 6:30pm-9:30pm daily, brunch 11:30am-2:30pm Sun.) offers a hefty spoonful of history along with its gourmet menu. Built in 1727 by John Harvey of the Bristol Cream clan, Fourways has been a private home, a restaurant, and a guesthouse over the years. Steeped in cedar and rife with antiques, narrow hallways, and low door frames, it retains a charming character and is a noted architectural landmark. The restaurant's award-winning kitchen has for decades garnered international accolades for its gourmet creations. With offerings such as premium Russian and American caviar, braised lamb shank ($38.95), roasted beet and fennel salad ($19.75), crab-crusted rockfish ($42.75), dark 'n' stormy soufflé ($13.50), fresh lobsters, herbs from the garden, and a wine list to get lost in, Fourways provides a dining experience you won't soon forget. It is not a cheap date, however; dinner for two with wine will cost at least $200. Patrons can choose to eat in the historic interior, where grandfather clocks and the Peg Leg Bar recall earlier times, or outside in the garden-fringed courtyard. Service is impeccable; dress code is smart-casual. The popular Sunday brunch is a good way to sample Fourways's menu with an eye toward cost-effectiveness. The brunch spread of sushi, roast meats, fresh fish, seafood, pasta, and omelets-to-order is $39.75 for adults, $20 children age four to 11, kids under three free.

Grocery Stores

Tucked behind Paget gas station, the small **A1 Paget Market** (Middle Rd. at Valley Rd. junction, tel. 441/236-0351, 8am-10pm Mon.-Sat., 9am-7pm Sun.) is a convenient stopping place for wines, liquors, fresh fruits and vegetables, frozen meals, deli meats, and baked goods. One of the stores in the MarketPlace chain, it is most popular for its rotisserie chicken and takeout chicken fingers, available near the back of the store. Friendly staff and easy parking attract a regular parish clientele.

The large, busy **Modern Mart** (104 South Shore Rd., tel. 441/236-6161, 8am-10pm Mon.-Sat., 9am-7pm Sun.) offers everything from groceries to foreign and local newspapers, greeting cards, toiletries, and pet paraphernalia. The store's ample wine selection is worth a visit. Modern Mart's butchers are particularly helpful and professional.

Burrows Lightbourn's **Corner Shop** (30 Harbour Rd. at Manse Rd., tel. 441/236-0355, 9am-6pm Mon.-Sat.) is tiny but well stocked, with wines, spirits, and beer, plus hot pizza, pies, and sub sandwiches on hand daily.

INFORMATION AND SERVICES

If you hear ambulance sirens in Paget, it's because the island's only emergency hospital is located here, on the northeast and western sides of the Bermuda Botanical Gardens. Bermuda's main health-care facility, the **King Edward VII Memorial Hospital** (7 Point Finger Rd., tel. 441/236-2345, www.bermudahospitals.bm), opened a $300-million Acute Care Wing in 2014 with state-of-the-art emergency, dialysis, oncology, and diagnostic imaging departments, five surgery theaters, and a total of 90 beds. The largest project of its kind undertaken in Bermuda's history, the new treatment center represents a major step forward for the island's health care; the original building was established in 1920. The brand-new wing has a modern gift shop, while the former building remains home to a public "Pink Ladies" cafeteria on the ground floor run by the volunteer group, and a second cafeteria on the first floor. The hospital vicinity, along Point Finger Road, Berry Hill Road, and The Lane, is lined with doctors' offices and headquarters for medical support services.

One of the islandwide Phoenix Stores chain, **Paget Pharmacy** (Rural Hill Plaza, 130 Middle Rd., tel. 441/279-5511, pharmacy tel. 441/279-5510, fax 441/236-9057, 8am-8pm Mon.-Sat., 10am-6pm Sun. and holidays) offers newspapers and magazines, makeup, beach supplies, candy, greeting cards, postcards, and a prescriptions counter.

Island Health Pharmacy (40 Point Finger Rd., tel. 441/236-8585, www.ihp.bm, 8:30am-5:30pm) is located inside a doctors' practice in this medical neighborhood, but the general public is welcome.

Located farther north on the same road is **Point Finger Road Pharmacy** (16 Point Finger Rd., tel. 441/236-3859, www.pharmacy.bm), a full-service operation that offers free blood sugar and blood pressure testing.

The cheery staff at pocket-sized **Paget Post Office** (108 Middle Rd., tel. 441/236-7429, 8am-5pm Mon.-Fri.) know all the locals, making this tiny outlet a hub of the parish community, especially during the busy Christmas season.

Rubis Paget Service Station (65 Middle Rd., at the corner of Valley Rd., tel. 441/236-1691, 7am-9pm Mon.-Sat., 9am-6pm Sun.) is run by a friendly team who know the regulars by name. The on-site shop sells newspapers, cold drinks, and baked goods.

Paget Dry Cleaners and Mailboxes Express (2 Lovers Ln. at Middle Rd., tel. 441/236-5142, 8am-7pm Mon.-Sat.) offers full dry-cleaning services, plus a DHL and TNT maildrop for overseas mail (documents only).

Clarien Bank (Paget Plaza, 161 South Rd. at Point Finger Rd., tel. 441/296-6969, clarienbank.com, 8:30am-4pm Mon.-Fri.), located at this corner shopping plaza, is the only bank branch in Paget and has full teller services and 24-hour ATM access.

ATMs can be found at Paget Plaza, Rural Hill Plaza, Modern Mart, and the hospital.

Public toilets are located at area restaurants and hotels, the Bermuda Botanical Gardens visitors center, and King Edward VII Memorial Hospital.

GETTING THERE AND AROUND

Buses

Paget is dotted with bus stops, making for easy public transport around the parish. Take the route 2 bus (hourly) through the parish center between Hamilton and Ord Road (north of Elbow Beach). To go to Sandys or the South Shore beaches farther west, hop on the route 7 bus (every half hour) or route 8 bus (every 15 minutes), which take South Shore Road and Middle Road, respectively, to the Royal Naval Dockyard. Travel within Paget qualifies for the three-zone tariff of $3 (exact change or tokens, tickets, or passes required).

Ferries

The quaint iron ferries *Georgia, Coralita,* and *Corona,* of the Paget-Warwick route, are worth experiencing, especially for the breezy harbor-hop to the ferry terminal in Hamilton. Paget has three very scenic stops along narrow Harbour Road, where you can either jump aboard or get off and explore. Farthest down the harbor is Lower Ferry (between Highwood Lane and Valley Road); Hodgson's Ferry opposite the Chapel Road junction is next, followed by Salt Kettle, situated at the foot of this charming old seafaring neighborhood. Corporate commuters use the service; in the mornings, you can see suits, skirts, and heels scampering along serpentine Harbour Road to catch the vessels en route from the city's ferry terminal. If you board in Hamilton, the short circuit out and back takes about a half hour; ferries leave Hamilton every 30 minutes or less at commuter times, otherwise every 45 minutes. Fares are $5 round-trip, $3 one-way (adults), $2.50 for kids five to 16. For information, call **Sea Express** (tel. 441/295-4506, www.seaexpress.bm) or check the schedules printed in the phone book.

Scooters and Bicycles

Paget is the headquarters for **Oleander Cycles** (6 Valley Rd., tel. 441/236-5235 or 441/236-2453, fax 441/236-1949, www.oleandercycles.bm, 8:30am-5:30pm daily), the island's largest scooter livery, with five other outlets around the island. Standard or deluxe (two-person) scooters can be rented by anyone age 16 or older; no driver's license is required, but instructors carry out a mini-tutorial on Valley Road before letting visitors loose on two wheels. Rates ($55 standard/$65 double for one day, $225 standard/$266 double per week, $17/$21 per day after seven days) include scooter delivery and pickup (or hotel

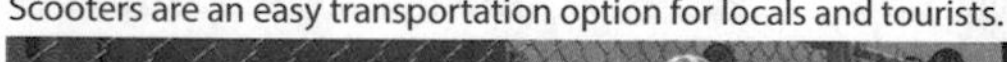
Scooters are an easy transportation option for locals and tourists.

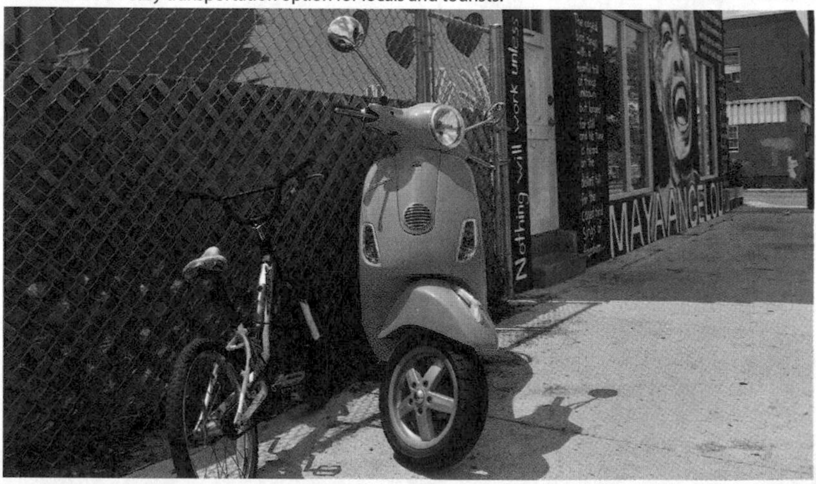

pickup), first tank of gas, helmet, lock, basket, $30 third-party insurance, and islandwide roadside service for breakdowns (24-hour helpline). Pedal bikes can be rented for $40 per day, or $175 per week.

Based at Paget's largest hotel, **Elbow Beach Cycles** (Elbow Beach Hotel, 60 South Rd., tel. 441/296-2300 or 441/296-8880, www.elbowbeachcycles.com) offers islandwide scooter delivery and pickup. Rates for gas scooters, from midsize to larger models able to transport two people, range from $46-81 per day to $208-286 per week; electric scooters are $41 per day or $249 for a week. Scooters and pedal bikes can also be rented here for as little as three hours. Check the website for deals, advance booking, and general information about touring Bermuda on two wheels. Midsized mountain bikes with 21 gears rent for $30 per day, and $114 per week. Hybrid (battery-powered) electric bikes, allowing easier travel through Bermuda's hilly terrain, cost $35 per day or $129 per week.

Eve Cycle Livery (114 Middle Rd., tel. 441/236-6247, www.evecycles.com) rents scooters starting at $48 per day and $210 per week, with free islandwide shuttle service and online advance booking. Mountain bikes can be rented for $30 per day, or $115 per week.

Taxis

There is a taxi stand outside the main entrance of the Elbow Beach Hotel. Otherwise, book a taxi via telephone. The main taxi companies are: **Bermuda Industrial Union Co-op** (tel. 441/292-4476, cooptaxi@fkbnet.bm), **Bermuda Island Taxi** (tel. 441/295-4141, www.bermudaislandtaxi.com), and **BTA Dispatching Ltd.** (tel. 441/296-2121, www.taxibermuda.bm).

Warwick and Southampton Parishes

Bermuda's most panoramically scenic parishes, with clifftop views of surf-tossed coastlines on one side and the Great Sound's archipelago on the other, Warwick and Southampton project the quintessential Bermuda experience.

The most recognizable images, those that sell the island in magazine layouts, TV ads, and postcards, are often captured here. Full-blast Waikiki-esque fun in the sun? Check. Secluded azure grottoes? Check. Kitesurfing, golf, tennis, scuba, spas? Ditto. Beaches, water sports, and big-resort indulgences are the key draws for these parishes, whether you're stopping off for a swim while driving west or choosing them as home base for a Bermuda stay. While shopping is limited to convenience stores, groceries, and retail outlets within hotels, and entertainment is almost exclusively of the outdoor variety, both parishes offer food, sports, and accommodations galore.

Sprawling westward between Paget and Sandys, Warwick and Southampton encompass undulating terrain scattered with residential neighborhoods, farmland, nature reserves, hotels, guesthouses, and national parks, to which the miles of south-facing beaches and coastal dunes belong. The two parishes are dotted with historic properties, as well as modest cottages tucked down meandering tributaries bearing soporific names like Sleepy Hollow Lane, Rose Glen, and Tamarind Vale.

When Bermudians talk about going "up de country," they mean heading west to Somerset through these parishes. There is a choice of routes to do this. Harbour Road on its northern boundary is one of Warwick's main arteries. It's a wall-hugging route reminiscent of narrow, sidewalk-free lanes in British seaside towns, meandering from the end of Hamilton Harbour around part of the Great Sound's southern rim. The serpentine journey poses a dilemma for scooter drivers: Sure, the scenery is alluring, but take your eyes off the road for a second, and you might miss the next hairpin turn—a somewhat common occurrence, based on the number of patched holes in the road's low wraparound wall. Harbour Road

Previous: Warwick Long Bay; Port Royal Golf Course. **Above:** Astwood Cove.

Look for ★ to find recommended sights, activities, dining, and lodging.

Highlights

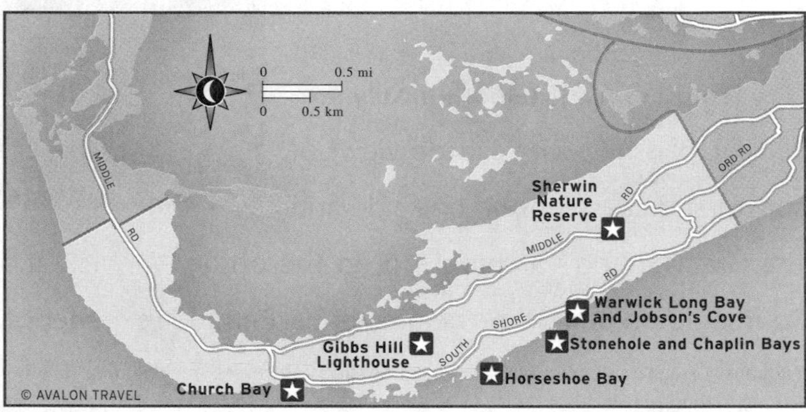

★ **Sherwin Nature Reserve:** Signage and cleared trails make this nature reserve, containing the second-largest freshwater pond in Bermuda, an attraction for anyone interested in ecowalks or island birdlife (page 120).

★ **Warwick Long Bay and Jobson's Cove:** As its name suggests, this is officially Bermuda's longest beach, its soft pink stretches typically less crowded than those of nearby Horseshoe Bay, to which it is connected by trails through the dunes (page 122).

★ **Stonehole and Chaplin Bays:** Romantics—and families with small children—will appreciate this postcard-pretty retreat from the hubbub of neighboring Horseshoe Bay. It's also a haven from the occasional force of breakers and rip currents (page 123).

★ **Gibbs Hill Lighthouse:** Even Queen Elizabeth II deigned to stop here (twice, in 1953 and 1975), and that was before gourmet meals were served. Today, a quaint restaurant, perched on the steep hilltop alongside the historic lighthouse, offers bird's-eye views and an inspired menu (page 132).

★ **Horseshoe Bay:** Bermuda's answer to Australia's Bondi Beach, this tamer version of surf and sand attracts crowds through the summer. Cruise ship passengers flock here during the week, but its beauty and access to miles of other beaches and coves make it worth a visit (page 134).

★ **Church Bay:** Boiler reefs located just a few yards from the rollers of this deeply soft beach make it one of the best snorkeling venues on the South Shore. Barracuda and parrotfish can be commonly seen. The fascinating architecture of the reefs themselves creates a true underwater wonderland (page 135).

represents one of the island's most sought-after addresses; hemmed by centuries-old mansions, the drive offers coveted water views and spectacular sunsets.

Near the Southampton border, Harbour Road connects via Burnt House Hill to Middle Road, which, as its name suggests, runs through the belly of the parish. The busy, low-lying route offers few pretty vistas but lots of local interest as traffic whisks Bermudians to and from sports clubs, grocery stores, schools, and residential neighborhoods. South Shore Road, with its wide curves and convenient hilltop pull-over areas, is the most dramatic vantage point from which to admire both parishes' tumbling dunes, sweeping beach views, and reef-dotted ocean expanses that reveal an intoxicating palette of blues, from swimming-pool turquoise to midnight navy. During the spring, migrating humpback whales—or at least their flukes and blowholes—are sometimes visible on the horizon beyond the inshore reefs.

South Shore Road continues west through half of Southampton before cutting north across the parish to Barnes Corner, where it ends at the harbor. From here, Middle Road becomes the only route west, running to Somerset Bridge in Sandys. Dissecting both parishes north-south are historic tribe roads—skinny, dead-straight, mostly pedestrian-only right-of-ways running shore to shore that were necessary for parish access before the days of larger thoroughfares and motorized vehicles. Indeed, early law dictated that the paths measured the width of a barrel, to allow transport of commodities like rum, foodstuffs, and gunpowder. Parallel to the main east-west roads runs the scenic old Railway Trail, accessible via the tribe roads and signposted points off Middle Road.

PLANNING YOUR TIME

If you're staying at a hotel or guesthouse in Warwick or Southampton, you will find yourself close enough to the beaches or Railway Trail for early-morning dips and evening strolls any season of the year. Most Bermudians swim strictly June-October, but visitors will find the ocean's average 65°F winter temperature quite balmy, especially if escaping winter snow. There are more than a dozen beaches, bays, and coves lining the southern side of both parishes, offering the island's best variety in swimming and beach venues. Depending on how much of a beach bum you are, you can enjoy a different spot every day of your trip. Outdoorsy types will enjoy activities like diving, whale-watching (in season), snorkeling, and horseback riding on the dunes.

The area is a magnet for golfers, thanks to four major courses in the two parishes, including the Belmont Hills Golf Club and the championship Port Royal Golf Course, which underwent a complete renovation in the 2000s and hosted the PGA Grand Slam of Golf for six years (2009-14).

Warwick and Southampton make convenient starting points for excursions to other parts of the island; they're well served by the island's buses, taxis, rental scooter outlets, and ferries. If you're staying elsewhere on the island, you will definitely want to visit both parishes, if only for the views. Beach aficionados can do what the locals do and make day trips to swim and sunbathe. Some of the best-known restaurants and spas, located in hotels and patronized equally by Bermudians and visitors, are also reason enough to visit. Travelers heading west on excursions to Somerset and the Royal Naval Dockyard can make the most of the panoramic scenery, various eateries, and sights like Long Bay and Gibbs Hill Lighthouse en route.

Warwick Parish

Warwick, like the county of Warwickshire in England's West Midlands, is properly pronounced WAH-rick, its silent, middle "W" usually proving confusing for American tongues. The parish was named for the Earl of Warwick, Sir Robert Rich, one of the original "adventurers" (London investors in the colony in the 1600s) and a key player in New World expansion during the Elizabethan Age.

Today, Warwick's residential neighborhoods are heavily populated and have suffered from crime and occasional gang violence. Yet the parish also contains beautiful national parks and rambling historic estates, often located cheek by jowl with lower-income areas. Perhaps as a result, there are no areas considered truly off-limits; aside from telltale groups of wall-sitters and graffiti in some places, a visitor would be barely aware of social problems beneath the pretty facade.

Warwick's key draws for visitors, like Southampton's, are its beaches (arguably Bermuda's best) and its wide assortment of accommodations within walking distance of the sand. For anyone whose chief aim is to relax, swim, and get a tan, there's no better area of the island. If you're staying here, the 20-minute drive into Hamilton for shopping and entertainment is hardly arduous, either.

SIGHTS

There are far fewer sights of specific interest in Warwick than those of general scenic beauty, and the best vistas can be appreciated by simply traveling along either **Harbour Road** or **South Shore Road** as you explore the parish (Middle Road is busier and less scenic). From the harborside, the expansive **Great Sound,** stretching from the harbor entrance to the fishhook of Dockyard, offers a pristine panorama, its waters sprinkled with mostly private smaller islands where Bermudians live full-time, keep summer cottages, or camp in August and September. Weekend yacht-racing and scheduled Bermuda dinghy-racing take place out here, as do impromptu public-holiday "raft-ups" of sometimes a dozen vessels or more, when local boaters tie up together at anchor for cockpit cocktails, picnics, and off-the-stern swims. Evening barbecue cruises to several islands can be arranged through Hamilton-based tour operators and boating outlets.

At **Darrell's Wharf,** the border of Paget and Warwick, ferries shuttle businesspeople and tourists to and from Hamilton, a 15-minute ride. This is a good spot to watch the cruise ships sail by twice a week; Monday mornings and Thursday afternoons, they dwarf the distant Pembroke shore and the Hamilton skyline. While mega-vessels stay put at Dockyard, tugboats escort smaller ships through the narrow channel of Two Rock Passage into Hamilton Harbour; at week's end they head out again to the North Shore channel. Harbour Road's tony properties, with brick drives, pergolas, spilling bougainvillea, and freesia-carpeted lawns, are also eye-catching.

Wide viewing spots on South Shore Road allow scooter motorists or taxis to pull over at particularly scenic vantage points along the route. Populated by whispering pines, baygrape trees, goldenrods, and dramatic white-flowering Spanish bayonets, this route is also popular with local runners and walkers. Its high vantage point gives a spectacular aspect of the whole shoreline, as well as the boiler reefs, which lie exposed at low tide.

Cobb's Hill Methodist Church

Among Warwick's specific sights is the seemingly nondescript **Cobb's Hill Methodist Church** (off Cobb's Hill Rd. on Moonlight Ln., tel. 441/236-8586, fax 441/232-4806, cobbshillmethodist@logic.bm, services 9:30am Sun.). With a steeple and tiny sanctuary dating back to 1827, the church "built by slaves in moonlight"—a truism proudly carried on its sign and in its literature—holds

Warwick Parish

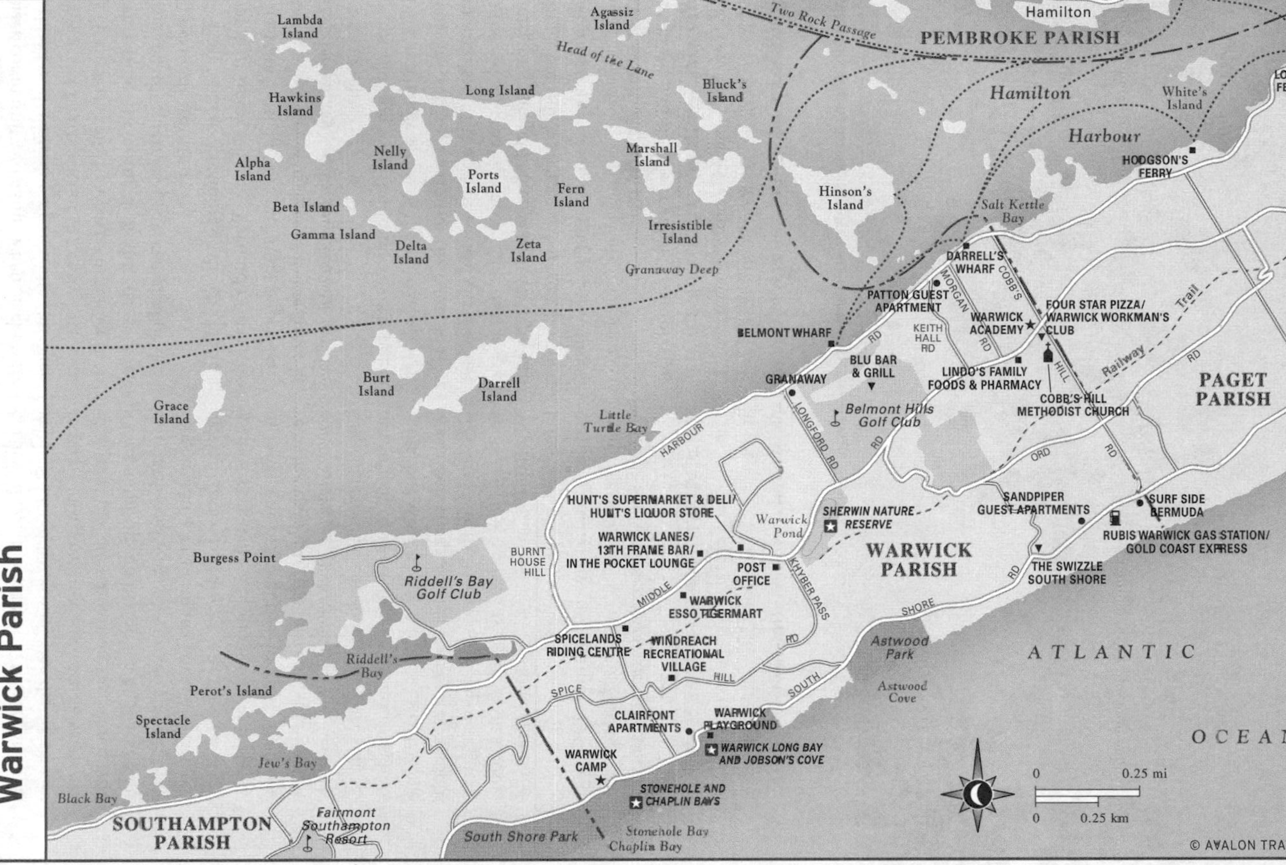
Lambda Island
Agassiz Island
Two Rock Passage
Hamilton
PEMBROKE PARISH
Head of the Lane
Hawkins Island
Long Island
Bluck's Island
Hamilton Harbour
White's Island
LOWER FERRY
Alpha Island
Nelly Island
Marshall Island
Ports Island
Fern Island
Hinson's Island
HODGSON'S FERRY
Beta Island
Gamma Island
Delta Island
Zeta Island
Irresistible Island
Salt Kettle Bay
Granaway Deep
DARRELL'S WHARF
MORGAN RD
COBB'S HILL
PATTON GUEST APARTMENT
FOUR STAR PIZZA/ WARWICK WORKMAN'S CLUB
WARWICK ACADEMY
KEITH HALL RD
BELMONT WHARF
BLU BAR & GRILL
LINDO'S FAMILY FOODS & PHARMACY
Railway Trail
Burt Island
Darrell Island
Grace Island
GRANAWAY
COBB'S HILL METHODIST CHURCH
PAGET PARISH
Belmont Hills Golf Club
Little Turtle Bay
HARBOUR RD
LONGFORD RD
ORD RD
HUNT'S SUPERMARKET & DELI/ HUNT'S LIQUOR STORE
SHERWIN NATURE RESERVE
Warwick Pond
SANDPIPER GUEST APARTMENTS
SURF SIDE BERMUDA
WARWICK LANES/ 13TH FRAME BAR/ IN THE POCKET LOUNGE
RUBIS WARWICK GAS STATION/ GOLD COAST EXPRESS
WARWICK PARISH
Burgess Point
BURNT HOUSE HILL
POST OFFICE
KHYBER PASS
THE SWIZZLE SOUTH SHORE
Riddell's Bay Golf Club
MIDDLE RD
WARWICK ESSO TIGERMART
SOUTH SHORE RD
SPICELANDS RIDING CENTRE
WINDREACH RECREATIONAL VILLAGE
Astwood Park
ATLANTIC OCEAN
Riddell's Bay
SPICE HILL
Perot's Island
Astwood Cove
CLAIRFONT APARTMENTS
WARWICK PLAYGROUND
Spectacle Island
WARWICK LONG BAY AND JOBSON'S COVE
Jew's Bay
WARWICK CAMP
0 0.25 mi
0 0.25 km
STONEHOLE AND CHAPLIN BAYS
Black Bay
SOUTHAMPTON PARISH
Fairmont Southampton Resort
South Shore Park
Stonehole Bay
Chaplin Bay
© AVALON TRAVEL

a symbolic spot in the hearts of the island's black community. At a time when blacks were banned from worshipping in white churches, slaves and free blacks of the early 19th century constructed their own church in their spare time, including at night, using block from nearby quarries. (Slavery was abolished in Bermuda in 1834.)

Thanks to its proud past, the church is a point of interest along Bermuda's African Diaspora Trail, but the building is open only during Sunday worship and Wednesday prayer evenings. Visitors are welcome to these weekly events.

An addition to the building was erected in 1967, and it now serves as the church hall. The most interesting section of the church from an architectural and historical perspective is the old sanctuary, where cedar beams and limestone slate and block were used to build a simple but sturdy structure that has withstood natural tempests and changing political times.

Warwick Academy

Bermuda's oldest surviving school, the **Warwick Academy** (117 Middle Rd., tel. 441/236-1917, fax 441/236-9995, www.warwickacad.bm), lies west of Cobb's Hill. It was established in 1662 by early settlers on property designated as school lands since the colony's earliest days. Bermuda's 17th-century surveyor, Richard Norwood, was the first headmaster. Once government-owned, it is now one of several private schools on the island, with a longstanding reputation for high academic standards and a racially mixed student body representative of Bermuda's own diverse population. Indeed, Warwick was the first of the white segregated institutions to admit blacks, in 1962. The original two-room schoolhouse remains visible in the current building, laid out around a small, shady quadrangle of palms. The cloakrooms, corridors, and curricula retain much of their British grammar school roots, but Warwick Academy's International Baccalaureate graduates today go on to both U.K. and North American colleges and universities. The school is open 8am-4:30pm Monday-Friday while in session September-June. The office is open 9am-2pm during holidays, including the summer. Tours can be arranged by contacting **Jane Vickers** (tel. 441/239-9465, jvickers@warwickacad.bm).

★ Sherwin Nature Reserve

The **Sherwin Nature Reserve** (Middle Rd. at the foot of Longford Rd., sunrise-sunset daily, admission free) stretches for nine acres

Migratory and native birds can be seen at the Sherwin Nature Reserve

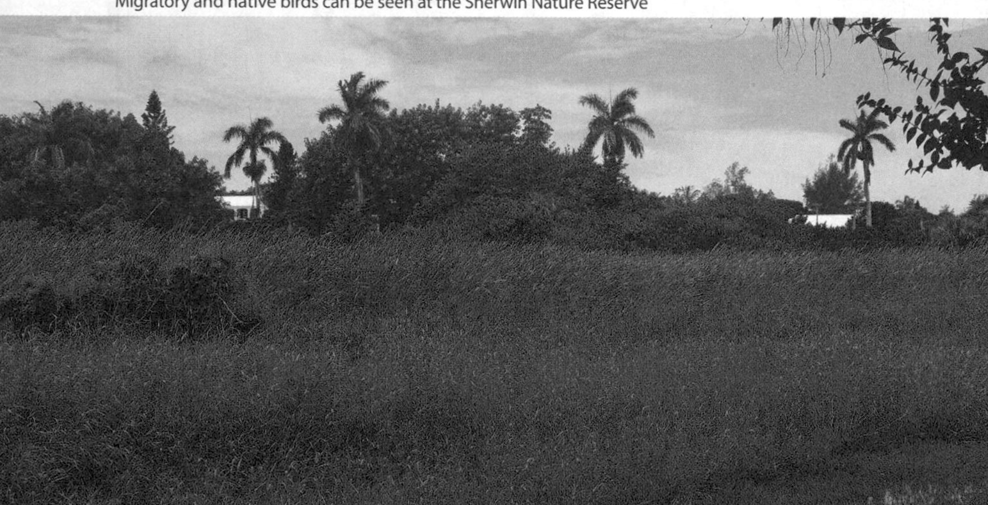

along Middle Road. Its marshy ponds, farm fields, and woodlands lie in a wide central valley coated by endemic Bermuda cedars and allspice trees. Recognized as a wetland of international importance by the World Conservation Union, the pond was once part of a chain of wetlands through Bermuda's center, linking Southampton to Spittal Pond in Smith's. It is Bermuda's second-largest freshwater pond (after Spittal) and a sanctuary for resident and migratory waterfowl, including barn swallows in the fall, common snipes in winter, and mourning doves year-round. You might also spot resident roosters.

Formerly called "Warwick Pond," the reserve was renamed in 2009 for the late Denis Sherwin, an ardent environmentalist and former president of the Bermuda National Trust. Interpretive signage along a circular path has made the reserve accessible to visitors, who can now appreciate different habitats (pond, marsh, forest) along with varied flora and fauna—even educating themselves on endemics versus invasives along the way. The pond's fertile wetland borders are rented from the BNT by farmers for cattle-grazing or agriculture. Warwick Pond's entrance is well marked by a BNT sign on Middle Road at the turnoff to Tribe Road 3 (opposite Longford Road) and also connects to the Railway Trail. For more information, contact the **Bermuda National Trust** (tel. 441/236-6483, www.bnt.bm).

Khyber Pass

You can cut through this dramatically named access route to get from Middle Road to the South Shore. At the foot of the steep hill, near a landmark rubber tree outside Warwick Post Office, a memorial commemorates the island's slaves. Formerly the site of a local slave market, the corner today is the staging area for the **Rubber Tree Market** (contact Roxanne Christopher, tel. 441/296-4339, www.bedc.bm, 9am-7pm Sat. year-round), a grassroots festival organized by the Bermuda Economic Development Association that brings scores of vendors selling crafts, jewelry, clothing, homemade jams, fresh fish, and baked goods. There are even fun castles and face painting for kids—and a house DJ.

To reach the beaches, continue over Khyber Pass, bordered by soaring limestone quarries used for past building works. Spice Hill Road, on the other side, winds down to South Shore Road.

Warwick Camp

Warwick Camp (1 South Shore Rd. at Camp Rd., tel. 441/238-1045), the headquarters of the Bermuda Regiment, covers a large property west of Warwick Long Bay and is opposite the entrance to Stonehole and Chaplin Bays. Although it's not generally open to the public, special tours or visits to the hillside site can be arranged. While the regiment itself was not formed until 1965 and marked its half-century anniversary in 2015, Warwick Camp was chosen back in the 1870s as a base for the British military due to its strategic location able to foil potential beach invasions. Today it comprises barracks, an officers' mess, a canteen, and firing range. Regiment recruits conduct training exercises on the nearby dunes, allowing passersby the rather incongruous scene of soldiers playing war while beach-lovers frolic in the surf a short distance away.

BEACHES

Warwick is synonymous with beaches, and where the parish may lack in shopping or five-star restaurants, it more than compensates with its glorious stretch of coastline. Walkers, runners, sunbathers, swimmers, kitesurfers, and volleyball enthusiasts will find all they need here. Lifeguards are posted at the most popular areas (including Horseshoe Bay) during the summer season, and Bermuda's Department of Parks ensures the soft, pink sand is combed of washed-up seaweed, jellyfish, and tar every morning. Do, however, watch for riptides, especially in pre-storm periods, and Portuguese man-of-wars. Warning signs are clearly posted during hurricane season, warning off swimmers when approaching storms bring dangerous swells—a big attraction to daredevil windsurfers and kitesurfers.

Astwood Cove

Annually battered by storm surge, this little beach is beautiful but a little tricky to get to. Still, if climbing down clifftop trails isn't a problem, you will find privacy once you get down to this, Warwick's first public beach as you head west. Surrounded by agricultural land and a scenic seaside park that's a favorite for family picnics and wedding photographs, the beach itself sits at the foot of steep cliffs that have been badly eroded but continue to be important nesting sites for Bermuda longtails. High surf perennially claims the sand, leaving just a field of underlying rocks, though seasonal tides return it every year. In the summer and fall, however, the cove is a very private and perfect place to spend the day, with thick, soft sand and a scattering of offshore reefs just yards from the surf to snorkel over. You can also wander eastwards along the coast, sprinkled with tidal pools containing trapped sealife and rock formations you can climb over. Picnic tables can be found in the park above, and ample parking is also available.

★ Warwick Long Bay and Jobson's Cove

Like neighboring Horseshoe, this is one of the island's most dramatic beaches, spanning a half mile of coast. The beach's thick, coral-sprinkled sand—perhaps Bermuda's pinkest—boiler reefs, and surrounding dunes and parkland make it a popular venue, yet it is never as crowded as Horseshoe, perhaps due to the lack of a café or very shallow bathing areas.

A few steps west of Long Bay, connected via the dune trails, is Jobson's Cove, a tiny gem of a swimming hole nestled between cliffs and boasting swimming-pool-clear water. Honeymooners and children make a beeline for this beach, though, so you may find it busy later in the day, especially when cruise ships are in port. A horseshoe of tall limestone cliffs creates this perfect swimming hole, no more than 40 feet across. Shallow water near the sand, plus reefs encircling the foot of the cliffs, makes it good for novice or young swimmers, and for snorkelers, too. Access Jobson's Cove via the signposted road down to Warwick Long Bay (park at the bottom and walk a few hundred yards along the west trail). Alternatively, you can go a little farther west on the main road and drive down the road to Chaplin and Stonehole Bays opposite Warwick Camp; a sandy dune trail leads east from Chaplin's equally beautiful setting to Jobson's Cove. Both also are an easy walk down from the main road bus stop.

Bermuda's "Pink" Sand

No need to don rose-colored glasses in Bermuda, at least on the beaches. The island's iconic pink sand, touted from brochures to tacky bottled souvenirs, is as mysterious to visitors as are tales of the Triangle.

The sand, most noticeable on the South Shore, especially on surf-heavy beaches like Warwick Long Bay, is the result of constant wave action on the nearby reef. Single-celled organisms called *Foraminifera,* or red foram, grow on the underside of Bermuda's reefs, their bodies peppered with holes through which they extend sticky threads to consume bacteria and other food. When they die, their bright red skeletons erode from the rock, drop to the seafloor, and wash up on beaches. Here they mix with white sand, composed of particles of shells, coral, seaweeds, mollusks, and other marine detritus.

While the phenomenon happens in the Caribbean and other reef areas worldwide, the result is most obvious on Bermuda's beaches, perhaps because the South Shore reef line, in particular, is so close to the shore. The island's sand is mostly soft and fine, though some patches are made gritty with larger particles of shell, coral, and foram.

Bermuda tourist trinkets have long incorporated the famous pink sand, and you can find tiny bottles of the stuff in souvenir shops around the island. Local artists and craftspeople also find inspiration in the beach sand, using it in souvenirs and artwork.

★ Stonehole and Chaplin Bays

These twin coves lie just west of Long Bay, again connected by the South Shore's public park system and an easy trail through the dunes. Chaplin sits on the Warwick-Southampton parish border below Warwick Camp, and beachgoers may sometimes spot Bermuda Regiment soldiers taking part in military training exercises on the dunes. Chaplin, like so many coves with soft limestone cliff faces along this stretch, is a very good spot to watch Bermuda's magnificent white-tailed tropicbird (longtail); these seasonal seabirds make their spring/summer nests on beachside cliffs, offering up-close viewing as they repeatedly exit and enter their nooks to soar with mates or scout food for nestlings. Both Chaplin and Stonehole offer good swimming and snorkeling areas and walkable access through dune trails to Horseshoe Bay in the next parish.

ENTERTAINMENT AND EVENTS

Warwick is weak on organized entertainment or events of any kind, and if you're staying in the parish, you will likely want to seek out nighttime activities at nearby hotels or head into Hamilton. There are a couple of bars, however, that attract crowds of locals and tourists, mostly on Fridays and Saturdays.

Nightlife

Warwick Workman's Club (42 Cobb's Hill Rd., tel. 441/236-7470, noon-midnight daily except Christmas Day, happy hour 5pm-8pm Wed.) is a favorite with local cab drivers, construction workers, and other area Bermudians, as well as its 100-plus-person membership. Friday afternoons are boisterous, when, as in many parish bars, the weekend starts early. But the atmosphere is always cordial.

13th Frame Bar (47 Middle Rd., tel. 441/236-5290, 6pm-11pm Mon.-Sat., 2pm-11pm Sun) is found inside Warwick Lanes, the island's only bowling alley. Friday happy hour starts at 4pm, and the bar also welcomes a busy Sunday night crowd.

The Swizzle South Shore (87 South Shore Rd., tel. 441/236-7459, www.swizzleinn.com, 11am-1am daily), the Warwick branch of Hamilton Parish's landmark Swizzle Inn, draws crowds of devoted regulars, who come for the namesake drink but also the convivial party-like atmosphere, including live music

Steep limestone cliffs overlook the breathtaking Astwood Cove.

Gombeys

Bermuda's cultural ambassadors are the gombeys, a name meaning "drums" given to African-inspired dance troupes adorned in elaborate outfits featuring feathers, beads, and sequins. Like tribal break-dancers in kaleidoscopic costumes, gombeys have long been adored by their Bermudian fans, but only in recent decades have they been officially recognized and even flown overseas by the government to represent the island at international events.

Gombeys derive from a grassroots tradition that borrows elements from Native American, British military, and Caribbean influences. Distinct family troupes evolved in the parishes over the centuries, and even today, gombey troupes consist of relatives and friends of specific families, and many include youngsters as young as two or three.

Their dance may appear to the uninitiated to be a free-for-all, but it is actually a structured art form with a beginning, middle, and end that dramatizes a popular Bible story or legend, such as that of David and Goliath. Gombey troupes used to appear mostly on Boxing Day (the day after Christmas), attracting crowds as they walked through parish neighborhoods, but they now perform at many cultural festivals through the year, including the Wednesday Harbour Nights in Hamilton. Tradition holds that spectators toss coins of appreciation on the ground, which are later gathered by a designated gombey.

The iconic dance is coupled with ornate costumes, which are works of art in themselves. Peacock feathers, beads, and sequins are painstakingly used to construct each outfit, with a mask attached to a tall, feathered headdress, and gloves, scarf, and boots. Accessories include drums, ornamental bows and arrows, braids, and tomahawks. Typically the troupe's captain uses a whip or whistle to orchestrate dance routines and storylines, keeping the other members in line.

Bermuda gombeys have performed at major events such as the Edinburgh Tattoo, the Smithsonian Folklife Festival in Washington, DC, and on the island with visiting Native American groups who hold strong familial ties with Bermuda's St. David's Island community.

on weekend afternoons and evenings. It offers a full menu of comforting pub grub (burgers, nachos, wings, spicy fries), as well as local seafood, pizzas, and veggie options.

SHOPPING

Shopaholics will find precious little to buy in Warwick, other than tie-dyed T-shirts and other items sold from roadside stands. There is a sparse collection of stores, most of them convenience marts.

The Sports Source (49 Middle Rd., tel. 441/236-9981, www.sportssource.bm, 10am-7pm Mon.-Thurs., 9am-8:45pm Fri.-Sat.), a branch of a Hamilton store by the same name, is a rare exception, offering urbanwear shoes and fashions with street cred (Nike, Adidas, Reebok, Puma, Jordan, and Pepe) to a loyal following. Parking is easy in the small adjacent plaza.

SPORTS AND RECREATION

Bowling

Warwick Lanes (47 Middle Rd., Warwick, tel. 441/236-5290, 6pm-11pm Mon.-Sat., 2pm-11pm Sun.) is the island's only bowling alley, and it always attracts a crowd, including club members and local teams, as well as novices and corporate groups enjoying a cheap night out, especially during the winter when league games are staged. It's a favorite for children's birthday parties, too. The air-conditioned facility is owned and operated by the Bermuda Bowling Club. It has 24 lanes, all computerized to take the work out of scoring. A bar and restaurant, serving hamburgers, fried chicken, sandwiches and soups, are also on-site. Fees are reasonable: $5.50 a game, children $3.50, shoe rental $3.50. Special opening hours can be arranged for events.

Golf

Warwick is home to two respected golf courses—one a time-worn country club, the other a multimillion-dollar redesign that features a super 14-bay driving range.

Tennis ace (and former Bermuda resident) Pat Rafter tested the links at **Belmont Hills Golf Club** (97 Middle Rd., tel. 441/236-6400, fax 441/236-0694, www.newsteadbelmonthills.com). Formerly the Belmont Hotel and Golf Course, the sister property to nearby Newstead boasts 18 holes and 6,100 yards of intense bunkering, with man-made water hazards galore. Designed by Algie M. Pulley Jr., the course includes a waterfall and two lakes, turf to meet USGA standards, and a tee-to-green irrigation system. Handicappers call it a "shotmaker's course," thanks to tricky pin placements and challenging greens, but you have to wait until the 17th and 18th holes for great ocean views. Greens fees are $120 (or book online via www.golfnow.com for $95), club rental $45-60, golf cart (mandatory until 3:30pm) $35, shoes $15. Lessons from the pro are $60 (half hour) or $100 (one hour), and a nine-hole playing lesson is $250 (18 holes $400). Dress code is strictly club-style: collared shirts and slacks for men, "Bermuda-length" shorts for men and women accepted. Soft-spiked shoes are obligatory. You can replenish your energy at a food and beverage cart, a snack shop, or the on-site **Blu Bar & Grill**. There is a ferry and private boat service to and from Hamilton from the Harbour Road dock.

Bermuda's oldest golf course, **Riddell's Bay Golf & Country Club** (Riddell's Bay Rd., tel. 441/238-1060, golf shop tel. 441/238-3225, www.riddellsbay.com, $135 for 18 holes before noon, $100 after noon, $79 twilight rate after 3pm, all include cart rental, club rental $45), dates back to 1922. A visit to its elegant Georgian clubhouse, set in a multimillion-dollar enclave, is like stepping into a tourist brochure of the 1950s or 1960s. The private club's golf course, which has seen the likes of crooner Michael Bolton and Olympian Jim Thorpe, is touted as a scenic challenge, with holes mapped out over an ocean peninsula that measures 600 yards at its widest point. At a total of 5,800 yards, the 70-par, 18-hole course falls short of the island's three championship courses (Mid Ocean, Tucker's Point, Port Royal), but its meticulously kept greens are challenging to mid-handicappers, particularly on windy days. It's best to commit to 18 holes, since the 9th hole finishes a good hike from the clubhouse. The club makes an effort to accommodate visitors. Call ahead to set a tee time.

Horseback Riding

Exploring the Railway Trail and beachside dunes can be a leisurely outing on horseback through **Spicelands Equestrian Centre** (50 Middle Rd., west of Warwick Pond, bus route 8, tel. 441/238-8212, www.spicelandsriding.com, 7am-7pm daily). The center runs several daily guided rides along shady trails to quiet beaches, but times vary according to season and sunrise time (summer's first ride usually starts at 7am, the last at 6pm). An hourlong group ride costs $90. Private rides are one hour for $140 per person. Special custom arrangements are also possible. Western saddles are used for comfort, but English-style tack is also available. Helmets are provided. Wear sneakers and pants or shorts. The facility, home to boarded horses and ponies, also offers riding instruction.

Bermuda Riding for the Disabled, at WindReach Recreational Village (57 Spice Hill Rd., tel. 441/238-2469, fax 441/238-7434, www.windreachbermuda.org), provides therapeutic riding free of charge to children with special needs. The nonprofit group, funded by public donations, has five horses and ponies and two full-time staff members at a dedicated equestrian center complete with stables and show ring on the 3.75-acre site, which also has a petting zoo and sensory room. Visits and rides should be arranged well in advance.

Self-styled cowboy (and former track star) Michael Watson leads popular Western-style trail rides from **Watson's Stables** (24 Tribe

Rd No. 2, off Middle Rd. opp. Belmont Hill Golf Club, tel. 441/747-7433, 90-min. ride $90 for group of up to six people, private rides $150).

Snorkeling

The coral reefs of the South Shore are arguably some of the most beautiful in the world, and close enough to shore to make them easily accessible. You don't even need to be a full-fledged scuba diver to enjoy them. Several beachside concessions, including an outpost at Warwick Long Bay during the summer, rent masks, snorkels, and fins, as well as ubiquitous polystyrene "noodles," allowing for hours of easy floating over boiler reefs and sea grass beds and around the edges of sheltered coves and bays. Here, you can watch exquisitely multihued parrotfish nibbling on the reef, ethereal angelfish, anemones, speckled morays, cheeky sergeants major, schools of jacks, and even endangered marine turtles in some areas.

Running and Walking

Walking enthusiasts will find plenty of off-road trails in Warwick, especially throughout the coast. On the dunes, twisting sand or dirt trails, hemmed by oleanders, baygrapes, prickly pears, and Spanish bayonets, are occasionally nosebleed-steep (one hill north of Chaplin Bay is dubbed "Kilimanjaro" by local runners). The trails are also pitted by knee-deep crab holes, so watch your step. **South Shore Road,** unlike many other major roads on the island, has ample grassy shoulders for safe walking and running.

Railway Trail (Warwick)

The Warwick portion of the Railway Trail stretches from the Cobb's Hill road crossing past Belmont Golf Club to Khyber Pass, a picturesque stretch of jasmine and fiddlewoods, towering limestone quarries, friendly neighborhoods, and rich farmland. It is frequented by runners, walkers, and cyclists, particularly in the evenings or weekend mornings. On Sunday mornings, listen for the clanging of the bell at St. Mary's Church.

For Kids

Children adore **WindReach Recreational Village** (57 Spice Hill Rd., Warwick, tel. 441/238-2469, fax 441/238-2597, www.windreachbermuda.org), a 3.75-acre oasis with an air-conditioned activity center, petting zoo, sensory trail, campground, and fully accessible playground and picnic area. The facility

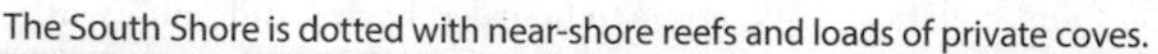

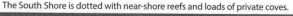

The South Shore is dotted with near-shore reefs and loads of private coves.

promotes activities for people of all ages with disabilities and special needs but has become a regular destination for all children on the island. The zoo, with its menagerie of guinea pigs, goats, parrots, miniature horses, rabbits, donkeys, and lambs, is especially popular. The playground, a shady, treehouse-style setup of slides, swings, stairs, and ramps under a giant poinciana, is also a must-visit. Wheelchair-accessible bathrooms are on-site. Tours and visits must be booked in advance.

Warwick Playground (South Shore Rd., east of Warwick Long Bay), one of a half dozen government-owned venues around the island, is a favorite, though its lack of ample shade makes it almost unbearable throughout the summer. Run by the Department of Parks, the dog-free playground is kept scrupulously clean and well maintained, with soft white sand surrounding equipment suitable for kids of all ages, from infants to 10-year-olds. Swings, slides, tunnels, poles, rope ladders, and a wooden fort and train are among the equipment. Kids also enjoy feeding and chasing the resident flock of chickens. A portable toilet and ample parking are available. A path on the playground's southern edge leads down to beachside parkland and Warwick Long Bay.

ACCOMMODATIONS

Under $200

Guests return again and again to ★ **Granaway** (1 Longford Rd., tel. 441/236-3747, fax 441/236-3749, www.granaway.com, rooms $190-230 high season with continental breakfast), the elegant 1734 manor-turned-guesthouse that offers lush mature gardens, a large pool surrounded by shady palms, and eye-popping views of the Great Sound from its five main house guest rooms. While it fronts busy Harbour Road, serenity can be had in the English-style gardens. All rooms have private bathrooms and air-conditioning, and breakfast is provided in the mornings. A separate cottage on the property (formerly a slave quarters) has a well-equipped kitchen, bathroom, and private garden and patio with views of the sound; the cottage is $300-325, with breakfast, during high season. Granaway is about a 10-minute walk from the nearest ferry stop (Belmont) on Harbour Road or the bus stop over the hill on Middle Road.

Plunge into the inviting lap pool at **Tim and Christine Patton's hilltop home** (Windy Ridge Rd. off Harbour Rd., tel. 441/505-5206, bookings for C47 via www.bermudarentals.com, $140 in high season for two adults, five-night minimum), where a warmly furnished rental apartment offers a taste of Bermuda life the way Bermudians experience it. Guests can be utterly independent in the unit, which has a separate entrance, two single beds (that can make a king) in the bedroom, plus a double Murphy bed and a single sofa bed in the living room, accommodating up to four adults. There is one bathroom and an eating area with table and chairs. The small, well-equipped kitchen has a refrigerator (with freezer), stove, microwave, and toaster, and guests can use an outdoor barbecue. Cable TV, wireless Internet, and air-conditioning are included. The quiet property is ringed by palms, cedars, frangipani, and a mulberry tree. The ferry stop (Darrell's Wharf) is just down Harbour Road, and the Middle Road bus stop is a seven-minute walk.

Clairfont Apartments (6 Warwickshire Rd., tel. 441/238-3577 or 441/334-8649, fax 441/238-3503, www.clairfontapartments.bm, $150-175) is spared the noisy main-road location of several of its competitors. Instead, the peachy complex, run as guest quarters for 30 years, sits high on a hill along a residential lane, a short walk from Warwick Long Bay, Jobson's Cove, and Warwick Playground. Eight self-contained units (six one-bedroom, two studios) include mounted hair dryers, voicemail, Internet connections, security locks and lights, credit-card safes, first-aid kits, and kitchen appliances. Spotlessly clean, modern, and airy, Clairfont offers an attractive alternative to pricier establishments that may have fewer amenities. Welcome letters, air-conditioning, maid service (except Sundays), cable TV, and a pool make guests feel pampered.

Sandpiper Guest Apartments (103 South Shore Rd., tel. 441/236-7093, fax 441/236-3898, www.sandpiperbda.com, studio $155 d, one-bedroom $195) suffers from its proximity to the noisy main road, but with simple, airy rooms, and a garden, pool, and hot tub, it's a good option for families, students, and anyone looking for affordable quarters near the beaches (it sits just a few minutes' walk from Astwood Cove). Fourteen rooms include five one-bedroom suites (with extra futons for additional guests) and studios with full kitchens. Barbecues are provided for poolside use.

Over $200

Location is everything for **Surf Side Bermuda** (90 South Shore Rd., tel. 441/236-7100, fax 441/236-9765, www.surfsidebermuda.com, starting at $325 d), which holds a panoramic perch over the South Shore stretch of reef line. With a pool and pristine private beach, the property has long been popular among honeymooners, wedding parties, and romantics. Oceanfront rooms range from basic bed and bath to penthouses with private lawn patios and cliffside suites offering living rooms, dining rooms, and fireplaces; while somewhat in need of an update, the rooms are clean and functional. Coin laundry and a mini spa are also on-site, though there is no longer a restaurant or bar. Surf Side sits directly on South Shore Road's bus routes, meaning easy access to Hamilton or points west.

FOOD

Cafés, Pubs, and Takeout

Opened in 2012 by the award-winning Little Venice Group, ★ **Gold Coast Express** (at Rubis Warwick Gas Station, 76 South Rd., tel. 441/232-2020, 6:30am-10pm daily) raises Warwick's culinary stakes with its delicious daily hot and cold buffets in this expansive, super-modern, and ultra-friendly gas station store. From specialty coffees (caramel iced cappuccino $6) and breakfast sandwiches (bacon-and-egg croissant $7.75), to a salad counter with Caesar and quinoa choices, to hot food specials (fried grouper on a baguette $9.95), Indian curries, Chinese cuisine, and pizza, you can find anything to satisfy hunger pangs here.

At Warwick Lanes, folks come to **In the Pocket Lounge** (47 Middle Rd., Warwick, tel. 441/799-4919, 6pm-11pm Mon.-Sat., 2pm-6pm Sun.) for the daily specials (fried chicken, Spanish rice, mashed potatoes) and the jovial goings-on around the lanes. Special opening arrangements can be made for parties and group visits.

For a quick "greeze" (grease), as Bermudians call their soul-food lunches, drop in to **Four Star Pizza** alongside **Warwick Workman's Club** (42 Cobb's Hill Road, tel. 441/232-0123, www.fourstar.bm, 11am-10pm Mon.-Thurs., 11am-11pm Fri. and Sat., noon-10pm Sun.). Line up with the local crowd for pizzas, pastas, calzones, subs, and salads at this longtime Warwick café now run by the efficient island-wide chain, which operates an Indian/Chinese grill in the same complex, serving curries, vegetarian dishes, and appetizers.

At **The Swizzle South Shore** (87 South Shore Rd., tel. 441/236-7459, www.swizzleinn.com, 11am-1am daily), popular fare includes Portuguese red bean soup ($7), nachos (including a veggie version, $15.75), conch fritters ($12.50), pizzas, burgers, and pub favorites, plus the infamous original Bailey's Bay Fish Sandwich—a huge grilled concoction with battered fish, melted cheese, and tartar sauce ($17.50). If you're not motoring by moped, wash it down with a signature rum swizzle. Barbecues through summer weekends offer pork ribs and steaks galore.

Buzz N Go (66 Middle Rd., inside Warwick Esso Tigermart, tel. 441/236-3021, 6am-10pm Mon.-Sun.) serves up the chain's full range of paninis, quesadillas, iced cappuccinos, and smoothies.

International

★ **Blu Bar & Grill** (25 Belmont Dr., Middle Rd., tel. 441/232-2323, fax 441/232-6464, www.blu.bm, dinner from 6pm daily, brunch buffet 11:30am-2:30pm Sun.) commands

Summer Snowballs

Summertime lineups at small roadside stands near the South Shore beaches usually mean just one thing: snowballs.

When temperatures soar and school's out, the crushed-ice-and-syrup confections sold June-September are a tempting way to cool off. Seasonal permit-holders—often students—set up carts daily to dole out the popular treat islandwide. Many choose spots along South Shore Road to catch traffic traveling to and from the beaches. After-work rush hour also sees a booming business, as locals snap up snowballs for the drive home.

Snowballs demand few tools or ingredients: ice cubes, an ice crusher, and special syrup, for which each vendor uses a different recipe of sugar and mix. Costing as little as $1, snowballs come in every flavor of the rainbow. If you want to taste the full gamut, ask for a Round the World—a combo of everything on hand, generally raspberry, strawberry, apple, cherry, and the all-time Island favorite, ginger beer.

panoramic views of the putting greens and Great Sound from the Belmont Hills resort's multistory clubhouse. Part of the Little Venice Group (which owns a half-dozen restaurants and runs the island's largest catering service), Blu draws a packed house year-round thanks to its mix of gourmet fare and comfort food—and its stunning vantage point, with several tables set out on a panoramic terrace overlooking the entire Great Sound. The dinner menu features a full sushi selection, plus faves like roasted figs with goat cheese fritters ($24), oyster tempura ($22), pizza and flatbread ($19-29), Asian dishes, a daily local fish special, grilled lamb chops ($44), and numerous vegetarian choices. An outstanding wine list, with close to 100 well-selected California vintages, is another good reason to stop by.

Grocery Stores

Bermudians flock to **Lindo's Family Foods** (128 Middle Rd., tel. 441/236-1344, www.lindos.bm, 8am-7pm Mon., Tues. and Thurs., 8am-8pm Wed., Fri. and Sat.), a large grocery stocked with pretty much everything, including wines and liquors, baked and frozen goods, and a butcher department often offering freshly caught Bermuda fish. There's also a pharmacy inside.

Hunt's Supermarket & Deli (49 Middle Rd., tel. 441/236-6343, 7am-8pm Mon.-Sat., 8am-7pm Sun.) is a small grocery stocked with all the staples, as well as fresh fruit, cold drinks, magazines, and a self-service deli offering island choices like baked chicken legs, macaroni 'n' cheese, salads, and sandwich fixings.

The adjacent liquor store, **Hunt's Liquor Store** (49 Middle Rd., tel. 441/236-8610, 9am-8pm Mon.-Sat, 9am-3pm Sun.) is a handy stop outside Hamilton.

INFORMATION AND SERVICES

Rubis Warwick Gas Station (76 South Rd., tel. 441/236-4158, 6:30am-11pm daily), which moved up the road into very large, renovated premises in 2012, makes a convenient stop not only for gasoline, but also for snacks and a wide assortment of grocery supplies, plus a visit to the large hot and cold deli, **Gold Coast Express,** inside.

The **Warwick Esso Tigermart** (66 Middle Rd., tel. 441/236-2595, 6am-10pm daily) sells a lot more than gas. The supersized facility includes a modern store with deli offerings, freshly baked pastries, and hot and cold snacks, as well as magazines, toiletries, and basic grocery items. There's an ATM and public washrooms, too.

Warwick Post Office (70 Middle Rd., just west of Khyber Pass, tel. 441/236-4071, 8am-5pm Mon.-Fri.) sells stamps and bus and ferry passes, and also offers free Internet access.

Lindo's Pharmacy (128 Middle Rd., tel. 441/236-0010, rxd@lindos.bm, 8am-7pm Mon., Tues., and Thurs., 8am-8pm Wed., Fri., and Sat.), located inside **Lindo's Family Foods,** is the only pharmacy between Paget and Somerset Village.

Mix with the locals at **Warwick Laundromat and Dry-Cleaning** (15 Ten Pin Crescent, behind Hunt's Supermarket, tel. 441/236-5403, 6:30am-9pm Mon.-Sat., 6:30am-6pm Sun.). **Ord Road Laundry** (44 Ord Rd., tel. 441/236-8699) is the parish's other venue.

ATMs are located at Lindo's Family Foods and at both Rubis Warwick Gas Station and the Warwick Esso Tigermart service station.

Public toilets are located at Rubis Warwick Gas Station, Warwick Esso Tigermart, Astwood Park, and Warwick Long Bay, as well as in area restaurants.

GETTING THERE AND AROUND

Buses

Buses are a convenient way to get up and down the South Shore Road between resorts and beaches (route 7, every 15 minutes) and along Middle Road (route 8, every 15 minutes), though bus routes do not include the parish's pretty Harbour Road. The three-zone tariff for both routes is $3 (exact change—rather than dollar notes—or tokens, tickets, or passes required).

Ferries

Ferries crisscross Hamilton Harbour throughout the day from the main ferry terminal in town to two stops in Warwick—Darrell's Wharf and Belmont Wharf. The scenic Paget-Warwick ferry route has kept its chugging, iron-clad veterans, *Corona*, *Georgia*, and *Coralita*, quaint throwbacks to the days before the advent of the speedy, air-conditioned, quieter vessels now used on longer routes such as Hamilton-Dockyard. The Paget-Warwick ferries provide service every half hour at commuter times on weekdays, or every 45 minutes at other times, including weekends. Fares are $5 round-trip, $2.50 one-way. For information, call **Sea Express** (tel. 441/295-4506, www.marineandports.bm).

Scooters and Bicycles

Scooters, both double-seaters and single-seaters, can be rented from livery outlets at major hotels (Fairmont Southampton and The Reefs in Southampton, or the Elbow Beach Hotel in Paget), as well as from liveries in Paget and Hamilton. It's an easy way to beach-hop independently, if you are a confident, safe biker. The cycle liveries also rent pedal bikes.

Taxis

Warwick has no set taxi stands, but many cabs move through the parish all day long to service Southampton's hotels. Contact these companies to arrange a pickup: **Bermuda Industrial Union Co-op** (tel. 441/292-4476, cooptaxi@fkbnet.bm), **Bermuda Island Taxi** (tel. 441/295-4141, www.bermudaisland-taxi.com), or **BTA Dispatching Ltd.** (tel. 441/296-2121, www.taxibermuda.bm).

Southampton Parish

Southampton lays claim to a close Shakespearean connection: Like the island's eight other parishes, it was named for one of the colony's original investors, in this case, the Earl of Southampton. Henry Wriothesley was a nobleman, soldier, and courtier, as well as a patron of William Shakespeare. In turn, Wriothesley had a poem dedicated to his generosity by the Elizabethan playwright, whose play *The Tempest* was supposedly inspired by the 1609 shipwreck that led to Bermuda's colonization by the English. If he had actually laid eyes on the parish, Shakespeare would not have been disappointed. Southampton is Bermuda's most sweepingly scenic region, a crescendo of breathtaking seascapes, azure reef lines, heartbreakingly beautiful beaches, and top-of-the-world lookouts like Gibbs Hill Lighthouse.

The parish is heavily populated with residential neighborhoods, many capitalizing on

Southampton Parish

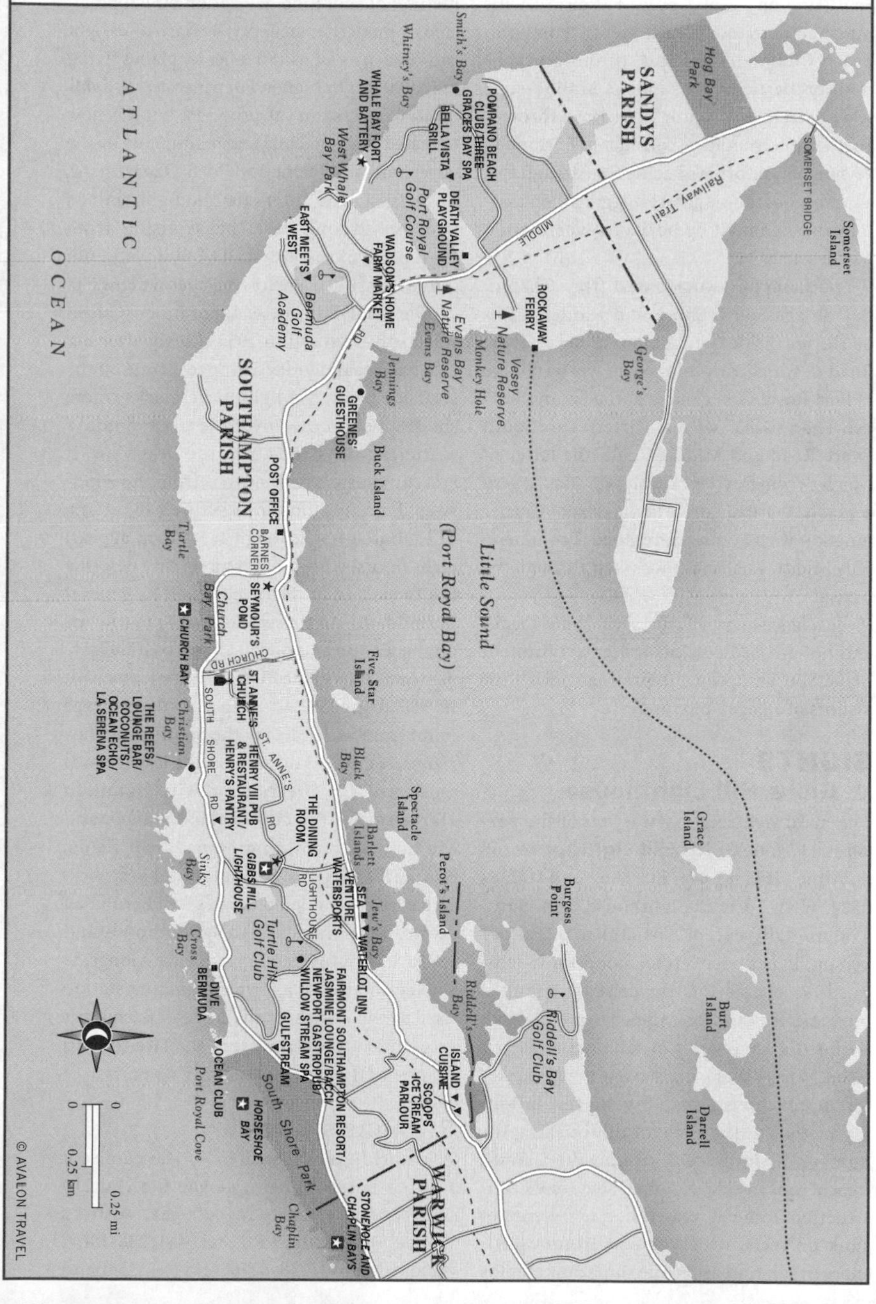

SANDYS PARISH
Hog Bay Park
Somerset Island
SOMERSET BRIDGE
Railway Trail
MIDDLE RD
Smith's Bay
Whitney's Bay
POMPANO BEACH CLUB/THREE GRACES DAY SPA
BELLA VISTA GRILL
WHALE BAY FORT AND BATTERY
West Whale Bay Park
DEATH VALLEY PLAYGROUND
Port Royal Golf Course
WADSON'S HOME FARM MARKET
EAST MEETS WEST
Bermuda Golf Academy
ROCKAWAY FERRY
Vesey Nature Reserve
Monkey Hole
Evans Bay Nature Reserve
Evans Bay
George's Bay
Jennings Bay
GREENES' GUESTHOUSE
Buck Island
SOUTHAMPTON PARISH
POST OFFICE
Turtle Bay
BARNES CORNER
SEYMOUR'S POND
Church Bay Park
CHURCH BAY
CHURCH RD
Little Sound (Port Royal Bay)
Five Star Island
ST. ANNE'S CHURCH
SOUTH SHORE RD
Christian Bay
THE REEFS/ LOUNGE BAR/ COCONUTS/ OCEAN ECHO/ LA SERENA SPA
HENRY VIII PUB & RESTAURANT/ HENRY'S PANTRY
ST. ANNE'S RD
THE DINING ROOM
Black Bay
Spectacle Island
Grace Island
Barlett Islands
GIBBS HILL LIGHTHOUSE
LIGHTHOUSE RD
VENTURE WATERSPORTS
SEA
Sinky Bay
Perot's Island
Burgess Point
Jew's Bay
WATERLOT INN
Turtle Hill Golf Club
Cross Bay
DIVE BERMUDA
FAIRMONT SOUTHAMPTON RESORT/ JASMINE LOUNGE/BACCI/ NEWPORT GASTROPUB/ WILLOW STREAM SPA
GULFSTREAM
Riddell's Bay
Riddell's Bay Golf Club
Burt Island
ISLAND CUISINE
SCOOPS ICE CREAM PARLOUR
OCEAN CLUB
HORSESHOE BAY
Port Royal Cove
South Shore Park
Darrell Island
WARWICK PARISH
STONEHOLE AND CHAPLIN BAYS
Chaplin Bay
ATLANTIC OCEAN
0 0.25 mi
0 0.25 km

the unrivaled views and rugged coastline. It is also home to a large chain hotel (the Fairmont Southampton Resort), as well as award-winning smaller resorts (The Reefs, Pompano Beach Club), all claiming stunning beachfront properties or precipitous Malibu-style real estate. In fact, South Shore Road through Southampton could be considered Bermuda's version of California's Pacific Coast Highway, a curvaceous thoroughfare hugging the shoreline and hemmed by horizons worthy of a movie set.

Southampton extends west from Chaplin Bay on the South Shore and Riddell's Bay on the northside Great Sound as far as Tribe Road 6, which runs along the western edge of Port Royal Golf Course at the Sandys border. The parish's two main arteries are South Shore Road and Middle Road, the latter of which becomes, after exiting Warwick, a very scenic harborfront drive to the Barnes Corner junction with South Shore Road. From here, only Middle Road continues west through the parish.

Beaches, scuba diving, spas, tennis, golf, and hotel-based cuisine and entertainment make Southampton the premier parish for visitors of all ages and interests.

SIGHTS

★ Gibbs Hill Lighthouse

The main sightseeing attraction of the parish is 117-foot **Gibbs Hill Lighthouse** (68 St. Anne's Rd., tel. 441/238-8069 or 441/238-0524, www.bermudalighthouse.com, 9am-4:30pm daily except Christmas, $2.50 per person, kids under 5 free), good for a dedicated visit or a stop on your drive west. Built of prefabricated cast iron shipped from England, the historic landmark's 26-mile lamp was first lit on May 1, 1846, as a navigational marker for approaching ships. It was a revolutionary method at the time for diminishing the number of shipwrecks around the island's treacherous necklace of reefs; before its construction, some 39 vessels had foundered or sunk on reefs, which extend 16 miles offshore in some areas. While ships now employ higher-tech navigation methods, such as GPS systems, the lighthouse offers a backup method of shoreline navigation still appreciated by modern mariners. The flash of its light can be seen as far as 180 miles by planes flying at 10,000 feet or higher. For generations, lighthouse-keepers ran the property, but it is now operated electronically and maintained by the government's Marine and Ports Department.

At 10-second intervals, the light emits a two-second-long flash that is visible from most parts of the island. Its 1,000-watt bulb is housed within a revolving beehive lens.

The whole hillside is panoramic—Queen Elizabeth II visited in 1953 shortly after her coronation, and today a bronze plaque on the roadside below the lighthouse marks where she stopped to gaze over the Great Sound's scattering of islands. But the best view, if you can muster the energy, is from the windswept balcony atop the structure's 185 stairs. The climb is not as tough as it might appear; eight floors, with mini exhibits that describe the tower's manufacture as well as general Bermuda history, provide resting platforms on the way up and down. Climb past the gargantuan lamp to the high-railed balcony with its 360-degree views—a spectacular vantage point from which to spy the South Shore horizons, the West End as far as the Royal Naval Dockyard, the Great Sound with Hamilton Harbour and the city in the distance, and the homes, swimming pools, farm fields, and seascapes of Southampton and Warwick. Indeed, the view demonstrates well Bermuda's crowding of residential neighborhoods and the lack of substantial greenbelts. Alongside the lighthouse, in a former signaling station used by the British Army, is one of Bermuda's most distinctive restaurants, the **The Dining Room,** and a gift shop selling souvenirs.

St. Anne's Church

A historic site responsible for the names of Church Bay (located opposite the church) and several vicinity streets, **St. Anne's Church** (13 Church Rd., tel. 441/238-1864, rectory tel. 441/238-0370, services 8am and

10:30am Sun.) makes a quaint stop en route west. One of the original parish church sites, St. Anne's today stands where a cedar version called "Port Royal Church" was built in 1620 by the first settlers. Structural additions over the years are said to have incorporated some of the original cedarwood. The nave and chapel were built in 1716-1717, while the west-end tower was added in 1905. Its new bell, replacing one from 1780, could be heard as far away as Hamilton in those days. The old bell can also still be seen in the vestry. The whitewashed building, one of the best examples of Bermudian ecclesiastical architecture, is surrounded by a picturesque graveyard that includes numerous tiny headstones marking the graves of infants and children. Park in the lot opposite the church on Church Road.

Seymour's Pond

Surrounded by marshland, with nearby pockets of woods and farm fields, tiny **Seymour's Pond** (sunrise-sunset daily, admission free) is tucked into the Barnes Corner junction of Middle and South Shore Roads. The half-acre reserve, owned and maintained by the Bermuda Audubon Society, is a natural freshwater pond, like Warwick Pond, and both belonged to the same connecting band of peat-marsh basins that once ran through Bermuda's central parishes. Described by Canadian biologist and author Dr. Martin Thomas as "the best example of a freshwater pond in Bermuda," the pond is known by nature-lovers as a good place to find a wide variety of animals and plants. Bird-watchers, in particular, will see many resident and visiting species. Coots, ducks, and common moorhens make their home here, and herons can also be spotted, usually sitting in trees and bushes around the pond edge. Dragonflies and damselflies swoop over the water, and diving beetles and other insects, including mosquitoes, hang out here—though large numbers of the eastern mosquito fish, a freshwater guppy look-alike, keep their numbers in check.

Whale Bay Fort and Battery

Whale Bay Fort and Battery, in **West Whale Bay Park** (at the end of Whale Bay Rd., sunrise-sunset daily, admission free), makes a beautiful sidetrack from a trip west. Once known as Fort Newbold for its commanding officer, Captain William Newbold, the half-moon-shaped fort was constructed in the mid-1700s, when several small coastal forts were built on the South Shore before the American Revolutionary War. Today, its actual walls are gone, but the flagstone gun floor where the fort once stood remains a spectacular vantage point, overlooking West Whale Bay and the dramatic sweep of ocean on the southern face of the island. Both the fort and nearby battery, built a century later, guarded the entrance to Hogfish Cut, a channel for small boats that was of value to local shipping as vessels traveled the western coast toward Dockyard. The battery's impressive walls, barracks, and underground magazine rooms are still standing and can be explored. Leave mopeds at the beach parking lot and climb the hill to the forts.

Evans Pond Nature Reserve

Access is difficult, but diehard naturalists will enjoy trekking around **Evans Pond Nature Reserve** (off Evans Bay Rd., sunrise-sunset daily, admission free), a small tract of private land containing one of the island's saltwater ponds that are connected to the sea by subterranean channels. The pond, nestled in woodland, is probably best viewed from a farm track off the busy main road. Fringed by black mangroves, this pond contains a rich ecosystem that often includes endemic species. Among the critters found here are giant toads, night herons, lizards such as the Jamaican anole, bonefish, bream, mullet, flatworms, sponges, seaweed, algae, and sea grass—though many of these are below the pond's surface and not immediately visible. Eels and green turtles find their way to the pond occasionally, clambering overland to get there. Turtles are only temporary visitors, though; while they feed as juveniles in Bermuda, they travel south to the Caribbean and Central America to breed.

Vesey Nature Reserve

Opened by the Bermuda National Trust and the local Audubon Society in 2013, this new reserve near the Southampton-Sandys parish border features two limestone quarries (inland and coastal), a natural limestone sinkhole, and a variety of habitats, from mangroves to woodland. The Trust installed walking trails, interpretive signage, benches, and an observation deck from which you can survey the panorama of the Great Sound. There's also a quarry exhibit showcasing an authentic five-foot-long quarry saw, which tradesmen once used to cut blocks to build island cottages (concrete block is used today).

BEACHES

★ Horseshoe Bay

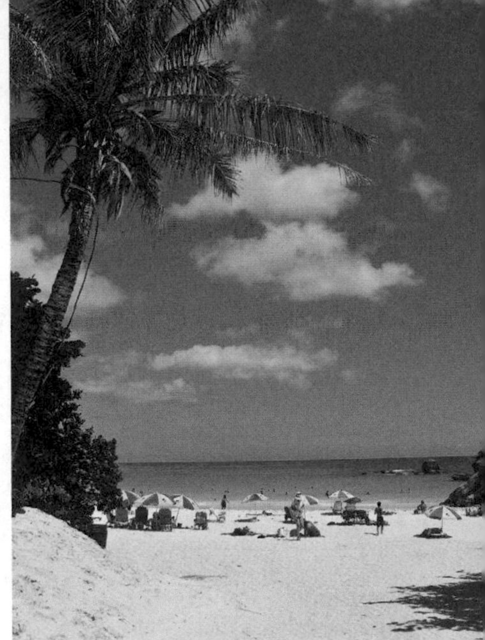

Horseshoe Bay

The most-photographed beach in Bermuda, **Horseshoe Bay** (South Shore National Park off South Rd., opposite the junction with Horseshoe Rd.) is equally popular among locals and visitors, its various moods appealing to a diverse range of beach-lovers. Arguably Bermuda's number-one tourist attraction, it welcomes shiploads of tourists daily during the summer cruise season; often they are taxied here the moment their vessel makes port. As a result, weekday afternoons May-October see the half-moon-shaped bay packed with bodies soaking up the soft sand, balmy water, and picturesque surroundings. Flotillas of cabs descend to ferry them back to Hamilton's docks around 4:30pm every day.

Staffed by lifeguards May-October, the beach itself is alluring, but its on-site services allow for a full day's outing. A concession at the entrance sells towels, beach mats, sunblock, sarongs, souvenirs, and flip-flops. Rentals beginning at 9:30am include lounge chairs ($10), umbrellas ($10), rafts ($12), and body boards ($8.50). A bonus of Horseshoe Bay is the café, where waterlogged beach bums can slake their thirst and heat with sodas and ice cream, as well as fast-food meals. Alcoholic beverages are served at an outdoor concession stand. Baby-changing facilities, showers, spacious sky-lit bathrooms, and outdoor showers and faucets for washing sandy feet before the ride home are also provided.

Locals head to Horseshoe Bay year-round at dawn on Saturday mornings to swim, run, and walk, enjoying the serenity of the beach and its dune trails before the day's later crowds. Horseshoe is a favorite hangout of Bermudian teens and twentysomethings on Saturday afternoons, when night owls nurse their hangovers with pizza, cheeseburgers, and eyefuls of beach-trotting fashionistas.

Families with young children also choose Horseshoe for its cliff-sheltered ends, which offer shade and wading pools. Horseshoe's beach has less of a steep surfside drop-off than next-door Warwick Long Bay's, lessening the undertow and allowing for wading farther out. There is also a kid-perfect adjoining cove, officially named Port Royal Cove but unofficially dubbed "the Baby Beach," to the west of the main stretch. A turquoise swimming hole encircled by cliffs that keep its waters flat, this little gem is a big draw for parents and nannies with toddlers or infants. Eastward, a handful of tiny, sheltered coves dot the shoreline between Horseshoe and Chaplin Bay, offering utterly scenic, private retreats.

★ Church Bay

Rounding the last bend off South Shore Road as you head west, Church Bay's clifftop park (South Rd., opposite the junction with Church Rd.) dazzles with views of divinely turquoise vistas that tempt passersby to make a pit stop. The park makes an incredibly scenic stop for a picnic, while the reef-protected bay below has long been considered the best snorkeling spot on the island. Moreover, the beach's deep, pink sand and sheltered, sun-soaked nooks and crannies make it one of the island's best-loved beaches.

A timber boardwalk and fence, erected after Hurricane Fabian's damage in 2003, lead down to the beach. A concession stand on the beach rents swimming and snorkeling gear, chairs, and umbrellas during the summer. The shady park at the top has a convenient pull-in and parking lot. Portable toilets are also on-site.

West Whale Bay

Surprisingly under-visited by locals or crowds of tourists, **West Whale Bay** (at the end of Whale Bay Rd., off Middle Rd.) is one of the island's best beaches, offering pristine pink sand, clear turquoise water, safe coves, and a sense of undisturbed privacy, as if it were a resort property rather than a public one. Follow Whale Bay Road to the end, where a quiet parking lot stands. A manicured lawn hemmed by whispering pines leads down to the beach under towering cliffs. Dramatic boulders, tumbled into the bay, separate the beach into a string of shady, private coves. Golfers can be seen down the distant shoreline, teeing off at the world-famous 18th green at Port Royal Golf Course. Portable toilets are located in the parking lot.

ENTERTAINMENT AND EVENTS

Good Friday brings the popular **Bermuda Kite Festival** to Horseshoe Bay, an Easter weekend spectacle not to be missed. The event, held noon-3pm, draws hundreds from all over the island for a colorful showdown of kites both store-bought and homemade in traditional island styles. Kite-flying is practically an art form in Bermuda, where traditionalists

Church Bay offers a sheltered beach, rock pools, and spectacular nearby reefs for snorkeling.

The Sargasso Sea

Sargasso weed *(Sargassum)* washes up in piles on Bermuda's beaches year-round, depending on wind direction, and is either carried back out to sea by high tides or swept clean by fastidious bulldozers the next morning. These floating mats of brown seaweed are found in the Sargasso Sea, a vast area of the North Atlantic Ocean in which Bermuda is the only landmass.

Fed by the warm waters of the Gulf Stream, the seaweed got its name from Portuguese mariners of the Age of Discovery, who dubbed it *sargaco* or "grape" since its air sacs and structure resemble the fruit. The weed comprises a self-sufficient food web that supports abundant small marinelife, including slugs, crabs, and shrimps, as well as juvenile fish, eels, and turtles.

Oceanographer Dr. Sylvia Earle has called the Sargasso Sea "the golden rainforest of the ocean" because the two-million-square-mile area provides habitats, spawning areas, migration paths, and feeding grounds to an immense assortment of flora and fauna—including numerous endangered species.

In 2011, the United Nations Environment Programme threw its support behind an international effort to make the Sargasso Sea, like Australia's Great Barrier Reef or the Florida Keys, a Marine Protected Area (MPA)—a level of protection similar to a national park. The difference, however, is that the Sargasso Sea lies beyond any one country's legal jurisdiction or 200-nautical-mile exclusive economic zone (EEZ). Leading the lobby is the **Sargasso Sea Alliance** (www.sargassoalliance.org), a partnership led by Bermuda's government in collaboration with scientists and private donors, which was formed in late 2010 to fight for legislation to protect this critical ecosystem—and in doing so, to pioneer a path toward high-seas governance worldwide.

If successful, the group's campaign could win protective measures against environmentally harmful activities in the Sargasso Sea, including fisheries and seabed mining.

turn tissue paper and sticks into kaleidoscopic flying contraptions, complete with tails and "hummers." Islanders come to check out the best designs (judged in various categories), fly their own kites, enjoy kids' games and music, and share Easter picnics of sticky hot-cross buns and codfish cakes. Kite-making demonstrations are often the highlight. Check www.gotobermudatourism.com for details in season.

Organized by the Chewstick Foundation, **Beachfest** (beachfestbermuda.com) celebrates Emancipation Day on the last Thursday of July, which also happens to be the kickoff to the island's biggest public holiday, Cup Match. The all-day beach party on Horseshoe Beach brings thousands of residents and visitors for dancing, drinking, and general merry-making in the sun.

The **Canada Day Beach Party** (at Warwick Long Bay, noon-5pm, www.canadians.bm), organized by the Association of Canadians in Bermuda (ACIB), has become an annual tradition on the Saturday nearest July 1. Even non-Northerners get into the mood, with Molson beer served up along with rum swizzles and a barbecue of burgers and hotdogs—while a DJ blasts the sounds of Rush, Neil Young, Barenaked Ladies, and The Tragically Hip. Entrance is gained through a $20 membership in ACIB, which garners you drink and food tickets.

Horseshoe Bay is the site for the annual **Bermuda Sand Sculpture Competition** (tel. 441/295-4597 or 441/295-0855, info@youthandsports.bm, 10am-4pm), sponsored by the Bermuda government and held at the end of August. The creative contest is free to enter and fun for both entrants and spectators, with five categories open to children, adults, families, teens, and tourists. Held in late August, the competition has in the past brought in the talents of professional American sand sculptors whose incredible creations wow the crowds of spectators.

Nightlife

Several bars in Southampton hotels offer live entertainment throughout the week. The parish also has a couple of popular pubs and bars.

At **Henry VIII Pub & Restaurant** (69 South Shore Rd., tel. 441/238-1977, www.henrys.bm, noon-10pm daily), local musicians perform 9:30pm-1am Friday, Saturday, and Sunday.

Guests of The Reefs cool their heels at the **Lounge Bar** (The Reefs, 56 South Shore Rd., tel. 441/238-0222, www.thereefs.com, 5pm-midnight daily), where 37 different cocktails and a dance floor get the party started. Live entertainment is featured daily during high season. Likewise, the **Jasmine Lounge** (Fairmont Southampton Resort, 101 South Shore Rd., tel. 441/238-8000, 7am-midnight daily) is a great way to kick off an evening out while enjoying a classic cocktail or glass of fine wine and live entertainment.

The Dock at The Waterlot Inn (Fairmont Southampton Resort, tel. 441/239-6623 or 238-8000, 5pm-10pm daily Apr.-Oct.) has become a very popular waterside venue for a chic evening out. If you can draw your gaze away from the spectacular sunsets this western-facing bay commands, you'll enjoy the alfresco lounge's menu of hip cocktails, including the notorious "Ridiculous Caesar and Bloody Mary Bar" concoction that's delivered to your table with a (yes, ridiculous) combo of wow-factor add-ons comprising mini-burgers, grilled shrimp, a lobster tail, an oyster, wagyu striploin, and more on skewers ($99). Or, create your own cocktail from à la carte options. Stellar service and tasty tapas bring crowds for Friday happy hour, when Bermudian Mike Hind plays his ukulele.

SHOPPING

Like Warwick, Southampton is hardly a shoppers' mecca, offering only hotel-lobby boutiques and the occasional souvenir outlet. Label-conscious travelers will appreciate Longchamp and Rolex at the **Fairmont Southampton Resort** (101 South Shore Rd., tel. 441/238-8000), home to a microcosm of Front Street's top-end retailers. The **Reefs Resort** also sells Bermuda-inspired gifts at a small boutique on its property.

The **Lighthouse Gift Shop** (68 St. Anne's Rd., 9am-5pm daily except Christmas) is good for postcards, disposable cameras, and tacky Bermuda memorabilia like clay ferries, baseball caps, and pirate flags.

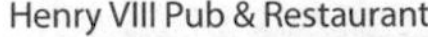

Henry VIII Pub & Restaurant

SPORTS AND RECREATION

Southampton is an outdoors enthusiast's nirvana, with great conditions and facilities for swimming, bodysurfing, kitesurfing, horseback riding, scuba, snorkeling, tennis, and golf. The large stretches of public parkland, including the Railway Trail, offer traffic-free space for walking, running, and mountain biking. Soccer and cricket fans can catch evening and weekend matches, in each sport's respective winter and summer seasons, at local sports grounds. Hotels have their own dive shops or liaisons with scuba outfits that operate off Southampton's reef line.

Scuba and Water Sports

Dive Bermuda (101 South Shore Rd., tel. 441/238-2332, www.bermudascuba.com) operates out of the Fairmont Southampton Resort, offering full PADI training in everything from introduction dives to open-water and rescue diver certifications, with guided outings to notable wreck sites. Its shop rents snorkel and scuba gear, double kayaks, floats, and airbeds and sells sunglasses, T-shirts, hats, and other gear. Staff have marked a "Snorkel Pathway" in Whaler Bay, noting points of interest such as corals and cannons with colored buoys.

Sea Venture Watersports (Fairmont Southampton Resort, Waterlot Inn Dock, Jews Bay, Middle Rd., tel. 441/238-6881, www.jetskibermuda.com) offers an adrenaline-packed way to see Bermuda from the water by Jet Ski, water skis, wakeboard, or tube. Ski-boat charters with a captain/instructor cost $220 per hour. Polaris and Yamaha personal watercraft rentals (the driver must be 16 or older) cost between $125 (one hour) and $330 (half day), with higher rates for two- and three-person vehicles. Two-hour and half-day personal watercraft tours around the West End, Great Sound, and myriad islands between can also be arranged. Instruction is provided for novices. Reservations are suggested, and rentals must be secured by credit card.

Golf

The executive 18-hole par-3 course at the **Turtle Hill Golf Club** at **Fairmont Southampton Resort** (101 South Shore Rd., reservations tel. 441/238-8000, pro shop tel. 441/239-6952, fax 441/238-8479, www.fairmont.com/southampton-bermuda/golf, $89 for 18 holes, includes cart) was designed by Ted Robinson, with a lofty, palm-studded layout rambling over the South Shore property. Its 2,684 yards (the longest hole is 215

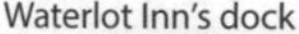

Waterlot Inn's dock

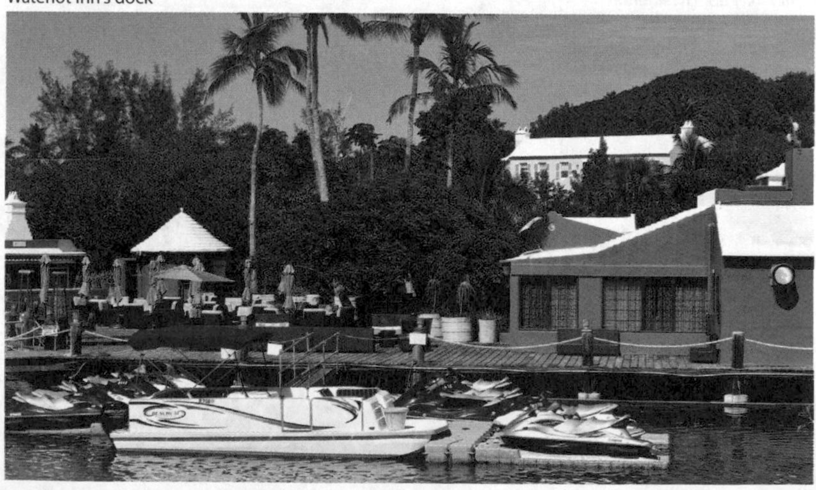

Whale-Watching

Whale-watching has become a spring ritual off Bermuda's South Shore, the migration route for humpbacks as they travel from the Caribbean to North Atlantic feeding grounds. Between March and April, pods of humpback whales can be spotted, even from the shoreline (you may see a line of motorists pulled over to ogle the distant spouts or flukes beyond the reef line).

Found throughout the world, most humpbacks follow regular migration routes. In the Atlantic, they tend to spend winters mating and calving in tropical zones, then move north to polar waters in the summer to feed. Unlike other species, they are highly acrobatic, breaching (throwing their whole bodies out of the water), swimming upside down with flippers raised in the air, or slapping the surface with their huge tails, called flukes. Scientists believe these may all be forms of communication between pod members, along with the species' characteristic singing.

Several conservation-focused nonprofits and charter boat companies organize whale-watching tours in these months; half-day and full-day tours offer spectacular offshore encounters with the whales, which can sometimes be seen frolicking with calves. You can compare tour details and prices and purchase tickets online through the **Island Tour Centre** (tel. 441/236-1300, fax 441/296-4661, www.islandtourcentre.com/whale-watching), which represents more than 20 vendors of ecotours and water sports. **Blue Water Divers & Watersports** (Robinson's Marina, Somerset Bridge, Sandys, tel. 441/234-1034, www.divebermuda.com) offers charters on request. **Bermuda Zoological Society** (tel. 441/293-2727, www.bamz.org) and **Bermuda Underwater Exploration Institute** (tel. 441/292-7219, www.buei.org) both offer whale-watching outings on their respective research/education vessels.

Bermudian Andrew Stevenson has spent several seasons filming whales for his **Humpback Whale Research Project** (tel. 441/777-7688, www.whalesbermuda.com). His award-winning 2010 documentary, *Where the Whales Sing,* describes the humpbacks' journey through the eyes of his six-year-old daughter, Elsa. DVDs of the film are on sale at several local bookstores and gift shops.

yards) include manicured hills, 60 bunkers, and three water hazards, making a course that takes an average 2.5-3 hours to play—appropriate for beginners or for couples who want to play together, or as a warm-up for longer courses. Unpredictable winds make it a highly challenging short course. Lessons, clinics, rentals, a practice putting green, and a pro shop offering lessons are on-site. Summer hours are 7am-6:30pm, winter hours are 7am-5pm daily.

Designed by Robert Trent Jones in 1970, the challenging, world-championship, 18-hole **Port Royal Golf Course** (5 Middle Rd., tel. 441/234-0974, fax 441/234-3562, www.portroyalgolf.bm, 7:30am-6pm daily, $180 high season, forecaddie service $50 per person with one-week advance booking) underwent a $14.5 million makeover to host the annual PGA Grand Slam of Golf starting in 2009. The 6,842-yard course is the island's longest, and with fairways that wind along dizzying clifftops and greens set against the ocean's dazzling turquoise, it was ranked one of the world's best public courses by *Golf Digest*. Greg Norman played here. Jack Nicklaus sang its praises. Hollywood's Samuel L. Jackson chose Port Royal to host his celebrity tournament for several years in the 1990s. And 2010 Grand Slam Champion Ernie Els called Port Royal's 16th hole "the toughest hole I've ever played in my life." Proper golf attire is required (no jeans, T-shirts, beach attire, track suits, or sneakers). The new **Bella Vista** restaurant at Port Royal's clubhouse serves lunch, dinner, and happy-hour cocktails.

The **Bermuda Golf Academy** (Industrial Park Rd., off Middle Rd., tel. 441/238-8800, fax 441/232-0034, www.bermudagolfacademy.com, 10am-10pm Mon.-Sat., 10am-9pm Sun.) is a good place for tuning up your tee game or simply having fun. The facility is home to an all-weather, 320-yard driving range featuring 40 practice bays, 25 of which are covered, and night lighting is offered. An 18-hole practice green, eight target greens, and a chipping/bunker play area also attract golfers, especially given the difficulty of landing tee times at favored clubs around the island. A bucket of 40 balls costs $6 daytime, or $5 after dark. Private lessons ($80 per hour, $45 per half hour) can be booked with three PGA pros. Children and adults also love the facility's mini-golf course, which has waterfalls, bridges, and Bermuda-style butteries. Mini-golf costs $12 for adults, $10 for children 10-16, $8 under 12. An **East Meets West** café is on-site, open 11am-11pm.

Tennis

The **Fairmont Southampton Tennis Club** (Fairmont Southampton Resort, 101 South Shore Rd., tel. 441/239-6950, witc@logic.bm), run by pro Mark Cordeiro, has six Plexi-pave hard courts, three lit for night play. Daily court rental for resort guests or any visitor to the island is $19 per person per day, or $15 per half day. Private lessons are $100 (one hour) or $50 (half hour) for up to two players. The club shop (8:30am-6:30pm daily in summer, 8:30am-5:30pm daily in winter) stocks one of the island's best selections of men's, women's, and kids' Nike tennis gear, along with other select brands. Clinics are available on request.

Four all-weather tennis courts are run by the **Port Royal Tennis Club** (5 Middle Rd., tel. 441/238-9430), which leases the facility from the government. Located on the Port Royal Golf Course property, the courts are not pristine but are safe and playable.

Soccer and Cricket

Football (aka soccer) fans enjoy the weekend action at **Southampton Rangers Sports Club** (1 Middle Rd., tel. 441/238-0058) all winter long. The same grounds convert to a cricket pitch May-September for the very competitive County matches, a series that pits teams in various zones of the island (Eastern, Central, Western) against each other, drawing spillover crowds throughout the summer.

Test your skills on the putting green at Bermuda Golf Academy.

Running and Walking

The wide, grassy shoulders of **South Shore Road** make it safe from traffic for walking and running. Fringed by spider lilies, goldenrods, and Spanish bayonets, the route sweeping high above the beaches makes for dramatically scenic territory. Down below, miles upon miles of beach dunes, with sandy trails that twist through seaside vegetation, are a great way to navigate on foot between coves, and also make for a challenging resistance workout away from main-road traffic for runners and walkers.

Railway Trail (Southampton)

Southampton's stretch of the Railway Trail includes some of the route's most deeply forested stretches, tunneling through spice tree and fiddlewood groves on a high ridge above Middle Road. It cuts across the Fairmont

Southampton Resort property and then meanders beneath Gibbs Hill Lighthouse (a tribe road cuts up from the trail to the lighthouse for easy access). A couple of breaks in the trail heading west mean you have to cross Middle Road and stay on the main road for a half-mile section after Barnes Corner before a paved stretch of the trail picks up again, leading into the rural beauty of Sandys.

Spas

The 15-room **Willow Stream Spa and Health Club** (Fairmont Southampton Resort, 101 South Shore Rd., tel. 441/239-6924, www.willowstream.com, day spa and fitness center 6:30am-9pm daily, salon 8am-7pm daily) is the island's biggest and most popular spa. One of six Willow Streams at Fairmont hotels around the world, it is one of the chain's most successful, thanks in big part to a devoted island clientele. Bermuda residents flock year-round for hot stone massages, rose hip body wraps, shiatsu, acupressure, and hydrotherapy treatments, as well as basic sports, aromatherapy, and stress-relief therapies, facials, manicures, and pedicures. Terraced gardens, outdoor hot tubs with ocean views, and an indoor pool with waterfalls add to the facility's understandable allure—and for non-hotel guests, the cost of any 60-minute treatment over $179 allows daylong use of all facilities, allowing spagoers a truly relaxing getaway.

The 31,000-square-foot spa has devoted male patrons as well, offering den-like lounges, sports massage treatments, a Gentleman's Barber Facial, and a Power Pedicure. Couples can enjoy mud and mask rituals together, then share lunch in robes and slippers by the pool and hot tubs, or downstairs in the hotel's **Jasmine Lounge.** Specialties include the Sea Splendor Body Oasis, with eucalyptus foot soak, exfoliation, aromatherapy bath, massage, and body wrap (80 minutes, $349); Couples' Side by Side (for couples, 60 minutes, $389); Stress Relief (one hour, $189); Bermuda Aromatherapy Facial ($189); and Power of the Sea Ritual (90 minutes, $269). The spa offers a hair and nail salon, steam room, sauna, women's and men's lounges, and a couples' lounge and treatment room. The fitness center has a full range of Cybex cardiovascular and weight-training equipment and a personal trainer. Spa products are for sale at reception. Spa guests must be 18 years or older, and use of cell phones and other PDAs is not permitted.

With one of the island's most jaw-dropping views of the navy South Shore horizon from its floor-to-ceiling glass lounge, **La Serena** (The Reefs, 56 South Shore Rd., tel. 441/239-0184, www.thereefs.com, 8am-8pm daily) is an utterly escapist retreat that makes you feel planets away from the hubbub of daily life. The spa has eight treatment rooms, including a spa suite for couples' massage, and a panoramic relaxation room. Choose treatments like Warm Bamboo Massage (90 minutes, $199); Reiki (75 minutes, $159); Oxygen Calming Facial (79 minutes, $159); Mother-to-be Massage (60 minutes, $139); or Frangipani Body Nourish Cocoon (60 minutes, $129). Special packages include daylong treatments with lunch at the resort restaurant ($279-449).

Three Graces Day Spa (Pompano Beach Club, 36 Pompano Beach Rd., tel. 441/234-0333, www.threegracesdayspa.com, 10am-7pm daily; public holidays 10am-3pm) is an oceanfront spa, with two of its three treatment rooms overlooking the dizzying turquoise shallows of the West End coastline. Therapists provide an assortment of hot stone facials and massage, manicures, pedicures, waxing, and mud treatments. Some of the more intriguing are the Chocolate Aroma Massage (50 minutes, $120); Citrus Salt Glow (50 minutes, $125); and Golfer's Delight (50 minutes, $135)—a nod to the next-door Port Royal Golf Course.

Tucked into a busy roadside plaza, **Nail Bar** (237 Middle Rd. at Heron Bay, tel. 441/232-0031, 10am-8pm Tues.-Sat, 10am-6pm Sun., closed Mon.) is a mini-spa, offering mani-pedis, facials, waxing, and massages. All treatments come with a glass of wine, juice, or tea while you get pampered.

For Kids

Southampton beaches are free, nonstop attractions for children—and usually offer more than enough to occupy all ages. Whether they're swimming, snorkeling, bodysurfing, building sandcastles, or simply puttering about between surf and sand, children seem to be perfectly content to spend days on end at the beach, even after their parents may have had enough. Horseshoe's main beach, its "Baby Beach," and shallow West Whale Bay a few miles west are all kid favorites. Memo to parents: Don't forget the sunblock!

Its unfortunate name notwithstanding, **Death Valley Playground** (Middle Rd., opposite the Esso Terceira's Port Royal Station) is a fun, safe place for kids to let off steam. Maintained by the Department of Parks, the small site entertains kids with swings, slides, and activity structures for toddlers as well as older children. Shady benches and a picnic table sit alongside, and a large playing field lies adjacent. Located next to the busy main road, there's no peace and quiet here, but the little ones don't seem to mind. There is plenty of parking space, but there are no public toilets.

Gibbs Hill Lighthouse is also a fun trek for kids old enough to hike up the tower's 185 steps. There are platform breaks, so it's not too arduous for children five and older. At the top, they'll enjoy spying on all the white-roofed cottages and trying to figure out where things are in the panorama far below.

ACCOMMODATIONS

Southampton is home to several high-end resorts. At Morgan's Point, the site of a former U.S. military naval base, plans are under way for a Ritz-Carlton Reserve with 84 rooms and 147 residences slated to open in 2016 in time for the following year's America's Cup. The parish also has more affordable cottage colonies and guesthouses. Check www.vrbo.com, www.airbnb, and www.bermudarentals.com for a wide range of affordable places to stay.

Under $200

Greenes' Guesthouse (71 Middle Rd., tel. 441/238-0834 or 441/238-2532, fax 441/238-8980, www.thegreenesguesthouse.com, $150 d, including full breakfast) is a family-run bed-and-breakfast in a panoramic property overlooking Jennings Bay and the Great Sound. Jane Greene and her son David have turned their very large house into comfortable, modern guest accommodations complete with ample lounges, a home theater area, and a large dining room for guests to enjoy

Gibbs Hill Lighthouse

the full breakfast Jane cooks up every morning (she also bakes gingerbread for afternoon tea). The six spacious rooms, each with a private bathroom, have air-conditioning, heating, telephones, refrigerators, and cable TV. The main kitchen is open for use by guests; Jane just asks that they clean up afterwards. While the sprawling property sits just a few yards off busy Middle Road, its rear side is serene with quiet lawns, patios, and a 40-foot pool overlooking the ocean. A public bus stop is just down the main road, though Jean often transports guests to nearby shops or the Rockaway ferry dock in her car. Notably, she hasn't raised her rates in many years.

Over $400

Encompassing 100 acres, the ★ **Fairmont Southampton Resort** (101 South Shore Rd., tel. 441/238-8000, toll-free reservations tel. 866/540-4497, www.fairmont.com/southampton, high season $399-2,900 d) is the island's largest luxury resort hotel property and a major conference center. Built in 1972 on a high ridge overlooking both the South Shore and Great Sound, the resort commands priceless views and easy access to all South Shore beaches as well as the West End. A free ferry service shuttles guests across the Great Sound to the dock at its sister hotel, the Fairmont Hamilton Princess. Major reinvestment over the past decade, including a $11.5-million upgrade of guest rooms and suites in 2013-2015, has kept it among the favorites of Bermuda destination properties.

If you enjoy large resort hotels and don't mind being 20 minutes from Hamilton, the Fairmont Southampton is the island's best choice. The resort boasts 593 accommodations, including 11 basic suites, 23 one- and two-bedroom suites, two split-level penthouse suites, and 74 Fairmont Gold rooms. All rooms have private balconies, in-room safes, air-conditioning, minibars, private baths, walk-in closets, cable TV, voicemail, computer dataports with Internet access, and hair dryers. All but the first of six floors are nonsmoking. The resort has six restaurants (including two earning AAA Four and Five Diamond Awards), two bars, and the 31,000-square-foot **Willowstream Spa.** It can accommodate convention groups of up to 1,500, with 16 meeting rooms and a multimedia amphitheater. Recreational amenities include two swimming pools (outdoor heated and indoor, both with hot tubs), an 18-hole par-3 golf course, 11 all-weather tennis courts, and a private beach. Other diversions include a cycle shop, a dive shop, Jet Ski rentals, and a year-round complimentary Kids Explorers Camp for children ages four and up.

★ **The Reefs** (56 South Shore Rd., tel. 441/238-0222, U.S./Canada toll-free tel. 800/742-2008, fax 441/238-8372, www.thereefs.com, high season $615-1,035, suites $650-1,099, Club Condos $1,299-2,325, cottages $635-1,839, rates include full breakfast, afternoon tea, and gourmet dinner) consistently rakes in international awards for privacy, professionalism, and its well-appointed property. Nestled in the cliffs above its own beautiful beach, the resort is owned by Bermuda's former tourism minister, David Dodwell.

The smoke-free Reefs surpasses many other Bermuda resorts by reinvesting in its coral-pink property. Accommodations range from guest rooms and suites, all with private balconies, to two- and three-bedroom Club Condos and cottages. Top-end "point suites" (with private outdoor hot tubs) exude an urbane decor reminiscent of a SoHo loft—a play on neutrals that makes a refreshing change from the worn wicker-and-floral epidemic afflicting many island accommodations. **La Serena Spa** is among the amenities, along with an infinity pool, its horizon blending with the South Shore's. Meticulous landscaping makes every planted palm appear freshly scrubbed and every lawn edge appear to have been trimmed with a razor blade. Honeymooners, families, and guests of every age bracket seem to enjoy the place equally. Bermudians flock here for weekend getaways in the off-season, and to the property's restaurants year-round. Wedding, honeymoon, and anniversary packages are offered. Three restaurants, a gym, pool, kayaks, croquet, shuffleboard, and tennis courts make this a property you might never want to leave.

Named for the schools of long-finned surf fish that swim offshore, **Pompano Beach Club** (36 Pompano Beach Rd., tel. 441/234-0222, toll-free 800/343-4155, fax 441/234-1694, www.pompanobeachclub.com, suites to townhouse units $550-1,500 d, four-night minimum stay in high season) commands one of the island's most dramatic seascapes. Ensconced in the cliffs of the southwest shoreline, the 75-room resort overlooks an atoll-like bay where low tide allows you to wade out some 250 yards over a shallow sandbar, called Pompano Flats, to the surrounding reef line. Sea turtles frolic here, and the wide-open azure horizons and rolling breakers give the illusion of looking out from the top deck of an ocean liner at sea.

Winner of numerous hotel awards, Pompano is a family-owned and -run property with a casual atmosphere that attracts kid-toting couples as well as honeymooners. Staff members boast about its high rate of repeat guests and the ultra-personalized service. Rooms have dated décor, with tiled floors, potted plants, floral prints, and pastel watercolors, but private balconies with uncommon surf views make up for the lack of interior inspiration. Golf, honeymoon, and anniversary packages are offered. The resort has a spa, fitness center, game room, oceanfront heated pool, kiddie pool, hot tubs, six tennis courts, and a glass-enclosed, 60-seat restaurant. A water-sports outlet offers guests kayaks, paddleboats, waterbikes, Hobie Cat sailboats, and windsurfing gear, and an exceptional golf experience can be had at the adjoining world-championship Port Royal Golf Course.

FOOD

Cafés and Takeout

For Bermudian favorites such as Sunday codfish breakfast, Portuguese kale soup, pan-fried rockfish, peas 'n' rice, and bread pudding, drop into ★ **Island Cuisine** (235 Middle Rd., tel. 441/238-3287, www.islandcuisine.org, 6am-9:45pm Mon.-Sat., 7am-2:45pm and 5pm-9pm Sun.). The bright blue roadside diner is run by mother-daughter team Audrey and Alicia Tucker, who offer affordable home-style food. All-day breakfast is served daily, and beer and wine are also available. Breakfast specials include banana pancakes ($6.50), omelets (11.50), and French toast. Lunchgoers can choose anything from peanut butter and bacon sandwiches ($5.50) to one of the best burgers ($4.75) on the island. The dinner menu features meatloaf ($16.75) and fish-cake dinner ($16.50). A menu for kids under 10 offers grilled banana ($2.75) and peas 'n' rice ($4.50).

Right next door to Henry VIII Pub is **Henry's Pantry** (69 South Shore Rd., tel. 441/238-1509, 10am-7pm Mon.-Sat.), which sells cold drinks, chocolate bars, snacks, batteries, and a few deli items like chicken legs, hot pies, beef patties, fish chowder, and sandwiches, along with its full wine, beer, and liquor selection. Manager Anthony Faries will fill you in on all Bermuda's need-to-know intel before you buy the daily newspaper.

East Meets West at the Bermuda Golf Academy (10 Industrial Park Rd. off Middle Rd., tel. 441/238-8580, eastmeetswestbm@yahoo.com, 11am-10pm daily, $3-19) satisfies golfers and drop-in customers with a takeout or eat-in menu of burgers, roti wraps, sandwiches, Asian noodles, and Indian dishes, including biryani, balti, and tandoor specialties, with nut-free and dairy-free options. Refreshing smoothies, milk shakes, lassi, and chai tea are also served.

Take a sweet timeout at **Scoops Ice Cream Parlour & Cupcake Café** (237 Middle Rd., Heron Bay, tel. 441/238-5382, scoopsbermuda.bm, noon-10pm daily) if you're passing through this busy neighborhood on your way west to Dockyard or east to Hamilton. The bright orange building is hard to miss at any rate, and its ice-cream flavors conjure scenes from the Little Golden Book *Good Humor Man*—peanut butter cup chocolate swirl, watermelon sherbet, black-raspberry truffle. A delectable menu of cupcakes also tempts a try, with lemon, chocolate mint, red velvet, chocolate hearts, vanilla, and apple strudel varieties.

Pining for pizza? **Heron Bay Pizza House** (Heron Bay Plaza, next to Heron Bay MarketPlace, tel. 441/238-2753, 11am-10pm Mon.-Sat., 1pm-8pm Sun., slice $4.50, pies $12-26) serves up fluffy pizzas with toppings galore by the slice or whole.

Horseshoe Bay Beach House (at Horseshoe Bay, 94 South Shore Rd., tel. 441/238-2651, 8am-6pm daily Mar.-Nov.) serves hamburgers ($5.50), veggie burgers, fish 'n' chips ($17), chicken nuggets, tuna sandwiches ($6.50), pizza, sodas, lemonade, ice cream, and snow cones ($4). Enjoy the outdoor patio with tables and shady umbrellas, or eat your picnic on the beach.

Tasty, tapas-style lunch or dinner can be enjoyed in the air-conditioned comfort of a hotel lobby bar at **Jasmine Lounge** (Fairmont Southampton Resort, 101 South Shore Rd., tel. 441/238-8000, www.fairmont.com/southampton, 7am-midnight daily), with all-day cocktails, gourmet sandwiches (prime rib $22), and an array of tempting tapas such as tuna melt sliders ($16) and mini cheeseburgers ($12), pulled pork tacos ($14), cobb salad ($16), and guacamole ($15), as well as afternoon tea (3pm-5pm, $35-44 per person). Watch the comings and goings of guests and golfers, including the occasional celebrity, as you nibble thin-crust pizza and garlic shrimp, or sip a martini.

Mediterranean

Bacci (Fairmont Southampton Resort, 101 South Shore Rd., tel. 441/238-8000 or 441/239-6966, www.fairmont.com/southampton, 6pm-10pm daily, closed Thurs.) is located next to the hotel's golf course, a good trek from the main entrance (take the hotel trolley or drive past the hotel to the golf club). Named for the Italian word for "kiss," Bacci is a casually elegant but family-friendly restaurant offering rustic crowd-pleasers such as fried calamari ($16), Tuscan meatballs ($18), and bean and artichoke salad ($14) as appetizers, homemade pastas and risottos ($21-30), pizzas ($20-25), and classic main courses such as veal marsala ($36), grilled tuna ($37), or strip loin with garlic herb butter ($35). Many vegetarian and gluten-free options are also on the menu. One of the most popular offerings is the antipasti bar, serving sun-dried tomatoes, sardines, grilled vegetables, bocconcini cheese, prosciutto, anchovies, and cured meats ($17).

Opened by the über-popular Rustico group in 2014, **Gulfstream** (117 South Shore Rd.,

East Meets West at the Bermuda Golf Academy

tel. 441/238-1897, www.dining-bermuda.com, gulfstream@logic.bm, lunch 11:30am-2:30pm Mon.-Wed., 11:30am-5pm Fri.-Sun., dinner 5:30pm-10pm daily) is a welcome newcomer to Southampton's restaurant scene; with its complete renovation and contemporary cuisine, it replaces the former Tio Pepe in the same location. Delicious paninis, pastas, pizzas, salads, and seafood are front and center. Appetizers include clams in white wine and garlic ($18) and Kobe beef sushi roll ($19); main dishes run the gamut from decadent lobster mac 'n' cheese ($26) and beef stir-fry ($26) to crab cakes ($32) and grilled fish of the day ($29). The extensive thin-crust pizza menu includes vegetarian options. Seating is in the coolly lit interior, or outside on the terrace.

Tucked into a historic cottage at the foot of Gibbs Hill Lighthouse, ★ **The Dining Room** (68 St. Anne's Rd., tel. 441/238-8679, thediningroom@northrock.bm, www.bermuda-dining.com, lunch 11:45am-2:30pm Fri.-Sat., dinner 6pm-10pm daily, breakfast/brunch 10am-2:30pm Sun.) is another member of the Rustico group. Its unique location—with 360 views out the quaint cottage windows—makes for memorable meals, but the menu is also attractive. Inventive dishes include thin-crust truffled mushroom pizza ($21), octopus carpaccio ($16), pumpkin ravioli ($18), and filet mignon with peppercorn sauce ($34). Lunch offers jerk-chicken and fish sandwiches ($16), lamb burgers ($24), salads, pizza, and rum-doused fish chowder. There's a broad cocktails, beer, and wine list, including more than a dozen wines by the glass.

Chef Livio Ferigo opened **Bella Vista Grill** (Port Royal Golf Course, 5 Middle Rd., tel. 441/234-0330, 11:30am-10:30pm daily) in late 2013, following years of success at Dockyard's Bone Fish Grill and Café Amici. Since then, it's won glowing reviews from visitors and locals guests who have sampled both its elegant menu and world-famous setting. Culinary creations here are original: salmon and asparagus pie ($18), Argentinian empanadas, tuna carpaccio and mussels ($18), and chicken Kiev ($26), along with pastas, burgers, and surf 'n' turf specials. In the summer, step out for a pre-dinner cocktail on the west porch; the venue overlooks Port Royal's panoramic back nine.

International

Seafood shines at the beachside **Ocean Club** (Fairmont Southampton Resort, 101 South Shore Rd., tel. 441/238-8000, www.fairmont.com/southampton, noon-9pm daily,

The terrace at Bella Vista Grill looks over the 18th hole at the Port Royal Golf Course.

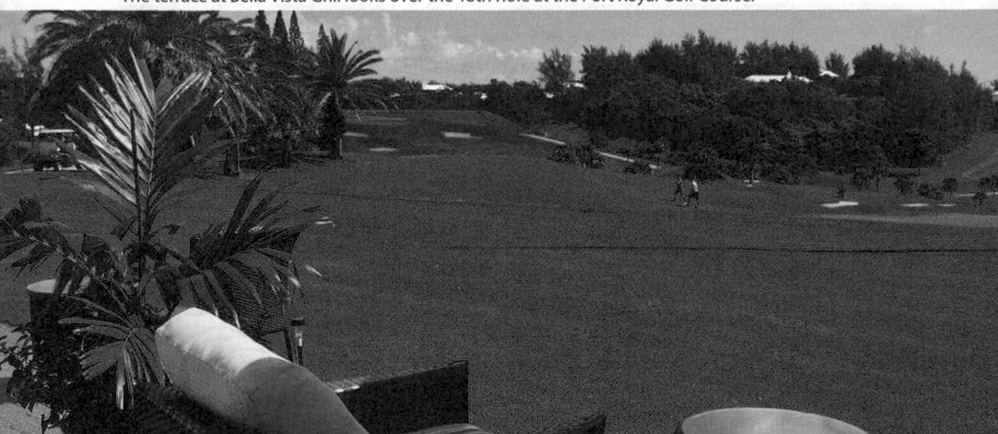

high season only). Located in the Fairmont Beach Club (accessible by hotel trolley), the seasonal restaurant overlooks the hotel's private beach and the South Shore breakers, its patio a perfect alfresco venue. The menu features fresh local catches (tuna, rockfish, wahoo), as well as oysters Rockefeller ($5 each), Maine lobster cocktail ($24), fish tacos ($16), steamed mussels ($20), bacon-wrapped scallops ($34), chowders, salads, and even a few meat and chicken dishes.

Inside the hotel, the **Newport Gastropub** (Fairmont Southampton Resort, 101 South Shore Rd., tel. 441/238-8000, 6pm-11pm daily) is the 2012 rebirth of legendary dining spot The Newport Room, but other than name, the two have nothing in common. Shedding its jacket-and-tie past, the new eatery is all about complete comfort—in both food and surroundings. Booths and TV screens showing live sports invite guests to sit back and relax while digging in to the fresh raw bar and charcuterie station, plus staples like fish 'n' chips ($27), shrimp 'n' grits ($25), burgers ($19), and pork ribs ($29). Draft beers are on tap, along with numerous bottled ales and lagers and a serious wine list.

Henry VIII Pub & Restaurant (69 South Shore Rd., tel. 441/238-1977, www.henrys.bm, lunch noon-4:30pm Mon.-Sat., pub fare noon-10pm Mon.-Sat., dinner 6pm-10pm daily, brunch noon-3pm Sun.) looks as if it might date back to Tudor times, though it's been a Southampton roadside fixture only since 1970. Permeated with the aroma of prime rib and spilled draught beer, the low-ceilinged eatery is Bermuda's best example of an English-style pub. A strong local following keeps the place lively even in the off-season, especially on Sunday nights when a raucous crowd enjoys dinner and live entertainment until 3am The kitsch plays to serious Anglophiles, but even if you don't delight in the sight of strolling minstrels in the dining room, the menu is heartily enjoyable. Highlights are the Bermuda rockfish ($34.95), Chateaubriand for two ($74.95), calf's liver with caramelized Bermuda onion ($33), steak and mushroom pie ($19.95), a sushi bar, and 14 different ales. Friday through Sunday there is live entertainment after 9:45pm

★ **Coconuts** (The Reefs, 56 South Shore Rd., tel. 441/238-0222, www.thereefs.com, lunch noon-3pm, dinner 6:30pm-10pm daily, Mar.-Dec.) wins the hearts of alfresco diners and numerous awards for the island's best lunch venue, most romantic restaurant, and best table with a view. Set on a treehouse-style covered deck below tumbling cliffs overlooking the surf, it has managed to be consistently competitive for more than a decade. Lunch offers light but creative dishes like blue crab guacamole, quinoa salad, grilled vegetable wrap, fish tacos, and baby back ribs. A typical dinner menu might include Bermuda snapper ceviche ($16), salt-and-pepper clams ($14), spice-rubbed sirloin ($38), and grilled octopus ($26). No matter how scrumptious the food, it will always be eclipsed by the spectacular thunder of the surf and the glittering turquoise reef line just a few feet away. For ultra-romantic occasions, celebrate with the sand between your toes as you feast: Dinner can be served at candlelit tables set right on the beach (7pm-8:30pm, five-course, prix fixe menu, $125 per person plus gratuities).

Bermudian brunchgoers park bumper to bumper along South Shore Road outside The Reefs every Sunday. The reason is **Ocean Echo** (The Reefs, 56 South Shore Rd., tel. 441/238-0222, www.thereefs.com, noon-3pm Sun., $45 for buffet brunch, $55 special holidays, half-price for children 5-12, dinner 6pm-10pm daily), the hotel's window-walled dining room, which tantalizes taste buds while wowing guests with eye-popping horizons. The curved dining room is the show-stopper, but the kitchen doesn't disappoint either. Dinnertime small plates include sesame-seared tuna ($18), crispy pork belly ($16), and thin-crust pizza ($14). Large plates ($22-48) range from swordfish to duck breast and lamb chop.

Fine Dining

Dating back to 1670, the historic ★ **Waterlot Inn** (Fairmont Southampton Resort, Jews Bay, Middle Rd., tel. 441/239-6623 or 441/238-8000, www.fairmont.com/southampton, dinner 6pm-10pm daily, closed Mon., brunch 11am-2pm Sun., dress "resort elegant") is a Bermuda landmark, beloved as much for its indulgent menu as for its resident ghost. Local lore says the spirit of pioneering owner Claudia Darrell still stalks the building that was home to generations of her seafaring ancestors as well as a blacksmith shop and parish post office over the years. In the early 1900s, Darrell inherited the house and converted it into an English-style tavern where she befriended visiting celebrities like Mark Twain, Eugene O'Neill, James Thurber, and Eleanor Roosevelt, becoming something of an island legend. Hamilton's flags flew at half-mast when she died in 1949. Owned today by the Fairmont Southampton Resort, the oceanfront Waterlot remains steeped in history, its cedar beams, thick limestone walls, and low ceilings converted to intimate dining rooms. Patrons often arrive by boat, and nothing is more bucolic than summer sunset cocktails and tapas at its updated waterside lounge, **The Dock.** An AAA Four Diamond Award winner, Waterlot aligns its menu with that of an upscale American steakhouse, despite its U.K. tavern appearance. So while the Caesar salads prepared tableside for two or more ($16 per person), oysters Rockefeller ($24), seared tuna ($42), and cedar-plank salmon ($34) may be scrumptious, the star attraction is the USDA steak, aged a minimum of three weeks: tenderloin, strip loin, loin chop, porterhouse, rib eye, and prime rib cuts ($44-89). Pick your accompaniments (seared foie gras, truffle butter, ginger beer sauce). Shared side orders ($9-12), such as garlic creamed spinach, truffled mac 'n' cheese, duck fat fries, and hand-cut onion rings, are worth splurging on, too.

Grocery Stores

Heron Bay MarketPlace (227 Middle Rd. at Heron Bay, tel. 441/238-1993, 7am-10pm Mon.-Sat., 9pm-7pm Sun.) is one of the larger members of the MarketPlace chain, stocking a large array of foodstuffs fresh and nonperishable, and including a bakery on-site. A small mall attached to the grocery has a pizza restaurant, a florist, and other retail outlets.

Markets

Wadson's Home Farm Market (at Wadson's Farm, 10 Luke's Pond Rd., tel. 441/238-1862, www.wadsonsfarm.com, 10am-6pm Tues.-Fri., 9am-1pm Sat.) is an organic mecca for area residents and anyone looking for some of Bermuda's best vegetables, lamb, chicken, pork, and sausages. Farmer Tom Wadson hails from a centuries-old Bermudian family and now focuses his energies on all things chemical-free. His Southampton farm, a good example of a sustainable organic operation, offers tours to visitors, by appointment.

INFORMATION AND SERVICES

The parish has one mail drop at **Southampton Post Office** (2 Church Rd., off Middle Rd., tel. 441/238-0253, 8am-5pm Mon.-Fri.).

Parish gas stations include **Terceira's Port Royal Service Centre** (31 Middle Rd., tel. 441/234-0090, 5:30am-11pm daily), a busy outlet with pleasant staff that sells newspapers and basics, along with hot dogs, fresh pies, sodas, and fruit drinks, and **Rubis Raynor's Service Station** (217 Middle Rd., near Heron Bay, tel. 441/238-3492, 6am-10pm Mon.-Fri., 8am-8pm Sat., closed Sun.), which has a convenience store. The station actually offers 24-hour service: Credit and debit cards can be used to access gas at any time.

ATMs are at Heron Bay MarketPlace (227 Middle Rd.) and Terceira's Port Royal Service Centre (31 Middle Rd.).

Public toilets are located at Horseshoe Bay and at the major hotels, restaurants, and golf clubs. In addition, portable toilets are located at Warwick Long Bay and Church Bay.

GETTING THERE AND AROUND

Buses

Catch the route 7 bus (Hamilton-Barnes Corner/Dockyard via South Shore) to get to the beaches or the lighthouse, or route 8 (Hamilton-Barnes Corner/Somerset via Middle Road) for points along the parish's harborside (buses on both routes run every 15 minutes most of the day). The fare to all points in the parish is $3.

Ferries

Busy with weekday commuters, the fast ferry service **Sea Express** (tel. 441/295-4506, www.seaexpress.bm) stops near the parish border with Sandys at Rockaway, Southampton. This ferry stop is accessible off Middle Road, opposite the Port Royal Golf Course. Weekday service offers an express route (20 minutes) to Hamilton leaving Rockaway at 7:20am. The evening's last ferry leaves Rockaway at 6:45pm, arriving in Hamilton at 7:20pm. The 4:30pm ferry departing Rockaway Monday-Saturday loops into the West End and Dockyard before returning to Hamilton. Ferries depart Hamilton every 15 minutes at peak commuter times, every 90 minutes at other times (no service Sun.). The fare is $4.50 adults, $2.50 children 5-16, kids under 5 free. No cash or change accepted; tickets or tokens only.

Scooters and Bicycles

Smatt's Cycle Livery (at Fairmont Southampton Resort, 101 South Shore Rd., tel. 441/238-7800, www.smattscyclelivery.com, 9am-5pm daily) rents single-seat ($50 per day) and dual-seat ($55) scooters ($225/$267 per week). Islandwide roadside assistance is part of the deal. Pedal bikes are also available for $55 per day or $160 per week.

Oleander Cycles (at The Reefs Resort, 56 South Shore Rd., 441/239-0189, www.oleandersycles.bm, 9am-5pm) rents standard single or double scooters. Rates ($55 standard/$65 double for one day, $225 standard/$266 double per week, $17/$21 per day after seven days) include scooter delivery and pickup (or hotel pickup), first tank of gas, helmet, lock, basket, $30 third-party insurance, and islandwide roadside service for breakdowns. Mountain bikes are $40 per day, $175 per week, $10 a day after seven days.

Taxis

There are always long taxi stands at the Fairmont Southampton, and often a few at Port Royal Golf Course and the Horseshoe Bay parking lot. To order a cab pickup, call **Bermuda Industrial Union Co-op** (tel. 441/292-4476, cooptaxi@fkbnet.bm), **Bermuda Island Taxi** (tel. 441/295-4141, www.bermudaislandtaxi.com), or **BTA Dispatching Ltd.** (tel. 441/296-2121, www.taxibermuda.bm).

Sandys Parish

The distinctive "fishhook" of Bermuda is the island's charismatic West End, Sandys—an undulating patchwork of geography, in which the rugged South Shore coastline on one side and the mirrorlike Great Sound bays on the other sandwich a rural bosom of onion fields, towering cedars, and loquat woods. The West End is all about peace and quiet; perhaps more than in any other parish, you can actually find loads of both here. Winding country lanes littered in oleander petals invite leisurely strolls past miles of red-earthed farms, avenued estates, and craggy islets where whalers once lived. You can watch old-time dinghies with billowing sails scoot across wide-open ocean or hang out with fishermen as they clean their catch in the afternoon. The fact that Sandys is so detached from the rest of Bermuda—a 40-minute drive from the bustle of Hamilton—lends serenity to any time spent in the parish. No wonder that a traveler would encounter places called Tranquillity Hill, Pinkhouse Lane, and Daisyfield Drive around here.

The parish name may conjure a delightful image of nonstop beaches—which wouldn't be deceiving—but Sandys (pronounced "Sands") actually is derived from Sir Edwin Sandys, one of the colony's first Virginia Company investors. To keep your bearings, it helps to remember that the parish comprises a string of five islands—plus a chunk of mainland bordering Southampton at Port Royal Golf Course—that curve around in an arc. That may help explain all those bridges you're crossing. From the west, the islands are: Ireland Island North, Ireland Island South, Boaz Island, Watford Island, and—the largest—Somerset Island, named for the English county. Somerset Island connects to the rest of the parish at its western tip via Somerset Bridge, the world's smallest drawbridge. Quaint Somerset Village is found on Somerset Island—a point of confusion when Bermudians talk about "Somerset." Sometimes, they may mean the village itself, but they could be referring to anything in the larger area. In fact, many locals tend to call all addresses

Previous: a horse and carriage tour; Fort Scaur. **Above:** Mangrove Bay.

Look for ★ to find recommended sights, activities, dining, and lodging.

Highlights

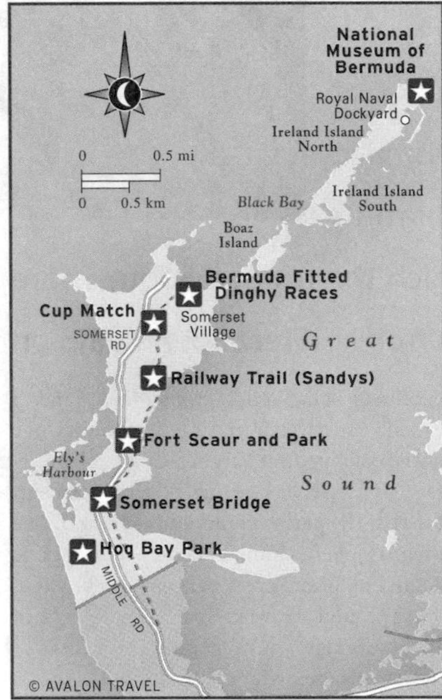

★ **National Museum of Bermuda:** The most-visited Bermuda attraction, the museum is housed inside the tall ramparts of the six-acre Keep, the Royal Naval Dockyard's citadel. Learn about the island's sea-swept history through exhibits on ancient shipwrecks, pirates, the Royal Navy, and the story of transatlantic slavery. Commissioner's House offers the island's best view (page 158).

★ **Bermuda Fitted Dinghy Races:** Somerset Village is the best place on the island to witness this hugely popular spectacle throughout the summer. Cute as a button, the pastel village on the shore of Mangrove Bay is itself worth a stop on a tour through Sandys, inviting languorous afternoons spent strolling its winding country lanes (page 169).

★ **Somerset Bridge:** Ferry service no longer stops at Somerset Bridge, but the world's tiniest drawbridge is worth driving or walking over nonetheless. Watch boaters navigate the skinny passage beneath its planks between Ely's Harbour and the Great Sound (page 174).

★ **Fort Scaur and Park:** Talk about lunch with a view! With panoramic views of the Great Sound and Dockyard, this fort and surrounding parkland make a great stop for a picnic or photo op. They also have access to the Railway Trail. Climb into the ditch leading from the 1870s fort right across Somerset Island (page 174).

★ **Hog Bay Park:** The island's third-largest park is a loner's paradise—38 acres of trails through farmland, woods, and coastal scrub. A pristine beach pops up on the shoreline at low tide, and snorkelers can wade out hundreds of yards to inspect reefs and sea grass (page 175).

★ **Cup Match:** Don't miss this annual cricket extravaganza if you happen to visit over the July-August cusp. Staged in Sandys every other year (it's held in St. George's in alternate years), the two-day festival represents an immediate initiation into island life. And don't worry if the game leaves you cold; the gambling, rum, fish sandwiches, and convivial crowds will more than make up for it (page 177).

★ **Railway Trail (Sandys):** Arguably the finest stretch of Bermuda's old railway bed to walk along is the section between the gates of the former U.S. Naval Air Station Annex at Morgan's Island and Somerset Village. The trail's cool cut-limestone walls, back-lane gardens, sweeping ocean views, and trails down to the rocky shoreline, where you can take a cooling dip, are unbeatable (page 179).

Sandys Parish

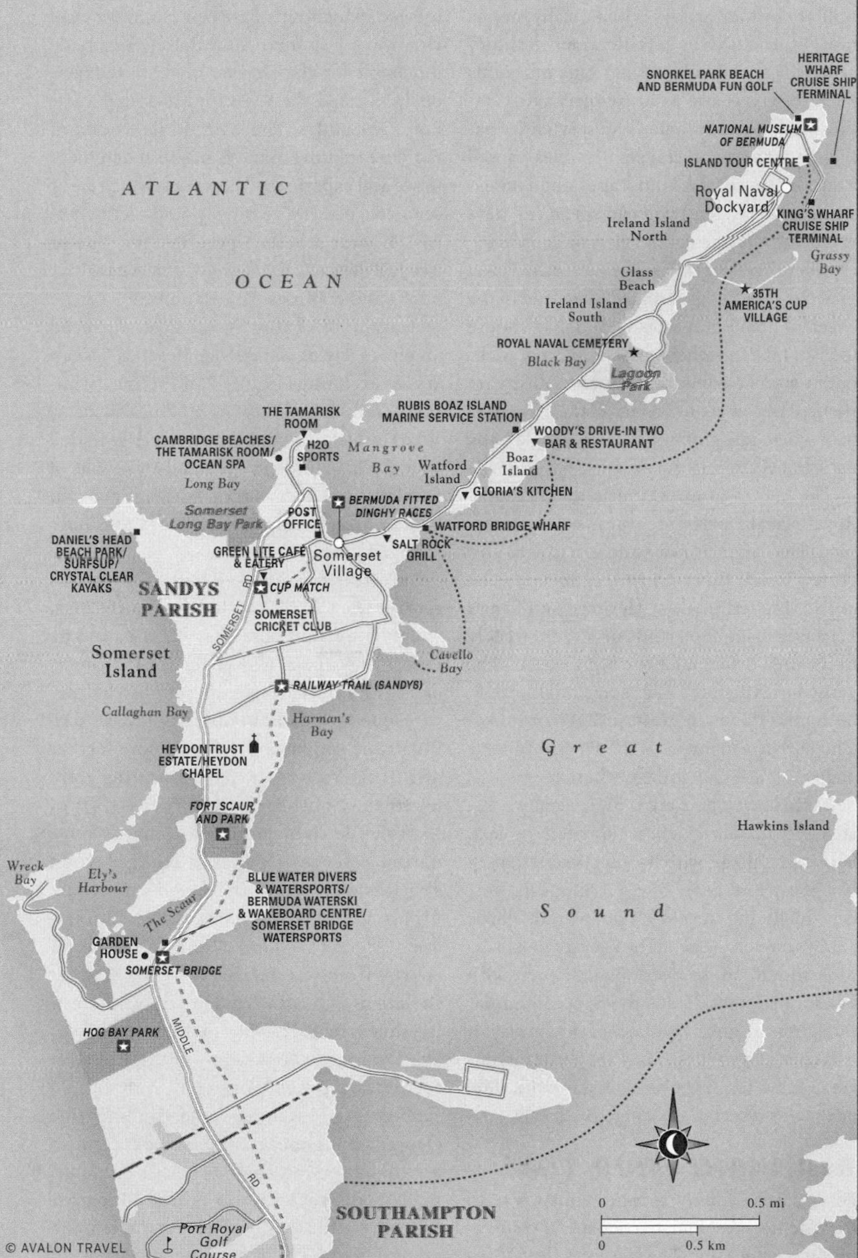

ATLANTIC
OCEAN
HERITAGE WHARF CRUISE SHIP TERMINAL
SNORKEL PARK BEACH AND BERMUDA FUN GOLF
NATIONAL MUSEUM OF BERMUDA
ISLAND TOUR CENTRE
Royal Naval Dockyard
KING'S WHARF CRUISE SHIP TERMINAL
Ireland Island North
Grassy Bay
Glass Beach
35TH AMERICA'S CUP VILLAGE
Ireland Island South
ROYAL NAVAL CEMETERY
Black Bay
Lagoon Park
THE TAMARISK ROOM
RUBIS BOAZ ISLAND MARINE SERVICE STATION
WOODY'S DRIVE-IN TWO BAR & RESTAURANT
CAMBRIDGE BEACHES/ THE TAMARISK ROOM/ OCEAN SPA
H2O SPORTS
Mangrove Bay
Watford Island
Boaz Island
Long Bay
BERMUDA FITTED DINGHY RACES
GLORIA'S KITCHEN
Somerset Long Bay Park
POST OFFICE
WATFORD BRIDGE WHARF
DANIEL'S HEAD BEACH PARK/ SURFSUP/ CRYSTAL CLEAR KAYAKS
GREEN LITE CAFE & EATERY
Somerset Village
SALT ROCK GRILL
SANDYS PARISH
CUP MATCH
SOMERSET RD
SOMERSET CRICKET CLUB
Somerset Island
Cavello Bay
RAILWAY TRAIL (SANDYS)
Callaghan Bay
Harman's Bay
HEYDON TRUST ESTATE/HEYDON CHAPEL
Great
FORT SCAUR AND PARK
Hawkins Island
Wreck Bay
Ely's Harbour
BLUE WATER DIVERS & WATERSPORTS/ BERMUDA WATERSKI & WAKEBOARD CENTRE/ SOMERSET BRIDGE WATERSPORTS
The Scaur
Sound
GARDEN HOUSE
SOMERSET BRIDGE
MIDDLE RD
HOG BAY PARK
SOUTHAMPTON PARISH
Port Royal Golf Course
0
0.5 mi
0
0.5 km
© AVALON TRAVEL

farther west than Somerset Bridge, including the other islands and Dockyard, Somerset.

Steeped in both early colonial and British military history, Sandys is historically important, as its stunning fortifications, military cemeteries, and cultural heritage museums will attest. It is also a nature-lover's destination, with two of Bermuda's most extensive national parks plus several smaller ones, as well as dramatic coastal landscapes and endless shallow reef systems you can spend full days exploring. Quintessential Bermudiana is everywhere here—in the village verandas, cricket matches, and cottage-fringed lanes, and in the cheerful homespun eateries you may choose to visit. Like the other parishes, it is not without its social troubles—gangs and graffiti are particularly overt on sections of the main road here where idle groups of young people hang out—but visitors are rarely affected.

The center of attention is the awesome Royal Naval Dockyard, an unbeatable combination of maritime endeavors, arts and crafts, beach fun, and hearty menus. The cruise ship terminals at Heritage and King's Wharves bring thousands of visitors weekly to the area throughout the high season. The arrival of America's Cup stage qualifiers in 2015, and the main event in 2017, promises a huge redevelopment of the Dockyard for a purpose-built Cup village where teams will be based and staging areas for spectators created through an 11-acre reclamation project. Somerset Village, with its infectious lethargy, is a West End gem. The surrounding parish—including the old Railway Trail, whose Sandys stretch is one of the island's most scenic—should not be overlooked, either; with memorable sights, loads to do, accommodations, restaurants, and laid-back whimsy, it will entice you to linger just that little bit longer. Sandys has few places to stay, with only one major resort (Cambridge Beaches).

PLANNING YOUR TIME

Ferries are a highly recommended way to travel to the West End, particularly if your vacation is a short one. The fast-ferry fleet of Sea Express revolutionized access to Dockyard and the way people visit the area, not to mention area residents' commute to work. The service, which zips between Hamilton and Dockyard in a mere 20 minutes, has made it possible for visitors who might have previously skipped the West End to spend a few hours in Sandys. That said, while Dockyard is a true treasure, Sandys has so much more to see and experience (the ferries, which carry scooters, also run to other points in the parish). If your schedule permits, give one or two full days to excursions to explore various nooks and crannies. For example, if it's utter relaxation you're after, you could easily spend an entire day at Cambridge Beaches' Ocean Spa, or exploring Hog Bay Park, hiking, swimming, and snorkeling at its pristine shoreline, where a little-known beach offers secluded beauty. Or soaking in the small-town vibe of Somerset's country lanes, where lunch can be had overlooking tranquil bays that have changed little in centuries.

In terms of must-see value, Dockyard rates at the top of the West End's offerings, worth a few hours at least. Next would be Somerset Village, with its charming shops, cafés, and backstreets, as well as the picturesque lanes leading off Mangrove Bay. Finally, if you have time to explore farther afield, the rest of the parish leading right up to the Southampton border is full of worthwhile sights and experiences—huge nature reserves (Hog Bay Park, Heydon Trust Estate), one of the island's most scenic forts (Fort Scaur), ultra-Bermudian eateries (Woody's, Gloria's), and myriad water sports, from waterskiing to scuba dives at the site of some of Bermuda's most interesting shipwrecks. Notably, the Sandys Railway Trail is a major highlight—one of the most scenic and peaceful stretches of the old railbed-turned-walking route, running from George's Bay Lane, at the parish border with Southampton, all the way to the Somerset Police Station at Somerset Village, Mangrove Bay. Along the way, walkers or cyclists can enjoy bucolic residential neighborhoods, tracts of farmland, soccer pitches, and trails leading down to quiet docks and picnic areas on the Great Sound (the very best stretch is from Somerset Bridge westward).

Dockyard is perfect for a family visit, with enough sights, attractions, and eateries to appeal equally to toddlers or seniors. The Hamilton-Dockyard ferry run allows scooters on board, so it's easy to explore Dockyard on foot, then drive out to see Somerset Village and the rest of the parish. There are several different transport combos you might choose to get to Sandys, around the parish, and back. You could take a one-way ferry from Hamilton, then ride the bus or drive a scooter back through the parishes. The bus ride to Hamilton takes about an hour, with numerous stops included; if you're traveling by scooter, count on a half-hour to 45-minute journey to the city or central parishes. Or, take the bus or drive out via Harbour Road or the South Shore beaches and ride the ferry back (driving both ways makes for a lot of scootering—unless you *really* want to). Another option would be to go by ferry, explore, and then take a Dockyard bus as far as Somerset Bridge to catch the Green Route Sea Express back to Hamilton. If you're on holiday without wheels, take advantage of the mini-train service from Dockyard that makes regular trips to Somerset Village and the Daniels's Head beaches and back; you can spend a few hours swimming, kayaking or paddleboarding, then hop on the train back to your ship or ferry. There's also a return bus service from Dockyard to Southampton's popular Horseshoe Beach.

Middle Road is the main parish artery for vehicles, continuing from Southampton. Its name changes as it passes through Sandys, becoming Somerset Road after Somerset Bridge, Mangrove Bay Road at Mangrove Bay, Malabar Road after Watford Bridge, Cockburn Road until Cockburn's Cut, and finally Pender Road to the Clocktower buildings (take Pender or the wharfside Freeport Drive on the way out).

Royal Naval Dockyard

Like the old town of St. George's in the East End, the Royal Naval Dockyard on Bermuda's western point is crucial to understanding what shaped the political and social history of Bermuda. It's also loads of fun to visit. The 24-acre area—the largest and best preserved of Bermuda's fortifications—is a functioning community with shops, restaurants, a marina, and working boatyards. It also embodies the fascinating maritime history of the island, including its 150-year Royal Navy connection. "Dockyard," as it's simply called by locals, sits on Ireland Island North, the westernmost of Sandys's five islands, its tip forming the entrance to the main shipping channel into the Great Sound. Towering stone pillars stand at its entrance on Pender Road, where the notorious—and now abandoned—Casemate Prison also looms. As Bermuda's primary cruise ship port, Dockyard's waterfront is a hive of activity through the summer months, with ferries coming and going, tourists pouring off ships at King's and Heritage Wharves, and charter fishing, snorkeling, sailing, and glass-bottomed boat operators at the ready. Two outlets of the **Island Tour Centre** now located near Dockyard's ferry stop make planning an action-packed itinerary a one-stop breeze—from scuba to Jet Ski, horseback riding to flyboarding, whale-watching to ecotours—and you can book activities offered by more than 20 vendors islandwide. Dockyard's sheltered marina is packed with local yachts and other pleasure craft, and myriad marine businesses operate out of historic former military buildings. Public washrooms and ATMs are located in the distinctive **Clocktower Building,** the air-conditioned home to a plethora of shops, a restaurant, and an ice cream bar. There are

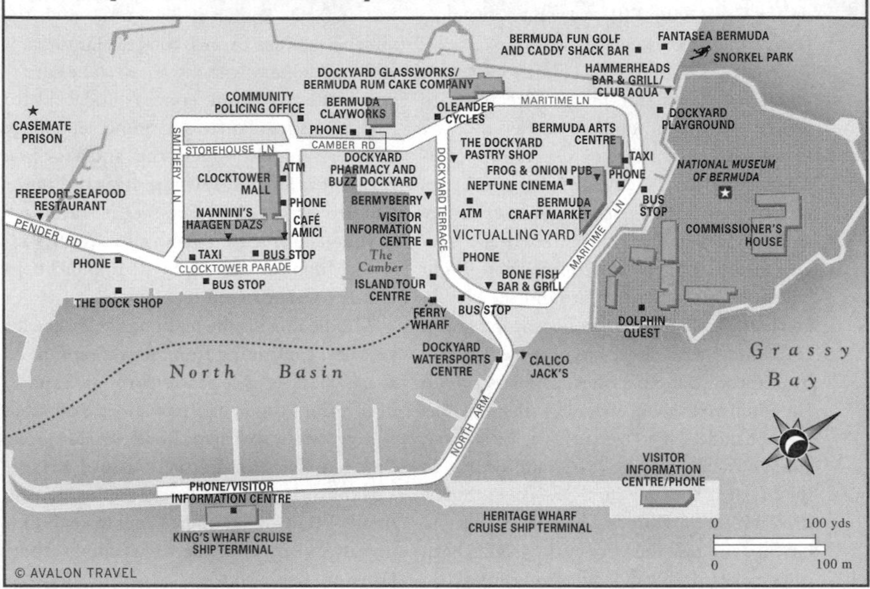

three **Visitor Information Centres,** at both cruise ship wharves (open only when ships are in port) and near the ferry dock, along with various means of transport—rental scooters, tour trains, Segway tours, buses—for exploring the area. Special evening festivals are held throughout the summer, with live musical entertainment, parades, gombey performances, vendors, and food and drink stalls. The 35th America's Cup event in 2017, along with its early-stage events in 2015, spurred plans for a massive land-reclamation project in the Dockyard, where Bermuda's government pledged to build a spectator complex and athletes' village inside the South Basin's existing breakwater on Cross Island. The project promises to revitalize the entire West End, not to mention the rest of the island.

HISTORY

On the heels of the United States' successful revolution against Britain in 1783, Bermuda's role in the maritime geopolitics of the day suddenly gained new stature. With the loss of its chain of North American ports (other than Halifax), Britain urgently needed a winter anchorage and dockyard to supply and repair its fleet, in the event of war with the United States or France. It also needed to protect its political and trade interests in the Caribbean. Efforts were begun immediately to transform once-sleepy Bermuda into a "Gibraltar of the West," transforming the island into a well-fortified western Atlantic British naval base and dockyard. Royal engineers designed breakwaters, boat slips, barracks, wharves, a victualing yard, and a fortified keep. Construction—including massive land reclamation—began in 1809 and continued through to the 20th century. Initially, this construction work was carried out by black slaves, but after emancipation in 1834, Britain shipped over thousands of convict laborers from England and Ireland. Housed in converted warships called prison hulks off Her Majesty's Dockyard, convicts quarried the region's hard limestone and, block by handsawn block, built what eventually became a

Spirit of Bermuda

In the "Age of Sail," Bermudians were renowned for innovative methods of boatbuilding and their sailing prowess. A nonprofit group is rekindling those talents in a new generation of Bermudians. The **Bermuda Sloop Foundation** (12 Wesley St., Hamilton, tel. 441/737-5667, www.bermudasloop.org) designed, built, and, in 2006, launched an 85-foot (107 feet with bowsprit) sail-training schooner, which is now inspiring maritime interest in young Bermudians and also teaching visitors about the island's proud past.

The design of *Spirit of Bermuda* is based on the rig of an actual vessel that sailed out of Bermuda in the mid-19th century. It features three heavily raked masts, the tallest in the middle, and a single boom on the mizzen. The main and foresail sheet like a jib, slightly overlapping the mast, and another jib is set forward on the schooner's long bowsprit. It has been adapted for safety reasons from the original Bermuda sloop design, which, while fast, challenged crews with its massive amount of sail—a huge, gaff-rigged mainsail and a square topsail. By contrast, *Spirit*'s design is nimble but more akin to the "Bermudian schooner" hull whose design evolved into the modern yacht.

Noted for their speed and durability, cedar-made Bermuda sloops were the envy of the Atlantic maritime world throughout the 18th century, with many countries adapting the rig for their own use. Such sloops were used for trade throughout the Caribbean and North Atlantic, for privateering, and for illicit pirating; in fact, they were often captured by pirates who coveted their getaway abilities.

Spirit of Bermuda was launched from a boatyard in Rockport, Maine, and now operates a full ocean sail-training program for Bermuda youth. Berthed at Dockyard near the ferry dock, the ship is also hired out for corporate team-building initiatives and private group charters (maximum 45 people). Various island stores also sell *Spirit*-monogrammed clothing and baseball caps.

self-contained "Little England" of military barracks, a prison, a hospital, warehouses, and munitions storage buildings, encircled by massive bastions, gun placements, and ramparts.

The payoff was immediate for Britain. In the War of 1812 with the United States, Britain launched its attack on Washington from the Bermuda Dockyard, its ships of the line successfully sacking and burning the city. Over the next century and a half, Dockyard's Grassy Bay anchorage and sheltered docks catered to Britain's greatest warships, which evolved from tall-masted men-of-war and ironclads armed with cannons to steam-driven dreadnoughts and diesel-turbine frigates bearing World War II torpedoes. The area also supported thousands of naval personnel and civilian staff.

The British operated an apprentice program at Dockyard in the 20th century, training a generation of Bermudians in the skilled trades of masonry, engineering, and electronics; some of these tradesmen are still alive today. The Royal Navy finally pulled up stakes in 1951, closing its operations at the Dockyard. The area became public land, but it was not until the 1970s and 1980s that a major renovation campaign transformed the Victorian military buildings into retail centers, restaurants, and artists' studios. Responsibility for the area now lies with the semipublic West End Development Corporation (WedCo), which has restored some of Dockyard's historic buildings, converting portions for loft-living and encouraging further revitalization of the peninsula.

The National Museum of Bermuda (formerly the Bermuda Maritime Museum), located in the six-acre fortress Keep at Dockyard's westernmost section, was opened in 1975. The museum's Commissioner's House, a landmark 1820s building made of limestone and prefabricated iron, was restored and opened in 2000 as a cultural heritage museum.

SIGHTS

The entire Dockyard, with its historic wharves and restored military buildings, is an attraction unto itself—even without its shops and museum. Feel free to stroll around the whole area, where tourist attractions sit cheek by jowl with working boatyards, sailmakers, and marine service centers. Most of the shops and visitors services hug the waterfront, along Clocktower Parade, the Camber Road, Maritime Lane, and Dockyard Terrace. You can watch glassblowing demonstrations, see ceramics being fired, and watch a cedar crafter work beauty from gnarled tree limbs. Walk out along **King's Wharf** or **Heritage Wharf,** where scores of vessels, from fishing craft to private sailing and motor yachts, sit in a marina near giant cruise ships at the West End throughout the April-November season. Opposite the entrance to the National Museum of Bermuda is the 1831 **Cooperage,** a historic building where barrels for preserving foodstuffs in salt were manufactured. Today it houses the Frog & Onion Pub. Two forges are on display in the atrium by the cinema and craft market. On the other side of the atrium lies the **Victualling Yard,** where high walls protected the Royal Naval fleet's food and drink from theft. Today, picnic benches near the wide-open lawns make it a good lunch spot.

★ National Museum of Bermuda

Bermuda's largest and most-visited attraction, the **National Museum of Bermuda** (The Keep, 15 Maritime Ln. at the northern point of the Royal Naval Dockyard, tel. 441/234-1333, fax 441/234-1735, www.bmm.bm, 9:30am-5pm daily, last admission 4pm, closed Christmas Day, $12 adults, children under 16 free) combines a spectacular property with historic buildings and fascinating exhibits, artifacts, and cultural heritage displays. Dolphin Quest is also based inside the property, allowing viewing of the dolphins even if you don't participate in its programs, which require advance reservations.

A National Museum of Bermuda exhibit showcases the legacy of shipwrecks.

The museum's property was expanded from 10 to 15 acres and renamed in 2009 when the Bermuda government approved the transfer of the historic Casemate Barracks (a prison during the 1960-80s) and adjacent buildings and fortifications at Dockyard's entrance to the formerly named Bermuda Maritime Museum. The move essentially restored the site to its 19th-century military footprint encompassing all the fortifications of the Dockyard and historic buildings within, including the dramatic Northwest Rampart, linking the Keep fortress with the Casemate area. Although the Casemate Barracks is closed for restoration over the next several years, the museum will eventually put exhibits in the newly acquired buildings and open the entire site to the public.

Until then, the museum remains headquartered in the Keep, a stronghold built within the fortified Dockyard to protect the entire Dockyard against attack by land or sea (though it never had to). The citadel has seven bastions and ramparts, reinforced by casemated gun emplacements with lines of sight sweeping the Great Sound and North and South Shores.

In the museum's lower grounds, the cavernous **Queen's Exhibition Hall,** where 4,860 kegs of gunpowder were once stored, has been updated with "Shipwreck Island," a compelling showcase of early shipwrecks, including artifacts from the *Sea Venture,* Spanish gold, and rare 17th-century ship rigging. The exhibit also explores life aboard ships, and underwater archaeology. Across the lawn is the **Boatloft,** where traditional Bermuda fitted dinghies are on display, along with other island craft. The famous pilot gig *Victory,* fully rigged, and the century-old racing yacht *Dainty* are prize maritime treasures. There are also exhibits on fishing and turtling in this building, distinguished by its clock tower. Children like to climb on the regal statue of Neptune, Greek god of the sea, out in the Keep Yard.

Kids will also love the **Museum Playground,** opened in 2014 behind the QEH, where a 21-foot lighthouse and slide—ensnared by a 70-foot green moray eel—will inspire loads of pint-sized adventures. An interactive playhouse with exhibits on local history is planned for 2015.

Leading to the upper grounds from the ticket office is an intriguing exhibit created inside the atmospheric **High Cave Magazine.** "Prisoners in Paradise" details the story of Dockyard's convict prisoners and Bermuda's Boer War prisoners, groups who left their legacies in the form of beautiful carved woodwork and stone artifacts.

The crown jewel of the museum, however, is **Commissioner's House** on the upper grounds, the grand home of the Dockyard's civilian commissioner. It's a building unlike any other in Bermuda, and one that—even if you're not interested in its exhibits—offers a spectacular vantage point. From the top-floor wraparound veranda, the sweeping panorama of the entire Dockyard is revealed, as well as the glistening turquoise seascapes of both the North and South Shores. The world's first cast-iron building, its girders, red brick, and flagstones were shipped from England in the 1820s, while its three-foot-thick walls consist of hard limestone quarried from the Dockyard. Restored in a mammoth 20-year campaign, the building reopened in 2000 as a museum. Three floors of exhibits fill Commissioner's House, from rooms of rare Bermuda maps to those showcasing notes and coins, including historic Hogge money—the island's first currency. Other rooms on the first floor are dedicated to exhibits detailing topics of cultural and social importance: the transatlantic slave trade and slavery in Bermuda; the Newport Bermuda Race; and the stories of Portuguese and West Indian immigrants. The second floor's dining rooms pay tribute to the various military in Bermuda, with both the British Navy and U.S. Navy highlighted with photographs and artifacts. Take a look also at the stunning 36-seat dining table in the Commissioner's Room, once a wartime mess hall, which now houses a collection of contemporary maritime art on loan from the Bank of Bermuda Foundation.

Downstairs on the ground floor, a dozen interlocking rooms contain the exhibit *Bermuda's Defence Heritage*, detailing the story of local defense, from the forts and cannons of the 17th century to Bermudian vets of World War II. Military uniforms, medals, and munitions vividly depict the role tiny Bermuda played on the world stage. A documentary film here includes interviews with local veterans. There's also the story of women at war: the island's female military members who served overseas and the famous "censorettes"—young Englishwomen headquartered at the Hamilton Princess Hotel who were trained to sift through incoming mail and telecommunications, checking for coded messages being sent to Germany.

And don't miss a towering mural in Pillared Hall (containing the rear interior staircase), where Bermudian artist Graham Foster spent three and a half years recreating Bermuda's history in 1,000 square feet of floor-to-ceiling detail. The artwork was officially opened by the Queen in 2009. Accessible from the first floor or ground floor, the hall is located in the northwest corner of the museum, an artistic spectacle that has won rave reviews for Foster's prodigious talent and spawned a 2011 coffee-table book.

A major player in the island's heritage protection scene, the National Museum is also home to a conservation center, where artifacts found on local shipwrecks or terrestrial sites are preserved. The museum coordinates with historians, archaeologists, and teams from abroad to organize joint field trips and dives throughout the year. Books published by the museum press are sold in island bookstores.

Museum visitors can explore the historic windblown ramparts and gun placements around the Keep's perimeter, where Bermuda's only flock of sheep graze—natural lawnmowers for the property. Museum admission also allows you to view the dolphins of **Dolphin Quest** (15 Maritime Ln., tel. 441/234-4464, fax 441/234-4992, www.dolphinquest.org, 9:30am-4:30pm), located at the Keep Pond on the lower grounds.

Casemate Prison

Looming over the southern side of Dockyard is the now-closed Casemate Prison, or Casemate Barracks, a former military barracks for Royal Marines built by convicts in the 1830s. The grim two-story structure is made of hard area limestone, its thick walls and vaulted roof built to sustain enemy cannon and mortar fire. When the British Navy left Dockyard in 1951, "Casemates," as it's called locally, became the island's main prison for housing convicted criminals over the next four and a half decades. Casemate Prison closed in 1995, when a new prison facility, Westgate, was built just outside the Dockyard gates on Pender Road. Casemates is not open to the public, but the National Museum of Bermuda has taken over management of the property with plans to turn it into heritage exhibit space.

BEACHES

Snorkel Park Beach (31 Maritime Ln., tel. 441/234-6989, www.snorkelparkbeach.com, 9am-6pm daily Apr.-Nov., entrance $5, children 12 and under free), the Dockyard's only beach, offers a fun-packed experience. Walk through the limestone tunnel at the northwest corner of Dockyard (alongside the public playground and fountain) to rent water sports equipment, snorkel gear, lounge chairs, and umbrellas, or eat and drink at **Hammerheads Bar & Grill,** the on-site eatery. The beach is small but clean, and its waters offer good snorkeling at the foot of the National Museum of Bermuda's towering ramparts. Reef areas farther out in the shallow bay are also teeming with marinelife. Kids love the pontoons for jumping into the water. A **Fantasea Diving** outlet situated within the park offers learn-to-scuba (two and a half hours, $100 per person), rentals of pedalboats, snorkels, and kayaks, plus aqua scooter adventures (two hours, $69 per person) and a Jet Ski Safari ($145, one hour). Snorkel Park has large bathrooms as well.

ENTERTAINMENT AND EVENTS

Nightlife

Laid-back resort by day, **Snorkel Park Beach** (31 Maritime Ln., tel. 441/234-6989, www.snorkelparkbeach.com, 10pm-3am Mon., Wed., Thurs., and Sat. in season, $10 cover charge for ages 18-plus only, valid ID required) turns nightclub when the sun goes down, attracting crowds of islanders and visitors with regular happy hours at its open-air **Club Aqua,** beach parties featuring top local DJs and live music, limbo dancers and gombeys, and special dance events that last until the wee hours and require smart-casual dress throughout the summer months. Closed November-April.

Floating bar **Calico Jack's** (tel. 441/504-5225, 11am-1am daily in season) looks like a beat-up pirate vessel—and that's the whole point. The converted ferry now doubles as a booze-cruise private charter that sometimes crashes the party in Hamilton, or an all-day bar when moored near the moongate outside Heritage Wharf. DJ nights and themes like Thirsty Thursday and Sunday Rumday have proved popular, and although walking the plank is optional, many patrons swear jumping off the bow between rounds is the highlight.

Cinema

Owned by Hamilton's Liberty Theatre group, **Neptune Cinema** (The Cooperage Bldg., Victualling Yard, 4 Maritime Ln., tel. 441/292-7296) is the West End's only cinema; it usually gets movies after they have shown at Hamilton's Liberty Theatre. The friendly staff sells popcorn and candy, but don't expect an IMAX-style screening.

Events

Heritage Nights (6:30pm-9pm May-Sept.) is the West End equivalent of Hamilton's Harbour Nights, a Thursday-night street-festival extravaganza of food, outdoor arts and crafts, and live entertainment. Ferries offer special service for the evening, and the Clocktower's shops stay open, too.

SHOPPING

Clocktower Mall

Clocktower Mall (9am-6pm summer, 10am-5pm winter daily, closed Christmas Day and Good Friday) is the West End's main shopping center, with more—and busier—retail outlets than Somerset Village, particularly on weekends and during the cruise ship season, when the mall gets swamped with passengers. Note that many stores here keep shorter winter hours, as the Dockyard reverts to quiet maritime enterprises once cruise season is over. There are ATMs, washrooms, and air-conditioning in here.

Beautiful kilim rugs, hanging lanterns, ceramics, shawls, and clothing from **Grand Bazaar** (tel. 441/234-4646, www.grandbazaarbda.com) are brought in from Turkey by husband-and-wife team Bulent and Teresa Ganal. Shipping to the United States, Canada, or U.K. can be provided.

Boyd and Muna Vallis also run a husband-and-wife operation, **Fair Trade** (tel. 441/234-5657), with carved wooden animals, wind chimes, jewelry, sarongs, and beautiful trinkets from Indonesia.

A few women's fashion outlets, such as **Orchid,** cater to West End fashionistas, and

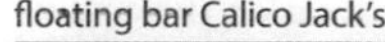
floating bar Calico Jack's

there are several stores—**Bermuda Triangle, Littlest Drawbridge, Dockyard Lines**—that sell Bermuda t-shirts, cedar trinkets, ornaments, and other island souvenirs.

Carole Holding Studio (tel. 441/238-7310, www.caroleholding.bm) carries the artist's painted mailboxes, postcards, cutting boards, and mugs based on her island watercolors.

New on the block is **Bermuda Fudge Company** (tel. 441/533-8343, www.bermudafudgeco.com), which opened in 2014 selling its own gluten-free fudge ($13 per half pound) in flavors from peanut butter crunch to mint chocolate swirl.

West End branch stores of Front Street's **A. S. Cooper** (tel. 441/234-4156), **Crisson** (tel. 441/234-2223), **E. R. Aubrey Jewellers** (tel. 441/234-4577), **Davison's** (tel. 441/234-0959), and **Calypso** (tel. 441/295-2112) are also located here.

Camber Road

On Camber Road, just around the corner from the Clocktower Mall, **Makin' Waves** (tel. 441/234-5319, www.makinwaves.bm, 9am-6pm daily) has the West End outlet of its popular swimwear and beachgear store. The large 2,000-square-foot space is a giant surf shop with everything for fun "in, on, or under the water," in the words of owner Stuart Joblin. This includes swimwear and shades by Maui Jim and Oakley; a full range of snorkeling equipment; souvenirs; casual wear from brands like Billabong, Rip Curl, Roxy, and Quiksilver; sandals, flip-flops, and board shorts; and skim and body boards, as well as large standup paddleboards.

Bermuda Clayworks (tel. 441/234-5116, fax 441/234-3136, www.bermudaclayworks.com, 9am-6pm or later daily in summer, 10am-5pm daily in winter) has a floor full of bright ceramics for sale and a worldwide shipping service so you don't have to lug breakables home.

You can watch free glassblowing and flame-working demonstrations at **Dockyard Glassworks** (tel. 441/234-4216, fax 441/234-3813, www.dockglass.com, 8am-9pm daily in summer, 9am-5pm daily in winter), where artists create beautiful art glass in the Venetian tradition. An adjoining retail gallery sells the rainbow of glassworks, which make elegant souvenirs and gifts, including Christmas ornaments. Adjoining the little factory is the **Bermuda Rum Cake Company** (tel. 441/234-4216, fax 441/234-3813, www.bermudarumcakes.com, 8am-5pm daily, or until 9pm when cruise ships are in port). Sample nine different flavors of the island's favorite dessert, including black rum, rum swizzle, dark chocolate rum, and banana rum.

Maritime Lane

Opposite the entrance to the National Museum of Bermuda, the 20-year-old **Bermuda Craft Market** (4 Maritime Ln., tel. 441/234-3208, fax 441/234-0823, 9:30am-5pm daily in summer, 10am-5pm daily in winter) is a co-op that sells the work of more than 60 artists, a collection that includes cedar crafts, candles, Christmas ornaments, needlework, quilts, ceramics, and batiks. There's also a section full of rare Bermuda books ("Bermudaphile treasures") and contemporary editions. Sample Bermuda food products like ginger beer or jam, and meet artists who give demonstrations of crafts such as banana doll-making or jewelry creation throughout the high season.

Next to the Bermuda Craft Market, with a cherry-red English phone box outside, is the **Bermuda Arts Centre** (tel. 441/234-2809, www.artbermuda.bm, 10am-5pm daily, admission free, wheelchair-accessible), one of the key venues for showcasing island artists. Regular seasonal shows (art is for sale), as well as a retail store and resident artists' studios, give visitors a true sense of the vibrant local arts scene. Landscape artist Jonah Jones keeps a studio/gallery here, as do plein air watercolorist Christopher Marson and oil painter Chris Grimes, and renowned cedar craftsman Chesley Trott. Drop into his sweet-smelling workshop, where rough boughs lie ready for transformation into polished works of art.

Trott, who teaches in the prison system, has an impressive collection of cedar pull-toys, including crickets and frogs. His public artworks are somewhat larger—an eight-foot totem pole, intricately carved with Bermudian icons, sits in the Arrivals Hall of L. F. Wade International Airport.

Dockyard Terrace

Island Outfitters (tel. 441/238-4842, 9am-5pm daily, 8am-8pm when cruise ships are in port), located in one of the old two-story naval buildings just steps from the ferry stop, sells T-shirts, tanks, jewelry, and Bermuda souvenirs, including duty-free rum, sherry peppers, and pepper jam (must be ordered by 1pm the day your of cruise ship's departure). It's a popular WiFi zone too, with tables outside for catching up on email, news, and social media.

SPORTS AND RECREATION

Water Sports and Tours

Your first stop upon arrival at Dockyard should be either of the two **Island Tour Centre** outlets (tel. 441/236-1300, www.islandtourcentre.com, 8am-6pm summer, 9am-4pm winter), one at the pink hut adjacent to the ferry stop, and the other upstairs at the Island Outfitters building just across the street. Here you can book any type of water or land tour that tickles your fancy; the center acts as a one-stop shop for more than 20 vendors not just at Dockyard, but islandwide (Jet Ski, paragliding, scuba, horseback riding, flyboarding, whale-watching, ecotours). Most of the charter boats operating from Dockyard book tours through the center. Advance bookings and payment can be made via the website. The **Dockyard Watersports Centre** is just a few yards away on the North Arm that connects Maritime Lane to both cruise ship wharves. Numerous vendors operate from this location and keep their vessels and water toys here; their services can be booked directly, or via the Island Tour Centre.

Located on the grounds of the National Museum of Bermuda, **Dolphin Quest** (15 Maritime Ln., tel. 441/234-4464, fax 441/234-4992, www.dolphinquest.org, 9:30am-4:30pm daily, entrance included with museum admission—$10 adults, $8 seniors, children under 13 free—prepaid reservations admitted free) is part of a U.S.-based for-profit group that runs interactive dolphin encounter programs on Big Island and Oahu in Hawaii, and in Bermuda. Different programs are geared to various ages, including young children, and

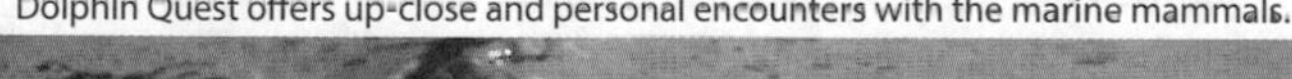

Dolphin Quest offers up-close and personal encounters with the marine mammals.

include programs where participants can get in the water and touch and swim with the boisterous mammals. The cost ranges from $215 for a 30-minute Dolphin Dip to $700 for a five-hour immersion as Trainer for a Day (10 and older). Reservations can be made two months in advance for the popular programs and can be booked online via the Dolphin Quest website, or through its central reservations office (tel. 540/687-8102 or 800/248-3316).

Fantasea Bermuda (two locations, Dockyard Watersports Centre on North Arm Dr., and inside Snorkel Park, tel. 441/236-3483, www.fantasea.bm, summer 8am-6pm daily May-Oct., www.fantasea.bm), the only PADI diving center in Dockyard, also offers snorkeling and sightseeing cruises, pontoon boat rentals, pedal bike Railway Trail excursions, standup paddleboarding, and ecotours. Tours are typically 3.5 hours, and range from $75 to $85 for adults, $55 per child. Dive instruction includes PADI Open Water certification ($600 for group session), as well as Rescue Diver, Divemaster, and EFR courses. Two-tank ($169 per person) and one-tank dives ($119) are four-hour excursions; if you have your own BCD and regulator, you receive a 25 percent discount. Snorkeling passengers can tag along for great reef viewing ($55), or just come for the boat ride itself ($35).

You can walk on the seafloor with **Hartley's Undersea Adventures** (tel. 441/234-2861 or 441/334-7607, toll-free tel. 866/836-3989, www.hartleybermuda.com, $95 adults, observer half-price), which has a pickup/departure point next to the moongate at Heritage Wharf. Morning and afternoon trips of 3-4 hours aboard dive boat *Rainbow Runner* offer shallow-water helmet diving, allowing even nonswimmers to go beneath the surface to see reefs and marinelife by wearing a helmet that receives fresh air pumped from the boat. No tanks, snorkels, or masks are needed, and you can even wear prescription glasses or contact lenses (your head stays dry). Tame angelfish and grunts, familiar with the helmeted visitors, come out to be fed on these expeditions.

Based at Dockyard, award-winning ecotour company **Hidden Gems** (tel. 441/704-0999, www.bermudahiddengems.com, bermyreef-explorer@gmail.com, book via www.island-tourcentre.com, summer 7 hours $150 per person, winter 5 hours $100, no children under 12) offers year-round excursions to different parts of the island, as well as private charter tours, and can also pick up at the Fairmont Southampton Resort and Botanical Gardens' south gate. Owned and run by former teacher Ashley Harris—a Certified Bermudian Ambassador—the company offers visitors a way to experience the "real" Bermuda, with an active itinerary that might include climbing to the top of St. David's Lighthouse, swimming in a crystalline cave, or literally jumping off a cliff. Harris provides each tourgoer with a backpack stocked with all necessary supplies, including snacks, water, a mask and snorkel, flashlight, and umbrella.

Mini-Golf

Commanding an acre of oceanfront property with 180-degree vistas alongside Snorkel Park is Best of Bermuda Award-winner **Bermuda Fun Golf** (tel. 441/ 400-7888, www.fungolf.bm, 10am-10pm daily in summer, 3pm-10pm Fri., noon-10pm Sat. and Sun. in winter, $15 adults, $12 children). The mini-golf complex has become a mecca for fans of the sport thanks to its 18 carefully designed holes that masquerade as some of the world's best: Number 7 at Pebble Beach, the island green at Sawgrass, the "Golden Bell" at Augusta, and the "Braid bravest" at Gleneagles—they're all here. Locals and visitors come for private parties or just a few hours of fun. Relax at the **Caddy Shack Bar** afterwards.

For Kids

Dockyard's tiny-town sort of feel is just the right scale for kids. Getting there is half the fun. The Sea Express fast ferry from the Hamilton ferry terminal ($8 return adults, $4 children 5-16, kids under 5 free) is a blast, even for grown-up kids. The 20-minute ride darts across the breezy Great Sound with lots of boats, houses, and skylines to take in.

At Dockyard, exit the ferry and head right, following the main road around to the **National Museum of Bermuda** (15 Maritime Ln., tel. 441/234-1333, fax 441/234-1735, www.bmm.bm, 9:30am-5pm daily, last admission 4pm, closed Christmas Day, $12 adults, children under 13 free), where kids can learn loads about pirates, shipwrecks, and gold treasure lost in Bermuda waters over the centuries. The lower floor of **Commissioner's House** appeals to young museumgoers with its cavelike maze of interlocking rooms, where exhibits feature giant cannons, forts, and local soldiers from the 1600s to the 1900s. Upstairs, kids can admire sweeping views of the entire North Shore from the building's king-of-the-mountain upper balcony. Just don't let them climb the railing! On the lower grounds, wrap up the visit with time at the **Museum Playground,** opened in 2014, where a zippy slide curves out of a play lighthouse entwined within a giant moray eel structure. An interactive **Playhouse** was to open here in 2015.

Dolphin Quest (15 Maritime Ln., tel. 441/234-4464, www.dolphinquest.org) is located on the southern part of the lower grounds. The mutual appeal of dolphins and kids is adorable, and while actually swimming with the clever mammals is a wonderful experience, just watching them cavort in the Keep Pond is almost as much fun. It's free with admission to the museum. Reservations for dolphin encounters need to be booked in advance; use the organization's website.

Outside, to the right of the museum gates, is the **Dockyard Playground** (admission free), complete with pirate ship apparatus to scramble aboard, captain's wheels to turn, and a tunneled slide to descend There are swings, too. Kids can spend a good chunk of time here, except in the heat of summer when it's grilling by midmorning. If they get too hot, there's a fountain designed perfectly for youngsters to get soaked in.

Through the adjacent gate is **Snorkel Park Beach** (31 Freeport Rd., tel. 441/234-6989, closed Nov.-Mar.), a great little cove for kids, with tons of amenities and playthings. Rent a noodle, mask and snorkel, or a floating chair. Adults like the beachside bar, just a few yards from the water's edge. There are large washrooms and a restaurant serving hot dogs, burgers, and other lunchtime staples sure to please waterlogged youngsters. Next door, **Bermuda Fun Golf** (tel. 441/ 400-7888, www.fungolf.bm, 10am-10pm daily in summer, 3pm-10pm Fri., noon-10pm Sat. and Sun. in winter, $15 adults, $12 children) is a hit with hackers of all ages; children's parties are often held here.

Alternatively, the **Frog & Onion Pub** (The Cooperage, Maritime Ln., tel. 441/234-2900, www.frogandonion.bm) serves up hearty pub grub inside or under umbrellas on the outdoor terrace. There's a large games room in the back, with coin-operated video games and a pool table. At Dockyard's entrance is **Freeport Seafood Restaurant** (1 Freeport Rd., tel. 441/234-1692, www.freeportseafood.com), with its tempting menu of authentic local fish cakes and fish sandwiches. If the family saves room for dessert, don't miss **Nannini's Häagen-Dazs,** a popular ice cream bar in the **Clocktower Mall.** Bermuda kids make Mom and Dad drive the length of the island just to come here for the two-scoop sugar cones, numerous rich flavors—and rainbow sprinkles.

Finally (if the kids are still awake), **Neptune Cinema** (4 Maritime Ln., tel. 441/234-2923) occasionally shows children's matinees, mainly during midterm breaks and Easter and summer holidays. Get some popcorn and candy and relax in the air-conditioned interior, which is smaller than some home theaters.

ACCOMMODATIONS

To date, there are no visitor accommodations in the Royal Naval Dockyard, though various historic buildings here have been converted to loftlike living spaces for locals.

FOOD

Cafés, Pubs, and Takeout

Now part of the Hog Penny-owned group, **Frog & Onion Pub** (The Cooperage, Maritime Ln., tel. 441/234-2900, www.frogandonion.bm, lunch 11:30am-4pm, dinner 5:30pm-9:30pm Mon.-Sat., lunch noon-4pm, dinner 5:30pm-9pm Sun., free WiFi), serves up much-loved pub grub to Dockyard locals and tourists alike. Starters include German pretzels ($9.95), nachos, and deep-fried pickles ($10.95); salads are inventive, with southwest chicken and blackened wahoo ($19.95). And old favorites never die: fish 'n' chips ($23.95), bangers and mash ($17.95), shepherd's pie, and chicken balti curry (both $19.95). The pub also offers quiz nights, happy hour specials, and live entertainment most evenings, plus kids' activities on Sunday afternoons (magic shows, free ice cream, kids' menus). The outside patio is a popular WiFi hot spot.

Situated in a former British naval officer's cottage, ★ **The Dockyard Pastry Shop** (12 Dockyard Terrace, at the entrance to the Victualling Yard, tel. 441/232-2253, 9am-5pm daily) serves up cappuccino, pastries, desserts, gourmet sandwiches, quiche, pies, and paninis. Customers can enjoy lunch on the little patio, or head indoors to the upstairs room. It also serves beer and wine. Anglophiles can enjoy afternoon tea 2pm-5pm with fresh-baked scones, clotted cream, and marmalade.

With its shady terrace overlooking a private cove, **Hammerheads Bar & Grill** (Snorkel Park Beach, 31 Maritime Ln., tel. 441/234-6989, www.snorkelparkbeach.com, 9am-5pm daily, bar 11am-3am daily, closed Nov.-Mar.) is popular for its burgers, sandwiches, fries, snacks, and cold drinks, including frozen alcoholic and virgin cocktails.

Fish sandwiches, fish cakes, fish 'n' chips—you get the picture, although **Freeport Seafood Restaurant** (1 Freeport Rd., just inside Dockyard's main gates, tel. 441/234-1692, fax 441/234-3605, www.freeportseafood.com, 11:30am-10pm daily, $6-19) serves burgers, pizzas, and sushi, too.

Nannini's Häagen-Dazs (Clocktower Mall, tel. 441/234-2474) has moved to new, larger premises at the mall's front entrance to accommodate the eager crowds who used to line up out the door for scoops of decadence (waffle cone $5.50). Still very popular, now with sit-down tables where you can chill out in the mall's welcome air-conditioning. It serves Starbucks coffee too.

Like its Hamilton outlet, **Bermy Berry** (Gazebo No. 2, Dockyard Terrace, tel. 441/292-3411, www.bermyberry.com, free WiFi) serves up fair-trade coffee and weekly-changing flavors of its delicious frozen yogurt, with toppings from fresh fruit to gummy bears.

Buzz Dockyard (Dockyard Pharmacy, 7 Camber Rd., tel. 441/279-5551, 8am-5pm Mon.-Fri., 10am-5pm Sat. and Sun.), one of several Buzz outlets throughout the island, is perfect for a takeout gourmet coffee, smoothies, cold drinks, or sandwiches.

International

Pizza and pasta are king at **Café Amici** (in the Clocktower Mall, 5 Freeport Rd., tel. 441/234-5009, www.amicibermuda.com, 9am-10:30pm daily April-Oct., 9am-5pm Mon.-Thurs. and Sun., 9am-9:30pm Fri. and Sat. Nov.-Mar.), the West End's only Italian restaurant. The family-style eatery is located in the western corner of the Clocktower Mall. Chef/owner Livio Ferigo has created a comfort-food menu based on his childhood favorites, including pastas ($19-24) and pizzas ($16-23). He goes local for Sunday breakfast, however, offering a spread of traditional Bermudian codfish and potatoes 9am-noon.

Sister restaurant **Bone Fish Bar & Grill** (6 Dockyard Terrace, tel. 441/234-5151, www.bonefishbermuda.com, lunch 11:30am-5pm, dinner 6pm-10:30pm Mon.-Sat., noon-6pm Sun., bar 11:30am-3am) serves up a wide menu of Bermuda seafood, pasta, steak, jerk chicken, salads, and sandwich specials. The front patio just steps from the ferry dock is a shady people-watching place in the afternoon, while the giant wooden deck commanding a large outside corner features live bands and DJs for nighttime entertainment, as well as salsa (Mon.), karaoke (Wed.), and reggae (Thurs.).

INFORMATION AND SERVICES

Dockyard has three **Visitor Information Centres:** Two operate in the cruise ship terminals (King's Wharf and Heritage Wharf) only when a ship is in port; the main outlet sits in Gazebo 2 near the ferry dock at **Dockyard Terrace** (tel. 441/542-7104, 8am-4pm daily, 8am-8pm when ships are in port). Each sells bus and ferry tickets and passes, and provides information and advice on local tours and attractions.

Dockyard's **Community Policing Office** (2 Sally Port Lane, North Basin, tel. 441/234-1010, 8am-8pm) was established in 2014 as an auxiliary police base in Sandys. The main police station is in Somerset Village.

At the area's only liquor store, you can find everything from cold drinks and coffee to fishing tackle and boating supplies. **The Dock Shop** (Pier 41, tel. 441/238-4141, 9am-5pm Mon.-Sat., 10am-6pm Sun.), located at the entrance to Dockyard on the waterside, has a marine gas station alongside; the facility provides berthing and bunkering services to vessels docked here and to those just passing through.

The Dockyard Pharmacy (7 Camber Rd., tel. 441/279-5410, 10am-6pm Mon.-Sat., noon-6pm Sun. and holidays) is a full-service pharmacy stocking prescriptions, international newspapers, beauty and fashion accessories, souvenirs, and a West End outlet of **Buzz** café.

ATMs are outside the western entrance to the Clocktower Mall, on Dockyard Terrace, and at the Visitor Information Centres.

Public toilets are located inside the Clocktower Mall, in a small building on Dockyard Terrace, outside Bermuda Craft Market, inside the National Museum of Bermuda's lower grounds, and on two upper floors of Commissioner's House.

The whole of Dockyard is considered a **WiFi** hotspot, though some areas such as restaurants and cafés may be better for getting online.

GETTING THERE AND AROUND

Buses

Bus service to Dockyard has suffered its share of challenges, as the system has faced a quantum leap in the number of visitors after Dockyard became a port for mega-ships. But when it's working properly, the bus system is efficient and frequent—it's also scenic if you take route 7, which goes via the South Shore beaches (route 8 also travels between Hamilton and Dockyard via Middle Road). Buses leave Hamilton every 15 minutes for the West End. The 14-zone journey ($4.50) takes about an hour. Bus stops are located in front of the National Museum of Bermuda and in front of the Clocktower Mall. For more information, contact the **Department of Public Transportation** (tel. 441/292-3851).

Ferries

The **Sea Express** (tel. 441/295-4506, www.seaexpress.bm) Blue Route operates regularly between Hamilton and Dockyard from morning (8:30am) to night on weekdays (the last ferry leaves Dockyard at 9pm), with less-frequent service on Saturdays, Sundays, and public holidays. The service runs every half hour throughout most of the day. Most runs are Hamilton-Dockyard direct (both ways). Along the way, you'll see: Front Street's facade; the lavish harborfront mansions of Pembroke's Fairylands and Point Shares neighborhoods; landmark Two-Rock Passage, where the liners come through; and the islands of the Great Sound. The breezy ride takes just 20 minutes; sit up on the sunny top deck (which features a salt spray on very windy days), or escape the heat in the main air-conditioned cabin. Cash is not accepted on ferries; buy tokens, tickets, or cost-effective one-day or multiday passes from the ferry terminal or Visitor Information Centres in Hamilton, St. George's, or Dockyard. Regular one-way fare to Dockyard is $4.50 adults, $2.50 children 5-16, kids under 5 free.

Scooters and Bicycles

Oleander Cycles (King's Wharf, Royal Naval Dockyard, tel. 441/234-2764, 8:30am-5:30pm daily) rents single- and double-seater scooters, as well as mountain bikes. Standard or deluxe (two-person) scooters can be rented by anyone aged 16 or older. Rates ($55 standard/$65 double for one day, $225 standard/$266 double per week, $17/$21 per day after seven days) include scooter delivery and pickup (or hotel pickup), first tank of gas, helmet, lock, basket, $30 third-party insurance, and islandwide roadside service for breakdowns (24-hour helpline). Pedal cycles can be rented for $40 per day, or $175 per week.

Taxis

If cruise ships are in port, there are usually lots of taxis in and around Dockyard. Taxis stands can be found outside the gates of the National Museum at Dockyard, and in front of the Clocktower Mall. Some operators are qualified tour guides—look for the special Blue Flag sticker or flag.

Tours

The Bermuda Train Company (6 Valley Rd., Paget, tel. 441/236-5972) operates a return shuttle ($15 May-Nov.) from the Dockyard Watersports Centre near the ferry dock to Daniel's Head National Park, home to several beaches, free WiFi, refreshments, and loads of water sports rentals. The 20-minute journey, which can be booked in advance through the Island Tour Centre, travels through Somerset Village en route.

The **Horseshoe Bay Shuttle** via bus ($16 return) is run by the Bermuda government and West End Development Corporation. The bus leaves the King's Wharf terminal regularly for the beach between 8:30am and 3pm, with a first stop at Church Bay; the last shuttle back to Dockyard is at 6pm.

You can see Dockyard aboard a Segway "human transporter" with the help of **Segway Tours** (tel. 441/504-2581, www.segway.bm or www.islandtourcentre.com, 10am-4pm May-Oct.). Look for the yellow double-decker bus parked at the Camber Road intersection with Dockyard Terrace; advance bookings also can be made online or at the

A courtesy shuttle carries cruise passengers to Dockyard's shops and eateries..

Island Tour Centre outlets at Dockyard or Hamilton. A 90-minute tour includes a video and training session to help you master the electric-powered, self-balancing scooter. The cost is $75, with weight and age restrictions.

Bermudian **Beau Evans** operates a blue-and-white free courtesy shuttle train that loops around Dockyard itself. If you want to take a load off, hop aboard for a ride between shops and restaurants.

Somerset Village

So small that you might whiz right by it if you're not paying attention, Somerset Village is a quaint, historic little community hugging picturesque Mangrove Bay. Mangrove Bay Road slopes through it to Dockyard. Pastel storefronts, wooden verandas, and the kind of old-time languor you thought the Internet had forever vanquished make Somerset a relaxing little community. Lanes like "Tween Walls," which run off on either side of Mangrove Bay Road, are worth strolling. Take a swim in the palm-fringed bay, where the surface looks like a mirror when the wind is right, or from the public dock, where freight was once offloaded from ships onto horse-drawn carts. Like Flatts Village, Somerset was a key maritime port for trade and boating around the island, in the days before roads and motorized vehicles linked the parishes. Illicit cargo was often taken to harbors like these to evade customs duties in Hamilton or St. George's. Today, Somerset doesn't seem capable of such energy. Your time here is best spent sampling the several eateries and moseying around the sleepy shops. As part of a West End tour, it only takes a few hours to experience the village properly, though you might end up staying longer.

BEACHES

Mangrove Bay Beach, with its line of coconut palms and pile of wooden dinghies, offers a taste of the way much of Bermuda used to be, and still is in these parts. Swim in the shallow, clear bay where schools of fry jump at dawn. There's plenty of parking in front of the post office.

ENTERTAINMENT AND EVENTS

Nightlife

There's not much of a nightlife scene in Somerset, aside from lively bars at two village establishments, **Somerset Country Squire** (10 Mangrove Bay Rd., tel. 441/234-0105, 11am-1am daily) and **Salt Rock Grill** (27 Mangrove Bay Rd., tel. 441/234-4502, bar tel. 441/234-4503, fax 441/234-4504, saltrockgrill@transact.bm, noon-11pm daily).

Non-Mariners Race

"Anything but a boat" is the battle cry of participants vying for honors in Mangrove Bay's annual July **Non-Mariners Race** (tel. 441/234-2248). Organized by the Sandys Boat Club, the Sunday afternoon affair features teams of Bermudians gussied up as pirates or in top hats, trying to sail across the bay in assorted craft made from anything you might least imagine had the ability to float. Needless to say, most end up in the drink. It's a laugh, for participants and the crowd of onlookers, many of whom arrive by boat and form party-style raft-ups that remain the entire day. Check out their "Non-Official" Facebook page.

★ Bermuda Fitted Dinghy Races

Mangrove Bay and its nearby shoreline provide some of the best vantage points from which to watch the Bermuda dinghy races. The much-loved tradition, featuring the island's trademark vessels vying for weekly honors amid mountains of sail and a flotilla of

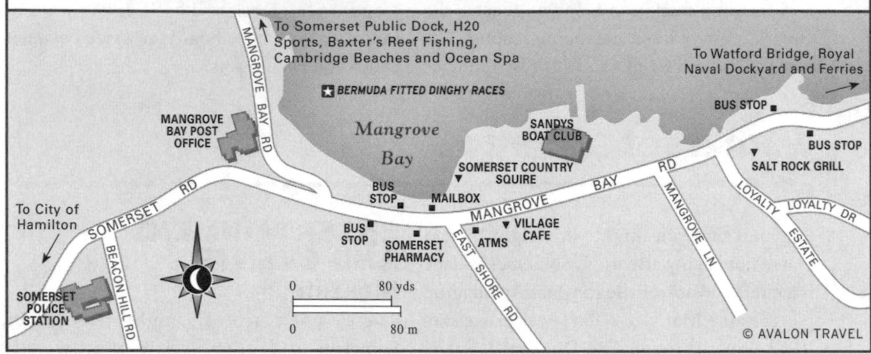

spectator boats, is one of the summer's highlights. Dinghy races are held every Sunday afternoon, alternating between different parts of Bermuda, namely St. George's Harbour, Granaway Deep in the Great Sound, and Mangrove Bay, where they sail from **Sandys Boat Club** (tel. 441/234-2248). The best part is when crew members jump overboard to lighten the load (they usually get rescued by passing friends or swim to raft-ups, where they can cheer on their boat with a beer or rum). Call the club for schedule details. Just around a few corners, on Watford Island, the **West End Sailboat Club** (tel. 441/234-1252, kitchen tel. 441/234-2523) organizes the annual East-to-West Comet Race.

SHOPPING

Platinum Entertainment (23 Somerset Rd., tel. 441/234-3737, 11am-9:30pm) sells DVDs, video games, a selection of reggae, soul, R&B, and urban hit music, as well as soaps, incense, and oils.

Knowledgeable, friendly staff make shopping a delight at **Somerset Pharmacy** (49 Mangrove Bay Rd., tel. 441/234-2484, sompharm@northrock.bm, 8am-6pm Mon., Tues., Thurs. and Fri., 8am-8pm Wed., 8am-5pm Sat., noon-2pm Sun.), which, aside from its dispensary and regular drugstore items, sells tourist items such as postcards, towels, and souvenirs. But its best items are the well-chosen toys, loads of them, for girls and boys of all ages, rivaling Hamilton stores of quadruple the size. Major-brand dolls, action figures, arts and crafts, balls, board games, baby toys—it's a child's heaven.

Genuine Bermuda linen-blend shorts (pink, yellow, red, $59.95) can be found at the Somerset branch store of **English Sports Shop** (Somerset Rd., tel. 441/234-0770, 10am-5pm Mon.-Sat.), along with linen and wool blazers ($250-275), Bermuda silk ties (sporting longtails, horse and carriage, and Hamilton's pastel skyline), and conservative women's fashions.

SPORTS AND RECREATION

Water Sports

Take to the water to explore by kayak, sailboat, or motorboat from **H2O Sports** (30 King's Pt., Mangrove Bay, tel. 441/234-3082, www.h2osportsbermuda.com, 9am-6pm daily May-Nov.). Single or double kayaks, paddleboards, fishing and snorkel gear, Sunfish ($40 first hour, $10 each extra hour), Hobie Cats ($60 first hour), and 17-foot sailboats and motorboats ($80 first hour, $30 each extra hour) can be rented along with snorkel and fishing gear. It's a perfect way to spend a day in the West End, because there are so many tiny coves, beaches, islands, and islets around this part of the island. Pack a picnic and go exploring the reef-laden South Shore flats or around Mangrove Bay and the Great Sound coastline.

Fishing

Baxter's Reef Fishing (tel. 441/234-2963 or 441/334-9722, www.bermudareeffishing.com, $100 pp, $600 for custom charters for up to six) departs daily from Mangrove Bay public dock at the foot of Cambridge Road. Captain Michael Baxter offers half- and full-day reef-fishing charters in his 32-foot Cape Islander, *Ellen B*. Typical catches are chub, grouper, triggerfish, snapper, porgy, shark, and barracuda; you can catch and release, or take your fish home for dinner. The boat can accommodate up to 10 people.

Spas

Cambridge Beaches' **Ocean Spa** (30 Kings Pt., tel. 441/234-3636, www.cambridgebeaches.com) has seven rooms and offers a full menu of face and body treatments for men and women, plus couples, as well as massage therapy. The De-Stress Muscle Release (80 minutes, $220) and Marine Breeze Facial (60 minutes, $140) allow clients to tap into the fountain of youth. Multihour packages, for example combining a facial with a massage and manicure (Ocean Spa Sampler $287), allow use of the whirlpool, sauna, steam room, lockers, showers, robes, and slippers. Upstairs, Aquarian Baths, a luxurious indoor heated pool with a retractable roof, is also available to spa clients. Half-day (10am-1pm or 2pm-5pm, $40) or full-day (10am-5pm, $65) passes are also a nice way to experience the resort and chill out on vacation.

ACCOMMODATIONS

Over $400

Historic ★ **Cambridge Beaches** (30 Kings Point Rd., tel. 441/234-0331, toll-free tel. 800/468-7300, fax 441/234-3352, www.cambridgebeaches.com, $450-1,300 d, minimum age 16) is one of the island's premier "cottage colonies"—resorts in which units are arranged around a central clubhouse, amid many other facilities. The five-star, 30-acre resort has 94 rooms, four private beaches, a putting green, a croquet lawn, tennis courts, a water sports center, two restaurants, two bars, and a spa. A pool with an infinity edge and waterfall feature is a highlight of the property. In the main house, a paneled library and stuffed floral sofas conjure the ambience of a grand English manse gone tropical. Accommodations range from rooms to suites to a cottage with a private pool. Old-style rooms and suites in

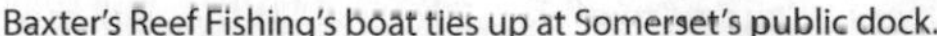
Baxter's Reef Fishing's boat ties up at Somerset's public dock.

cottages, or contemporary condo-style units overlooking Mangrove Bay, are furnished in an island-chic style—mahogany, sisal rugs, rattan, and bold florals leading the way. Amenities include cable TV, Internet hookups, air-conditioning, and king-size beds. Bette Midler, Kenny G, and Natalie Cole have all stayed here over the years. An adults-only resort, it is a favorite for honeymoons, anniversaries, and other couples escapes. It also has a useful dine-around exchange agreement with other West End properties that allows guests to enjoy meals at The Reefs Resort or Bella Vista at Port Royal Golf Course, with the only cost being transportation and beverages.

FOOD

Cafés and Pubs

Home turf of yachties and other neighborhood regulars, the **Somerset Country Squire** (10 Mangrove Bay Rd., tel. 441/234-0105, lunch 11:45am-2:30pm Thurs.-Sat, noon-4pm Sun., dinner 5:30pm-9:30pm daily, $6-25) has a cavelike bar and dining room downstairs that's used throughout the winter, and an alfresco bar and terrace, where fish dinners, fresh lobster, burgers, steak and kidney pies, and filet mignon are popular fare all summer long. A children's menu is offered, too. Live TV sporting events, including NASCAR races and English soccer matches, draw a crowd of locals.

Cambridge Beaches (30 Kings Point Rd., tel. 441/234-0331, www.cambridgebeaches.com) has two casual alfresco cafes: **Breezes** (lunch noon-3pm daily, dinner 7pm-9pm Thurs.-Sat., $9.50-40) is on Long Bay Beach, but open only through the high season (May-Oct.); **Shutters,** at the resort's poolside, is open for lunch year-round (noon-3pm daily, $6-22).

Sandra and Venette run a tight ship at the pocket-size, roadside **Village Café** (29 Mangrove Bay Rd., tel. 441/234-3167, 7:15am-4pm Mon.-Thurs., 7:15am-3am Fri. and Sat.), efficiently whipping up a tasty early-morning breakfast (bacon, egg, toast, coffee $10, omelets $11, Johnny bread $2.75) until 10:30am weekdays, before serving a wide-ranging lunch menu—chowder, burgers ($5.25), corned beef hashcakes, grilled cheese, and Bermuda fish entrées ($15)—to a lineup of locals who appreciate the home-style cooking and easy-on-the-pocket prices, especially in weekend mornings' wee hours. A codfish and potato breakfast is available on alternate weekends.

International

The view—as well as the menu—is a crowd-pleaser at **Salt Rock Grill** (27 Mangrove Bay Rd., tel. 441/234-4502, bar 441/234-4503, fax 441/234-4504, www.saltrockgrillbda.com, lunch noon-5pm, dinner 5:30pm-10pm daily). Wide-open views of Mangrove Bay from its hilltop location bring boaters across the Great Sound for weekend brunches. Sushi (served daily except Mon.) is a big draw, along with pastas ($20), teriyaki, surf and turf, and a catch of the day ($30.75).

Fine Dining

Candlelight dinners are served in ★ **The Tamarisk Room** at Cambridge Beaches (30 Kings Point Rd., tel. 441/234-0331, toll-free tel. 800/468-7300, fax 441/234-3352, www.cambridgebeaches.com, 7pm-9:30pm daily), where cedar-steeped surroundings, dark coral walls, and silver service make for a formal treat. Jacket and tie are optional for male guests, but "elegant-casual" is the suggested dress code. The gourmet, five-course menu changes daily, along with recommended selections from the vintage wine cellar. Appetizers include sparkling pineapple soup ($9), truffle-marinated portobello ($13), and beet-cured wild salmon with banana mousse ($14), while entrées range from turbot fillet ($33) to rack of lamb ($36). For dessert, try the deep-fried Coca-Cola maraschino cherries ($14.50).

INFORMATION AND SERVICES

Mangrove Bay Post Office (55 Mangrove Bay Rd., tel. 441/234-0423, 8am-5pm Mon.-Fri.) offers snail-mail and Internet service. It is the island's most picturesque post office, in a restored historic building a few feet from the sand of Mangrove Bay Beach.

Somerset Pharmacy (49 Mangrove Bay Rd., tel. 441/234-2484, 8am-6pm Mon.-Fri., 8am-5pm Sat., noon-2pm Sun.) offers a dispensary and regular drugstore items, as well as postcards, beach towels, and lots of toys.

One of few independent pharmacies on the island, **Caesar's Pharmacy** (30-32 Somerset Rd., tel. 441/234-0851 or 441/234-0987, fax 441/234-0783, caesarpharm@tbi-net.bm, 9am-7pm Mon.-Sat., 2pm-6pm Sun.) has an efficient dispensary and all the drugstore basics in its small store.

Somerset Police Station (3 Somerset Rd., atop the hill entering Mangrove Bay, tel. 441/234-1010 or 441/234-1011, www.police.bm) is the regional detachment with responsibility for the West End.

Two retail banks have branches in Somerset Village: **Butterfield Bank** (45 Mangrove Bay Rd., tel. 441/234-0048, 9am-4pm Mon.-Fri.) and **HSBC** (31 Mangrove Rd., tel. 441/295-4000, 9am-4:30pm Mon.-Fri.). **ATMs** are located outside both bank branches.

Bud's Wines & Spirits (10 Mangrove Bay Rd., tel. 441/234-1740, 8:30am-8pm Mon.-Sat.), on the main village street alongside the Somerset Country Squire, stocks ice, cigars, bait, beer, and wine.

Public toilets are available at restaurants, Mangrove Bay Post Office, and next to Somerset Police Station.

GETTING THERE AND AROUND

Buses 7 and 8, which travel every 15 minutes between Hamilton and Dockyard, service the village.

The Watford Bridge stop is the closest to Somerset Village, served by the Sea Express Blue Route **ferries** with five scheduled stops throughout the day. The fare is $4.50 (adults), $2.50 (children 5 to12) one-way (tokens or tickets required, no cash or change accepted).

Oleander Cycles has an outlet at Cambridge Beaches (30 Kings Point Rd., tel. 441/234-0331), renting single- and double-seat scooters.

Around Sandys

The environs of Somerset Village and points east as far as the Southampton border encompass a wonderful array of places to leisurely let time pass. Swim at the countless little coves, hike through the several beautiful parks, ogle spectacular ocean views on both shores—and let the hours slide easily by. The region is best seen in a flexible timeframe; even a day of tooling around on a scooter or walking the Railway Trail will give you a truer sense of real life "out West."

SIGHTS

Lagoon Park and the Royal Naval Cemetery

Beyond Dockyard's gates and over one-vehicle-wide Grey's Bridge on Ireland Island South is **Lagoon Park** (sunrise-sunset daily, admission free), a large, quiet chunk of parkland that has a spectacular islet-sprinkled coastline on the Great Sound. Named for the central lagoon, which attracts birdlife, insects, toads, and frogs, the park has lots of picnic tables and grassy lawns, as well as coves and bays for swimming. Nestled alongside the parkland is a large meadowy valley that contains the Royal Naval Cemetery. The early-19th-century graveyard contains intriguing headstones and above-ground cemetery plots, where the lives (and often unfortunate deaths) of naval officers, crewmen, and their families are honored with touching inscriptions. Easter lilies pop up here around Easter, and wildflowers are scattered over the hillside.

Somerset Long Bay Park

Lovely **Somerset Long Bay Park and Nature Reserve** (Daniel's Head Rd. off Cambridge Rd., sunrise-sunset daily, admission free) is co-owned by the Bermuda National Trust and the Bermuda Audubon Society. This coastal mangrove area is a sanctuary for resident and migratory birds. A plot of adjoining private land was purchased to expand the protected zone, which now includes a stretch of pristine coastline. Restoration of the reserve included culling invasive species and replanting endemics, as well as clearing garbage and debris. Located on a quiet stretch far from the noise of road traffic, the grassy park, equipped with a playground set, is a shady place to relax, and the shallow beach, with turtle grass and reefs just a few yards out, is a good spot for snorkeling. It's a popular local beach, too: Bermudian families congregate here for picnics, swimming, and games throughout the summer.

★ Somerset Bridge

The smallest drawbridge in the world, **Somerset Bridge** (Somerset Rd. at Robinson's Marina) has become a quintessential Bermuda icon, featured on postcards and the island's banknotes for almost a century. The bridge's central plank can be raised, an opening just wide enough to permit a yacht's mast to be eased through by someone standing above, thereby allowing vessels to pass between the Great Sound and Ely's Harbour (though this is a rare occurrence in modern times). Built in the 17th century, the structure is one of the most historic points in the parish, connecting Somerset Island to the mainland. A roadside park sits alongside the bridge, a good place for a picnic while watching boats pass through the waterway. The park also connects to the Railway Trail.

★ Fort Scaur and Park

One of the region's loveliest views can be had from a quiet bench atop **Fort Scaur** (Scaur Hill, Somerset Rd., sunrise-sunset daily, admission free), overlooking the whole Great Sound and Dockyard. A telescope allows you to see as far as Fort St. Catherine and St. David's Lighthouse. The West End fort and its surrounding 22 acres of parklands comprise one of the island's most scenic and well-preserved fortifications. Built in the 1870s, the fort was intended to guard the crossing at Somerset Bridge—and to thereby protect against a landward approach by an enemy toward the Dockyard. It was used through

Somerset Bridge is the smallest drawbridge in the world.

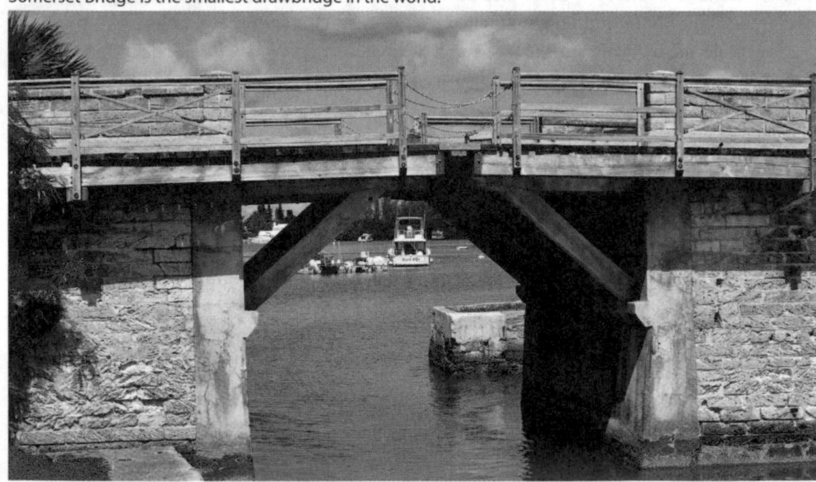

Buy Back Bermuda

A Somerset Long Bay property was the lightning rod for a populist campaign to win back open space for Bermudians.

Bermuda National Trust and Bermuda Audubon Society joined forces in 2004 to launch the "Buy Back Bermuda" campaign, an effort to inspire Bermudians to fight for land that would otherwise fall into the hands of developers—an all-too-common scenario amid the island's ultra-hot real estate market. When a three-acre Sandys property was made available by its owner for a friendly price of $1.7 million—half what it might have won on the open market—Bermudians rallied to raise the money. The land lay next to Somerset Long Bay, an Audubon nature reserve and national park, and its addition would protect the length of the shoreline, creating a public park of almost 10 acres.

In less than a year, the campaign had achieved its goal—and sparked such grassroots enthusiasm that organizers set about looking for other sensitive properties to target under the Buy Back banner. More than 400 people, including schoolchildren, took part in the drive. "We believe it shows the high value Bermudians put on preserving open space," said a BNT spokesman. Since then, Buy Back Bermuda has raised more than $4.5 million to save a total of 14 acres of open space for posterity.

the 1920s; later the American 52nd Coast Artillery mounted two eight-inch railway guns at Scaur Park. The fort, with ramparts, cannons, and gun placements, is surrounded by a defensive ditch, which extends across the length of Somerset Island. There is a steep trail leading eastward through the woods to the Railway Trail on the shoreline below. You can also walk into the galleries flanking the hillside and go through the sally port into the ditch, itself an impressive feat of engineering. Picnic tables and lawns invite relaxation in the adjoining park.

A property on the left as you descend the other side of Scaur Hill, heading out of the West End, is **The Parapet,** the mustard-colored home where artist Georgia O'Keeffe stayed during her visit to Bermuda in the early 20th century. O'Keeffe was recovering from depression at the time, but her charcoal drawings of a banyan tree and banana flowers helped restore her creative energies.

Heydon Trust Estate

Open to the public, the privately owned, 22-acre **Heydon Trust Estate** (Heydon Dr. off Somerset Rd., sunrise-sunset daily, admission free) is a natural enclave of protected woodland, farmers' fields, a couple of private homes, and the charming **Heydon Chapel** atop the hill. Turn in off the main road and follow the country lane all the way to the tiny whitewashed building, which overlooks the Great Sound. It dates back to a 1616 survey of Bermuda, and today it is still used for religious services. Nearby, a walled rose garden contains numerous Chinas, teas, and mystery species; it's considered one of Bermuda's best collections. There are also trails rambling through the extensive cherry forests around the property. The land is a noted birding location.

★ Hog Bay Park

One of Bermuda's most spectacular wild parks, government-owned **Hog Bay Park** (sunrise-sunset daily, admission free) comprises some 38 acres of open space, leading from a roadside parking lot on Middle Road to the coast. Between, there are undulating, shady dirt trails that lead past an ancient limekiln near the entrance, rise past numerous tracts of agricultural fields and cherry, loquat, and spice tree forests, and descend to serpentine seaside trails past prickly pears and the silvery skeletons of Bermuda cedars. While it is Bermuda's third-largest park, and one of its most untamed, Hog Bay is underused; you can find remarkable solitude exploring it in any season, though because of the steep hills, you need to be fairly fit. Follow the main trail down to the shoreline, where there's a beach area at low tide and a beautiful spot for swimming. Sea grass attracts turtles here, and rock pools contain crabs and sergeants major. You can actually explore a long section of the coastline here, with the wide-open horizon of the South Shore flats stretching out as far as you can see. At low tide, the shallows extend for about 1,000 feet, good for snorkeling.

The park, which is used occasionally for cross-country races and mountain biking, is named for Bermuda's wild hogs, which roamed the island when the first settlers arrived in the early 17th century. It's believed that in years prior, passing mariners had offloaded the animals to multiply and create a natural larder at Bermuda that might feed castaways wrecked on the island's treacherous reefs. The former Hog Bay, where settlers found a large herd of the swine in the West End, is now called Pilchard Bay.

BEACHES

The West End's **Glass Beach,** on Ireland Island South, is a repository for washed-up sea glass of all shapes, sizes, and colors. Unlike other coves where you can find sea glass, however, it is entirely composed of glass, with so much piled up that you can't even see the underlying sand. That wind chime-like tinkling you hear as you approach is the glass pieces being turned over by gentle waves rolling in. The beach, not signposted, is located on the southwest shoreline (not the Great Sound side) outside the pillars at the bridge leading into Dockyard. Follow Cochrane Road back from Cockburn's Cut about 650 feet, and you'll find a trail through the casuarina woods (look for the historic stone tower). The beach lies at the foot of the trail.

Black Bay, also on Ireland Island South, opposite the Royal Naval Cemetery, has a gem of a beach that appears only at low tide. Night herons can sometimes be seen standing like statues on the coastal rocks—until they dart for crabs in the shoreline rock pools. Throughout most of the summer, it's a good place for a shallow, calm swim, and there are picnic tables nearby, too.

Somerset Long Bay (turn off Somerset Rd. on to Cambridge Rd. which leads down to the park and shoreline) is the perfect place to cool off, far from traffic and the crowds who frequent the larger South Shore beaches (including Warwick Long Bay) most weekdays. On weekends and public holidays, Somerset Long Bay sees lots of local families come for picnics and swimming.

Daniel's Head Beach Park (turn off Somerset Rd. on to Long Bay Lane, then left

The Sandys coastline is peppered with bays and beaches you can enjoy.

Rules of Cricket

More popular even than Christmas among Bermudians, Cup Match is a two-day public holiday celebrating the game of cricket. Held on a Thursday and Friday at the close of July or start of August, Cup Match incorporates Emancipation Day and Somers Day—the first of which marks the end of slavery in Bermuda in 1834, while the second commemorates the founding of Bermuda by English admiral Sir George Somers. While respect is paid to both milestones, and many Bermudians take the midsummer break to go camping, boating, and beaching around the island, the focus of holiday fervor is cricket, namely the annual showdown between the east and west ends of the island.

For weeks leading up to the match, residents flaunt their favorite team's colors—baby blue and navy for St. George's (east), navy and red for Somerset (west). The match is held in alternate years at Somerset or St. George's Cricket Club, drawing crowds of thousands—from politicians to pundits—to cheer on their chosen club. Attendees often spend both days at the cricket grounds, soaking up the food, fashions, and festive atmosphere—not to mention the game itself.

For those unfamiliar with the somewhat confusing intricacies of Britain's (and Bermuda's) national summer sport, here are a few basic insights:

- The game is played between two sides, each with 11 players; as in baseball, each team takes turns hitting and pitching a ball (called "batting" and "bowling"), and the team with the most runs wins.
- Each side has a captain who nominates his players before a coin toss; if a captain wins the toss, he chooses whether to bat or bowl first.
- A match can last one or two "innings" (when a team bats).
- The team batting tries to score as many runs as possible up and back a narrow 22-yard "pitch" between batter and bowler, while hitting the ball around the oval field.
- The team bowling (always overarm) can get the batsman out by catching the ball or knocking two wooden "bails" from the top of the "stumps" with the ball; stumps are three vertical wooden posts making up the "wicket," situated at each end of the pitch.
- To novices, cricket is best known for its arcane terminologies—oddities such as "googly" (a screwball pitch designed to fake the batter), "double century" (an individual batter's score of 200 runs or more), "chinaman" (a left-handed spin bowler), "maiden over" (six pitches in which no runs are scored), "leg-break" (a pitch that breaks into a batter's body off the bounce), and "sticky wicket" (a field that is partly wet and dry, causing uncertain bounce conditions that confuse batters).

along the shore to the end of Daniel's Head Rd.), comprises 17 acres of coastal green space, including two public beaches with pristine bays perfect for snorkeling, kayaking or standup paddleboarding. Vendors are on-site during the summer season, along with a café. Just offshore is the *Vixen* shipwreck, a fish magnet that's a mecca for snorkelers.

ENTERTAINMENT AND EVENTS

★ Cup Match

The biggest event in Sandys—Cup Match—happens every other year. Bermuda's favorite public holiday is held the last Thursday and Friday of July or the first Thursday and Friday in August; it celebrates **Emancipation Day,** marking the freedom of Bermuda's slaves, followed by **Somers Day,** in honor of island founder Sir George Somers. With the weekend tacked on, Cup Match makes for a four-day extravaganza loosely revolving around a historic and hotly contested cricket match. For over a century, St. George's and Somerset Cricket Clubs have battled for victory—and major bragging rights—in a two-day tournament that draws thousands of spectators to either end of the island (teams alternate years playing host).

But Cup Match is so much more than cricket. Many attend the game at **Somerset Cricket Club** (6 Cricket Ln., tel. 441/234-0327), whose team colors are red and navy, or St. George's Cricket Club (navy and baby blue) simply to socialize with friends and family or feast on the piles of homemade treats—mussel pie, fish sandwiches, peas 'n' rice—sold from stalls dotting the grounds. Others come to try their luck at Crown & Anchor, an old British Navy dice game, during the only two days of legalized public gambling the government permits. The weekend presents a who's who of Bermuda and a slice of true island life, making it imperative to experience if you're vacationing here at that time.

SPORTS AND RECREATION

Water Sports

Blue Water Divers & Watersports (Robinson's Marina, Somerset Bridge, tel. 441/234-1034, www.divebermuda.com) has been leading dive expeditions for more than 30 years. Its qualified guides lead a two-tank dive ($125), which departs at 9am daily, followed by a single-tank dive ($80) in the afternoon. Scuba enthusiasts often want to do both, with a soup lunch at the marina in between. Dive packages can also be arranged. There are numerous interesting shipwreck dives off the West End, many in shallow reef-laden waters, including the 1881 *North Carolina*, the 1943 *Hermes*, and the *Maria Celestia*, a U.S. Civil War blockade-runner that sank in 1864 (the vessel's paddlewheels remain intact).

Somerset Bridge Watersports (Robinson's Marina, Somerset Bridge, tel. 441/234-0914, www.bdawatersports.com) rents 13-foot and 15-foot Boston Whaler motorboats (13-ft. for 4 adults two hours $95, four hours $145), kayaks ($25 single, $30 double per hour, $60/$75 for four hours) and Jet Skis (75 minutes: single $125, double $135). All three options are great for exploring the West End by water.

Bermuda Waterski & Wakeboard Centre (Robinson's Marina, Somerset Bridge, tel. 441/234-3354 or 441/335-1012, www.islandwindsbermuda.com) is run by Bermudian über-athlete Kent Richardson, an accomplished triathlete and expert skier. He gives group or individual water-ski and wakeboarding lessons aboard his *Ski Nautique* in

Boats and watercraft pass beneath Watford Bridge between the Great Sound and Mangrove Bay.

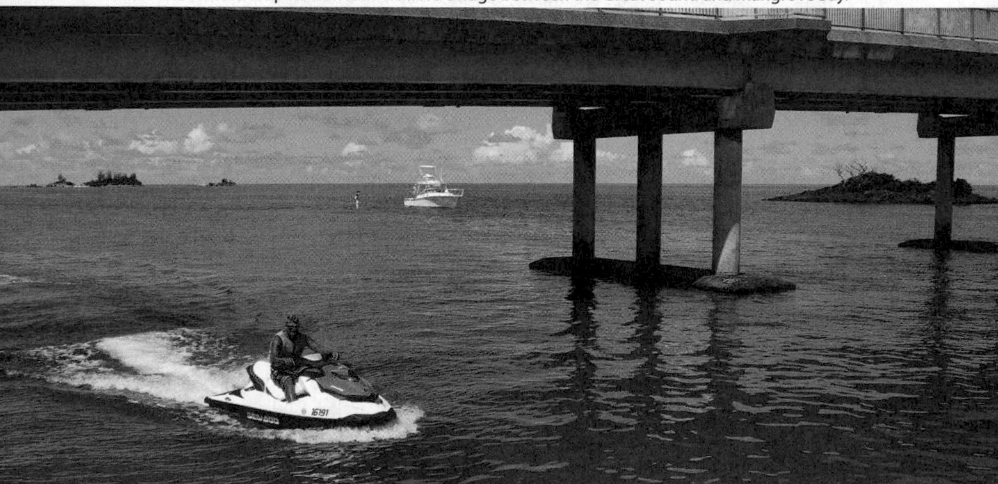

the Great Sound or off the West End, depending on the weather. Lessons are $200 for an hourlong session (up to six people). Richardson also offers cliff jumping, general sightseeing, and snorkel tours aboard his speedboat.

When the 9 Beaches Resort shut down in 2010 at **Daniel's Head Beach Park,** entrepreneurial local vendors moved in to rent paddleboards, kayaks, and beach gear on one of the area's most beautiful coastlines. The park has a laid-back surfer vibe, the kind of place where you want to cool your heels for days—or at least several serene hours. On-site vendors include **SurfsUp** (4 Long Bay Lane, tel. 441/300-1000, www.surfsupbermuda.com, 10am-5pm April to Sept., by appointment Oct-Mar., free WiFi), which rents standup paddleboards ($30 per hour), Zayak sea sleds ($15 per hour), and snorkeling gear ($15 all day); and **Crystal Clear Kayaks** (tel. 441/595-2925, www.crystalkayaks.com, 9am-sunset April to Sept., by appointment Nov.-Mar., $30 per person per hour), which offers sit-atop kayaks and also runs 70-minute tours ($40), including private arrangements.

★ Railway Trail (Sandys)

The Railway Trail in outer Sandys Parish is one of the nicest stretches to walk of the whole island, with a flat shady trail passing farmlands, residential neighborhoods, forts, and dramatic seascapes. Get on at George's Bay Road, at the former U.S. Naval Air Station Annex; the trail leads all the way to Mangrove Bay. From the former Somerset Bridge ferry stop westwards, the trail hugs the Great Sound shoreline, with wonderful views and tributaries that allow you to break off, take a refreshing swim, or visit sights along the way, like Fort Scaur. Be careful of locals on speeding motorbikes along the tarmacadam sections; while the trail is supposed to be off-limits to motorized traffic, area residents are allowed access, but many take advantage of that loophole to break the speed limit while off the main road.

ACCOMMODATIONS

Outer Sandys has no major resorts and only one guesthouse, although it is a good one. Short-term rental units can also be found on www.airbnb.com, www.vrbo.com, www.bermudarentals.com, and www.bermudagetaway.com.

Under $200

Garden House (4 Middle Rd., tel. 441/234-1435, fax 441/234-3006) is a true gem, tucked up a limestone drive just footsteps from Somerset Bridge. For more than three decades, owner Rosanne Galloway has rented a two-bedroom, two-bath cottage ($200 d) and a poolside studio unit ($115 d). Both have full kitchens. The three-acre property's manicured gardens surround the home. Persian carpets, antiques, TV, and private phone lines make guests feel quite at home.

$480-600

Bermudian Tina Stevenson rents a standout, family-friendly three-bedroom, three-bathroom **cottage** (49 Wreck Road, tel. 441/236-0267, www.vrbo.com/432886, sleeps 6-8) that commands panoramic views of the ocean. The home has air conditioning, TV, WiFi, and an expansive open-plan kitchen and living room. Two docks and an outdoor patio allow guests to enjoy the West End serenity of both Ely's Harbour and the western waterfront.

FOOD

Cafés, Bars, and Takeout

Tucked behind the legendary Somerset Cricket Club (home of Cup Match every other year), **Green Lite Café & Eatery** (15 Cricket Ln., tel. 441/234-1211, 8:30am-9pm Mon-Thurs., 8:30am-11pm Fri. and Sat., 10am-7pm Sun.) is a rarity in Bermuda—a vegetarian and vegan establishment. But Shawnette Simmons Smith's brainchild is attracting a loyal following of healthy eaters eager for its lentil and chickpea burgers, spinach lasagna, breaded broccoli, stir-fried cabbage, apple crumble, split pea soup, and salad and smoothie bar.

You'll find Gloria (Smith) cooking up a storm at **Gloria's Kitchen** at West End Sailboat Club (Watford Island, tel. 441/234-1252 or 441/234-2523, 11am-3pm Mon.-Sat., 5pm-10pm Fri. and Sat.), including loads of fresh fish, chicken, salads, and peas 'n' rice, among other daily dishes.

Standing on the edge of a harborside inlet where convict laborers were once held in jails, popular local watering hole **Woody's Drive-In Two Bar & Restaurant** (1 Boaz Island, tel. 441/234-2082, restaurant tel. 441/234-6526, 11am-1am daily) offers typical Bermudian comfort food. Most popular are its wicked fish sandwich (one of the island's best), fish cakes, and burgers. The outdoor bar attracts area locals.

Four Star Pizza (65 Somerset Rd., tel. 441/234-2626, 7am-11pm Mon.-Thurs., 7am-midnight Fri. and Sat., 7am-10pm Sun.) has a wide-ranging menu of takeout or delivery subs, wraps, Indian curries, and Asian rice dishes, in addition to its popular pizza.

Misty's Takeout (54 Main Rd., tel. 441/234-2449) is popular for its fish sandwiches and burgers—ideal for an authentically Bermudian lunchtime picnic.

Grocery Stores

The aroma of whole rotisserie chicken draws folks to the **Somerset MarketPlace** (48 Somerset Rd., tel. 441/234-0626, 8am-10pm Mon.-Sat., 9pm-7pm Sun.), the area's largest grocery store and part of an islandwide chain. A full array of frozen and dry goods are sold, along with wines, beer, spirits, dairy, meat, and deli products.

Arnold's Supermarket (41 Somerset Rd., tel. 441/234-2237, 7am-10pm Mon.-Sat., 7am-midnight Sun.) sits just down the road east of MarketPlace but offers a much smaller selection of goods. The next-door **Arnold's Liquor Store** (tel. 441/234-0963) does a roaring trade.

Maximart (42 Middle Rd., tel. 441/234-1940, 6:30am-midnight daily) is a small modern supermarket, owned by the Arnold's group. It has lots of parking and all the basics, including fresh fruits and vegetables.

INFORMATION AND SERVICES

Rubis Robinson's Marine Service Station (178 Somerset Rd. at Somerset Bridge, tel. 441/234-0709, robinsons1@logic.bm, 6:30am-10pm Mon.-Thurs. and Sun., 6:30am-10:30pm Fri. and Sat.) is a year-round hub of visitor and local activity. The small station shop sells shades, fishing supplies, cold drinks, and snacks. The plaza outside is home to several water sports outfitters and deep-sea fishing operations, and the dock is also used by area anglers.

Rubis Boaz Island Marine Service Station (28 Malabar Rd., Boaz Island, tel. 441/234-0128, 6:30am-8:30pm Mon.-Sat. in summer, 7am-7pm Sun.) sells cold drinks, cookies, potato chips, and some canned goods. There is also a marine service area on the waterfront for boat fuel refills.

Sandys Esso Service Station (37 Somerset Rd., tel. 441/234-1542, 6:30am-8pm Mon.-Sat., 8am-5pm Sun.) is a handy little outlet on the main road into the West End.

Two laundries within a half mile of each other are **Sandys Laundromat** (at the MarketPlace Plaza, off the main road, tel. 441/238-3200) and **Somerset Laundromat** (57 Middle Rd., tel. 441/234-3361).

ATMs are located outside Maximart and Somerset MarketPlace grocery stores.

Public toilets are located at Hog Bay Park and at area gas stations and restaurants.

GETTING THERE AND AROUND

Buses

Routes 7 and 8 run via Middle Road through Sandys every 15 minutes throughout the day, with the first bus leaving Hamilton at 7am and the last departing Dockyard at 10:20pm Monday-Friday; on Saturday the first bus is at 9:30am and the last departs Dockyard at 11:59pm. Sunday and public holidays schedules run every half hour 9:30am-6pm

Ferries

The **Sea Express** (tel. 441/295-4506, www.seaexpress.bm) Blue Route runs between Hamilton and Watford Bridge and Cavello Bay, in the early morning, late afternoon, and evening. While Hamilton-Dockyard service operates every half hour, ferries travel to these outer parish stops only during commuter periods. The 6:30 ferry from Hamilton stops in at Dockyard before returning to the city. One-way fare is $4.50 adults, $2.50 children 5-16, kids under 5 free (no cash or change accepted; tickets or tokens only).

Smith's and Hamilton Parishes

Stamped with some of Bermuda's most rugged scenery, Smith's and Hamilton Parishes will appeal to outdoors enthusiasts seeking Bermuda's less-manicured facets, as well as history buffs, birders, naturalists, and beachgoers.

Families with children will find plenty of activities to entertain youngsters, from caves and beaches to playgrounds and the island's only aquarium and zoo.

Two beautiful bodies of water shape the contours of these parishes—Harrington Sound and Castle Harbour. Each is ringed with stunning homes, often hidden from the main road, and a honeycomb of limestone caves, including two open for public tours. Both parishes feature sections of the South and North Shores, scenic stretches of the Railway Trail, wide farmland tracts, beaches, swimming coves, nature reserves, historic sites, and must-see attractions.

There are several routes to travel through the two parishes, the most scenic being South Shore Road and Harrington Sound Road. In Smith's, South Shore Road leads east from Collector's Hill, up McGall's Hill, and past the wooded splendor of Spittal Pond Nature Reserve to John Smith's Bay and Mangrove Lake, Bermuda's largest saltwater pond. Continuing east on the South Shore, you enter a small chunk of Hamilton Parish, most of it cushioned by the undulating greens of the world-famous Mid Ocean Club. Briefly crossing the parish boundary (into Tucker's Town, St. George's), it's necessary to cut through Paynter's Road to return to Hamilton Parish via picturesque, serpentine Harrington Sound Road.

From the eastern reaches of Hamilton Parish, you can take the Causeway into St. George's or explore North Shore neighborhoods, such as Coney Island, Bailey's Bay, and Crawl. North Shore Road also hugs the cove-sprinkled coast through Smith's to the border of Flatts Village, before linking to a narrow, postcard-pretty stretch of Harrington Sound Road—another pleasant way east, particularly on dead-calm days when the North Shore horizon looks like a lake, and arriving cruise ships can be seen following the distant

Previous: John Smith's Bay in Smith's Parish; Flatts Village. **Above:** Bermuda Aquarium, Museum & Zoo.

Look for ★ to find recommended sights, activities, dining, and lodging.

Highlights

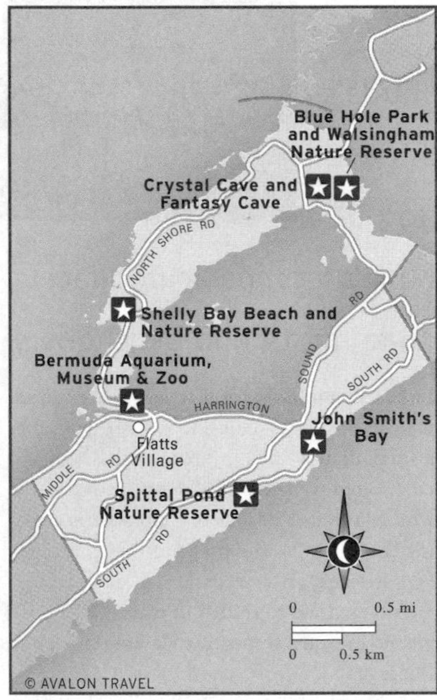

★ **Spittal Pond Nature Reserve:** Explore the sprawling 34-acre bird sanctuary—the island's premier nature reserve. Rolling coastal trails with unparalleled outlooks over the South Shore, plus numerous local and migratory birds, make it well worth a hike (page 188).

★ **John Smith's Bay:** A family favorite, this small half-moon bay is good for a day's retreat or just a dip while touring the eastern parishes. It is one of the few beaches with lifeguards on duty through the summer (page 191).

★ **Bermuda Aquarium, Museum & Zoo:** Long Bermuda's most-visited attraction, this waterfront facility's lush, exotic grounds and modern exhibits offer an up-close look at Bermuda's diverse marinelife, plants, and conservation projects, not to mention intriguing creatures from oceanic islands around the world. Kids of all ages will love the activity rooms (page 197).

★ **Blue Hole Park and Walsingham Nature Reserve:** For a rejuvenating escape to nature, head to the little-visited forest reserve commonly known as Tom Moore's Jungle, with winding trails through cherry bushes, mangroves, and sunken caves. Fish and turtles can sometimes be seen in one of its pocket-sized lagoons—a delightful swimming hole connected to the sea (page 199).

★ **Crystal Cave and Fantasy Cave:** Discovered in the early 1900s, Crystal Cave and Fantasy Cave are but two grand examples of a honeycomb that riddles the parish. The caves themselves offer spectacular interiors, but their garden estate's royal palms and behemoth Indian laurel trees are equally fascinating (page 201).

★ **Shelly Bay Beach and Nature Reserve:** There's nothing more beautiful on a summer day than the mirror-flat turquoise shallows of this roadside beach. Surrounded by sports fields, a playground, a grassy picnic area, and a nature reserve, it's popular with families, romantics, and, when the breeze picks up, kiteboarders (page 203).

channel into the Great Sound. Middle Road is a third route through Smith's, traversing the parish's residential interior, where schools, a riding stable, farm fields, and grazing pastures reveal Bermudians' busy daily lives. Interconnecting roads like precipitous Harrington Hundreds, St. Mark's Road, farm-dotted Verdmont Road, and Knapton Hill, with its moongates and modern, middle-class spreads, are also worth meandering if you have the time.

PLANNING YOUR TIME

Both Smith's and Hamilton Parishes are full of attractions—historic, eco-oriented, and recreational. You could spend several days' outings exploring this region, particularly since some sights, such as the Bermuda Aquarium, Museum & Zoo, Spittal Pond Nature Reserve, Crystal Cave and Fantasy Cave, and certain beaches, offer hours of possible exploration and enjoyment. Any of these could also be visited as part of a drive east to St. George's, since all are easily accessible from the main roads. Cafés, restaurants, and ice cream parlors, like those at Flatts Village, Collector's Hill, Crawl, or Bailey's Bay, offer many options for libation and meals en route. Kayak and sailboard rentals, scuba, snorkeling, and sailing charters can also be arranged through several operators located here.

Beginning in Flatts, a whole day's outing could be tailored to a circuit of Harrington Sound itself, encompassing visits to Bermuda Aquarium, Museum & Zoo, the caves, parks, beaches, or historic sites like Holy Trinity Church, and any number of restaurants or cafés along the way. Shopping and organized entertainment in both parishes, however, are slim pickings, with only a handful of retail outlets, mostly tiny stores inside key attractions. Accommodations are also few, so it's likely you would venture here from other parishes. Mopeds, taxis, and buses are efficient ways to get around; well-marked bus stops are outside most of the main sights.

As elsewhere, the Railway Trail offers lovely out-of-the-way views, coastal serenity, and glimpses of genuine Bermudian life, though the trail is interrupted by main roads at a couple of points. Several of Bermuda's best swimming areas are located in these parishes, a mixture of South Shore's surf and sand and North Shore's calmer, sometimes beachless rocky coves, snorkeling areas, and deep swimming holes.

Smith's Parish

The dramatic lookouts, diverse plants and animals, and the coastal trail of Spittal Pond Nature Reserve alone would be enough to make Smith's worth visiting, but the parish has much more, including a historic—some say haunted—house that's now a museum, beautiful beaches on both shores, panoramic stretches of the Railway Trail and Harrington Sound, and a few good restaurants. The parish is named for London power broker Sir Thomas Smith, a key figure in the colonization efforts of London's East India Company, Russia Company, and North West Passage Company, as well as a stakeholder in early Bermuda. Smith's is largely residential, with a busy community hub at Collector's Hill, offering a grocery, pharmacy, restaurants, and essential services like gas and ATMs.

The parish also claims a large farming community, with substantial parcels of land producing onions, strawberries, carrots, and other seasonal produce sold in island supermarkets. A dairy farm, one of just two on the island, sits next to Spittal Pond Nature Reserve. Smith's is home to many Portuguese residents, some of them newly arrived Azorean contract workers, others naturalized immigrants; many more are full-fledged Bermudians whose families have been here for generations.

Smith's Parish

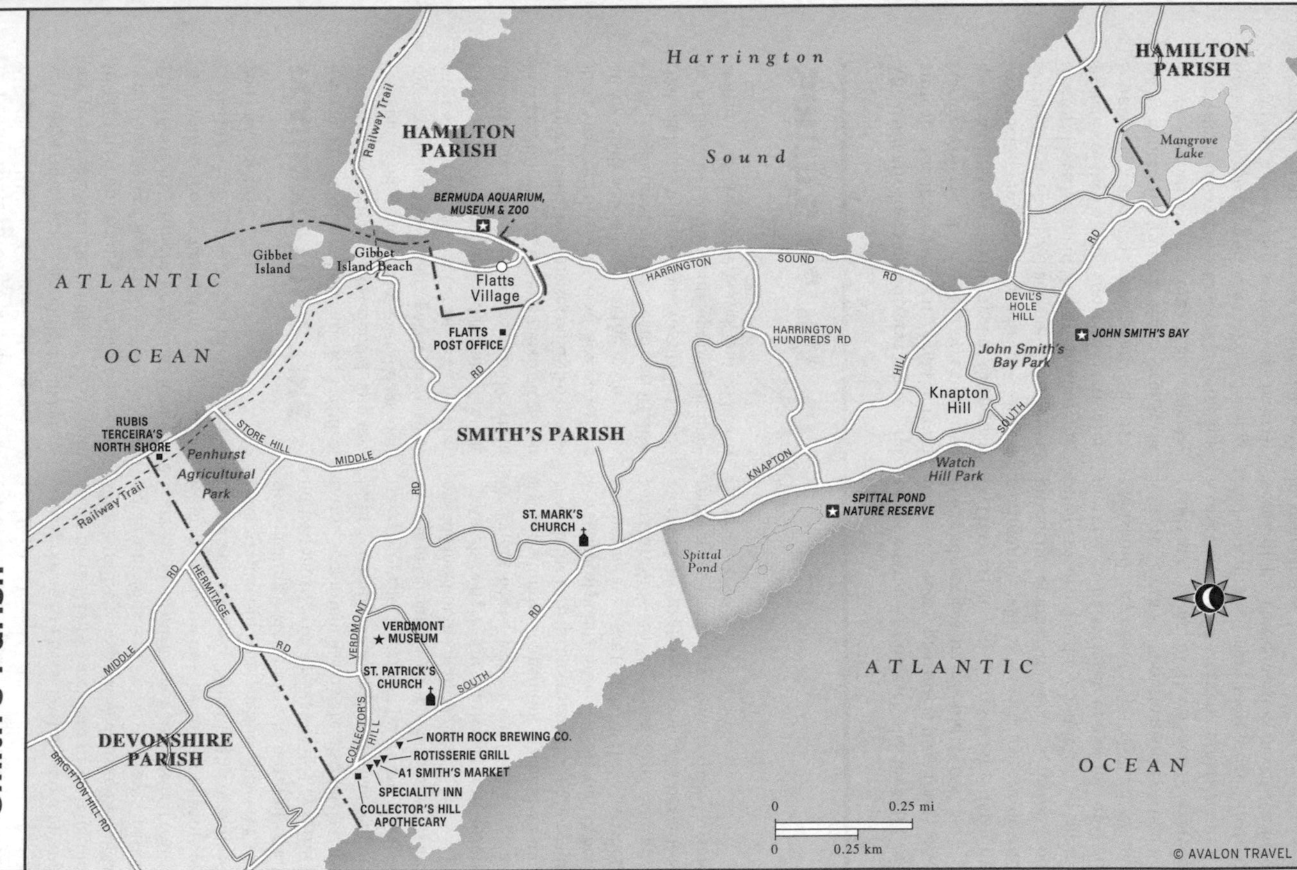

The historic St. Mark's Church is a Smith's Parish landmark.

Driving through the rolling parish, you can't help but be wowed by spectacular views of all kinds: Longtails arching from sheer cliff faces. Red dawn lifting over the glass-like surface of Harrington Sound. Sapphire depths of a favorite swimming hole. Smith's has as much to offer as any of the parishes, yet, without a single big-buzz attraction, the parish maintains an out-of-the-way quietude, a rural modesty that lets one imagine Bermuda as it used to be.

SIGHTS

Verdmont Museum

High on a hill overlooking the South Shore, **Verdmont Museum** (6 Verdmont Ln. off Collectors Hill, tel. 441/236-7369, www.bnt.bm, 10am-4pm Wed.-Fri. May-Oct., Wed. only Nov.-Apr., $5 adults, or $10 combo ticket for three BNT museums, $2 children 6 to 18) is a historic home that offers a glimpse of old-time colonial life—as well as a neck-prickling ghost legend. Flanked by sentry-like palmettos and surrounded by rambling lawns and rose beds leading up its garden paths, this treasure of the Bermuda National Trust sits at the end of a quiet lane off heavily trafficked Collector's Hill. The home's distinctive architecture, with four grand chimneys and a fine cedar staircase, excites historians, for it incorporates elements of both 17th- and 18th-century building design. Unlike most Bermudian houses, which typically exhibit a hodgepodge of structural add-ons, Verdmont has remained structurally unchanged for 300 years.

Historians guess Verdmont was built around 1710. The home's English-influenced layout includes a formal drawing room and parlor on the ground floor and a charming nursery at the top of the house, displaying a rocking horse, Victorian dollhouse, and other time-worn toys. The home's collection of furniture, assembled by the Bermuda National Trust in the 1950s, is impressive; fine Bermuda cedar cabinets, desks, and a Chippendale-style tallboy with marching legs are among the standouts. Several imported furnishings were brought to the island by early sea captains, including Chinese porcelain and English hurricane shades. Portraits of several former Verdmont owners hang throughout the house.

Some believe the phantom of one 1930s resident, Spencer Joell, remains in the house. Several tour guides over the years have reported experiencing strange feelings, finding furniture inexplicably moved around, and sensing an odd chill in various rooms, including the attic nursery. Visitors, too, often ask whether the house is haunted. One incident involved a New Jersey couple who took a snapshot of the nursery in 1976, and later mailed back the photo, along with an alarmed letter, to Verdmont's then-curator. The room was empty, they said, when they took the picture, yet the photo showed a man sitting at a table. The curator, so the story goes, recognized the figure immediately, because she had known him well—it was Joell.

In recent years, archaeological digs have been carried out on the property and exhibits added to interpret the story of Verdmont's slaves. The gardens are also worth exploring, peppered with herbs, roses, and fruit trees.

St. Patrick's and St. Mark's Churches

Continuing from Collector's Hill along South Road in the McGall's Hill area, the Portuguese influence is strong. The large, circular Roman Catholic church, **St. Patrick's** (23 South Shore Rd., tel. 441/236-9866, stpats@logic.bm), incorporates Portuguese elements into readings and songs of its 9am Sunday service. Gardens carefully planted with Easter lilies, vegetables, or brilliantly hued flower beds speak to the community's agricultural legacy, and the names of so many neighborhood residents—Moniz, DeSilva, Cabral, Furtado—reflect the waves of Portuguese immigration to Bermuda over the past 150 years. Azoreans were invited to the island in the mid-1800s to help spur a farming revival; within a couple of years, Bermuda was benefiting from the influx in laborers, as well as innovative farming methods and equipment. By the 1870s, annual exports of Bermuda onions (70,000 barrels and 350,000 crates), arrowroot, potatoes, and tomatoes to U.S. East Coast cities had revitalized the island's economy and begun paving the way for Bermuda's cultural face to change.

At the top of McGall's Hill sits **St. Mark's Church,** a quaint parish landmark built in 1847 whose spire can be seen down the valleys on both sides. Inside, its cedar altar and pulpit are good examples of Bermudian workmanship. The graveyard, draped with riotous bougainvillea at certain times of year, and filled with tombstones of seafaring, old-family islanders dating back a century and a half, is also worth a wander.

★ Spittal Pond Nature Reserve

The rugged, 34-acre **Spittal Pond Nature Reserve** (sunrise-sunset daily, admission free), co-owned by the Bermuda National Trust and the government, has two entrances along South Shore Road. Both have parking lots and lead to the circuitous trail around the park, though the eastern entrance offers a more direct entry and faster access to some of the most dramatic viewing spots. The reserve is the island's premier nature reserve, a sprawling sanctuary that includes a valley cradling the large brackish pond, several freshwater ponds, and surrounding marsh and woodland through which meandering trails

The Spittal Pond Nature Reserve offers a welcome habitat for migrant and resident birdlife.

climb to spectacular outlooks over the South Shore. Notably, the reserve's varied habitats provide a refuge for resident and migratory birds, including woodland cardinals, finches, mallards, turnstones, sandpipers, cliff-nesting longtails, blue herons, white egrets, occasional visiting hawks, and the ubiquitous yellow-crowned night herons, which devour crab populations throughout the island.

The park's highlights include the "Portuguese Rock"—a historic carving on an exposed rocky cliff face, believed to have been left by Portuguese mariners before the island's colonization. The inscription, now cast in bronze, includes letters that look like "RP" (possibly for *Rex Portugaliae,* referring to Joao III, Portugal's monarch) and the date 1543. Historians believe the markings were the work of 32 castaways who escaped their shipwreck off Bermuda that year and spent time on the island fashioning a new vessel from cedar timber. Up here, atop cliffs tumbling down to frothy boiler reefs below, the flat rock face surrounded by a cedar fence gives a breathtaking view of the whole southern coastline. Assorted contemporary graffiti has been carved in the outlook's limestone.

Just down the trail from Portuguese Rock is "Jeffrey's Hole," a cave with an overhead entry hole; the cave, according to local lore, once served as a temporary shelter for an escaped slave. Another oddity, at the western end of the park, is the "Checkerboard"—a large, flat square rock surface near the water's edge bearing crosshatch markings. Experts can't decide whether it was crafted by human hands or the sea, which sprays over the edge and pounds the rock on stormy days.

Descending from Spanish Rock, follow a skinny coastal trail edged by prickly pears and baygrapes to a wind-battered promontory—a salt-licked plateau over the roiling surf where parrotfish can sometimes be seen nibbling the reef edges. Turning inland past a small pond where egrets nest and ducklings learn to paddle, the woodland trail is laced with banks of Kermit-green flopper plants, a succulent whose lanternlike flowers bob by the hundreds over assorted ferns and wild blossoms. Continuing past fiddlewood groves, aromatic spice trees, and sugarcane, the trail leads past a dairy farm to the western parking lot; exit onto South Shore Road and follow the grassy verge east for about 150 feet until a set of wooden steps leads under a hedged arch back into the reserve. The woodland trail continues around the large pond's northern rim back to the east parking lot.

Hurricanes periodically send towering waves over the cliffs into the valley and pond, the salt leaving a swath of dead vegetation. Hurricane Fabian's terrific storm surge ate away chunks of the South Shore limestone cliffs in 2003, and the erosion from this and other tempests is still evident. Government Department of Parks crews continually cull invasive species and replace them with hardy endemics like palmettos and cedars.

The park's steep trails and hourlong circuit restrict access to the able-bodied, but good views of the South Shore can be had from the wooded trailhead alongside the eastern parking lot. There is a portable toilet here, too.

Watch Hill Park

Just east of Spittal Pond, looking out over one of Bermuda's most dramatically spectacular stretches of coastline visible from the main road, tiny **Watch Hill Park** (sunrise-sunset daily, admission free) offers a peaceful stopping place for a picnic or rest while heading east. Anglers come here after work and on weekends, casting their lines for pompano and "good-eating" reef fish like snapper, rockfish, triggerfish, and hogfish. The park is located on a peaceful stretch of South Shore Road, where traffic is generally very light. The main road east from here is the quintessential "scenic route," leading far from rush-hour destinations—to leisurely Tucker's Town and its private golf courses.

Penhurst Agricultural Park

When actor Michael Douglas's Bermudian mother, Diana Dill Darrid, married President Nixon's former Treasury chief of staff Donald

Bermuda's Portuguese

On November 6, 1849, a sailing ship made port in Hamilton carrying 58 men, women, and children—the first Portuguese immigrants to Bermuda. "We sincerely trust this importation of laborers will answer the end contemplated," read a dispatch in *The Royal Gazette,* "and we hope they will be the means of inducing the cultivation of the wine more extensively than at present."

Vineyards never did become a thriving enterprise in Bermuda, but those first farm workers from the island of Madeira were the vanguard of waves of Portuguese immigration to the island. Their journey would be repeated by thousands of Portuguese, mostly from the remote Azores Islands, who headed to Bermuda to fill a dire need for agricultural expertise and carve out a better life for themselves. Their efforts paid off, and farming—and the export of onions, arrowroot, tomatoes, and other products—became a lucrative economic generator for the island in the second half of the 19th century. Today, as lawyers, bankers, and tenacious entrepreneurs, generations of Portuguese Bermudians have called the island home; their community makes up an estimated 25 percent of the population.

It wasn't always smooth sailing for Portuguese immigrants. Bureaucratic and social discrimination relegated them to the status of second-class citizens, even into the 1960s and 1970s. Strict government regulations attempted to bar the immigration of whole families and restricted job classes to menial labor. Like blacks until desegregation in the 1960s, the Portuguese were banned from many of the island's social clubs. But the community was a strong and self-supportive one; established Portuguese helped new immigrants find their footing and lobbied for their rights. In the 1980s, the Portuguese-Bermudian Association pressed the case of long-term residents, including numerous Portuguese who had lived or even been born in Bermuda but had no legal right to stay on the island. The group's efforts finally nudged the government to grant long-

Webster in 2002, the bride and groom asked guests to donate toward the preservation of **Penhurst Agricultural Park** (Middle Rd., west of Store Hill, sunrise-sunset daily, admission free) in lieu of wedding gifts. They held a publicized ceremony to plant cedar saplings on Christmas Eve inside the 14-acre reserve, which rambles from Middle Road down across the Railway Trail to North Shore, encompassing farm fields and dense woodland that few Bermudians have ventured to explore. Visible from the park entrance area are the communications tower and giant satellite dish on the next-door property of Cable & Wireless, on which the lion's share of Bermuda's telecommunications depends. The park gives easy access to the Railway Trail in Smith's; south of the trail, it descends to a grassy spread where a bench overlooks the North Shore. Bluebirds, cardinals, mourning doves, and finches can all be seen and heard here, amid the fiddlewoods, palmettos, and cedars. Department of Parks crews have culled invasive species, such as Mexican pepper bushes, and planted replacement endemics.

Harrington Sound

This inland sound, favored by boaters and anglers, is considered by naturalists to be biologically unique in the world, because of its necklace of underwater caves, tidal currents, submerged notches, and the abundance of marinelife found here. Calico clams, black mussels, purple urchins, harbor conches, squids, and spiny lobsters can all be seen, not to mention rays that occasionally lift out of the water like speckled stealth bombers before coming down in a loud splash—a heart-pumping experience for any nearby swimmer.

Measuring some three square miles, the sound is deep, extending down to 80 feet in some places, and ringed by steep cliffs and sheer shores, the highest point being Abbot's Cliff in Hamilton Parish. Below these, numerous caves provide fascinating exploration for

term residency to many people of all nationalities who have made a significant contribution to Bermudian society.

Portuguese Bermudians keep their culture vibrantly alive on the island, linking the island to the vast diaspora of Portuguese civilization around the world. Their club, the **Vasco da Gama Club** (51 Reid St., Hamilton, tel. 441/292-7196), has been a social and political hub for both new immigrants and later generations. Portuguese is now considered a second language on the island, and in recent years, government departments, banks, and some businesses have begun to provide translated signs and customer information on official forms, websites, and in retail centers. The **Portuguese Cultural Association** promotes beloved age-old traditions by teaching dances, cooking, and other arts to younger generations, who perform at national events such as the May 24 Bermuda Day Parade.

Religious *festas* also make colorful public spectacles throughout the year, with ornate costumes and processions in which church elders and citizens walk on carpets of petals to celebrate important Roman Catholic saints and the Holy Trinity. In the procession of Santo Cristo, held on the fifth Sunday after Easter, hundreds gather at St. Theresa's Cathedral in Hamilton for a solemn march through the city's streets to seek miracles for the sick and needy. In June, Portuguese Bermudians celebrate the **Festa do Espiritu Santo** (Festival of the Holy Spirit) in King's Square, St. George. An elaborate pageant paying tribute to the legendary charity of Queen Isabel includes a feast for participants who are served bowls of *sopa* (soup) and *pao dolce* (sweet bread).

Portugal has established a **Portuguese Consulate** office in Bermuda (Melbourne House, 11 Parliament St., Hamilton, tel. 441/292-1039), headed by Honorary Consul Andrea Moniz DeSouza, an associate lawyer who works as a liaison between the Bermuda and Portuguese governments and the Portuguese national community.

cave divers, kayakers, and snorkelers, though the mouths of some, such as Green Bay Cave on the western shore, lie underwater. (Inside this particular cave, however, stalactites hang from the ceiling above the surface.) Another example is Shark Hole Cave, in the emerald-hued southwest corner, which extends under the traffic of Harrington Sound Road. Swimmers can often feel patches of cool water throughout the sound, as seawater from the outer shore enters through hundreds of fissures.

Scattered around the sound are various private islands (Rabbit Island, Cockroach Island) where Bermudians keep summer cottages. Sporting events such as Zoom Around the Sound (a run/walk/cycle event), the Round-the-Sound Swim, and the Trunk Island Swim also take advantage of the sound's scenic loop and its mostly calm waters in the summer and fall. Flatts Bridge is a great vantage point to view most of the sound, and swimming is popular off the rocks at Shark Hole—the only soft landing is a small beach on the property of the Palmetto Gardens condominiums, at the three-way junction of North Shore, Middle, and Harrington Sound Roads. But the high cliffs and private properties encircling much of this body of water prevent easy access, unless by boat.

BEACHES

★ John Smith's Bay

The lifeguard station posted at this crescent-shaped cove attests to its popularity, particularly among families with children. Nestled between two promontories, the beach—named for pioneer Captain John Smith of the Virginia Company, which administered early Bermuda—is usually fairly protected from high waves and winds and has an adjoining little park.

Ample parking, toilets, and a friendly daily lunch wagon that doles out drinks, burgers, fish cakes, and fries to hungry swimmers make John Smith's a top beach choice for locals and anyone who wants a change from the beach crowds of Warwick and Southampton.

Coconut palms and baygrapes frame the beach, where jutting rocks have created convenient mini-coves that provide a measure of privacy even when the beach gets busy. Tucker's Town's sweep of surf along the private Windsor and Mid Ocean Beaches can be seen in the distance. On Sunday mornings, the beach attracts a group of recreational swimmers who meet for spiritual gatherings at dawn throughout the year. Easter Sunday also sees a special beachside service.

Gibbet Island Beach

The beauty of Gibbet Island and its idyllic facing coves belies an ugly past. Its name refers to the gallows post that once stood on the island, a site where slaves and criminals were hanged, their bodies on public display as a warning to passing maritime traffic. Such history remains a sore spot for the island's black—and white—communities in the ongoing effort to foster harmonious race relations more than 170 years after emancipation in Bermuda. Today, the property is owned by a private family trust, so the beach is officially off-limits, though the public Railway Trail runs through the land to Flatts Inlet, which also offers a refreshing dip. Here, a bridge once carried the train on to Shelly Bay and points farther east; eight massive stone pylons remain in the inlet. To recoup the trail, you need to retrace your steps, walk through Flatts Village and around the inlet, and follow North Shore Road into Hamilton Parish.

SPORTS AND RECREATION

Railway Trail (Smith's)

The Smith's Parish portion of the Railway Trail is short in comparison with stretches in Paget, Warwick, and the West End, but it offers views of the North Shore, a shady fairyland of forest, and easy access to the Penhurst Agricultural Park. Banks of nasturtium and asparagus fern line the muddy path, hemmed by steep limestone walls where the trail was cut through the hillside. This stretch of trail is a popular route for equestrians on their daily outings from nearby Hinson Hall Stables. Enter halfway up Store Hill. You can walk west to adjoining Penhurst, or about a half mile east to Gibbet Island, where the trail breaks at the water's edge. Follow North Shore Road east and pick up the trail again in Hamilton Parish. For a longer excursion, experience the other

John Smith's Bay is a postcard-pretty beach in Smith's Parish.

Bermuda Shorts

If you really want to blend in among Bermuda society, remove those white socks, sneakers, gold sandals, and baseball cap—and go native. There's no more Bermudian a uniform (for men anyway) than Bermuda shorts. But you have to get it right. As one retailer opined, "a lot of people don't understand the difference between Bermuda shorts and shorts bought in Bermuda."

Genuine Bermuda linen-blend shorts can be found for under $60 at the **English Sports Shop** (tel. 441/295-2672), which has branches in Hamilton, Somerset Village, and St. George's. Key to the shorts' authenticity is length, which should be no less than one inch above the knee, and cut in a particular way, stiffly creased down the front and held up by a belt. **The Authentic Bermuda Shorts (TABS)** (www.authenticshorts.bm), founded by Bermudian Rebecca Hanson, sells its high-quality cotton twill styles online (international shipping charges apply, or compliementary delivery in Bermuda), and at A. S. Cooper in Hamilton and Southampton, and Coral Beach & Tennis Club, Paget.

Fabrics can vary from Madras prints to lemon yellow and pastel pink (matched with same-color ties and knee socks if you *really* want to look the part). Don't worry about sticking out in such unusual hues—you won't: Just look around Hamilton any weekday, and you'll find yourself comfortably swimming in a rainbow sea of males parading up and down the busy streets as if there was nothing at all outlandish about robin-red shorts, matching knee socks, a dress shirt, natty tie, and blazer. In fact, the shorts are perfect attire for the hot, humid climate, which leaves many a visiting Wall Street "suit" looking like a fish out of water.

two-thirds of the western North Shore stretch by starting in Devonshire, where the trail can be accessed from Barker's Hill or Palmetto Road. Try an out-and-back walk from here, returning for lunch at Ocean View Golf Club.

ENTERTAINMENT AND EVENTS

Amphibious athletes take to the waters of Harrington Sound for the marathon **Zobec Round-the-Sound Long-Distance Swimathon,** held in mid-October. The charity event, organized by the Bermuda Open Water Swimming Association (tel. 441/238-0652, www.roundthesound.bm, jjproduce@transact.bm, registration via www.racedayworld.com), is competitive, with staggered starts beginning at 10am for five distance categories ranging from 0.8K to 10K. The joint finish is at the private Palmetto Bay Beach on Harrington Sound Road. The event awards trophies for speed, position, and money raised from pledges, but visitors to the island can participate by simply paying the entry fee. Kayaks, paramedics, and police keep participants safe.

ACCOMMODATIONS

After several years in receivership, the parish's only hotel property (the 13-acre former **Pink Beach Club,** dating back to 1947) was bought in 2014 by Canada-based Sardis Development; the group has since razed the site to make way for a new boutique hotel and condos. The $51.5-million plan promises a 34-room hotel with two restaurants, six guest condos, two guest suites, a new beach club, gym, spa, and two swimming pools.

FOOD

Cafés and Pubs

The Collector's Hill neighborhood at the intersection of South Road and Collector's Hill has a handful of busy eateries popular with area residents and passersby.

A local favorite, ★ **Speciality Inn** (4 South Shore Rd., tel. 441/236-3133, fax 441/236-2929, speciality@northrock.bm, 6am-10pm Mon.-Sat.) serves up home-style comfort food, including the creamiest mac 'n' cheese, in a casual, cafeteria-style diner/pizzeria where the folks are friendly and fast.

Lori Woolfe rules the roost at the checkout counter, cajoling clientele with dollops of "Dahlin'" and "Sweetheart." The down-home ambience brought Clint Eastwood here during a golfing holiday in 1996, as well as Jimmy Carter and his son Jack, a former Bermuda resident—all are paid tribute to on a kitchenside wall of fame. Grab a barstool in front of the grill for a quick Bermudian-style breakfast (bacon, egg, and cheese on a coffee roll). The wide-ranging lunch and dinner menus offer everything from burgers ($4.60) served on freshly baked rolls to sandwiches ($5.25-12.75), pizzas (starting at $11), calzones, and stromboli, plus a separate kids' menu. A full sushi menu is also available, prepared at a separate bar by dedicated sushi chefs. Home-baked loaves of banana bread and gingerbread are often sold at the checkout counter. The only thing missing is a liquor license.

Roadside diner **Rotisserie Grill** (8 South Rd., tel. 441/232-7444, 11am-10pm Mon.-Sat., 7:30am-8pm Sun., $13-22) does a roaring trade with its comfort-food menu of pasta, pizza, local fish, pot roast, daily specials, and family-sized dinners of roast chicken or ribs, with biscuits and sides of mashed potatoes. Eat in or take out, including Sunday morning breakfasts.

Named for the rocky outcrop located 10 miles off Bermuda's North Shore, Bermuda brewpub **North Rock Brewing Co.** (10 South Shore Rd., tel. 441/236-6633, fax 441/236-2288, lunch 11am-3pm, dinner 6pm-9:30pm daily) is a British-style pub, complete with a dark-hued interior, booths, and a bar. The menu is pricier than your corner Limey pub, mind you, but varied. Seafood, burgers, sandwiches, curries, pastas, ribs, and pub staples like steak-and-ale pie ($22.50), bangers and mash ($18.95), and fish 'n' chips ($22) are all available. Bermuda fish and lobster (in season) are also offered.

Groceries

At the hub of routes east, west, and north, **A1 Smith's Market** (10 South Shore Rd. at Collector's Hill, tel. 441/236-8763, www.marketplace.bm, 8am-10pm Mon.-Sat., 9am-7pm Sun.) is a busy little grocery that stays stocked with most of the basics. One of seven groceries that belong to the islandwide MarketPlace chain, it has Bermudian bakery items, a full dairy and butcher's counter, fresh fruit and vegetables, and a wide, well-priced wine selection. Cheerful checkout clerks make it a busy neighborhood stopping place.

Serving the billionaires of Tucker's Town and the nouveau riche of Knapton Hill, **Harrington Hundreds Grocery & Liquor Store** (99 South Shore Rd., opposite Spittal Pond's east entrance, tel. 441/293-1635, fax 441/293-3136, 8am-8pm Mon.-Sat., 8am-2pm Sun.) is a foodie oasis far from Hamilton. The store has a superior selection of Bermuda-grown fruit and vegetables (sweet local strawberries, ripe on-the-vine tomatoes, melt-in-your-mouth melons) and a wide selection of organic fare, including specialized items for vegans and folks with wheat allergies and other dietary challenges. The store carries a good wine selection (from California to the Continent), fresh-baked stick loaves, and Ben & Jerry's ice cream. Who could want more?

Intermezzo Wines & Spirits (5 Park House, Middle Rd. at Verdmont Rd., tel. 441/293-0656, noon-8pm daily) makes a convenient parish stop for wine, beer, and liquor.

INFORMATION AND SERVICES

Collector's Hill Apothecary (7 South Shore Rd. at Collector's Hill, tel. 441/279-5513, prescriptions tel. 441/279-5512, www.phoenixstores.com, 8am-8pm Mon.-Sat., 11am-7pm Sun.) is well stocked with makeup and toiletries, sweets and snacks, toys, gift cards, newspapers and magazines, and a large pharmacy offering online prescription refills.

Smith's has just one gas station, with a small convenience store attached: **Rubis Terceira's North Shore** (2 North Shore Rd., tel. 441/292-5130, 6:30am-8pm Mon.-Sat., 9am-4pm Sun.).

Flatts Post Office (65 Middle Rd., next to Whitney Middle School, tel. 441/292-0741, 8am-5pm Mon.-Fri.) is a tiny parish landmark and convenient mail drop.

ATMs are located outside Collector's Hill Apothecary (7 South Shore Rd. at Collector's Hill) and at Harrington Hundreds Grocery (99 South Shore Rd. opposite Spittal Pond's east entrance).

GETTING THERE AND AROUND

There are no scooter rental outlets or ferry services in Smith's. Scooters can be rented elsewhere and are a good way to scoot around the parish, especially off the main thoroughfares. Buses are also an efficient way to travel the main arteries of Smith's. Bicycles, rentable from hotels and liveries, are great for exploring the Railway Trail. To arrange a pickup by cab, contact **Bermuda Industrial Union Co-op** (tel. 441/292-4476, cooptaxi@fkbnet.bm), **Bermuda Island Taxi** (tel. 441/295-4141, www.bermudaislandtaxi.com), or **BTA Dispatching Ltd.** (tel. 441/296-2121, www.taxibermuda.bm).

Buses

Buses travel all three routes through the parish: South Shore Road, North Shore Road, and Middle Road. Take route 1 for South Shore Road destinations (Hamilton-Grotto Bay/St. George's, buses run every half hour). Take route 3 for points on Middle Road (Hamilton-Grotto Bay/St. George's, every half hour); it also travels through Flatts Village and along picturesque Harrington Sound Road. Routes 10 and 11 are your buses for North Shore Road (Hamilton-St. George's, every 15 minutes). Fares from Hamilton to points throughout Smith's are $3 for adults, $2 for children 5-16, and kids under 5 ride free. Exact change, tokens, tickets, or passes required.

Hamilton Parish

Though it carries the same name as Bermuda's capital, Hamilton Parish is totally distinct from the City of Hamilton, which lies about six miles away, in Pembroke Parish. The two Hamiltons are not named for the same person, either; the parish, like the other eight, took the name of an early investor, in this case, James Hamilton, the second Marquis of Hamilton, while the city was named for Governor Henry Hamilton nearly 200 years later. The Bermudian lexicon distinguishes clearly between the two: When someone says, "Let's go to Hamilton," they mean "Town," or the city. By contrast, locals normally describe Hamilton Parish locations within their neighborhood context ("Bailey's Bay," "Crawl," "Harrington Sound"). Indeed, historically, Hamilton Parish was simply known as Bailey's Bay by most islanders, since the North Shore community was a hub of trade and travel (by boat) around the island in its early colonial days.

Today, Hamilton Parish, wrapped like a half-doughnut around Harrington Sound, is largely residential, with impressive, mostly hidden waterfront homes, as well as several public parks, one large resort (Grotto Bay Beach Resort), and popular attractions such as the Bermuda Aquarium, Museum & Zoo and the caves. Unless you are staying in St. George's, your tour of the parish will begin immediately after arrival, since you have to travel from the airport through Hamilton Parish to reach any other part of the island.

SIGHTS

Flatts Village

Flatts Village (North Shore Road), or "Flatts" as everything in the general vicinity is known in the local lingo, has enjoyed a renaissance of sorts in the 2000s, with a tasteful renovation of its smattering of shops and

Hamilton Parish

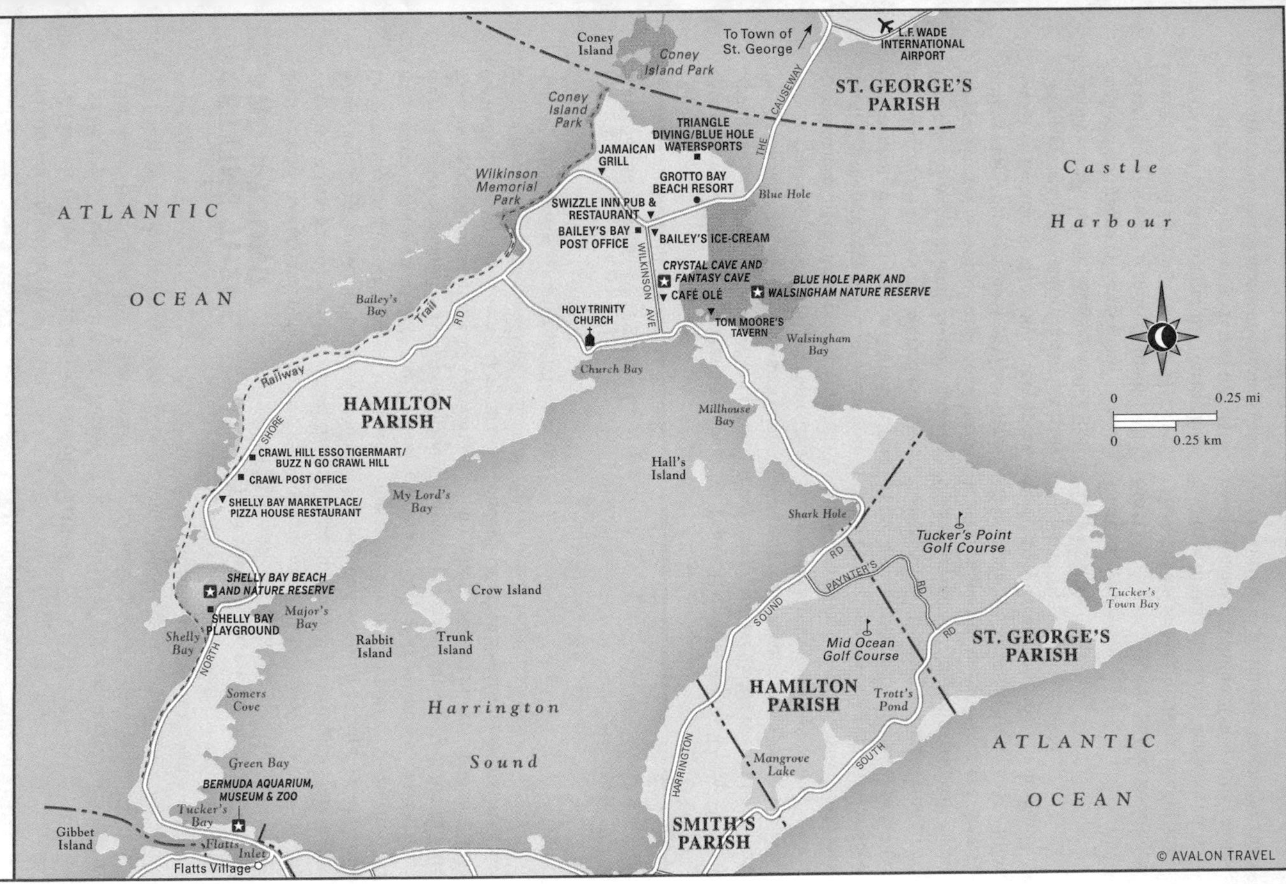
Coney Island
Coney Island Park
To Town of St. George
L.F. WADE INTERNATIONAL AIRPORT
ST. GEORGE'S PARISH
THE CAUSEWAY
Coney Island Park
TRIANGLE DIVING/BLUE HOLE WATERSPORTS
JAMAICAN GRILL
GROTTO BAY BEACH RESORT
Castle Harbour
Wilkinson Memorial Park
ATLANTIC
SWIZZLE INN PUB & RESTAURANT
Blue Hole
BAILEY'S BAY POST OFFICE
BAILEY'S ICE-CREAM
WILKINSON AVE
CRYSTAL CAVE AND FANTASY CAVE
BLUE HOLE PARK AND WALSINGHAM NATURE RESERVE
OCEAN
Bailey's Bay
Trail
RD
CAFÉ OLÉ
HOLY TRINITY CHURCH
TOM MOORE'S TAVERN
Walsingham Bay
Church Bay
Railway
HAMILTON PARISH
Millhouse Bay
0
0.25 mi
0
0.25 km
SHORE
CRAWL HILL ESSO TIGERMART/ BUZZ N GO CRAWL HILL
CRAWL POST OFFICE
Hall's Island
SHELLY BAY MARKETPLACE/ PIZZA HOUSE RESTAURANT
My Lord's Bay
Shark Hole
Tucker's Point Golf Course
SHELLY BAY BEACH AND NATURE RESERVE
Crow Island
RD
PAYNTER'S
RD
Tucker's Town Bay
SHELLY BAY PLAYGROUND
Major's Bay
SOUND
Shelly Bay
Rabbit Island
Trunk Island
Mid Ocean Golf Course
RD
ST. GEORGE'S PARISH
NORTH
Somers Cove
Harrington
HAMILTON PARISH
Trott's Pond
ATLANTIC
Green Bay
Sound
HARRINGTON
Mangrove Lake
SOUTH
BERMUDA AQUARIUM, MUSEUM & ZOO
OCEAN
Tucker's Bay
Gibbet Island
Flatts Inlet
SMITH'S PARISH
Flatts Village
© AVALON TRAVEL

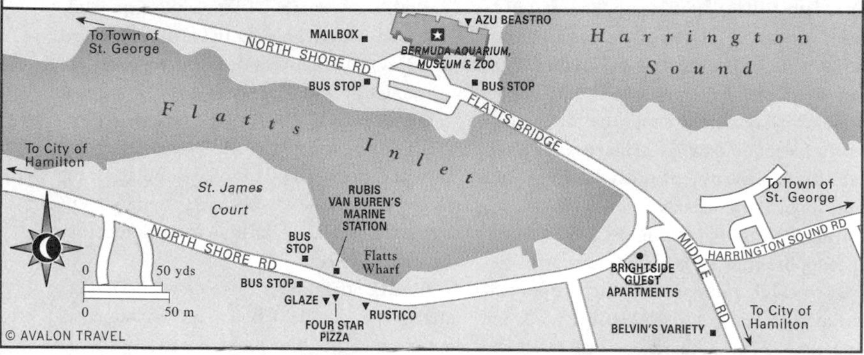

architecturally interesting cottages, as well as the addition of new restaurants, much-needed sidewalks, and a revamped marina. The tiny community lies on the eastern band of Flatts Inlet, a finger of shallow-edged turquoise harbor that links Harrington Sound to the ocean. Directly opposite Flatts on the inlet lies the Bermuda Aquarium, Museum & Zoo, the area's main attraction. Aside from the few restaurants and a bakery, there's virtually nothing to do in Flatts Village itself except ogle the tide as the ocean sweeps in and out of the pristine sound twice a day, the two-knot current creating the nearest thing to river rapids for wannabe white-water kayakers. Sport anglers return to port at sunset, while those with less high-tech accoutrements simply cast their lines over Flatts Bridge and nearby docks when weather permits. Fishing off island bridges is supposedly illegal, but the rule seems to be widely ignored and, judging by the pastime's popularity, rarely enforced. Line fishing is allowed from the rocks beneath the bridge, however, and containers for disposing of old fishing line—a hazard for turtles and other marinelife—have been installed here. Jumping and diving off the bridge into the rushing tide is a favorite summertime activity of daredevil youth. In the early mornings or evenings, spotted eagle rays and larger manta rays can be seen swooping beneath, as they commute between the sound and the shore beyond.

The area is historically important, since Flatts was one of Bermuda's earliest and busiest settlements of the 17th and 18th centuries, when travel and communication between the parishes was primarily by boat. Like other sheltered harbor settlements, including Crow Lane, Ely's Harbor, and Riddell's Bay, Flatts became a center for trade—and a refuge for smugglers fleeing customs duties levied by Hamilton and St. George's. "Later, when Bermudians turned to shipbuilding and overseas trading, these villages took on the significance of home ports," wrote historian William Zuill in his 1946 parish tour, *Bermuda Journey.* The sleepy whimsy formerly found in Flatts has been mostly lost in the noise and speed of today's nonstop traffic, which flows through the village via North Shore Road—as well as summer's marine rush hour at day's end in the inlet.

★ Bermuda Aquarium, Museum & Zoo

Bermuda's best-known attraction, the **Bermuda Aquarium, Museum & Zoo** (BAMZ, 40 North Shore Rd., tel. 441/293-2727, fax 441/293-3176, www.bamz.org, 9am-5pm daily except Christmas Day, last admission 4pm, gift shop 10am-4pm, $10 adults, $5 seniors and children 5-12, kids under 5 free, wheelchair-accessible) sits opposite Flatts Village on the facing shore of Flatts Inlet, attracting crowds of visitors and locals alike. Some 15 percent of Bermuda's population are members, and more than 100,000 people visit annually. Supported by the nonprofit Bermuda Zoological Society (BZS), the facility is government owned and attracts both public and private funding. While it is a fun, recreational venue, BAMZ, through its support charity, is also a hub for important research and conservation programs—protecting marine turtles, coral reefs, and endangered skink lizards, among other species. Environmental education is also a core goal: Through BZS educators, the center supplements the science curricula of more than 6,000 students annually, offering marine and terrestrial field trips, school visits, holiday camps, and outreach programs. Through exhibits in the aquarium and zoo, BAMZ and BZS work to raise awareness about fragile oceanic islands—not only the delicate balance of Bermuda's own flora and fauna, but also that of Australasia, the Caribbean, Madagascar, and other threatened ecosystems. The facility has been accredited by the Association of Zoos & Aquariums (AZA) since 1993.

Opened at the present site in 1928, BAMZ was born of a collaboration between the Bermuda government, island environmentalists, and American scientists from Harvard and New York Universities who, together, set up a biology and zoology research station at Flatts as early as 1903. After various relocations during the two World Wars, the aquarium and the Bermuda Biological Station for Research became established as separate entities, though they continue to work together on many projects.

BAMZ offers an up-close look at Bermuda's marinelife, especially that of its precious coral reefs—some of the most northerly in the world. The aquarium's main hall, renovated in 2014, displays large moray eels, schools of silver minnows and squid, spiny lobsters, gigantic groupers, beaked parrotfish, an octopus, and a total of 200 species of fish and invertebrates. The pièce de résistance is the 140,000-gallon North Rock Exhibit—the first living coral reef exhibit of its scale in the world. Occupying the whole western side of the main aquarium building, the tank is actually two interlocking tanks naturally lit from above, cleverly mimicking what you might see by diving on North Rock, a reefy outcrop some 10 miles north of the facility

A pufferfish is one of many local species on display at Bermuda Aquarium, Museum & Zoo.

shallow bay in Blue Hole Park and Walsingham Nature Reserve

on the North Shore. Inside the smaller front tank, tiny jewel-like reef fish dart among anemones, queen angelfish sway like ballerinas, and sponges, corals, and sea fans all can be seen up close. Behind this, the larger tank offers floor-to-ceiling viewing of sharks, barracudas, schools of pompano, golden-frilled triggerfish, and a mammoth black grouper, nicknamed "Darth Vader." Benches are provided, and children—even babies and toddlers—can commune at floor-level with the various curiosities, making this a popular place for playgroups and family outings.

The lively seal exhibit, with western Atlantic harbor seals, is located near the entrance. You can watch daily feedings at 9:30am, 1:10pm, and 4pm. Beyond the aquarium's front entrance, in an outdoor pool next to the bus stop, swim a collection of green turtles, some rescued after being injured in boating accidents.

The on-site Natural History Museum explores the geology and biodiversity of Bermuda with audiovisual and interactive exhibits, as well as lab-style drawer displays of preserved animals. Outside, the zoo contains more than 300 birds, mammals, and reptiles in exhibits that aim to teach about the habitats found on oceanic islands. Redbrick paths, rest areas, lookouts over Harrington Sound, and beautifully landscaped gardens featuring some of Bermuda's most exotic flowering plants and trees encourage a leisurely visit that can easily span a couple of hours. A flock of 65 pink flamingos lives in a large open area at the zoo, where the birds have bred successfully.

The Australasia Exhibit recreates the humid interior and landscape of a rainforest for the menagerie of tree kangaroos, wallabies, and a python that live here. Parrots squawk loudly in the cliff-style rock faces above them. In the Caribbean Exhibit, cardinals and other birds dart freely among bamboo and other tropical forest plants, along with pairs of golden lion tamarins. The monkeys are part of an international conservation program, the Species Survival Plan (SSP), which links Bermuda to an organized effort to boost the populations of endangered animals. Bred in captivity, many tamarins are released back into the Brazilian rainforest. You will also see spoonbills, scarlet ibises, a two-toed sloth, and endangered Haitian sliders (terrapins) in this exhibit.

Madagascar: Land of Mystery and Wonder opened in 2011 and features a predatory, catlike fossa, as well as a troupe of lemurs that leap around a large free-flight area featuring a waterfall and tsingy-style rock formations. There are also gem exhibits showcasing the vibrant beauty of tiny tomato frogs and chameleons.

The Bermuda Zoological Society gift shop sells eco-friendly items, and an on-site café opened on the Harrington Sound waterfront in 2013.

★ Blue Hole Park and Walsingham Nature Reserve

This vast property (sunrise-sunset daily, admission free), held largely by a private family trust but open to the public, incorporates coast and forested land from Blue Hole Park to

Tom Moore's Jungle (as Walsingham Nature Reserve is more frequently called). Of the whole area, government-owned Blue Hole Park is the only designated public park, with the best access and parking. Although each area of interest can be accessed by its respective entrance—a half mile or so apart—all are linked, so they can be explored on foot from any entry point.

Tom Moore's Jungle (Walsingham Ln., off Harrington Sound Rd.) is a tangle of cherry forests, crystalline caves, and mangroves surrounding Tom Moore's Tavern, a four-star restaurant housed in a 1652 waterfront inn. Both the tavern and jungle take the name of Thomas Moore, an Irish poet and bon vivant whose mediocre romantic verse during a brief stay as court registrar (January-April 1804) managed to keep him very much alive in local legend. A highlight of the so-called jungle are the swimming grottoes, fed via subterranean tunnels by the tides of Castle Harbour; turtles and fish can often be seen in the turquoise depths. The Castle Harbour coastline here is also perfect for snorkeling; the shallow bays, reefs, and mangroves invite hours of exploration. Bird-watchers will enjoy spotting not only the many herons that stalk crabs on the shore, but also finches, cardinals, and doves. Caves honeycomb the woodlands, like a children's fairy story. Part of this chunk of land, the 1.25-acre Idwal Hughes Nature Reserve, is owned by the Bermuda National Trust and contains indigenous palmettos and cedars, along with unique geological formations.

The region is also riddled with underwater caves, including the most famous, Crystal Cave and Fantasy Cave, which are open to the public. Tom Moore's Jungle connects to Blue Hole Park through a woodland trail leading under diminutive bush archways, quaint enough to have been fashioned by elfin folk. Blue Hole Park, home to a popular dolphin show in the 1970s, is honeycombed with caves, including a cave mouth called Causeway Cave and caverns along the shoreline filled with seawater. Bermuda's oldest rock, a very hard limestone estimated to be 800,000 years old, can be found at the surface in the Walsingham area.

Bermuda's most famous tree, a calabash, is located here. Tom Moore sat in its generous shade to compose his poems, and on November 4, 1844, members of the nascent Royal Bermuda Yacht Club held their first meeting and a celebratory lunch under its branches; the iconic club has celebrated key anniversaries at the spot ever since. Tragically, Hurricane Emily in 1987 nearly destroyed the tree, but cuttings were replanted and it has now sprouted to several feet in height. Follow the trail left of the tavern about 200 yards to a clearing, where you will see the surviving sapling.

Holy Trinity Church

With a picture-perfect setting, **Holy Trinity Church** (Trinity Church Rd., off Harrington Sound Rd. or North Shore Rd.) also happens to be historically important. The current building, or at least part of the nave, dates back to 1660-1670, but historians believe there was an even earlier stone structure on the site that bore a palmetto-thatch roof. Regardless, Holy Trinity is one of the oldest church buildings in the Western Hemisphere, having survived hurricanes, storm damage, and numerous alterations and additions over the centuries.

Perhaps the church's most notable feature is its array of 28 stained glass windows, most of them English and installed since the 1890s. Five of these were designed by Sir Edward Burne-Jones, a noted pre-Raphaelite artist who designed for the William Morris Company. Experts have declared the quintet the best collection of his work anywhere in the world. Holy Trinity's furnishings are also impressive, including its mahogany pulpit, the 200-year-old Bevington-built organ, and a bronze baptismal font made in the 1970s by a resident sculptor (the original 1840s stone font can be seen in the churchyard). The church's silver collection is valuable, with the oldest piece, a handsome tankard, dedicated to "the church of Hambleton Tribe, 1677." Outside,

Beebe's Bathysphere

In August 1934, Bermuda made global headlines when two scientists achieved a pioneering feat that stunned the scientific community and captured the public imagination: They descended a record-making 3,028 feet (a nautical half mile) off the island encased in a steel contraption called a bathysphere. Naturalist William Beebe, a former assistant curator of birds at the New York Zoological Society, and bathysphere inventor Otis Barton had spent several years in area waters, establishing the Bermuda Oceanographic Expedition in 1928. The island made an ideal laboratory thanks to its biodiversity, year-round mild climate, and easily accessible depths of more than 12,000 feet. It was the perfect testing ground for the steel pod, which was lowered by steel cable from a ship at the surface into the black reaches of the deep ocean, where two tall men curled up like spiders would stare from a glass porthole at the most wondrous specimens the world had ever seen.

"Here I was privileged to peer out and actually see the creatures which had evolved in the blackness of a blue midnight which, since the ocean was born, had known no following day," later noted Beebe in his 1934 book, *Half-Mile Down.* Electricity and a phone line were run into the bathysphere, allowing Beebe's observations to be relayed to an artist at the surface who made fantastic drawings of the iridescent fish, silvery eels, flying snails, and mists of crustaceans for the world to ogle. "We are still alive," was his comment to the anxiously waiting team at the surface when the pair dipped for the first time to a depth of a quarter mile.

Beebe, who had switched his scientific focus from birds to tropical studies in the 1920s and begun his diving quest with a homemade helmet, had an uncanny ability to describe the eerie netherworld of the deep in a way that was entirely factual, yet read like science fiction.

"To the ever-recurring question, 'How does it feel?' I can only quote the words of Herbert Spencer: I felt like 'an infinitesimal atom floating in illimitable space,'" he noted. "No wonder my sole contribution to science at the time was: 'Am writing at a depth of a quarter of a mile. A luminous fish is outside my window.'"

Beebe continued his research in Bermuda through World War II, carrying out scores of dives in the submersible chamber. He also wrote numerous popular works on his discoveries, inspiring laypersons and scientists alike with his detailed descriptions of "the last frontier." Life-sized replicas of his 5,000-pound bathysphere—which measured just four feet, nine inches in diameter—can be found at both the Bermuda Aquarium, Museum & Zoo and the Bermuda Underwater Exploration Institute.

wander through the churchyard with its roses and royal palms, and view gravestones bearing the names of this parish's hallmark families and seafarers—Outerbridge, Trott, Vesey—many of whose descendants still live in the area. The church is open on Saturdays while it is being cleaned and on Sundays during services (10:30am), but contact the parsonage (tel. 441/293-5366 or 441/293-1710) if you would like to arrange a visit at another time.

★ Crystal Cave and Fantasy Cave

While the group tour experience can sometimes be kitschy, the actual geological phenomena visible in these two dramatic caves is worth the price of admission. Superstar Beyoncé loved them so much during a 2008 visit, she chose to stage a fashion shoot inside the caverns. While **Crystal Cave and Fantasy Cave** (Wilkinson Ave., tel. 441/293-0640, www.caves.bm, 9am-5pm daily, by guided tour only, last tour 4:30pm) are but two of hundreds of caverns around Harrington Sound and Castle Harbour, they are the largest and the only ones open to the public. Guided tours are carried out every 20 to 30 minutes throughout the day; in the winter, when visitor numbers dwindle, you might be lucky enough to get a private viewing. Admission to each cave is $22 ($30 both caves) for adults and $10 ($12) for children ages 5-12

Bermuda Turtle Project

In the summer of 2005, a handful of baby turtles hatched from eggs on an East End Bermuda beach and laboriously wobbled their way down to the nearby surf. Not so exceptional, perhaps, for waters frequented by marine turtles, except for the fact that it was the first time in almost a century that eggs had actually been laid and successfully hatched on the island. The phenomenon was celebrated by local naturalists involved in the Bermuda Turtle Project (www.conserveturtles.org), one of the world's longest-running tagging and research programs, established in 1968, which today partners with the Sea Turtle Conservancy.

While the baby turtles in question were loggerheads, the Bermuda Turtle Project is mainly focused on the critically endangered green turtle *(Chelonia mydas)*, once so plentiful on the island that colonists would gather hundreds of eggs at a time and capture 40 adults per boat per day. The species diminished almost immediately as a result; as early as 1620, the Bermuda Assembly moved to prevent turtle killing. Modern threats, despite legal protection, are no less severe. Turtles fall victim to boat collisions as well as to ocean debris such as plastics, Styrofoam, tar, and balloons, which fatally clog their digestive tracts. Entanglement in fishing gear, including discarded nets and lines, also kills marine turtles.

The Bermuda Turtle Project, through the Bermuda Zoological Society and the Bermuda Aquarium, Museum & Zoo, works to educate Bermudians about these dangers, as well as to gather and share vital information on turtles' life history. Green turtles are carried by ocean currents for the first years of their lives, until they mature enough to feed off the bottom in inshore habitats. Bermuda's green turtles are such juveniles, who spend up to 15 years in this "developmental" stage, grazing on lush sea grass beds amid the coral reefs in the island's surrounding atoll. Once adult, and averaging 300 pounds, green turtles migrate south to foraging and mating grounds.

Ultimately, the Turtle Project hopes to encourage a return of nesting populations on the island. In the 1970s, more than 25,000 green turtle eggs were brought to Bermuda from Costa Rica and buried on isolated beaches. Some 16,000 turtles hatched and swam away. Since turtles are known to return to nest at the beach where they were born, scientists hope that when these offspring reach maturity (age 50 in green turtles, whose lifespan reaches a century), they will come back to Bermuda.

Green turtles tagged or recorded in Bermuda have been traced back to origins in Costa Rica, Florida, Mexico, Suriname, and Venezuela, showing the vast ocean ranges covered by the species. Unfortunately, the size of its habitat poses dangers: Many turtles mature safely in Bermuda only to be slaughtered in the Caribbean or Central and South America—a problem the project is working to change. Each summer, the project invites students, scientists, and resource managers from turtle-visited countries such as Costa Rica, Nicaragua, Panama, and the United States to take part in a 10-day field course. Participants visit sea grass beds on the Bermuda platform and net turtles who feed there to learn methods of gathering data—including turtle growth rates, movement patterns, and even the genetic composition of turtles found around Bermuda. Project scientists are also teaching the use of satellite telemetry to track movements of turtles.

(kids under 5 are free). If you visit just one cave, Crystal Cave is the most eye-popping and features a greater variety of formations.

Island folklore tells how Crystal Cave was discovered in the early 1900s by two boys playing a game of cricket. When they lost their ball down a hole, they found a subterranean wonderland beneath their feet. A 25-minute tour leads 80 feet down into the earth by way of a steep set of stairs cut into the hard limestone rock. At the bottom, the well-lit series of caverns opens up to expose a sapphire-bottomed lagoon, some 55 feet deep, over which a "floating trail" of pontoon bridges has been erected. Walk across the water, past soaring stalagmites and spearlike stalactites dripping like incessant taps into the pool. The water is incredibly inviting, especially in the torpor of summer, but swimming is not allowed.

A brief "nature walk" leads through an

avenue of royal palms and down a redbrick path through the estate gardens to Fantasy Cave. Avocado trees, sprawling Indian laurels, a fiddlewood forest, and mature cherry groves nearly drown out the traffic at the busy intersection beyond. This cave's 88 steps wind down to another subterranean wonder, an open area dense with crystalline columns and more stalactites and stalagmites. Narrow walkways allow you to explore various underground nooks and crannies before climbing back to the surface, a 30-minute adventure.

The property has picnic tables under awnings, a popular café, a gift shop selling (imported) gemstones, rock crystal, and quartz, and pristine public bathrooms.

Crawl, Bailey's Bay, and Coney Island

A trio of North Shore neighborhoods leads from Shelly Bay to the Causeway in Hamilton Parish. Peppered with gospel halls, a rainbow of cottages, and essential services like gas stations, variety stores, and coin laundry centers, they are totally local in focus, without important attractions or fancy restaurants—or even signposts letting you know when you've passed from one into another. But all give a good sense of regular Island life. The Railway Trail is the perfect way to traverse each area, via the rocky coastline. Bicycles, scooters, and mopeds would also allow you to explore the region easily. It also sits on the main bus route. Crawl is essentially a neighborhood hillside leading up past Shelly Bay as you head east. Artist Otto Trott's gallery sits here, and Dub City Variety stocks snacks and sundries. The Railway Trail leaves Shelly Bay, following the coastline to Burchall Cove, before leading past craggy limestone formations, inlets, and bays into Crawl. This is one of the trail's most beautiful sections, exposing seaside cottages and charming old butteries as it hugs the ocean on its way to the dramatic island-dotted seascape of Bailey's Bay. While the noisy main road runs parallel nearby, the thick limestone walls of the railway bed shut out most of civilization, allowing for a tranquil escape. Crawl ends at Bailey's Bay, a sheltered harbor for small boats surrounded by hilly residential pockets and farmland. Eastward around the corner, turn into Coney Island Park, a rugged peninsula incorporating parkland, beach coves, a cricket club, and various government outposts such as the Fisheries Department. There's a Jamaican Grill restaurant here, and usually a cricket match on summer weekends.

BEACHES

North Shore Road's rocky shoreline throughout Hamilton Parish—from Flatts Inlet to Coney Island—provides plenty of quiet coves, fishing spots, and swimming holes for adventurous travelers. The beauty of this shoreline is the lack of beach crowds (for there are few beaches). Instead, deep pristine water falls away from low rocks, from which the daring can dive. The shoreline, calmest when the wind is blowing from the south, is blanketed in reef life, making it ideal for snorkeling or kayaking.

★ Shelly Bay Beach and Nature Reserve

Incorporating a lovely beach, a first-rate playground, a cricket pitch, soccer fields, and a protected nature reserve, this chunk of coastal Hamilton Parish invites hours of recreation. It is a favorite spot for family get-togethers and children's parties on weekends throughout the spring and summer months.

The soft white sand and gentle slope of the beach make it a perfect spot for small children or swimmers who lack confidence. Although the busy North Shore Road is all too near, the beach's beauty on a summer morning is enough to tune out any traffic noise. Due to its easy access, the beach is also a magnet for windsurfers when the breeze swings around to the northwest. Picnic tables are situated on the grassy lawns adjacent to the beach to the east. Bordering the park is a nature reserve, home to biodiverse mangroves.

Shark Hole

A dock at the ominously named Shark Hole (there's virtually no risk of the toothy reality) allows easy access to swim or snorkel in the emerald waters of this corner of the sound. Encircled by cliffs and bypassed by a hairpin section of Harrington Sound Road, the inviting grotto is also the site of a cave that extends beneath the main road. If you venture inside, you can hear the passing traffic above.

SPORTS AND RECREATION

Hamilton Parish offers a world of outdoor spaces and pursuits, from organized underwater tours to trails and parks for independent exploration. Soccer fields and cricket pitches are at Shelly Bay Beach Park and the charming Sea Breeze Cricket Oval on Coney Island. Both are good spots to watch island teams of both sports (depending on the season) and mix with avid local fans, who are usually more than happy to explain the complexities of the games.

Scuba and Water Sports

Get your blood racing with a wakeboarding outing aboard John Martin's **AXIS Adrenaline Projects** (Flatts Inlet, tel. 441/537-1114, www.axisadrenaline.com, $200 per hour for groups up to 10). Armed with Ronix and Radar gear aboard his custom Tige RZ2 speedboat, he'll calmly teach you the basics—then let you jump the wake and fly. Based in Flatts Inlet, he can pick up islandwide.

Triangle Diving (Grotto Bay Beach Resort, 11 Blue Hole Hill, tel. 441/293-7319, www.trianglediving.com) is a five-star PADI dive center, offering certification and advanced courses, night dives, one- and two-tank dives, and private charters. The facility also sells diving equipment. Its location allows for excursions to the many East End dive sites, including Spanish shipwreck *Cristobal Colon,* some 10 miles offshore near North Rock Beacon, and the popular "Cathedral," a towering coral reef preserve you can swim through, situated just off the St. David's Island shore. Rates include a one-tank dive for $95, a two-tank dive for $135, and 10 dives for $575.

Blue Hole Water Sports (Grotto Bay Beach Resort, 11 Blue Hole Hill, tel. 441/293-2915 or 441/293-8333, ext. 37, www.bluehole-water.bm) has a wide assortment of stress-free water sports, including paddle-your-own Sunkats, sit-on-top kayaks, and snorkel gear, as well as Sunfish sailboats, sailboards, and small motorboat rentals (13-foot Boston whalers). Sailboards and sailboats are $35 an hour, motorboats $150 for four hours. All are perfect ways to explore the turquoise calm of Ferry Reach and Castle Harbour.

Ana Luna Adventures (at Grotto Bay Beach Resort dock, tel. 441/504-3780, analunaadventures.com) runs sailing charters May through August aboard its 45-foot French-built catamaran, including afternoon snorkel outings ($69), glow-worm tours ($69), sunset champagne cruises ($59), and history tours ($59) past the UNESCO-protected forts around St. David's and St. George's Harbour. All departures from the Grotto Bay Beach Resort dock. Private charters can also be booked ($69 per person for three hours, minimum 10 guests).

Railway Trail (Hamilton Parish)

Pick up the Railway Trail in Hamilton Parish on North Shore Road, after crossing Flatts Bridge and passing the Bermuda Aquarium, Museum & Zoo. Rounding the next corner as you head east, you can pull in on the left, where there is a space to park scooters looking out toward the ocean. Access to and through the Shelly Bay area is easy and scenic, thanks to a boardwalk linking the Railway Trail with the beach, a half mile away. The wooden walkway allows walkers, runners, and bikers to stick to a safe, coastal path that runs parallel to busy North Shore Road. The trail continues through a protected nature reserve, northeast of Shelly Bay's picnic park, which contains mangrove-fringed tidal pools and many indigenous plants. Continue on the trail

Old Rattle and Shake

The onetime Bermuda Railway was a short-lived initiative that nonetheless offered a popular mode of transport in the years before private cars were allowed on the island.

Opened in October 1931, the train—whose common nickname was "Old Rattle and Shake"—carried passengers in first- and second-class carriages across the length of the island. At a time of racial segregation, the higher-priced sections were outfitted with wicker chairs and reserved for whites, while cheaper seats, for blacks, consisted of simple benches. Thirty-three bridges linked Bermuda's islands along the 22-mile line, an end-to-end journey that gave passengers accustomed to horse-and-carriage, bicycle, or boat travel a whole new perspective of the island.

The privately financed venture suffered from continual delays, breakdowns, and other snafus, however, running up large debts and eventually becoming unworkable. Notably, the train's key components—iron and diesel—were found utterly incompatible with Bermuda's rust-inducing climate, and the cost of shipping fuel to the island was prohibitive. The Bermuda government took over the line for a few years but finally closed it down in 1948, selling it off to British Guyana.

The advent of automobiles in Bermuda was the final nail in the railway's coffin. After high-profile protests, including a petition signed by Mark Twain and Woodrow Wilson (both Bermudaphiles), led to a government ban on cars early in the 20th century, automobiles for private use were finally made legal and available in 1946, along with taxis. Though legislators assumed that duties and licensing would restrict vehicle numbers, they underestimated the American-style consumer tastes of Bermuda residents; before long, the once-peaceful crushed-coral roads had been asphalted, and locals were enjoying their newfound speed and mobility.

Neglected for decades afterwards, the old rail line was rehabilitated by the Bermuda government in the 1990s as a pedestrian walkway through the island as part of the public parks system. The Railway Trail has since become a highly popular route with walking clubs, joggers, horseback riders, and mountain bikers. Former parish stations, housed in trailside cottages, can be seen en route. Over the past couple of years, new interpretive signage has been erected along the trail, making the route easier to navigate. The project was sponsored by Catlin End-to-End (www.bermudaendtoend.bm), a nonprofit group that hosts a springtime St. George's-to-Dockyard fundraising walk that attracts thousands of participants and, since 1988, has raised more than $4 million for island charities.

through the Crawl neighborhood, where, hugging the craggy coastline, it offers beautiful marine views but also a glimpse of Bermudian life as you wander past shoreline cottages. The Bermuda government and a nonprofit, Friends of Bermuda Railway Trail, reconnected the Crawl trail with its Bailey's Bay continuation in 2014 through construction of several wooden bridges across the water via the original stone pylons. The project allows pedestrians and pedal cyclists to avoid the busy main road and keep to the shore-based trail instead.

ENTERTAINMENT AND EVENTS

Runners, walkers, and cyclists turn out for the Bermuda Zoological Society's **Zoom Around the Sound** (tel. 441/293-2727 ext. 130, volunteers.bzs@gov.bm), a 7.2-mile circular course around Harrington Sound via Harrington Sound Road and North Shore Road. Held in March to raise money for the Bermuda Aquarium, Museum & Zoo, the race starts and finishes at BAMZ. The entry fee is $20. Refreshments are served, and T-shirts and goody bags go to all participants.

Open (free admission) days, kids' storytime (11:15am Fri.), yoga classes, lectures, and themed events are held regularly at **Bermuda Aquarium, Museum & Zoo** (40 North Shore Rd., Flatts, tel. 441/293-2727, www.bamz.org).

SHOPPING

Hamilton Parish shopping is limited to small gift and souvenir stores inside several of the main attractions and restaurants, including the Swizzle Inn, the caves, the Grotto Bay Beach Resort, and the Bermuda Aquarium, Museum & Zoo. The latter is probably the most interesting, with its eco-friendly inventory, such as stuffed toys and quality plastic animal toys for kids (including dinosaurs and endangered species); soothing classical and world music CDs; and a good collection of Bermuda books, including the comprehensive coffee-table edition of *The Natural History of Bermuda,* by Canadian biologist Martin Thomas, and diver/photographer Ron Lucas's *Bermuda Reef Portraits,* both published by the Bermuda Zoological Society.

ACCOMMODATIONS

Under $200

Brightside Guest Apartments (38 North Shore Rd., Flatts Village, tel. 441/292-8410, www.brightsidebermuda.com) has been a fixture of Flatts since 1979. The family-run property commands the southwest portion of so-called Lazy Corner—the busy junction of Middle Road, North Shore Road, and Harrington Sound Road—so tranquility is not its biggest drawing card. However, the guest units are cushioned by beautifully landscaped gardens, and there's a large swimming pool in the center of the complex. Units, all with basic decor, range from a room with double bed ($145) to a cottage accommodating four people ($455). A new addition to the property is a three-bedroom, three-bath poolside cottage ($720). All rooms have a microwave, refrigerator, coffee pot, phone, cable TV, and air-conditioning. The location is handy for sights (the aquarium, the caves, St. George's), restaurants, beaches, and bus routes.

Over $300

The 21-acre **Grotto Bay Beach Resort** (11 Blue Hole Hill, tel. 441/293-8333, toll-free U.S. tel. 800/582-3190, fax 441/293-2306, www.grottobay.com, oceanview/waterfront suites $389-439 d, minimum three-night stay) covers a lush hillside above the Causeway, giving panoramic views of Castle Harbour, Coney Island, Ferry Reach, and the airport, less than a mile away. The resort's many yards of coastline encompass sheltered coves, an east-facing main beach, and a dock with a water-sports center offering scuba, snorkeling, waterskiing, sailing, windsurfing, pedal boating, and parasailing. The property claims its own crystal cave, nestled in landscaped grounds; a small spa; a pool; and four tennis courts, two lit for night play. The casual atmosphere, coupled with a playground and children's program during the high season, makes the resort a good choice for family vacations.

The large Great House lobby is reminiscent of a comfortable hunting lodge, or possibly a Polynesian loft, with open-beamed ceilings, solid oak floors, knotty pine columns, a cozy winter fireplace, and numerous nooks and crannies on two floors for reading or meeting friends. Two dining rooms—one formal, the other laid-back tropical—are located off the lobby. Many of the 201 suites, outfitted in tropical prints, are somewhat boxy, with tiny bathrooms, but have lovely views of the bay below.

FOOD

Cafés and Pubs

Parents, kids, and zoogoers love **AZU Beastro** (at Bermuda Aquarium, Museum & Zoo, tel. 441/296-2429, www.bamz.org, 9am-4pm daily) for the made-to-order sandwiches, paninis, and wraps ($6-12). The grill menu ($4-13.50) includes burgers, beef franks, tandoori chicken breast, tuna burgers, and fish tacos, and you can also create your own pizza with healthy toppings like arugula, peppers, and goat cheese. The kids' menu delivers junior treats such as grilled cheese and fish nuggets. Licensed for beer and wine, it's a handy rest stop for moms and dads while the little ones keep busy in the nearby zoo playground.

Pizza House Restaurant (at the Shelly Bay MarketPlace, North Shore Rd., tel. 441/293-8465, fax 441/293-1290, 11am-10pm daily, $4.50-26) is one of a three-outlet chain (also at Southside and Heron Bay) offering pizza slices, pizza trays for parties, sandwiches, subs, burgers, salads, cold drinks, and snacks. **Buzz N Go Crawl Hill** (at the Esso Tigermart gas station, tel. 441/293-0777, www.buzzcafe.bm, 6am-10pm daily) is the Hamilton Parish branch of the successful chain of delis, offering sandwiches, paninis, salads, smoothies, and specialty coffees.

Jamaican Grill's Coney Island outlet (1 Duck's Puddle, tel. 441/293-8899, 11am-10pm Mon.-Wed., 7am-midnight Thurs.-Sat., 7am-10pm Sun., $10-13) serves up West Indian favorites like jerk chicken, coconut fish, and cocoa bread.

Run by the efficient, cheery Barbara Outerbridge, ★ **Café Olé** (8 Crystal Cave Rd. off Wilkinson Ave., tel. 441/293-7865, 9am-4pm for the grill, until 5pm for snacks daily) attracts taxi drivers and other local clientele by offering breakfast and opening on Sundays. Service is super-friendly and fast, the restaurant spotless, and the menu tasty. Breakfast includes a choice of eggs, bacon, or a combo sandwich, while the lunch menu has fish sandwiches, hot dogs, homemade hamburgers ($7), ice cream ($3.50 a scoop), sandwiches, cookies, and other snacks. The property is a perfect place to stop for lunch while heading east. Quaintly tiled, powder room-style bathrooms are located a few steps from the café.

A local institution, the ★ **Swizzle Inn Pub & Restaurant** (3 Blue Hole Hill, tel. 441/293-9300, www.swizzleinn.com, 11am-1am daily) is as much a Bermudian hangout as a tourist magnet, thanks to its lively social calendar, satisfying menu (including all-day breakfast), and deadly pitchers of rum swizzle. The Swizzle's caloric masterpiece, the Bailey's Bay Fish Sandwich ($17.50), seems to have reached legendary proportions, and regular visitors commonly stop for lunch on their way to or from the airport, which is just a few minutes away. "I have missed this so much, I couldn't leave the island again without one," confided a former resident, who now lives in Los Angeles, during a pit stop for the Dagwood-sized creation (chunks of battered local fish fillet, topped with melted cheese, tartar sauce, lettuce, and tomato, stuffed precariously inside pieces of white toast). The swizzle, made from an artful combination of Gosling's Black Seal Rum, Gold Rum, and fruit juices, is the sort of refreshing but potently mind-liberating concoction that makes it dangerous to get on a scooter afterwards. Take a cab to lunch and back instead. The Swizzle offers nightly entertainment, including live bands, trivia nights, and Mardi Gras, St. Patrick's Day, and (American) Thanksgiving celebrations. The on-site Swagger Out Gift Shop is popular for hangover souvenirs, and is accessible for online shopping via the pub's website.

Bailey's Ice-Cream (2 Blue Hole Hill, tel. 441/293-8605, 11am-10pm daily in summer, noon-6pm Mon.-Thurs. and noon-8pm Fri.-Sun. in winter) is a hot spot throughout the summer months, thanks to its 40-odd flavors of Bermuda-made cool stuff, namely award-winning ice creams, yogurts, and sorbets. In the summertime, people wait in long lines for scoops of chocolate-chip cookie dough, butterscotch crunch, Oreo sweet cream, and mango-passion fruit—all available by the tub in several island supermarkets that stock Bailey's products. Sit in the air-conditioned interior or outside on the brick patio. The 20-year-old eatery also serves snacks and sandwiches, as well as hot dogs and chili.

Bermuda's only pizza-delivery chain, **Four Star Pizza** (6 North Shore Rd., Flatts Village, tel. 441/292-9111, www.fourstar.bm, 11am-10pm Mon.-Thurs, 11am-11pm Fri.-Sat., noon-10pm Sun., $10 minimum order, $2 delivery charge) delivers deep-dish, low-carb, and 10- and 14-inch specialty pizzas, as well as calzones, sub sandwiches, salads, chicken wings, breadsticks, and desserts. Dine-in and takeout is also available. If you're accustomed to North American fast food, you might be shocked by the steep prices ($25 for a 14-inch pizza, gratuities not included).

Part of the same complex, **Glaze** (6 North Shore Rd., Flatts Village, tel. 441/292-3988,

8am-5pm daily) bakes its own breads daily, including whole wheat, raisin, and baguettes. It's also well known for special-occasion cakes and a wide assortment of pies, including mussel, beef, curried chicken, and vegetarian varieties, which are also sold at grocery and convenience stores and gas stations islandwide.

International

Tucked into a busy, curb-edge site, ★ **Rustico** (8 North Shore Rd., Flatts Village, tel. 441/295-5212, fax 441/296-6686, www.bermuda-dining.com, lunch 11:45am-2:30pm, dinner 6:15pm-10pm daily) is one of Bermuda's most popular and consistently top-quality restaurants. Sister to The Dining Room at Gibb's Hill Lighthouse, and Gulfstream, both in Southampton, Rustico offers take-out or eat-in service—either inside its cozy dining room or alfresco, where a tent-room tucked into the limestone cliffside is heated with lamps during the winter. Lovers of Mediterranean cuisine will not be disappointed here. A well-chosen wine list and menu staples like crisp calamari, escargots, inventive salads, lamb shank ossobuco ($35), grilled duck breast ($30), pastas ($16-21), thin-crust pizzas (starting at $14), and vegetarian dishes incorporating vine-ripened tomatoes, lots of garlic, polenta, and porcini and portobello mushrooms create high demand for parking spots on the narrow street outside. Devotees swear by the efficient service and tasty, carefully crafted dishes.

Fine Dining

★ **Tom Moore's Tavern** (Walsingham Ln. off Harrington Sound Rd., tel. 441/293-8020, fax 441/293-4222, www.tommoores.com, open for lunch on request, dinner 6:30pm-10pm daily, closed Cup Match Thursday, Christmas Day, and the month of January) is a AAA Four Diamond restaurant housed in a historic setting deep in the forested Walsingham Nature Reserve. The intriguing waterfront building, an old homestead built in 1652, became an inn during the 19th century and is named for Irishman Thomas Moore, who lived on the property briefly in 1804 and penned a collection of love poems beneath a calabash tree. The restaurant, colloquially referred to as "Tom Moore's," still inspires romanticism; its silver service, elegant multicourse menus, and hushed interiors make it a favored spot for very special nights out. If you pine for a $1,600 bottle of Chateau

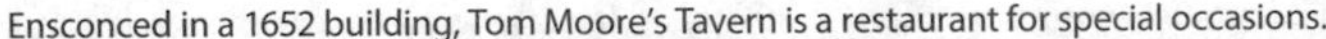
Ensconced in a 1652 building, Tom Moore's Tavern is a restaurant for special occasions.

Lafitte-Rothschild 1999, a $110 glass of dessert wine, or fountains of Armand de Brignac champagne, general manager Bruno Fiocca will make it happen. In addition to Prince Charles, who ate lunch here on an October 1970 visit to the island, the restaurant's perennial celebrity guests include oil magnate Ross Perot, former New York City mayor Michael Bloomberg, and former Italian prime minister Silvio Berlusconi, all three of whom own homes in Tucker's Town.

Canadian executive chef Robert Nicolle's menu has appetizers like caramelized sea scallops ($22), carpaccio of the day ($19), and rum-soaked fish chowder ($12); main courses range from blue cheese-stuffed pork tenderloin ($36) to slow-roasted salmon ($38) and a fish of the day ($41); and desserts include dark chocolate tart ($12), banana mousse cake ($13), and made-to-order soufflés. Ports, cognacs, and liqueurs are available. Your pocketbook will undoubtedly groan (17 percent gratuities are added to your bill), but the experience is memorable. The restaurant seats up to 160 in five rooms on two floors, making it a top choice for weddings and group parties, as well as intimate dinners-for-two. (Special bookings are not restricted by the dinner-only schedule.) In recent years, Tom Moore's has followed the island trend and relaxed its strict dress code to "elegant-casual," with no jacket required.

Groceries

Teetering halfway up Flatts Hill, **Belvin's Variety** (5 Middle Rd., tel. 441/292-4583, 6am-midnight daily) would be easy to miss were it not for all the truck drivers, cabbies, and neighborhood residents angling for a parking spot outside. The pocket-sized convenience store is perfect for picking up a daily newspaper, cream bun, cat food, or any assortment of other basic necessities.

Long checkout lines during weekends and evenings are the only downside of **Shelly Bay MarketPlace** (110 North Shore Rd., tel. 441/293-0966, 8am-10pm Mon.-Sat., 9pm-7pm Sun.), a superstore with everything you could want for food or drink, as well as toys, kitchen supplies, beachware like towels and coolers, party balloons, and many other products.

INFORMATION AND SERVICES

Hamilton Parish has three gas stations: **Rubis Van Buren's Marine Station** (3 North Shore Rd. at Flatts Village, tel. 441/292-2882, 7am-9pm daily); **Crawl Hill Esso Tigermart** (North Shore Rd. at Crawl Hill, tel. 441/293-6491, 6am-10pm daily), and **Rubis Causeway Service Station** (15 Blue Hole Hill, tel. 441/293-0621, 6am-10pm Mon.-Fri., 7am-10pm Sat., 8am-8pm Sun.).

Hamilton Parish has two post offices: **Crawl Post Office** (42 Radnor Rd., tel. 441/293-1400), and **Bailey's Bay Post Office** (2 Wilkinson Ave., tel. 441/293-0305). The last is a stamp-sized outlet at the North Shore junction—and a convenient place to post your mail on the way to the airport. They are all open 8am-5pm Monday-Friday.

ATMs are located outside Four Star Pizza (6 North Shore Rd.), Rubis Causeway Service Station (15 Blue Hole Hill), Shelly Bay MarketPlace (110 North Shore Rd.), and Crawl Hill Esso Tigermart (North Shore Rd. at Crawl Hill).

GETTING THERE AND AROUND

Buses

Buses are an easy way to travel through Hamilton Parish, with frequent, well-marked stops at all the major attractions, including the Bermuda Aquarium, Museum & Zoo, Shelly Bay, the caves, and Grotto Bay Beach Resort. Take route 1 (via South Shore Road, Tucker's Point, and the caves) every half hour or route 3 via Harrington Sound Road every 15 minutes (both run from the city of Hamilton-Grotto Bay/St. George's). Buses 10 and 11 travel North Shore Road (via the aquarium and Shelly Bay) every 15 minutes, between City of Hamilton and St. George's. The parish, like St. George's and Sandys, qualifies as a 14-zone area, with a tariff of $4.50 from Hamilton.

Scooters and Bicycles

Oleander Cycles (Blue Hole Hill next to Grotto Bay Beach Resort, tel. 441/293-1010, www.oleandercycles.bm, 8:30am-5pm) rents standard single or double scooters. Rates ($55 standard/$65 double for one day, $225 standard/$266 double per week, $17/$21 per day after seven days) include scooter delivery and pickup (or hotel pickup), first tank of gas, helmet, lock, basket, $30 third-party insurance, and islandwide roadside service for breakdowns. Mountain bikes are $40 a day, $175 per week, $10 a day after seven days.

Taxis

There are taxi stands at Grotto Bay Beach Resort and cabs can also be found in the parking lots at Crystal Caves and Swizzle Inn. Contact **Bermuda Industrial Union Co-op** (tel. 441/292-4476, cooptaxi@fkbnet.bm), **Bermuda Island Taxi** (tel. 441/295-4141, www.bermudaislandtaxi.com), or **BTA Dispatching Ltd.** (tel. 441/296-2121, www.taxibermuda.bm) if you need to arrange a ride.

St. George's Parish

Look for ★ to find recommended sights, activities, dining, and lodging.

Highlights

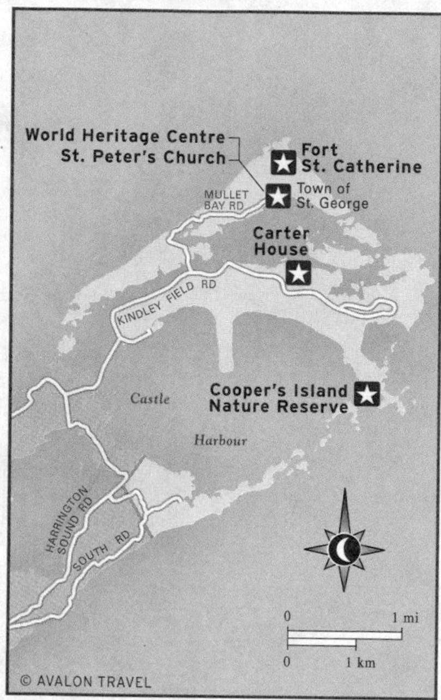

★ **World Heritage Centre:** Any tour of St. George's and the East End logically begins here, where modern exhibits, maps, brochures, and informed guides can give you Bermuda's history in a nutshell and help plan your tour of the old town and parish (page 218).

★ **St. Peter's Church:** Although its wooden predecessor was destroyed by a 17th-century hurricane, this remains the oldest continually used Protestant church site in the New World. The church's segregated graveyards—one for slaves, one for white dignitaries—are fascinating (page 221).

★ **Fort St. Catherine:** Peer over the ramparts at the very stretch of ocean the first castaways saw after escaping the shipwrecked *Sea Venture*. This large fort has exhibits on early Bermuda and military life, and replicas of the Crown Jewels (page 233).

★ **Cooper's Island Nature Reserve:** The newest addition to Bermuda's public parkland, this was once the site of a NASA tracking station. Opened to the public in 2008, the 44-acre peninsula comprises pristine beaches, coastline, and woodlands (page 244).

★ **Carter House:** This 300-year-old home-turned-museum tells the intriguing story of St. David's, from the neighborhood's days of whaling and harvesting Easter lilies to the advent of the U.S. military base (page 245).

Bermuda's old-time soul can be found in St. George's Parish, landing point of the first settlers and home to the oldest permanent English town in the New World. Wandering its shady backstreets, where peeling pastel walls, hidden gardens, and signs such as Old Maid's Lane and Featherbed Alley invite soporific afternoons, visitors get a sense of traditional island life a world away from Hamilton's bustling sidewalks and corporate milieu.

Both the parish and the old town are called St. George's. The 400-year-old town, seat of Bermuda's government for two centuries, is a UNESCO World Heritage Site, along with the parish's fortresses. The parish encompasses parkland and residential areas around the town, plus areas farther afield such as the airport, Southside, St. David's, and Tucker's Town. All of these sit on an amalgam of islands joined by bridges to form the eastern chunk of Bermuda's mainland—the so-called East End. The town and its immediate environs, as well as Ferry Point National Park, sit on St. George's Island. The parish's other main islands are St. David's Island, which is attached to a former U.S. military base, now called Southside, and Cooper's Island, a 44-acre wooded peninsula that was once a NASA site—with seven pristine beaches, it was opened to the public as a nature reserve in 2008. Scattered offshore islands and islets also belong to the parish, including Smith's, Paget, Hen, and Governor's Islands in St. George's Harbour, and Nonsuch and Castle Islands spanning the channel into Castle Harbour.

Exploration of the parish should begin in the old town, whose tangle of skinny streets, including the original town grid of the early 1600s, juxtaposes immensely historic sites with the contemporary homes of St. Georgians tackling 21st-century lives. In a nation where consumerism is king, St. George's stands apart as an anachronistic getaway, offering amusements that often demand neither transport nor a fat wallet. A stroll around its harborside square evokes images of the rowdy days of American Civil War smugglers, whose latter-day counterparts are laid-back yachties

Previous: street in St. George's; Well Bay on Cooper's Island Nature Reserve. **Above:** St. Peter's Church, the old town of St. George.

St. George's Parish

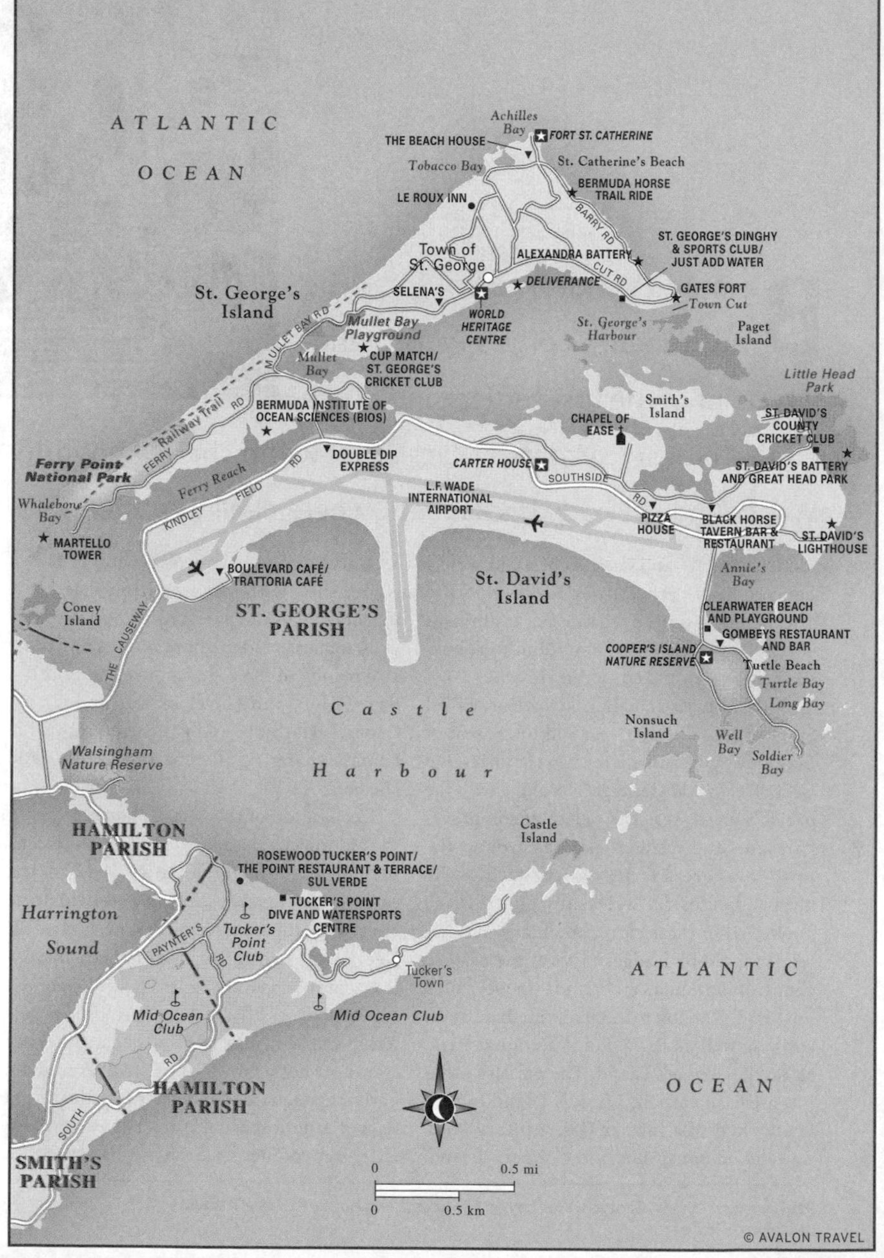

on their way to a winter in the Caribbean. The old town is the kind of place where one can idle away the hours without achieving more than some serious people-watching and enjoying an ice cream cone.

While the parish may be a treasure trove of sights for adventurous visitors, residents of the old town are still looking for their golden goose. They have spent years awaiting long-promised hotel developments to pan out to save struggling restaurants and retail outlets. Due to the town's narrow harbor mouth, most modern mega cruise ships must bypass St. George's (and Hamilton) for Dockyard. Talks of blasting out a larger passage have been slammed for environmental reasons; St. Georgians prefer the idea of attracting more smaller ships and relying on better ferry service to get passengers to their end of the island.

In the meantime, visitors who do make the trek to the East End—by scooter, taxi, bus, or ferry—will not be disappointed. In fact, to properly understand Bermuda's roots, a visit here is a must-do. That it has beautiful beaches, innovative restaurants, and some cute boutiques is just a bonus.

An interactive World Heritage Centre on the harborfront at Penno's Wharf highlights the area's fascinating history and guides modern explorers to points of interest in St. George's and beyond. Key attractions include the old town, Tobacco Bay, Fort St. Catherine—perched above the beach where shipwrecked *Sea Venture* castaways rowed to safety—and Ferry Point National Park, a national reserve where Easter lilies and cherry hedges line the eastern stretch of the Railway Trail. Then there's St. David's, a quirky community long detached from the rest of Bermuda, which remains quite unto itself, both physically and as a state of mind. Once home to Native American slaves whose descendants today proudly trace their lineage to Pequot roots, St. David's swirls with tall tales that linger from a heyday of whaling and pirating, its residents still innately tied to the sea.

Indeed, it is wholly understandable why the air pervading St. George's harks back to another time; it was only during the Victorian era that the parish was finally linked to mainland Bermuda by a half-mile causeway—and even that connection has proven at times tenuous. In 2003, when Hurricane Fabian's surges swept over the winding roadway, killing four Bermudians who were on it, St. Georgians were confined to the parish and were once again forced to fend for themselves. Government plans for a new bridge to replace the 135-year-old structure were shelved in 2008 with the onset of several recent recessionary years.

Despite perennial problems with youth gangs and petty crime, the parish remains a distinct society where neighbors generally know everyone's business and the rhythms of life invite small-town generosity, candid opinion, and an utterly fatalistic humor.

PLANNING YOUR TIME

St. George's may be your first point of contact with Bermuda, whether or not you plan to visit the parish: L. F. Wade International Airport is located here, occasional cruise ships berth in the old town, and private yachts arriving at Bermuda are required to clear Customs at the East End. Visitors tend to fall into two distinctly different categories in terms of how they spend their time. Cruise passengers of the summer and fall flock to the town's beaches; winter visitors tend to seek out the town's historic and natural highlights—its forts, museums, churches, and parks. With a few days to play with, it's easy to combine the best of both worlds.

The old town alone is worth at least a full day's exploration if you intend to properly visit its landmark buildings and stroll intriguing backstreets, not to mention its landmark forts. Exploring on foot is the best strategy. Within the town, the *Deliverance* replica, St. Peter's Church, the State House, Tucker House, and the Bermuda National Trust Museum's Rogues & Runners exhibit are vital to understanding the colorful past of St. George's.

Grand Fort St. Catherine and its beach should not be missed, either, and along the way are Alexandra Battery and the compact Gates Fort, teetering over the pencil-thin Town Cut, where liners pass, sometimes precariously, into St. George's Harbour from the open sea. Tobacco Bay's unique volcanic structures—and beachside café—make it one of Bermuda's best places to snorkel. With more time, you should expand your tour of the whole parish; if nothing else, a hike through Ferry Point National Park—home of the 1820s Martello Tower and two other forts, a lovely beach, and a scenic stretch of the Railway Trail—and a fish sandwich or lobster feast in St. David's are well worth the sidetracks. You can get to St. George's by fast ferry from Hamilton (a 45-minute journey), by scooter (a 25-minute ride from the center of the island), or via several bus routes from the capital (1, 3, 10, and 11). Don't disregard the possibility of staying in the East End; in addition to two area resorts (Grotto Bay Beach Resort and Rosewood Tucker's Point), there are several well-run bed-and-breakfasts plus self-catering apartment rentals, allowing travelers to experience St. George's overnight and soak in more of its living history.

The old town revamped itself after winning UNESCO World Heritage status in 2000. New signage was posted, and many of the most historic streets were bricked over to enhance the old-time feel. The World Heritage Centre on historic Penno's Wharf is a logical starting place for any tour of the parish, with interactive exhibits, informational booths, and helpful staff.

Weekly walking tours and historical reenactments, beach parties, and town markets on Sunday afternoons bring out locals and visitors to buy arts and crafts and listen to local entertainment. St. George's is a very festive place to visit over the end-of-year holiday season; the Bermuda National Trust Christmas Walkabout in early December—a buzzing Friday night street festival attended by thousands—is one of Bermuda's favorite events. And on New Year's Eve, you can watch a mammoth onion drop into King's Square as the old town jauntily mimics Manhattan in lively fashion.

The Old Town of St. George

Bermuda's first capital, St. George's has remained a living town from its earliest days. Never ruined or relocated, like Virginia's Jamestown, it has retained the look and feel of its 17th-century origins, representing an impressive 400 years of domestic, religious, and military architecture. Because the town was the island's major port and capital for nearly 200 years, the story of St. George's is essentially the story of early Bermuda and the island's drastic reversals of fortune that alternately shaped St. George's as a boomtown or backwater.

HISTORY

The town was named for England's patron saint and dragon slayer, Saint George, by an English admiral who claimed Bermuda for the Crown in 1609. Sir George Somers headed the English relief fleet, which in July 1609 was crossing the Atlantic with supplies for James Fort, Virginia, when it was hit by a hurricane. The flagship *Sea Venture,* carrying Somers and 150 men, women, and children, wrecked off St. Catherine's Beach. Miraculously, no one perished in the disaster, nor did the ship sink. Wedged on reefs, *Sea Venture* and her contents were salvaged by the survivors, who spent the next 10 months as castaways, fashioning two new ships of island cedar, *Deliverance* and *Patience.* The wreck's remains eventually sank and today are buried beneath sand.

All but three men continued their journey to the New World in 1610, Somers among them. But when the admiral later sailed back

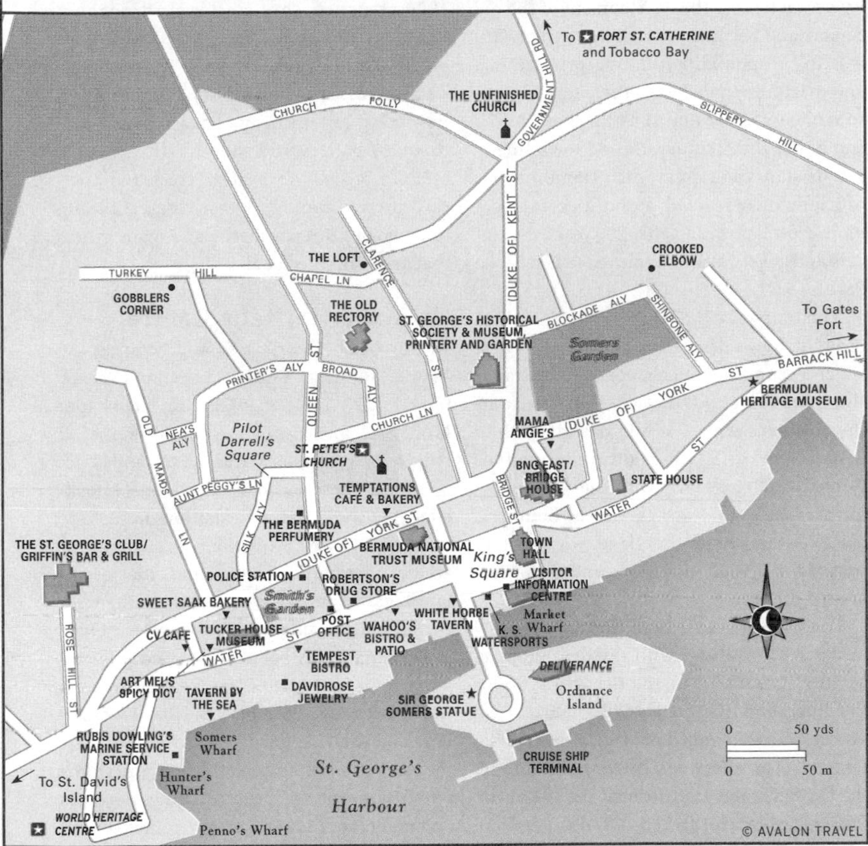

to Bermuda to gather more supplies for the starving Virginia settlers, he died, purportedly after eating contaminated meat. His body was returned to his birthplace, Lyme Regis in Dorset, England—now also a World Heritage Site and the sister city of St. George's since 1996. The admiral's heart was buried in what now is the site of Somers Garden, near the town center.

The physical town began as a collection of palmetto-thatched wooden huts built by the first official settlers, who sailed from England in 1612 aboard the *Plough*. Erected around a market square, the community was dubbed New London. The colonists had to learn how to adapt to life in the tropics, and improvise building methods and materials; by the close of their first century, colonists' huts had been replaced by sturdier limestone buildings and bridges linking Bermuda's main islands.

More than half of Bermuda's 90 fortifications were erected here, surviving virtually intact as the earliest English masonry forts of the New World (most in the Americas were constructed of timber). Bermuda never actually came under enemy fire, however. Today, the UNESCO site comprising the town and surrounding forts is considered "a place of cultural heritage of the greatest importance for humanity."

A pattern of economic stagnation interspersed with periods of immense prosperity characterized the development of the old capital, and Bermuda as a whole. In the 1700s, whaling, shipbuilding, piloting, privateering, and maritime trade built a thriving economy as St. George's became a bustling port. At the end of the 18th century, the old town finally lost its status as capital when Hamilton was officially incorporated; authorities wanted a more central port, and after 200 years, the seat of island government was moved to Pembroke Parish.

The four-year U.S. Civil War (1861-1865) brought boom times back to St. George's, which became a strategic port for the transshipment of goods between Britain and the Southern states. While the island, like Britain, was officially neutral, Bermudian sympathies lay heavily with the South; cotton ("white gold") was carried by Southern blockade runners to the island, where it was traded for British munitions and European luxury goods.

Tourism proved a boon for St. George's in the 20th century, with the development of ritzy Tucker's Town and the arrival of the first liners and flying boats to Bermuda. Later, World War II changed the face of the parish forever. A land-lease deal between Britain and the United States transformed the islands of Castle Harbour into a U.S. Naval Air Station whose airbase later became Bermuda's civilian airport. The U.S. military pulled out in 1995, and the East End baselands were renamed "Southside" and opened for public use. Beaches, an emergency medical center, and sports areas sit on the land, which has also been used as a site for affordable housing.

SIGHTS

The old town has a plethora of public museums and historic sites open to visitors most of the year, but bear in mind as you stroll around that the entire community lays claim to the World Heritage designation. As a result, the bank where you get your cash advance, the store where you buy a cashmere sweater, and the home where your bartender lives may all be immensely historic as well. Scores of pre-1800 structures are scattered throughout the town, and many are marked with their own World Heritage plaques. These include **Stockdale,** a private home on Printer's Alley; **Esten House** on King's Square, now home to an art gallery and shops; **Stiles House,** HSBC's branch on Water Street; the postcard-pretty **Fanny Fox's Cottage** at the top of Duke of Clarence Street; and many others that aren't marked at all.

★ World Heritage Centre

A tour of St. George's should begin at the **World Heritage Centre** (19 Penno's Wharf, tel. 441/297-5791, www.sgf.bm, 10am-4pm Mon.-Sat., museum admission $5 adults, $2 children, kids under 5 free, handicapped-accessible), where audiovisual exhibits, knowledgeable staff, and information on history, tours, sights, and attractions throughout the area can be found. The ground-floor orientation gallery provides an entertaining walk through Bermuda's early history, including comparisons between St. George's and Jamestown, the tale of the *Sea Venture,* and the island's key role in both the Revolutionary War and the U.S. Civil War. Also detailed is the story of whaling and other local maritime pursuits, along with eye-catching dioramas and models of the early town—complete with miniature buildings, people, and domestic animals. Voices of key characters in St. George's history help explain milestone events. A children's area invites kids to learn about life in early Bermuda with hands-on exhibits and a dress-up section where they can mimic soldiers, sea captains, and colonists. In the lobby, maps and brochures on attractions and tours are available. A "time-tree" highlighting historic episodes guides visitors upstairs, where changing exhibits relating to the Island's East End heritage are on display and a short film introducing the old town's attractions and history plays in a small amphitheater. Computer touchscreens and interpretive panels here detail the story of St. George's, St. David's, their

a replica of *Deliverance,* Cooper's Island

fortifications, and why both communities are so important to the UNESCO site. A charity shop in the building, Second Hand Rose, sells books, CDs, jewelry, china, and other trinkets, with all proceeds going to the nonprofit St. George's Foundation.

King's Square

Like every other market square in the world, King's Square has long been the hub of its community's life. Emblazoned with the town crest, the **Town Hall** (tel. 441/297-1532, 9am-4pm Mon.-Fri., admission free) is the meeting place of the mayor, aldermen, and town councilors who represent the Corporation of St. George's (whose offices are housed in modern premises on Ordnance Island). The building is furnished in cedar, and its walls pay tribute to past mayors, their portraits gazing down on visitors. On the northern edge of the square, you can't miss a couple of **stocks and pillories**—contraptions used in past times to publicly embarrass citizens found guilty of minor transgressions ranging from petty theft to adultery. Tourists typically pose for photos here, their necks and arms stuck through the now easily liftable wooden frames to mimic 17th-century citizens who would have been pelted with rotten fruit or eggs by a rowdy crowd. Near the water's edge, the historic **ducking stool** dunked women accused of being "nags and gossips." Popular 15-minute reenactments are held several times a week for the amusement of modern-day tourists.

Attached to the square by bridge is **Ordnance Island,** once the British military's storage place for munitions, as well as a gallows site. Now it is home to a cruise ship wharf and small harborfront park, where a bronze statue of Bermuda's founder, ***Sir George Somers,*** by Bermudian sculptor Desmond Fountain, throws its arms to the sky in apparent relief at reaching land at the island in 1609.

Deliverance

Ordnance Island is also home to a replica of ***Deliverance*** (www.sgf.bm, 10am-4pm Mon.-Sat., admission $3 adults, $2 children 5 to 16, no handicapped access)—the ship built by Sir George Somers and the other shipwrecked *Sea Venture* castaways in order to sail on to Jamestown, Virginia. The life-sized model, with cabins and stairways that demonstrate the claustrophobic nature of life aboard such vessels, underwent a complete renovation of its woodwork and rigging before it reopened in 2009 with audiovisual exhibits telling the 40-foot *Deliverance*'s dramatic story. Included throughout are interpretive panels about "The Ship That Saved America" as well as an animatronic figure of William Strachey, a 17th-century Englishman who survived *Sea Venture*'s crash landing; his detailed diaries describing the epic shipwreck and survival were widely read in London and only inspired a contemporary—another William (Shakespeare)—to write his famous last play, *The Tempest.* Exhibits describe the epic hurricane that wrecked the *Sea Venture*, the castaways' ingenious survival on Bermuda, and their escape aboard two hand-hewn ships, one of which was *Deliverance,* to Jamestown—where

African Diaspora Trail

Bermuda's black heritage and the 200-year legacy of slavery on the island is remembered through a chain of monuments and museums. The African Diaspora Trail belongs to an international group of heritage sites by the same name, all officially designated UNESCO Slave Route Projects. There are a dozen points of interest throughout the island, each marked by a bronze plaque. Six of these are located in St. George's, so a half-day tour of trail sites in this parish is recommended. If you dedicate a full day, you could begin at the National Museum of Bermuda at Dockyard in Sandys, then take the fast ferry to St. George's and bus or scooter back through the central parishes. Here are some of the key sights and points of interest along the trail.

The West End's **Commissioner's House,** at the National Museum of Bermuda, contains exhibits and compelling artifacts detailing the island's part in the transatlantic slave trade, as well as slavery in Bermuda. Ships carrying slaves often smashed on Bermuda's reefs, leaving telltale artifacts such as iron manacles, glass beads, and cowry shells belonging to the human cargo. Many Bermuda families can trace their roots to slaves who worked as farmers, ship pilots, whalers, or carpenters on the island before slavery was abolished here in 1834.

Warwick Parish's **Cobb's Hill Methodist Church** was built by slaves and free blacks, who often toiled "by moonlight" in the after-hours allowed by their masters. A Chief Justice permitted a piece of land to be released for the project, and the church was finished in 1827. Today, it is located on Moonlight Lane, and its congregation includes descendants of those who labored to build it.

Barr's Bay Park, on the City of Hamilton waterfront, is included on the trail, as it was the place where an American schooner named the *Enterprise* landed in 1835. Sent off course by a storm, the ship was carrying a cargo of 78 slaves—an illegal activity in Bermuda a year after abolition. Local officials refused to clear the vessel, and members of a Bermuda "Friendly Society" took the captain to court. The slaves eventually were allowed to choose whether to stay in Bermuda or return to the United States. All but one woman and her five children opted to remain on the island; the descendants of those 72 slaves can still be found in Bermuda.

A Bermuda National Trust property, **Verdmont Cottage,** alongside the historic house in Smith's Parish, was once a slave quarters. Slaves would have helped build the main house, living in the outroom and buttery. Later, they worked as laborers or domestic help. Verdmont Cottage was the property's original kitchen, and archaeologists believe it also served as slave quarters.

Site of a dedicated slave graveyard, **St. Peter's Church** in the Town of St. George hosts a special ceremony each Emancipation Day (late July/early August) to remember Bermuda's slaves. Inside the church, a gallery on the western end was built in the early 1700s to allow free blacks and slaves to attend services in the segregated society. The slave graveyard is located outside the gallery, separated from the main gravesite of many of the early town's white citizens. An interesting artifact in the church is a baptismal register for 1834, in which a line drawn at the month of August indicates when blacks no longer had to be entered as "slave" or "free."

Opened in 1994, the **Bermudian Heritage Museum** in the Town of St. George celebrates achievements of black Bermudians, including personalities in music and sports, the gombey tradition, and members of "Friendly Society" lodges who helped blacks adjust to life after emancipation.

For more information on the African Diaspora Trail, contact the **Department of Cultural Affairs** (tel. 441/292-9447), or Bermuda's Visitor Information Centres throughout the island.

food supplies they had gathered on the island helped starving settlers hang on to America's first colony. Children, particularly, will enjoy experiencing history on this climb-aboard monument, which also makes for great photo ops of the surrounding old town.

Bermuda National Gallery East

Ensconced in an historic National Trust property, **BNG's St. George's gallery** (Bridge House, 1 Bridge St., 11am-4pm Mon.-Sun., free admission) opened in 2014, with changing exhibits of painting, sculpture, photography, and installation pieces that often have a more contemporary flavor than shows at the gallery's City Hall, Hamilton headquarters.

State House

On a hilltop over King's Square stands the distinctive white **State House** (corner of King St. and Princess St., 10am-4pm Wed., except holidays, admission free), the 17th-century colony's first stone building—and the only structure of the period that survived. Built in 1622, it was used alternately as a munitions storage depot, a courthouse, and home of the world's oldest parliament outside of Britain. For 200 years, the State House was the seat of government for the colonial General Assembly's meetings. It is constructed of sturdy limestone blocks set in a mortar of turtle oil and lime; it's believed that some of the island's first Caribbean slaves may have helped to build it, introducing new methods at a time when cedar-framed structures were the norm. An original third story used for holding gunpowder was removed during 1730 renovations. It was restored in 1969. Most notoriously, the State House was the venue for more than two dozen witch trials during the colony's first century, which, as in similar instances throughout Europe and the United States, resulted in the public hanging, burning, or torture of innocent women. Since 1816, the State House has been rented for the annual sum of a single peppercorn by Bermuda's oldest Masonic lodge, St. George No. 200 of the Grand Lodge of Scotland. The paltry due is paid at a colorful public ceremony in the town square every spring, attended by the governor and the Bermuda Regiment.

★ St. Peter's Church

One of Bermuda's most famous hallmark buildings, **St. Peter's Church** (Duke of York St., tel. 441/297-0216, friends@stpeters.bm, 10am-4:30pm Mon.-Sat., 11am service Sun.) is a favorite venue for local weddings and funerals, where attendees crowd into the cedar-packed interior. The original church on this site was made of wood and thatched in palm fronds by the first settlers in 1612. It was here that the first meeting of the fledgling Assembly was held on August 1, 1620, two years before the State House was built as the government's dedicated headquarters. Among the items on that inaugural agenda: a ban on both "idle and unprofitable persons" and the slaughter of turtles. Although the first structure did not survive, St. Peter's is built on the same site, qualifying it as the oldest Protestant church in the New World. St. Peter's was rebuilt in stone in 1713, and its tower was added in 1814. Inside, its exposed cedar ceiling beams and pews, cedar communion table, and dole cupboard (used to store donations of bread for the parish poor) are all excellent examples of early craftsmanship; the furniture is believed to be the oldest on the island. St. Peter's collection of communion silver is also notable; the St. George's Chalice was given to the church by the Bermuda Company in 1625, while the communion set bears the royal arms of William III, who had it made and sent to St. Peter's in 1697. On its 400th anniversary in 2012, the old royal title "Their Majesties Chappell," given to authorize the chalice's delivery to the island, was restored to St. Peter's. There is also a rare piece of 1616 Hogge money on display, an example of the island's earliest coins, decorated with the iconic image of the wild pigs that roamed Bermuda in the early years of settlement.

The church graveyards are almost as fascinating. In the eastern graveyard, notable townsfolk are buried alongside modern VIPs; an example of the latter is Sir Richard Sharples, a Bermuda governor who was assassinated in 1973. He lies here alongside his aide-de-camp, Captain Hugh Sayers of the Welsh Guards, who was slain by the same gunman in the same attack. Under the shade of coconut palms, a second, separate graveyard holds the bodies of town slaves and free blacks. Even after the Slavery Abolition Act took effect on August 1, 1834, Bermuda's black and white societies remained divided until official segregation was outlawed in the 1960s. A

Return of the Cahow

The Bermuda petrel or cahow *(Pterodroma cahow)* is the island's most famous endemic species. Its return from the brink of extinction is the stuff of a Hollywood comeback classic.

Gadfly petrels are specific to a single oceanic island or group of islands—in the cahow's case, Bermuda. While they nest on land, the powerful, agile fliers spend most of their lives at sea, returning to lay eggs and hatch a single chick that spends the first eight years of life far from land over the open ocean. In the 1500s, the nocturnal birds were so abundant, their high-pitched courtship calls scared off passing mariners, who believed the islands inhabited by devils. "A kind of web-footed fowl there is, and hovering in the air and over the sea, made a strange hollow and harsh howling," wrote shipwrecked English colonist William Strachey in his epic 1610 account. Fossil remains indicate that up to a half-million pairs were nesting on Bermuda, inhabiting rock crevices or burrows on the forest floor. Tragically, however, castaways and wild hogs deposited on the island by passing ships nearly destroyed the cahow population. By the time colonists arrived a century later, with rats and domestic animals, they fed off the tame birds in such large quantities that, according to historical reports, cahows were almost nonexistent within a decade.

In January 1951, after an absence of more than 300 years, seven breeding pairs were discovered by Robert Cushman Murphy, curator of birds at the American Museum of Natural History, and Bermudians Louis S. Mowbray and David Wingate. The trio found the gray-and-white birds living on the East End islets of Castle Harbour, which were immediately declared wildlife sanctuaries. "It was kind of like rediscovering the dodo," remembers Wingate, a 15-year-old student at the time, who made the cahow his life's work. After graduating from Cornell University, he returned to Bermuda, where he was named the island's first conservation officer in 1966, a post he held until he retired in 2000. During that time, he was almost solely responsible for the cahow's return, creating a "living laboratory" of endemic species at Nonsuch Island, as well as overseeing cahow nests on other isolated islets and even creating artificial burrows to encourage nesting.

Today, another Bermudian, Terrestrial Conservation Officer Jeremy Madeiros (cahowman@yahoo.com), continues the work. In 2011, cahow numbers reached a record 98 breeding pairs, including 10 pairs at a newly established nesting colony on Nonsuch, and 57 successfully fledged chicks. Madeiros has been painstaking in his efforts to ensure such a comeback, hand-feeding chicks when necessary to keep survival rates high.

Cahows have been the subject of numerous documentaries and media coverage in recent decades, including a feature-length 2006 film, *Rare Bird,* by Bermudian filmmaker Lucinda Spurling. The birds remain exceedingly rare, but conservationists are confident that if protective measures continue, the bird once thought to be gone for good will flourish again.

solemn walk and ceremony is held at this site every year on the eve of Cup Match, whose Thursday public holiday in late July or early August celebrates Emancipation Day.

The Bermuda National Trust Museum

Few Americans realize the strategic role tiny Bermuda played in the U.S. Civil War (1861-1865). **The Bermuda National Trust Museum** (Globe Hotel, King's Square, tel. 441/297-1423, 10am-4pm Mon.-Thurs. and Sat., closed Fri. and Sun., $5 adults, $2 children 6-16, under 6 free) tells the dramatic story of blockade runners, spies, and international subterfuge when the town was a hotbed of Southern sympathies, Union authorities, and British cotton smugglers. Four years of war activity brought a torrent of unprecedented wealth to St. George's, marking a heyday in its history. The Globe Hotel dates back to around 1700, when the island's governor, Samuel Day, sparked a bitter court battle when he tried to claim it for his own; he later died in prison. The building became the headquarters of Confederate agent Major Norman Walker, who lived here with his wife Georgiana and their three children while he masterminded the flow of guns and war supplies through Union blockades. The museum's exhibit, *Rogues & Runners*, details the complex web of loyalties in Bermuda in that era and how the town became a major port for Southern captains and a transshipment center for U.K.-bound cotton. Included in the admission is a brief film about Bermuda and St. George's. The museum shop sells Bermuda books, souvenirs, and arts and crafts.

Bermudian Heritage Museum

A tribute to black Bermudian history, the **Bermudian Heritage Museum** (Samaritans Lodge, corner of Duke of York St. and Water St., tel. 441/297-4126, 10am-3pm Tues.-Sat., closed holidays, $4 adults, $2 children, under 5 free) opened in 1998 in a historically relevant building. The 19th-century lodge belonged to the Grand United Order of Good Samaritans, one of the largest so-called "Friendly Societies," which aided newly freed blacks before and after their emancipation in 1834. The museum records the story of slavery and these societies, as well as related symbols and other folklore, such as the gombey tradition and the origins of Cup Match. One of the recommended stops on the African Diaspora Trail, the museum highlights historical milestones of black pride, notably the 1959 Theatre Boycott, a protest by black moviegoers that brought about the end of official racial segregation in restaurants, hotels, and schools. Black entrepreneurs, sporting figures, and politicians are also honored.

Tucker House Museum

Built as a merchant's house, this simple whitewashed building takes its name from Henry Tucker, one of the colony's most important figures as president of the Governor's Council. Walking through its elegant interior takes you back to the time of candlelit chandeliers, brick ovens, and four-poster beds. **Tucker House Museum** (Water St., at the junction of Barber's Alley, tel. 441/297-0545, 11am-3pm Wed.-Sat., $5 adults, $2 children 6-16, under 6 free) is a treasure trove of priceless antiques, including English mahogany and Bermudian cedar furniture, family portraits by American artist Joseph Blackburn, and domestic items such as hand-sewn quilts and kitchen utensils. On the lower floor, visit the archaeological display, which chronicles recent years' excavations and the artifacts found below the cellar floor. Also

The Bermudian Heritage Museum showcases the story of abolition and black enterprise.

particularly notable is the kitchen, where Joseph Hayne Rainey, a freed South Carolina slave and later the first black member of the U.S. House of Representatives, operated a barbershop for several years. The adjoining **Barber's Alley** pays tribute to Rainey and his seamstress wife, who both escaped to Bermuda during the U.S. Civil War and set up successful businesses before returning to the United States. Off this alleyway, there is a pocket-sized public garden, **Smith's Garden,** which Princess Anne officially opened in 1991.

Somers Garden

For a tranquil break between museum tours or a shady lunchtime picnic, visit **Somers Garden** (sunrise-sunset daily, admission free), the town's largest public park. Bordered by Duke of York Street, Shinbone Alley, Blockade Alley, and Duke of Kent Street, the park has a fine collection of palms and other plants amid its manicured lawns and flowerbeds. Teddy bear picnics and art-in-the-park events are sometimes held here. The oasis is named for Sir George Somers; his heart is buried here, commemorated by a stone monument in the park's center.

St. George's Historical Society & Museum, Printery, and Garden

Tucked away in the backstreets, the headquarters of the **St. George's Historical Society** (Featherbed Alley, tel. 441/297-0423, 10am-4pm Mon.-Sat., $5 adults, $2 children under 12) is home to an intriguing little museum, a historic printery, and a pretty garden. The building itself is an 18th-century gem, complete with a traditional "welcoming arms" stairway. Like Tucker House, its rooms are full of interesting possessions that give a sense of life long before email, television, and motorized transport. The building's lower floor is especially historic: It was the site of the island's first printing press, operated by the King of England's printer, Joseph Stockdale, to produce the colony's original newspaper. Inside is a working replica of a 15th-century Gutenberg printing press, like the one Stockdale used.

The Old Rectory

The Old Rectory (Broad Alley, behind St. Peter's Church) is a Bermuda National Trust property rented as a private home. With one of the most photographed facades on the island, the quaint homestead featuring rose-dotted

Owned by the Bermuda National Trust, The Old Rectory is now rented to tenants.

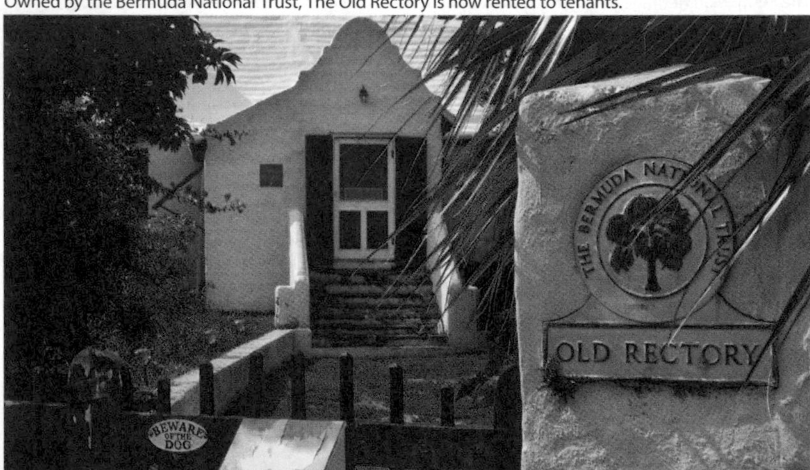

gardens is one of Bermuda's oldest buildings, dating back to 1699. It once belonged to an infamous Bermudian pirate, Captain George Dew, and later to Parson Alexander Richardson, who was nicknamed the "Little Bishop."

The Unfinished Church

Like Gaudi's unmistakable Sagrada Familia Cathedral in Barcelona, Bermuda's **Unfinished Church** (Government Hill Rd., at top of Duke of Kent St., admission free) is a story of half-done architectural artistry. Leased by the Bermuda National Trust, the Victorian Gothic structure was the victim of financial problems, infighting among its congregation, and a series of vicious storms. When construction began in 1874, the church was intended as a grand replacement for St. Peter's Church but was never completed. The structure's soaring arches, cruciform shape, and imposing—but roofless—tower give a hint of the grandeur the architects hoped to achieve. It was declared off-limits to visitors (to walk through) in 2011, until it can be renovated for public safety.

ENTERTAINMENT AND EVENTS

Festivals and Events

Top hats and bonnets come out amid full pomp and regalia for the annual **Peppercorn Ceremony,** held in mid- to late April. The tradition dates back to 1815, when the seat of the island's government finally moved to the new capital, Hamilton. As a conciliatory gesture, the Assembly, which was vacating its longtime home at the State House, symbolically passed the building on to the mayor, aldermen, and councilors of the new Corporation of St. George. The yearly rent requested for Bermuda's oldest Masonic Lodge, St. George No. 200 of the Grand Lodge of Scotland, was one peppercorn. Every year, government dignitaries drive to the East End en masse to join the governor, who, in feathered helmet, presides over the official handover ceremony in King's Square. A 17-gun salute heralds the governor's arrival, and the Bermuda Regiment's Band Company and Corps of Drums also perform. The 45-minute spectacle, watched by schoolchildren and crowds of curious tourists, includes the high-decibel proclamations of the town crier of St. George's, who rings his bell and yells loudly enough to bring the entire congregation to immediate silence. The peppercorn is presented on a velvet cushion laid out on a silver platter, like the princess's pea of the Hans Christian Andersen fairy tale. For annual dates, contact the Corporation of St. George (5 Ordnance Island, tel. 441/297-1532).

Held the first Friday evening in December, the Bermuda National Trust's **Christmas Walkabout** in St. George's has become a calendar institution. Thousands pour into the old town after work to sip cider and meet old friends while strolling the historic streets, strung with festive illuminations. Stores stay open late to sell Christmas gifts, candlelit museums offer free admission, and carolers fill King's Square with song. For information, contact the BNT (tel. 441/236-6483, www.bnt.bm).

Other holiday events in the town include the annual **Santa Claus Parade,** with majorettes, elves, and St. Nick, and the **New Year's Eve** celebrations at King's Square, complete with the dropping of a giant (fake) Bermuda onion.

Throughout the April-October high season, Sunday **Old Towne Market** celebrations (Water St., 2pm-6pm) are held. Crowds meander along a festive walkway of local food and arts and crafts, as well as a peddlers' market selling everything from old china to jewelry.

Pretend you're a 17th-century plebeian at the weekly **ducking stool** reenactments on King's Square (noon on Mon., Tues., Wed., Thurs., and Sat. in high season). The bellowing town crier calls everyone to order at 11:45am before the volunteer "wench" gets her due in the harbor to the delight of onlookers at the stroke of noon. The 15-minute demonstration harks back to the days when women were punished for crimes like gossiping and nagging.

SHOPPING

St. George's has a fraction of Hamilton's shops, and many are branch stores, but several new boutiques have opened in recent years, so there is retail therapy to enjoy. Shops around King's Square sell T-shirts, perfume, and souvenirs, while Water and Duke of York Streets offer clothing, shoe stores, toy shops, and a bookstore. Somers Wharf, west along Water Street, has a quaint shopping complex on the waterfront.

The Bermuda Perfumery (Stewart Hall, 5 Queen St., tel. 441/293-0627, www.lilibermuda.com, 9am-5pm Mon.-Sat.) is located in history-steeped Stewart Hall, a Bermuda National Trust property. The building houses a production center and retail outlet, where the world-famous bottles of White Oleander, Frangipani, Pink, and other varieties of perfume are sold. There are also talcum powders and body creams in the same hallmark scents. Free tours are given to visitors interested in how the fragrances are made.

Designer perfumes can be found at **Peniston Brown** (6 Water St., tel. 441/297-1525, 10am-4pm Mon.-Sat.), many of them at U.S. prices. Guerlain makeup products are also sold here.

The stunning harbor views outside floor-to-ceiling picture windows mirror the décor within at **Davidrose Jewelry** (20 Water St., tel. 441/293-7673, www.davidrose.bm, summer 10am-5pm Mon.-Sat., winter closed Sun. and Mon., call for private appointments). The fashionable turquoise boutique is owned and run by Bermudian David Zuill and his wife Avrel Rose, who met as university students in Toronto and decided to open a jewelry shop here in 2012. The couple uses diamonds, gemstones, and precious metals to fashion bridal and engagement jewelry, statement pieces, custom creations, and a luxury silver line that includes Bermuda-themed pendants, for a local and international clientele.

Mother-daughter team Kelli and Roseclair Thompson are behind **Saltwater Jewellery** (29 Water St., tel. 441/519-9906, 10am-4pm Mon.-Sat., noon-3pm Sun.), where they have transformed their love of Bermuda sea glass into one-of-a-kind bracelets, necklaces, and earrings. The pair also work Venetian glass, freshwater pearls, and semiprecious stones into their creations.

Enjoy a glimpse of island panache inside

The town of St. George includes a mix of Bermuda and West Indian gingerbread architecture.

Gregory Nelmes Interior Design (8 York St., lower terrace level, tel. 441/704-7740, 11am-4pm Mon.-Sun.), where the award-winning Bermudian designer displays some of his hallmark shelter treasures for sale—lamps, vintage bottles, blue-and-white crockery, artworks, Bermuda-themed cushion covers, traditional furniture with contemporary upholstery. The array is so tempting, you might have to arrange for shipping some home.

Bermudian glassblowers create colorful works of art for sale at **Dockside Glass** (3 Bridge St., tel. 441/297-3908, www.dockglass.com, www.bermudarumcakes.com, 9am-6pm daily). Vases, exotic glass fish, and plates—all featuring a swirling rainbow of hues—can be purchased here. Rum cakes in nine flavors and three sizes are also for sale.

Vera P. Card (22 Water St., tel. 441/295-1729 or 441/297-1718, vcard@ibl.bm) left Hamilton for the old town in 2008, an elegant retail addition to Water Street. The well-known store, now located alongside the Tempest Bistro, carries fine jewelry, watches, crystal, clocks, and china by Lladro, Swarovski, and other designer brands.

The Book Cellar (Tucker House Basement, Water St., tel. 441/297-0448) stocks fiction, including British best sellers, classic literature, coffee-table editions, gift books, and a small kids' section. The standing-room-only space, squeezed beneath Tucker House Museum, also carries a selection of Bermuda books.

Aside from the expected toiletries and candy, **Robertson's Drug Store** (24 York St., St. George's, tel. 441/297-1828, pharmacy tel. 441/297-1736, 8am-7:30pm Mon.-Sat., 2pm-6pm Sun.) also stocks a wonderful array of well-chosen toys, beach gear, children's and Bermuda books, pulp fiction, magazines, newspapers, greeting cards, and children's art supplies.

A branch of its popular Hamilton stores, **The Island Shop** (Somers Wharf, tel. 441/297-1514, www.islandexports.com) carries beautiful ceramic and linen products designed by local artist Barbara Finsness. It is the perfect place to find Bermuda-inspired gifts—whether cushion covers or Christmas ornaments—all with colorful tropical themes like butteries and Bermudiana blooms.

Cigar-lovers will want to seek out **Churchill's** (27 Duke of York St., tel. 441/297-1650, fax 441/297-0814, churchills@myoffice.bm, 8am-9pm Mon.-Sun.), home of fine Cuban cigars and a good selection of wines, spirits, and gift items, including an array of wine-bottle openers and other bar essentials.

SPORTS AND RECREATION

Scuba and Water Sports

Operators of water-sports outfits mostly moved to Dockyard with the advent of the mega ships, but some still operate from St. George's Harbour. You can also rent kayaks, sailboats, motorboats, and snorkel equipment from Hamilton Parish outfits to explore the many bays, coves, and islands of the East End—from St. George's Harbour to Castle Harbour, Ferry Point to Coney Island. Traveling by water brings a whole new perspective, even for Bermudians. Paddling a kayak is a particularly good way to get around; the wildlife, including turtles, is least disturbed by this vessel, and you'll see things the Jet Ski speed demon won't. You can book excursions islandwide through the **Island Tour Centre** outlets at Dockyard and Hamilton, or make a reservation and pay in advance via its website (www.islandtourcentre.com).

K. S. Watersports (8 King's Square, tel. 441/297-4155, kswatersports.com, 9am-6pm daily) offers Jet Ski tours (90 minutes, $120 single, $130 double, May-Oct.), plus rentals of kayaks ($20 single per hour, $25 double), 16-foot Boston Whalers ($185 for four hours, $340 full day, up to six people), 23-foot pontoon boats ($400 for four hours, $700 full day, up to 13 people) and standup paddleboards. Rentals and tours are booked online or by phone via **Island Tour Centre** (tel. 441/236-1300, www.islandtourcentre.com).

Nonsuch Island

Its evocative name is alluring enough, but what the East End's Nonsuch Island represents in the environmental world is akin to a scientific miracle. Starting in the 1960s, David Wingate, the island's first conservation officer, almost single-handedly recreated Bermuda's original habitats on Nonsuch Island, bringing back the cahow, or Bermuda petrel, from near-extinction in the process.

The island is the largest of several that sit off Castle Harbour, including Governor's Island, Castle Island, and Southampton Island (where the first settlers built landmark forts in the 17th century). In the 1930s, Nonsuch served as the marine research station headquarters for American deep-ocean pioneer William Beebe's expeditions off Bermuda. But it was in 1951 that Nonsuch and the other islets won world renown when they were found to be the last nesting habitats of the cahow.

Nonsuch at the time was covered in invasive plant species, though introduced animals such as toads and rats had not made it across the bay from the mainland. Through Wingate's efforts, Nonsuch was immediately declared a protected nature reserve, and over subsequent decades, with much culling and replanting, it was transformed into a "living laboratory," in his words, of the island's indigenous flora and fauna. Wingate—whose daughter Janet recounts life as a 12-year-old on the island in her 2005 memoir, *Nonsuch Summer*—recreated pristine wetlands, mangroves, cedar, and palmetto forests, as well as shoreline coastal habitats and bird-viewing areas. Nonsuch has remained an oasis for nature amid Bermuda's drastically changing environment.

Ecotours to Nonsuch are sometimes organized by the Bermuda Zoological Society or Bermuda Institute for Ocean Sciences. Special visits can also be arranged by appointment only through the **Department of Conservation Services** (tel. 441/293-2727).

Spas

Tranquil Hair and Beauty (Somers Wharf, tel. 441/297-0026, 9am-6pm Mon., Tues., Fri., and Sat., 9am-8pm Wed. and Thurs., 2pm-6pm Sun.) offers well-priced face and body treatments for men and women, including massage (one hour, $95), pedicure ($55), and waxing and hair services.

ACCOMMODATIONS

A number of very reasonable, family-run bed-and-breakfast accommodations and self-catering apartment rentals offer travelers an inexpensive but comfortable way to experience living in St. George's. Also check www.airbnb.com, www.vrbo.com, www.bermuda-rentals.com, and www.bermudagetaway.com, which lists several St. George's rentals, including a few in historic town buildings.

Under $200

St. Georgian Susan Oatley has been providing travelers with a comfortable, cost-effective place to stay in the old town for quite a few seasons now. A studio apartment attached to her home, **Gobblers Corner** (1 Turkey Hill, tel. 441/297-2519 or 441/335-3429, oatley@northrock.bm, $110 s, $130 d) has a queen bed, a large bathroom with shower, air-conditioning, cable TV, free WiFi, washer and dryer, and a kitchen with refrigerator, stove, and microwave. A private backyard has a barbecue for self-catering. Located just two minutes away from the town center, in the picturesque backstreets, the apartment makes a handy little pied-à-terre for travelers who don't seek resort-style amenities.

Architectural technologist Philip Seaman restored a 200-year-old carriage house owned by his family into a guest property he called **The Loft** (7 Duke of Clarence St., tel. 441/232-2243 or 441/537-7337, $165 d summer, $135 d winter). The labor of love not only energized his passion for Bermuda's tourism industry, but has also won praise from the steady stream of guests who have adored the quaint structure that boasts modern amenities such as a full kitchen with stainless appliances, a modern bathroom, and a sleeping loft with double/full bed. Seaman won an award from the

Bermuda National Trust for his careful transformation of the building.

It's worth staying at **Crooked Elbow** (5 Shinbone Alley, tel. 441/297-0898, www.bermudagetaway.com, $150 d) for the address alone. Resident Anne Rowe rents out the lower apartment of her historic home, which has a private entrance. Included are an air-conditioned bedroom with queen bed, living room, full kitchen, bathroom, and dining room, plus free WiFi.

Over $300

The St. George's Club (6 Rose Hill, tel. 441/297-1200, fax 441/297-8003, www.stgeorgesclub.com, one-bedrooms $475, two-bedrooms $600, plus 9.75 tax and $10 per person housekeeping charges) is a cottage complex time-share facility that also offers short-term rentals for travelers, space permitting. Cut into the hillside, the resort's one- and two-bedroom cottages have spectacular views of the old town. The club has a total of 25 air-conditioned cottages, all with cable TV and fully equipped kitchens. Guests enjoy the use of a private beach club, three freshwater pools (one is heated), an on-site convenience store, three tennis courts, and a putting green. There is also a business center with Internet access, photocopier, fax machine, and FedEx services.

FOOD

Cafés, Pubs, and Takeout

All day Wednesdays and on Saturday mornings, the scent of cinnamon buns wafts down York Street, beckoning town residents to ★ **Sweet SAAK Bakery** (16 York St., tel. 441/297-0663, www.sweetsaak.com, 8:30am-3pm Tues.-Sat.), a business run by the Cannonier family siblings. The super-popular bakery also whips up cupcakes, scones, cakes, marshmallow chocolate-chip cookies and other decadent treats.

At the foot of the stairs leading up to St. Peter's Church, **Temptations Café & Bakery** (31 York St., tel. 441/297-1368, 8:30am-4pm Mon.-Sat.) serves up sinful treats in its simple interior, including cakes, pastries, and muffins, as well as sandwiches, hot soups, coffee, and cold drinks. Sit at banquettes with views out to Duke of York Street, or farther inside at tables. Be careful when you step outside, though; the sidewalk is so narrow, you risk falling into the busy thoroughfare's traffic.

Quirky ★ **CV "Conscious Vibes" Café** (8 York St., lower, off Water St., tel. 441/297-0208, 10am-4pm Mon.-Sat.) does a booming little business with its organic teas, juices, lattes, and specialty fair-trade coffee, delicious waffle breakfasts, and lunches of paninis ($8.95), sandwiches, and salads ($6.75). Seating is indoors on comfy sofas or outside on the patio.

★ **Art Mel's Spicy Dicy** (14 York St. off Water St., tel. 441/297-3965, noon-10pm Tues.-Fri., noon-8pm Sat.) enjoys the kind of reverence reserved for Michelin Star establishments elsewhere, so East Enders were ecstatic when the legendary Pembroke café, renowned for its gargantuan fish sandwiches, opened a St. George's outlet in 2013. The menu mainstay starts at $11 (plus whichever toppings—cheese, fried onions, coleslaw, lettuce, tomato—you choose to make it yours).

Mama Angie's (48 Duke of York St., tel. 441/297-0959, 8am-3pm Mon.-Thurs., 8am-2:30pm and 5pm-10pm Fri., 8am-noon Sat., closed Sun.) is the kind of place where time slips effortlessly away. Tucked into the busy main street, the tiny eatery serves up java and plenty else, including Western omelets, sandwiches, macaroni 'n' cheese, chicken legs, fish cakes—and lots of local atmosphere. Try the juicy homemade burgers ($4.50).

White Horse Tavern (8 King's Square, tel. 441/297-1838, www.whitehorsebermuda.com, all-day breakfast and lunch 11am-5pm Mon.-Fri., breakfast 9am-11am Sat.-Sun., dinner 5pm-9:30pm daily, $11-29) is a waterside sports bar offering a codfish breakfast on Sundays. It specializes in pub and seafood dishes, and takeout is available.

Tavern by the Sea (14 Water St., tel. 441/297-3305, fax 441/297-3227, tbts@therock.bm, 11am-10pm daily, happy hour 5pm-7pm Mon.-Fri., $11-20) provides a perfect spot to sit outside on the harbor's edge and watch visiting yachties load provisions or work on their boats. The menu offers local, reasonably priced specialties and pub favorites, including nachos, fish chowder, satisfying hot and cold sandwiches, grilled wahoo, fish 'n' chips, burgers, pizzas, salads—and swizzles, if you *really* want to relax. There are vegetarian and children's menus, and takeout service.

The view is the main attraction at **Griffin's Bar & Grill** (St. George's Club, 6 Rose Hill, tel. 441/297-4235 or 441/297-1200, lunch noon-3pm Mon.-Sat., dinner 6pm-10pm Mon.-Sat., breakfast 9am-11:30am Sat. only, brunch noon-4pm Sun., $20-31), a lively sports bar-style restaurant with a popular Sunday brunch buffet.

Chinese

Wong's Golden Dragon Restaurant (13 Duke of York St., tel. 441/297-0408, 11am-10pm Mon.-Sat., 2pm-9pm Sun., $10-14) offers a range of Mandarin and Szechuan specialties, including fried rice and noodles, lo mein, foo young, chop suey, and sweet-and-sour beef, chicken, and pork, as well as many vegetable dishes.

Mediterranean

★ **Wahoo's Bistro & Patio** (36 Water St., tel. 441/297-1307, www.wahoos.bm, 11:30am-9:30pm Tues.-Sun., 11:30am-5pm Mon.) wins high ratings for its scrumptious menu, which can be enjoyed inside, in a bistro-style dining area, or out on the harborside deck or terrace. For lunch, try Austrian owner/chef Alfred Konrad's award-winning fish chowder ($7), caprese or canelli bean salad ($9.50), or curried fishcakes ($12); dinner choices include fresh rockfish ($35), Bermuda lobster when in season, cowboy steak ($39), wiener schnitzel ($25), and daily pasta specials. Named for Bermuda's deliciously meaty gamefish, the restaurant devotes an entire section of its menu to wahoo specialties—wahoo pâté, chowder, nuggets, tacos, even a wahoo burger.

Fine Dining

Replacing the long-closed Carriage House Restaurant, ★ **Tempest Bistro** (22 Water St., tel. 441/297-0861, lunch 11:30am-2pm Tues.-Sun., dinner 6pm-onwards Mon.-Sat.) brings contemporary culinary flair to an 18th-century wharfside building once used as a warehouse serving the busy shipping trade. Vaulted ceilings, exposed brick, and wooden floors in the main dining room, coupled with a creative menu and very capable service, make meals here a special treat. There is also the option of eating alfresco on the harborside veranda. The beloved venue was brought back

fish sandwich at Art Mel's Spicy Dicy

to buzzworthy life by the folks who run the award-winning Mad Hatter's in Pembroke. After opening the East End eatery in 2014, it fast became the go-to for St. George's gourmands. Enjoy steak frites ($20), panko-crusted fish 'n' chips ($15), or a Niçoise salad ($19) for lunch; the dinner menu includes mussels, crab cakes, panzerotti ($16), river trout ($26), and New York strip steak with bacon shallot butter ($35).

Grocery Stores

Owned by Hamilton's Supermart group, **Somers Supermart** (41 York St., tel. 441/297-1177, fax 441/297-0827, www.supermart.bm, 7am-9pm Mon.-Sat., 8am-7pm Sun.) has sat at the same busy intersection for decades, the only grocery store in town. The small store offers all the basics, though if you're looking for deli items or more variety, Southside Supermarket (logically located in Southside), a new modern food mart, is a better option.

INFORMATION AND SERVICES

Created in 1995, **The St. George's Foundation** (15 Duke of York St., tel. 441/297-3370, fax 441/297-2479, www.stgeorgesfoundation.com) is the independent nonprofit group that drove the UNESCO campaign; since then, it has raised funds and orchestrated capital improvements to the old town. The group, which works with St. George's residents and businesses to stimulate tourism in the area and encourage educational projects, has partnered with numerous related overseas entities, including the Colonial Williamsburg Foundation, the Jamestown/Yorktown Foundation, and the Historic Charleston Foundation.

The old town's **Visitor Information Centre** (7 Market Wharf, King's Square, tel. 441/297-0556, 10am-4pm Mon.-Sat. depending on cruise ship schedules) was moved and renovated in 2014. Manager Phillip Anderson provides tour and general information, and sells ferry and bus tokens and tickets. Free WiFi is offered for 10 minutes; a $5 charge applies for longer usage.

St. George's Police Station (22 Duke of York St., tel. 441/297-1122 or 441/297-1124, fax 441/297-0461, sgps@bps.bm) is on the main drag just around the corner from King's Square.

St. George's Post Office (11 Water St., behind St. George's Police Station, tel. 441/297-1610, 8am-5pm Mon.-Fri.) is housed in a historic building near the center of town.

St. George's Esso Service Station (2 Rose Hill, tel. 441/297-1622, 7am-7pm Mon.-Sat.) is near the entrance to town, on the drive leading up to the St. George's Club. **Rubis Dowling's Marine Service Station** (12 Water St., tel. 441/297-1914, 6:30am-9pm Mon.-Fri., 6:30am-7pm Sat. and 7am-6:30pm Sun.) sits along the harbor next to Tavern by the Sea.

HSBC (tel. 441/297-1812, 9am-4:30pm Mon.-Fri.) and **Butterfield Bank** (tel. 441/297-1277, 9am-4pm Mon.-Fri.) are conveniently located near each other at King's Square and the junction with Water Street.

ATMs are at bank branches on King's Square and Water Street.

Public toilets are on King's Square and at area restaurants.

GETTING THERE AND AROUND

Buses and Ferries

Several bus routes from Hamilton serve St. George's Parish, and a few daily fast ferries from Hamilton via Dockyard provide the scenic option of getting there by water. **Buses** 1, 3, 10, and 11 travel between the capital and the Town of St. George daily. Bus 1 runs every half hour, the other routes every 15 minutes.

Sea Express fast ferries run four daily trips weekdays only from Hamilton via Dockyard to St. George's April-October (leaving Dockyard at 9:30am, 11:30am, 2pm, and 4:30pm). From Hamilton or Dockyard, one-way fares are $4.50 for adults, $2.50 children 5-16, kids under 5 free (take a free transfer from Hamilton). You can take your scooter for an extra charge of $4. Buy tickets, tokens, or passes in advance (at the ferry terminal or select stores), as cash is not accepted on board.

Scooters

Oleander Cycles (26 York St., tel. 441/297-0478, www.oleandercycles.bm, 8:30am-5:30pm daily) rents single- and double-seater 50cc scooters and mountain bikes.

Eve Cycles (1 Water St., tel. 441/236-0839, www.evecycles.com, 8am-5:30pm daily) is housed in a historic building that attracts nonstop photos thanks to the Penny Farthing bicycle outside. Eve's rents 50cc scooters and pedal bikes and offers pickup and delivery service.

Both companies have representatives at St. George's wharves when cruise ships are in port. Scooter rental rates start at around $50 per day. Major credit cards including MasterCard, Visa, and American Express are accepted.

Taxis

There is a taxi stand outside the White Horse Tavern in King's Square, but it may be necessary to call for pickup in the winter; there are always cabs at Bermuda's airport, located in the parish, so wait time should not be excessive. The main companies are: **Bermuda Industrial Union Co-op** (tel. 441/292-4476, cooptaxi@fkbnet.bm), **Bermuda Island Taxi** (tel. 441/295-4141, www.bermudaisland-taxi.com), and **BTA Dispatching Ltd.** (tel. 441/296-2121, www.taxibermuda.bm).

Tours

Old Towne Railway Tours (King's Sq., tel. 441/297-5001) operates regular shuttles to three St. George's-area beaches ($15), as well as 45-minute history tours of the town ($20 adults, $10 children 5 to 16, under 5 free) two or three times a day May-October.

Around the Old Town

The environs of St. George's Parish beyond the old town are not part of the World Heritage Site—except for the many interesting forts—but its parkland and various neighborhoods are worth visiting and can be covered in any daylong visit to the East End. Most visitors will at least explore the rest of St. George's Island north and east of the town, a circular loop that heads up Cut Road and along Barry Road, incorporating three important fortifications—Gates Fort, Alexandra Battery, and Fort St. Catherine. Continuing on, Coot Pond Road meanders past Achilles Bay and Tobacco Bay (a prime snorkeling spot) on the North Shore, then back to the town's exit via Government Hill Road.

West of the town, past Mullet Bay, is the extensive Ferry Point National Park, home to a nature reserve, hiking trails (including a scenic stretch of the Railway Trail), and three forts—the Martello Tower, Ferry Island Fort, and Burnt Fort. Across the Swing Bridge, there's the large St. David's and Southside community to explore. And there's also a section of the parish completely removed from the rest due to the vagaries of land division and the layout of islands; crossing Longbird Bridge and the Causeway into Hamilton Parish, a chunk of St. George's lies west of Shark Hole on Harrington Sound, encompassing most of the golf-coursed splendor of the exclusive Mid Ocean Club and Rosewood Tucker's Point. Tucker's Town continues east along South Road past mansions and private beaches to the tip of Frick's Point, where Castle Island, Nonsuch Bay, and other rocky guardians of Castle Harbour lie in a chain all the way back to St. David's.

SIGHTS

Gates Fort and Alexandra Battery

Two easy-to-visit forts that belong to the World Heritage Site are Gates Fort and Alexandra Battery (sunrise-sunset daily, admission free), located within a few hundred yards of each other along Barry Road, on the easternmost flank of St. George's Parish. Perched on the picturesque **Town Cut**—the main shipping passage into the harbor—sits tiny Gates Fort, named for Sir Thomas Gates, a key figure aboard the ill-fated *Sea Venture* who went on to become deputy governor of Virginia. The original fort was built in the 1620s and rebuilt in 1700 as a parapet for guns. Down the road, Alexandra Battery overlooks Frobisher's Bay, where Gates supervised the construction of the ship *Deliverance* in 1610. The fort was built in the 1840s, though various subsequent reconstruction efforts created a concrete emplacement for four guns.

★ Fort St. Catherine

If you only see one fort in Bermuda, **Fort St. Catherine** (15 Coot Pond Rd. at St. Catherine's Point, tel. 441/297-1920, 9am-4pm Mon.-Fri., $7 adults, $5 seniors, $3 children 5-15, kids under 5 free) should be the top choice. (Fort Hamilton is a close second.) Fort St. Catherine's historic, well-preserved interior, exhibits, and artifacts make it well worth an hour's stop on your East End tour. The fort has recently undergone a complete makeover of exhibits and facilities. On the northern tip of St. George's Island, the fort stands above St. Catherine's Beach on one side and Achilles Bay on the other. Built during the year of settlement in 1612, its ramparts gaze over the stretch of ocean where the *Sea Venture* hit reefs in 1609, causing England to finally claim Bermuda for its own. Enter by a wooden drawbridge over a dry moat to a reception area and ticket office. Inside the renovated lobby, interpretive exhibits detail the fort's evolution over the years, and how it fits into the time line of Bermuda's military history and chain of forts. Guides point the way down steps and tunnels leading into the bowels of the fort, where magazines have displays and even uniformed mannequins to illustrate the mechanisms of military life inside a fort. Other rooms have replicas of the Crown Jewels, as well as various armaments, including swords, muskets, pistols, and giant rifled muzzle-loaders weighing 18 tons each. A short film details the significance of this and other Bermuda forts. The fort saw military use by the British Army

Gates Fort commands a key vantage point overlooking the Town Cut.

Risky Business

Bermuda engineered the unlikely pairing of scientists and insurance companies in the mid-1990s, when the Risk Prediction Initiative (RPI) was established at the East End's Bermuda Institute for Ocean Sciences. The program brings together the latest findings on climate change, weather patterns, and disasters by the world's leading scientists with corporations whose business it is to insure the risk of hurricanes, tornados, tsunamis, and earthquakes.

The benefits work both ways: Scientists at top institutions around the globe receive funding for research on destructive weather phenomena, while sponsor companies get back cutting-edge data that allows them to better value and package risk as a commercial commodity and determine future payouts. Specifically, weather research helps provide insurers, governments, and others with a vested interest in more accurate estimates of the probability and path of future catastrophes. In return, scientists see their years of study help communities in very practical ways. Days before Hurricane Katrina's arrival along the U.S. Gulf Coast in 2005, for example, hurricane forecasters, including members of RPI, had pinpointed its trajectory and most likely point of impact, allowing corporations and government agencies to brace for the onslaught. "Those of us watching felt an intense dread because the hurricane was by then a recipe for disaster," noted the RPI's Dr. Kerry Emanuel, a professor at the Massachusetts Institute of Technology, which runs a Program in Atmosphere, Oceans, and Climate.

Among other projects, RPI scientists have developed a computer program that uses current and past data to plot trends and make predictions on the likelihood of weather phenomena striking particular locations around the globe. Their data is also being used to assess whether such catastrophes are the result of global warming or pure chance.

Bermuda remains a perfect forum for such synergy between science and commerce, given its reinsurance juggernaut and its location smack-dab in the path of hurricane alley. Workshops held on the island bring together the two fields to discuss their findings and new areas where further research could be useful.

and through World Wars I and II, when local forces were trained here. Incidentally, Fort St. Catherine's main terrace—a lofty plateau rimmed by ramparts overlooking the parrotfish-nibbled reefs below—has been the setting for several theatrical displays, the most notable by Hollywood's Charlton Heston in a 1950s production of *Macbeth*.

Bermuda Institute of Ocean Sciences (BIOS)

Located on the north shore of Ferry Point, and visible from Kindley Field Road, the **Bermuda Institute of Ocean Sciences** (BIOS, 17 Biological Ln., tel. 441/297-1880, fax 441/297-8143, www.bios.edu, free tour 10am first Wed. of every month only) was established in 1903 in Flatts. Scientists from Harvard and New York Universities, together with the Bermuda Natural History Society, decided Bermuda was a fitting place to set up a marine research facility, due to its balmy climate, biodiverse reefs, and relatively easy access to ocean depths of 12,000 feet. The BIOS has been at its present location since 1932, after receiving an endowment and facilities provided by the government and the Rockefeller Foundation. Today, it is a world-renowned nonprofit center for pioneering marine science and regularly hosts visiting scientists and student interns who join local counterparts in projects ranging from global warming studies to research on possible medical applications of sealife. The station also runs a popular year-round Road Scholar (Elderhostel) program for senior travelers, who get an inside look at "Science in Bermuda Shorts" going on around the station and island.

The Wednesday tour gives visitors a look inside the station's many laboratories, where they can meet international scientists who have achieved breakthrough discoveries here, in fields such as pharmaceutical research and climate studies. When in port, the BIOS research vessel, RV *Atlantic Explorer*, a live-aboard, deep-ocean marine laboratory, features onboard labs, high-tech machinery, living areas, and captain's bird's-eye views. Scientific lectures and a marine science open house are held throughout the year.

The atmosphere at BIOS these days is akin to a college campus; in effect, the facility acts as one. Undergraduate and graduate internships, distance-learning programs, and a panoply of research projects are all carried out here, along with summer courses and workshops. Notably, the station is one of two centers for studies on the impact of the ocean on climate change, and in 1998 it established the International Center for Ocean and Human Health. Under that program, scientists are involved in a range of cutting-edge research, including studying marine uses in pharmaceuticals and what the genetic makeup of corals and sea urchins can tell us about curing cancer and Alzheimer's disease, and learning more about the human aging process. The Risk Prediction Initiative, a partnership with the global reinsurance industry, is also based here.

Ferry Point National Park

For hikers and history buffs, **Ferry Point National Park** (Ferry Rd. off Mullet Bay Rd., sunrise-sunset daily, admission free) is one of Bermuda's treasures. It is named for its westernmost tip, Ferry Point, where a boat used to ply back and forth across Ferry Reach in the 1800s, carrying passengers from Coney Island to St. George's Island before the Causeway bridge was built, finally connecting the East End to the rest of Bermuda. The stretch of the Railway Trail here is one of the most remote, far away from main-road traffic and the hustle of residential neighborhoods. The trail runs beside the North Shore, bordered by a nature reserve, mangroves, and a brackish pond called Lovers Lake. Easter lilies and silver cedar skeletons pepper the landscape, and on stormy days sea spray washes across the dirt path. In the western section of the park, three forts—**Martello Tower, Burnt Point Fort,** and **Ferry Island Fort**—belong to the World Heritage Site. Visits to the tower can be arranged through the Department of Parks (tel. 441/236-5902) or by calling park rangers at Fort St. Catherine (tel. 441/297-1920), who will open the tower. You can cross the small drawbridge over the ditch and climb up the 1820s structure, made of hard Bermuda limestone. Inside, exhibits detail the tower's military importance and the daily lives of the British garrison soldiers who manned it. Burnt Point Fort is older, built in the 1600s to defend the western approach to Bermuda. Ferry Island Fort, built in the 1790s, is named for the boat service that used to carry St. Georgians to the mainland at Coney Island, before bridges linked the parish to the mainland.

Tucker's Town

Created in the 1920s when 500 acres of land were forcibly bought from a rural black community, Tucker's Town quickly became the enclave of the rich and famous. The exclusive Mid Ocean Club demands an initiation fee of $30,000, and members include those who own multimillion-dollar homes on the manicured peninsula dubbed "Billionaire's Row": Texas billionaire Ross Perot, former Italian prime minister Silvio Berlusconi, and former New York mayor Michael Bloomberg among them. Of course, most of what lies here is off-limits to visitors, including the breathtakingly beautiful Windsor and Mid Ocean Beaches (a manned roadblock forbids nonresidents). But you can visit the public dock on Tucker's Town Bay to get a view of the Beverly Hills-like neighborhood—and Bloomberg's lavish spread on an opposite hillside. The dock is a nice picnic spot, and you can even swim in the sheltered bay, where area boaters keep their craft moored. Take Paynter's Road to cut through the Rosewood Tucker's Point property, an enclave of palm-flanked golf course, then follow Harrington Sound Road through Hamilton Parish to its junction with North

Shore Road. Once this meets the Causeway, you have once again entered St. George's Parish.

BEACHES

St. Catherine's Beach, Achilles Bay, and **Tobacco Bay** are the three main beaches of St. George's, all located north of the town. St. Catherine's is the largest, a stretch of white sand below the fort. Tiny Achilles Bay and Tobacco Bay—which has a popular café—are known for snorkeling; the latter, with its natural stone columns rising from the bay, is one of the best areas in Bermuda for watching fish and reef life in a clear setting. Vendor **Beach Boys** took over operations here in 2014, renting SUPs ($15 for two hours), kayaks ($25 for two hours), snorkeling equipment, and a chair/umbrella combo ($20 all day). There is also a licensed bar, and a café that offers burgers, chicken tenders, fish sandwiches, and fries.

St. Georgians know **Buildings Bay,** beside Alexandra Battery, is one of the island's best glass beaches, with a constantly changing collection for the taking.

Farther afield, **Whalebone Bay** at Ferry Point National Park also has good sea glass collections, depending on tides and currents. Its shallow water, glassy calm when the wind is blowing from the south, is good for children and novice swimmers.

ENTERTAINMENT AND EVENTS

Nightlife

The Beach House (Fort St. George, 6 Rose Hill next to Fort St. Catherine, tel. 441/297-1400, www.stgeorgesclub.com, noon-9pm Tues.-Sun., Apr.-Nov. only) is a perfect place to while away the sunset hours after a day of snorkeling in Achilles Bay below. Owned by the St. George's Club, it is one of Bermuda's few beachside bars.

The handsome **Tucker's Bar** (Rosewood Tucker's Point, 60 Tucker's Point Dr., tel. 441/298-4010, 11am-11pm daily) adjoins The Point Restaurant & Terrace at the resort. Overlooking the pool, it makes for a sophisticated pre-dinner cocktail or post-golf refreshment.

Cup Match

Thousands pour into St. George's every other summer for the cricket showdown and carnival atmosphere of Cup Match. The island's favorite holiday sees club teams from both ends of the island, St. George's and Somerset, meet

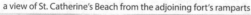

a view of St. Catherine's Beach from the adjoining fort's ramparts

for a two-day contest, held in alternate years at each club's headquarters. **The St. George's Cricket Club** (56 Wellington Slip Rd., tel. 441/297-0374, www.stgeorgescricketclub.com, www.bermudacupmatch.com) welcomes the masses, who fill bleachers and enjoy a festival of local food and drink provided by vendors selling island favorites like mussel pies, conch fritters, rum swizzles, and fish sandwiches. Gambling, in the form of Crown & Anchor game tables, is legalized for the occasion, and tens of thousands of dollars change hands at the so-called "Stock Market"—along with gallons of rum and other spirits. Amid the blazing heat, Cup Match draws everyone from politicians to schoolchildren to celebrate the century-old festival.

SHOPPING

For last-minute purchases of black rum (Gosling's Black Seal, $13.50 for one-liter bottle), cigarettes ($39.85 a carton), makeup, perfume, or candy, visit the three **Bermuda Duty Free** shops (U.S. and International Departures Halls and Arrivals Hall, L. F. Wade International Airport, tel. 441/293-2870, 6:30am-4pm, reopens for evening flights) before flying home.

SPORTS AND RECREATION

Golf

The crème de la crème of Bermuda golf courses, the revered **Mid Ocean Club** (tel. 441/293-0330, fax 441/293-8837, www.themidoceanclubbermuda.com, greens fee $250 per person) is *the* place to play, a highly challenging 18-hole championship course. PGA great Ben Crenshaw called it one of the best small courses in the world. Though it's a private club, guests of members are allowed to play on Monday, Wednesday, and Friday, including guests of several hotels on the island (check with your concierge to see if arrangements can be made). Designed in 1921 by Charles Blair Macdonald, considered one of the world's top designers, the course was altered slightly by Robert Trent Jones in the 1950s. It boasts spectacular views of the reef-dotted ocean, its rolling greens and immaculately maintained fairways teetering over the South Shore cliffs. You might run into Jack Nicholson or Catherine Zeta-Jones at the Colonial-style clubhouse. Over the years, players have included Babe Ruth, Dwight Eisenhower, Winston Churchill, the Duke of Windsor, and George H. W. Bush. The annual PGA Grand Slam of Golf was held here in 2007 and 2008. The club atmosphere is very formal: Jacket and tie attire is expected for dinner.

Rosewood Tucker's Point (golf pro shop tel. 441/298-6970, www.tuckerspoint.com, non-member greens fee $130 weekdays, $180 weekends, $100 seniors), like Mid Ocean, is an 18-hole championship course open to members, guests of members, and guests of certain island hotels. It also welcomes guests of Rosewood Tucker's Point. Great vistas, a par-70 course with TifEagle greens and high elevations over Harrington Sound and Castle Harbour, plus bells-and-whistles service make playing here a very memorable experience. Walking is discouraged. A state-of-the-art pro shop offers shoe-cleaning, well-kept locker rooms, and coffee and orange juice stations. There is also a driving range, a 10,000-square-foot practice putting green, and a short-game area. The hilltop clubhouse houses the popular Grille Room & Bar, which serves lunch to players daily.

Horseback Riding

Bermuda Horse Trail Ride (Moran Meadows, 7 Salt Spray Lane, tel. 441/537-0400, www.bermudahorsetrailride.com, bdatrailride@gmail.com, Mon.-Sat. only, ages 7-plus) is one of only three horseback-riding operations islandwide, and the only one near the East End. Private rides (1 hour $130, 1.5 hours $170) are offered for groups of two or three family or friends, along coastal routes near Fort St. Catherine, Tobacco Bay, and the St. George's Club golf course, as well as along the St. George's parish beaches in winter.

Water Sports

Launched in 2014 at the dock of the old town's yacht club, **Just Add Water** (St. George's Dinghy & Sports Club, 24 Cut Rd., tel. 441/707-5000, www.justaddwaterbda.com, 8am-8pm daily Apr.-Oct., 9:30am-5pm Wed.-Mon. Nov.-Mar.) promises free-wheeling adventures for all ages—from ATX paddleboard and kayaking expeditions (90 minutes, $70) and Jet Ski tours (90 minutes, $120) to cycle and snorkel tours (three hours, $90) and cost-effective motorboat rentals (four hours, $195), along with other water sports. The company's shop sells U.K. surfer brand Animal, as well as T-shirts, hats, and accessories.

You don't have to be a guest to use the Rosewood resort's **Tucker's Point Dive & Watersports Centre** (tel. 441/298-4050, www.divinginbermuda.com, watersports@tuckerspoint.com, 8:30am-5pm daily), which rents kayaks, sailboats (Hobies and Snarks), and motorboats (2 hours $140, half-day $445) that come equipped with snorkel equipment, towels, snacks, and water. Reservations are recommended, especially on summer weekends when locals make use of the facility too.

Sailing

Both local and out-of-town yachties congregate at **St. George's Dinghy & Sports Club** (24 Cut Rd., tel. 441/297-1612, www.stgdsc.bm). The club is far smaller than its Hamilton cousins, the Royal Bermuda Yacht Club and the Royal Hamilton Amateur Dinghy Club, but it is very involved in the area's sailing scene and acts as local host for several international events, including a cruising rally from Virginia.

Running and Walking

The parish has perhaps more open space than any other for enjoying runs or long hikes. Ferry Point National Park and Cooper's Island Nature Reserve offer tens of acres of both trails and paved roadways set amid stunning natural scenery.

Railway Trail (St. George's)

This parish's section of the Railway Trail in Ferry Point National Park is far removed from main roads or even large residential neighborhoods, lending it a deep serenity not found on the trail's other stretches. It is also very scenic, with a mile-long stretch of unpaved trail running parallel to the North Shore, high above spray-washed rocks and azure bays. An out-and-back route means you could start or finish with a swim at pretty Whalebone Bay. Tangents along the way can lead you past mangroves, through steep casuarina forests, or into historic sites such as graveyards and forts. The only modern disturbance is the occasional jet soaring away from Bermuda from the nearby airport—North American flight paths are directly overhead, but luckily there are only a handful of takeoffs each day.

For Kids

Mullet Bay Playground (on the southern edge of Mullet Bay Rd. leading into St. George's) is a popular stop for neighborhood and visiting children. Cradled in a grassy park near the moored boats of Mullet Bay, the playground has a wide assortment of climbing frames, swings, and slides, usually well maintained. There is a parking lot at the site. **Fort St. Catherine** is also a must-see, for its labyrinth of tunnels, climbable cannon, and spectacular vantage points for pretend pirates.

ACCOMMODATIONS

Accommodation choices in St. George's Parish are sparse, but they range from a boutique hotel, the tony Rosewood Tucker's Point, to bed-and-breakfasts in private homes. Check sites such as www.airbnb.com, www.vrbo.com, www.bermudarentals.com, and www.bermudagetaway.com for good options. The government has had longtime plans to develop a former Club Med site overlooking St. Catherine's Beach, but that project will take years to happen.

Rooms look out over Castle Harbour at Rosewood Tucker's Point.

Under $200

Mike and Debi Montgomery's **Le Roux Inn** (14 Secretary Ln., tel. 441/292-9212 or 441/338-2952, monty@logic.bm, $120 d) was, indeed, a *ruin* when they bought their property, hence the play on words. But today, guests will find utter home-style comfort in the refurbished, cute-as-a-button cottage, where almost every need has been thought of. Games, linens, a library of Bermuda books, and even staples have been provided by the couple, who have been renting out the inn to travelers since 2001. The studio-style cottage, which sits apart from the main house, has a high open-beamed ceiling; Mexican-tile floors; air-conditioning (and heat for the winter); a kitchenette with small fridge, toaster oven, hot plate, and microwave; a queen bed; a bathroom with shower; an eating area; and a grill. Only cash and travelers checks are accepted.

Born-and-bred St. Georgian Bernard Oatley and his wife, Lily, rent out a well-equipped studio, **Brae Apartment** (2 Secretary Ln., tel. 441/297-0629, www-bermudagetaway.com, $120 d), attached to their hilltop home on the North Shore side of the old town of St. George. The apartment, with private entrance, has a double bed plus a double sofabed; a kitchen area with stove, fridge, microwave, and washer and dryer; a bathroom with tub and shower; and cable TV, a VCR, a fan, and air-conditioning. Sliding glass doors open onto a patio with views of the sea. Dishes, sheets, towels, and WiFi are all provided.

Over $500

★ **Rosewood Tucker's Point** (60 Tucker's Point Dr., tel. 441/298-4010, www.rosewoodtuckerspoint.com, $875-2,305 d), opened in 2009, is Bermuda's newest resort, situated on a stunning coastal property that was home for decades to the historic Castle Harbour, later a Marriott. The site has a championship golf course and high-end fractional ownership residences.

The hotel incorporates a 2,000-square-foot spa and fitness center, two 25-meter infinity pools, four tennis courts, a croquet lawn, a water-sports center, a 5,000-square-foot conference center, a five-star restaurant and bar, and 88 guest rooms, including 68 deluxe rooms (poolside units come complete with daybeds) and 20 elegantly outfitted suites, all units boasting dramatic views, Kohler bathrooms, wet bars, gilt mirrors, walk-in closets, Persian rugs, and English-manor decor. Accommodations range from rooms with balconies to one- and two-bedroom suites and villas, some waterfront or poolside; all have flat-screen TVs, iPod docking stations, Egyptian linens, twice-daily housekeeping, and panoramic views of either Castle Harbour or Harrington Sound.

The building's cedar-steeped interiors include marble surfaces and fireplaces at every turn, lush carpeting, retail spaces with resortwear and jewelry, chandeliers, "view corridors," and a giant spiral gold staircase leading up to the eye-popping spa terrace, whose chalet-style treatment rooms overlook carefully landscaped gardens with yoga areas and jasmine-covered pergolas, forested hillsides, and the turquoise horizons of Harrington Sound. Free WiFi and cost-saving VOIP telephone service are offered throughout the property. Guests also have access to the golf, beach, and tennis clubs. The beach club, with another restaurant, infinity pool, and gorgeous reef-dotted South Shore strand, is located a mile away on the exclusive Tucker's Town peninsula next to the Mid Ocean Club.

FOOD

Cafés and Pubs

Tobacco Beach Bar & Grill (1 Coot Pond Rd., Tobacco Bay, tel. 441/705-7263, 9am-6pm daily in summer), launched by vendor Beach Boys in 2014, brings fish sandwiches, frozen cocktails, and DJ entertainment to the popular swimming hole.

Beach House (Fort St. George, 6 Rose Hill next to Fort St. Catherine, tel. 441/297-1400, www.stgeorgesclub.com, lunch noon-4pm and dinner 6pm-9pm Tues.-Sun. Apr.-Nov.) serves up pub grub such as Cannon Balls (jumbo scallops, $13.95), burgers, conch fritters ($12), chowders, soups and salads, and entrées such as a seafood platter ($22.95) and rack of lamb ($31.50).

Mediterranean

★ **Sul Verde** (Rosewood Tucker's Point, 60 Tucker's Point Dr., tel. 441/298-6983, www.rosewoodhotels.com, lunch noon-3pm, dinner 6pm-9pm, bar 11am-10pm, dress code: smart casual) is an unabashedly Italian family-style restaurant, but an elegant one, with a magnificent antipasti buffet (focaccias, cold cuts, house-made pickles, $19.50 appetizer, $26.50 main course), a mozzarella bar ($15), a full selection of pizza and pasta ($22-28), an extensive wine list and infused grappas, and substantial mains, from meatballs with spaghetti ($26) to pork tenderloin medallions ($32). The setting, the upper floor of the resort's grandly proportioned golf club, overlooks the velvet golf course—appropriately, its name translates as "on the green"—and blue horizons of Castle Harbour, making it a great choice for family gatherings.

Fine Dining

With its elegant steakhouse atmosphere, ★ **The Point Restaurant & Terrace** (Rosewood Tucker's Point, 60 Tucker's Point Dr., tel. 441/298-4010, opening days/hours vary by season, jackets suggested for men) is fashioned after New York's award-winning Gramercy Tavern. Low lighting, fireplaces, plantation shutters, and vintage oil-on-canvas murals once owned by Pan American Airlines and depicting the major ports of the world lend an aura of old-school quality. The menu is designed to impress, boasting appetizers like crispy duck egg ($17) and lobster and swordfish carpaccio ($21), and entrées such as Berkshire pork ($38), Amaretto-crusted lamb loin ($40), and goat cheese and a trio of vegetarian tarts ($31). A prix fixe "360 Menu" offers a 5-, 7-, or 10-course gourmet journey ($85-135) created by Chef Guido Brambilla and inspired by destinations depicted in Gerard Henderson's murals—Beirut, Canton, Istanbul, and Rio de Janeiro. With a fireplace and floor-to-brick-vaulted ceiling backdrop of 3,000 bottles, the Wine Room offers an unforgettable private dinner party setting within the restaurant.

At L. F. Wade International Airport

Fresh sushi and a full bar are the draw at **Boulevard Café** (Lower Concourse, L. F. Wade International Airport, tel. 441/293-1321, www.diningbermuda.com, 8:30am-8pm daily), the last stop for travelers to snack with relatives before heading through security to the airport's upstairs departure lounge for Canada or UK flights. St. Georgians also like the café for takeout on their drive home. The café stays open until the evening British Airways flight leaves. Sit inside or out in the hallway terrazzo, a busy people-watching perch.

Like its sister restaurant in Hamilton,

Trattoria Café and the nearby **Sports Bar** (Upper Departure Lounge, tel. 441/293-0254, www.diningbermuda.com, restricted to U.S.-bound air passengers, 6:30am-4pm, or until last flight leaves, daily) has hot and cold dishes, including pizza and daily pasta specials. It also offers takeout to travelers who prefer not to dine on airlines' mystery chicken. The bar has TV screens and views of Castle Harbour.

On Mullet Bay Road

Many Bermudians swear by the fish cakes at **Selena's** (123 Mullet Bay Rd., tel. 441/297-2979, 11:30am-9:30pm Tues.-Sat., 9am-7pm Sun., closed Mon.), where the fast food is deliciously homemade. Burgers, fried chicken, baked goods, daily soup specials, oxtail, and barbecued ribs are also on the menu. The restaurant is run by Selena Minors, who serves up her goodies daily to a full house, including takeout, with efficient and friendly style.

Friendly **Cousins Variety** (123 Mullet Bay Rd., tel. 441/297-1752, 8am-10pm daily) is located in the same building as Selena's on the north side of the winding main road out of town. Hands of freshly picked Bermuda bananas and baked goods, including gingerbread, are among its best offerings.

INFORMATION AND SERVICES

The **Airport Mail Facility** (2 Kindley Field Rd., tel. 441/293-1767) is a handy post office for passengers at L. F. Wade International Airport.

The **Airport Police Station** (tel. 441/293-1940) services L. F. Wade International Airport.

St. David's Island and Southside

"You got your passport?" locals jokingly rib Bermudians who stray from other parishes into the distinctive neighborhood of St. David's—for fresh lobster, sightseeing, or rum-rich nights out at the parish's single tavern. Indeed, St. David's, like its southwest Wales counterpart, stands out for feeling utterly apart from the rest of Bermuda, even to born-and-bred residents. Even areas farther east in St. George's don't manage to evoke such a quirky sense of individuality, stoic humor, and catchy turn of phrase as St. David's folk seem to have. Maybe it's because the island was disconnected from the main part of Bermuda until the 1930s. Today a perimeter road leads off airport-hugging Kindley Field Road, past Southside, and finally into the serpentine collection of country lanes that bear curious names such as So Far Drive and Tranquillity Lane. Here, the sea-swept hillsides are peppered with pastel homes.

St. David's begs one to slow down, linger, hang out, and ease into the community mindset. It's a corner of St. George's Parish that many visitors either skip completely or gloss over, but for those who look beyond the rather tatty surface of the neighborhood, the rewards are rich. It is the people who make St. David's a unique community, and it is they who have fueled the folklore and legends of the original 500-acre island. It is a community where far-fetched tales—and everyone here has one—sometimes turn out to be absolutely true. St. David's folk cherish their family heritage and love to share their neighborhood with "outsiders," whether in the form of a fish sandwich or a tall tale about their ancestors. Either way, sit back, relax, and soak it in; there's every chance you'll never stumble upon such an unusual community again.

With Carter House, St. David's Lighthouse, St. David's Battery, and Great Head Park, not to mention the Black Horse Tavern, a down-home bar and eatery that might snare you for several hours, you could easily while away

Forts and Guns

Fort St. Catherine's structure, armaments, and exhibits make it a must-see.

Anyone touring Bermuda's surviving forts can trace the rise and fall of the British Empire. Built from 1612 through the 1950s, the structures tell us much about world history, Bermuda's changing role over the centuries, and the evolution of global superpowers. The fascinating chain of defense also reflects the metamorphosis of military warfare itself, since historic artillery for which specific forts were made has also weathered the test of time.

Bermuda once counted a total of 90 fortifications throughout the parishes, but today many of these exist only as buried archaeological remains or are inaccessible to the public because of overgrown vegetation or trash-dumping. Over the past decade, the Department of Parks has gradually restored some of these historic sites to their former glory, enhancing cultural tourism in the process.

A dozen impressive examples of forts scattered through the main island are in good condition and open to the public. From the east, around the Town of St. George, these include: **Fort St. Catherine, Alexandra Battery, Gates Fort,** and **Fort George.** At nearby Ferry Reach, the **Martello Tower, Burnt Point Fort,** and **Ferry Island Fort** are all worth visiting, as is the park where they are located. In St. David's, the dramatic **St. David's Battery,** with its cannon and cliffs, makes a panoramic place for a picnic, and **Fort Popple** next to St. David's Cricket Club is also scenic. In Hamilton, don't miss a visit to **Fort Hamilton,** one of the best-kept forts, with moat gardens, dungeons, and a plateau of lawns overlooking the city. Farther west, **Whale Bay Fort and Battery** commands views of the South Shore's turquoise horizons, while **Fort Scaur**'s benches give a peaceful vantage point over the Great Sound. At Bermuda's westernmost point, the island's largest fortress—the cannon ramparts, casemates, magazines, and bastions of the **Royal Naval Dockyard,** including

a day here, but an afternoon would suffice. Take route 6 from the Town of St. George, or transfer from any of the Hamilton-St. George's routes (1, 3, 10, and 11) onto route 6 after Kindley Field Road.

HISTORY

Named for the patron saint of Wales (though there's no trace of Welsh culture here), St. David's swirls with maritime legends that can be traced back to the community's immersion in whaling, boatbuilding, fishing, and piloting—the practiced art of guiding ships into port safely through the skinny channels between reefs. There's the story of Tommy Fox, who climbed into a whale's belly to prove he could. Or the tale of "wreckers" who cheered a "turtle in the net"—their euphemism for luring ships onto reefs with coastal fires in order to plunder them. Residents believe to this day that some of that treasure is buried beneath the soil of farmers' fields in the neighborhood. Lily farming was a major industry here in the late 19th and early 20th centuries, when the fragrant white blooms were shipped overseas by the thousands at Eastertime.

St. David's also stands apart due to its Native American links. Indians from various tribes were shipped to the island as slaves, starting in the 17th century. Many ended up living in St. David's, marrying Bermudians and gradually becoming part of the social and ethnic mix of the area. Today, many St. David's residents claim Native American

the six-acre Keep of the National Museum of Bermuda—are perhaps the island's most notable historical landmarks.

A couple of the early forts built on the outer islands of St. George's are considered immensely valuable in heritage terms. **Fort Cunningham,** on Paget Island in St. George's Harbour, and **King's Castle** on Castle Island, at the entrance to Castle Harbour, are accessible by boat, though a tour boat and guide are advised, since Castle Island is very difficult to land at, and Fort Cunningham can only be reached via a tunnel (flashlight required). **Southampton Fort** and **Smith's Fort** lie on protected nature reserves and are therefore out of bounds. A handful of other forts, including **Fort Victoria** in St. George's and **Fort Prospect** in Devonshire, are in disrepair and are therefore currently inaccessible, but that may change if restoration continues.

The forts encompass an interesting variety of ages and styles that reveal much about the era in which they were built. The first forts were small limestone constructions, most of them built on outer islets of St. George's Parish in the 1600s. They were intended primarily for local defense (against pirates, for example), since Bermuda was not considered valuable property from a 17th-century geopolitical perspective. That changed radically, however, after the close of the American Revolutionary War (1783), when Britain lost all her U.S. ports between Halifax and the Caribbean. Bermuda then became a strategic possession, and fortifications were considered vital for Britain's empire-building. Fortified commands were put up throughout the length of the island, and the Royal Naval Dockyard was built as a mid-Atlantic hub for the British fleet. By the mid-1800s, "Fortress Bermuda" had become a bastion of the British Empire.

"The 'enemy' up to the first decade of the 1900s was the United States," writes Dr. Edward C. Harris, director of the National Museum of Bermuda, in *Bermuda: Five Centuries*. "With [one exception], all the great forts built in the 19th century were intended to hold Bermuda from an American conquest. That the Americans ended up assuming the coastal defence of Bermuda forts from 1941-45 is perhaps the greatest military irony of our history."

The impressive legacy of Bermuda's fortifications includes gun placements, historic cannons, and other artillery. St. David's Battery, for example, was built in 1910 and kept in use as late as 1957, when the British military finally pulled out of the colony. Today, a pair of 1890s rifled breech-loader guns manned in both World Wars still point out to sea here—a telling tribute to the importance of the island's coastal defenses even in modern times.

family roots, particularly among the Pequot tribe of New England. Over the past decade, the St. David's community has made strong efforts to revive these links, forging cultural alliances with U.S. Native American groups whose members have visited the island several times to attend festivals and exchange genealogical history.

But World War II would change St. David's drastically, in both physical and less tangible ways. The island's original size was expanded by 150 acres when the U.S. Army descended in 1941 to undertake a gargantuan project: obliterating Cooper's Island, Longbird Island, and a large part of St. David's Island to form Fort Bell and Kindley Field, later called Kindley Air Force Base and then U.S. Naval Air Station Bermuda. The Severn Bridge, which had linked St. David's to the mainland in 1934, was dismantled, and once again, St. David's, tucked behind the new sprawling foreign entity, was separated from the rest of Bermuda.

The lands were returned to St. David's in the late 1990s and renamed Southside. In 2008, the adjoining Cooper's Island peninsula was declared a national park and nature reserve and opened to the public. Part of this impressive open space was used as a NASA tracking station from 1960 until 2000. One of organization's 18 radar and telemetry outposts around the world, it provided vital communications links between the Kennedy Space Center at Cape Canaveral and the astronauts on various space missions. The European

Space Agency used the site in 2011, and NASA returned to Cooper's Island in 2012, signing a four-year agreement to deploy a temporary mobile tracking unit used to support satellites in low-Earth orbits and also monitor rockets launched from Wallops Flight Facility in Virginia to the International Space Station and beyond.

While St. David's belongs to St. George's Parish, its separate identity is recognized by the fact it claims its own electoral constituency.

SIGHTS

Until 1995, the large tract of St. David's land now called **Southside** belonged to the U.S. Naval Air Station and was not open to the general public. When the U.S. military pulled up stakes in 1995, locals finally got access to the lands bordering L. F. Wade International Airport. While the whole area still has the look and feel of a military base (wide concrete avenues, military-style building construction) rather than a typical Bermudian aesthetic, Southside offers much-needed recreational space for East Enders and all Bermudians. It's home to a bowling alley, launderette, and fast-food restaurant, but most locals flock to the neighborhood for its beaches (Clearwater Beach and Turtle Beach), its recreational areas (noisy go-karting clubs come to let off steam here), and for Clearwater Playground.

★ Cooper's Island Nature Reserve

The Cooper's Island Nature Reserve, long a birding habitat, is the most exciting addition to Bermuda's public open spaces in recent years, and a definite must-see for anyone who appreciates pristine beaches, coastline, woodland, and a serene outdoors hike in any season. The 44-acre park is, above all, environmentally important; its outlying islets are nesting sites for the endangered Bermuda petrel, called the cahow, and in 2005, scientists discovered one of the beaches was a nesting ground for at least one loggerhead turtle. The park is a wonderful place to spend a day sampling beautiful, usually empty, beaches. Four additional beaches now join Clearwater and Turtle Beaches on the park's outskirts: Turtle Bay and (yet another) Long Bay face southwards, while Soldier Bay and Well Bay sit on the edge of Castle Harbour. Much of Bermuda's marine and terrestrial wildlife can be found here. Breeding pairs of long-tailed tropicbirds, or longtails, nest in cliffs and can be seen swooping over the bays. Spotted

Soldier Bay sits on the west-facing coast of the Cooper's Island Nature Reserve.

sandpipers dart along the beach, and great blue herons and snowy egrets are birder favorites. Goldfinches, catbirds, and white-eyed vireos nest in the woods. Rare land hermit crabs make their homes on the coastline. Sea grass beds in the coves support juvenile turtles, black grouper, spiny lobsters, yellowtail snappers, and queen conch. No private transport is allowed inside the reserve; park at the gate and walk in. Park rangers do patrol.

★ Carter House

The oldest dwelling in St. David's, **Carter House** (Southside Ave., tel. 441/293-5960, 10am-4pm Tues., Wed., Thurs., and Sat. in summer, Sat. only in winter, $2 adults, children under 12 free) is believed to have been built around 1640. With its sloping limestone roof, original hand-cut cedar beams, buttresses, and "welcoming arms" stairs, the whitewashed cottage looks completely out of place amid the sterile development of the former baselands. It was built by the descendants of Christopher Carter, a member of the *Sea Venture* crew who stayed behind in Bermuda when the other colonists continued on to Virginia. Carter's descendants lived in the home for centuries, and, as was custom in rural areas, many were buried on the land. When the U.S. military took possession of the property, these graves were exhumed and moved to the Chapel of Ease church in St. David's. Carter House was used as a home for military officers, but after the base was closed, it was renovated and returned to the St. David's community in the late 1990s. Today, it is run by the St. David's Historical Society as a museum to celebrate the history of the unique community, including traditions of whaling, piloting, fishing, boatbuilding, and farming. In 2013, the society built a thatched hut on the grounds of Carter House using materials and construction methods akin to those of the first settlers.

Chapel of Ease

Down the pretty lane bearing the same evocative name, the **Chapel of Ease** (near the junction with Tranquillity Ln., tel. 441/297-1231, 9am Sun.) captures the maritime history of this East End community. The simple Anglican church is decorated nevertheless with stunning stained glass windows portraying Bible stories and figures linked to the sea. The whitewashed graves outside hold the remains of sailors, soldiers, and maritime pilots and the surnames of centuries-old Bermudian families—Lamb, Fox, Hayward, and Pitcher.

St. David's Lighthouse

Like its Gibbs Hill counterpart in Southampton, **St. David's Lighthouse** (Lighthouse Hill Rd., Department of Parks, tel. 441/236-5902, 7:30am-4pm daily, admission free) is a landmark to guide ships safely past the island's treacherous reef line. Built in 1879, the structure rises 55 feet to a fixed-light lantern. It was purportedly erected here as a foil against St. David's "wreckers"—nefarious locals who would purposely lure ships onto the reefs to loot their cargoes. If you think the view from its base is good—overlooking the windswept pastel cottages of St. David's—just wait until you climb the 85 steps to the top.

St. David's Battery and Great Head Park

St. David's Battery at Great Head Park (southeast end of St. David's Island off Battery Rd., sunrise-sunset daily, admission free) commands one of the most dramatic vantage points in Bermuda—and for good reason. The clear sightlines from this clifftop park, with views across the entire East End, were chosen so that this 1910 fortification could help defend the Narrows Channel in conjunction with Alexandra Battery across St. George's Harbour. The last major fortification to be built in St. George's Parish, the battery was manned for coastal defense until 1957, including stints by the Bermuda Militia Artillery during World War II, when Bermuda was a strategic mid-Atlantic base for the Allies. Four large gun emplacements, with two British breech-loading guns still in situ pointing out to sea, sit above magazines and storerooms, which unfortunately have been marred by modern graffiti and garbage. The 9.2-inch guns had a range of about seven miles, easily capable of stopping an enemy vessel before it ventured too near the island. But despite the neglect, the park, towering over the eastern cliffs where you can watch longtails soaring over the reefs, remains a top-of-the-world place for a picnic or a photo opportunity. A bronze memorial to Bermudians lost at sea sits here; the 16-foot-tall monument, by Bermudian sculptor Bill "Mussey" Ming, depicts an upturned rowboat attached to symbolic sea-related items such as a life jacket, paddle, hourglass, and nautical dividers (navigational plotting instruments).

BEACHES

Clearwater Beach and adjacent **Turtle Beach** are highly recommended for swimmers of all abilities, including children. This is one of a handful of beach areas with government lifeguards on duty throughout the summer season. The wide bay of Clearwater is shallow and usually calm throughout the summer, its long arc of white sand facing southeast toward the islets guarding Annie's Bay. Just across the lawn, **Clearwater Playground** has boldly colored climbing frames, ropes, tunnels, swings, and slides that make it a hit with kids of all ages. The on-site concession, **Gombeys Restaurant and Bar,** (193 Cooper's Island Rd., tel. 441/734-0858, 10am-onwards daily) rents out snorkeling gear, as well as kayaks, paddleboats (one hour $30), umbrellas, and snorkeling gear.

Walk through the gates of the new Cooper's Island Nature Reserve, and four more lovely beaches are open to the public: Turtle Bay, Long Bay, Soldier Bay, and Well Bay. A lifeguard is posted at Long Bay, and there are restrooms next to Turtle Bay. Because access is only by foot, these beaches tend to remain fairly quiet, even during the busy summer season. Boating access is also restricted, keeping out noise and overcrowding, and protecting the peninsula's reefs and sea grass beds.

ENTERTAINMENT AND EVENTS

Nightlife

Get "shipwrecked" at **Black Horse Tavern Bar and Restaurant** (St. David's Rd., tel. 441/297-1991, noon-10pm Tues.-Sun.), where owner Gary Lamb, of centuries-old St. David's stock, has been known to drive folks home if they end up having too many dark 'n' stormies. The waterside bar, overhung with assorted fishing

Turtle Bay is one of several pristine swimming spots at Cooper's Island Nature Reserve.

tackle and stuffed game-fish prizes from Gary's expeditions, is *the* life of the parish, attracting locals as well as a devoted flock from "the rest of the country" on Friday and Saturday nights.

Gombeys Restaurant and Bar (193 Cooper's Island Rd., tel. 441/734-0858, 10am-onwards daily) is a licensed bar, drawing a late party crowd on weekends through the high season, plus special events (like its New Year's Eve party) year-round.

SPORTS AND RECREATION

Cricket is a big passion in this parish neighborhood, home of the loftily named **Lords Oval** at **St. David's County Cricket Club** (52 Great Bay Rd., tel. 441/297-0449). Located on a plateau below Battery Park, where the ocean breeze whips in from the cliffside, the club welcomes visitors to watch hotly contested games before a knowledgeable crowd during the sport's summer season. County cricket tournaments against rival island clubs are exciting to watch—even if you're clueless about the ins and outs of the game.

Four asphalt tennis courts compose the **Kindley Community Tennis Courts** (Southside, northeast of the Clearwater turnoff, tel. 441/295-0855), which formerly belonged to the U.S. military and are now open to the public free of charge. There's an adjacent basketball court as well.

FOOD

Cafés and Pubs

Near the busy junction of Kindley Field Park, Swing Bridge, and St. David's Road, **Double Dip Express** (1 Kindley Field Rd., tel. 441/293-5959, 10am-11pm daily in summer, 11:30am-9pm in winter) does a roaring trade, selling ice cream ($3 a scoop) of all flavors, fish cakes ($6), hot dogs ($4.25), baked goods, chicken legs, and other short-order treats for passersby.

The canteen at **St. David's County Cricket Club** (52 Great Bay Rd., tel. 441/297-0449) serves up a small menu of fresh fish sandwiches, fish cakes, and burgers during cricket tournaments, football (soccer) games, and other community events on the panoramic oceanfront field. Call the club for schedule information.

At the site of a U.S. Naval Air Station McDonald's franchise that closed when the U.S. forces left Bermuda in 1995, **Pizza House** (106 Southside Rd., tel. 441/293-5700, 10:30am-9pm Mon.-Wed., 10:30am-10pm Thurs.-Sat., noon-9pm Sun.) serves up burgers ($5), fries, pizza by the slice or box ($4-26), and soft drinks.

Gombeys Restaurant and Bar (193 Cooper's Island Rd., tel. 441/734-0858, 10am onwards daily) cooks up burgers, hot dogs, fish sandwiches, fries, chicken wings, shrimp, and conch fritters for hungry swimmers. It is also a licensed bar, drawing a late crowd on weekends.

Bermudian

Tuna steaks, rockfish, and sweet lobster just a half hour out of the ocean are what bring the crowds to Gary Lamb's ★ **Black Horse Tavern Bar and Restaurant** (101 St. David's Rd., tel. 441/297-1991, noon-10pm Tues.-Sun.), a fixture of St. David's quirky social scene for decades. The waterfront, family-friendly restaurant pleases celebrities and common folk alike with its no-frills decor and down-to-earth service. You can sit inside amid the noisy chatter or at picnic tables next to the water on the grassy lawn out back—a prime spot on summer evenings. Bermuda spiny lobsters, half or whole, are available in season (Sept.-Mar.), baked in butter and served on the shell. Other house specialties include curried mussels with rice ($25), conch fritters ($14.50), Bermuda fish chowder ($6.75), shark hash ($26), and pan-fried rockfish steak ($38). Service may take a while, but that's beside the point. The onsite bar is a hive of activity on Friday and Saturday nights, when area partygoers and Bermudians from the rest of the island come for rum—and lots of it.

INFORMATION AND SERVICES

Southside Police Station (2 Stokes Point Rd., tel. 441/293-2222) services the whole parish.

The **Lamb Foggo Urgent Care Centre** (1 Hall St., tel. 441/298-7700, 4pm-midnight Mon.-Fri., noon-midnight Sat.-Sun.) offers medical assessment and treatment for minor injuries or illnesses, including cuts, bruises, sprains, colds, and earaches.

The friendly staff, easy access, and community-friendly hours make **Southside Laundromat** (103 Southside Rd., tel. 441/297-3419, 7am-9pm daily) a well-used service in the area.

St. David's Variety (tel. 441/297-0475, 6am-10pm Mon.-Sat., 8am-8pm Sun.) is the area's mini-grocery-cum-corner store, located just past the Black Horse Tavern.

GETTING THERE AND AROUND

Exploring different parts of St. David's and Southside is best done by scooter, given the distances between points of interest in this section of St. George's Parish. Visiting St. David's Lighthouse and Cooper's Island Nature Reserve, for example, would take a while to travel between by bus. If you're planning to spend the whole day at Southside beaches, however, a bus trip from Hamilton or St. George's would be more practical, saving the cost of a rental when most of your time will be spent swimming or sunbathing.

Scooters

The St. George's outlet of **Oleander Cycles** (26 York St., tel. 441/297-0478, www.oleander-cycles.bm, 8:30am-5:30pm daily, $55 per day) rents single- and double-seater 50cc scooters. Also with an presence in the old town, **Eve Cycles** (1 Water St., tel. 441/236-0839, www.evecycles.com, 8am-5:30pm daily) is housed in a historic building marked by a Penny Farthing bicycle standing outside. The livery rents scooters starting at $48 per day and $210 per week, with free islandwide shuttle service and online advance booking.

Buses and Ferries

Routes from Hamilton include bus numbers 1, 3, 10, and 11; they travel between the capital and the Town of St. George daily. The number 1 bus runs every half hour, the other routes run every 15 minutes. Bus number 6 runs between the old town and St. David's (including Southside); a transfer lets you board another bus at Southside's first gate to travel to Clearwater Beach and back every half hour.

Sea Express fast ferries have four daily trips in high season from Dockyard to St. George's (9:30am, 11am, 2pm, and 4:30pm). The one-way fare from Dockyard (get a free transfer for that leg if you set off from Hamilton) is $4.50 for adults, $2.50 for kids. You can take your scooter for an extra charge of $4. Buy tickets, tokens, or passes in advance (at the ferry terminal or select stores), as cash is not accepted on board.

Background

The Landscape

An archipelago arranged as a fishhook, Bermuda comprises a total of more than 100 islands encircled by a collar of coral. Wary Spanish mariners of the 16th century dubbed them *Las Islas de Demonios* (Islands of Devils), while the English preferred the more benign moniker "The Summer Islands." Today, eight of the largest islands—St. George's Island, St. David's Island, Bermuda Island, Somerset Island, Watford Island, Boaz Island, Ireland Island South, and Ireland Island North—are connected by bridges and a causeway to form a single entity, which locals simply call "The Island." Within the many picturesque harbors, bays, and sounds are scatterings of smaller islands and islets, some public, others privately owned, many just rocky uninhabited outcrops lacking structures or vegetation. The main island is relatively small at 21 square miles (22 miles end to end, and never more than two miles wide), with the hook's western third curling around to the northwest. But due to its varied and hilly—though not mountainous—terrain, Bermuda from the ground is rather deceptive, leading one to believe that, just around the next corner, there might be more than the sum of its compressed vital statistics. An aerial view is more revealing: As you descend for a landing at the East End airport, sweeping from violet deep-ocean across reef-dotted aquamarine shallows, the island appears almost fragile in its entirety—an oceanic oddity whose geographic isolation has shaped a distinct survival.

Bermuda's unique, seemingly contradictory characteristics have long intrigued scientists. A subtropical island about 650 miles from the nearest mainland (Cape Hatteras, North Carolina), it bears little resemblance to its Caribbean cousins in climate, biota, or geology. Instead, Bermuda is bathed by the balmy Gulf Stream, which exerts a moderating influence on its climate, just as the easterly trade winds do down south. Yet, unlike the tropical Indies, Bermuda's winters are damp and storm-wracked. There is no typical wet or dry season; indeed, the island's weather habits are so capricious that a thunderstorm can let loose on one parish while sparing all the others.

Geologically, the island's core is soft, white limestone, despite violent volcanic origins. There are no rivers, lakes, or streams. The topography is neither towering nor dangerously low (Town Hill in Smith's Parish is the highest point of land at 259 feet above sea level). And though tiny, Bermuda's landmass holds an astonishingly diverse range of natural habitats—from marshland to sand dunes and cedar woodland—that support an equally varied ecology.

Visitors, of course, are tantalized by such offerings. Bermuda's geologic permutations have left a place characterized by mostly welcoming temperatures; by floral eye candy found throughout the island's undulating length; by soft, rosy-hued beaches and turquoise swimming holes; by saltwater sounds that provide perfect natural harbors; by pastel homes hewn from the very rock they sit on; and by a necklace of biodiverse coral reefs—the most northerly in the world.

Except for the ferocity of its storms, including seasonal hurricanes, Bermuda's environment is indeed charmed. Immune to natural disasters such as earthquakes, volcanoes, mudslides, or floods, devoid even of dangerous plants or animals, its appearance conjures a manicured country garden rather than a mid-Atlantic atoll.

Previous: passion flower; Elbow Beach.

GEOGRAPHY

Bermuda lies at 32°17' N, 64°46' W, along the latitude of Savannah, Georgia. The nearest point of land is Cape Hatteras, North Carolina, 650 miles to the northwest. Roughly the size of Manhattan, Bermuda is 2,100 miles west of the Azores and 910 miles north of the Bahamas. There are no distinct topographical regions on the island, but rather a variety of natural habitats, all of which can be found in most of the nine parishes.

Bermuda consists of a limestone cap sitting at the pinnacle of a submerged volcanic seamount. Its geological origins can be traced back 110 million years to the Mid-Atlantic Ridge, a volatile, mostly submerged division between the divergent American and European tectonic plates. Scientists believe "Mount Bermuda" was the byproduct of a massive volcanic eruption just west of the ridge, which moved slowly westward over the next 80 million years. A second eruption caused the volcano to enlarge into the Bermuda Seamount, incorporating a trio of peaks: the Bermuda Pedestal (on which the island now sits), the Challenger Bank, and Argus Bank. Of these, only the 13,000-foot Bermuda Pedestal now extends above sea level. The seamount moved an additional 500 miles west in the following 30 million years, leaving the island currently situated in a stable area of the earth's crust.

The seamount's limestone cap was formed biologically over the last million years as seaweeds, algae, corals, and other shallow-water marine organisms laid down deposits. A 350-foot-deep layer of calcium carbonate was formed, and as sea levels fell, about 100,000 years ago, this layer was exposed to air. The result was the formation of many tons of sand, which wind blew across the island to form rolling dunes that eventually hardened into what geologists term aeolian limestone, meaning "created by wind." Remnants of these old dunes, sometimes even dunes atop dunes, can be seen along the shoreline of Bermuda or in road cuts such as the dramatic Blackwatch Pass in Pembroke. Soft, porous limestone rock now makes up Bermuda's entire surface and has been quarried over the centuries for roof slate and building blocks used for Bermuda's characteristic island homes.

The porous nature of the limestone helped shape Bermuda's geological identity. It allowed rain to soak into the surface rock, deterring freshwater runoff that would have created streams, rivers, and lakes. Instead, rainwater burrowed deep into the earth, forming a network of twisting underground tunnels, caverns, and caves, which still honeycomb certain parishes and give Bermuda one of the highest concentrations of caves in the world. Some are found underwater, becoming refuges for rare species. In the best known, you can find stalactites and stalagmites, columns, flow stones, and soda straws.

Bermuda's biological history begins about 800,000 years ago—the date of the oldest terrestrial fossils, belonging to a petrel (a tube-nosed seabird), found in Hamilton Parish. But climatic changes and the dramatic rise and fall of sea levels over time created havoc for the habitats, animals, and plantlife that may have lived on an ancient Bermuda far larger than its current form. As Canadian research scientist Dr. Martin Thomas points out in his book, *The Natural History of Bermuda,* observations from deep-ocean submersibles examining the Bermuda Pedestal have revealed former beaches at a depth of 315 feet—a fascinating clue about the island's previous life. It was not until about 10,000 years ago that rising sea levels stabilized and Bermuda took its present shape. Marine and terrestrial organisms then arrived as larvae, spores, or adults, transported by wind or carried on debris propelled by the powerful Gulf Stream. Against big odds, these first forms of life would slowly spawn the rich environment to which Bermuda is home today.

Beaches

Bermuda is renowned for its scores of beaches, which vary considerably around the island. Those responsible for most of the rave reviews are located on the South Shore, where

The Bermuda Triangle

If there's one thing most everyone knows about Bermuda—even if they've never set foot on the island—it's that the archipelago lies in the maw of a spooky phenomenon dubbed the "Bermuda Triangle." Bermudians who live or travel overseas get peppered with questions about the popular myth, and it is a favorite topic of discussion among tourists, but locals tend to dismiss it with humor and skepticism. Despite the Triangle's perennial appearance in books and science-fiction TV series, scientists agree it is nothing more than an enduring legend fueled by deadly coincidence.

Conspiracy theorists have devoted seas of ink to explaining why ships and aircraft have sunk, caught fire, or vanished without a trace within an area of Atlantic Ocean spanning Bermuda; San Juan, Puerto Rico; and Miami, Florida. Some believe these were the victims of paranormal occurrences, blaming malevolent sea creatures, time warps, UFOs, aliens, and the lost city of Atlantis. Others speculate that natural sources such as fog fields, magnetic anomalies, or methane bubbles popping up from the sea floor might have caused planes' instruments to malfunction or vessels to sink.

Empirical data suggests a far simpler explanation—that such "mysteries" aren't really mysterious at all. Given the fact that many Triangle incidents took place during raging storms or in the 1940s and 1950s before the advent of high-tech navigation equipment such as global positioning satellites (GPS), basic human error or the whims of Mother Nature could easily account for the disasters. In fact, Lloyd's of London accident records have shown that the Triangle's geographic area is no more dangerous than any other part of the ocean—a conclusion confirmed by the U.S. Coast Guard.

Yet the world's fascination with the Triangle continues, particularly with the story of Flight 19, the unsolved disappearance of five Avenger torpedo bombers on December 5, 1945. The Triangle's best-known tale describes how the aircraft left Fort Lauderdale's Naval Air Station on a routine practice mission with 13 student pilots, accompanied by their commander, Lt. Charles Taylor. The flight plan called for a test bombing run followed by a triangular course east and north, a distance of 120 miles. But about 90 minutes after leaving the base, the squadron found itself in trouble. Taylor sent a radio transmission reporting that his compasses were malfunctioning, and it soon became clear he was hopelessly disoriented. As night fell and a storm approached, communications faded and finally stopped, presumably when the planes ran out of fuel and plunged into the sea.

One of two Martin Mariner search planes that went to look for the missing squadron also disappeared; there were reports of an explosion after it took off, and airplane debris was spotted nearby. Nothing was seen of Flight 19, however. The Navy, pressured by Taylor's family, cited "causes or reasons unknown" for the disaster, rather than pilot error. In subsequent decades, the story of Flight 19 became the focus of Triangle speculation, which heightened after Charles Berlitz's sensational bestseller of 1974, *The Bermuda Triangle.* Flight 19's planes and pilots even enjoyed a reappearance in Steven Spielberg's 1977 UFO classic, *Close Encounters of the Third Kind.*

One of the most lauded books on the Triangle attempts to lay such fantasies to rest. *The Bermuda Triangle—Solved* was written by Arizona librarian Larry Kusche, who in 1975 decided to investigate claims put forward by the plethora of articles and books on the Triangle's unsolved mysteries. Digging into contemporary accounts and other primary sources, he discovered factual material other writers had overlooked or ignored, much of it pointing to entirely rational explanations for unusual events. His book catalogs his findings, offering in-depth detail about some of the myth's highlights and ultimately refuting many outlandish claims.

Surprisingly, Bermuda has never made much of the legend, even as a potential tourist attraction. Eponymous cocktails took the name, and several island companies pay tribute to the folklore with Triangle monikers, including retail stores, a printing house, and a scuba outlet. Bermuda Department of Tourism officials seem to have qualms about marketing the Triangle to the world at large, despite calls from some in the industry for Triangle-themed travel ads, a museum, or boat tours.

Bermuda's Beaches

Bermuda's beaches are world-renowned, and there are hundreds of them around the island. Whether you're staying at a dedicated beach resort, or at an inland guesthouse, you are never far from the shore. Although some are officially private, belonging to resorts or restricted neighborhoods, most of Bermuda's beaches are open to the public from sunrise to sunset, from the water's edge to the high-tide mark.

You can swim all year round (though Bermudians don't). Water temperatures in summer can reach a balmy 85°F or more; winter temperatures dip to an average 65°F. The first official beach day is May 24, when boaters take to the water to kick off the season, but most locals wait until June or July to make their first beach foray. Midsummer's Cup Match holiday is the ultimate beach extravaganza, with practically every inch of shoreline occupied by family outings and elaborate seaside camping parties. Care to spend Christmas Day at the water's edge? Hardy expatriate residents have long celebrated the morning of December 25 with a dip and champagne toast at Elbow Beach; some don Santa hats and bring miniature trees, complete with ornaments, for the festive occasion.

Concessions—for boogie boards, noodles, masks and snorkels, hair-braiding, umbrellas, and refreshments—can be found at several major beaches, particularly those along the South Shore. Hard-core surfing is rare, because Bermuda's rollers are usually not large enough, hurricane season excepted. However, kitesurfing—in which a rider, hooked by harness to a power kite, skims waves on a board—is popular among local thrill-seekers; the far more sedate passion for standup paddleboarding has also taken off in recent years, and you can rent boards from several outlets. There are no nude or topless beaches, and baring all on this conservative island will only land you in trouble with the law.

Government lifeguards are posted on just a handful of the most popular strands, identifiable by their white huts with posted flags that indicate daily danger levels. Be careful of riptides and undertow on the South Shore, especially during hurricane season, when swells propelled by approaching storms surge against the coast.

sweeping tracts of coral-tinted sand are pounded by turquoise surf populated by iridescent parrotfish and schools of pompano and amberjack. The surf is relatively gentle, thanks to the protection of reefs that lie a stone's throw from shore (a mere few yards in some areas) on this side of the island.

The North Shore, including areas of the Great Sound and St. George's, though less of a tourist attraction, is just as beautiful for swimming, snorkeling, kayaking, and scuba diving. In contrast to the sand and surf of the South Shore, this side of the island is punctuated by small rocky coves and azure bays, some without beaches at all, and there is no surf. Local youngsters practice their high-diving here, and deep grottoes invite plunging in. The reef line exists, but since it sits 10 miles offshore, it is barely visible, and divers need a boat to get out there.

All the island's beaches are covered in the same white or pinkish sand, scattered with shells and seaweed, but with none of the pebbles or dark grit of Caribbean volcanic islands such as Montserrat or Guadeloupe. In the winter, prevailing northeast winds can make the North Shore choppy, but throughout most of the summer northern horizons are as calm as a lake.

CLIMATE

Bermuda's climate is subtropical and influenced by two major factors: the Gulf Stream and the Bermuda-Azores High. Like a giant security blanket, the Gulf Stream flows northeast from the Gulf of Mexico—from which it takes its name—through the Straits of Florida to an area northeast of Bermuda, channeling warm equatorial water northward on its journey. The Gulf Stream moderates temperature, bringing mild weather throughout the year and preventing Bermuda from getting as hot or cold as mainland areas of the same latitude. Frost is not found here, though winter gets the occasional hailstorm.

The Bermuda-Azores High is a high-pressure zone, which also exerts a welcome influence on Bermuda's climate. In the summer, the zone lies east of Bermuda, bouncing storm systems north of the island and causing light southerly winds to blow throughout the season. In the winter, though, the high sits too far southeast to make a difference, allowing northerly gales to pummel the island with cooler temperatures. Unlike the Caribbean, Bermuda has no trade winds or monsoons, and its isolated position brings a lower risk of hurricanes.

Bermuda's hurricane season runs from June to November.

Seasons

Officially, Bermuda has two seasons—summer and winter—which have defined the tourism industry. Summer, the "high" season for visitors, runs April-October, while winter, once snubbed as the "off" or "low" season, runs November-March.

Most Bermudians, however, would argue the island actually does enjoy four seasons like its mainland counterparts. Locals can immediately discern the first breath of fall in the second week of October, when temperatures dip from the torpor of summer, or the sweet calm of spring in early April after the windy barrage of New Year storms.

The island has no rainy season; instead, rain tends to be spread throughout the year, with January being the wettest month on average, with 150 millimeters, or six inches of rain. Typically, even torrential rainstorms peter out after an hour or two, and rare are the days when the sun does not make a single appearance. The hour-by-hour changes can prove challenging to packing clothes for a Bermuda holiday in any season; choose a mix of outfits and layers to accommodate the unexpected.

True summer can be counted on May-September, with temperatures peaking in July and August. Relative humidity (ranging between 75 and 85 percent all year, but occasionally spiking to 90 in midsummer) makes Bermuda feel uncomfortably like a greenhouse, draining energy—and buckets of sweat—in the summer. Hydration is key to doing anything active in these months, and swimming is the most refreshing way to cool off. October-December marks one of the most pleasant times of the year, when cool breezes prevail, but the sun can be hot enough that you'll want to swim. The windy season usually takes control after Christmas, bringing storms, cold winds, rain, and damp days and nights from January to March; this is, perhaps, the most unpredictable season, for there can often be long spells of sunshine amid the tempestuousness. Ignore the euphemistic descriptions on tourist brochures, though; it can get *very* chilly by Bermudian standards, and many homes and hotels have no heating, aside from fires and electric heaters. Remember, too, that a modest 60°F can feel downright frigid if you happen to be driving a scooter on a windblown winter's night; wear gloves like Bermudians do. Spring signals a drop

Preparing for a Hurricane

Bermudians can reel off the dates and names of worst-offending hurricanes like a list of wayward relatives they would have preferred had not visited: Emily (a Category 1 hurricane that caught the island off guard on September 24, 1987, causing $35 million in damage); 1995's Felix (which swept away surfside restaurants and swiped the Island back and forth three times); and Fabian (a Category 3, which scored a rare "direct hit" on Bermuda on September 5, 2003, killing four people, closing several hotels, knocking out power for several weeks, and causing an estimated $300 million in damage).

While most hotels and guesthouses will make safety and logistical arrangements for guests in the event of a hurricane, it helps to be prepared if you're staying in a private home or renting an apartment. A hurricane checklist should include candles, canned goods (including pet food for any animals you may be taking care of), flashlights, propane lanterns, batteries, battery-powered AM/FM radio, propane stove, tarpaulin (in case roof slate blows off), and a bucket and rope for hauling freshwater from the tank. Secure all moveable objects from the garden or yard (garbage cans, garden furniture). Secure storm shutters, and tape or board up windows. Clear out roof gutters and put strainers in downspouts to keep debris out of drinking water. Make sure pets are kept indoors. Stock up on emergency supplies, including medications. Fill the bathtub to enable flushing of toilets. Make sure vehicles have full gas tanks.

Weather updates and community news are provided by the Government Emergency Broadcast Facility on FM 100.1 MHz.

During a storm, do not go outside, and stand clear of the windows in case flying debris smashes the glass. If you must go out, watch for falling branches and power lines. When the eye of the storm passes over the island, the weather will calm down dramatically, but do not assume that the hurricane is over. Remain inside, because the storm will resume from the opposite direction.

After the storm, report any fallen trees or downed power lines and do not drive unless absolutely necessary. To save food for as long as possible, try not to open the fridge or freezer for long periods.

Call 911 for an emergency, or 955 to report a power outage.

in winds and a resulting rebirth in garden growth and blossoms, as calm, sunny weather prevails and temperatures begin their inevitable rise toward the end of May. Bermuda Day (May 24) is the traditional first day of summer, though islanders usually refuse to swim until at least a month later.

Temperatures

Bermuda's summer and winter temperatures differ considerably, though the yearly average is a balmy 76°F. Monthly variations are more telling: Average temperatures range from 66°F in February to 85°F in August, the effects heightened considerably by summer's humidity. Annual lows and highs normally range from 55°F to 95°F.

Seawater temperatures hover around 65°F in the winter but warm to a bathlike 83°F by August. Visitors often swim and scuba dive year-round, however.

Rainfall

Bermuda's rainfall is fairly evenly distributed throughout the year, with no true rainy season, though rain is more likely to intrude on outdoor activities if you visit between January and March. Even then, Bermuda rainfall tends to come in the form of a quick downpour rather than daylong drizzle, so barring a hurricane, weather rarely ruins a Bermuda vacation. Indeed, it's possible to have torrential rain in Paget while St. Georgians simultaneously bask in the sun.

Hurricanes

The hurricane season officially runs six months, June-November, but Bermudians consider themselves safe until the seawater temperature hits 85 degrees, usually in July, and after it starts to dip again, by mid-October.

Bermuda escapes most of the annual roster of storms, the majority of which miss the island due to its tiny landmass, though severe storms have scored direct hits—on average every half-dozen years. One of the worst on record was the Category 3 Hurricane Fabian, in 2003. But even more memorable was the double-whammy the island got in mid-October 2014 when Category 1 Hurricane Fay and Category 3 Hurricane Gonzalo slammed roofs and vegetation in the space of a week. More common are huge storm swells off the beaches, which whip up surf and prohibit swimming, and heavy rain and wind when hurricanes are in the vicinity. Storms have also spawned tornadoes that twist across isolated areas of the island, ripping off roofs before vanishing out to sea.

Hurricane near-misses, when these violent vortexes sideswipe the island, have occurred some seasons; very rarely, hurricanes bounce back eastward after first careening toward the U.S. East Coast. Particularly after the fury of Fabian, however, Bermudians are highly aware of a hurricane's destructive force and monitor the track of every single storm during this season, no matter how large, small, or apparently distant.

The government and media communicate the details of approaching storms, and Bermuda's Emergency Measures Organization is well prepared to orchestrate recovery and cleanup efforts in the event of severe damage. After Fabian killed four Bermudians, the government cracked down with stricter storm preparations, including closing the mile-long Causeway to St. George's when big storms draw too close. Yet, Bermuda generally fares far better than Caribbean islands in the event of a direct hit, thanks to its sturdy limestone and cement-block buildings, well-developed infrastructure, and modern communications system. Most householders stock up every summer with hurricane supplies (tarps, flashlights, batteries, and buckets).

Hurricane Strength

Bermuda uses the American Saffir-Simpson Hurricane Scale to judge the strength and property-damage potential of approaching storms.

- **Category 1:** winds 74-95 miles per hour (minor damage)
- **Category 2:** winds 96-110 miles per hour (roof, window, vegetation, and small-craft damage)
- **Category 3:** winds 111-130 miles per hour (structural damage to homes, vegetation)
- **Category 4:** winds 131-155 miles per hour (extensive damage)
- **Category 5:** winds 155-plus miles per hour (catastrophic damage)

The **Emergency Measures Organisation** (tel. 441/295-0011) broadcasts police, government, and media alerts via 100.1 FM, when other stations are knocked off the air during power outages. Weather warnings, including marine forecasts, are broadcast by the **Bermuda Weather Service** (tel. 977, www.weather.bm) or via Bermuda Harbour Radio (tel. 441/297-1010, www.marineandports.bm, click on Marine Operations Centre). During hurricane season, both the **National Weather Service** (www.nws.noaa.gov) and **The Weather Channel** (www.weather.com) track developing storms and their movements through the Caribbean and Atlantic with satellite images and forecasts.

Another useful site to visit to learn about hurricanes and Bermuda folklore is www.sharkoil.bm, named for the homespun meteorological indicators many locals still consult when bad weather looms. Even in the 21st century, orthodox science sometimes takes a backseat to these traditional barometers—sealed bottles

Residents catch rainwater on white roofs that channel it into underground storage tanks.

of fatty hydrocarbons extracted from a shark's liver. For centuries, Bermudians have hung "shark oil" in a sheltered spot outdoors, where they check its contents to predict a storm's ferocity. While younger generations now turn to CNN, old-timers swear the bottle's contents turn cloudy during disturbances, and if a hurricane actually looms, a spiraling plume will be visible inside.

ENVIRONMENTAL ISSUES

Bermuda may look like a pristine paradise, but pollution, pesticides, and overdevelopment are wreaking havoc on the island's ecosystems.

Warning signs are causing scientists to become alarmed; they note that reductions in plant and animal species, as well as the ebbing health of some species, are important barometers of environmental degradation. Since 1997, the island's sea grass beds—vital habitats for conch, sea urchins, rockfish, turtles, and spiny lobsters—have drastically declined; marine biologists say 20 percent of the 5,100 acres have been eradicated in the last decade alone. Leaching cesspits and dredging are blamed for the loss, and authorities promise sea grass beds will be added to the list of protected areas of the island.

Disposal of waste, including sewage, is one of Bermuda's biggest problems and one of the most prominent on the minds of environmentalists, who have worked in recent years to make sustainable development a public debate. The island burns its garbage at an incinerator constructed for $64 million in 1992; its tower, at Tynes Bay, Devonshire, is visible along the North Shore. Sewage waste, dissolved and pumped out to sea, has caused a growth surge in marine weeds that choke slower-growing corals—an ecological imbalance scientists are monitoring.

Pollutants in ponds and nature reserves—evident in the resulting populations of deformed toads—are also raising concern. A large part of the problem may be the lackadaisical attitude Bermudians have long held toward pesticides. For decades, householders liberally sprayed bug-killers such as Baygon and Raid, and environmental organizations now push for the use of less-toxic alternatives.

Even Bermuda's air quality is susceptible to modern contaminants. Large numbers of high-emission motorbikes, as well as cars, have raised air pollution to dangerous levels in some areas around the City of Hamilton, even exceeding annual readings of some European cities, scientists report. These are issues Bermudians must grapple with and find solutions to as island development, traffic, and population—along with their ugly fallout—seem only certain to increase.

Water Conservation

Rainwater is at a premium on an island, as households depend on it as their main source of freshwater—at least to run faucets, showers, baths, and toilets, if not for drinking. Large water tanks are built under every home, and rain is caught as it has been for centuries—on traditional white limestone slate roofs, whose pipes and gullies channel it to a subterranean tank. From there, water is pumped into domestic plumbing systems. There are also large public water-catchments for government use. Not surprisingly, water conservation is the rule amid chronic droughts. The first five months of 2011, for example, brought just 12.32 inches of rain—nearly half the average precipitation for that period, causing severe water shortages.

Conservationists have sounded warnings about the problem of increasing water consumption on the island, particularly the pressure it exerts on underground lenses, which supply larger private users, such as hotels, as well as the City of Hamilton. Bermuda residents consume an estimated 1.58 billion gallons of water annually; each cruise ship consumes up to 50,000 gallons daily in port. The island has just one reverse-osmosis plant, to supply the hospital and offset shortages, but experts argue several more plants are needed to avert future crises.

Cruise Ships

The extent to which the cruise industry benefits Bermuda has generated much debate on the island, but perhaps even more controversial is the question of whether Bermuda's infrastructure can support the advent of far bigger ships. The world's cruise liners are estimated to have nearly doubled in size every decade. The current generation of Panamax vessels launching from shipyards are longer (965 feet), wider (106 feet), and have a deeper draft (39.5 feet) than conventional ships; they are named for an enlarged superstructure design that fits the maximum lock dimensions of the Panama Canal. Such ships can carry 3,000-4,000 passengers, double that of standard ships. Critics question whether Bermuda can absorb so many cruise visitors without a negative impact on other tourists and residents. Larger ships have already caused transport issues, forcing the government to ensure more buses, ferries, and taxis are available. Other concerns include pressure on garbage, sewage, and water systems, given that ships in port make liberal use of those services. Heritage Wharf, alongside King's Wharf at the Dockyard, has been the docking spot for mega-vessels since it was built in 2009. Far smaller and, typically, older ships make port in Hamilton, with occasional stops in St. George's.

Plants and Animals

HABITATS

The island's habitats are not as numerous or exotic as those found in pure tropical regions like the Caribbean and Central America. Yet Bermuda's ecosystems are interesting in their more subtle variety, as well as in their increasing fragility due to rampant development. The main habitats are the rocky shore; beaches and dunes; inland forest; marshes, ponds, and mangroves; karst and caves; sea grass beds; and coral reefs. All these areas can be seen and explored at sites around the island. Interpretive displays complete with audio are found at the Natural History Museum (part of the Bermuda Aquarium, Museum & Zoo) at Flatts, in Smith's Parish, and describe habitats and common species found in each.

The Rocky Shore

Some of the most impressive aspects of wild Bermuda are its rocky shore and coastal environments. Climbing up and down the spray-bashed coast, where biodiverse tide pools are often large enough to swim in, you can imagine the natural setting that greeted the castaways who reached Bermuda's shores. When the first humans arrived on the island's shoreline in the 1500s, they encountered a reef-necklaced oasis of endemic cedar forests and palmetto palms, both of which were beneficial to survival in myriad ways: for timber to build huts and ships, for roof thatch, for berries to mull wine, and for hearts of palm, which shipwreck survivors roasted or baked.

The rocky shoreline is home to a wealth of plants and animals, a unique bridge between marine and terrestrial environments. Algae, lichens, and rockweeds drape the intertidal zone, where they have adapted to a hybrid environment with features such as attachments, or "holdfasts," to the rock. The band lying between the lowest tide and the spray zone is darkened and made slippery by bluegreen bacteria, which provide a larder of food for other animals. Among the various species found here, rainbow-hued parrotfish can be found grazing, gnawing on reef and rock with their hallmark beaked mouths. Crabs, snails, urchins, anemones, and seaweeds also thrive. The banded West Indian top shell *(Cittarium pica)* can sometimes be found; it's a protected species, and removing this creature is illegal. Growing profusely atop the wind- and sea-eroded limestone shore are hardy, salt-resistant succulents, such as the sea purslane, coast spurge, and seaside oxeye, whose vibrant yellow flowers dot the landscape. Prickly pears, spiky Spanish bayonets with luxuriant towers of white blossoms, baygrape brushes, fennel, and fields of seaside goldenrod, waving feathery, butter-colored wands, cover areas above the tidal shore.

Beaches and Dunes

Sand dunes harbor a similarly tough variety of plants, whose growth effectively serves to anchor the dunes and prevent sand masses from shifting too far. Dune vegetation is peppered with the types of bright blossoms that are so striking in desert environments, although here, they are totally different varieties; these include the purple-flowered vine, seaside morning glory, wild stock, sea lavender, and the buttercup-like seaside evening primrose. Land crabs dig long burrows in dune areas to escape the prying beaks of hunting night herons; be careful when hiking the dunes not to twist your ankle in their exit holes.

Inland Forest

As a result of residential and urban development, Bermuda's original woodland comprising endemic cedars, palmettos, and olivewood has been whittled down over four centuries to mere remnants of its former expanse. Today, true remains of the old forest are almost nonexistent, since woodland is now dominated by introduced species. Many have proven detrimental to endemics; examples such as the Mexican pepper, whispering pine or casuarina, and the Chinese fan palm have competed for space and nutrients with cedars and palmettos—usually successfully. Yet inland forests covering uplands and interior valleys contain dense evergreen coverage, providing vital breeding and nesting areas for birds, insects, and other species.

Surviving native trees include the Bermuda cedar *(Juniperus bermudiana),* the palmetto *(Sabal bermudiana),* the yellow wood, olivewood, and hackberry. Nonendemic fiddlewoods, allspice, Surinam cherry, and Indian laurel trees are much more common and can be found in forested hillsides and valleys and in the woodland tracts of most nature reserves. The East End's Nonsuch Island Nature Reserve, which can be visited through special tours, is the only area of the island where endemic forest has been totally restored over the past three decades. The government's Department of Parks has embarked on an islandwide restoration effort in many other protected areas to replace invasives with endemic and native saplings, a program that will take many years to achieve maturity.

Marshes, Ponds, and Mangroves

Peat marshes, freshwater and salt ponds, and mangroves are some of the most fascinating natural environments for amateur or professional biologists to explore. Such wetlands provide a vital feeding ground for bird species and also nurture insects, toads, lizards, and other animals. Bermuda's mangrove swamps—wet forests that can tolerate saltwater—are the Atlantic's most northerly.

The Bermuda Cedar

The Bermuda cedar *(Juniperus bermudiana)* is a symbol of survival for islanders, who have depended on the sturdy evergreen from the first days of human habitation on Bermuda. The endemic cedar, along with the palmetto and olivewood, covered the island in thick woods during the 1500s and early 1600s, and later sustained generations of English colonists. They used its timber for constructing homes, churches, and forts after colonization in 1612. They chose cedar for building light, rot-resistant Bermuda sloops—vessels that fueled a whole maritime industry for over a century in the 1700s. The cedar tree's aromatic, red-hued wood was much sought-after for crafting cabinetry and fine furniture, including chests, tables, and four-poster beds, much of which graces modern Bermudian homes. Early Bermudians even produced liquor by fermenting the cedar's blue-gray berries and had medicinal uses for its dark-green foliage and hairy bark.

With salt-tolerant foliage and long roots anchored in the island's limestone-rich soil against hurricanes, cedars were so abundant that islanders squandered the wood, burning cedar forests in vain attempts to rid the island of rats. Colonists also shipped it carelessly overseas in the form of expendable crates to hold exports. Bermuda cedar was soon in such short supply that it became immensely valuable. Indeed, by the 18th century, island properties were valued by the number of cedars growing on them. Protection laws enacted over the years bear testimony to the iconic worth of the beloved cedar in the eyes of local residents.

But Bermuda's landscape changed drastically in the 1940s, when an environmental tragedy nearly wiped out the cedar. An invasion by two scale insects, the oystershell scale and the cedar scale, spread a virulent form of cedar blight that eradicated 90 percent of the island's cedar trees within a mere decade. As the infestation continued, Bermudian officials tried to curb the pests with introduced species such as the ladybug, but efforts were ineffective and too late. Silvery hillsides of skeleton trunks—some of which remain—underscored the enormity of the outbreak; by the time authorities had a handle on the problem, just 1 percent of the original forest remained.

It has taken the species decades to recover, but the cedar is slowly making a comeback, thanks to strong reforesting efforts by the island's Department of Parks and conservation

Red and black mangrove trees, with a dense tangle of roots, many submerged, thrive in coastal swamps such as Hungry Bay on the South Shore, Blue Hole Park, and Ferry Point National Park. There are also brackish pond mangroves at Spittal Pond and Walsingham Nature Reserves. Bees and other insects are attracted to the yellow or white flowers of mangroves. Black mangroves have air-breathing roots, which rise like alien fingers from the water. These atmospheric environments are home to numerous species of snail, mollusk, and crab, as well as lizards, crab spiders, large hurricane spiders, dragonflies, tiny whistling frogs, and giant toads. Birdlife includes herons, kiskadees, migrating warblers, and waterfowl. The only plant to avoid when exploring nature reserves, particularly swamp forests, is poison ivy *(Rhus radicans)*, a red-veined crawling vine that can leave a nasty rash after contact with skin.

Karst and Caves

Scientists have discovered diverse plant and animal life inside the island's honeycomb of marine and terrestrial caves. Most are located in Smith's and Hamilton Parishes, where karst scenery is characterized by limestone terrain containing sinks, underground caves, and pinnacle rock. The dark, still, isolated environment inside caves has fed interesting biological adaptations and fostered endemic forms of life, some of which may have evolved from deep-sea creatures that inhabited Bermuda's seamount in prehistoric times. Unusual crustaceans, similar to shrimp, have been found in marine caves, and numerous more common biota, including sea squirts

services, using insect-resistant trees. Every September, Bermudian schoolchildren are encouraged to gather the tree's bluish-green berries to grow cedar saplings for dispersal around the Island. The government is also pushing ahead with a long-range program to replace invasive species with cedars and palmettos in national parks—an effort to reclaim the look of Bermuda's first forests.

Cedars still hold a special place in Bermudian hearts. Planting a cedar tree on your property remains a popular wedding tradition, symbolizing the growth of the bride and groom's relationship. Bermuda cedarwood is coveted in the construction industry for doors, window frames, and beams—though it is now so hard to get, and therefore so expensive ($42 a board foot), that many homeowners opt for Virginian cedar instead. (Indeed, cedar trees are in such demand, they have been illegally cut down and stolen from nature reserves.)

Sturdy Bermuda cedars can withstand even hurricanes.

Visitors can find carved cedar trinkets for sale around the island, either in stores or from outdoor vendors (at Dockyard, for example). But the best examples of Bermuda cedar are found at auction. Check the daily paper; if your visit happens to coincide with one of the annual major auctions of contents from grand island homes, exquisite cedar heirloom chests or coffee tables will no doubt be among the offerings. Be prepared to put your pocketbook up against those of local aficionados, however; genuine Bermuda cedar treasures may appear the epitome of rustic beauty, but they cost the crown jewels.

(sea cucumbers), sponges, and mollusks, also make their homes here. Cave mouths on land have helped keep alive many endemic species and are populated by ferns, herbs, and mosses.

Sea Grass Beds

Many of Bermuda's bays and shallow offshore areas are covered by sea grass beds, which are prime nurseries and feeding grounds for fish, turtles, invertebrates, and other species. Flounders, crabs, and crustaceans—and often, protected green turtles—can be spotted feeding on sea grass. The mud underlying sea grass beds is home to marine worms and other species. Snorkeling over sea grass beds can be fascinating, but watch out for spiny sea urchins if you put your feet down in these shallow areas.

Coral Reefs

The marine equivalent of rainforests, coral reefs are precious ecosystems whose rich biodiversity of plants and animals supports a complex web of interdependence. Coral reef organisms, including hard and soft coral species, construct their own environment and thrive in areas near the Equator that receive even temperatures and sunlight year-round. Fed by the warm Gulf Stream, Bermuda's coral reefs are the world's most northerly; thanks to legislative protection, they have not been destroyed like so many in other regions.

Bermuda's coral reefs take various forms. Rim reefs encircle the island inside a shallow plateau that drops off beyond to the deep ocean. This reefy necklace, the bane of ships over the centuries, lies fairly close to the South Shore coastline, several hundred feet off in places; on the North Shore, by contrast, rim reefs are located about 10 miles out. Patch reefs are scattered across the shallow plateau, covering some 290 square miles around the island. Boiler reefs are "micro atolls"—wine-glass-shaped structures that rise from the sea floor and harbor coral-based ecosystems in miniature. They are particularly visible just a few yards off the entire length of the South Shore and West End. At low tide, boiler reef rims can sit just above the surface. At high tide, you can actually swim down inside these mushroom-like formations to investigate various plant and animal life within.

Bursting with life, coral reefs are continually decaying and rebuilding naturally, as organisms such as stony corals create the framework that other limestone-skeletoned creatures like forams, sea mosses, and bristle worms cement together. Anemones, sea fans, and soft corals then fill in the gaps—in turn, providing food on which other creatures come to graze. Boring clams, sponges, and barnacles undermine the reef structure in the meantime, a process that sees honeycombed chunks break off, providing fresh surfaces for new growth.

PLANTS

Bermuda's manicured environs are the product of its hothouse climate, a subtropical mixing bowl of high humidity, loads of sunlight, and brief, torrential rainfall that makes green thumbs of even neophyte gardeners. Not much is difficult to grow here, and garden clubs and horticultural societies devoted to raising roses, orchids, cacti, island endemics, and other dedicated plant varieties have flourished as a result. Yet, while gardens thrive, Bermuda's wild spaces are few. More than 75 percent of the island's landmass is developed; of that, over 10 percent is covered by concrete, roads, and buildings. Open space in the form of nature reserves and national parks makes up just 7 percent of all of Bermuda's land and is therefore strictly protected. It is in these reserves that various habitats, including inland forest, mangroves, and coastal zones, can be witnessed as they have existed for centuries. But mixed-use areas such as agricultural land, hotel properties, forts, and golf courses—though designed for different purposes—are also important breeding and nesting areas for bluebirds and other species and are home to many different types of both wild and planted flowers, bushes, and trees.

Flora blossom throughout the year (there is no autumnal fall of leaves here), infusing the island with deep color and scent. Lanes lined with the prolific oleander *(Nerium oleander)* turn pink with perfumed petals starting in June. Midsummer carpets of flaming royal poinciana *(Delonix regia)* splash the landscape red in July. Riotous magenta bougainvillea vines paint parks and gardens showily year-round, while waxy frangipani trees *(Plumeria rubra* and *Plumeria alba)* and lady-of-the-night turn evenings sweet with fragrant flowers throughout the summer. Morning glory vines laden with blue-violet blossoms creep over walls and fences, and banks of red, yellow, and orange nasturtiums hem the roadsides. Trumpet lilies tumble onto sidewalks in October like a pile of golden goblets. And hedgerows of ubiquitous hibiscus *(Hibiscus rosa sinensis)*, hillsides of February freesias *(Freesia refracta alba)*, and Bermuda Easter lily *(Lilium longiflorum)* fields stretching as far as the eye can see are iconic to the landscape.

Bermudiana

Come springtime, carpets of purple wildflowers cover rocky hillsides and sandy shores around the island. Bermuda's national flower, the Bermudiana *(Sisyrinchium bermudiana)* is also known as Bermuda iris or blue-eyed grass. It grows wild in dry, sunny, windswept, seemingly harsh areas, such as Spittal Pond Nature Reserve. Standing about eight inches high, its slender stem and leaves are waxy and grasslike, its small flowers sporting violet petals and yellow centers. Though related to North American species, the Bermuda variety is endemic—it does not grow wild elsewhere.

Bermuda has 17 surviving endemic (or unique) plant species; some 150 native, or naturally occurring, species; 1,000 introduced species; and an estimated 900 cultivated plants. Such abundance has always entranced visitors. Former Beatle John Lennon was so taken by a particular species of yellow freesia he encountered in the Bermuda Botanical Gardens during a June 1980 sojourn—six months before his murder—that he gave his last album the same name: *Double Fantasy.* (Staff later planted a lily, suitably named Strawberry Fields Forever, where the freesia had once grown, though, predictably, the sign noting this vanished almost immediately.)

Much of Bermuda's plantlife can be seen without special visits to nature reserves—it's found along city streets, hemming roadways, and on public properties and attractions. The island's 130 miles of roadsides alone offer an eclectic mix of most island plants, from wildflowers to aloes and agaves, from bamboo thickets to herbs and exotic trees. Similarly, Hamilton's streets are lined with ornamental trees, including flamboyantly hued varieties such as the lilac jacaranda *(Jacaranda mimosifolia),* the cassias (golden and pink showers), and the African tulip tree. Reid Street's parade of sweet-smelling black ebony sends down cascades of fragrant powder-puffs in early summer. Outside the Bermuda Library on Queen Street, a centuries-old Indian laurel welcomes visitors to Queen Elizabeth Park; it looks like a tree from a storybook, thanks to its vast canopy, wide-stretched limbs, and gnarled spread of roots. In Flatts, a similarly historic mahogany tree stands at the junction of Middle Road and Harrington Sound, while a gargantuan banyan tree spreads over nearly an acre of land at the Southlands property in Warwick. Many of these landmarks are protected by law under tree preservation orders. Hamilton's Victoria Park and Fort Hamilton properties are also beautifully planted; the latter's highlight is a circular moat garden accessed through limestone dungeons and boasting a bedded jungle of towering ferns, sprawling vines, locust and wild honey (or "Swiss cheese") plants, elephant ears, bromeliads, life plants or "floppers," and other shade-loving species.

Bermuda's natural harvest of wild fruit is just as impressive. At different times throughout the year, roadsides, reserves, gardens, and trails are littered with abundant piles of fruit, lots of it collected by locals and used for making preserves—or eaten on the spot. Surinam cherries, produced twice a year, in the spring and fall, can be seen thick on evergreen bushes bordering many properties; the fruits are good to eat, though more sour than most North American cherry varieties. Loquat trees are heavy with fat, yellow fruit in January and February—a favorite after-school treat for passing children. Guava plums and prickly pears, though difficult to pick from thorn-infested plants, are commonly eaten or boiled for jams. Bay grapes ripen in the autumn on their waxy-leafed coastal bushes. Summer storms shake down plump avocados en masse. Towering pawpaw trees, palmlike in appearance with large, round yellow fruits that are good for baking and renowned as a meat tenderizer, can be found everywhere. Local bananas also grow abundantly; small and thin, they are sweeter than imported counterparts.

Roses

Bermuda's British inclinations are nowhere so beautifully on display as in the parishes' many rose gardens. Indeed, the island has been proclaimed "a living museum of roses" by one garden historian, with more than 140 different varieties noted. Tea roses, Chinas, bourbons, noisettes, hybrid musks, climbers, ramblers, and miniatures—old garden roses are prolific on the island. Perhaps the most intriguing group is the so-called mystery roses, whose original names and provenance are not known. Instead, these sometimes-unusual blooms have been given the name of the place or owner of the garden where they were found, and most commonly are simply labeled "Bermuda roses."

Roses have been part of the Bermuda landscape since early settlement. In 1639, a visiting

Spaniard noted that many gardens were full of roses, and since then, numerous references point to the popularity of the rose here through the centuries. The **Bermuda Rose Society** (P.O. Box PG 162, Paget, PG BX, tel. 441/236-0215 or 441/292-4575), founded in 1954, today is affiliated with similar societies in Britain, North America, Australia, and New Zealand and is a member of the World Federation of Rose Societies. Its 100 members work to encourage the cultivation of roses, conserve old garden roses, and import others suitable to the island's climate and conditions.

Society members propagate hundreds of rose bushes for sale every year and also care for several dedicated rose gardens around the island, where all varieties can be appreciated free of charge. These include the rose garden at the Bermuda Botanical Gardens in Paget; another at the Heydon Trust Estate in Sandys; and the Heritage Rose Garden at Waterville in Paget, the Bermuda National Trust headquarters. Old garden roses can often be found in sheltered church gardens, too, such as Old Devonshire Church or St. Peter's in St. George's. Somers Garden in St. George's is another showcase for almost two dozen types of Chinas, teas, and mystery roses. The flowering season for most roses in Bermuda is October-May, though, depending on weather conditions, some varieties bloom throughout the year.

Interestingly, through the exchange of cuttings between society members and overseas colleagues, Bermuda roses such as the Smith's Parish, Emmie Gray, Miss Atwood, St. David's, and Bermuda Kathleen have taken root around the world, including several U.S. locations: Huntington Botanical Gardens in San Marino, California; the Antique Rose Emporium in Brenham, Texas; and the Brooklyn Botanic Garden in Brooklyn, New York.

Medicinal Plants

Island folklore has enshrined the healing and nutritive value of many Bermuda plants. The practice of herbalism dates back to the colony's earliest days, including the use of poisonous species as a form of revolt by black slaves against their owners. Nontoxic plants also fueled a plethora of uses: The large red leaves from match-me-if-you-can bushes were soaked in whiskey or vinegar and wrapped over the body to relieve measles and fevers; plantains were believed to heal sexually transmitted diseases; allspice leaves were used as antioxidants; a bath of chicory and herbs

Goblet-like cereus flowers bloom only at night.

could combat eczema and diabetes; the raw pulp of prickly pears was said to stop diarrhea; and cedar berry syrup was a common cold remedy.

A small medicinal garden, planted next to the kitchen beds behind Camden House, can be found at Bermuda Botanical Gardens. Herbalist Juliet Duncan lectures and writes on the therapeutic value of local plants. Her publication, *Historic and Edible Herbs & Berries of Bermuda,* can be found at some related retail outlets, including Brighton Nurseries (12 Brighton Ln., Devonshire, tel. 441/236-5862, brighton@logic.bm).

Gardening Clubs

Gardening clubs include the **Bermuda Botanical Society** (tel. 441/236-5291); **The Garden Club of Bermuda** (tel. 441/232-1273); the **Bermuda Rose Society** (P.O. Box PG 162, Paget, PG BX, tel. 441/236-0215 or 441/292-4575); the **Bermuda Orchid Society** (P.O. Box HM 3250, HM PX, tel. 441/293-2035); and the **Bermuda African Violet Society** (P.O. Box HM 1112, Hamilton, HM EX, tel. 441/236-5669 or 441/234-1050). Most clubs meet once a month through most of the year and welcome visitors.

ANIMALS

Like any isolated oceanic island, Bermuda is a biologist's nirvana, not because of the number of species or habitats (for there are fewer than in many Caribbean islands), but for the interesting way its ecology has evolved. Separated from natural competitors and predators that wiped out mainland counterparts, numerous marine and terrestrial species that arrived in Bermuda thousands of years ago have weathered the ages and today count as precious endemics, unique to the island.

The island has long drawn scientists to its mid-Atlantic location, unique marine habitat, geological phenomena, mild climate, coral reef accessibility, and unusual forms of marine and terrestrial plant and animal life. The island lays claim to more than 8,300 known species, half of which are marine. About 3 percent are endemic. Bermuda's biologically isolated ecology has posed intriguing questions to naturalists, particularly those interested in the development and survival of endemic species.

By its very geography, separated from the mainland by vast stretches of ocean, Bermuda's biological character is unique. From its earliest days, the Gulf Stream acted as a massive conveyor belt, carrying seeds, plantlife, and marinelife to the limestone-covered former volcano; animals able to swim or fly from mainland habitats also arrived, and life gradually took root. Cut off from predators and other factors that shaped the evolution of mainland counterparts, plant and animal life, along with the habitats they clung to, survived or developed differently. Before humans arrived on the island in the early 1500s, abundant turtles, cahows (Bermuda petrels), and fish made the archipelago an idyllic natural larder. Rats and hogs arrived with the first passing sailors, who, it is believed, offloaded swine to multiply for future provisioning. Rodents, domestic animals, cockroaches, and other pests multiplied with the waves of English colonists who followed, from 1612 onwards, setting loose a domino effect of natural destruction that has continued into the 21st century.

Today, Bermuda's wildlife remains under the international microscope. The **Bermuda Zoological Society** (BZS; www.bamz.org) and the **Bermuda Institute for Ocean Sciences** (www.bios.edu) attract world-class scientists who use the island as a laboratory for global investigations, including studies on climatological risk prediction and the use of certain species, such as sea sponges, in pharmaceuticals. The Bermuda Zoological Society also funds conservation research projects on endangered creatures such as seahorses, turtles, and toads. The Bermuda Biodiversity Project, established through BZS in 1997, has generated important baseline studies of the island's species and habitats, with a focus on those considered critically endangered.

Protecting Vanishing Species

Bermuda has a checkered past when it comes to protecting its natural heritage. Destruction of habitats and species began as soon as humans began arriving in the 16th century. The "Isle of Devils" was actually a lifesaving larder for castaways and passing mariners, who feasted on everything from turtles and cedar berries to fat petrels, or cahows, which were captured and killed to the point of near-extinction. Hogs that had been previously set ashore to multiply foraged the early forest floor, while rats, cockroaches, and domestic animals brought disease and destruction.

After settlement, legislative measures were taken as early as 1615 to control the exploitation of species such as the green turtle, and later, the native Bermuda cedar *(Juniperus bermudiana)*, a staple for shipbuilding and furniture. In later centuries, cultivation, overdevelopment, and pesticide use have had a severe effect on the island's fragile ecosystem. Human efforts to intervene have more often than not resulted in a spectacular comedy of errors. Such was the case with the Jamaican anole, a lizard brought to Bermuda in 1905 to combat the Mediterranean fruit fly. The anole quickly adapted but preferred ladybugs to fruit flies, setting off a destructive domino effect. A belated attempt in the 1950s to control the lizard with the great kiskadee was similarly disastrous; the raucous birds may have nibbled on reptiles, but they also attacked the nests of bluebirds and other natives.

The Bermuda government took decisive action in 2003 to protect and restore disappearing species and habitats, passing the Protected Species Act, which created a recovery plan and made it a crime to harm or capture certain listed plants and animals. The legislation is vital to endangered species, particularly those that live outside national parks and have never been protected. Those with special status include the white-tailed tropicbird (Bermuda's graceful harbinger of spring, also called a longtail), the skink (a rarely seen lizard), the land hermit crab, and the cahow, whose fragile population is being nurtured with special nesting habitats on off-lying islands.

Among other aims, its scientists work to record data on caves, coral reefs, and other special habitats; define major threats to the island's ecosystems; and develop education and public awareness programs.

Birds

Bermuda's fearsome early reputation as a haunted "Isle of Devils" is blamed on the eerie cry of the nocturnal cahow *(Pterodroma cahow)*, or Bermuda petrel, which populated the island in the 1500s. Sailors heard the plaintive call of the large oceanic birds and believed the island was home to supernatural creatures. Unfortunately, the endemic cahow's placid nature and lack of agility when not in flight made it so easy to catch that early colonists were able to literally pluck the birds from nests by the thousands, pushing cahows to the brink of extinction within a scant decade of their 1612 settlement.

While the cahow is undoubtedly Bermuda's most famous avian resident, the island claims 22 breeding bird species (3 of which are seabirds, not year-round residents). Migrants and vagrants bring the tally to 360 species, though only an estimated 132 are commonly seen, according to author Andre Raine in his 2003 publication, *A Field Guide to the Birds of Bermuda*. Bird-watching enthusiasts will find plenty to marvel over. The gracious longtail, or white-tailed tropicbird *(Phaethon lepturus)*, is Bermuda's national bird, featured on the local quarter; it can be seen swooping elegantly from nests in South Shore clifftops throughout the spring and summer. The raucous kiskadee, whose yolk-colored chest and bossy behavior makes it perhaps the most noticeable local bird, is entertaining to watch. Pairs of melodic northern cardinals or redbirds *(Cardinalis cardinalis)* frequent gardens and parks; the male's crimson plumage with tufty crest is unmistakable, as is its repetitive trilling song (females are smaller and more brown than red, but both have red beaks). Another treat is a shy beauty, the eastern

Hurricane Fabian drove home the importance of encouraging endemic species. After 120-mile-per-hour gales blasted the island for 24 hours on September 9, 2003, flowering trees and ornamental plants were ravaged, while areas of sturdy cedars and palmettos stood virtually intact. As residents stocked up on tarps, roof slate, and generators in the aftermath, they also began investing in more down-to-earth gardening choices: cedar saplings and palmetto berries.

The Department of Conservation Services now works actively with resident and visiting scientists to protect Island species and habitats. Successful initiatives include installing moorings at popular dive sites to minimize anchor damage on coral reefs, and erecting canisters at coastal fishing areas so that anglers can properly dispose of nylon line—a major killer of sea turtles.

Bermuda's conservation organizations actively work to protect vanishing species, manage nature reserves, preserve open spaces and landmark buildings, and educate the public, particularly school students. The **Bermuda Zoological Society** (16 North Shore, Flatts, tel. 441/293-2727, fax 441/293-4014, membership.bzs@gov.bm) supports the Bermuda Aquarium, Museum & Zoo and related education and species conservation programs. The **Bermuda National Trust** (BNT, Waterville, 2 Pomander Ln., Paget, tel. 441/236-6483, fax 441/236-0617, www.bnt.bm) preserves historic homes and buildings, manages nature reserves, and raises funds to buy tracts of undeveloped land for public use. The **Bermuda Audubon Society** (P.O. Box HM 1328, Hamilton HM FX, tel. 441/292-1920 or 441/238-3239, www.audubon.bm) keeps several nature reserves, runs birding tours, educates on birdlife, and works to protect wildlife habitats. **Greenrock** (tel. 441/747-7625, www.greenrock.org) is an energized nonprofit focused on lobbying for green lifestyles and sustainable development. **Keep Bermuda Beautiful** (P.O. Box HM 2227, Hamilton HM JX, tel. 441/295-5142, www.kbb.bm) organizes annual trash cleanups and education campaigns.

bluebird *(Sialia sialia).* The only other endemic species is the small greenish-yellow Bermuda white-eyed vireo, whose chirpy song mimics its nickname, "chick-of-the-village." Common sparrows, barn owls, mourning doves, sandpipers, finches, moorhens, herons, and numerous species of waterfowl can all be frequently spotted. Most originated from the eastern and central United States, as well as the Caribbean.

Spring and fall are the most popular birding seasons. Thousands of migratory species travel north in the spring and south in the fall in these months, either using Bermuda as a convenient stopover or wintering on the island. Migrants can be seen as early as February. The aftermath of storms and hurricanes sometimes finds more exotic species from further afield, having been carried off course by prevailing wind patterns. After the frantic 2005 season, for example, when Hurricane Katrina wreaked havoc on the U.S. Gulf Coast, scores of large frigate birds were suddenly spotted gliding high over the island—a species rarely found in the area.

Sadly, the bluebird—which flashes vivid cornflower as it flits between trees—is becoming something of a rare treat to see. Sightings usually occur near shady lawns or meadow areas of quiet parks such as Devonshire's Arboretum or Ferry Point National Park in St. George's. It also feeds and nests around golf courses. Flocks of bluebirds were once common throughout the island, nesting in cedar trees. In recent decades, Bermudians have rallied to protect the declining species (an estimated 500 birds remain), which has fallen prey to domestic and feral cats, has lost vital habitat to development, and has had to compete with the more adaptable sparrow for food and nesting sites. A widespread campaign distributes wooden bluebird nest boxes, with entry holes small enough to deter larger intruders, such as the pushy starling or kiskadee. Bluebird nest boxes can be seen islandwide, in gardens and parks and along trails at hotels and golf courses.

Some of the island's best bird-watching locales include Spittal Pond Nature Reserve in Smith's Parish, whose range of habitats attracts diverse species from oceanic birds to waterfowl; Hog Bay Park in Sandys, a large tract of isolated land that includes coastline, wooded hillsides, and agricultural areas; Paget Marsh, with its endemic cedars and palmettos; and the undulating Arboretum. The **Bermuda Audubon Society** (P.O. Box HM 1328, Hamilton, HM FX, tel. 441/292-1920, www.audubon.bm) leads birding field trips, including sea-watching tours, throughout the year at parks and nature reserves. Check the society's website for tour details. *A Birdwatching Guide to Bermuda* (2002), by society president Andrew Dobson, is another good source of information on Bermuda bird species.

Insects and Spiders

The island has a robust population of creepy-crawlies, with more than 1,200 insects and over 1,000 other arthropods. Some are irksome, like mosquitoes, fleas, and mites, but none are very dangerous—though one rarely seen spider, the brown widow, is venomous.

The cockroach is one of the more conspicuous local insects. Bermuda has 11 species, including the large American cockroach *(Periplaneta Americana)*. They're harmless and can be found absolutely everywhere—from garbage dumps to the swankiest homes, where they fly in on summer nights like some kind of bizarre windup toy.

Bermuda's butterflies are perhaps not so exotic as those of more tropical areas, but there are some beautiful varieties that frequent flower-packed gardens throughout the island. The gulf fritillary, cloudless sulphur, buckeye, cabbage white, and monarch are all fairly common. Some 200 moths seen on the island include the great gray sphinx or frangipani hawkmoth, whose large red-and-black caterpillars feast on the fragrant frangipani trees.

Beekeeping is popular in Bermuda, and honeybees are found buzzing in gardens and park beds—though their numbers have declined in recent years along with bee populations worldwide. Delicious Bermuda honey is sold in supermarkets and at the weekly winter farmers market in Hamilton. Other common insects include beetles, wasps, dragonflies, damselflies, grasshoppers, ladybugs, church worms, and centipedes—the largest of which is the St. David's centipede, or giant centipede, which can grow to a foot in length.

Some 59 different spiders can be found on the island. Of these, the colorful, spiny-bellied orb weaver, or crab spider—beloved by children for its clownlike red spines and black polka-dots—can be seen in trees and bushes. More dramatic is the golden silk spider, or hurricane spider, a hand-sized bright yellow creature that drapes diaphanous webs in woodland areas. Island folklore says that when these webs are spun close to the ground, a hurricane is imminent.

Frogs, Toads, and Lizards

Bermuda's treefrog, the common whistling frog *(Eleutherodactylus johnstonei)*, came from the Lesser Antilles in the 1800s. A second whistling frog species that also arrived from the Caribbean has not been seen in recent years, and scientists believe it may now be extinct. Treefrogs are delicate creatures, less than an inch long, with large black eyes and suction pads on their toes. Hidden away in damp areas of forests or gardens during the day, they emerge on balmy nights or during rainstorms, singing loudly, their echoing call aptly described by naturalist Martin Thomas as "a bell-like 'gleep-gleep.'" It is one of the most distinctive sounds of Bermuda.

Whistling frogs are among the two amphibians and eight reptiles, all introduced species, that now inhabit Bermuda. The giant toad, also called the cane toad or Surinam toad *(Bufo marinus)*, is an iconic resident of all parishes, and unfortunately often is seen splayed on the macadam as roadkill. Both whistling frogs and Surinam toads are insectivores. Declining numbers of frogs and toads have worried scientists over the past two decades; amphibians are considered barometers of environmental health, as their permeable skin allows contaminants to pass through. Tissue samples of both frogs and toads indicate the creatures are absorbing significant amounts of metals, pesticides, and petroleum hydrocarbons from Bermuda wetlands. The Bermuda Amphibian Project, sponsored by the Bermuda Zoological Society, is now trying to determine the source of these contaminants and their general risks to the environment.

Four lizard species live in Bermuda, including the critically endangered skink, or rock lizard, which has been on the island so long that it is now considered endemic. The bronze skink is easily recognizable, with shiny, scaled skin and clawed feet, but its numbers have been so drastically reduced that you may never see one. Just a few decades ago, skinks were found in most coastal and wooded areas but are now confined to remote sections of the shoreline with low-lying vegetation, such as the islets of Castle Harbour or forested parks like Spittal Pond Nature Reserve. They are also found in larger numbers on Nonsuch Island. Skinks do not climb trees like other lizards; by contrast they scramble along coastal rocks or underbrush, burrowing and feeding on fruit and arthropods, including beetles, spiders, and crustaceans. The reasons for their demise are not completely known, though cats and kiskadees are considered major culprits, along with overdevelopment and the impact of humans on their habitat. Roadside trash, for example, creates lethal traps for the clawed skinks, who crawl into empty bottles and soda cans but cannot escape the slippery interiors. An education campaign funded by the Environment Ministry and geared toward educating Bermudians about skinks appears to be succeeding, and scientists hope these efforts—plus the animal's protected status, established in 2003—will help halt any further deterioration of skink populations.

Among the other three lizards, all originally from the Caribbean, is the blue-green Jamaican anole, which was brought in to control the insect infestation of cedar trees but soon moved on to other prey like bluebird eggs and ladybugs. Males put on a decorative courtship display, each extending a large orange lobe from his throat while bobbing on walls and tree trunks. The yellow-green Barbados anole, at a maximum length of 14 inches, is the island's largest lizard, and

Bermuda has four common lizard species.

its numbers are increasing; the aggressive creature feeds on bird eggs and insects. The coppery Antiguan anole is far more shy, preferring deeply shaded areas.

Whales and Dolphins

Humpback whales migrate north to the U.S. east coast and Canada in the springtime. Their pods can sometimes be seen from land along the South Shore on a clear day. Ecotours run by the Bermuda Institute of Ocean Sciences (BIOS), the Bermuda Zoological Society (BZS), the Bermuda Underwater Exploration Institute (BUEI), and charter boat companies take passengers out on whale-watching expeditions in March and April. Check the daily newspaper for advertisements, or the websites of **BIOS** (www.bios.edu), **BZS** (www.bamz.org), and **BUEI** (www.buei.org) for details. The **Humpback Whale Research Project** (www.whalesbermuda.com), started by Andrew Stevenson in 2007, films and gathers research on humpbacks as they migrate past Bermuda. Pilot whales, sperm whales, minke whales, and Cuvier's beaked whales are also seen in local waters. Wild dolphins occasionally are found offshore, including the common ocean dolphin, but rarely venture within the reef line to beaches or bays.

Marine Turtles

There's nothing more magical, when kayaking around West End sea grass beds or dropping anchor in the sheltered chain of bays between Great Sound islands, than hearing a turtle flipper slap the surface or catching the glint of its shell in the sunset as it dives back down again. Turtle populations are now a fraction of what they were in centuries past, before human exploitation for meat and shells devastated nesting populations, particularly those of the green turtle. Today, all species of marine turtle in Bermuda waters are protected under law.

Five species are found here; the most common are the olive-brown green turtle, which grazes on sea grass beds, and the smaller, ornately shelled hawksbill, which feeds on reef sponges. The large reddish loggerhead, which lives in the Sargasso Sea for its first years of life, occasionally ends up in coastal waters; by contrast, the deep-diving leatherback never ventures into shoreline areas, but Bermuda happens to lie on the edge of its oceanic migratory route and breeding ground. Kemp's ridley, a rare and critically endangered species usually found in the Gulf of Mexico, occasionally makes its way to Bermuda waters.

Tragically, motorboats have killed and maimed numerous turtles in recent years, though some injured animals have been rehabilitated and released back into the wild by staff at the Bermuda Aquarium, Museum & Zoo and Bermuda Zoological Society.

Sharks and Sportfish

Bermuda's waters are spawning grounds for several larger fish, including commercial species such as yellowfin tuna, white marlin, blue marlin, wahoo, dolphin fish, and swordfish, making the island a popular deep-sea fishing destination. Of all the gamefish, marlin and swordfish are the most powerful speedsters, able to exceed 70 miles per hour (faster than a cheetah). Slashing their pointed bills to stun schools of fish, they pass Bermuda on annual summer migrations.

More than 20 shark species, including tiger sharks and dusky sharks—and docile whale sharks, the world's largest at 40 feet long—have been recorded off Bermuda, though divers do not usually see them. Sharks tend to frequent the reef platform at night, though many stay in deep ocean beyond the reef line. They are rarely seen inshore or off beaches, although old or sick sharks seeking easy meal pickings occasionally have followed cruise ships into port. Shark attacks in Bermuda, however, are all but unheard of. Since 2005, the **Bermuda Shark Project,** headed by veterinarian Dr. Neil Burnie and videographer Choy Aming, has gathered valuable data via satellite tagging of tiger sharks off the Bermuda reef platform; research to date has demonstrated the sharks, the top predator in Bermuda's marine ecosystem, routinely travel thousands of miles between the island, the Caribbean, and points around the mid-Atlantic.

Other Fish, Shellfish, and Reef Life

Bermuda is renowned for its coral reefs and abundant fish and crustacean species. More than 430 marine species have been recorded from the island, and simply donning a mask and snorkel reveals the rich diversity of fish. Spend a few hours floating over reefs, and you will discover a symphony of shapes and colors, from jewel-like wrasses and tangs to elegant blue angelfish and spotted butterfly fish, iridescent turquoise parrotfish, gliding silver barracudas, and inquisitive bee-striped sergeants major. Amid the delicate beauty of sea fans, corals, and anemones, you will frequently see trumpetfish, clownlike cowfish, moray eels (green and spotted varieties), groupers, snappers, red hinds, triggerfish, hogfish, spiny lobsters, and many more varieties.

Prized for its sweet meat, the Bermuda rockfish is a reef inhabitant and a staple of local seafood menus. The longsnout sea horse used to be another common reef-area inhabitant, but its numbers have declined recently. You may see it, tail wrapped like an anchor around seaweed or sea grasses. Sheltered bays are home to peacock flounders, odd-looking puffers, balletic squid, urchin-eating porgy, Bermuda chub, grunts, and bottom-feeding bream. Spotted eagle rays, some measuring six feet in length, make for a dramatic sight as they sweep under Flatts Bridge into Harrington Sound. And common, but no less breathtaking, are the schools of thousands of tiny "fry" or minnows, which leap in unison to create silver arcs as they try to evade predators. Fishers typically set nets to catch fry for bait.

Portuguese man-of-wars are probably the most dangerous species you'll encounter. Warnings are posted on some South Shore beaches when onshore winds are bringing in large numbers of these long-tentacled jellyfish. Look out for their distinctive blue-purple balloons, with purple tentacles attached, washed up on the tideline. Where there is one, there are usually lots more in the water, being blown in from the same high-seas area.

After a severe decline in fish stocks over the 1970s and 1980s, the Bermuda government slapped a ban on the use of fishpots, which succeeded in increasing threatened populations. Spearfishing within the reef line or with scuba gear is also banned. You can see examples of most local fish species in the fascinating tanks at the Bermuda Aquarium, Museum & Zoo in Hamilton Parish.

History

Bermuda's history is the story of unlikely survival—and remarkable economic success—against daunting odds. Geography was the first immense hurdle for this tiny speck of land isolated from the rest of the world by 600 miles of ocean. Perhaps as a result of such distance from the North American mainland, Bermuda had no indigenous people; its first inhabitants were shipwrecked English colonists of the early 17th century. Although Spanish mariners discovered Bermuda more than a century before the English ever set foot on the island, it was the English who eventually claimed the island. Bermuda's destiny and heritage could have been far different, had the Spanish considered the island useful enough to colonize.

How did Bermuda evolve from such a minuscule mid-Atlantic outpost into one of the world's wealthiest countries? A mixture of very good luck and islanders' ability to take advantage of any and all opportunities. Living by their wits, Bermudians dabbled in piracy and privateering, benefited from the conflicts between larger warring nations, developed successful export farming, and later traded

The Legacy of Juan de Bermúdez

Bermuda's discovery date has long been a point of intrigue and uncertainty among historians, and the man who discovered and lent his name to the island is just as much of an enigma.

What is known is that Spanish seafarer Juan de Bermúdez was a pioneer during the Age of Discovery, a golden era of exploration and colonization by Spain and Portugal throughout the 1500s. Bermúdez, born in 1449 in the port of Palos on Spain's east coast, came from a seafaring family. Though he did not participate in the iconic 1492 voyage to the Americas by Christopher Columbus, he was a seasoned navigator who distinguished himself even among other mariners of the time through the sheer number of his pioneering transatlantic voyages. Between 1495 and 1519, he made a total of 11 crossings, back and forth between Europe and the West Indies; in ship records, he is named in expeditions of 1495, 1498, 1502, 1503, 1505, 1509, 1511, 1512, 1513, and 1519, when he finally died in Cuba.

It was on one of his journeys that Bermúdez first spotted Bermuda and named the island—but all concrete evidence ends there. The date of the milestone is unclear, though historians have recently tried to nail it down through a process of elimination. The mystery owes much to the fact that so little is known about Bermúdez himself. Like many mariners of the time, he was probably illiterate and left no letters, diaries, logbooks, or written testimonials—at least none that have been found. Nor does there exist a portrait, written description, or any physical image of the man to whom Bermuda owes its nomenclature.

Historians in the United States, Britain, and Bermuda now lean toward 1505 as the most likely date of discovery. Using Spanish sources, experts have analyzed the dates of Bermúdez's trans-

on their small landmass's natural beauty and offshore tax laws. Bermuda's course through 500-plus years of history, from discovery through the first decade of the 21st century, was not without failures, periods of pestilence, or turbulent growing pains. But the society, economy, and standard of living that resulted are today one of the globe's most envied. Bermudians are well aware of their collective serendipity and unique identity.

THE AGE OF DISCOVERY

Bermuda's early reputation was that of a fearsome devils' haunt, likely owing to tropical storms, animal shrieks, and the necklace of treacherous reefs. Yet those who did manage to make it safely ashore were uniformly surprised by what they found: a peaceful paradise with a rich supply of seabirds, turtles, fish, fruit, and wild hogs—believed to have been set ashore by passing mariners as food for castaways. "All the island and keys are covered with cedar forests and tufted palmetto palms," noted Spain's Diego Ramirez in 1603 after his galleon ran aground. "There are great droves of hogs in the island which have overrun it and trodden wide paths like well-travelled roads to the watering places."

After Italian pioneer Christopher Columbus forged the way to the New World in 1492, numerous mariners began traveling back and forth between Europe and the Americas on state-funded voyages. It was one such captain, Spaniard Juan de Bermúdez, who happened upon Bermuda by accident in 1505 and gave his name to the island. Although Bermúdez is not known to have actually landed, several subsequent transatlantic captains and crews did, by accident or necessity. During the 1500s, mariners usually made every effort to avoid Bermuda, the "Isle of Devils." England's maritime hero Sir Walter Raleigh noted his Spanish counterparts feared fictitious spirits and "durst not adventure [there] but called it *Demoniorum Insulam.*"

"It almost always rains there, and thunder is so frequent, that it seems as if heaven and earth must come together . . . the waves as high as mountains," wrote French explorer Samuel de Champlain in 1600. Gradually,

atlantic crossings, matching them with the voyages of one particular vessel, *La Garza*. It was this ship, a caravel, of which Bermúdez was said to have been captain when he sighted the island—and 1505 was the only year he sailed the vessel. A telling clue comes from a 16th-century courtier, Gonzalo Fernandez de Oviedo y Valdes, who wrote the first history of the West Indies. "I sayled above the island Bermuda, otherwise called Garza," he wrote in *La Historia General y Natural de Las Indias*, "being the furthest of all the islands that are found at this day in the world." Unfortunately, although Oviedo noted Bermúdez had given his name to the island, he failed to provide a date.

Bermúdez would have been 56 in 1505, and in the prime of his career. It is thought he stumbled on Bermuda by venturing too far north during a return voyage to Europe. While Bermuda did not appear on a map until 1511, the island became a key navigational marker for homeward-bound mariners throughout the rest of the century.

Spanish and Portuguese castaways, and at least one Englishman, landed on the uninhabited island during the 1500s, but no one claimed Bermuda for another 100 years. Historians attribute the paucity of interest to the island's lack of freshwater and natural resources, compared to the allure of gold and silver in other parts of the New World. Bermuda's reef line also posed daunting navigational challenges, which, coupled with superstitions of the time, earned it the nickname "Isle of Devils." It was not until 1609 that Admiral Sir George Somers recognized the colony's potential, after shipwrecking en route to Jamestown, Virginia. Before long, the tiny outpost would become one of Britain's most valued possessions.

after Ramirez's account filtered back to Spain, the archipelago became better known as a useful stopover for provisions by anyone who dared land there. Bermuda was also used as a navigational landmark for ships homeward-bound to Europe; vessels would venture north from the Americas and the Caribbean until they spotted the island, then veer east, carried home by prevailing winds.

Ramirez's false assumption that Bermuda's waters were rich in pearls raised the island's allure. Yet its lack of natural resources such as freshwater or gold made Bermuda far less attractive to conquistadors of the time than the wealth-laden territories farther west. As a result, Bermuda sat virtually untouched until 1609, when the first English colonists arrived—and then only by profound accident.

THE FIRST COLONISTS

"We found it to be the dangerous and dreaded islands of Bermuda . . . the Isle of Devils, and are feared and avoided of all sea travelers alive, above any place on earth," commented Englishman William Strachey, secretary-elect of Virginia and a passenger aboard the ill-fated *Sea Venture*. The 300-ton, 108-foot vessel, flagship of the Third Supply relief fleet to Jamestown, became separated from the rest of the fleet after encountering a ferocious hurricane off Bermuda. Its crew and passengers battled the storm for several days until it drove the ship onto rocks less than a mile off the island's East End, at the point now called St. Catherine's Beach. Admiral Sir George Somers and Sir Thomas Gates orchestrated the safe escape of all 150 survivors: men, women, and children who had left behind middle-class lives in southern England to live out New World dreams.

Like a real-life episode of *Survivor*, the castaways stripped the *Sea Venture* of rigging, weapons, food supplies, and timbers, something settlers would continue to do until the wreck sank from sight many years later. They fended for themselves over the next 10 months, building temporary shelters and constructing two new ships of Bermuda cedarwood to continue the voyage they had originally planned. "The Bermooda is the most plentiful place that I ever came to, for fishes, hogs and fowl," Sir George Somers would write. After much bickering among the group, all but three left Bermuda in 1610 aboard the newly built *Deliverance* and *Patience* for Jamestown, where the supplies they'd gathered from the island proved salvation for the American colony's starving residents. Sir George returned to Bermuda for more goods but died here later in 1610. His heart was buried in St. George's.

It was not until 1612 that England's first official settlers arrived aboard the *Plough*, after a decision by the Virginia Company to include Bermuda among its American enterprises. London-based investors, called "Adventurers," realized that the new acquisition, with its safe harbors and lack of inhabitants, might prove advantageous for their New World exploits. Sixty people arrived at Bermuda, among them a carpenter named Richard Moore, selected by the Virginia Company to be Bermuda's first governor. Bermuda was dubbed "Virginiola" and, later, the "Somers Islands" or "Summer Islands," after Sir George Somers as well as its balmy climate. The first settlement was initially called "New London," but its name was later changed to St. George's. The fact that Jamestown fell into ruin and did not endure makes St. George's the oldest surviving English town in the Americas.

The first settlers laid the foundations for a colony that would develop into one of England's key possessions over the next 400 years. They fashioned palmetto huts and dug wells, creating a community around a market square at the East End, which, despite the subtropical setting, was as English as any in the motherland. The colony's laws and government were English, along with its judicial system, Church of England religious beliefs, education methods, and loyalty to King James. Great pressure was laid on Moore and the settlers to produce riches like pearls, silk, tobacco, and ambergris (a highly prized substance derived from whales' intestines and used in medicines and fragrances) to send back to the London investors, little of which ever materialized. Instead, the Virginia Company, and later the Crown, had to support the struggling colony with constant shiploads of food and supplies for most of the century.

Ironically, Bermuda's inhabitants were restricted from becoming self-sufficient by a monopolistic regimen; they were forced to trade only with Virginia Company ships and were barred from whaling or shipbuilding. Forts and bridges were built, and the main island was divided into "tribes," or privately owned parishes, creating Bermuda's first infrastructure. But the colonists felt stifled by the oppressive rules laid down by the company, and as a result, they rebelled. Finally, in 1684, trade restrictions were lifted when the company of investors was dissolved and Bermuda became a genuine Crown colony. Commercial independence was encouraged, and Bermudians looked to the sea to forge a lucrative livelihood that would endure for the next 200 years.

MARITIME TRADITIONS

Bermuda's residents quickly forfeited lackluster farming efforts to undertake all things maritime instead. Shipbuilding, piloting, whaling, and trade with nations to the south and east allowed entrepreneurial talent to flourish in the 1700s, and the colony finally began to thrive. In an era of constant wars among European nations, Bermudian privateers had the approval of the island's royal governors to prowl shipping lanes in search of enemy vessels to capture. Many of the island's most prominent families—Frith, Trimingham, Cox, Durham, Joell—were engaged in privateering, though sometimes their attacks on foreign vessels were simply in defense of shipping interests.

Native cedar was used to innovatively craft speedy sloops that became the envy of larger maritime nations. The vessels were heavily used for seaborne commerce; of Bermuda's 8,000-strong population in the early 1700s, a third of local men were constantly at sea. Unlike refuges in the Caribbean and Far East, Bermuda never became a hotbed of pirates,

Hogge Money

Named for the wild boars early settlers found roaming Bermuda in the first decade of the 1600s, "Hogge money" was among the colonists' first currency, along with tobacco. The money is renowned for having been the very first of English colonial coins, and today the few remaining artifacts are valuable collectors' items. In September 2011, a Hogge money shilling realized more than $65,000 at auction. Rare specimens can be seen in the Commissioner's House, at the National Museum of Bermuda.

The currency was shipped out from England in 1616 to pay workers employed by the Bermuda Company. Settlers were prohibited from exporting the coins, which were minted from copper or silver-plate in shillings (twelvepence, sixpence, threepence, and twopence pieces). Each bore the image of a hog on one side and a sailing ship on the other.

Hogge money was scoffed at by the settlers. They gave it the derogatory nickname because they preferred to use tobacco, bartered goods, or English or Spanish gold or silver for trade. Indeed, the coins became so unpopular, they remained in circulation for only a few decades, vanishing around 1650.

though it's easy to argue that Bermudians exhibited more than a modicum of buccaneering behavior in many of their pursuits. "Wrecking," for example, was a nefarious pastime in which islanders would lure passing ships onto reefs with strategically placed fires aimed at disorienting them; salvagers would then row out to plunder the stricken vessels. The island also boasted a handful of homegrown bandits who became notorious for committing wicked deeds in other regions.

Most maritime ventures were aboveboard, however. Salt production and trade from the Turks and Caicos Islands became a major industry for Bermudians and their ships in the 1800s. Bermudian captains would journey south for summers in the Turks, then spend the winter trading their haul of salt for grain, tobacco, or meat in American ports. Whaling was a tough but profitable enterprise of the period, one that demanded talented seamanship. Humpback and sperm whales were hunted offshore for their "sea beef," oil from blubber, and occasional ambergris.

Bermuda became a marine hub of utmost importance to the British after the empire's defeat in the American Revolutionary War stripped the Crown of a string of ports between Halifax and the Caribbean. Britain decided Bermuda was a strategic location for a Royal Naval Dockyard—a fortified harbor where the royal fleet could anchor and reprovision. Work began on the facility at Bermuda's West End in the early 1820s and continued for several years, using mostly convict labor brought from Ireland and England. Forts throughout the island were enhanced or added to over the century, and the fortified Dockyard, a penal station for 40 years, became a military gem nicknamed "Gibraltar of the West." The Royal Navy remained there until 1951.

SLAVERY IN BERMUDA

Slavery existed in Bermuda for some 200 years, beginning in the early days of colonization—when blacks and some Native American slaves were brought from the Caribbean and the Americas—and lasting until the Slavery Abolition Act took effect in 1834. It evolved from the insidious roots of indentured servitude into full legal enslavement. Though the culture of Bermuda slavery differed greatly from the plantation system of the Americas' sugar and cotton economies, the prejudices that allowed its existence were the same. Slaves frequently rebelled against their owners, staged revolts, and ran away in protest.

Bermuda's slaves were natives of the Caribbean, Central America, and Africa, who arrived at the island through various circumstances. Some were sold off by sea captains to pay debts when they made port. Most were brought from the Caribbean. Female slaves were generally kept busy with domestic work, including the care of children of white families; male slaves commonly worked as house servants, gardeners, or farmers. Slave families were housed in cottages or cellar-like quarters attached to the main houses of Bermudian estates. Slaves were also master artisans and crafters. Notably, many of Bermuda's ship crews were black—whether slaves or free men, they worked in overseas maritime trade, or as pilots trained to guide ships through reef-lined channels. Sometimes, slaves who excelled at such work were granted their freedom in exchange. After slave emancipation was legally established in 1834, many slaves continued to work in maritime trades, running their own businesses and participating in the Atlantic trade network.

In the 1700s, draconian laws were laid down to control Bermuda's slaves, who by then made up a third of the population. Banishment to other islands was not uncommon for certain crimes, including any form of rebellion, and men, women, and children were sold, hanged, and punished at public venues such as King's Square in St. George's.

Due to its geographical location, Bermuda was intimately tied to the transatlantic slave trade. The island's reefs are a graveyard of ships, including those of slavers traveling from Africa's Gold Coast via the infamous Middle Passage. In recent years, items found at these wreck sites have included shackles used to restrain captives on voyages and beads and other artifacts used for barter in the slave trade. Many of these are now on display at heritage institutions such as the National Museum of Bermuda, which also serves as a site on the island's African Diaspora Trail.

By the 1800s, blacks had established their own churches, graveyards, and schools, some of which were run by Methodist missionaries who came to the island. Britain abolished the slave trade in 1807, and after a massive humanitarian lobby effort by the Anti-Slavery Society, finally outlawed slavery itself in 1833. Bermuda followed suit the next year, and the island's blacks celebrated Emancipation Day on August 1, 1834. Freedom brought its own challenges, however, and blacks heavily relied on their communities' "Friendly Societies" as a social network to help raise funds, facilitate lending, and encourage education and arts. Long after slavery ended, racial friction and legal segregation continued in Bermuda until the 1960s—still a sore point in black-white relations.

BACK TO THE EARTH

Emancipation was the final nail in the coffin of Bermuda's dependence on maritime activities. The island had lost control of the salt trade in the Caribbean, along with its monopoly on the carrying trade after conflicts between Britain and America eased and North American traders were allowed back into West Indian ports. The advent of steam power in the 19th century also helped to put Bermuda's sloops out of business. When slave labor dried up, it was time for Bermudians to find another way of life.

Agriculture, long abandoned in favor of nautical pursuits, became the new focus. Progressive governors advocated that immigrants from farming societies in Madeira and the Azores revitalize local farming in Bermuda. From 1849 onward, the arrival of Portuguese, with their strong work ethic and generations of agricultural know-how, changed the face of Bermudian society and the direction of its economy. Potatoes, arrowroot, tomatoes, and the world-famous Bermuda onion fast became lucrative exports to winter markets in New York and other East Coast centers. Over the second half of the 1800s, farming drove Bermuda's fortunes. The Easter lily also became a popular crop, and springtime harvests of the waxy white bloom were shipped overseas for sale.

Farming exports began to decline at the start of the 1900s, thanks to protective American tariffs and new competition from mainland farmers. Exports collapsed, though small-scale sales of lilies continued into the 20th century. Once again, Bermuda needed to reinvent itself.

TOURISM TAKES OFF

The island's saving grace came in the form of tourism, as wintering Victorian visitors proved the vanguard of a whole new industry. Travel as a recreational pursuit was a fairly new idea, but the island's quiet beauty attracted artists, writers, and the rich and famous, who traveled to the island for months at a time to escape the snowbound East Coast. Mark Twain, Woodrow Wilson, Babe Ruth, Winslow Homer, Georgia O'Keeffe, the Rockefellers, and the Vanderbilts lent cachet to the tiny island that sat just a few days' steamship cruise from New York. "What a contrast to the icy mountains and valleys of drifted snow," enthused early American visitor Julia Dorr after an 1883 sojourn. Over the first decades of the 20th century, Bermudian merchants set about investing in new hotels, restaurants, golf courses, and tennis courts, and the seeds of a century-long industry—as well as a new way of life for Bermudians—were sown. The era also brought the novelties of electricity, telephones, and elevators, technology that Bermuda embraced to improve the visitors' experience.

Bermuda forged agreements with major steamship lines to bring foreigners to the island through the 1920s and 1930s, when the industry truly came of age following the close of World War I. Bermuda was marketed as an upscale paradise. During the era of Prohibition in the United States, Bermuda was "one continual carousal," according to one British visitor. The advent of air travel and luxury cruises following World War II dramatically opened Bermuda to the masses; inside the island, the motor car was finally permitted for residents, and new technology like televisions, record players, and washing machines became must-haves in Bermudian homes as islanders embraced "the American Dream." Tourism would continue to drive the economy nearly exclusively through the late 1980s, when international business took over as the primary economic generator for the remainder of the century. Tourism never recovered its heyday, but today business travelers contribute heavily to overall visitor numbers.

MILITARY INFLUENCES

The British and American militaries have played a large part in Bermuda's evolution, security, and economic success over the centuries. The Royal Navy ran its business at Dockyard through the first half of the 20th century, pouring a welcome sum into the island's coffers. British military forces manned island defenses during both World War I and II, though an attack on Bermuda never came. Bermuda's own militia groups, divided by race, also took part in fighting overseas in both conflicts. In World War II, some 500 local men and women left the island to join British, American, and Canadian forces in fighting around the world. Bermuda became a bastion of Allied defense in these years also, when the government signed a 1941 deal to provide America with 99-year leases for two baselands—one in the East End, the other in Southampton. A massive land reclamation project by the U.S. Army created a military airfield and naval base in these areas. Antiaircraft artillery were installed, and antisubmarine patrols used the island as a base from which to scour the Western Atlantic. Bermuda also became a headquarters for the British Imperial Censor in the war years, as "censorettes" intercepted coded Nazi messages.

After the Royal Navy and British Army garrison pulled out of Bermuda in the 1950s, the American and Canadian militaries continued to operate from the island. During the Cold War, Bermuda became a refueling station for U.S. nuclear bombers, and U.S. forces carried out aircraft missions from the island. Americans remained on the island until budget restrictions forced the bases' final closure in 1995.

TURBULENT TIMES

Despite its peaceful facade, Bermuda has suffered its share of social and racial conflicts.

In the 20th century, women led a decades-long campaign for equality, seeking specifically the freedom to vote. Suffragettes, like their American and British counterparts, held rallies, marches, and protests in a bid to force lawmakers to grant them voting rights, which, in an archaic island system, were restricted to male owners of land of a certain value. While British women won suffrage in 1919, their Bermudian sisters had to battle old-fashioned notions for another quarter of a century. When island women finally won their fight in 1945, their victory opened the door for universal adult suffrage in Bermuda later in the century, though black Bermudians had a long fight for full social and economic equality ahead of them.

The first labor union, formed by black teachers in 1919, was the vanguard of a bitter civil-rights struggle that would last many decades. Activists, including labor hero Dr. E. F. Gordon, spent the 1950s and 1960s agitating for change, inspired by the rhetoric of Malcolm X, Martin Luther King Jr., and the black civic-lobby campaigns in Britain and North America. Bermuda's white establishment continued to hold the bulk of power and wealth, and black resentment built up to a boiling point. The black-led Bermuda Industrial Union took shape in the late 1940s, representing the rights of mostly black blue-collar workers for the next several decades. In 1959, blacks staged the "Theatre Boycott," a successful stand against racial segregation in cinemas, which also spread to restaurants, hotels, churches, and schools. As a direct result of the protest, discriminatory racial practices gradually ended, and blacks finally won the right to vote in 1963. However, black Bermudians continued to be largely shut out of economic power-sharing until the 1980s and 1990s.

Riots in 1965 and 1968 underscored the racial unrest, as did the violent upheavals of the 1970s, when Governor Sir Richard Sharples and his aide-de-camp, Hugh Sayers, were assassinated in 1973 while walking on the grounds of Government House. Two black Bermudians were convicted and hanged, sparking an overflow of racial tensions in the form of violent street riots in 1977, and British forces were brought in to quell the disturbances. Capital punishment remained on the island's law books until 1999, though no one was ever hanged again.

The national crisis took a toll on Bermuda—financially, and in far more lasting ways—but change, while slow, did result, along with government promises to heal the island's social wounds. Royal commissions looking into the unrest pointed to gross racial inequality and recommended better housing, education, and more support for black businesses. Bermuda evolved into a more democratic and inclusive society, though members of the black community argue that it will take many more decades to achieve true economic equality.

MODERN PROSPERITY

From the 1980s until the global recession of the late 2000s, Bermuda enjoyed economic boom years fueled by international offshore business, and to a far lesser degree, tourism. The result has been an enviable standard of life with per capita income—in 2013 at $86,000—that is the world's highest, according to the World Bank. Bermudians of all races and backgrounds travel overseas frequently; attend top universities in the United States, Canada, and the United Kingdom; and benefit from Bermuda's need for highly skilled labor in the island's law firms, accounting practices, banks, insurance companies, and other fields.

Bermuda has become part of the global community, and while social pressures continue—ironically, some of which are aggravated by the island's own success—it prides itself on being a progressive, peaceful, and stable democracy.

Government

Politically stable and largely self-governing, Bermuda has the oldest Westminster-style government outside of Britain. Established by the island's English governor and colonists in the 17th century, the first legislative assembly met on August 1, 1620; among the 15 laws passed in its inaugural session was a ban on "idle and unprofitable persons" being shipped to the colony—a credo that has paved the way for Bermuda's capitalistic pursuits ever since.

One of the last remaining British Overseas Territories, Bermuda nevertheless manages most of its own affairs—including the passage of all laws. Despite the island's significant autonomy on national matters, the Queen of England remains the titular head of state, and responsibility for Bermuda falls to the Foreign & Commonwealth Office in London, which appoints a resident governor, approved by the queen. As the Crown's voice on security, defense, and international issues, the governor—who lives in Bermuda at Government House, a grand, rambling old property with a towered mansion on the North Shore in Pembroke—acts as a liaison between the Bermuda and U.K. governments. He also appoints the judiciary and police service, though these positions are truly selected by the government; the governor's signature, over the last century at least, has been nothing more than a rubber stamp. While many of the governor's day-to-day duties are purely ceremonial, he is a key diplomatic figure as a go-between for Bermuda and London, particularly as the island wrestles with the notion of cutting ties with Britain.

Bermuda participates in the United Nations through British delegations, and the Bermuda government is consulted on all international decisions affecting the island—though relations between Government House and the perennially pro-independence Progressive Labour Party (PLP) have been frosty at times. Bermuda's interests in the United States are represented by the United Kingdom via its Washington, D.C., embassy, but the U.S. Consul General in Bermuda is also very active in the area of United States-Bermuda diplomacy. Robert Settje, a career diplomat in the U.S. Foreign Service, has held the post since 2012.

For almost a half-century, the island has had an elected government formed under a two-party system. The Bermuda Constitution was drawn up on June 8, 1968, and updated in 1989 and 2003. In the Westminster tradition, the government is three-pronged, with executive, legislative, and judicial branches. The executive hierarchy is headed by the Queen of England, whose role is carried out by the governor; the governor is followed by a premier—leader of the party winning the most seats in a general election—and a 13-member cabinet nominated by the premier from among members of parliament. The 36-seat Legislature or Parliament has two legislative chambers: the House of Assembly, whose members are chosen by eligible voters in general elections held at least every five years, and the appointed 11-member Senate, or upper house of Parliament. All laws must be passed by the House of Assembly and approved by the Senate and the governor. The Senate's 11 members are named by the governor, the premier, and the leader of the opposition.

Bermuda's legal system is its own, dating back to 1612, though it is based on English common law. The judiciary, which enforces laws, is three-tiered: Magistrates Court, or lower court, rules on lesser criminal offenses; Supreme Court, or high court, decides more serious criminal cases, as well as civil issues; and then there's the Court of Appeal. Judgments have the right of final appeal to the House of Lords in London. A chief justice, appointed by the governor, heads the Supreme Court, where English tradition goes full-tilt with judges in robes and powdered wigs. All judicial entities are based in Hamilton, with the largest Supreme Court room and the House of Assembly occupying separate floors of the Sessions House on the hill overlooking Parliament Street. Magistrates Court is just yards away, in the modern Dame Lois Browne Evans Building on Court Street.

The political parties represented in Parliament are the Opposition Progressive Labour Party (PLP) and the governing One Bermuda Alliance (OBA)—created in 2011 after the merging of the historic United Bermuda Party (UBP) and upstart Bermuda Democratic Alliance (BDA). The OBA won power after 14 years of PLP rule in a 19-17 December 2012 victory. Bermuda's government is the island's largest employer, with an estimated 15 percent of the population working in its various ministries and departments.

Bermuda has nine parishes—St. George's, Hamilton Parish, Smith's, Devonshire, Paget, Pembroke, Warwick, Southampton, and Sandys—each further divided for electoral purposes into 36 single-seat voting districts (Pembroke North, Devonshire South, etc.) that each elect a Member of Parliament (MP). These constituencies measure roughly half a square mile and hold about 1,000 voters each. The Corporations of Hamilton and St. George's largely run the affairs of their respective municipalities, based in Pembroke and St. George's, and parish councils act as local advisory groups. All Bermudian citizens over the age of 18 have the right to vote.

British-style pomp and pageantry accompany the official convening of a new Parliamentary session every November (MPs break for three months over the summer). MPs decked out in lounge suits and Ascot hats ascend the steps to the Sessions House for the reading of the Throne Speech—a rundown of the government's policy plans for the coming year. Visitors can visit Parliament every Friday when in session (upstairs in the House, at Parliament St. and Church St.) to watch island politicos harangue each other over issues ranging from serious (gang violence, government debt, poor public education standards) to purely trivial (whether to allow personalized vehicle license plates). In a society where appearance tops nearly all else, the latter motion was easily passed.

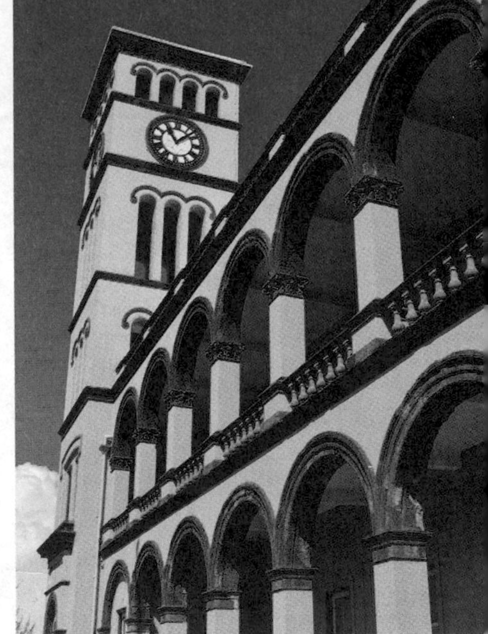

Bermuda is self-governing, with a Parliament of 36 elected members.

POLITICAL PARTIES

Although it went 35 years without winning an election, the **Progressive Labour Party** (www.plp.bm) is Bermuda's oldest political party, formed by black activists in May 1963 with a mandate to improve quality of life for the island's blacks. While its socialist-leaning platform called for better health care, education, and housing, the PLP's main target was electoral reform and the eradication of racial discrimination. Until the late 1960s, voting rights in Bermuda were restricted to property owners, which eliminated the majority of the black community, as well as most women of both races.

Equal voting and universal adult suffrage finally came about on May 22, 1968, when Bermuda's first election was held. The now-defunct United Bermuda Party, founded in 1964 and loosely based on the British Conservative party, formed the first government under the island's new constitution, winning 30 of 40 seats. The party held on to power for eight successive electoral victories, finally losing to the PLP in 1998 in a landslide 26-14 defeat. With a founding power base of white, old-family merchants, the UBP was long perceived as a party dedicated to representing the interests of Bermuda's whites; indeed, Bermudians only half-jokingly refer to the virtual "cabinet meetings" held in the Royal Bermuda Yacht Club, a whites-only male bastion comprising Front Street's "Forty Thieves"—wealthy shopkeepers who shaped the island's destiny. Such history proved hard to shake—despite the fact that in later decades the party's ranks were bolstered by middle-class blacks, women, and conservative Portuguese, and two of its leaders were black; in 2011, an unpopular UBP was finally forced to merge with the Bermuda Democratic Alliance, a new party composed of many UBP defectors. The new entity relaunched as the **One Bermuda Alliance,** or **OBA** (www.oba.bm) in May 2011.

Given the emotive path of party politics, the PLP's decisive 1998 victory, which claimed 54 percent of the popular vote and catapulted the party into power for the first time, was a euphoric milestone for Bermuda's 60 percent black majority population. The election result also won support from whites who believed democratic change would help heal long-held racial frictions. Yet, under four successive leaders, the PLP government was increasingly criticized by both whites and blacks for overspends that pushed the island's national debt over $1.4 billion, or 28 percent of gross domestic product by 2012. The PLP was reelected in 2003 and 2007, but in 2012 lost to OBA supporters anxious for an economic turnaround amid increasing job losses during a five-year recession. In its debut term, the OBA made it a priority to hike GDP and bring back foreign exchange in order to trim the debt; it began by ending restrictive immigration policies such as six-year term limits on work permits that had been highly unpopular in the international business sector. The government also created two private-public agencies: one to run tourism, the other to pursue proactive business development for Bermuda. With the next election due in 2017, and only incremental signs of an economic recovery evident two years after taking office, the OBA team has its work cut out for it.

Bermudians love talking politics, and everyone from the multinational CEO to the horse-and-buggy driver has a viewpoint, which they usually are more than eager to share. Tune in to Bermuda talk radio daily to hear what Bermudians feel about the issues of the day. Declining tourism, increasing crime, systemic problems in public education, and environmental destruction continue to be the most substantial national problems facing the government. With growing calls for public policy that nurtures more sustainable development, it looks likely these will remain Bermuda's fundamental challenges in the years to come.

THE REGIMENT AND POLICE

As a British territory, Bermuda's security is the domain of the United Kingdom in the event of serious civil disturbances, terrorism, or other external factors. When street riots erupted in 1977, for example, Britain jetted in 250 Royal Regiment of Fusiliers soldiers, who quickly put an end to the visible chaos. Similarly, Scotland Yard police officers are sometimes called upon to investigate serious crimes on the island.

In most circumstances, however, the island's part-time army and police forces handle internal security issues. Since its establishment in 1965, the 600-strong Bermuda Regiment has held a mostly ceremonial role, marching with its Band Company and Corps of Drums in "Beating the Retreat" displays and other traditionally British events, such as the Queen's Birthday Parade, Remembrance Day, and Parliament Throne Speech. One area in which it has been more hands-on is

Hamilton police station and court rooms are located on Court Street.

hurricane relief after debilitating storms; marine service is also proposed as a useful role in the future. But its policy of conscription—under which males aged 18 to 25 are recruited for three years of compulsory part-time service—is outdated, say detractors, and the OBA government has promised to end it. With the governor acting as commander-in-chief, the battalion currently has 27 full-time staff. Female service is voluntary. Back in the 1960s, the regiment's inception brought an end to racial segregation of local forces by amalgamating a white rifle corps and a black militia. Today, it is affiliated with Canada's Lincoln & Welland Regiment, as well as several in the United Kingdom.

The Bermuda Police Service, established in 1879, has nearly 500 officers, including plainclothes detectives, marine patrols, and narcotics and forensics teams. Headquartered in Prospect, Devonshire, ever since the British Army garrison withdrew in 1958, the police force has stations in Hamilton, Somerset, St. George's, and the airport, as well as marine detachments in Hamilton and St. George's.

As gangs and gun crime increased through the 2000s, some Bermuda Police units on patrol began carrying guns for the first time. By contrast, their old-time ties remain steadfast; officers sometimes wear traditional British "Bobby" hats—to the amusement of North American visitors—as well as flat-capped versions, with both caps emblazoned with the force's silver crest and royal cypher. One of the island's most photographed sights is the Front Street "Birdcage"—a blue-and-white-spoked kiosk in the center of the road at Heyl's Corner, near the Queen Street junction, where an officer is occasionally posted to direct traffic, and also to pose for innumerable snapshots.

Economy

If Bermuda's wealth of past centuries was generated in large part by pirates and privateers, today's pursuit of capitalistic rewards from these 21 square miles is no less ambitious. Bermuda's per-capita GDP sits at around $86,000, and it remains a society of no-holds-barred entrepreneurial spirit; islanders, no matter their job field, are ever ready to grasp shifting opportunities or run with a good idea. Money—making it, spending it, and, very often, flaunting it—is the linchpin of island life, and you need relatively more of it here to pay for everything from restaurant tabs and groceries to rent and transport. Because practically all goods must be imported—food, clothing, household wares, animals, machinery—and prices reflect high government customs duties, the cost of living in Bermuda is among the world's highest. That is even without traditional sales, income, or wealth taxes, though there exists a 14 percent payroll tax split between employer and employee.

Yet despite Bermuda's traditional ability to weather economic storms elsewhere, the five-year recession that began in 2008 had a sobering effect on the island. After two decades of boom times driven by a near-constant influx of capital-rich companies, Bermuda experienced a stark reality check. Driven by sharp declines in financial services, international business, hotel and restaurant spending, and construction, the island's gross domestic product (GDP) experienced net year-over-year shrinkage, with 2013 figures indicating a drop of between 2 and 2.5 percent from the previous year. That compared to a pre-crisis (2003-2008) average of 2.8 percent annual growth. The shortfall underscored the vulnerability of Bermuda's small economy to external shocks. By 2014, however, the economy was stabilizing, foreign investment was slowly returning, and signs of a gradual turnaround were recorded; GDP growth by the end of that year was estimated to be relatively flat, around 0.5 percent, with the international business sector remaining the primary driver of Bermuda's economy and accounting for 26 percent of overall GDP. Notably, the government projected that Bermuda's winning bid to host the 35th America's Cup in June 2017, along with the regatta's run-up, the America's Cup World Series in October 2015, would attract at least $250 million of on-island spending, and be a catalyst for an upsurge in tourism and major investment in infrastructure and hotel properties.

Until the 2014 America's Cup announcement, the result of a frailer economy has meant leaner times for most Bermudians—and the rarity of true unemployment, estimated at around 8 percent in 2013, with the loss of 5,700 jobs since 2008. As well, a gradual exodus of an estimated 2,000 foreign workers between 2008 and 2013—due to company relocations and uncertainty over government policies—had a perceivable impact on the local economy, particularly retail, restaurants, construction, and real estate. Landlords who in the late '90s and early 2000s were charging $30,000 a month for executive home rentals were left scouring the island for corporate tenants willing to pay two-thirds or less that amount. Seniors struggling to pay for medications or families sharing apartments to get by are no longer rare scenarios, and belt-tightening has been the buzzword rather than the profligate spending of past years. The shift has served to illustrate how tightly Bermuda's well-being is in sync with that of the United States—"When America sneezes," goes the aphorism, "Bermuda catches a cold."

International business has maintained its position as the island's largest employer. Industries that support the business sector, such as financial and legal services, IT, and accounting, have fared best even amid tougher markets. This sector alone has sustained a

Real Estate on "The Rock"

Bermuda has long claimed some of the priciest real estate in the world, nearly equivalent to North American urban centers such as New York or Los Angeles. The global recession of the early 2010s, which saw thousands of expatriate workers leave the island over five years, has cooled both Bermuda's sales and rental markets. Some would argue it simply brought down to earth a decade-plus period of sky-high prices that saw "executive" rentals average up to $30,000 per month, a tiny cottage routinely snag $1.2 million, and two-bedroom condominiums sell for $900,000.

Today, condos remain popular options for Bermudians looking to buy a piece of "The Rock," and numerous landowners have cashed in to develop properties for income. Hotels have led the trend, building luxury time-share villas for foreign clientele. Foreign purchase of Bermuda property has always been curtailed by a price floor of about $2 million on homes offered to non-Bermudians, coupled with sky-high taxes.

While Bermuda buyers and renters may finally benefit from the market's cool-down, the island's perennial housing crunch has caused pressures of many kinds—social, economic, environmental—as politicians grapple with how to make local housing affordable. While real estate prices may now be more achievable for young couples or fresh graduates, for example, leaner times and inherently fewer jobs mean many still hold out little hope of buying property unless they inherit or are helped by family members or employers.

longtime labor shortage in Bermuda that attracts thousands of foreign workers to provide "intellectual capital" to fill often highly specialized white-collar jobs in the finance, IT, or reinsurance industries.

Despite recent concerns, Bermuda from a historical perspective remains a textbook example of unbridled economic success—all the more impressive given its geographic remoteness. From tobacco farming to shipbuilding to the sale of winter vegetables, the island's economy flip-flopped from one pursuit to another over the better part of three centuries. In the 1900s, Bermuda reinvented itself twice. With no exportable natural resources, no heavy industry, and few viable exports other than onions, the island cashed in on its physical beauty, launching an enviable tourism industry in the early 20th century that became its economic pillar. An even more dramatic economic makeover was to follow: After the end of World War II, Bermuda simultaneously began to attract foreigners interested in the island for its offshore business benefits—and a behemoth second fiscal mainstay was born. Thousands of insurance "captive" companies, trusts, mutual funds, and most importantly, multibillion-dollar reinsurance firms, flocked to the island in the 1970s, '80s, '90s and early to mid-2000s, turning Bermuda into a blue-chip financial center. International business quickly surpassed tourism as Bermuda's major cash cow, and today, the island's insurance sector ranks as one of the world's four major markets, alongside London, Switzerland, and Ireland.

The resilience of "Bermuda, Inc."—as the number-one industry is dubbed—is reassuring to all Bermudians because the trickle-down effect sustains an entire economy. Yet the widening gap between those who benefit directly from corporate largesse and those who do not is widening, supporting a two-class system that feeds racial rifts and social pressures. Undereducated young black men, particularly, feel shut out of the prosperity enjoyed by the international business sector.

Such fragility of the island's economy, and the fact the sector's labor shortage in specialized financial fields means it is largely driven by non-Bermudians, are the downsides of what, on the surface, seems a win-win scenario for the island. But Bermudians appear determined to weather the tough years and encourage the wave of corporate opportunity for as long as possible. As for what comes next, their economic spirit seems content to embrace the stoicism of Bermuda's national motto, emblazoned on the island's flag: "Whither the Fates Carry Us."

INTERNATIONAL BUSINESS

Insurance derivatives trader. Reserving actuary. Catastrophe modeler. Structured finance credit analyst. The arcane job descriptions for international business posts on the island fill most of the employment pages in the daily paper—a visible testament to the extent of the island's economic mainstay.

What brings so many foreign companies to the island? One of the most business-benign regulatory environments in the world, along with a tax-neutral environment and political stability, are the main attractions, along with a handy location that's connected to key urban centers like New York and London via a simple direct flight. "Exempt" or "permit" corporations—which differ from local companies in that they can be owned by non-Bermudians as long as their business is overseas—are not taxed on their worldwide earnings, and there are no taxes on interest, dividends, unearned income, or capital gains. The island also offers a professional workforce, a sophisticated commercial infrastructure, and cutting-edge telecommunications. While Bermuda has benefited hugely as a result, it has also managed to hone a reputation as a respected and transparent offshore financial center, untarnished by the rampant money-laundering, corruption, and dubious bank-secrecy laws that plague many other so-called tax havens. Yet, the specter of Congressional crackdowns on offshore companies is a persistent bugbear for the industry—along with local headaches like xenophobic attitudes toward expats.

The international business sector comprises a variety of enterprise: heavily capitalized reinsurance companies (firms insuring against underwritten loss); insurance captives (offshore subsidiaries offering insurance within the parent company or mainland group); financial services firms; mutual and hedge funds; trusts; investment managers; shipping corporations; and commercial traders. The largest class of new company registrations since 2009, however, have been "special purpose insurers" such as insurance-linked securities (ILS) firms; these entities leverage sophisticated financial instruments like catastrophe (cat) bonds and collateralized reinsurance to allow investors to wager on insurance risks. In addition, all the "Big Four" accounting firms—PricewaterhouseCoopers, Deloitte, KPMG, and Ernst & Young—have major offices in Hamilton. Banking, investment, and management services; advertising firms; printing houses; computer and data consultants; and many other Bermudian-owned businesses also support and benefit from the industry.

Reinsurance Juggernaut

The reinsurance market has been king in Bermuda since the mid-1980s and plays a vital role in the global community, underwriting an estimated 8 percent of all reinsurance business and providing a third of total financial relief after major disasters. Figures indicate over the past dozen years Bermuda-based reinsurers have contributed a combined $35 billion in catastrophe claims payouts to U.S. clients—including $2.5 billion after the World Trade Center attacks, $17 billion for Hurricane Katrina, $2 billion after tornadoes in 2010-2012, and $3 billion in losses after Hurricane Sandy. A. M. Best Co. has rated the Bermuda market well prepared to meet claims from future catastrophic events, thanks to its ready pool of capital and claims-paying track record.

The sector is changing rapidly, and, along with recent global regulatory challenges, has experienced economic pressures as the lines between traditional reinsurance and the capital markets collide. This phenomenon has seen billions of dollars in new third-party "convergence capital" pumped into the market over the past few years by alternative reinsurance companies such as hedge fund-backed reinsurers and ILS entities, driving down rates while allowing new capital—including hedge and pension funds—to take on underwriting risks to diversify their portfolios. The worldwide catastrophe reinsurance capacity was estimated at around $300 billion in 2014, of which the top 10 ILS funds control 12 percent and growing. An increasing number of these are Bermuda-based: by the end of 2014, the Bermuda Stock Exchange recorded a record 100-plus listings of insurance-linked listings, amounting to nearly $16 billion and representing 60 percent of the worldwide stock of ILS. Observers believe this trend of new risk-transfer mechanisms will revolutionize conventional reinsurance models—forcing traditional companies to evolve and changing the fundamental ways in which catastrophe reinsurance is transacted.

Islanders themselves depend heavily on the international business sector, particularly reinsurance, directly or indirectly. Foreign companies bring foreign exchange that fuels the economy: in 2014, Bermuda's insurers and reinsurers contributed almost $900 million to the island's coffers, employing more than 1,500 people. Corporations pay for the privilege of an offshore jurisdiction through certain fees, including payroll tax, and by bringing business visitors to the island, providing jobs and revenue to local businesses, and fueling the need for construction. The trickle-down is felt even on the grassroots level: Companies help support island charities, including museums and art galleries; fund summer camps, conservation initiatives, and social projects; even pump cash into private-school budgets. The good news for Bermuda is that although perennial problems such as work-permit controversies and U.S. tax crackdowns—plus the politically divisive ramifications of independence from Britain—have the potential to drive international business to competing jurisdictions like Zurich, Dublin, or the Cayman Islands, the immediate future of the industry appears strong.

TOURISM

Golden Years

Missionaries and military officers were Bermuda's first visitors, their impressions of the island ranging from euphoric descriptions of an earthly paradise to indictments of a disease-ridden backwater. It was not until the late 19th century that the concept of travel as "vacation" was born. It took the 10-week winter sojourn of Queen Victoria's daughter, Princess Louise, in 1883, to officially launch tourism in

All the "Big Four" accounting firms have a presence on the island.

Bermuda. Following glowing media coverage of her visit, America's elite—politicians, socialites, artists, and writers—began to travel to the island to escape North American winters. Woodrow Wilson, Rudyard Kipling, Mark Twain, and Frances Hodgson Burnett were among the most celebrated early visitors, and as hotels and clubs sprang up to accommodate tourists like them, Bermudian officials marketed the island as a lotusland for wealthy urban Americans. In 1911, the first guidebook extolled the offerings of Bermuda as "Nature's Fairyland" and the "Isles of Rest"—euphemisms that fixed the island in foreign imaginations as a romantic escape from the real world.

That image—of candy-pink cottages, blossom-sprinkled lanes, and private azure bays—has been Bermuda's calling card ever since, a magnet that made the island the private playground of the super-rich and gradually built a significant industry. The timing was perfect, as Bermuda desperately needed an economic lifeline. Agriculture in the early 1900s was starting to wane, and the chance for a makeover through tourism was welcomed. Early visitors attended garden parties, dances, and military displays, traveling around by bicycle or horse-drawn carriages on unpaved roads (cars were banned until the postwar years). Croquet, tennis, and golf became popular, as well as the popular new pastime of swimming.

Gradually the island became both a winter and summer resort, with ocean liner service to and from the U.S. East Coast, whose residents made up 85 percent of the trade. A steady influx of year-round visitors began to pour into the island. Critics worried the influx would spoil Bermuda's quaint character, but there was no stopping it. Between the two world wars, the tourism industry became more developed, and Bermuda's appeal, especially to the glitterati, grew. Visits by Vincent Astor, William Vanderbilt, Charlie Chaplin, and playwright Eugene O'Neill underscored the island's self-perpetuated image as a place for the rich and famous.

Tourism's heyday came in the post-World War II years, thanks to the new civilian airport, built during the war by the U.S. military. The airport opened the island for the first time to large numbers of mainstream visitors from gateway cities. Bermuda was no longer the realm of the elite. The island had modernized, too, allowing private cars and investing in large new hotels. By the mid-1960s, some 200,000 visitors were traveling to the island annually, including many thousands on cruise ships during the summer season. The industry's golden years throughout the 1970s and 1980s saw that figure catapult to a peak of 630,000 in 1985. Tourism employed thousands of Bermudians and represented not only the country's economic lifeblood, but also its sense of identity and national pride.

It was not to last, however. Competing destinations, especially bargain resorts in the Caribbean, coupled with rising costs triggered a slow but steady slump in the industry throughout the 1990s and the first decade of the 2000s. By 2011, full-year air visitor numbers totaled about 235,000, while cruise visitors were close to 415,000. More alarming to the industry was the continued drop in visitor spending; retailers blamed fewer air arrivals compared to cruise passengers, a demographic that traditionally spends less than those who fly to the island.

Modern Pressures

Several well-known hotels have closed in the past quarter-century, including Club Med, the Belmont, Lantana, the Palmetto Hotel, the Inverurie, Wyndham Sonesta Beach Resort, the Marriott Castle Harbour, and Pink Beach Club. Most recently, Waterloo House in Hamilton and Horizons in Paget—both part of the same Relais & Chateaux group—shut down, the former sold and leveled to make way for corporate offices and waterfront condominiums, the latter seeking to raise reinvestment capital. The Hamilton-based Bermudiana Hotel, where Woodrow Wilson once slept, was sold in the 1980s to become the headquarters of Bermuda's largest reinsurers. Other former hotel properties have developed upscale time-share and condominium units, with a promise to the government to include a certain number of hotel rooms in the future. Labor is another challenge: From the mid-1980s onward, the industry has been hemorrhaging young Bermudians to better-paying careers in international business.

Tourism remains Bermuda's second-largest industry, however, and to a large extent business and tourism are codependent on each other, with increasing numbers of business visitors needing accommodations, attractions, and visitor-geared recreation. Indeed, many of the most successful hotels and guesthouses now claim business clientele as their major source of income. But the global recession has not done the industry any favors, and several long-planned redevelopments remain in limbo, awaiting financing. Lantana was purchased with plans for a spa resort, though to date no ground has been broken. And ambitious plans to build a business hotel in Hamilton and a golf resort in St. George's have yet to leave the starting gates.

As international economies strengthen, however, there are positive signs. Rosewood Hotels & Resorts took over management in 2011 of the 88-room boutique Tucker's Point Hotel & Spa (situated on the historic former Marriott Castle Harbour property in Tucker's Town, St. George's), after the government controversially approved expansion of the resort's fractional ownership properties. Canada-based Sardis Development purchased Pink Beach Club for $51.5 million in 2014, razing it for construction of a five-star, 34-room boutique hotel property. The Bermuda-based Green family bought the Fairmont Hamilton Princess Hotel in 2012 and promptly launched a $90 million upgrade of the historic "Pink Palace" to be complete by 2015; the family also bought the former Sonesta site with plans for a Princess beach club And the new owner of Lantana went on to buy the Newstead-Belmont Hills Resort in 2014, taking it out of the limbo of a four-year receivership.

Aggressive new marketing efforts, particularly digital campaigns, were launched in 2012 when the OBA government dismantled the former Department of Tourism and created a public-private "Bermuda Tourism Authority," with a mandate to revitalize the industry and hike tourist numbers. The new agency created a National Tourism Plan that made increasing air arrivals, encouraging smaller, high-end cruise ships, delivering high-quality visitor attractions, and promoting Bermuda more robustly on social media its priorities, among other initiatives.

Cultural and Events-Oriented Tourism

The majority of Bermuda's visitors still hail from North America, mostly Americans (72 percent), followed by Europeans (12 percent) and Canadians (13 percent). The difference is that more now come from farther afield—the U.S. Midwest and the West Coasts of both Canada and the United States—and the island is starting to attract people from newer markets such as continental Europe. Generally, Bermuda visitors of all nationalities are affluent (making at least $100,000 a year) and mature (air visitors' average age is between 35 and 54; cruise ship passengers are slightly older), and many are "repeat" customers. The island has always enjoyed a solid market of repeat visitors—Bermudaphiles who come year after year for decades. Leisure travelers make up 62 percent of the market, business visitors 20 percent, and those who come to visit families and friends who live and work on the island account for 16 percent. Shopping, soft adventure, cultural pursuits, and the more typical beach experience are the norm.

There are constant calls from industry watchers for Bermuda to offer better service to match prices, and lower airfares to attract more visitors—something that discount carriers such as JetBlue and Canada's WestJet are now offering. Having evolved from a winter resort to a midsummer escape in the 20th century, Bermuda is today a multiseasonal destination challenged to offer attractions and events that appeal to visitors looking for more than sunburns and rum swizzles. While travelers still seek relaxation, they also want to know more about the destination they choose, a worldwide trend.

Bermuda has focused on developing cultural and events-oriented tourism, with an emphasis on island heritage, grassroots traditions, and community involvement. While the PGA Grand Slam of Golf announced it would return to the U.S. in 2015 after eight years in Bermuda, the island's much-celebrated winning bid to host the 35th America's Cup in 2017, along with its preliminary World Series races in 2015, promises to more than make up for the loss of the PGA Grand Slam of Golf.

The Department of Parks has revamped some of the centuries-old forts throughout the island, and weekly outdoor markets and other events help bring a buzz to the UNESCO World Heritage Site of St. George's. At the island's other end, the handicrafts of Bermudian artisans—including cedarwork by inmates at the nearby prison—are sold at weekly Heritage Nights that showcase everything from cricket to Crown & Anchor gaming. North Hamilton has also caught the celebratory spirit, holding occasional street festivals where local cuisine, games, and music attract a family atmosphere.

The BTA is also encouraging Bermudian entrepreneurs to pitch their ideas for innovative new tours, activities, and events to appeal to visitors. Ecotourism is another facet of the industry with largely untapped potential, though there has been growing interest in activities such as whale-watching trips, reef snorkeling, birding tours, and other outdoor pursuits.

People and Culture

Bermudians grapple with their national identity, which, combining British colonialism, American capitalism, West Indian roots, and dashes of Portuguese and Native American culture, is sometimes incredibly difficult to pin down. Aside from the complicated ethnic and cultural mix, there's the deeper question of how to characterize islanders as a people—stuck somewhere, physically and philosophically, between the sophistication of the world we belong to and the insular self-complacency engendered by living on a remote island.

If generalizations can be made, Bermudians represent a rather quirky combination of small-town vice (islanders love nothing better than to gossip, and it's easy because everyone knows everyone) and cosmopolitan sophistication (most have traveled overseas, many have attended mainland colleges and universities). As survivors in the broadest sense—of the sea, of hurricanes, of economic fragility and an unlikely history—Bermudians have evolved as an enigmatic and sometimes contradictory breed, both greedy and freely giving, open-minded and terribly bigoted, standoffish and disarmingly friendly. They are also an assimilation of many people and cultures over the centuries, creating a diverse society.

The perennial debate over political independence has strong social overtones for Bermudians as a people. If we cut our ties to Britain, do we lose or gain? Would Bermudians then have a stronger sense of identity? Can such a small society so far removed from others make it alone . . . and should we try? While many Bermudians would gladly keep hold of the motherland's apron strings, others feel ready to take the leap. Whatever's decided, it's fair to say that the Bermudian character—stoic, proud, ultimately charming, and resilient through many storms—will remain intact.

DEMOGRAPHICS

From its earliest days, Bermuda has been a home to immigrants. Unlike many Caribbean nations, there were no indigenous people when the first English colonists arrived in the early 17th century, likely due to the island's isolated position in the mid-Atlantic. Since then, empire-building, more than two centuries of slavery, and labor shortages have brought waves of immigration to the island—notably large numbers of British whites, West Indian blacks, and Azorean Portuguese. The official language has always been English, though Portuguese is spoken within a restricted community.

According to the 2010 census, the population stands at roughly 64,000, of which 60 percent is black. Sixty-seven percent of the population is Bermuda-born, while 29 percent is foreign-born. U.K. immigrants made up 25 percent of the immigrant population, Americans 20 percent, Canadians 15 percent, Caribbean 12 percent, and Portuguese/Azorean nearly 10 percent. Until a cap on immigration in the latter half of the 20th century, the most recent immigrants were British teachers, police officers, pharmacists, and nurses in the 1950s and 1960s. Caribbean immigration began arriving en masse in the late 1890s when citizens of Jamaica, St. Kitts, Barbados, and Trinidad were fleeing economic depression. Development of the Royal Navy Dockyard demanded the region's skilled workers, and many West Indian Bermudian families can trace their roots back to this period. More Caribbean workers were recruited in the 1920s to build the Bermuda Railway, and later Caribbean police were sought to help balance the racial mix of Bermuda's police force. Portuguese have also had a large impact on Bermuda's demographics and culture since the first Azoreans were brought to the island in 1849 to revitalize agriculture. In the past 20-plus years, Bermuda's Asian- and African-born community has developed; this is partly due to a high demand for Filipino guest workers as housekeepers, nannies, and caregivers, as well as demand for Indian, Indonesian, and Thai nationals by restaurants seeking cheaper labor than Bermudians are willing to provide. Even today, though immigration laws are far stricter, Bermuda depends on foreign labor to survive, and inevitably many expatriates marry locals and end up living on the island forever.

RACISM AND SOCIAL TENSIONS

The island's mix of races, cultures, and immigrants has not developed without bitter tensions. Slavery—from the earliest record in 1616 to emancipation in 1834—along with its socioeconomic fallout, has proven the most divisive and emotionally fraught issue among Bermudians, right up to the current day. Slavery in Bermuda was domestic in nature, and very different in scale from the plantation system of the Caribbean or U.S. South—mainly because the islands had no sugarcane or cotton. Bermudian colonists used slaves to farm their land, crew their ships, and look after their homes and children. In a system of conflict and compromise, island whites and blacks influenced each other's lives heavily and shaped the culture and look of modern Bermuda—the generally lighter skin color of Bermudians compared to Caribbean or African blacks is an obvious example.

It took until modern times, even up to the 1980s and 1990s, for Bermudians to start openly discussing race and racial tensions in their society. That is largely due to the fact that racial segregation here ended just a generation ago, in the early 1960s. One of the biggest issues for the black community remains the ongoing struggle to achieve economic equality, after decades in which even getting a mortgage from a white-owned bank was impossible. Racist views still exist in Bermuda, though with a large and growing black middle class, and increasing Bermudian youth receiving higher education in multiethnic urban centers, it continues to recede. If racist sentiments are ever expressed, they are often subtler than in the United States. "Bermuda's blacks and whites mix very well nine-to-five, and at big community events," comments Charles Barclay, former editor of *Bermuda Business Visitor* magazine. "But among some in the older white community, there flourishes what might be described as a benign bigotry; a casual, condescending bias which one could laugh off as the folly of a fading era—were it not for the fact that they retain significant wealth and power."

Complicating the situation is the influx of "expats"—mostly white expatriate workers, many of whom are hired at higher salaries than Bermudian counterparts, black or white. Common resentment against foreign workers is difficult to separate from the issue of race, though more often than not, economic factors are to blame.

Regardless of color or salary, there is a definite pecking order in Bermudian society. At the top of the heap in terms of social acceptance are "Born Bermudians," though those with 300-year-old families rather than second-generation status are preferred. Next come the spouses of Born Bermudians, who are accorded respect almost grudgingly, and still commonly discriminated against, socially at least. So-called "Paper Bermudians"—foreign-born individuals who have won their status, either decades ago, when it was straightforward, or as newly recognized long-term residents—are next down on the list of social importance.

Finally, at the bottom of the heap, come the foreign workers, the expats. They have no voting rights, their children born in Bermuda are not granted citizenship—and they even have to stand in a different line than Bermudians at the airport when returning to the island. They consider themselves, correctly in most cases, to be standing on shaky ground in a much larger sense. Thanks to Bermuda's work-permit system—which allows one-year or three-year permits to workers in most categories, excluding key personnel at large companies—the expat population remains a largely silent one. Most foreign residents prefer not to speak out publicly about issues of any kind, let alone controversial topics like race or political independence; most feel they would be jeopardizing their chances of remaining on the island. Some Bermudians dislike foreigners because they are seen to consider the island as a place to make loads of money with little care for its people or culture. As a visitor, you will usually be unaware of such complicated social undercurrents, but they do exist and affect daily life for all residents.

RELIGION

Bermuda is often cited as the place that has more churches per square mile than anywhere else in the world, something that will readily become apparent as you spot innumerable places of worship around the parishes—from Anglican spires and Roman Catholic grandeur to African Methodist Episcopal congregations and simple gospel halls. Some churches stand on the site of 17th-century origins; others are modernist creations of the new millennium. Baptists, Seventh-Day Adventists, Christian Scientists, Lutherans, Ethiopian Orthodox, Jews, Evangelicals, even nondenominational churches—they are all well represented. The Religion pages in the weekend edition of the *Bermuda Sun* or the Churches listing in the phone book are proof of the island's deep religious roots, as well as the substantial power wielded by church lobby groups.

Visiting Bermuda's churches, either when they're empty or during services, is a fascinating lesson in local history and social studies. Most churches are open to the public at different times during the week. Check schedules with respective church offices or pastors.

Essentials

Transportation

GETTING THERE

By Commercial Airline

Bermuda has no shortage of direct daily flight service from major cities on the U.S. East Coast, as well as from London and Toronto. Eight commercial airlines flew round-trip schedules from 14 destinations to the island in 2014.

Bermuda's airport was renamed **L. F. Wade International Airport** (2 Kindley Field Rd., St. George's, tel. 441/293-2470, www.bermudaairport.com, airport code BDA or TXKF) in 2007 to honor former Progressive Labour Party leader L. Frederick Wade, who died three years before his party formed the government for the first time in 1998. The airfield, built by the United States military in 1941, is located in the East End, in St. George's Parish, which is linked by a half-mile causeway to the rest of the island. It's a half-hour drive to central hotels.

Travelers flying back to America from Bermuda will appreciate one of the tangible benefits the island reaps from its long, amicable relationship with Uncle Sam. Under a special arrangement made in the 1970s, the U.S. Customs pre-clearance at Bermuda's airport—a process of a few minutes—basically allows passengers to be treated as domestic arrivals once they reach their American airport destination, thereby avoiding the long lines of TSA and Immigration and Customs Enforcement checks at mainland airports.

The airport has benefited from numerous improvements in recent years, and today has several restaurants, cafés, bars, and retail and duty-free shops in all departure terminals, as well as updates like self-service kiosks and on-site airline ticket purchases. Free WiFi access is offered throughout the airport's departure lounge area, and powered seating allows passengers to charge electronic devices. Porters are on hand to help passengers with luggage, and an executive lounge, located in U.S. Departures, is open to first- and business-class passengers traveling on U.S.-bound flights.

RESERVATIONS AND FARES

Bermuda tourism's biggest problem has long been the stratospheric cost of air travel to and from the island. Industry officials and locals recognize the high cost as probably the biggest single reason for the slide in visitor numbers over recent decades and have labored to try to find ways to bring flight prices down.

Bermuda's problem can be attributed to geography and supply-and-demand economics. It is not a major urban center, so airlines serving the island can wield complete monopolies on various gateways. As a result, Bermuda has become something of a cash cow for carriers; the island rates as one of the highest-yield destinations in the world, and the Bermuda government has to cough up in weak travel years, under minimum revenue agreements with airlines.

Luckily for travelers, including Bermuda residents, more airline and gateway choices have emerged—including money-saving options. JetBlue launched competitive fares with daily service from New York's JFK, and followed up with seasonal service from Boston. Discount airline WestJet upped the competition for Air Canada, meaning lower fares to Toronto. Fare sales remain the most cost-effective way for leisure travelers to get to Bermuda, particularly in the peak summer season. If you happen to narrowly miss out on

Previous: pink bus touring the parishes; ferry service from Hamilton to the West and East Ends.

Airlines

- **Air Canada:** tel. 441/293-1777 or 888/247-2262, www.aircanada.com
- **American Airlines:** tel. 441/293-1420 or 800/433-7300, www.aa.com
- **British Airways:** tel. 441/293-1944, 44-844/493-0787, www.ba.com
- **Delta Air Lines:** tel. 800/221-1212, www.delta.com
- **JetBlue Airways:** tel. 441/293-3608 or 800/538-2583, www.jetblue.com
- **United Airlines:** tel. 441/293-3092 or 800/864-8331, www.united.com
- **US Airways:** tel. 800/622-1015, www.usairways.com
- **WestJet:** tel. 441/293-0550 or 888/937-8538, www.westjet.com

For airport information, including lost and found, call L. F. Wade International Airport (tel. 441/293-2470, 9am-5pm Mon.-Fri.). For U.S. Customs and Border Protection, call 441/293-8127. For the Bermuda Department of Civil Aviation, contact 411/293-1640 or bcaenquiries@gov.bm (8:30am-5pm Mon.-Fri.). For Bermuda Immigration, call 441/293-2542; for HM Customs, call 441/293-2424. Check www.bermudaairport.com for airlines' daily arrivals and departure schedules, cancellations, and flight numbers.

a seat sale after booking a ticket, some airlines will honor the lower price and offer a refund.

Seat availability diminishes (and prices rise accordingly) during the peak summer months and over Christmas, when Bermudians fly home en masse from London, Toronto, and U.S. East Coast cities. Generally, though, you will pay more April-October than during the quieter November-March "off" season. Midweek fares are also less expensive than weekend options, as demand is higher Friday to Sunday, especially holiday weekends, when North American travelers tend to fly to the island for brief doses of subtropical R&R. Prices from the same gateway city can vary dramatically, depending on all these factors. A ticket on American Airlines from New York City to Bermuda, for example, can range anywhere from $250 (during a seat sale) to well over $1,000 if booked last-minute.

The Bermuda airport's code is BDA (IATA) or TXKF (ICAO); it's the island's only airport. If you search for fares online, try checking different departure airports to win a cheaper fare. Rates from the New York area to Bermuda vary, for instance, depending on whether you fly American Airlines from JFK or US Airways from LaGuardia. Similarly, if you plan to travel from Britain and don't mind stopping, fares from London via New York are sometimes cheaper than Gatwick-Bermuda direct.

One stringent rule about flying to Bermuda: You must have a return ticket. Airlines normally will not sell one-way fares to foreign countries without proof of residency, and if you land here, you will not be permitted through Bermuda Immigration and Customs without proof of return. Even if you are leaving the island by alternative transport (as a crew member on a private yacht, for instance), it is best to buy an unrestricted round-trip ticket, then get the return refunded.

A valid, machine-readable passport is also required.

A $35 departure tax is charged to all air passengers to Bermuda, both visitors and residents. The charge is incorporated into the airfare and collected in advance. Children younger than two are exempt.

Two local travel agencies, both based in Hamilton, are **Worldview Travel** (35

Church St., tel. 441/292-3033, fax 441/292-3205, www.worldviewtravel.bm, 8am-5pm Mon.-Fri.) and **Watlington & Conyers Travel** (The Armoury Bldg., 1st floor, 37 Reid St., tel. 441/295-3815, watlingtonandconyers.com, 9am-5pm Mon.-Fri.). Both are IATA-accredited agencies.

FROM THE UNITED STATES

There are five commercial airlines serving Bermuda from the United States. **American Airlines** flies direct from New York (JFK) and Miami daily. **Delta Air Lines** offers daily direct flights from Boston and Atlanta. **US Airways** flies nonstop daily from Philadelphia, with seasonal service from Charlotte, Orlando, Boston, and Washington, D.C. **United Airlines** serves Bermuda daily with a direct flight from Newark. **JetBlue** offers daily service from New York (JFK) and from Boston (except on Tues. and Thurs.).

FROM CANADA

Air Canada and **WestJet** fly direct daily to Bermuda from Canada, to and from Toronto.

FROM THE UNITED KINGDOM

British Airways flies direct to and from London's Gatwick airport daily. A British Airways Executive Club is located in the International Departures Lounge.

FROM OTHER COUNTRIES

New York, Boston, Atlanta, Miami, London, and Toronto are key gateway cities for connecting flights to Bermuda from most other points of departure, including other U.S. and Canadian destinations, the Caribbean and Latin America, continental Europe, Africa, Asia, and Australasia.

Private Aircraft

The use of private jets by corporations and deep-pocketed individuals worldwide skyrocketed after late 2001, a timesaving trend fueled by the desire to bypass long security lines endured by commercial airline passengers. Often, civilian aircraft use smaller airports, allowing passengers to avoid the congestion of major hubs and access suburban business centers more easily. In Bermuda, the leasing and purchase of private jets can be attributed to the growth of the island's reinsurance market after 9/11.

If the billions of dollars in insurance capital isn't actually visible to the average Bermudian, the daily lineup of sleek Gulfstreams, Hawkers, and Learjets along the airport's

Direct flights to Bermuda's airport travel from the United States, Canada, and Britain.

northern perimeter presents undeniable evidence of the wealth injection. Resident and visiting celebrities (Michael Douglas, John Travolta) have always traveled this way, and today a handful of Bermudians count themselves among such high-income globetrotters. The bulk of private arrivals are corporate, as CEOs of Hamilton-based multinational corporations zip between meetings in New York, Zurich, and London, or host on-island gatherings. While many Bermuda-headquartered companies own executive aircraft, more are opting for lease arrangements, "air shares," or other forms of joint ownership.

Passengers arriving by private jet still have to be checked by Customs and the Department of Immigration, but they are quickly processed in a small, separate terminal at L. F. Wade International Airport in an efficient operation run by a private company, **Bermuda Aviation Services** (BAS, tel. 441/293-5067). Pilots of private planes liaise with BAS prior to departure from mainland airports.

A Bermudian company, **Longtail Aviation** (tel. 441/293-5971, www.longtailaviation.bm), offers executive charter flights aboard Bermuda-registered aircraft based on the island. Established in 1999, the company offers service to North America, the Caribbean, Western Europe, and beyond, aboard its various jets, including a transoceanic Falcon 900, a six-passenger Clifford Citation light jet, and King Air 350 and 200 models.

Cruise Ship

Cruising to Bermuda has been a popular mode of getting to the island since the wintering elite used to journey here aboard elegant steamships from snowbound U.S. cities in the late 1800s. Today, cruise ship passengers to Bermuda are typically American budget travelers, and the season has long switched to summer (avoiding the North Atlantic's fierce winter storms—though hurricane season can still make for turbulent passages). Due to the efficiency of Hamilton-based port agents **Meyer Group of Companies** (35 Church St., Hamilton, HM 12, tel. 441/295-4176 or 441/296-9798, www.meyer.bm) and the well-organized slate of shore excursions, cruising is a good way to experience Bermuda's highlights in just a handful of days.

Cruising is popular, as it offers an all-inclusive package vacation, with transport, meals, and lodging included in a single price. Passengers sleep on board the ship during their Bermuda stopover, and most also eat on board—though flexible dine-around programs are now offered. The cruise ship industry contributes an estimated $90 million to the Bermuda economy through government taxes, on-island purchases by passengers and crew, and shore excursions.

Most excursions from U.S. ports take the form of weeklong cruises, with three and a half days spent in Bermuda. Cruise ships visiting the island have hailed from dozens of different ports in recent years, including Baltimore, Boston, New York, Charleston, Fort Lauderdale, the Azores, Cuba, Puerto Rico, and other Caribbean islands. Of these, a select few serve Bermuda weekly through the summer season, though ships and schedules change each year.

Most cruise ships visiting Bermuda no longer berth at Hamilton or St. George's, but at Dockyard, where the Heritage Wharf and King's Wharf terminals were built in 2009 to accommodate the trend toward larger vessels.

In 2015, some 135 cruise calls were projected, with 366,000 cruise visitors arriving via both occasional callers and regular contract ships. The latter included: ***Summit*** from Cape Liberty, New Jersey (Celebrity Cruises, www.celebrity.com); ***Liberty of the Seas*** from Cape Liberty, New Jersey, and ***Grandeur of the Seas*** from Baltimore (Royal Caribbean International, www.royalcaribbean.com); and ***Norwegian Breakaway*** from New York and ***Norwegian Dawn*** from Boston (Norwegian Cruise Line, www.ncl.com). Ships such as ***Veendam*** (Holland American Line, www.hollandamerica.com), along with cruises by the Premium Ocean Cruises line, Luxury's Regent Seven Seas Cruises and Silversea

Cruises, MSC Cruises, Princess Cruises, and Carnival Cruise Line were all scheduled to make occasional visits with smaller ships, docking in Hamilton or St. George's.

Numerous other cruise ships, many of them European vessels sailing transatlantic voyages or 10-day or two-week excursions to or from the Mediterranean, schedule briefer stops at Bermuda, typically a one-day or overnight call. These occasional visitors have also included ships of American lines. For updated cruise schedules, with information on specific ships and ports of call, check the **Bermuda Maritime Operations Centre** website (www.marops.bm or www.marine-andports.bm) or contact **Bermuda Tourism Authority** (tel. 800/237-6832, www.gotobermuda.com).

Regularly visiting cruise ships arrive in Bermuda on either Monday or Tuesday morning and depart on Thursday or Friday afternoon. Technology has automated the Customs and Department of Immigration checks; these departments receive the passenger manifests in advance and electronically review them before ships make port. Upon the ship's arrival, Customs officials board for a 30-minute inspection process, including a walk-through with drug-sniffing dogs, before passengers are free to go. Passengers need their ship's identity card—also usable as a credit card and cabin key on some vessels—plus personal ID, such as a driver's license, to reboard the ship.

Shore excursions (including golf, kayaking, snorkeling, yacht charters, walking tours, and bus tours to the Bermuda Aquarium, Museum & Zoo and Crystal Cave) may be booked online via cruise ships' websites or arranged after boarding through vessels' shore excursion desks. Alternatively, visitors can independently book tours and activities when they disembark at Bermuda, including sports or sightseeing options that may not be available on the ship's prearranged slate. If you prefer doing your own thing, this is the best way to go, but be warned: If you have not prebooked your excursions, you run the risk of sold-out tours and zero tee times.

Private Yacht

Bermuda is a strategic port for private yacht traffic sailing and motoring between North America and the Caribbean. Boats head south from all points on the Eastern Seaboard in the early fall, in preparation for key industry boat shows in St. Thomas, Tortola, Antigua, and other islands, and the start of the winterlong charter season in the West Indies. A similar migration occurs in the spring, when yachts return en masse to North American harbors from Florida to Nantucket for the summer. Bermuda is a convenient halfway point on both annual journeys for refueling, provisioning, making repairs, and taking on crew.

Hundreds of yachts also descend on the island for international races held between May and July, either annually or every other year. These include the Charleston Bermuda Race (Charleston, South Carolina, to Bermuda) in May of odd years; the Bermuda Ocean Race (Annapolis, Maryland, to Bermuda) in June of even years; the Newport Bermuda Race (Newport, Rhode Island, to Bermuda) in June of even years, and the Marion Bermuda Race (Marion, Massachusetts, to Bermuda) in June of odd years. The Argo Group Gold Cup in October and International Race Week in June also attract scores of yachters for world-class match racing and International One Design events. Skippers of boats visiting the island during these times but not involved in any of these events should make advance arrangements for berthing and other needs.

Anyone traveling to the island by yacht needs to be acutely aware of ocean safety for the Atlantic crossing and also well attuned to the particular dangers of Bermuda's reef-strewn waters. Centuries of shipwrecks attest to the dangers of the area's tricky channels and necklace of reefs, which, extending up to 10 miles north of the island, are not taken lightly even by veteran mariners.

MAPS AND COMMUNICATIONS

British Admiralty Hydrographic Office charts for the Bermuda area are available from yachting supply or map and travel outlets throughout the United States and Canada. On the island, contact **PW's Marine Centre** (110 Woodlands Rd., Pembroke, tel. 441/295-3232, fax 441/292-5092, www.pw-marine.bm). All charts have been revised and electronically aligned so that satellite positions can be plotted. At the very least, all mariners should have charts depicting offshore beacons and reef areas, as well as major eastern approaches (the Narrows Channel and St. George's Harbour).

The island has one marine radio communications facility. **Bermuda Maritime Operations Centre,** which encompasses the Rescue Coordination Centre (RCC Bermuda) and Bermuda Radio/ZBR (tel. 441/297-1010, fax 441/297-1530, www.marops.bm, INMARSAT C AOR [East] 581-431010110, or INMARSAT C AOR [West] 584-431010120). Duty officers are in 24-hour contact with the U.S. Coast Guard and other sea-air rescue centers in North America, Europe, and the Caribbean, and they maintain a continuous listening watch on international distress frequencies of 2182 kHz, 4125 kHz, marine VHF Channels 16 and 27, and digital selective call frequencies 2187.5 kHz and Channel 70 VHF.

Bermuda Radio also broadcasts navigational and weather warnings and information by voice and Navtex to an internationally published schedule. Radio broadcasts are initially broadcast on 2182 kHz and Channel 16 VHF, before switching to 2582 kHz and Channel 27 VHF. Continuous weather information is also available on VHF Weather Channel 2 (WX 02), frequency 162.4 MHz. Channel 16 VHF is reserved for distress calls, or call and reply. Be sure to stay off VHF Channels 12 (used by piloted ships), 10 (port operations), 22 (Bermuda Marine Police Section), and 70 (digital selective calling). There are no VHF radio-telephone link calls from Bermuda.

Offshore Safety

The **Maritime Operations Centre,** managed by the government's **Marine and Ports Department** (www.gov.bm), advises all ocean-going yachts to stow the following safety equipment onboard:

- An emergency position-indicating radio beacon (EPIRB), preferably one that operates on frequency 406 MHz
- A VHF radio-telephone transceiver capable of 25 watts power output
- A single sideband (SSB) radio-telephone transceiver operating on medium and high frequencies, or satellite telephone
- An ocean-ready life raft designed to hold the total number of crew aboard your vessel, and a survival or "panic" bag containing prepacked rations and other essential items
- A radar reflector
- Parachute rockets, smoke flares, and dye markers
- Some form of auxiliary power
- Sufficient battery power to keep navigation and communication systems operating for several days to cover engine or generator failure

ARRIVING IN BERMUDA

During an approach to Bermuda, all vessels should make and maintain radio contact with Bermuda Radio beginning at 30 miles from the island; duty officers can assist when necessary. Buoys and beacons mark Bermuda's channels, in keeping with international marking systems. Port Hand markers are even-numbered green can buoys, which flash green when lit. Starboard Hand markers are odd-numbered red conical buoys, which flash red when lit.

Private vessels arriving at Bermuda have to obtain clearance (available 24 hours) from **Customs, Immigration, and Health** (eastern end of Ordnance Island, St. George's, tel. 441/297-1226, VHF Channel 16) in St. George's Harbour before venturing to any other part of the island. Fly code flag Q (the yellow quarantine flag) until Customs clearance is granted. The Customs boarding officer, who caters to all three departments, brings aboard all necessary clearance documents and collects a passenger tax of US$35 per person. A valid, machine-readable passport is required.

ANCHORING AND BERTHING

There are safe anchorages in both St. George's and Hamilton Harbours; Bermuda Radio will provide anchorage and berthing instructions, and clearance must be given to shift berth or sail. The **St. George's Dinghy & Sports Club** (24 Cut Rd., St. George's, tel. 441/297-1612, www.stgdsc.bm) can accommodate up to a dozen 100-foot yachts berthed in a Mediterranean mooring style (stern to dock), offering water, electricity, showers, laundry, Internet access, and garbage and waste oil removal. Yachts anchoring in St. George's Harbour are also offered full access to club facilities and can come alongside to fill water tanks ($0.15 a gallon). In Hamilton and the West End, modern facilities, plus water, ice, electricity, and trash disposal are offered by **King's Point Marina** (Dockyard, tel. 441/234-0300), the **Royal Bermuda Yacht Club** (Albuoy's Point, Hamilton, tel. 441/295-2214, www.rbyc.bm), **The Waterfront Marina** (96 Pitt's Bay Rd., Pembroke, tel. 441/295-1233), the **Royal Hamilton Amateur Dinghy Club** (25 Pomander Rd., Paget, tel. 441/236-2250, www.rhadc.bm), and the 59-berth **Princess Marina** (Fairmont Hamilton Princess, dock manager David Carey, tel. 441/705-7431, david.carey@fairmont.com), which opened in late 2014 with state-of-the-art integrated pump-out facilities, custom-metered electrical service, and water distribution for vessels from 30 to 75 feet. Trash pickup can also be arranged through the Corporations of Hamilton (tel. 441/292-1234, docks manager Earl Francis) or St. George's (tel. 441/297-1532). **The Mariner's Club** (22 Richmond Rd., Hamilton, tel. 441/295-5598, fax 441/292-1519) has facilities for naval personnel and other mariners, including a chapel.

MARINE SERVICES AND INFORMATION

Having arrived safely at Bermuda, you will find a wealth of marine services in the ports of Hamilton, St. George's, and Dockyard. Harbour Radio can arrange for emergency repairs. **Fuel** (diesel or gasoline/petrol) is easily available at several waterfront marinas, including **Rubis Dowling's Marine** (1 Penno's Dr., St. George's, tel. 441/297-1914), **Rubis Boaz Island Marine** (Boaz Island, Sandys, tel. 441/234-0128), and **Rubis PW's Waterfront Marine** (Barr's Bay, Hamilton, tel. 441/295-3185). For bulk fuel orders, contact **Rubis of Bermuda** (tel. 441/297-1577, www.rubis-bermuda.com) to supply duty-free fuel via dockside pipeline or tank truck to its all-weather bunkering facility at Ireland Island, Sandys. Canvas repairs are done by **Dockyard Canvas Co.** (Royal Naval Dockyard, tel. 441/234-2678) and **Ocean Sails/Doyle Sailmakers Bermuda/Ocean Electronics** (60 Water St., St. George's, tel. 441/297-1008, fax 441/297-8330, www.oceansails.com). Rigging is handled by **Triangle Rigging** (tel. 441/297-2155, www.trianglerigging.com). Engine and other repairs can be handled by **West End Yachts** (10 Smithery Ln., Royal Naval Dockyard, Sandys, tel. 441/234-1303 or 441/703-1307, www.westendyachts.com), **PW's Marine Centre** (Pembroke, tel. 441/295-3232, www.pwbda.com), **Bermuda Marine Supply & Services** (72 Pitts Bay Rd., Pembroke, tel. 441/295-9950, www.marinelocker.bm), **Anfossi Marine** (17 Mill Creek Rd., Pembroke, tel. 441/292-8001, anfossimarineltd@ibl.bm), **Offshore Yachting & Maintenance** (83 Harbour Rd., Red Hole, Paget, tel. 441/236-9464, www.oymbermuda.com) and **Mills Creek Marine** (17 Mill Creek Rd., Pembroke, tel. 441/292-6094, www.millscreekmarine.bm).

Bermuda Yacht Services (Mark Soares, 9 Ordnance Island, St. George's, tel. 441/297-2798, www.bermudayachtservices.com) offers a 24-hour offshore emergency service and is also a one-stop shop sought out by visiting sail and motor yachts for arranging everything from marine salvage, towing, and yacht-sitting to fuel-brokering or provisions; check its website for anchorage charts, weather forecasts, and pre-arrival questionnaires for download.

The Customs clearance center for yachts on Ordnance Island in St. George's provides four-day forecast charts, tropical warnings, and Gulf Stream analysis. Pre-sail weather briefings can be booked from the **Bermuda Weather Service meteorologist** (tel. 441/293-5067). For emergencies in port, contact Bermuda Radio or call 911 for police, fire, or ambulance services. A detailed outline of marine regulations and resources can be found in Ralph Richardson's *Bermuda Boater,* published in 2004. The **Bermuda Tourism Authority** (tel. 441/296-9200, www.gotobermuda.com, contact@bermudatourism.com) also publishes a comprehensive resource booklet for private yacht travelers.

GETTING AROUND

"This is one of the last refuges now left in the world to which one can come to escape such persons," read a 1908 petition against allowing cars (and their drivers) in Bermuda. The petition was signed by Mark Twain and Woodrow Wilson, among other Bermudaphiles, who staged a successful lobby against the noisy onslaught of 20th-century transport. Alas, such quaint hopes for tranquility are long gone from Bermuda's now-frantic roads. The influence of celebrity visitors managed to keep out automobiles until as late as 1946, but since then, Bermudians have proven as hungry for four-wheeled convenience as anyone else. There are certain restrictions, including a limit of one car per household and a maximum vehicle size, though the government has stretched the limits to allow bulkier SUVs and Cabriolet convertibles. Given the ever-increasing congestion, it's understandable that the island has always denied car rentals to visitors.

The rule poses challenges, however, for movement around the island, particularly for families traveling with babies or small children, or anyone who dares not risk the next best option, mopeds and scooters. But public transport via buses and ferries is comfortable, safe, and mostly efficient, and allows a far more leisurely appreciation of Bermuda's picturesque scenery than could be had negotiating hairpin turns and dodging local road hogs.

Taxis

Your first experience with Bermuda-style transport will most likely be a taxi ride from the airport to your hotel or guesthouse. Taxi drivers have all airport flights covered like clockwork, so there is rarely a problem getting a cab to where you need to go. When you exit Customs, you will be directed through glass sliding doors to the Arrivals Hall, where taxis line up outside at the curb. (If a resident is collecting you, he or she will be waving at you from the small corral at Arrivals, parked through the door on the right leading from the hall.) All taxis are metered; the government sets the rates, which are as steep as anything else on the island. A 45-minute ride to the hotel-peppered parish of Southampton, for instance, will set you back at least $30. A tip of 15 to 20 percent of the fare is appreciated—and expected, if there's heavy luggage to schlep. Rates are held by law at $6.40 (for up to 4 passengers) or $8 (5-6 passengers) for the first mile and $2.25 (or $2.80) for every additional mile. There is also a surcharge of $1 per piece of luggage. Fares are between 25 and 50 percent higher between midnight and 6am and all day on Sunday and public holidays.

Bermudian taxi drivers are friendly and knowledgeable for the most part, and usually fastidious about cab cleanliness. Some drivers are specifically registered as official tour guides (look for a blue flag atop the vehicle or in its front window, or make a special request from a taxi company or your hotel concierge). For travel to business meetings, the airport, dinner reservations, or any other time-sensitive appointment, prearranging rides hours in advance, or the night before an early flight, is absolutely advisable. Taxis can take eons to arrive for last-minute reservations islandwide, particularly when it's raining or during peak periods such as Friday and Saturday nights. If you need a taxi in parish extremities such as St. George's or Sandys, calling early is again wise. The island's taxi industry agreed to the installation of global positioning systems (GPS) in vehicles in 2005, but some companies and cabs have since reneged.

If you are touring the parishes, hailing cabs along roadsides rarely succeeds, because most of the ones passing you will already be on calls. Flagging down a passing taxi in Hamilton is more rewarding, and there are also specific cab stands in the city (mainly along Front Street) and at King's Square in St. George's in the busy season. Major hotels always have taxis on hand, and Hamilton's Bermudiana Road, Bermuda's "Restaurant Row," is a sure bet for cabs on Friday and Saturday evenings.

The **Bermuda Taxi Association** (tel. 441/296-2121, www.taxibermuda.com) lists many of the island's major cab companies on its website, including: **Bermuda Industrial Union Co-op** (tel. 441/292-4476, cooptaxi@fkbnet.bm), **Bermuda Island Taxi** (tel. 441/295-4141, www.bermudaislandtaxi.com), and **BTA Dispatching Ltd.** (tel. 441/296-2121, www.taxibermuda.bm).

Transport can be prearranged with reliable independent operators like **Nevis Barboza** (tel. 441/334-8239, prbarboza@logic.bm), **Quinton Bean** (tel. 441/335-4689, quianreu@logic.bm), and **Robert Powell** (tel. 441/337-1558), all Qualified Bermuda Tour Guides; as well as **Gladstone Brown** (tel. 441/734-7377, gladstone51@hotmail.com); **Lloyd J. Smart** (VIP Taxi Service, tel. 441/534-8688, lsmart@northrock.bm); **Roger Vanderpool** (tel. 441/334-7665, rajav2k4@yahoo.com); **Nesbitt's Taxi Service** (tel. 441/333-0156 or 441/337-3411, cnesbitt@logic.bm); and **Hodgson's Taxi Service** (tel. 441/534-8095). **First Step Taxi Service** (tel. 441/735-7151, rogersberlyn51@hotmail.com), with driver Berlyn Rogers, has a wheelchair-accessible vehicle.

Two companies cater specifically to airport transportation: **Bermuda Triangle Tours** (tel. 441/293-1334 or 441/293-5806, fax 441/293-1335, www.bermudahosts.bm) offers airport meet-and-greet, golf tours, restaurant drop-off and pickup, and three- and six-hour sightseeing trips, with minibuses able to handle groups. **Bee Line Transportation Bermuda** (tel. 441/293-0303, 9:30am-5pm daily, www.beelinetransportltd.com) offers shuttles and bus and taxi tours. John Powell of **Island Transfers** (tel. 441/734-8260, fax 441/236-0074, islandtran@ibl.bm) caters to special prearranged transport requests, particularly those of visiting corporate travelers, with his fleet of six-seater vans, many chauffeured by ex-police or prison officers. He also has wheelchair-accessible vans, able to transport groups of up to nine passengers in wheelchairs.

Buses

Aside from perennial complaints about a few drivers' unfortunate lack of people skills, the island's bus service generally wins positive reviews from visitors and is also well used by locals, including resident schoolchildren, who can ride free. Routes cover the main roads and neighborhoods of the entire island, and vehicles are well maintained and air-conditioned. Strollers can be stowed in a rack at the front, and drivers are usually more than willing to alert you to your desired stop.

The candy-pink diesel fleet operates from the **Hubert W. "Sparky" Lightbourne Central Bus Terminal** (Washington St. at Church St., Hamilton, tel. 441/292-3851 weekdays), where passes, tokens, and books of tickets, plus routes and fare information, can be found. From here, buses travel east and west with numerous stops along the way. If you want to save time, opt for the fast ferries instead; buses take an hour between Hamilton and Dockyard, for example, compared to a breezy 20-minute journey across the Great Sound. But buses offer a slice of workaday Bermudiana you won't necessarily find on customized tours or taxi rides. Local custom demands Bermudians boarding the bus call out an all-inclusive "good morning!" or "afternoon!" to the driver and seated congregation as they choose their seat. Students in their various school uniforms pile on board later in the afternoon, as buses take them home or to Hamilton. And views of the South Shore beaches and other scenic areas are worth the long journeys and sometimes-lurching movement as buses stop and start their way through the parishes. For more peaceful trips, avoid the rush hour and travel between 9am and 3pm or after 5:30pm

For foreigners confused by the island's drive-on-the-left rule, bus stop poles offer color-coded clues to let you know which side of the road to stand on. Neon pink poles indicate a route inbound to Hamilton; the electric blue ones mean passing buses are headed out from the city. One rule all drivers enforce: Exact fare (coins only) is needed, so no change is given. Passes, tokens, and tickets are more economical if you plan to make frequent use of the bus or ferry to get around during your stay. The useful Transportation Pass is available for one day ($15), two days ($25), three days ($35), four days ($44), seven days ($56), one month ($55), or three months ($135) of unlimited use, allowing you to get on and off buses and ferries as many times as you wish. These are also sold at the ferry and bus terminals, and other authorized outlets.

There are 11 routes covering the island, on most of which buses run every half hour throughout the day. Morning start times vary according to route, but service begins as early as 6:15am and generally runs until around 6:30pm weekdays. The exceptions are routes 7, 8, and 11, serving Southampton, Dockyard, and St. George's, which keep running until 10pm or 11pm There are curtailed schedules and fewer buses on weekends and holidays. Fares are based on 14 zones and priced accordingly (each zone is about two miles long). Fares are either $3 or $4.50 (for Hamilton to Dockyard, St. George's, or Hamilton Parish), but special passes and books of tickets cost less per ride. Children under five, resident seniors, and local school students ride free. Routes, fares, schedules, and running times can be found in public transport brochures available at Visitor Information Centres, or contact the **Public Transportation Board (PTB)** (26 Palmetto Rd., Devonshire, DV 05, tel. 441/292-3851 weekdays, fax 441/292-9996). **Tours and group charters** (tel. 441/292-6704, prowland@ptb.bm) can also be arranged.

Ferries

Bermuda's ferry service, **Sea Express** (www.marineandports.bm), is fast and efficient, encouraging an increasingly large number of locals to use the boats to commute to work. Four "fast ferries"—two-tier air-conditioned, hovercraft-like vessels—practically fly over the Great Sound to Dockyard and along the North Shore to St. George's. For the nostalgic, the clunky old iron black-and-white ferries, *Georgia, Corona,* and *Coralita,* still chug along the Hamilton/Paget/Warwick route, while the veteran *Deliverance* and *Patience* make occasional scenic milk runs along the Somerset shore several times a day in the summer.

The four ferry routes are divided by color: The popular and busiest Blue Route (which also takes scooters aboard) runs between Hamilton and Dockyard; the Pink Route serves the quieter stops of Paget and Warwick; the Green Route, an express service geared mainly to West End commuters, serves Rockaway, Southampton; and the Orange Route travels between Hamilton, Dockyard, and St. George's. The latter represents a wonderfully scenic—and hassle-free—way to do a day trip to the East End. You can take your scooter on board for an extra $4, allowing you to explore the parish by scooter once you get there. Due to budget cutbacks, high-season departures to St. George's were cut to just three daily May-November from Hamilton via Dockyard and back. In the winter, an early-morning ferry travels from Hamilton to St. George's direct and returns in the evening.

The cost of a single fare varies by route; an adult one-way fare to St. George's (via

Dockyard) is $8, from Hamilton to Dockyard it's $4.50, and across the harbor to Paget and back it's just $3. As with the buses, cost-saving transportation passes ranging from one day to three months offer unlimited ferry use. Books of 15 tickets ($30) are also cost-effective for longer vacations. While buses accept exact change, as well as tickets, tokens, or passes, ferry passengers will not be able to board using cash; purchase tickets, tokens, or passes in advance. Children under five and resident seniors ride free. Information, advice, schedules, tokens, tickets, and passes are available at the **Hamilton ferry terminal** (8 Front St., tel. 441/295-4506, 6:30am-8pm Mon.-Fri., 7:30am-6pm Sat., 8:30am-6pm Sun. and holidays). Passes, tickets, and tokens are also sold at the central bus terminal in Hamilton, and at sub-post offices, hotels, and guesthouses.

Scooters and Mopeds

They are fun, fast, and offer the utmost freedom to explore, but you should not underestimate the very real dangers associated with renting mopeds and scooters. Scores of visitors every year end up in the hospital's emergency room for treatment of grazes and gashes—"road rash" in local parlance—which can ruin a vacation. More serious injuries, such as broken limbs and head and back injuries, even fatalities, also occur—nine people were killed on Bermuda's roads in 2013, and a record 17 in 2008—meaning the decision to rent scooters should not be made lightly. The problem is such that cruise ships no longer recommend rental scooters to passengers for liability reasons, though livery reps continue to offer their services at dockside.

For those visitors who choose to rent motorized bikes, note that children under 16 years may not drive motor scooters, though they can sit on the back as passengers—a highly risky proposition for youngsters. All scooter drivers and passengers are required by law to wear safety helmets securely fastened at all times.

Most gas stations are open 7am-7pm daily, though some remain open later. The only 24-hour gas station is **Esso City Automarket** (37 Richmond Rd., Hamilton, tel. 441/295-3776).

RENTALS

There are four liveries. The largest, **Oleander Cycles** (6 Valley Rd., Paget, tel. 441/236-5235, fax 441/236-3916, 24-hour answering service, www.oleandercycles.bm), has several satellite locations: 15 Gorham Road, Hamilton (tel. 441/295-0919, fax 441/292-7336); The Reefs Hotel & Club, South Shore Road, Southampton (tel. 441/238-0222); King's Wharf, Royal Naval Dockyard (tel. 441/234-2764); Blue Hole Hill next to Grotto Bay Beach Resort (tel. 441/293-1010), and 26 York Street, St. George's (tel. 441/297-0478). All are open 8:30am-5:30pm daily. **Smatt's Cycle Livery** (74 Pitts Bay Rd., outside the Fairmont Hamilton Princess, tel. 441/295-1180, fax 441/295-2539, www.smattscyclelivery.com, 8am-5pm daily) has two other outlets—at the Fairmont Southampton Resort (tel. 441/238-7800) and the Rosewood Tucker's Point (tel. 441/298-4085).

Eve Cycles (tel. 441/236-6247, fax 441/236-6996, www.evecycles.com) has three outlets: in Paget (114 Middle Road, tel. 441/236-6247), St. George's (1 Water St., tel. 441/236-0839), and the airport (tel. 441/293-6188). All are open 8am-5:30pm daily. **Elbow Beach Cycles** (Elbow Beach Resort, 60 South Rd., tel. 441/296-2300 or 441/296-8880, www.elbowbeachcycles.com) is based in Paget, but offers scooter delivery and pickup anywhere on the island, including Dockyard's cruise ship wharves.

All liveries offer a free shuttle between their outlets and locations where visitors are staying, and also pick up clients left stranded by broken-down vehicles. They usually have representatives at wharves in Dockyard and St. George's when cruise ships are in port. All scooters and mopeds have 50cc engines with electric start and automatic gears. Rates vary, usually starting at around $50 per day, with special rates for longer rentals, but prices are fairly competitive between the companies and

Scooter Safety

Road traffic accidents (RTAs) are far too common in Bermuda, affecting both locals and visitors. Before you end up a victim of "road rash"—painful grazes after skimming macadam—or far worse, consider these basic safety tips.

- Drive on the *left*, and remember the left-hand rule when turning into junctions and navigating city streets. (Roundabouts, or traffic circles, routinely confuse the uninitiated; to negotiate them without a problem, be sure always to give way to traffic approaching on your right.)
- Wear the helmet provided with your scooter rental. It's the law, but it may also keep you alive in an accident. If you forget, as visitors sometimes do, you will notice locals flagging you down, waving their arms, and pointing at your bare head.
- Bermudians rarely do this, but keep to the speed limit of 35 kilometers per hour (about 22 miles per hour). Take corners especially carefully, and drive defensively at all times: You never know when a local is about to cut across a lane of traffic or throw a car door open in your path. Look out for blind entrances and sharp turns.
- Do not turn around to look at motorists or sights behind you. In a group of scooters touring together, let the slowest driver go in front.
- When it rains, take extra care, as mopeds and scooters skid and slide easily on slick roads. Drive slowly and brake gradually in these conditions, touching the rear brake first. The same goes for areas with sand or oil on the road.
- Many scooter and motorbike riders suffer bad calf burns because their legs touch the muffler. When you dismount your scooter after driving, stay clear of the muffler, which becomes dangerously hot; you should also avoid those of parked scooters when walking between bikes.
- Secure all possessions either inside the scooter compartment or tied with a bungee cord on the rear basket. Bag thefts from bikes are one of the most common island crimes, and you provide an easy target for thieves on bikes if your belongings are not obviously strapped down.
- Park only in legal spaces and lock the scooter, both with its ignition lock and the wheel lock provided. The rental rate insures against accidents, but not theft (though visitors generally do not get nailed for stolen bikes).
- If you do come off and suffer scrapes, Dr. Edward Schultz, head of Bermuda's Emergency Department, recommends treating road rash as you would a second-degree burn: Cleanse gently with saline or clean water, then use cream dressings, changed frequently. Don't use Vaseline or leave wounds open and dry. Swimming, long considered by Bermudians to be a healing factor, actually risks infection, says Schultz. Keep injured areas out of the sun, also, as the skin is more prone to damage.

include delivery and pickup, a basket accessory, mandatory third-party insurance ($20-30), and the all-important helmet and lock.

Bicycles

Bicycles up the adventure quotient for travelers who want exercise with their sightseeing—just bear in mind the high heat and humidity of Bermuda in midsummer and the island's hilly terrain. Nevertheless, increasing numbers of visitors are exploring Bermuda by bicycle, including off-road enthusiasts who enjoy the ever-popular Railway Trail. **Bicycle Works** (13 Tumkins Ln., Hamilton, tel. 441/297-8356, www.bicycleworks.bm) has road bikes (Felt 95, $70 one day, $250 seven days). All the liveries also rent pedal bicycles.

Train Tours

Bermuda lost its railway in the 1940s, but you will still see trains tootling around on the main roads. **The Bermuda Train Company**

(6 Valley Rd., Paget, tel. 441/236-3130, www.bermudatrain.com), owned by Oleander Cycles, uses colorful mini-trains, like large kids' toys, to conduct tours around the City of Hamilton and the Royal Naval Dockyard April-November. Bookings can be made via the **Island Tour Centre** (www.islandtourcentre.com), through your cruise ship, or independently through Oleander. Hour-long historical tours are run from Hamilton (Front Street Flagpole to Bermuda Botanical Gardens and back, $25), and 20-minute shuttles travel from Dockyard to the beaches of Daniel's Head Park (return $15). The open-air carriages allow great sightseeing. Private tours for a minimum of eight passengers can also be booked.

Visas and Officialdom

Air passengers arriving at L. F. Wade International Airport must pass first through Department of Immigration and then Customs controls. There are three separate lines—for Bermudian status-holders, Bermuda residents, and arriving foreigners—all of which can be long and tedious. Criticism is perennially leveled at airport officials and staff of both Customs and Department of Immigration operations. Patience, a friendly demeanor, and the correct paperwork will usually get you through. Know that the island's authorities and its legal system do not differentiate between drug dealers and those who carry small amounts of banned substances for personal consumption; for those who are caught, the penalties are stiff.

DOCUMENTS AND REQUIREMENTS

Passports and Visas

Travelers to Bermuda need a valid, machine-readable passport and a return or onward ticket, or other proof of transportation off the island to a country where right of entry has been granted. Open returns may have a time limit imposed on their length of stay by island Department of Immigration officials. Women traveling under a married name, but with identification documents stating a maiden name, should also bring a marriage certificate or certified copy.

Know the name of your hotel or guesthouse, or the street address of the private home where you'll be staying. Keep the name and address of your accommodation handy for officials. If you are staying at a private residence, don't be surprised if the Department of Immigration officer personally knows your host. As you'll soon find out, the island is a *very* small place.

In 2014, the Bermuda government removed the need for entry visas or visa waivers, assuming visitors carry multi reentry visas (MRVs) for the U.S., Canada, and the U.K., where needed. The change has made for a far smoother immigration process for tourist and business visitors of all nationalities. Check www.immigration.gov.bm or www.gotobermuda.com for updates.

Traveling Children

As well as the relevant travel documents, children who are not traveling with their parents must show a letter from their parent(s) authorizing the child to be accompanied by another adult. Parents traveling with adopted children should bring proper documents for their adopted children. Children entering Bermuda for adoption must carry Department of Immigration paperwork.

Length of Stay

The maximum amount of time a visitor may stay in Bermuda is six months, but only through exceptional circumstances; the standard limit is 90 days. If you wish to extend your length of stay (for example, owners of timeshare or fractional ownership properties), you must apply in person either to

Secondary Immigration Control upon arrival at the airport, or to an Immigration Inspector at the **Department of Immigration Headquarters, Government Administration Building** (30 Parliament St., Hamilton, tel. 441/295-5151, 9am-noon Mon.-Fri.). Travelers cannot enter Bermuda to live, work, or look for work without work permits or other official documentation, nor will they be allowed in for an indefinite period, nor without a return ticket. For more information, check www.immigration.gov.bm.

TAXES AND CUSTOMS

All visitors must fill out a Customs Traveller Declaration (CTD) Form 98, citing any goods and gifts that will be left in Bermuda. Duty is payable on any goods not covered by the island's duty-free allowance. Once you pass through Immigration and collect your baggage, there may be long lines of visitors waiting to clear the Customs Department, especially when several flights arrive at similar times or when crowds of Bermudians are carting back suitcases full of foreign purchases. Make sure you have completed your Customs declaration form. A uniformed officer will either give you the all-clear and wave you through to the exit and ground-transportation stands, or will direct you to the baggage inspection desk.

Taxes

Residents and visitors are equal under Bermuda's Passenger Tax Act, passed in 1972. Passenger taxes are $35 for all air travelers (included in the airfare) and up to a maximum of $60 for cruise ship passengers (collected in advance by cruise lines). Children under the age of two are exempt in both cases.

Duty Free

Visitors are allowed to enter the island with personal clothes and belongings, including sports equipment, cameras, golf bags, 50 cigars, 200 cigarettes, 0.5 kilogram of tobacco, one liter of liquor, one liter of wine, and $30 worth of gifts. Duty of 25 percent will be levied on more than 20 pounds of meat and other foodstuffs brought into the island. There are strict rules governing the importation of plants, fruits, and vegetables, and these require an import permit. Live marine animals are not permitted, but fresh, frozen, or cooked fish or shellfish may be brought in, as long as it contains no algae or seaweed. For more information, visit www.customs.gov.bm.

Animals require proper documentation or they will be returned to their point of origin, since there are no quarantine facilities on the island. They must be accompanied by an import permit issued in advance by the **Department of Environmental Protection** (tel. 441/236-4201, fax 441/232-0046, www.animals.gov.bm),.as well as a health certificate issued within 10 days of the visit by a licensed vet in the animal's home country. For more details on document requirements, contact the department.

Returning Home

Bermuda visitors are allowed to take home duty-free merchandise purchased on the island. U.S. Customs has a pre-clearance facility at L. F. Wade International Airport, so declaration forms must be filled out in Bermuda before your journey home. Forms are available at airlines and travel agencies. **U.S. citizens** (www.cbp.gov) are usually permitted $800 goods allowance after 48 hours, including 200 cigarettes and 100 non-Cuban cigars. The allowance is good every 30 days.

Canadian citizens (www.cbsa.gc.ca) are allowed $50 after 24 hours, $400 after 48 hours, or $750 after seven days. **U.K. citizens** (www.hmrc.gov.uk) can take back £390 worth of purchases from non-EU nations.

Different countries have varying rates of duty on goods carried back above the duty-free limits. Plants should not be taken back without permission from your own country.

FOREIGN CONSULS

Since Bermuda remains a British dependency, no foreign embassies are located here. Instead, relevant business is conducted through

British Embassies in Washington, D.C. (3100 Massachusetts Ave. NW, Washington, DC 20008, tel. 202/588-6500, fax 202/588-7870) and other centers.

British nationals seeking their country's assistance can contact **Government House** (11 Langton Hill, Pembroke, HM 13, tel. 441/292-3600, fax 441/295-3823).

The **United States Consulate in Bermuda** (Crown Hill, 16 Middle Rd., Devonshire, tel. 441/295-1342, fax 441/295-1592, duty phone 441/335-3828 for life-and-death emergencies, http://hamilton.usconsulate.gov, 8am-4:30pm Mon.-Fri. except Bermuda and U.S. public holidays) serves Americans living in and visiting Bermuda, as well as Bermudians and foreign nationals who wish to visit the United States. Photo identification is required to enter the consulate. A small parking lot is located on the adjacent property.

The **Honourary Canadian Consul** in Bermuda is **Heather Conyers** (73 Front St., fourth floor, Hamilton, tel. 441/292-2917, fax 441/292-9307, www.canadians.bm). Bermuda-related matters are also handled by the **Consulate General of Canada in New York** (1251 Avenue of the Americas, New York, NY, 10020-1175, tel. 212/596-1628, fax 212/596-1666, cngny-cs@international.gc.ca).

The **Portugal Consulate** office (Melbourne House, 11 Parliament St., Hamilton, HM 12, tel. 441/292-1039, mail@cnham.dgaccp.pt) is headed by Honorary Consul Andrea Moniz DeSouza, an associate lawyer who works as a direct liaison with Lisbon, processing passport renewals, ID cards, and paperwork authentication. An estimated 10 percent of Bermuda's population is of Portuguese origin, most born in the Azores or to Azorean immigrants or guest workers. Many of Bermuda's Portuguese are children who were born in Bermuda but lack Bermudian status (citizenship) because their parents are not Bermudian—a quandary that confronts any child born on the island to non-Bermudian residents. There is also a steady stream of Azorean contract workers coming to Bermuda, as well as Portuguese Bermudian families on the island who maintain strong links to relatives in the Azores, Madeira, and Portugal.

Eighteen other nations, including Norway, Ireland, Belgium, Austria, Germany, France, Italy, Ghana, Mexico, and Jamaica, are represented by honorary consuls, who maintain diplomatic links with Bermuda via Britain's Foreign & Commonwealth Office. Honorary consul positions are awarded to resident Bermudians who are natives of or have strong links to represented countries.

Conduct and Customs

ATTITUDES AND ETIQUETTE

Perhaps due to its British past, the island projects an air of entrenched conservatism, at least on the surface. Loud public demonstrations, big-L liberal sentiments, and overly revealing clothing—or a lack of adequate clothing altogether—do not go down well with most Bermudians. Men and women, both black and white, tend to project a polite reserve upon initial contact—until they've sized you up, anyway. Like their iconic onions, they prefer to reveal themselves gradually.

Generally, things tend to change slowly in Bermuda, including attitudes and the adoption of new ideas. Outsiders are suspect—at least at first. A certain pace and ritual is expected in social encounters: The omission of a requisite "good morning" or "good afternoon" (passkeys to any conversation with locals) can mean the difference between terse unhelpfulness and beaming cooperation. Indeed, there's a darkly humorous local joke that describes how (fictitious) Bermudian air-traffic controllers let a plane crash because the pilot forgets to greet them properly as he makes his descent.

Mostly, playing by the rules goes a long way toward really fitting into the island's sometimes oddball environment—just don't expect Bermudians to consistently do the same. They can be flagrant scofflaws, and nowhere is that more apparent than on the island's roads. Local drivers break all speed limits, double-park to have a chat or grab a takeout, dump trash out their car windows, and overtake on blind hairpin bends at 70 miles per hour. These are the same folks who'll shake their heads and tut-tut in disapproval if someone tells a bawdy joke too loudly in a restaurant or happens to walk down the street in a bikini top.

Punctuality is not as big a problem in Bermuda as it is in more laid-back island nations to the south, but, aside from the corporate circles of Hamilton, locals often tend to avoid being overly fastidious about time. Nor are they too worried about returning phone calls or emails immediately, turning up when they said they would, or delivering what was promised. Yet jobs get done, people make a good living, and the economy ticks around. But when 5 o'clock tolls, Bermudians head for the door. Don't try to achieve anything important toward the end of a workday afternoon, particularly in bureaucratic environments. That goes triple if it's a Friday afternoon before a public holiday weekend. Islanders *love* their holidays, and it really doesn't matter whether it's Christmas or Cup Match (although the latter sees Bermudian frivolity at the extreme); locals are like children in a candy store in the run-up to such festivities. Driving through Hamilton at such times reveals a free-for-all, a cheerful camaraderie that reverberates through "Town," as people wave, shout, honk their horns at each other—and load up on groceries as if Armageddon were about to arrive.

FESTIVALS AND EVENTS

January

Bermuda Festival of the Performing Arts: This six-week evening festival running from mid-January through the end of February brings international dance, drama, comedy, music, and even circus performers to City Hall and Arts Centre, Hamilton, and the Ruth Seaton James Centre for the Performing Arts, Devonshire (www.bermudafestival.org).

Bermuda Marathon Weekend: Hundreds of locals and visitors take part in this mid-January weekend's quartet of

Flying homemade kites is a Good Friday tradition.

events: an international marathon, half-marathon, 10K run and charity walk, and an invitational mile. The 10K starts and finishes at Devonshire's Bermuda National Sports Centre; all other events take place on Front Street, Hamilton (tel. 441/296-0951 or 441/236-6086, www.bermudaraceweekend.com, www.bnaa.bm).

Bermuda Regional Bridge Tournament: More than 200 players fly in for this prestigious seven-day test of bridge skill, hosted by the Bermuda Bridge Federation and held in the last week of January at the Fairmont Southampton Resort (tel. 441/293-5432, www.bermudaregional.com).

February

Bermuda Festival of the Performing Arts: The festival continues through another month in the City of Hamilton and Devonshire (www.bermudafestival.org).

March

Zoom Around the Sound: Organized by the Bermuda Zoological Society, this 7.2-mile walking, running, and bicycling loop race is held mid-month and travels around Harrington Sound to raise money for the Bermuda Aquarium, Museum & Zoo (www.bamz.org).

Bermuda International Film Festival: Award-winning films from around the world are screened at island cinemas for 10 days starting mid-month, along with celebrity appearances and filmmaking workshops. Tickets can be purchased online or from the BIFF box office in Hamilton (www.biff.bm).

April

Bermuda Kite Festival: Kite-flying contests, fish cakes, gombeys, face-painting, bouncy castles, and tug-of-war make for traditional island fun the Friday before Easter at Horseshoe Bay, Southampton (www.gotobermuda.com).

Bermuda Annual Exhibition: Held at Bermuda Botanical Gardens in Paget during the last week of April, this three-day cultural and agricultural showcase, featuring equestrian events, acrobats, and school displays, has become a beloved institution (tel. 441/239-2351, fax 441/236-4182, www.bdaexhibition.bm).

Open Houses and Gardens: The Garden Club of Bermuda's open-house tour is held every Wednesday afternoon for four weeks in a row during April and May, allowing a rare inside look at some of the island's most impressive properties (tel. 441/236-7321).

May

Open Houses and Gardens: The Garden Club of Bermuda's Wednesday afternoon open-house tour continues through May (tel. 441/236-7321).

Bermuda Day Parade: Enjoy Bermuda's daylong version of Caribbean Carnival, held throughout the City of Hamilton on May 24, with highlights being a historical half-marathon and an all-out parade of floats, dancers, and marching bands. Bermuda Day also marks the official first day of summer boating for Bermudians.

Harbour Nights: Evening street festivals in the City of Hamilton (7pm-10pm Wed.), St. George's Market Nights (7pm-10pm Tues.), and Heritage Nights in Dockyard (6:30pm-9pm Thurs.) run through May and June (www.bermudachamber.bm or www.cityhall.bm).

Bermuda Fitted Dinghy Races: Traditional dinghies vie for weekly honors throughout the summer. Races take place every Sunday afternoon in St. George's Harbour, Mangrove Bay, and Granaway Deep (www.rhadc.bm).

Bermuda International Invitational Race Week: Five classes of boats—J105, J24, Lasers, Etchells and International One Designs (IODs)—race for honors in this hotly contested regatta organized by the Royal Bermuda Yacht Club and pitting visiting sailors against local counterparts in the Great Sound (www.biirw.bm).

Public Holidays

New Year's Day	January 1
Good Friday	late March or April
Bermuda Day	May 24
National Heroes Day	mid-to-late June
Cup Match	last Thursday and Friday in July or first Thursday and Friday in August
Emancipation Day	last Thursday in July or first Thursday in August
Somers Day	last Friday in July or first Friday in August
Labour Day	first week of September
Remembrance Day	November 11
Christmas Day	December 25
Boxing Day	December 26

Public holidays falling on a weekend result in public closures of shops and offices on the following weekday. Government offices are closed on public holidays and weekends. For more information on public holidays, contact the **Bermuda Employers Council** (tel. 441/295-5070).

June

Newport Bermuda Race/Marion Bermuda Race: The Newport Bermuda Race, a 107-year-old blue-water sailing contest from Newport, Rhode Island, to St. David's, brings a fleet of maxi-yachts to Hamilton and St. George's Harbours (www.rbyc.bm, www.bermudarace.com). The Marion Bermuda Race, from Buzzard Bay, Massachusetts, to St. David's is for amateur cruising yachts (www.rhadc.bm, www.marionbermuda.com). Run in alternate years, both races bring hundreds of competitors to the island.

National Heroes Day: Different Bermudians who have made history are selected to be honored in this public holiday's parades and tributes.

Harbour Nights: Evening street festivals in the City of Hamilton (7pm-10pm Wed.), St. George's Market Nights (7pm-10pm Tues.), and Heritage Nights in Dockyard (6:30pm-9pm Thurs.) run through the month (www.bermudachamber.bm or www.cityhall.bm).

July

Harbour Nights: Evening street festivals in the City of Hamilton (7pm-10pm Wed.), St. George's Market Nights (7pm-10pm Tues.), and Heritage Nights in Dockyard (6:30pm-9pm Thurs.) run through the month (www.bermudachamber.bm or www.cityhall.bm).

Bermuda Fitted Dinghy Races: Traditional dinghies continue their summerlong Sunday afternoon series at harbors throughout the island (www.rhadc.bm).

Canada Day: Canadians gather at Long Bay, Southampton, on July 1 for barbecues, games, and music to mark Canada's birthday (www.canadians.bm).

Bermuda Big Game Classic: A three-day, big-fish team event in mid-July offers cash and prizes, including a top prize to the largest blue marlin catch (www.bermudabiggameclassic.com).

August

Harbour Nights: Evening street festivals in the City of Hamilton (7pm-10pm Wed.), St. George's Market Nights (7pm-10pm Tues.), and Heritage Nights in Dockyard (6:30pm-9pm Thurs.) run through the month (www.bermudachamber.bm or www.cityhall.bm).

Bermuda Fitted Dinghy Races: Sunday afternoon races at various harbors around the island continue throughout August (www.rhadc.bm).

Beachfest (beachfestbermuda.com) is an all-day beach party organized by the Chewstick Foundation to celebrate Emancipation Day on the last Thursday of July—the start of the island's biggest public holiday, Cup Match. It's an all-day party on Bermuda's most popular beach, Horseshoe Bay, Southampton.

Cup Match (Emancipation Day and Somers Day): This two-day holiday honoring both the abolition of local slavery and Bermuda's founder, Sir George Somers, stages a historic showdown between St. George's and Somerset Cricket Clubs, complete with island-wide campouts, boating, and parties galore.

Bermuda Sand Sculpture Competition: Grownups and kids can get creative and win prizes at this daylong creative contest of hand-crafted architecture at Horseshoe Bay in Southampton, organized by the Bermuda government (tel. 441/295-4597 or 441/295-0855, info@youthandsports.bm, 10am-4pm). Prizes for locals and visitors.

September

Harbour Nights: Evening street festivals in the City of Hamilton (7pm-10pm Wed.), St. George's Market Nights (7pm-10pm Tues.), and Heritage Nights in Dockyard (6:30pm-9pm Thurs.) run through the month (www.bermudachamber.bm or www.cityhall.bm).

Labor Day March and Celebration: Participants including gombeys and majorettes march to Bernard Park in Hamilton for a daylong festival honoring Bermuda's labor movement and organized by the Bermuda Industrial Union (tel. 441/292-0044).

October

TEDxBermuda: Promoting "ideas worth spreading," an annual slate of international and local speakers follow the world-popular TEDTalks format that celebrates cutting-edge concepts in technology, entertainment, and design. Launched in 2011, the independently organized event is held at the Fairmont Southampton and attracts an audience of about 1,000 for the five-hour Saturday afternoon mindfest (www.tedxbermuda.com).

Argo Group Gold Cup: This international event brings the world's top yacht match-racing competitors to vie in a showdown of spinnakers for the sport's oldest trophy, the King Edward VII Gold Cup, in Hamilton Harbour and the Great Sound (www.bermudagoldcup.com).

Zobec Round the Sound Long-Distance Swimathon: Open-water swimmers compete in 10K, 7.25K, 4K, 2K, and 0.8K swims in scenic Harrington Sound, Flatts (tel. 441/236-9586, www.bermudatiming.bm).

November

Queen of Bermuda Triathlon: Launched in 2014, this event (www.memracing.com) attracts local and visiting women, from elites to novices, to compete as individuals or teams in a sprint triathlon comprising an 800-meter swim, 20K ride, and 5K run along the scenic South Shore, as well as a duathlon (1-mile run, 20K bike, 5K run).

World Rugby Classic: International former top rugby players compete in 11 matches in this highly popular weeklong event held at the Bermuda National Sports Centre in Devonshire (tel. 441/295-6574, www.worldrugby.bm).

Remembrance Day Parade and Ceremony: The Bermuda Regiment and Band Company join war veterans in a solemn march down Front Street in the City of Hamilton on November 11, a public holiday.

December

Bermuda Goodwill Golf Tournament: The island's top four golf clubs team up to host this event, which brings golfers from the United States, Canada, and the U.K., with teams made up of one professional and three amateurs (www.bermudagoodwill.org).

Bermuda National Trust Christmas Walkabout: This festive evening street festival takes place the first Friday in December in the Town of St. George. Crowds flock to mingle with friends, sip hot cider, and listen to strolling carolers (www.bnt.bm).

Christmas Boat Parade: Head to Hamilton Harbour to see beautiful illuminated boats of all sorts vie for prizes as they loop the waterfront (www.bermudaboatparade.bm).

Bermuda Musical & Dramatic Society Pantomime: An annual treat for children, the annual BMDS pantomime at Hamilton's City Hall and Arts Centre features the island's amateur actors in a British-style theatrical extravaganza (www.bmds.bm).

New Year's Eve Festival: Revelers ring in the new year at King's Square, St. George's, where live music and a street-festival atmosphere climax with fireworks and the dropping of a giant disco ball-style onion.

Recreation

Bermuda is a recreational playground, thanks to its temperate, year-round climate, well-maintained sports facilities, organized clubs, and spectacular outdoor spaces. Bermudians are devout fans of every sport and hobby—from triathlons to bowling to motocross to soccer, along with trendier activities like paddleboarding, wakeboarding, and beach tennis. While the island, like many other developed countries, suffers its fair share of diet-related ailments, including diabetes and heart disease, much of the population is extremely health-conscious, as is evident by the number of fitness centers, gyms, outdoor fields, pitches, pools, tennis courts, and organized sports events around the island. A few of the latter are international affairs—such as November's World Rugby Classic and January's Bermuda Marathon Weekend—welcoming hundreds of international athletes and spectators annually. Sports fans can check out www.islandstats.com for information and results about local teams in a panoply of sports, including basketball, squash, volleyball, netball, athletics, cricket, soccer, field hockey, darts, softball, rugby, and mountain biking. Bermuda Tourism Authority's website (www.gotobermuda.com), www.bermuda.com, and www.nothingtodoinbermuda.com all carry updated calendars of monthly events.

PARKS AND NATURE RESERVES

Bermuda's open spaces give a fascinating opportunity to enjoy outdoor exercise while viewing eye-popping surroundings and wildlife. National parks and nature reserves throughout the island, owned by the **Bermuda National Trust** (BNT, tel. 441/236-6483, www.bnt.bm) and **Bermuda Audubon Society** (tel. 441/292-1920, www.audubon.bm), offer ocean scenery, woodlands, farm tracts, birdlife, insects, and geology. Contact either of these groups for seasonal information on birding tours and other ecotour schedules. Public parks are open from dawn until dusk, and demand no permits or admission fees. Remember to take only pictures, not plant or animal samples. For more information, contact the Department of Parks (tel. 441/236-5902).

LAND AND MARINE TOURS

If you're considering any type of land or marine tour or activity, your first stop should be the offices or website of the **Island Tour Centre** (Albuoy's Point, 5 Point Pleasant Park, City of Hamilton, tel. 441/236-1300, fax 441/296-4661, www.islandtourcentre.com, 8am-6pm daily summer, 9am-4pm daily winter, plus two outlets in the Royal Naval

Dockyard). The center operates as a centralized booking agent for scores of activities islandwide, from scuba to horseback riding to party cruises and parasailing. Check out the assortment of brochures and flyers at its three outlets, or view, reserve, and pay online.

There's no better way to soak up the essence of Bermuda than on foot. Free organized walking tours are offered in the City of Hamilton, the Town of St. George, and the West End. To check departure times and schedules for all seasonally organized tours, call the **Department of Cultural Affairs** (tel. 441/292-9447) or the **Bermuda Tourism Authority** (tel. 441/292-0023, www.gotobermuda.com). Independent guides also offer a year-round slate of organized and custom tours to suit varied interests, from birding to geology, medicinal plants to architecture. A fourth-generation Bermudian and Certified Bermuda Ambassador, Ashley Harris wins rave reviews for her company, **Hidden Gems** (tel. 441/704-0999, www.bermudahiddengems.com, 7 hours $150, 12 years-plus) which leads all-inclusive, year-round ecotours that take adventurous visitors from jungles to cliff-jumps to caves and the top of a lighthouse. Trekkers are given a backpack with any needed equipment, including lunch, snacks and water.

Byways Tours (tel. 441/535-9169, www.bermudafootsteps.com) is run by Heidi Cowen, a fifth-generation Bermudian and granddaughter of a lighthouse keeper. Accompanied by her spaniel, Buddy, in a mini-bus that can transport eight, she offers all kinds of explorations, including an end-to-end Island Tour with picnic lunch and a beach or park stop (about 5 hours, $100 per person, $50 for kids ages 6 to 10, lunch included, cash payment only). Family tours, history tours, and a Bermuda flora tour are other favorites (1.5 to 2 hours, $50 per person); many include stops for snacks or photos at places only a true Bermudian would know. She posts her daily observations on Facebook.

Antiques dealer, natural history buff, and former schoolteacher Tim Rogers of **Bermuda Lectures & Tours** (tel. 441/238-0344, trogers@northrock.bm) takes visitors on custom tours around the island. The U.K. native, a Bermuda resident for 20-plus years, is knowledgeable about Bermuda's plants, animals, architecture, and cultural history. He often uses the Railway Trail for tours to explore all these topics. Standard hourly fees are $80 for a maximum group of six people.

Educator Robert Chandler of **Discovery Walking Tours** (tel. 441/335-4944, rkchandler@ibl.bm, all tours two hours, $45 per adult for groups of more than four people; $80 per hour for fewer than four) leads islandwide guided walking tours, flora and fauna tours of national parks, cultural tours, and custom tours by request. With an environmental focus, his tours include Hog Bay Park, Blue Hole Park, and the South Shore beaches and dunes as favorite sites.

For those who prefer to do their own thing, most of the island is easily walkable—though certain areas are short on sidewalks. To get away from main roads, hike the **Railway Trail,** today part of the National Parks System, or meet up with the **Walking Club of Bermuda** (contact Laura Gorham, tel. 441/737-0437, www.walk.free.bm), which gets together every Sunday morning at a different location for a six- to seven-mile hike, with cut-off points for those who don't want to go the full distance.

Don't forget that much of Bermuda's biodiversity is marine, not terrestrial; half-day and full-day marine tours can be arranged through several museums, conservation groups, and respected outfitters. The **Bermuda Zoological Society** (tel. 441/293-2727, ext. 2138, http://bamz.org) offers whale-watching and turtle-spotting tours, nighttime glowworm outings, and boat trips to North Rock and other spectacular seamount reefs for snorkeling.

SCUBA AND SNORKELING

Fantasea Bermuda (tel. 441/236-1300, fax 441/236-8926, www.fantasea.bm) offers snorkel, kayak, reef-fishing, and glass-bottomed boat excursions departing from Dockyard, along with one- and two-tank dives as a five-star PADI center.

Blue Water Divers and Watersports (www.divebermuda.com) organizes boat dives and snorkel charters from its Somerset Bridge Dive Centre, Robinson's Marine, Sandys (tel. 441/234-1034).

In the East End, **Blue Hole Watersports** (Grotto Bay Beach Resort, 11 Blue Hole Hill, tel. 441/293-2915 or 441/293-8333, ext. 37, www.blueholewater.bm) rents paddleboats, kayaks, snorkel gear, sailboats, and motorboats—all the ingredients for a fun day out around Ferry Reach or Castle Harbour.

Triangle Diving (Grotto Bay Beach Resort, 11 Blue Hole Hill, tel. 441/293-7319, www.trianglediving.com) is a five-star PADI dive center offering certification and advanced courses, night dives, one- and two-tank dives, and private charters.

Perhaps the island's most stunning snorkeling site is at **North Rock,** about nine miles off the North Shore, where an area of extremely shallow (4- to 30-foot deep) reef extends from a rocky outcrop that supports a large beacon warning off approaching ships. Swim down through wide avenues of reef, populated with giant sea fans, corals, anemones—and crowds of every kind of Bermuda fish species. The site inspired a 140,000-gallon tank exhibit by the same name at the Bermuda Aquarium. To protect the reef, just two moorings are located here and several operators take trips throughout the summer. One great expedition is organized by the **Bermuda Zoological Society,** which schedules four-hour weekend afternoon outings to North Rock and back aboard its research vessel, *Endurance* (check www.bamz.org or www.islandtourcentre.com for details).

For details on more individual operators, see the **Bermuda Tourism Authority**'s website (www.gotobermuda.com). The compact size of the island allows you to maximize your exploring by land or by sea; you can float over parrotfish in the morning, inspect mangrove dragonflies in the afternoon, and still have time to enjoy a spa treatment or some retail therapy.

Most operators rent all the equipment you need, but if you want your own, pay a visit to **CB Dive Shop** (15 Burnaby Street, Hamilton, tel. 441/292-3839, 9am-5pm Mon.-Sat.) for water shoes, masks, fins, snorkels, and wetsuits by top brands.

DEEP-SEA FISHING

Bermuda lies in the path of migrating schools of many species of fish, including tuna and wahoo. More than 27 varieties of game fish, including yellowfin and blackfin tuna, mahimahi, wahoo, great barracuda, amberjack, shark, and marlin can be found in local waters. From June through September, blue and white marlin are plentiful; blues can range up to a whopping 1,350 pounds. Wahoo tend to run early (May), while schools of marlin and tuna arrive later (September and October).

Located off the island's southwest end, Argus and Challenger Banks are remnants of volcanic peaks that formed Mount Bermuda millions of years ago. The sides of these banks, dropping from 30 to 600 fathoms in just a few hundred feet, create a plentiful fishing ground, particularly the shallow plateaus where small baitfish come to feed—attracting larger fish seeking prey near the edges of the banks. Weather and tide action determine the type of fishing here, but bottom fishing, trolling (with depth sounders and "fish finders"), and drift fishing are all practiced. One of the more unusual fishing methods is blue-water fly-fishing, in which flying fish bait is rigged to a kite, popping the fish in and out of the water—a tempting lure for tuna.

Numerous sport-fishing vessels operate in Bermuda. Details can be found in the Bermuda Yellow Pages (www.bermudayp.com), or through the Bermuda Tourism

Authority (www.gotobermuda.com), the **Bermuda Sportfishing Association** (tel. 441/295-2370), **Seahorse Anglers Club** (David Pantry, tel. 441/236-8451, www.seahorseanglers.com), **Blue Water Anglers Club** (28 E. Broadway, tel. 441/292-5529, info@bwac.bm), or **Bermuda Anglers Club** (tel. 441/293-0875, www.bermudaanglersclub.com). Three events in July, the **Bermuda Billfish Blast** (www.bermudabillfishblast.com), the **Bermuda Big Game Classic** (www.bermudabiggameclassic.com), and the **Billfish Tournament** (www.bermudatriplecrown.com) bring scores of fishing buffs to the island thanks to trophies and cash prizes for winning catches.

Local sportfishers support tag-and-release programs for sharks, tuna, and billfish. Restrictions control minimum weights and lengths for pelagic species like tuna and marlin. Longline fishing is currently not permitted, though the government has suggested it might be in the future. Fishpots are banned; protected species such as turtles, rockfish, and certain grouper cannot be taken; and recreational fishers may not sell fish or lobster. For more information, contact the **Department of Environmental Protection** (tel. 441/293-5600).

You can also line-fish off the rocks on the North or South Shores, or with a rod and reel, though anglers agree there are fewer "big ones" now than there were just decades ago.

Fly Bridge Tackle (26 Church St., Hamilton, across from the central bus terminal, tel. 441/295-1845, fax 441/292-0131, 9am-5pm Mon.-Sat. in summer, closed Mon. in winter) is well stocked with rods, reels, line, bait, tackle, and nets, as well as books on island fishing. Staff are well versed in the tricks of the trade. Bait is also sold at a few waterfront gas stations, including Robinson's Marina at Somerset Bridge and the marina at Flatts Village.

GOLF

Bermuda is one of the world's most golf-dense destinations, thanks to its seven courses—many boasting breathtaking ocean views and championship layouts. For eight years (2007-2014), the island hosted the PGA Grand Slam of Golf, but you don't have to be a world champion to enjoy the game. Balmy temperatures year-round bring golfers of every breed, and even duffers can enjoy the emerald fairways, turquoise horizons, and postgame rum swizzles in history-steeped clubhouses. Renowned golf-course architect Robert Trent

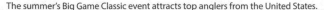

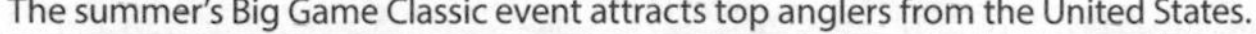
The summer's Big Game Classic event attracts top anglers from the United States.

Jones designed four of Bermuda's courses, including Tucker's Town's premier **Mid Ocean Club,** a par-70, 6,666-yard course over ocean bluffs that's rated one of the world's best links. It was here that Babe Ruth was said to have lost a dozen golf balls attempting to hit a tee shot over Mangrove Lake on the infamous fifth hole, a 433-yard par 4.

While just two of the courses are public, hotel concierges usually have no problem securing tee times for nonmembers at the island's private clubs. Lessons, for adults and kids, can also be arranged. The island also has a couple of driving ranges, plus a 10,000-square-foot practice putting green and short-game area at the tony **Tucker's Point Club.**

Greens fees at Bermuda clubs range from about $80 to $200 and up. Proper golf attire is required, including shirts with collars and sleeves. Women's and men's right- and left-handed golf club sets are available at all courses; balls start at $40 per dozen. Use of golf carts is mandatory at some clubs or on weekends and holidays; caddies are available only at Mid Ocean. Visit www.gotobermuda.com to tour links, learn about tournaments, arrange vacation packages, or schedule a tee time up to a year in advance.

SAILING

Sailing is a time-worn tradition in Bermuda, and young islanders continue to make their mark in international competitions every year. Local associations for different boat types stage regattas and races featuring International One Designs, Fitted Dinghies, Lasers, Optimist Dinghies, Etchells, Bytes, Comets, J-24s, and J-105s from March to November in Hamilton Harbour and the Great Sound. Hundreds of foreign and local yachts also race to Bermuda—from Newport, Rhode Island, or Marion, Massachusetts—on alternate years in a pair of historic events.

International Race Week in June attracts top skippers from all over the world. The Argo Group Gold Cup in October brings professional sailors to compete for the oldest match-race trophy in the world in an exciting weeklong showdown.

Local yacht clubs include the **Royal Bermuda Yacht Club** (tel. 441/295-2214, www.rbyc.bm), the **Royal Hamilton Amateur Dinghy Club** (tel. 441/236-2250, www.rhadc.bm), the **St. George's Dinghy Club** (tel. 441/297-1612, www.stgdsc.bm), and **Sandys Boat Club** (tel. 441/234-2248, www.sandysboatclub.com).

For details on races, contact any of the clubs or the **Bermuda Sailing Association** (tel. 441/295-7935, www.bermudasail.bm).

HORSEBACK RIDING

Taking a horseback ride through parkland, tribe roads, and across beaches can be a leisurely way to see Bermuda. Warwick's **Spicelands Equestrian Centre** (50 Middle Rd., west of Warwick Pond, tel. 441/238-8212, www.spicelandsriding.com) offers lessons and horseback outings. For harness-racing excitement, visit the **National Equestrian Centre** (48 Vesey St., tel. 441/234-0485 or 441/505-0903, www.bef.bm) in Devonshire on Sunday afternoons through the winter season, when pony-trap owners vie for bragging rights.

Former track star Michael Watson's other love has always been horseback riding, specifically Western saddle, and he appears regularly at island equestrian competitions in full cowboy regalia. His tours, through **Mike Watson's Western & English Horse Riding** (tel. 441/234-6773 or 441/747-7433), take visitors along the Railway Trail and through the maze of beach dunes in South Shore National Park.

In the East End, **Bermuda Horse Trail Ride** (Moran Meadows, 7 Salt Spray Lane, tel. 441/537-0400, www.bermudahorsetrailride.com, bdatrailride@gmail.com, Mon.-Sat. only, ages 7-plus) offers private rides (1 hour $130, 1.5 hours $170) for groups of two or three family or friends, along coastal routes near Fort St. Catherine, Tobacco Bay, and the St. George's Club golf course, and along the parish beaches in winter.

TENNIS

Bermuda boasts more than 100 clay and hard-surface tennis courts, making the sport a true national pastime. Indeed, Bermudian Mary Outerbridge went down in the history books for introducing the game to America in 1874; she took a racquet, balls, a net, and rulebook with her on a visit to New York and was allowed to design a tennis court on the grounds of the Staten Island Cricket Club, the first such court in the nation.

Most Bermuda hotels have courts, many lit for night play, as well as resident pros who offer clinics and private lessons (average rate is $50 per half hour). Proper tennis attire is required at most courts. Racquets can be rented and restrung at several centers.

Players will find September through June to be the best months for play, as heat and humidity make midday play, at least, debilitating throughout the summer. A panacea might be beach tennis—a fast-paced combo of tennis and volleyball played out on the sand—which made its island debut in 2008, with international stars competing and demonstrating the sport.

The government-owned W. E. R. Joell Tennis Stadium in Pembroke is a popular venue for lessons, games, and local tennis championships. For more information, contact the **Bermuda Lawn Tennis Association** (tel. 441/296-0834, fax 441/295-3056, www.blta.bm).

ATHLETICS AND TRIATHLONS

Running clubs took root in Bermuda in the 1970s, and the sport has been going strong ever since. On an island where some sports tend to split the population by race, it is also one of the few whose events have always brought together Bermudians of all ethnic and socioeconomic backgrounds. Visitors are always welcome, too. Road races are held September-June, usually on Sunday mornings, most of them sanctioned by the **Bermuda National Athletics Association** (BNAA, 15 Brunswick St., Hamilton, P.O. Box DV 397, Devonshire, tel. 441/296-0951, www.bnaa.bm), an affiliate of the International Association of Athletics Federation (IAAF). Race dates and details are posted on the websites of the Bermuda National Athletics Association (BNAA), as well as the **Mid-Atlantic Athletic Club** (MAAC, www.maac.bm), which also organizes evening and weekend fun runs, and **Bermuda Timing Systems** (tel. 441/236-9586, www.racedayworld.com).

Bermuda runners comprise all abilities, from joggers seeking a sociable outing to former elite Olympic Trials competitors. Many take part in major events overseas, including the Boston, New York, Marine Corps, Chicago, Toronto, and London marathons, and ultra distance events.

The highlight of the racing calendar is January's **Bermuda Marathon Weekend** (www.bermudaraceweekend.com), which incorporates a Friday mile event on Front Street, followed by a Saturday 10-kilometer race and a Sunday half-marathon and marathon.

Triathlon is also a highly popular sport in Bermuda, with weekend events throughout the fall and spring, kids' training clubs, and local athletes competing in Ironman events worldwide. Two Bermudians, Tyler Butterfield and Flora Duffy, are also currently competing on the world pro circuit; Butterfield placed seventh in the 2013 Ironman World Championship in Kailua-Kona, Hawaii, while Duffy won the 2014 X-Terra World Championship in Hawaii. For more information on events, contact the **Bermuda Triathlon Association** (www.bermudatriathlon.com).

SPECTATOR SPORTS

Even if you don't participate in Bermuda's recreational scene, you're spoiled for choice as a spectator. From road races to cycling, fitted dinghies to pony-racing or kitesurfing, you can enjoy any number of sporting events from the sidelines year-round. The island's truly "national" sports are soccer and cricket, and you can savor the essence of Bermudian life at any weekend game, where a festive atmosphere prevails.

Cricket matches featuring local teams are played on weekends from April to mid-September all over the island. The highlight, of course, is the annual Cup Match, played over two days in July or August since 1902. For more information, contact the **Bermuda Cricket Board** (tel. 441/292-8958).

Introduced by British military garrison soldiers in the 1800s, the game of **football (soccer)** has become the island's winter obsession. Matches are played on weekends and some weeknights in season (Sept.-Apr.). Contact the **Bermuda Football Association** (tel. 441/295-2199, www.bermudafa.com) for details.

Rugby (Bermuda Rugby Football Union, tel. 441/338-2952, www.bermudarfu.com) is also a highly popular sport, and weekend matches are well attended. The not-to-be-missed World Rugby Classic every November features former top players from around the world playing in 11 international matches.

The **Bermuda Bicycle Association** (tel. 441/291-5435, www.bermudabicycle.org) organizes road races, mountain bike trail races, time trials, and other special events throughout the year. Amateurs and visiting professionals compete in September's Bermuda Grand Prix, with a weekend of events including a time trial, circuit race, and criterium.

For a more leisurely spectator experience, drop by Elbow Beach in Paget or Shelly Bay Beach in Smith's on a windy day and watch daredevil **kitesurfers** catching air in apparent slow motion as they crisscross the rollers for hours on end.

Accommodations

Travelers to Bermuda have a choice of luxury resorts, quaint cottage colonies, guesthouses, self-catering apartments, or bed-and-breakfasts. The range of accommodations is only matched by the vast price range, from as low as $100 a night for a double room in high season to a $7,500 boutique suite. Generally, most of the resort hotels offer average rooms in the $300-400-a-night price bracket, compared to the $175-250 range of smaller, independent properties. Summer's rates (high season, Apr.-Oct.) are higher than winter's (Nov.-Mar.). There has been a constant demand over the years for more affordable places to stay in Bermuda, and that call is now increasingly being met by local residents who are renting out rooms, attached apartments, or separate cottages on their properties for far more reasonable rates than those charged by the hotel industry. Some of these are in beautiful homes or historic landmark properties, including several owned by the Bermuda National Trust. Visitors who seek something more private or unusual than a standard hotel, or who don't mind staying in less-than-five-star surroundings, should check www.airbnb.com, www.vrbo.com, www.bermudarentals.com, or www.bermudagetaway.com, which all list scores of well-managed guest accommodations ranging from private villas with swimming pools to pullout-sofa studios. Most of these fall below the radar of the Bermuda Tourism Authority's official listings or permit designation (only properties with six or more units require government inspection and licenses).

The global recession hit hard at the island's existing hotels and also shelved several plans for new resorts or redevelopments due to financing woes. Yet some projects have moved forward, notably a $90 million refurbishment of the Fairmont Hamilton Princess and a new boutique venture on the site of the former Pink Beach Club.

The key to choosing a place to stay in Bermuda lies in recognizing the type of vacation you want, as well as the style of accommodations you prefer. Because it's easy to

Camping Out

Crowds of locals lounging under roadside tarpaulins, blasting their stereos and barbecuing four-course meals—no, it's not squatters or a sudden outbreak of homelessness, just the start of camping season, Bermudian-style.

The island may lack North America's natural drama and absolute serenity of the great outdoors, but camping is a beloved summer ritual nonetheless. True, it's difficult to retreat far from the madding crowd on an island with so little undeveloped land, but for islanders, that's not really the point. Bermudians simply enjoy the change of scenery and routine, coupled with the camaraderie of outdoor living, even if they do take all the comforts of home with them—everything including the kitchen sink.

"I saw one guy with his laptop and a 52-inch TV, which he was running from the battery of his dump truck," recalls Craig Burt, of the Department of Parks. "Bermudians don't like to leave anything behind."

Come July and August, particularly the four-day Cup Match public holiday that falls between these months, Bermudians set up camp all over the island—in public parks, on roadsides, and along the South Shore dunes. At the height of camping season, virtual tent villages sprawl along the North Shore waterfront, along Kindley Field Road at Ferry Reach, between Warwick Long Bay and Horseshoe Bay, and everywhere in between. Whole families turn out, with camping accoutrements and picnic fare galore, to swim, rest, spend time with friends and relatives, wave to passing traffic, and generally enjoy time off work.

Camping is, however, restricted to Bermuda residents; all island visitors must be registered at a local hotel, guesthouse, cruise ship, or private residence—though, perhaps, if a visitor was staying with locals at a private residence, they could partake in this beloved ritual and join the bevy of tents under the subtropical stars.

cover the whole island, regional preferences are perhaps less important than, say, whether you plan to spend every day on the beach or shop till you drop. Most Bermuda properties are on Facebook, or have websites featuring photos of rooms and amenities, rates, and full descriptions of facilities.

Reservations

Early reservations are highly recommended for all accommodations. Popular hotels and resorts book quickly in the summer months, especially thanks to the phenomenon, typical for Bermuda, of repeat visitors who stake a claim on their accommodations up to a year in advance. Smaller properties or tiny rentals with just one or two rooms also get booked up quickly. For large properties, you may encounter better deals, including air-and-hotel package options, online; family-run properties with just a few rooms are best contacted directly. Check the Bermuda Tourism Authority's website (www.gotobermuda.com) and www.bermuda.com for full listings of most of the island's major hotels and guesthouses.

Rates

Rates go up during the high season (Apr.-Oct.), typically by a third, but sometimes are double the winter rates (Nov.-Mar.). With smaller properties, check whether quoted rates are double occupancy or per person. Beyond the quoted room rate, expect to pay a government tax of 9.75 percent and a 10 percent gratuity or a housekeeping or service charge. Other extra fees might include an extra-person charge, if you're adding a bed, or an extra charge for children, though most kids sleep free. Properties have different deposit requirements and cancellation policies; make sure you know the details before booking. All resorts and major hotels, and most guesthouses, accept major credit cards. Some private residences or apartment rentals only accept cash or travelers checks.

ACCOMMODATION TYPES

Bed-and-Breakfasts

A very cost-effective way to enjoy a Bermuda vacation, bed-and-breakfasts usually comprise a room in a private home or a historic property, with either a private or a shared bathroom. Breakfast is included in the rate and ranges from continental croissants to "FEB" (full English breakfast; for example, bacon and eggs). Eating out is normally required for other meals, so this type of accommodation is best suited for short stays.

Private Residences

This is the way to see Bermuda if you are want to live like the locals. Staying in a private home, whether it's a studio apartment beneath the main house or a separate cottage across the lawn, lends a touch of island authenticity you don't get to experience in resorts. More and more residents are offering rentals, including long-term rentals to visiting businesspeople. Don't be surprised to find properties with pools, waterfront docks, beautiful gardens, or historic legacies. Like the larger hotels, these nearly always offer amenities such as air-conditioning (a must in the summer months), self-catering kitchens, barbecues, ironing boards, and cable TV. The downside is that no matter how private the place, it is part of the owner's home, so total freedom and anonymity may be limited.

Inns and Guesthouses

Bermuda has many inns and guesthouses, some in historic or picturesque neighborhoods, others on the water or featuring a pool. Doubles with king- or queen-size beds and private bathrooms inside a large homestead are the norm. Some allow for self-catering with kitchenettes (mini-fridge, microwave, toaster oven, and hot plate); others allow guests to share kitchen facilities. Breakfast, baked goods, and afternoon tea are sometimes served.

Apartments and Cottages

The island has numerous apartment and private cottage rentals that are not part of a local family's property, thereby offering total privacy. Some are stand-alone cottages located on estates in tony neighborhoods—upscale rentals in the $300-400 range for summer double occupancy. Others are less expensive, with several apartments arranged around a pool. All are self-catering, with kitchens and barbecues, but maid service is usually included.

Cottage Colonies

These quaint throwbacks to the elegant vacations of the 1950s and '60s are fast disappearing. The successful ones are upscale properties, with on-site spas, pools, putting greens, beaches, dining rooms, and concierge services. They feel almost like a private club and often lay claim to beautifully manicured estates dating back many decades. The more casual, cost-saving variety are regrettably a thing of the past.

Small Hotels

Repeat visitors swear by the island's small hotels, which often seem to offer as much in the way of luxurious amenities as their bigger counterparts. Spas, high-end restaurants, and designer bathrooms are slowly becoming the norm for many of these. Yet they retain an intimate feel and connection with staff and other guests, which many visitors to the island like to experience.

Resort Hotels

Bermuda's major resort hotels are almost all beachfront or harborfront—or, at the very least, have impressive views of the ocean. Most offer pools, tennis courts, putting greens, spas, beauty salons, social desks or concierges, multiple restaurants, room service, porters, nightclubs, entertainment, scuba and water-sports centers, and kids' activity clubs during the high season. Some have a golf course on-site, or rights at sister properties. Failing all else, the concierge can arrange pretty much anything.

Food and Drink

BERMUDIAN CUISINE

Is there a true Bermudian cuisine? Gourmands might snigger at such a proposition, but Bermuda has claimed its repertoire of hallmark dishes—usually a melting pot of items from other places adapted for local menus. The amalgam of British, West Indian, African, and Portuguese cultural influences has created a somewhat eclectic collection of local dishes. Many are pure comfort food, and probably not the best for waistlines or arteries, but they are usually delicious. British cuisine has donated fish 'n' chips, shepherd's pie, steak pies, and teatime desserts like scones, pound cake, trifle, and lemon meringue pie. Slavery's legacy is seen in dishes once rejected by Bermudian white society for their poor-man simplicity but now embraced in the fanciest restaurants; these include cassava and farine pie (made from root vegetables), peas 'n' rice and johnnycakes (common in the Caribbean), fried chicken legs, fried fish sandwiches (made with local catches like grouper or rockfish), butter-baked lobster, macaroni 'n' cheese, and sweets like macaroons, gingerbread, and coconut cake. The immigration of Azoreans over the past 150 years has entrenched certain dishes and snacks into the island's culinary lexicon. Portuguese chourico (spicy sausage) and *malacadas* (deep-fried doughnuts) are the most common examples, found islandwide at corner stores where hot snacks are served.

Restaurants dedicated to these assorted nationalities are good places to sample such dishes. Café Acoreano (Hamilton) is owned and staffed by Portuguese Bermudians. Jamaican Grill (with branches in Bailey's Bay and North Hamilton) is a very popular family-run café-style eatery with jerk meats and West Indian curries. For the ultimate in British fare, head for any of the numerous pubs throughout the island—Henry VIII Pub & Restaurant, in Southampton, and Hog Penny in Hamilton set the standard—or attend an afternoon cream tea served at tearooms like the Heritage Court at the Fairmont Hamilton Princess, Pembroke. Down-home Bermudian restaurants are becoming sparse these days, as upscale eateries take over, but holdouts like The Spot (Hamilton) and Black Horse Tavern Bar and Restaurant (St. David's) remain favorites.

Interestingly, there's been a movement among top chefs over the last decade toward adapting favorite local ingredients and everyman dishes into a more innovative interpretation of Bermudian cuisine on the pricier menus. As a result, there are few top-notch restaurants nowadays that don't serve a gourmet version of Bermudian fish cakes, banana or loquat chutneys, onion tarts, or rum cake. A recent example is star chef and author Marcus Samuelsson, of Harlem's Red Rooster fame, who is incorporating his twist on iconic island dishes into the menu of his panoramic new restaurant opening in 2015 in the Fairmont Hamilton Princess.

Bermuda fish is excellent, from the sweet fillets of snapper and rarer rockfish, to the steaks of fresh-caught tuna, wahoo, and swordfish. Lobsters (the spiny variety) are in season September-March; fishing laws are strict, so you'll see only imported lobster on the menu over the summer months—at least in restaurants. There are no local shrimps, oysters, mussels, clams, or conch, so any of these on local menus have been imported.

Fresh local produce is worth seeking out in season, mainly because imported fruit and vegetables can't compare with straight-from-the soil versions sold in grocery stores and roadside stands. Large bananas imported from the United States and Central America, overripe by the time they arrive, can't compete with Bermuda's own tiny sweet hands of fruit. Similarly, Bermuda carrots, tomatoes, and potatoes are well worth buying if you're staying in a self-catering unit or simply want to try the local harvest.

Wild fruits are also popular, namely the Surinam "Bermuda" cherry (a sour cherry), which has several harvests throughout the year, and the loquat, which hangs heavy on trees throughout the island in January and February. Help yourself to a taste from trees in local parks or on public land along the Railway Trail. At the height of cherry or loquat season, you often see drivers pulling over to gather a roadside haul or schoolchildren dangling out of trees as they collect a fresh snack. Similarly, Bermudians gather bags of avocadoes to share among friends when the local trees drop their heavy harvests.

In the supermarkets, there has been a growing movement among some local farmers to supply organic fare, including organically raised chickens, vegetables, and salad greens. Locally grown products can be found in most large groceries, particularly The Supermart, on Front Street in Hamilton, and Tom Wadson's farm store in Southampton. Saturday roadside stands in most parishes are also well stocked with fresh fruit and vegetables in season.

Fishers sell their daily catch, including spiny lobsters in season, at roadside stands islandwide. Sometimes, this is simply a guy with a cooler. The best places are at the foot of Scaur Hill in Sandys; Devonshire Dock and Devonshire Bay in Devonshire; Blue Hole Hill in Hamilton Parish; and at the top of Trimingham Hill in Paget, leading out of Hamilton.

The best occasions, outside of restaurants, to sample Bermudian cooking and specialties are public festivals and holidays such as Cup Match, when alfresco gatherings or street fairs usually have food stalls selling fish sandwiches, fish cakes, homemade pies, and other goodies.

RESTAURANTS

Eating out is a favorite island pastime, and many residents, particularly those who work in Hamilton, and especially young expatriates, frequent local bars and restaurants several evenings a week. With Bermuda's steep tabs, that could bankrupt you pretty easily. Like everyone else, restaurants have to import the majority of their ingredients, a reality reflected in menu prices. On top of that, almost all charge an automatic 17 percent gratuity included on the bill. If you *really* enjoyed the food and service, you can leave an extra 10 percent, but otherwise the built-in surcharge will suffice. Check your tab to make sure it's included.

Bermudians would admit the quality of fare, even at the priciest restaurants, is inconsistent, and food and service do not always compare with the offerings of similarly priced establishments in urban centers such as New York or London. But generally, the standard is fairly high, with menus created by award-winning Bermudian and foreign-born chefs. Many Bermuda restaurants now connect with their clientele via Facebook, Twitter, and other social media.

BARS

Bermudians love to drink—there was even a song with that title released by a local artist in 2005. They also love to drink and drive, though media pressure and police crackdowns in the past 20 years have somewhat curtailed the habit. Don't be tempted to hop on a scooter after a few black rums or Elephant beers; many visitors (and locals) have been killed or badly injured over the years doing just that. But *do* enjoy Bermuda's bars; they must rank among the most lively in the world, particularly in the busy crush of summer. Happy hours are prevalent, with cheaper drink prices offered for a couple of hours after work, usually on Friday. A full wine list and a good choice of beers, cocktails, and liqueurs can be found at most drinking establishments and licensed restaurants. National favorites Black 'n' Coke (black rum—preferably Gosling's Black Seal—and Coca-Cola) and Cockspur 'n' Coke are party staples.

Travel Tips

WHAT TO TAKE

Bermuda's summer heat demands flip-flops, leather sandals, or boat shoes for comfort. Breathable cotton outfits are recommended for all seasons; layer up when it gets chilly. A waterproof, windproof anorak is always useful. Hats and shades are a must. Waterproof sunblock is also necessary, and mosquito repellent is advised.

TRAVELING WITH CHILDREN

There's no end to child-friendly fun in Bermuda, and, best of all, a lot of it is absolutely free. Beaches, public playgrounds, gombey dances, and the serenade of treefrogs—kids fall in love with the island even faster than their parents. Traveling to Bermuda poses no special health risks; the island has a standard vaccination program for infants and children, so there are few serious communicable diseases. Bermuda is also rabies-free, and water from the taps is usually safe. The short flight from U.S. East Coast cities—a mere couple of hours—is doable for kids (daytime flights from London are about seven hours). Many of the major hotels have special kids' camps during the summer high season; inquire about their activities and age restrictions when you book accommodations. Some hotels and guesthouses can also arrange babysitting.

Most child-care products are easily available on the island at drugstores and supermarkets, including diapers, wipes, shampoos, vitamins, sunblock, and children's pain relievers. The majority stock North American brands, except for The Supermart's popular English Waitrose grocery line; if you're traveling from Europe and will miss a favorite product, you might want to bring it with you.

There are numerous toy stores and kids' clothing outlets, though prices generally run at least a third higher than in the United States.

Generally, local eateries are more than willing to try to make young diners happy, with kids' menus, high chairs, and cheery waitstaff.

The best public playgrounds are located at Mullet Bay in St. George's; Shelly Bay in Hamilton Parish; Parson's Road in Pembroke; South Shore Road in Warwick (just east of the entrance to Warwick Long Bay); Death Valley, Middle Road, in Southampton; and inside the National Museum of Bermuda at Dockyard. All are equipped with regulation climbing frames, tunnels, swings, and slides, for both toddlers and older children.

WOMEN TRAVELERS

Women will find Bermuda a far more benign traveling environment than many places in the Caribbean, Central America, or even a typical North American city. Bermudians pride themselves on the safety of their island, and violent, arbitrary crime is extremely rare. Female travelers should nevertheless use common sense and practical measures to keep safe, especially at night and if alone or in more remote areas.

Generally, Bermuda is conservative and modern in its attitudes toward women, and women won't notice any gender issues they wouldn't encounter in London or Los Angeles. Women doing business on the island will be treated with the same respect as their male colleagues (the local and international business communities count a growing number of women in top corporate jobs). And women need not feel unsafe or out of place touring most areas of the island, or eating alone in restaurants. They need not expect to encounter unwanted harassment, either, although Bermudian men have the habit of issuing a surreptitious hiss to catch your attention. Whether you smile, wave, or have no reaction, there's rarely any further approach. The exception may be on the beaches, where local men sometimes try to chat up foreign women.

Women take part in most sports and clubs on the island, and a few annual sporting events are geared to them, such as the **PartnerRe Women's 5K Run & Walk** (www.partnerre5k.bm) in mid-October and the **Queen of Bermuda Triathlon** in early November. Top female match-race teams compete in an annual championship qualifier for the prestigious **Argo Group Gold Cup** International One Design competition, also in October.

Should you need help or advice, the **Women's Resource Centre** (25 Point Finger Rd., Paget, tel. 441/295-3882, fax 441/295-9833, 9am-5pm Mon.-Fri., 24-hour crisis hotline 441/295-7273, www.wrcbermuda.com) is the island's prime advocacy group; its services include emergency response, counseling, assistance for victims, and a crisis intervention hotline. Other women's support and networking resources include the **Business & Professional Women's Association of Bermuda** (21 Somerset Rd., Sandys, tel. 441/238-3685, bpwabermuda@yahoo.com) and the **Bermuda Junior Service League** (tel. 441/332-2575, www.bjsl.bm).

GAY AND LESBIAN TRAVELERS

While Bermuda has a general tolerance for homosexuality on a grassroots level, politically, the island lags far behind North American and European societies. The Human Rights Act became law in 1981, yet gay sex was illegal in Bermuda until 1994. The House of Parliament eventually decriminalized sexual relations between consenting gay men after a private bill was introduced that year (no former law had outlawed lesbian relations).

In more recent years, the island's gay community, led by grassroots lobbyists like **Two Words and a Comma** (www.twowordsandacomma.com) and supported by Amnesty International (Bermuda), battled for human rights legislation that would prevent discrimination based on sexual orientation. In 2013, Bermuda's Parliament voted in favor of landmark legislation, the Human Rights Amendment Act, that finally added sexual orientation to the list of prohibited grounds of discrimination. However, the island's Matrimonial Causes Act continues to void same-sex marriages.

Gay tourists will probably not experience any overt discrimination, but bear in mind the island is a very conservative society, and open displays of affection even among heterosexuals are frowned upon, so subtlety is valued.

There is not a true "gay scene" in Bermuda compared to livelier urban centers, but Hamilton has a number of gay-friendly venues. These include Café Cairo and Casey's Cocktail Lounge on Fridays. Funky coffeehouse Rock Island Coffee is also gay-friendly, with a very mixed crowd. The Little Venice Wine Bar and nearby nightclub The Club on Bermudiana Road also support all clientele equally.

Bermuda hotels and guesthouses noted for being welcoming and respectful to gay guests include the Fairmont Southampton Resort and Fairmont Hamilton Princess, The Reefs, and Royal Palms, among others.

TRAVELERS WITH DISABILITIES

Bermuda is far from ideal as a perfectly accessible destination for travelers with disabilities, of whom many travel to the island by cruise ship. But improvements have been made in recent years. Many more attractions, city sidewalks, restaurants, nightclubs, and public buildings have been made wheelchair accessible over the past decade. However, many places, including retail stores and restaurants, and even some cruise ship ramps, pose great physical challenges to people with disabilities. While the fast ferries and ramp-fitted ferry terminal are a breeze, public buses are not equipped at all for disabled access. Lobby groups have also complained that too few taxis accommodate wheelchairs.

The WindReach Recreational Village (57 Spice Hill Rd., Warwick, tel. 441/238-2469,

Tie the Knot

Planning to say "I do"? Bermuda is a top wedding destination, thanks to its heart-stopping scenery, proximity to North America, and relatively easy marriage requirements. The island dotes on long-held wedding traditions, including romantic moongates (kiss beneath one and a long marriage is assured), horse-drawn carriages, his-and-hers gold and silver cakes, and locations like historic churches, public gardens, clifftops, and beaches that promise highly memorable nuptials.

Scores of visitors get married in Bermuda every year, so everyone—from local wedding planners to clergy and hotel staff—is ready to ease prospective brides and grooms through the process. Many guesthouses and hotels have special **wedding packages,** churches offer chaplains for off-site locations, and even Bermuda's sometimes burdensome bureaucracy has honed the business of getting married into a painless to-do list.

Couples must have their "Notice of Intended Marriage" published in Bermuda's newspapers. You can download the form from www.gotobermuda.com (must be printed on white legal-size paper, 8.5 by 14 inches) or request one from the **Registry General** (Government Administration Building, 30 Parliament St., Hamilton HM 12, tel. 441/297-7709 or 441/297-7707, www.registrygeneral.gov.bm). No blood tests or health certificates are needed, but copies of divorce decrees or death certificates must be submitted with the completed form, along with a cashier's check or bank draft for $354.. After the notice is published, a license to marry is granted. It is valid for three months and can be collected from the Registry General office.

Civil ceremonies can be performed weekdays or Saturday mornings (10am-11:30am) in the Registry's Marriage Room for $300 (plus $30 for certificate). For more information, call Registry's Kim Minors, or email kminors@gov.bm. Justices of the Peace cannot perform marriages in Bermuda. You must have two witnesses over the age of 18 to any wedding ceremony; these can be provided by the Registry General's office Monday-Friday only.

Churches can be booked for a fee, and officiating clergy can be arranged to perform the ceremony on-site or elsewhere. **Catholic churches** in Bermuda will marry nonresident Catholics if baptismal certificates and other documents are provided in advance (for details, visit www.catholicbermuda.org and click the International Marriages link). Couples seeking marriage blessings or renewal of vows need to provide copies of their original Catholic church marriage certificate.

Professional wedding planners in Bermuda have a good reputation for efficiently coordinating all the details, from flowers and photographers to accommodations and catering. For information, contact **Bermuda Bride** (tel. 441/232-2344, www.bermudaweddings.com); **Bermuda Event Solutions** (tel. 441/236-9469, www.weddingsolutions.bm); **The Bridal Suite** (tel. 441/292-2025, www.bridalsuitebermudaweddings.com); **A Wedding in Bermuda** (tel. 441/238-6362, www.aweddinginbermuda.com); **To Have and To Hold Wedding and Event Planning** (tel. 441/236-7473, www.tohaveandtoholdbermuda.com); or **Kreative Koncepts** (tel. 441/537-2237, www.kreativekoncepts.biz).

One of the best resources to help prospective brides and grooms pull together all the details of their big day is the Bermudian Publishing Company's website (www.bermudianweddings.com). It carries advice from wedding planners; contacts for flowers, fashions, cakes, and rentals; bridal blogs sharing useful resources; plus photo features on real Bermuda weddings.

fax 441/238-2597, www.windreach.org) is a nonprofit community group located on a quiet chunk of rural property surrounded by agricultural fields and residential neighborhoods. It offers special-needs services and activities, including a petting zoo, a wheelchair-accessible playground, and a fully accessible camping area with wheelchair-accommodating cabins, bathrooms, and shower facilities. Located on the same property, **Bermuda Riding for the Disabled** (tel. 441/238-7433, brd@ibl.bm) provides therapeutic riding lessons and programs for children and adults with disabilities.

The **Bermuda Physically Handicapped Association** (Summerhaven, South Shore

Rd., Hamilton Parish, tel. 441/734-8260, summerhaven@northrock.bm) is located on a quiet stretch of South Shore Road, opposite scenic John Smith's Bay.

The **Bermuda Red Cross** (Charleswood, 9 Berry Hill Rd., Paget, tel. 441/236-8253, www.bermudaredcross.com) rents equipment such as walkers and wheelchairs. Other resources include the **Association for the Mentally Handicapped** (tel. 441/292-7206); **Bermuda Islands Association of the Deaf** (tel. 441/238-8116, biad@therock.bm); and **Bermuda Society for the Blind** (Beacon House, 3 Beacon St., Hamilton, tel. 441/292-3231).

SENIOR TRAVELERS

Bermuda has long been a favorite destination for older travelers, particularly in the wintertime, when golf, ecotours, and cultural programs take center stage. While scores of substantial discounts—on public transport, museums, and groceries—are offered to resident seniors, unfortunately these are not available to visitors. However, the island's moderate temperatures, easygoing lifestyle, and numerous accessible leisure activities make it popular among senior travelers, and costliness is often not a deterrent to this increasingly active and well-heeled demographic.

The best dedicated program for senior travelers to the island is **Road Scholar,** educational adventures created by nonprofit Elderhostel Inc. and run through the **Bermuda Institute of Ocean Sciences (BIOS)** (17 Biological Ln., Ferry Reach, St. George's, tel. 441/297-1880, fax 441/297-8143, www.bios.edu). Based at the station for the past quarter-century, the year-round program includes accommodations, cafeteria-style dining, field trips, lectures, and evening entertainment for $200 a day. Five weeklong courses range from a study of Bermuda birds to local history and heritage to an inside look at the cutting-edge global "science in Bermuda shorts" that goes on at the world-famous station, encompassing topics such as the ocean's influence on climate change. All participants should be able to walk at least a mile, enjoy a long bus tour, and feel comfortable on short, smooth boat trips. Access to the lecture hall and dining area is up a single flight of stairs. To register or find out more, contact the Road Scholar coordinator in Bermuda (kaitlin.baird@bios.edu), visit www.roadscholar.org, or call Road Scholar at 617/426-8056.

The November-March period offers a program of daily events geared to visitors of all ages, though these are particularly popular with seniors. Included are glass-blowing demonstrations, bagpipe skirling ceremonies, gombey revues, guided walking tours of Hamilton, St. George's, and Somerset Village, and historical reenactments in St. George's. In any season, older travelers who wish to steer clear of scooters should opt for a multiday transportation pass that allows unlimited use of ferries and buses within the designated time frame. One-day, three-day, seven-day, and monthlong passes can be purchased at Visitor Information Centres and the Hamilton bus or ferry terminals.

VOLUNTEERING

Bermuda's charities and nonprofit organizations depend heavily on volunteers to carry out much of their day-to-day workload. Very often, unpaid volunteers are retired or wealthy Bermudians, or the spouses of expatriate workers who don't hold work permits themselves and are looking for social and professional interaction after they move to the island. From walking the canine residents of the SPCA to providing CPR instruction to staffing the front desk at an art gallery, volunteers keep the island running smoothly. If you are visiting Bermuda for an extended period and would like to get involved, check the charities' listings in the Bermuda Yellow Pages (www.bermudayp.com), or contact the **Centre on Philanthropy** (Sterling House, 16 Wesley St., Hamilton, tel. 441/236-7706, fax 441/236-7693, www.centreonphilanthropy.org) to find out which organizations are in need of extra help.

Health and Safety

With one of the highest standards of living anywhere, Bermuda poses none of the health risks found in many exotic destinations, particularly those in the Caribbean or Latin America. Sanitary standards are excellent, and health care is modern and professional. The island's freshwater, rain caught on the limestone-coated roofs and channeled into tanks below every home, is nearly always potable—except after hurricanes and severe storms, when consuming water that's been exposed to rotting foliage and other debris in the tanks can lead to stomachaches and intestinal problems. Bottled water is available in all grocery stores, gas stations, drugstores, and restaurants. Bermuda is subtropical, and therefore has no common tropical diseases, such as malaria. Vaccinations are unnecessary.

BEFORE YOU GO

Bring all prescription medications you may need with you, including enough for an extra day or two in case flights are canceled or travel is delayed for any reason. Wear a medical-alert bracelet if you have a health problem, to help medical staff treat you properly in an emergency. Eyewear prescriptions and meds, left in their original containers for easy passage through customs, are best packed in carry-on luggage in case bags go missing. Keep a detailed written list in your purse or wallet as a backup. Meds are often the last thing packed, and therefore frequently forgotten; put them in an obvious place as you pack so you don't overlook them as you leave home.

Travel and Medical Insurance

Any industry veteran will tell you travel insurance—while often deemed unnecessary—is a prudent investment, particularly if your regular health insurance does not cover overseas expenses or treatment. As well, primary insurers can sometimes take up to two weeks to verify a patient's policy details—an unworkable delay in an emergency. Bermuda's hospital cannot treat overseas patients who are not covered by insurance, unless they are able to pay on the spot. In an emergency, traveler's health insurance avoids logistical nightmares, allowing for confirmation of an overseas hospital bed and immediate air-ambulance transport. Take time to review your health-care plan before leaving home to find out exactly what is covered, as well as any restrictions that might affect the choice of hospital in an emergency. Remember, it's not just the patient who may need help in an emergency but also relatives or companions who may have to find accommodation or make other travel plans while a patient is in the hospital.

MEDICAL SERVICES

Good medical services are provided by the island's main health center, **King Edward VII Memorial Hospital** (7 Point Finger Rd., Paget, tel. 441/236-2345, fax 441/236-2213, www.bermudahospitals.bm), which was modernized with a $300 million Acute Care Centre in 2014. The hospital provides round-the-clock emergency care and islandwide ambulance service; it is equipped with maternity facilities, a children's ward, a hyperbaric recompression chamber for divers and diabetics, and intensive care, dialysis, oncology, OR, ER, and cardiac diagnostic units, as well as other specialty services. Emergency air-ambulance service, organized by the hospital, provides access within 24 hours to U.S. and Canadian cities for treatment of serious conditions, including severe burns and spinal, neurological, and coronary problems. The hospital's East End clinic, the **Lamb Foggo Urgent Care Centre** (1 Hall St., Southside, St. George's, tel. 441/298-7700, 4pm-midnight Mon.-Fri., noon-midnight Sat.-Sun.) treats minor injury or illness.

A second local hospital, the **Mid-Atlantic**

Wellness Institute (formerly St. Brendan's Psychiatric Hospital, 44 Devon Springs Rd., Devonshire, tel. 441/236-3770, www.bermudahospitals.bm), offers professional counseling and treats patients suffering from mental disorders.

Well-stocked pharmacies and drugstores are located throughout the island. Pharmacists can issue a maximum five-day refill of a prescription, including a one-cycle pack of birth-control pills, providing they approve that the medications and doses are accurate. If a longer supply is needed, you'll have to visit a local doctor who can write a new prescription. Pharmacies do not accept prescriptions from overseas doctors, so any phone call to Bermuda that your home physician might make on your behalf would be wasted. If you need to see a doctor, appointments can be made via your hotel, guesthouse, or host. Most major resorts and hotels have a physician on call who can arrange treatment or phone prescriptions directly to a pharmacy, sometimes without an office visit. Cruise ship passengers can visit local pharmacies, but it's usually simpler to contact their ship's doctor, who can write a five-day prescription, fillable at an island pharmacy by the ship's agent.

MEDICAL EMERGENCIES

King Edward VII Memorial Hospital has an effective protocol in place for emergency treatment of visitors who may need to be flown off the island for specialized treatment—as long as health insurance or upfront funds are provided. An air-ambulance journey from Bermuda to the U.S. East Coast costs $10,000-15,000. Keep on hand your information about any preexisting medical condition, as well as the name and contact number of your primary doctor, so that if air-ambulance transport is necessary, hospital staff can arrange for your doctor to be the receiving physician at the destination.

Among their myriad tasks, "Pink Ladies" and "Pink Men" volunteers (whose title refers to their rosy uniforms) help families find emergency accommodation if a relative or traveling companion ends up having to stay in the hospital. Limited space in the nearby nurses' residence is available for such a scenario at minimal cost, about $75 a day. Many island hotels and guesthouses also try to accommodate visitors during emergencies.

Patients who have been checked into the hospital need a "fit-to-fly" document signed by a local doctor in order to leave. The other possibility is for patients or their families to sign an "against medical advice" form, or AMA, but departure from the island's airport under such circumstances ranges from difficult to impossible. For cruise ship passengers checking out of the hospital, doctors will confer with the ship's physician to ensure all necessary equipment (oxygen, for example) is aboard the vessel before it leaves port.

The U.S. Consulate General (Crown Hill, 16 Middle Rd., Devonshire, tel. 441/295-1342, duty officer 441/335-3828, fax 441/295-1592, http://hamilton.usconsulate.gov) can aid American citizens when things go awry, particularly those lacking travel insurance. Staff may sometimes contact relatives or credit card companies to help pay out-of-pocket expenses.

HEALTH PROBLEMS

Sunburn and Dehydration

Bermuda's high humidity, coupled with blistering summer temperatures—in the high 90s for much of July and August—can lead to severe sunburns, dehydration, and sunstroke. Regardless of your skin tone, wear sunscreens with high SPF content; some brands, such as Australia's Bullfrog, make waterproof sunblock of SPF 30 or higher, which protects your skin from harmful UVA and UVB rays for hours, even if you're sweating or in the water.

If you're not accustomed to the heat, cover up. Wear light clothing of natural fibers like cotton or silk that covers easy-to-burn or overexposed areas. Arms, hands, and shoulders can burn while driving a scooter, and even moped passengers end up sporting lobster-red knees and feet after sitting in the same position under scorching skies. Protect

Emergency Contacts

Ambulance, Fire, Police, and Marine	911
King Edward VII Memorial Hospital	441/236-2345
King Edward VII Memorial Hospital Emergency Room	441/239-2009
Bermuda Police Service	441/295-0011
Fire Services Headquarters	441/292-5555
Electricity Power Outage	955
Telephone Repair Service	441/295-1001
Harbour Radio	441/297-1010
Weather Forecast	977
Women's Resource Hotline	441/295-7273
Physical Abuse Hotline	441/297-8278
Crime Stoppers (calls are anonymous)	800/623-8477
Government Emergency Radio Broadcast	FM 100.1 MHz

your face, including eyes and lips, with shades, a sun hat, and lip balm with sunblock. If you do get too much sun, slather on aloe creams or place paper towels soaked in vinegar on the affected region (an island remedy to draw the heat out). Then try to skip a day or two's beaching to let your skin recover; visit a museum or go shopping instead.

Stay hydrated in hot weather by drinking lots of water throughout the day, especially if you're exercising. Bermuda's humidity, regularly in the 80-90 percent zone, can make it feel like you're moving around inside a greenhouse. Dehydration's onset—including heavy sweating, cramps, and dizziness—means it's time to get out of the sun to let your body rest. Heat stroke, a potentially fatal condition, happens when the body's self-regulating thermometer shuts down completely. Symptoms include severe headaches and delirium. Get emergency aid and keep heat-stroke patients as cool as possible. Bermuda's hospital emergency department has intravenous treatment to speedily rehydrate and reenergize heat-stroke victims with electrolytes and water.

Keep children well protected from the sun, especially toddlers, who are often oblivious to the sun, or youngsters who may not complain about burns until the damage is done. Reapply sunscreen often, particularly if you are swimming, and take a large water bottle to the beach. Many adults and kids in Bermuda wear UV-protective clothing, including hats, bodysuits, and long-sleeved, high-necked tops made of swimsuit fabric to guard against months of destructive sun exposure at the beach or on the water. One local company, **Groovy UV** (tel. 441/232-0527, www.groovy-uv.com), operated by Bermudian sailors Debbie and Adam Barboza, offers a full range of colorful outfits for all ages, including UV goggles and board shorts.

Sexually Transmitted Diseases

An estimated 300 people were living with AIDS/HIV on the island in 2014, according to the Department of Health. Less severe sexually transmitted diseases such as gonorrhea, syphilis, and genital warts are also the focus of periodic public health campaigns. Condoms can be purchased in all the island's drugstores. Confidential HIV screening and counseling are available at the **Communicable Disease**

Control Clinic at the Hamilton Health Centre (67 Victoria St., tel. 441/292-6777, 8:30am-4:45pm Mon.-Thurs.). The Hamilton Health Centre also offers information regarding **sexual health services** (tel. 441/278-6442 or 441/236-0224, ext. 229 or ext. 242, 2pm-4pm Mon.-Fri.).

Insects and Poison Ivy

Bermuda has no truly dangerous wildlife—no scorpions, snakes, nor even sharks close to shore. (Sharks do frequent local waters but are seen rarely inshore. As a result, there has not been a reported shark attack in more than 50 years.) The few hazards that do exist are not serious, and mostly of the insect variety.

Mosquitoes are irritating outdoor pests on summer evenings, and during the day in areas where they breed. Wear a repellent in areas near ponds or marshland, for example, and after dark when the insects are prevalent. Bermuda's subtropical climate is also conducive to flea infestations; responsible pet owners treat cats and dogs regularly with prescription flea-killers that stop the little parasites from infestation. Bermuda has no ticks.

American cockroaches (the large, flying type)—euphemistically dubbed "palmetto bugs" in Florida—can be seen everywhere at night throughout the hot summer months, even on the walls inside elegant homes. They are rather frightening apparitions upon first encounter, but they are harmless; window screens usually serve to keep them outdoors. Savvy scooter riders appreciate shades or, better still, helmets with visors to keep wayward flying insects from face collisions.

Ants by the thousands are a byproduct of summer and are especially apparent after severe storms or hurricanes. Again, they are harmless, but a nuisance. To keep their numbers down, avoid leaving dirty dishes around, including pet bowls, and conquer invasions with a simple household tool: the vacuum cleaner. Some also swear by lemon sprays and baby powder.

The St. David's centipede, or giant centipede, which can grow to a foot in length, is rarely seen these days, but it can inflict a mild bite, so avoid it if you happen to spot one.

Poison ivy *(Rhus radicans)* grows wild in parks and brush areas of the island, including off-trail parts of Paget Marsh and other nature reserves. Stay on boardwalks or main trails to avoid it. Rash, blisters, and itchiness break out once you have been exposed to the plant, but they usually disappear without treatment within a couple of weeks. Use cool compresses or an antihistamine to soothe the itching.

BEACH HAZARDS

Rip Currents and Undertows

Other than the risk of scooter accidents, the sea poses the greatest danger to Bermuda visitors, particularly rip currents and undertows found off the South Shore beaches. Drownings are infrequent—and often caused by neither phenomenon. Bermuda has very few "dangerous surf" days, except around hurricanes, which tend to occur at the season's end in September and October. But inexperienced swimmers should check beach conditions carefully before entering the water and know what to do if they encounter risks.

Rip currents, also called riptides (though they are not tidal), are found at the world's surf beaches, such as those on Bermuda's South Shore. They occur as water dumped by breakers at the shoreline returns to the deep sea, "ripping" past natural structures such as rocks, reefs, or sandbars. They are intensified by onshore winds coupled with storm conditions. A rip current is recognizable as a sandy stream of fast-moving water flowing seaward, sometimes splashing as it hits incoming waves. It moves at right angles from the beach—a bottleneck of water stretching up to 200 meters. Swimmers trapped in its movement feel helpless as the surge carries them away from the beach. If you find yourself in a rip current, the number-one rule is: Keep calm. Swimming against the outward-flowing water is exhausting and unproductive, even for strong swimmers. Instead, try to swim across it, parallel to the beach. Rip currents aren't very wide, so a swimmer can usually reach the current's edge, escape its pull, and then swim back to safety. If you can't, don't panic. The current will eventually release you and will not pull you under.

Undertows or "runbacks," sometimes mistakenly called rip currents, occur by contrast in the rolling surf at the edge of steep beaches, posing a risk to weak swimmers. As a wave is about to break, water from the beach edge is sucked back beneath it. The force of gravity can be strong enough to sweep swimmers off their feet and beneath the crashing surf. The cycle repeats as more waves break, disperse, and break again. The phenomenon, intensified by the angle of a beach, can make even practiced bodysurfers feel a sense of lost control. If you get swept into a series of waves, try to stand up, climb out, or call for help.

May-October, lifeguards are stationed 10am-6pm daily at a few popular and family beaches around the island, including Horseshoe Bay, John Smith's Bay in Smith's, and Clearwater, Turtle Beach, and Long Bay in St. George's. They are on the lookout for swimmers in trouble; wave an arm or call out if you need help. Avoid swimming alone or in rough conditions or storm swells; bodysurfing in hurricane surf, for example, can cause spinal fractures and other injuries. Warning signs and flags are posted in particularly stormy conditions at popular beaches, including Horseshoe Bay and Warwick Long Bay. A yellow flag crossed by a black diagonal stripe is a warning: See on-duty lifeguards or read information boards posted at the beach entrance. A red flag, for example, around a hurricane's approach and aftermath prohibits swimming. A flag atop the lifeguard tower indicates that a lifeguard is on duty.

Cliff-Diving

Shallow water and submerged rocks near favorite swimming holes have over the years left Bermudians paralyzed, in comas, or dead. Accidents commonly occur over the summer holidays as daredevils show off to friends or spectators from the picturesque overhangs at the edge of popular beaches such as Horseshoe Bay on the South Shore or Admiralty Cove on the North Shore. Travelers would be ill-advised to try high-diving from any points around the island where they are not entirely sure of water depth or the possibility of concealed reefs, sunken objects, or other hazards.

Portuguese Man-of-Wars

A translucent, frilly-edged, violet balloon, the jellyfish known as the Portuguese man-of-war might be considered exquisitely beautiful—if it wasn't such a menace.

This invertebrate marine animal *(Physalia physalis)* has a gas-filled, purple-blue float topped by a crest that catches the wind and carries the organism over the ocean. But what you see at the surface is just a fraction of the creature, whose severely poisonous tentacles stretch many feet below. Found in the Gulf Stream and in tropical oceans worldwide, Portuguese man-of-wars travel in schools of hundreds or thousands and can be a swimming hazard on Bermuda's South Shore year-round, depending on wind direction and other conditions. Onshore winds blow them in. Look for their balloons washed up on the beach (they are difficult to spot on the sea surface) before you enter the water.

Avoid getting stung by the man-of-war's clinging blue tentacles, which can cause intense pain and occasional blistering, and leave red welts on the skin. The impact is rarely more serious, though small children, the elderly, and those with allergies face a greater risk of severe reaction. Notably, the jellyfish is not only harmful when intact, but also when its myriad tentacles are broken into particles by the surf, causing rashes and irritation. Out of the water, the sting is no less severe, so don't be tempted to pick one up.

The best remedy if you do get stung? Treatment and opinion among medical professionals has evolved over the past 20 years, advising everything from meat tenderizer to urine, and there is still no absolute consensus. The key, says Dr. Edward Schultz, director of Bermuda's ER, is to deactivate the venom-firing cells, called nematocysts, released by tentacles on to the skin. Schultz recommends that jellyfish victims:

- Remove any visible bits of tentacle (wipe off with a towel or gloved hand)
- Rinse with seawater
- Soak the area in vinegar (acetic acid soothes pain and reduces inflammation)
- Shave the affected area to remove stinging particles
- Apply a warm compress or immerse in hot water

Lifeguards on Bermuda beaches will assist you with first aid if you get stung. While a hospital visit isn't usually necessary, go to the ER immediately if you have difficulty breathing, feel lightheaded or weak, or if the rash spreads. For emergency aid, call 911.

Fire Coral

Fire coral *(Cnidaria Phylum)*, a reddish-brown spongy-looking mass on the island's reefs, can deliver a stinging, burnlike sensation. Related to the jellyfish rather than the coral family, it can also scrape the skin. Rule of thumb on the reefs: Don't touch anything—for your comfort, as well as the reef's longevity (real corals can die when touched).

Other Marinelife

Fish to avoid include the porcupine-like lionfish, a poisonous species usually found in Australasia, but which has infiltrated Bermuda's waters in recent years. The fish usually avoids human contact, but if touched it releases venom from its puncturing spines.

The great barracuda's menacing profile is deceptive; despite its ugly, toothy grin, this large fish is usually harmless, though barracudas have been known to snap at shiny metal objects, so keep watches and jewelry out of sight. Moray eels may look fearsome, but they mostly avoid human contact—unless you shove a hand into one's lair.

Do not touch the flat red bristleworm or the related fireworm; their needles leave a rash. Most corals, sea anemones, and jellyfish deposit a poisonous zap on human skin, so try not to touch them. Spiny sea urchins hidden in sea grass also pose a hazard; wearing fins or surf slippers helps avoid such dangers, as well as nasty reef scrapes and coral cuts.

CRIME

Against Bermuda's bucolic backdrop, the specter of crime—even the petty variety (handbag snatches, break-ins)—may seem out of place. But it is an unfortunate reality of modern life. Every parish has its share of neighborhoods plagued by perennial drug problems, the catalyst for most of the island's criminal activity; gangs and drug abuse appear to be the biggest factors driving an increase in violent crime in modern Bermuda. For the visitor, this flip side of local life is usually barely visible, but it is there nonetheless, and sensible measures should be taken to guard against opportunistic crime.

Closed-circuit surveillance cameras are installed in several Hamilton locations, including North Hamilton's Court Street and Pembroke's Pitts Bay Road—two economically divergent neighborhoods, yet both areas where police have recorded a high number of crimes, ranging from bag-snatchings to assaults and drug-related incidents. Cameras in other parts of the city have reduced the number of bike thefts, bag snatches, and public nuisances.

Bag-Snatching

Protect your belongings and use the same street sense and practical judgment you would anywhere else in the world. The most common crime is bag-snatching, from beaches, scooter baskets, or, on rare occasions, from scooter riders wearing bags over one arm—sometimes leading to traffic accidents and injuries. Visitors are not the only victims; Bermuda residents are also targets, though most have learned to lock away handbags, knapsacks, or shopping items in compartments attached to the back or under the scooter seat, or to strap down belongings in a rear basket with bungee cords looped through bag handles. Thieves have also targeted tourists strolling through Hamilton's streets at night, notably in quiet, seemingly safe, upscale neighborhoods, where numerous hotels and guesthouses are located.

Take cabs at night if you are traveling alone. Be aware of your surroundings, keep wallets or purses out of sight, and wear long-strapped bags across your body, or hold them firmly to avoid becoming easy prey. On beaches, don't leave belongings unattended, or if you do, don't carry valuables and money. It is not unusual for swimmers to come back from a swim to find belongings gone or bags missing contents.

Break-Ins

Break-ins and home burglaries do occur throughout the parishes, and again, Bermudian householders face a similar risk. Indeed, although leaving doors unlocked was the oft-touted neighborhood habit of decades past, well-informed residents rarely leave their homes unlocked anymore when they're out. Most locals also lock doors and windows overnight when they're sleeping. Tourist properties, particularly guesthouses and rental cottages outside the more secure confines of a hotel, are frequently targeted. Thieves know that windows and sliding-glass doors at holiday properties are often left open through ignorance or to let in the breeze if there's no air-conditioning. Easy-to-cut screens are no deterrent. Thieves commonly break into rooms and residences when inhabitants are sleeping, though break-ins have rarely turned violent. Use hotel property safes to store valuables, and lock your room or house at night and when you're not around.

Motorcycle Theft

Scooters are favorite targets of thieves, who usually go for joyrides or scavenge for spare parts before dumping the remains on the roadside. Lock up your scooter or moped whenever you leave it. Scooters sometimes have both an ignition lock and a provided U-lock to place on the back wheel. It's a drag to have to fiddle with several times a day, but well worth the effort. Other bikes are safe as long as the ignition key is removed. If your rental scooter or bike is stolen, contact the livery, which will usually collect you if you're stranded and notify the police.

Crimes Against Women

Violence against women in Bermuda has increased in recent years, along with violent crime in general. The Bermuda Police Service advises women traveling alone to choose well-lit routes and areas, to check vehicle gas regularly so you don't find yourself stranded, and to carry a cell phone, flashlight, or warning device such as a small air horn.

Stay alert if you are walking or running alone—for example, along remote stretches of the Railway Trail or in large parks such as Spittal Pond Nature Reserve or Hog Bay. If possible, women should avoid exploring or traveling alone in these areas; for safety, try to join organized groups of runners, walkers, or hikers, or take along a companion.

Harassment

Travelers tired of harassment in the Caribbean will appreciate being left alone in Bermuda; rarely are drugs offered or sold in public, and purveyors of services such as hair-braiding generally do not actively solicit clients, foreigners included. In recent years, Hamilton has experienced a minor problem with panhandling, but those who beg are typically harmless and less dogged than in many other places.

SMOKING

Smoking is banned in Bermuda's enclosed public places and work areas under a 2006 law that included bars, restaurants, shops, cinemas, or any enclosed workplace—in line with similar rulings in North America and Europe. The law also prohibits cigarette vending machines on the island and the sale of cigarettes to anyone under age 18. Penalties for smokers who defy the law are $250, or $1,000 for repeat offenders.

Information and Services

TOURIST INFORMATION

The website of the **Bermuda Tourism Authority** (www.gotobermuda.com) offers a well-researched rundown on immigration rules, wedding resources, daily activities, seasonal events, islandwide accommodations, and group and incentive tours, along with a mechanism to book trips online, including air-and-hotel packages.

The **BTA** (22 Church St., Hamilton, tel. 441/296-9200, contact@bermudatourism.com) is based in the City of Hamilton. For information on traveling to Bermuda, you can also call its North American headquarters toll-free at 800/BERMUDA (800/237-6832) or email travel@bermudatourism.com.

Once on the island, a first stop should be any of three **Visitor Information Centres (VIC),** which provide free maps and brochures and advise on day trips, tours, shows, and other activities. They are located at Dockyard, in a gazebo near the ferry stop, as well as in the King's Wharf and Heritage Wharf cruise terminals when ships are in port; in Hamilton, alongside the ferry terminal building on Front Street; and in St. George's on King's Square. All are staffed, with varying opening hours.

The pocket-sized *Handy Reference Map,* an easy-to-read, east-to-west depiction of sights and attractions produced by the Bermuda Tourism Authority, can be picked up at the VICs, or at information booths at cruise terminals, the Clocktower Mall in Dockyard, and other points, along with bus and ferry schedules and brochures on restaurants, shopping, water sports, nature reserves, and the Railway Trail. Bus and ferry schedules, tokens, and passes can be purchased at the ferry terminal or the Hubert W. "Sparky" Lightbourne Central Bus Terminal, both in Hamilton.

MONEY

Bermuda's currency, formerly based on the sterling system of shillings, pounds, and pence, went decimal in 1970, adopting colorful dollars and cents issued by the Bermuda Monetary Authority (BMA). Today, Bermuda's money is pegged to the U.S. dollar and interchangeable with it anywhere on the island.

In 2009, Bermuda released a new set of banknotes, even more striking in their design and color scheme than the originals. Incorporating cultural icons and island landmarks, including flora and fauna, plus numerous innovative security features, the notes will no doubt be sought after by collectors. The currency includes banknotes in denominations of $2 (turquoise, bluebird), $5 (violet-red, blue marlin), $10 (indigo, angelfish), $20 (green, whistling tree frog), $50 (yellow-orange, longtail), and $100 (red-orange, cardinal).

Coins are similarly artistic, especially the penny, manufactured in bronze with the image of a wild hog on the back—a tribute to the distinctive and now very rare Hogge money forged for use by settlers in the colony's early years, when tobacco-bartering was also common. Other coin

Visitor Information Centres

Covering the capital and both ends of the island, there are three staffed Visitor Information Centres open all year—plus two additional ones in each of Dockyard's cruise ship terminals that are open only when a ship is in port. All offer advice and resources on events, activities, dining out, and transport options for visitors.

- **City of Hamilton** (Front St., next to the ferry terminal, tel. 441/295-1480, 9am-4pm Mon.-Sat. year-round)
- **Royal Naval Dockyard** (Gazebo 2, Terrace Pavilion, in front of ferry dock, tel. 441/542-7104, 8am-8pm daily when a ship is in port, 8am-4pm otherwise)
- **St. George's** (7 Market Wharf, King's Square, tel. 441/297-0556, 10am-4pm Mon.-Sat. depending on cruise ship schedules)

denominations, in nickel, include: 5 cents (angelfish), 10 cents (lily), 25 cents (longtail), and $1 (in gold, Bermuda fitted dinghy). The latter was introduced in 1988, when a $1 note was discontinued and a $2 introduced. Since her coronation in 1952, all notes and coins have featured Queen Elizabeth II, though in the latest note series, her image is simply a small profile posted on the front bottom-left corner. Because Bermuda notes and coins are restricted to use on the island, U.S. currency is used by all island-based international companies and their non-Bermudian employees, who are paid in U.S. dollars and hold local U.S.-dollar accounts at Bermudian banks.

Changing Money

Travelers are advised to bring credit cards or travelers checks (both are widely used throughout the island), plus a minimum amount of cash for their Bermuda holiday. Since Bermudian currency cannot be exchanged at foreign banks, ask stores for U.S. change where possible before leaving the island (many merchants are happy to comply); HSBC's Harbourview Centre (37 Front St.) and Church Street branch (64 Church St.), both in Hamilton, have handy U.S. cash ATMs, as do the Butterfield locations (65 Front St. and 11 Bermudiana Rd.). Visitors with passports can exchange travelers checks for U.S. cash at any branch of the three licensed retail banks: **HSBC** (37 Front St., tel. 441/295-4000, www.hsbc.bm), **Butterfield Bank** (65 Front St., tel. 441/295-1111, www.bm.butterfieldgroup.com), or **Clarien Bank** (19 Reid St., tel. 441/296-6969, www.clarienbank.com). Mondays and Fridays are busiest, especially during lunch hours when Bermuda residents do most of their banking; the advent of online banking in recent years, however, has cut down on long bank lines.

Personal checks drawn on U.S. banks may be used for purchases at more than 200 establishments on the island. United States checks may be cashed at some hotels or local banks by arrangement. ATM machines, open 24 hours, are located at each bank's Hamilton headquarters and throughout the island at bank branches, gas stations, and supermarkets. Butterfield Bank introduced the first multicurrency ATM in 2014 in the airport's refurbished International Lounge; it dispenses Canadian dollars, British pounds, and euros. The bank also was working to install a U.S. dollar ATM in the U.S. Departures Lounge.

The island's ATMs issue a maximum of BM$2,500 per day (or much less, depending on your home bank's policy, which can be as low as US$250 per day) and charge a 1.5 percent transaction fee of the dollar amount withdrawn, with a minimum fee of $2.50. Bermudians can buy foreign currency, including U.S. and Canadian dollars, British pounds, euros, and special-order currencies, from all the banks. Bank hours vary, but most are open 9am-4:30pm (Somerset, St. George's, and airport branches have restricted hours).

Travelers Checks

Most international travelers checks (Visa, American Express, Barclays) are accepted on the island, but travelers are advised to bring U.S.-dollar checks rather than any other currency. Individual stores and hotels set various limits on amounts that can be cashed at any one establishment. A passport is usually necessary as valid photo ID to cash travelers checks, which must be in the visitor's own name.

Credit Cards

All major credit cards (Visa, MasterCard, American Express) are accepted at most hotels, restaurants, liveries, and retailers and can be used for cash advances at all bank branches. ATMs open 24 hours around the island also distribute cash advances for Visa, MasterCard, American Express, Cirrus, and Plus cards (know your PIN number). The American Express representative is **Bermuda Financial Network** (British-American Building, fourth floor, 133 Front St., Hamilton, tel. 441/292-1799), which offers free phone calls and emergency AmEx card-replacement services. AmEx cardholders can also make payments on their cards at this office. It also allows money to be received or sent in minutes via Western Union money-transfer services.

Lost or stolen major credit cards can be reported to these contact numbers (800 numbers are not toll-free from Bermuda):

- American Express: tel. 800/528-4800
- MasterCard: tel. 800/307-7309
- Visa: tel. 800/847-2911
- Visa Gold/Business: tel. 800/847-2911

Costs

Despite the lack of sales tax, Bermuda rates as one of the priciest destinations in the world, and many visitors are shocked by the high cost of island living, particularly restaurant tabs (which slap on an automatic 17 percent gratuity) and grocery bills. But budget-conscious travelers can save money in a number of ways during a Bermuda vacation.

Booking an apartment or studio via websites such as www.airbnb, www.vrbo, www.bermudarentals.com, or www.bermudagetaway.com can save the great expense of a resort vacation and allow you to live like a local. Shopping—wisely—at grocery stores instead of breaking your budget at pricey restaurants every day can also rein in costs. Shop like Bermudians do: Farmers' roadside stands or fishers' catch of the day deliver the freshest local ingredients in season at very fair prices.

Traveling by bus and ferry is cheaper than renting a moped or taking taxis. Buying passes for public transport saves money, too: A three-day pass allows you to hop on and off buses and ferries all day long. A book of 13 tokens saves money on each ride if you plan to stay a while.

Currency

Bermuda launched a set of striking new banknotes in 2009 to coincide with the island's 400th anniversary of settlement. It marks the first redesign since Bermuda went decimal and introduced the Bermuda dollar (on par with its U.S. counterpart) in 1970.

The colorful notes are distinctive and popular among collectors—most notably, perhaps, for their shape: They are vertically oriented. They also feature bold designs that incorporate the island's iconic flora and fauna—tree frogs, cardinals, longtails, angelfish, and bluebirds—along with enhanced anticounterfeiting elements such as new watermarks, iridescent bands, see-through features, and serial numbers that increase in size.

The notes, released by the Bermuda Monetary Authority (BMA), are available in collector sets, along with special coin releases of the past, from the **BMA offices** (43 Victoria St., tel. 441/295-5278, www.bma.bm, 9am-4pm Mon.-Fri.).

As far as sights and activities go, much of what Bermuda has to offer is free: Explore the chain of forts, trek the Railway Trail and national parks, swim at umpteen beaches, wander the backstreets of Hamilton, St. George's, and Somerset—you will not only save money, but you'll leave Bermuda with a truer picture of island life than anyone sequestered in an all-inclusive cruise or fancy resort.

Tipping

Bermudians in the service industries are fond of their tips. Taxi drivers expect a 15 to 20 percent tip on rates, more if heavy luggage or official touring is involved. In nearly all restaurants, a 17 percent gratuity is automatically added to your bill, so there is no need to leave a tip at these establishments unless you feel the service or food is exceptional enough to deserve more; in such circumstances, islanders may leave an extra $10 or $20. Smaller, homespun eateries tend not to build a tip into the tab; check the menu or bill slip to confirm. In hotels, bellhops and door porters should receive $5 or more. Room service warrants a $5-10 tip. Depending on your length of stay and service, housekeepers typically get $3-5 per day. Bermudians tip gas-station attendants $2 or more for a fill-up (all of Bermuda's stations are full-serve).

PHOTOGRAPHY AND DIGITAL SERVICES

Just as it is to artists, Bermuda is a never-disappointing muse to photographers both amateur and professional. Lensfolk rhapsodize about the unique softness of the island's light, the diffusion of water and air, the multi-turquoise hues of its ocean, the cornucopia of pastel shades at every turn.

Digital photo printing is expensive in Bermuda (85 cents each for 4x6 prints, $1 for 5x7), so you might prefer to wait to do it at home, but there are several efficient, good-quality outlets that offer a speedy turnaround. **P-Tech Photo** (5 Reid St., Hamilton, tel. 441/279-5419 or 441/295-5496, www.ptech.bm, 9am-5pm Mon.-Sat.) has a full-service digital mini-lab so customers can order lab-quality prints and create greeting cards. Photo files can be uploaded online and prints collected from the store. **Kodak Express** (corner of Church and Queen Streets, Hamilton, tel. 441/295-2519, www.kodakexpress.bm) offers digital printing to order, and also has four self-service kiosks, two of which can print sizes of up to 8x10 while you wait.

For fine art digital printing, photo enlarging, and pre-press services, Loris Toppan at **Colourlab** (second floor, Somers Bldg., 15 Front Street, Hamilton, tel. 441/799-6180) is a maestro.

Beware the effect of heat on cameras—do not store equipment inside parked cars or in the ovenlike canisters on the back of rental mopeds. Bring a polarizing UV lens filter to take the shine off ocean shots, in particular, and be careful of sand and salt exposure at the beach or on the water (keep cameras covered when not in use). Avoid shooting in the harshness of midday if possible; Bermuda's intense sunlight 11am-2pm fills photos with deep contrasts, burnout, and shadows; dawn or early evening will provide the most alluring light conditions, not to mention soft pink sunrises and sunsets.

Wedding photo specialists include **Sacha Blackburne** (tel. 441/234-5089, www.sachablackburne.com); **Alex Masters** (tel. 441/705-2868, www.alexandermasters.com); **Amanda Temple** (tel. 441.236-2339, www.amandatemple.com); **Becky Spencer Photography** (tel. 441/238-5236, www.beckyspencer.com), Gavin Howarth (441/532-3234, www.gavinhowarth.com); Mark Tatem and Ally Lusher of **Two and Quarter** (tel. 441/541-0214, www.photo214.com); **Moongate Productions** (tel. 441/300-5005, www.moongateproductions.com); and **Ernie McCreight** (Visual

Impact Photography, tel. 441/295-4755, www.ernestmccreight.com).

LookBermuda's digital photographic services (tel. 441/295-3555, www.lookbermuda.com) include shooting special events and panoramas. For more contacts and portfolios, check www.bermudaphotographers.com.

ELECTRICITY

Power losses, both brief and of the lengthier variety, are unfortunately an integral part of island life. Bermuda relies on one power plant, BELCo, on Hamilton's outskirts in Pembroke, to serve the island's electricity needs. When something goes awry or a bad storm hits, Bermudians are made acutely aware of their tenuous connection to modern comforts.

Heavy winter storms and summer hurricanes usually take Bermudian homes and businesses off the grid at least temporarily. Few Bermuda homes are without flashlights, matches, lighters, candles, or batteries—the essential tools for any semblance of life after dark during power outages. Major hotels, both hospitals, and many businesses and private residences also own gas- and propane-fueled generators, which can be switched on to run basic electrical needs such as showers, water pumps, stoves, and refrigerators.

Power surges are common, so make sure to unplug laptops, phones, faxes, and other sensitive equipment after an outage; when the power returns, it sometimes shuts on and off a couple of times during testing before being fully restored. Bring a surge protector with you, or purchase one at **The Complete Office** (17 Reid St., Hamilton, tel. 441/292-4333, www.tco.bm) or **Red Laser** (8 Bakery Ln., Pembroke, tel. 441/296-6400, www.redlaser.bm). Call 955 to report outages via a recorded phone-in system that matches the caller's telephone number with the affected neighborhood address.

Like North America, Bermuda operates on 110-volt AC, 60 cycles, with U.S. flat-blade (two-pin) plug outlets, so any U.S.-manufactured appliances such as hair dryers and curling irons will not require voltage converters or adapters. European visitors, however, can either bring adapters with them or purchase them at stores such as **Unlimited Supplies** (7 Elliott St., Hamilton, tel. 441/295-9229) or **P-Tech** (5 Reid St., Hamilton, tel. 441/295-5496).

BUSINESS HOURS

Most Hamilton offices follow their North American and English counterparts, with an official eight-hour workday Monday through Friday. Staff in retail outlets start winding down at 4:30pm, in readiness for a prompt 5pm exit. The "rush hour"—a misnomer, since it is more a motorized crawl through the parishes—typically runs 7:30am-9:15am weekday mornings and 5pm-6:15pm evenings, as residents make their way to and from Hamilton en masse. Traveling to and from the East End in these hours is usually not too difficult. Try to avoid being caught up in the western flow of traffic, however; all three arteries to and from Hamilton (Harbour Rd., Middle Rd., and South Shore) are crammed with bumper-to-bumper cars, with scooters zipping down the center line to get ahead.

Major Front Street stores stay open during the summerlong Harbour Nights street festival (7pm-9pm). Stores throughout Hamilton usually keep longer Friday hours (until 9pm) during the Christmas period.

As a conservative, religious society with more churches per square mile than nearly anywhere, Bermuda has been slow to embrace Sunday shopping. The law was finally amended in the late 1990s, and since then, most supermarkets are open 1pm-6pm, though you will see their liquor departments roped off (it remains illegal for stores to sell alcohol on Sundays). Most bars stay open until 1am, though nightclubs and a few private after-hours clubs wait to shut their doors until 3am.

TIME

Bermuda is on Atlantic standard time, one hour ahead of Eastern Standard Time (Toronto, New York, and U.S. East Coast cities) and four hours behind Greenwich mean time. Daylight savings time is observed, with clocks jumping forward an hour each spring and back in the fall. DST was brought in line with U.S. energy-saving measures in 2007, starting in mid-March and ending in early November. Dawn varies between 6:15am in the summer and 7:30am in winter, and dusk falls between 5:15pm and 8:30pm depending on the time of year.

MEASUREMENTS

Although Bermuda adopted the metric system for measurement in the second half of the 1900s (just as it went decimal in its currency), the conversion was far from universal on the island. As in Britain, imperial measures are found just as commonly in Bermuda as metric ones, both in private and government use, though United Nations reporting guidelines are typically followed by public agencies. Therefore, you'll see ubiquitous references in both official literature and local conversations to the island's size of 21 square miles or 21-mile-per-hour speed limit, police reports describing individuals' height and weight in feet and pounds, newspaper ads for 10K running races, trade statistics in kilograms, and pool lengths by the meter. In this guidebook, the imperial system is used to refer to most measurements.

Communications and Media

Bermudians, isolated 650 miles from the nearest landfall (Cape Hatteras, North Carolina) take their communications very seriously. Thanks to a well-developed infrastructure, albeit threatened by seasonal hurricanes, the island provides modern telephone, fax, Internet, wireless, and wireless-roaming services. The mail service is mostly efficient, there's no shortage of couriers, and the island is bombarded with up-to-the-minute media—print, digital, and broadcast.

MAIL AND COURIER SERVICES

Airmail travels to and from the island daily. Mail received by 9:30am at the **General Post Office** (56 Church St., Hamilton, tel. 441/297-7893, gpo@gov.bm) is sent out the same day but may take several days to reach its destination. Mail sent internationally via the sub-post offices in the parishes must first go to the General Post Office, sometimes taking a day or two to exit the island. Stamps for a postcard to the United States and Canada cost 70 cents; to Europe, 80 cents; to Africa, Asia, and Australasia, 90 cents. Letters weighing 10 grams are 5 cents more, plus up to 50 cents on top for each additional 10 grams. The General Post Office is open 8am-5pm Monday-Friday, 8am-noon Saturday. Parish post offices are open 8am-5pm Monday-Friday. Surface mail is airlifted to and from Bermuda frequently. **International Data Express** (tel. 441/297-7802), a service offered through the General Post Office, is a 48-hour mail service delivering to most international destinations; it requires mail be posted by 10:30am for same-day dispatch.

Local company **Mailboxes Unlimited,** at three locations, offers mail and courier services, including boxing and wrapping, as well as full-scale moving services for larger items. The main office (48 Par-la-Ville Rd., Hamilton, tel. 441/292-6563, fax 441/292-6587) sells boxes, envelopes, bubble wrap, labels, tape, and pens. There are also Mailboxes Unlimited outlets in Hamilton (12 Church St., tel. 441/296-5656) and Paget (2 Lovers Ln., tel. 441/236-5142).

All major international courier services have offices in Bermuda, in some cases several outlets. They include **FedEx** (3 Mill Creek Rd., Pembroke, tel. 441/295-3854); **DHL Express** (14 Burnaby St., Hamilton, tel. 441/294-4848; 16 Old Ferry Rd., St. George's, tel. 441/294-4838); **International Bonded Couriers** (IBC, 10 Park Rd., Hamilton, tel. 441/295-2467, fax 441/292-7422, www.ibc.bm); **UPS** (10 Park Rd., Hamilton, tel. 441/295-2467); and **Best Shipping** (6 Addendum Ln. S., Pembroke, tel. 441/292-8080, www.best.bm).

TELEPHONES

Bermuda's phone, fax, and wireless data services, like its Internet capabilities, are modern and efficient, though more costly than in North America or Europe. Travelers to Bermuda usually bring their own cell phones or wireless handhelds. Most North American models operate normally here. However, calling via a phone linked to an overseas network can be outrageously expensive. To avoid large roaming charges, an alternative (for GSM phones only) is to purchase prepaid SIM cards. **Digicel** (22 Church St., at the Washington Mall, tel. 441/500-5000, www.digicelbermuda.com) sells $20 cards and will remove and later put back your own SIM card, providing the phone is unlocked or attached to AT&T or T-Mobile networks. **CellOne** (18 Church St., Hamilton; 18 York St., St. George's; Heron Bay Plaza, 227 Middle Rd., Southampton, tel. 441/700-7000, www.cellone.bm) offers the same service. Mobile phones can be rented from **Bermuda Cell Rental** (Armoury Building, 37 Reid St., Hamilton, tel. 441/232-2355, www.bermudacellrental.com).

Public phones are located around the island, though often are in a shabby state or out of order—a problem most Bermudians, with their surgically attached mobiles, don't seem to notice or care about these days.

Phone boxes are still in operation in Bermuda.

For international calls, **TeleBermuda International** (1st floor, Victoria Pl., 31 Victoria St., Hamilton, tel. 441/296-9000, info@telebermuda.com, 9am-4:30pm Mon.-Fri.), has a retail center in Hamilton, where prepaid phone cards can be purchased.

Bermuda's international access code is "1" followed by "441" (area code) and the phone number. To dial the United States or Canada from Bermuda, simply dial "1" plus the area code and number. For operator-assisted calls, dial "00." For U.S. or Canada directory assistance, dial "1" plus the area code plus "555-1212." To make U.K. calls, dial "011" followed by "44," plus a city area code and a phone number. Caribbean nations take "1" or "011" as international access codes, depending on their nationality, with European islands requiring the latter.

INTERNET ACCESS

Bermuda has been cyber-crazy ever since Internet service was first offered here in the early 1990s. Most hotels and guesthouses offer free WiFi to visitors. Larger properties cater to laptop-toting business travelers with high-speed connections in rooms, lobby areas, and dedicated business centers. There are also numerous cybercafés and restaurants around the island, and most of the City of Hamilton and the Sandys Dockyard is a WiFi zone. Free online access is also offered via kiosks at parish post offices, and free wireless Internet can be had at L. F. Wade International Airport.

Computer and communication supplies are extremely expensive to purchase in Bermuda, so try to come equipped, or be prepared to pay two to three times the price you would at home.

Bermuda's Internet domain is .bm, though some Bermuda-based websites have .com URLs for higher visibility.

PUBLICATIONS

Tourist Publications

Destination Bermuda (tel. 44/19-35816142, www.destinations-magazines.com, ralstonpub@aol.com) is an annual magazine published in the United Kingdom and distributed free of charge to Bermuda-bound airline passengers at check-in at Gatwick, London; New York; Toronto; and other major North American gateways. Photos and features highlight cultural attractions, activities, history, shopping, and business services.

Experience Bermuda, a glossy, hard-backed advertorial-heavy publication backed by the Bermuda Hotel Association, can be found in hotel rooms islandwide. Included are photo features and write-ups on things to see and do, wining and dining, and weddings and honeymoons. Check its companion website (www.experiencebermuda.com) for seasonal deals on accommodation packages.

This Week in Bermuda (www.thisweek.bm) and ***Bermuda.com guide*** (www.bermuda.com) are both free booklets packed with ads and information on seasonal events, tours, cultural sights, restaurants, and shopping highlights. Find them at major hotels, bookstores, airport and cruise ship terminals, and Visitor Information Centres. The latter is an interactive print guide with augmented reality features allowing video clips, photo galleries, and other digital content via smartphone, tablet or iPad with the download of a free app, Layar App.

Newspapers

Bermuda has one daily newspaper, *The Royal Gazette*, available at island newsstands and hotels and costing $1.

The Royal Gazette (tel. 441/295-5881, www.royalgazette.bm) dates back to 1828 and is owned and printed by Bermuda Press Holdings. While the professionalism of its writing and design ebbs and flows, it is a morning must-read for most locals, even those who perennially criticize the paper for its white roots and conservative slant on social issues. Indeed, the *Gazette* is an essential ingredient of life in Bermuda, where staying atop national truths and small-town gossip is considered imperative for dinner-party conversation.

The *Gazette* covers local news, sports, the arts scene, and the business community, its pages padded by wire stories covering overseas events. Aside from the funeral listings, the *Gazette*'s best-read section is the daily "Letters to the Editor," on page 4, where views of all persuasions—sometimes signed, more often not—wax loudly on everything from political scandals to scolding over traffic violations.

For visitors, the *Gazette* is a barometer of island life. It also offers concrete resources including movie listings, a community calendar listing events, activities, shows, and art and museum openings, plus advertisements for auctions, end-of-season sales in Hamilton stores, and other services. The otherwise slim Saturday paper provides a rundown of restaurants and other businesses open on Sunday. If you are planning a trip and want to get a sense of what's making headlines, check out the *Gazette*'s online edition before you arrive.

Local Magazines

For such a small market, Bermuda has a plethora of glossy magazines, all fighting for a diminishing pot of advertising dollars. ***RG*** magazine, published six times a year and distributed free inside *The Royal Gazette,* offers newsy features, profiles of local personalities, and a comprehensive calendar of seasonal events. ***The Bermudian*** ($6.90), launched in 1930 in the vein of *The New Yorker,* downsized after its 75th anniversary in 2005 from a monthly to a quarterly. Produced by the Bermudian Publishing Company, it features Bermuda history, architecture, and traditions, and a well-perused party section. The magazine's popular "Best of Bermuda Awards" issue each summer provides a well-vetted insider's list of the island's favorite shops, attractions, and services—a very useful resource for visitors.

Other magazines include Bermuda Media's annual ***New Resident*** ($4.95), a resource for newcomers to the island; ***Who's Who,*** a listing of Bermuda personalities; and ***Bermuda Real Estate Handbook,*** which offers advice on buying and selling property in Bermuda and advertises local realtors.

Business travelers should pick up a copy of ***Bermuda:Re*** magazine, which counts many of the island's CEOs as subscribers; and ***Bottom Line,*** the Royal Gazette's free quarterly assessment of domestic and international company news, including in-depth corporate profiles.

International Publications

Major American, Canadian, and British newspapers are available at the large **Phoenix Centre** (3 Reid St., near the Queen St. junction, Hamilton, tel. 441/295-3838, phoenixstores.com, 8am-6pm Mon.-Sat., noon-6pm Sun.), and at some of its islandwide outlets, though the cost of flying them in makes for elevated prices. Some American dailies do not end up on shelves until the afternoon. Weekend editions of Canadian papers are available Sunday afternoons. British editions come to the island aboard British Airways' evening flights, appearing in stores the following morning. Some resort hotels fly in copies of *The New York Times, Wall Street Journal, Financial Times,* and *USA Today* on afternoon flights to Bermuda, or distribute condensed versions of those publications downloaded daily from their respective websites.

Magazine racks at the Phoenix Centre and The Bookmart at Brown & Co., as well as other pharmacies and most large grocery stores, display weekly editions such as *People, Time, Newsweek, US Weekly, New York,* and *The New Yorker*—though typically a week late. All the major monthly U.S. glossies, from fashion to home decor magazines, as well as a few Canadian ones, are also sold at these stores, along with U.K. counterparts. Prices, particularly for the British editions once translated back into dollars (*British Vogue,* $16), can be daunting for magazine junkies.

BROADCASTING

Television

North American—mostly U.S.—television fare is on the menu; major U.S. networks are affiliated with Bermuda stations, which air their programming daily, and the island's two cable companies offer hundreds of mainly American channels.

Three broadcast stations represent the U.S. television networks and also offer some local, though amateur-quality, programming. Established in 1947, **Bermuda**

Broadcasting Company (Fort Hill, Devonshire, tel. 441/295-2828) today has two commercial TV stations: ZFB-TV channel 7 (cable channel 2) is the affiliate of ABC, while ZBM-TV channel 9 (cable channel 3) airs CBS network programming. Both stations also air locally produced daily evening news, talk shows, and sports programs. Two companies offer digital and standard cable television service islandwide. **Bermuda Cablevision** (19 Laffan St., Hamilton, tel. 441/292-5544) offers nearly 200 24-hour channels from the United States, Canada, and Portugal. Newcomer **WOW (World on Wireless) TV** (Washington Mall, Church St., Hamilton, tel. 441/292-1969) has 110 channels, 84 of which are available in digital.

Several channels offer Bermuda-produced programming, though often of poor quality. **The Bermuda Channel** (channel 77) carries visitor-oriented features on sightseeing, sports, transportation, shopping, and restaurants. The Bermuda government channel **CITV,** or Community Information Television (channel 2), presents 24-hour coverage of government events, cultural programming, interviews, and local human interest features. **Look TV** (channel 1) offers local segments on island personalities, traditions, and major cultural and sporting events. **Fresh TV** (channel 3) broadcasts music videos, local events, and interviews with Bermudian personalities. The **Bermuda Weather Channel** (channel 4) airs weather warnings, storm advisories, and hurricane tracking.

Radio

The island has 10 radio channels, with eclectic, sometimes homespun announcers, DJs, reporters, and programming.

For locals and visitors, daytime talk shows—featuring call-in segments and vociferous debates about all things Bermuda—are a highly entertaining slice of island life. **Gold AM (VSB-1) 1450 AM,** with host Shirley Dill, carries such programs throughout the afternoon, along with country music, while **ZBM-2 1340 AM,** with host David Lopes, also broadcasts lively local chitchat. Other AM channels include: **VSB-2 1280 AM,** which offers religious and gospel programming, **ZFB 1230 AM,** offering an easy-listening mix and local programming, and **VSB-3 1160 AM,** the British Broadcasting Corporation (BBC World) feed.

FM channels include **ZBM 89.1 FM,** with piped-in syndicated programming from the United States, including mellow chart favorites from the 1970s onward, plus afternoon call-in shows to local hosts; **VSB-4 106.1 FM (Mix 106),** which has a popular morning host ("The Captain") and broadcasts a mixture of old and new rock, along with teen pop and rap hits; and **ZFB Power 95 FM,** which carries a mix of reggae, rap, and R&B.

Hott 107.5 FM, targeting the island's young black population, offers the most slickly produced programming, thanks to its Chicago connections—one of its founders was the former program director of WGCI there. Sister station **Magic 102.7 FM** carries adult contemporary soul, R&B, and light rock hits from the 1970s, '80s, and '90s.

Resources

Suggested Reading and Films

ISLAND LIFE AND TRAVEL

Barritt, Fred, and Peter Smith. *Bermewjan Vurds: A Dictionary of Conversational Bermudian.* 7th ed. Bermuda: Lizard Press, 2005. Hilarious collection of amazing-but-true local idiom and slang, updated periodically.

Berg, Daniel, and Denise Berg. *Bermuda Shipwrecks: A Vacationing Diver's Guide to Bermuda's Shipwrecks.* East Rockaway, New York: Aqua Explorers, 1991. An A-to-Z rundown of legendary wrecks discovered off Bermuda, with a brief history, plus photos of wreck sites, artifacts, and the divers who found them.

Caswell, Tracey. *Tea with Tracey: The Woman's Survival Guide to Bermuda.* Bermuda: Print Link, 1994. A cockroaches-and-all view of Bermuda by a resident expat whose introduction to island life is a highly entertaining read for anyone interested in what it's really like to live in a so-called paradise.

Emery, Llewellyn. *Nothin' But a Pond Dog.* Bermuda: Bermudian Publishing Company, 1996, reprinted 1999. Businessman, cedar craftsman, and author Emery paints both a humorous and poignant portrait of back o' town life as a child in the 1950s.

Richardson, Ralph. *The Bermuda Boater.* 2nd ed. Bermuda: Pyro Press, 2004. Written by a seasoned Bermudian navigator and boating enthusiast, this edition is an extremely useful resource for yachties and commercial or recreational boaters in Bermuda. Complete with navigation and safety basics, local chart references, and island knowledge on weather, tides, emergency resources, and other tips.

Smith, Molly. *Discovering Bermuda with Paintbrush and Bike.* Bermuda: Bermudian Publishing Company, 2005. An island tour through the eyes of Bermudian watercolorist Smith, whose sketches, paintings, and observations along the way—including recipes, herbal remedies, and poems—paint a rich portrait of a whimsical island.

Watlington, Frank. *Bermuda Kites: How to Make and Fly Them.* Reprint. Bermuda, 1960. A 101 primer on tried-and-true methods to create the colorful tissue-paper concoctions that grace island skies over the Easter weekend. Easy-to-follow diagrams describe basic designs, papering, and looping tricks that have become a beloved Bermudian tradition.

HISTORY AND FOLKLORE

Bermuda's Architectural Heritage Series. Devonshire, St. George's, Sandys, Hamilton Parish, Smith's, Paget. Bermuda: Bermuda National Trust, 1995-2005. In-depth parish histories researched and written by local historians, full of photos and illustrations.

Bernhard, Virginia. *Slaves and Slaveholders in Bermuda, 1616-1782*. Columbia: University of Missouri Press, 1999. Historical analysis of the complex relationship between slavery and racism in the second-oldest colony of the New World.

Cox, John. *Bermuda's Favourite Haunts*. Bermuda: John Cox, 1991. Spooky chronicle of haunted houses around the island and the ghosts that inhabit them.

Deichmann, Catherine Lynch. *Rogues & Runners: Bermuda and the American Civil War*. Bermuda: Bermuda National Trust, 2003. Companion booklet to the fascinating exhibit in the Bermuda National Trust Museum at the old Globe Hotel building in St. George's.

Grearson, Don. *USS Bermuda: The Rise and Fall of an American Base*. Bermuda: Great Dog Publishing, 2009. An inside look at the controversial 1995 closure of the U.S. military bases in Bermuda and the local and international politicking that followed.

Harris, Edward Cecil. *Bermuda Forts: 1612-1957*. Bermuda: Bermuda Maritime Museum Press, 1997. Harris, who is an archaeologist, historian, and the director of the National Museum of Bermuda, provides a comprehensive overview of the island's chain of fortifications, detailing their history and archaeology. It is especially topical now that the local government plans to restore many of these decaying landmarks as cultural attractions.

Jones, Rosemary. *Bermuda: Five Centuries*. Bermuda: Panatel VDS, 2004. Full-color, reader-friendly history of the island from its discovery in 1505 to the 21st century. A companion to a DVD series by the same name, the book contains time lines, contemporary accounts, and more than 360 historic images from private and public collections.

Jones, Rosemary. *Bermuda: Five Centuries for Young People*. Bermuda: Panatel VDS, 2009. Adaptation of Bermuda's narrative history for a primary-to-middle-school readership. Redesigned with new images and color-coding for easy navigation, the book has end-of-chapter questions and activities for school/home-school use.

Jones, Rosemary, and Dr. Edward Harris. *Royal Bermuda*. Bermuda: National Museum Press, 2014. A pictorial history, showcasing the island's four centuries of connections to the British Crown, including Queen Elizabeth II's seven visits since 1953.

McDowall, Duncan. *Another World: Bermuda and the Rise of Modern Tourism*. London: Macmillan Education, 1999. Canadian history professor and longtime Bermudaphile McDowall describes the economic makeover that tourism gave Bermuda in this highly readable, anecdotal work.

Slayton, Marina I., ed. *Four Centuries of Friendship*. Bermuda: Bermuda Maritime Museum Press, 2009. A colorful historical overview of diplomacy and relations between the United States and Bermuda from the 1600s to today.

Woodward, Hobson. *A Brave Vessel: The True Tale of the Castaways who Rescued Jamestown and Inspired Shakespeare's The Tempest*. New York: Viking, 2009. A detailed and compelling narrative of the 1609 *Sea Venture* shipwreck on Bermuda, its survivors' subsequent rescue of starving colonists at Jamestown, and the tale's creative impact on history's most famous playwright. By an associate editor of the Adams Papers at the Massachusetts Historical Society.

Zuill, W. S. *The Story of Bermuda and Her People*. 3rd. ed, London: Macmillan Caribbean, 1999. Concise paperback history of the island, written by a former editor of *The Royal Gazette*.

NATURE AND THE ENVIRONMENT

Bermuda Rose Society, The. *Roses in Bermuda*. Bermuda: Bermudian Publishing Company, 1997. Packed with color photos to make identification easy, this edition highlights the wealth of roses and where to find them throughout the island, from ramblers and hybrid teas to the so-called mystery varieties. One section even details where to find Bermuda roses in the United States.

Dobson, Andrew. *A Birdwatching Guide to Bermuda*. Shrewsbury, England: Arlequin Press, 2002. A detailed birding guide written by the president of the island's Audubon Society.

Frith, Kathleen, Jonathan Frith, James Constable, Jennifer Constable, and James Cooper. *Sporty Little Field Guide to Bermuda*. Bermuda: 2 Halves Publishing, 1997. A comprehensive paperback guide to the island's main plant and animal life, with artful illustrations accompanied by brief, informative text.

Lucas, Ron. *Bermuda Reef Portraits*. Bermuda: Bermuda Zoological Society, 2008. A full-color photographic guide to the island's marinelife, useful for divers and snorkelers.

Phillips-Watlington, Christine. *Bermuda's Botanical Wonderland: A Field Guide*. London: MacMillan Education, 1996. Whimsically illustrated edition with renditions of typical island habitats and the abundant flora within them.

Sterrer, Wolfgang. *Bermuda's Marine Life*. Bermuda: Bermuda Zoological Society, 1992. A comprehensive, and highly readable, look at all forms of island sealife by a former curator of the Bermuda Zoological Society's Natural History Museum in Flatts.

Stevenson, Andrew. *Whale Song: Journeys into the Secret Lives of the North Atlantic Humpbacks*. Lyons Press, 2011. Stevenson's beautiful photographs of humpbacks off Bermuda are the result of a four-year project to learn more about these migrating mammals.

Thomas, Martin L. H. *The Natural History of Bermuda*. Bermuda: Bermuda Zoological Society, 2004. Comprehensive full-color coffee-table edition by a Canadian professor and research scientist who studied the island's flora and fauna for more than 30 years. Photos and detailed text on marine and terrestrial habitats and wildlife, along with coverage of threats to the island's delicate ecosystem. Available at the Bermuda Aquarium, Museum & Zoo shop, as well as bookstores in Hamilton and St. George's.

Thomas, Martin L. H. *A Naturalist's Field Guide to Bermuda*. Bermuda: Bermuda Zoological Society, 2009. A condensed version of the author's larger work, in the form of a portable, full-color, pocket-sized field guide.

Wingate, Janet. *Nonsuch Summer*. Czech Republic: Janet Wingate, 2005. An evocative memoir written by the daughter of Bermudian naturalist Dr. David Wingate about her idyllic childhood summers spent on Nonsuch Island in Castle Harbour, where her dad spent a career recreating original habitats for a "Living Museum" project. Winner of a Bermuda Literary Award in the Young Adult category.

COLLECTORS

Williams, Malcolm, and Peter T. Sousa, eds. *Coins of Bermuda*. Bermuda: Bermuda Monetary Authority, 1997. A history of island coinage, from the first Hogge money and sterling coins to the decimal system.

ART AND ARCHITECTURE

Calnan, Patricia. *The Masterworks Bermudiana Collection*. Bermuda: The Bermudian Publishing Company, 1994. Lavish edition showcasing the repatriated island artworks of Winslow Homer, Georgia O'Keeffe, and other art-world luminaries, as collected by Bermuda's Masterworks Foundation.

Foster, Graham, and Rosemary Jones. *Hall of History: Bermuda's Story in Art*. Bermuda: National Museum of Bermuda Press, 2011. A visual feast, this oversized coffee-table edition showcases artist Foster's epic mural at the Commissioner's House, Dockyard. Annotations detail the history captured in each image, from the 1500s to modern day. Included are sections on Foster's often humorous details, and essays chronicling how he completed the 1,000-square-foot masterpiece.

Masterworks at 25. The Masterworks Foundation, 2012. Large-format edition tracing the art charity's mission to repatriate Bermuda art over the past quarter century and its success in bringing home works by Homer, O'Keeffe, Gleizes and other world-renowned artists who had been inspired by the island.

Shorto, Sylvia, and Ian MacDonald-Smith. *Bermuda Gardens & Houses*. New York: Rizzoli International, 1996. Informative coffee-table volume written by Bermudian art historian Shorto and photographed by much-published island lensman MacDonald-Smith.

FOOD

Bottone, Edward. *Spirit of Bermuda: Cooking with Gosling's Black Seal Rum*. Bermuda: The Bermudian Publishing Company, 1998. Vibrantly illustrated cookbook by Philadelphia chef and former resident Bottone, with all the island's favorite recipes (codfish cakes, cassava pie), as well as colorful descriptions of holiday traditions and culinary folklore.

Island Thyme: Tastes and Traditions of Bermuda. Bermuda: Junior Service League, 2004. Collection of recipes, menus, and table settings from island residents and restaurants in a full-color volume produced to raise money for one of Bermuda's core social agencies.

Ming, Fred. *Bermuda Favourites*. Bermuda: Fred Ming, 2004. A compendium of recipes from one of the island's best-known chefs and cooking teachers, including red snapper fillets, red bean soup, and nasturtium salad.

Wadson, Judith. *Bermuda: Traditions and Tastes*. Bermuda: Judith Wadson, 1998. A history of Bermudian holidays, including Cup Match and Good Friday, and the typical dishes that accompany the celebrations.

PHOTOGRAPHY

Airey, Theresa, and Edward Marshall. *Bermuda: The Quiet Years, 1883-1953*. Bermuda: Theresa Airey and Edward Marshall, 2004. A fascinating collection of 147 restored nitrate negatives published for the first time, this book portrays the island before the advent of automobiles. Photographs taken by a handful of the island's professional photographers capture street scenes, city restaurants, lily festivals, the railway, and pristine landscapes many Bermudians would barely recognize anymore.

MacDonald-Smith, Ian. *A Scape to Bermuda*. 3rd ed. Bermuda: Ian MacDonald-Smith, 2004. All-season Bermuda, with studies of clouds, rocks, flower-strewn lanes, architecture, rainbows, and Christmas lights.

Skinner, Roland. *Picturesque Bermuda I and II*. Bermuda: Roland Skinner, 1996 and 1999. Landscapes, seascapes, and aerial shots of Bermuda by prolific lensman Skinner, a former Bermuda News Bureau staffer who now owns one of the largest Bermuda stock photo libraries and sells large-scale prints of his work.

Spurling, Ann. *Nine Parishes*. Bermuda: Ann Spurling, 2003. Pricey ($80) but satisfying photographic tour of the island by the island's premier homes-and-gardens photographer. Entertainingly written and laden with informative captions and parish intros, its lush spreads feature Bermudian homes, people, cultural traditions, and pastimes. For its scope and local knowledge, it is one of the best Bermuda pictorials available.

BUSINESS

Duffy, Catherine R. *Held Captive: A History of International Insurance in Bermuda*. Toronto: Oakwell Boulton, 2004. Definitive 516-page tome outlining the creation of "Bermuda, Inc." in detailed CEO interviews, photos, glossaries, and corporate profiles.

Stewart, Robert. *A Guide to the Economy of Bermuda*. Toronto: Oakwell Boulton, 2003. An analysis of why Bermuda has been one of the most successful economies in the world for the past half century. It's written by an economics teacher and former Shell Group CEO who now is the director of several international Bermuda companies and investment funds.

CHILDREN

For such a small island, Bermuda boasts a surprising number of well-produced children's books, which local and visiting kids enjoy for their stories about island animals, icons, and traditions, including tree frogs, cedar trees, and sailboats. They make great souvenirs for kids back at home, too.

Booth, Mark. Illustrated by Patricia DeCosta. *Bermuda's Sidney the Sailboat*. Bermuda: Bermudian Publishing Company, 1994. Compelling Cinderella tale of a neglected sailboat and its adventures. Perfect for ages four and up.

Cooper, Dana. *My Bermuda ABC*. New York: Worzalla Publishing Company, 1991. Bermudian commercial artist Cooper's whimsical counting and alphabet guide, inhabited by tropical touchstones like loquats, limestone, and lizards.

Donkin, Andrew. *Bermuda Triangle*. New York: Dorling Kindersley (DK), 2000. Eerily illustrated and vividly told, this DK Readers Program book, with large text for easy reading, is a kid-pleasing synopsis of the legendary phenomenon.

Jacobs, Francine. *Bermuda Petrel: The Bird that Would Not Die*. New York: William Morrow & Co., 1981. The story of the endemic Bermuda petrel, or cahow.

Jones, Rosemary. *Bermuda: Five Centuries for Young People*. Bermuda: Panatel VDS, 2009. This spin-off of the adult edition was created for young readers, with kid-friendly text and a redesign loaded with images, time lines, and breakouts.

Karwoski, Gail Langer. *Miracle: The True Story of the Wreck of the Sea Venture*. Plain City, OH: Darby Creek Publishing, 2004. Very professionally produced edition by Georgia-based writer Karwoski that's sure to captivate young imaginations with the story of Bermuda's first colonists. Kid-friendly design includes scores of illustrations, photos, and graphics, along with digestible, yet historically detailed text and provoking sidebars on early navigation, island traditions, birds, and animals. A great buy for inquisitive kids of all ages.

Mulderig, A. Elizabeth. *Tiny the Treefrog Tours Bermuda*. Bermuda: Bermudian Publishing Company, 1992. A charmingly illustrated rhyme about a quixotic tree frog and his Bermuda sightseeing exploits.

Stevenson, Kevin. Illustrated by Helen Daniel. *The Story of the Bermuda Cedar Tree*. Bermuda: Bermudian Publishing Company, 1997. Artfully illustrated with gouache plates, the book tells the story of Bermuda's iconic tree and its multiple uses throughout the centuries.

RARE OR OUT-OF-PRINT BOOKS

Some of the best books on Bermuda are now out of print, but copies can be found for sale at various stores around the island, including Bermuda Bookstore and Bermuda Craft Market at Dockyard. Or, contact dealers directly: **Anthony Pettit** (by appointment, tel. 441/292-2482, fax 441/295-5416, www.anthonypettit.com), **Twice-Told Tales** (34 Parliament St., Hamilton, tel. 441/296-1995). Some rare editions often can be found online for competitive prices at sites like eBay, Alibris, and other rare-book sites.

Beebe, William. *Half Mile Down*. New York: Duell, Sloan & Pearce, 1951. In his own words, the story of deep-ocean pioneer Beebe's underwater explorations in a revolutionary bathysphere off Bermuda in the 1930s.

Dorr, Julia. *Bermuda: An Idyl of the Summer Islands.* New York: Charles Scribner & Sons, 1884. Amusing Victorian travelogue written by a wintering American at the time of tourism's debut in Bermuda, her island sojourn coinciding with that of Princess Louise.

Hutchings Smith, Louisa. *Bermuda's Oldest Inhabitants: Tales of Plant Life*. Sevenoaks, England: J. Salmon Ltd., 1963. Gardeners and naturalists will enjoy this beautifully illustrated account of the island's flora, with nine color plates by artist May Middleton.

Winchester, Simon. *Outposts: Journeys to the Surviving Relics of the British Empire.* London: Sceptre, 1986. Witty observations of journalist Winchester's 1970s visit to Bermuda, among other remaining British colonial "pink" spots on the map.

BERMUDA ON FILM

The Bermuda Depths, Rankin-Bass, 1978. A made-for-TV motion-picture adventure written by Arthur Rankin Jr., a Bermuda resident and Canadian cartoon producer of *Rudolph the Red-Nosed Reindeer* and *Frosty the Snowman.* Directed by Shussei Kotani, the film stars Burl Ives, Leigh McCloskey, Carl Weathers, and Connie Sellecca in a ghost yarn about scientists terrorized by a giant turtle as they investigate the Bermuda Triangle. McCloskey and Sellecca's kid versions are played by Bermudian children.

Bermuda: Five Centuries, Panatel VDS, 1999. Six-part documentary series using contemporary interviews and historic and modern footage to trace the island's history via major social themes over 500 years. With companion book.

The Deep, Columbia Pictures, 1977. Peter Benchley's underwater thriller, directed by Peter Yates and starring Nick Nolte, Jacqueline Bisset, and Lou Gossett Jr., was inspired by Benchley's visits to the island and was filmed in Bermuda. A romantic interlude turns to adventure when a couple discovers gold coins and mysterious glass ampoules on a sunken World War II wreck. The film features many familiar sights—including lots of Bermudian extras. Based on Benchley's 1976 book of the same title, one of its hallmark elements was the theme song, sung by Donna Summer.

The Lion and the Mouse, Lucinda Spurling, Afflare Films, 2009. Narrated by former Bermuda resident Michael Douglas, the documentary explores the four centuries of strong connections between Bermuda and America, from early colonial days to modern times.

Mr. Happy Man, Matt Morris, 2010. Award-winning 10-minute documentary by U.S. director Morris about Bermuda's Johnny Barnes and his longtime morning ritual of waving joyfully to local commuters as they drive to work, Barnes's bid to make the world a happier place.

Neptune's Daughter, Warner Studios, 1949. This Oscar-winning musical-comedy-romance directed by Edward Buzzell and starring aquatic goddess Esther Williams, Red Skelton, and Ricardo Montalban was filmed at a pool on Agar's Island, in Bermuda's Great Sound. The production was fraught with problems, but the film ended up as the 10th highest-grossing movie of that year, propelled by the popular song, "Baby, It's Cold Outside."

Rare Bird, Lucinda Spurling, Afflare Films, 2006. Spurling's documentary details the fascinating story of the endangered Bermuda petrel, or cahow, from believed extinction to rediscovery in the 1950s, and its gradual comeback today.

Where the Whales Sing, Andrew Stevenson, 2010. An award-winning documentary featuring Stevenson's young daughter Elsa, in which she and her father try to discover the secrets of migrating humpback whales on their journeys past Bermuda to Canada and the Caribbean. The film traces Stevenson's four years of research on humpbacks (www.whalesbermuda.com).

Internet Resources

GENERAL INFORMATION

Bermuda.com
www.bermuda.com

Boasting the most hits of any Bermuda site, this comprehensive portal is owned and run by a local printer, the Bermuda Press. Thorough but advertising-driven listings for accommodations, dining, and activities understandably read like a tourism brochure.

Bermuda Tourism Authority
www.gotobermuda.com

The easy-to-navigate Bermuda Tourism Authority website offers facts, figures, and useful resources for travelers, including events, sights, Department of Immigration and Customs rules, licensed accommodations, wedding how-to info, activities, and a reservations system.

Bermuda4u
www.bermuda4u.com

This concise independent guide to Bermuda by former resident David Mottershead, who is now based in the U.K., offers a frank and witty overview of Bermuda life, services, attractions, and regulations for visitors, along with a trip-booking facility.

Bermuda Online
www.bermuda-online.org

Comprising a portal linking to 128 websites, plus a digital library compiled by local resident and author Keith Forbes, the regularly updated website is now owned and supported by *The Royal Gazette.* Overwritten and cumbersomely designed, it remains a useful repository of information—from census figures to resources for new residents.

Central Intelligence Agency (CIA) World Factbook
www.cia.gov/cia/library/publications/the-world-factbook/geos/bd.html

The Central Intelligence Agency's online factbook is crammed with constantly updated information on Bermuda, including land-use, population, literacy, and electricity-consumption statistics.

Nothing to Do in Bermuda?
www.nothingtodoinbermuda.com

Contradicting its ironic title, this site by

resident Claire Hattie, which she now manages for the Bermuda Press, rebuts island naysayers by showcasing the full slate of weekly events, activities, nightlife, sports, and artistic pursuits Bermuda offers to keep boredom—or "rock fever"—at bay. Included are links to expat groups, plus loads of fun stuff to keep kids amused, too.

U.S. Department of State
www.travel.state.gov

The U.S. Department of State's website posts a Consular Information Sheet on Bermuda, which gives an accurate overview of crime, communications, traffic safety, and customs issues, as well as links relevant to U.S. travelers.

GOVERNMENT

Corporation of Hamilton
www.cityhall.bm

The Corporation's website carries news and traffic advisories for the City of Hamilton, along with details of upcoming events, services, cruise ship schedules, and links to local resources from attractions to ferry fares and the yellow pages.

L. F. Wade International Airport
www.bermudaairport.com

L. F. Wade International Airport's website gives flight, check-in, Customs, Immigration, retail, and restaurant details, plus airport telephone numbers for airlines that serve Bermuda, with links to airlines' URLs.

Official Bermuda Government Website
www.gov.bm

The official Bermuda government website is a portal to all ministries, departments, and related bodies, including the National Anti-Money Laundering Committee (NAMLC).

ISLAND LIFE AND EVENTS

Bermemes
www.bermemes.com

Bermuda's most popular masters of social media, the Bermemes crew dish continual LOLs on the vagaries of local life via Facebook and Twitter daily. This site captures the ones gone viral, plus blogs on favorite Bermudian food, dry humor, and offbeat comments on upcoming weather, events, traditions, or funny local names, and links to the wittiest of grassroots websites (#badparking Bermuda), including video and animation. A revealing insight into the real Bermudian character.

Bermynet.com
www.bermynet.com

Covering the home-from-college scene, this site features photos from Hamilton happy hours, as well as the summer club scene, beach parties, DJs, and live web radio.

Box Office Tickets
www.bdatix.bm
www.premierticketsglobal.com (www.ptix.bm)

Buy tickets online to all Bermuda's major entertainment events or movies via these sites, all of which are well used by island residents.

E-Moo
www.e-moo.bm

A morning must-see for thousands of residents, this classifieds website carries information on public events, yard sales, and stuff for sale galore, from jewelry and pianos to boats and furniture.

ACCOMMODATIONS

airbnb.com and vrbo.com (Vacation Rental By the Owner)

Global websites carrying information on unique accommodation in hundreds of countries, including Bermuda. Many local residents post quality home and apartment rentals on both sites, allowing a more cost-effective way to visit the island, not to mention experiencing a taste of what it's really like to live here.

Bermuda Accommodations
www.bermudarentals.com

Toronto-based Bermudian Fiona Campbell is a broker for a list of islandwide vacation properties of various sizes and rates, including historic homes and long-term rentals. A map shows where they are on the island, and numbered links connect with the property's information page. Most are studios or apartments attached to local homes. Prices range from under $100 to $300 a night for a double room. It also contains useful contacts and links to activities and services, from hiring a gourmet chef to scuba tours and grocery deliveries.

Bermuda Vacation Rentals
www.bermudagetaway.com

This website provides a listing of information, photos, and contacts for a select group of highly rated Bermuda vacation rentals, located on an island map, including beachside cottages and historic buildings. The site allows prospective renters to check availability by date and to send reservation inquiries to the property owners.

WEDDINGS

Getting Married in Bermuda
www.bermudianweddings.com

As a favorite wedding destination, Bermuda makes getting married here a breeze. *The Bermudian* magazine's dedicated wedding website rounds up all the resources prospective brides and grooms will need, along with photos of island nuptials and blogs by experts. Individual wedding planners also have their own sites, and each can arrange every detail—from paperwork and photographers to flowers, cakes, and surfside ceremonies:

www.tohaveandtoholdbermuda.com
www.sweetdreamsbermuda.com

MEDIA

The Bermudian
www.thebermudian.com

Launched in 1930, *The Bermudian* magazine is a veritable institution on the island, but one that has evolved with the times. Today's editions are sleek and contemporary in look and lifestyle content, and its website is too. It carries features about island life and residents, history, homes, even recipes. One great resource, with its own tab on the website, is the company's popular Best of Bermuda Awards, which laud the standouts in categories like shopping, restaurants, events, people, and places. Previous award-winners are archived here too.

Bernews
www.bernews.com

Often scooping the local newspaper (*The Royal Gazette*) with its speedy round-the-clock postings, Bernews has gained an impressive number of devotees, becoming *the* place locals go for fast-breaking island stories, news updates, even environmental and history features.

The Royal Gazette
www.theroyalgazette.com

The online edition of Bermuda's daily paper carries current-day headlines, features, sports, columns, commentary, classifieds, TV listings, and online reader polls, but the site is often slower to post daily breaking news than Bernews, and its daily edition isn't posted until midmorning.

BUSINESS INFORMATION

Association of Bermuda Insurers and Reinsurers
www.abir.bm

Headquartered in Hamilton, ABIR represents the interests of Bermuda's international insurers and reinsurers. The site contains news, facts, figures, and history about the island's insurance sector, details on Bermuda tax exchange agreements and trading partners, and links to ABIR's 20-plus members, multibillion-dollar global companies that underwrite the world's biggest disasters.

Bermuda Business Development Agency
www.bda.bm

The BDA promotes the island as a premier offshore business center, supports locally based international companies, and helps companies that want to move operations to the island or launch start-ups in Bermuda. As a public-private partnership, the agency connects prospective business leaders with industry professionals, government contacts, and regulatory officials.

Bermuda Chamber of Commerce
www.bermudacommerce.com

The Bermuda Chamber of Commerce's website represents its members, from e-business to construction companies. Included is information on how to acquire permits to sell and showcase products on the island, as well as details on cruise ship schedules and weekly Harbour Nights summer street festivals in Hamilton, Dockyard, and St. George's.

Bermuda Monetary Authority
www.bma.bm

The official website of the Bermuda Monetary Authority (BMA), the island's main regulatory body, which supervises the financial services industry, approves incorporations, oversees licenses to financial institutions, and issues banknotes and coinage. The site offers text of public legislation, and a "warning" list of bogus companies not licensed to do business on the island.

Bermuda Stock Exchange
www.bsx.com

The website of the Bermuda Stock Exchange, which, established in 1971, bills itself as the largest offshore electronic securities market. The site features market highlights, news, a daily trade report for the domestic market, plus links to trading members.

REAL ESTATE

Propertyskipper.com
www.propertyskipper.com

Don't want to leave Bermuda? This site helps house hunters find their dream home, acting as a centralized clearinghouse for the island's rental and for-sale markets, including commercial and land listings. A quick-search mechanism lets you narrow your search by parish and also carries property-related news and a clickable listing of local real estate brokers.

TELEPHONE DIRECTORIES

Bermuda Yellow Pages
www.bermudayp.com

Using the Yabsta platform, the searchable Bermuda Yellow Pages website lists thousands of island businesses, community agencies, and services, also provides free classifieds, event listings, weather updates, an airline arrivals schedule, blogs, and a visitor section with links to bus and ferry schedules, restaurant menus, wedding planner resources, and a video tour of the island.

WEATHER

Bermuda Weather Service
www.weather.bm

The official site of the Bermuda Weather Service offers current conditions, weeklong forecasts, marine conditions, climate data—and live satellite and three-hour loop radar imagery showing the approach and size of rain bands, hurricanes, and other area disturbances.

SharkOil.bm
www.sharkoil.bm

A succinct, well-designed site (named for the homespun storm predictor) that details everything from Bermuda hurricane folklore to a homeowner's hurricane prep list. It includes Atlantic storm synopses and satellite storm-tracking imagery, including video buttons with current satellite imagery or archived tracking of past storms.

LIVE WEBCAMS

Bermuda Cahow Cam Project
www.blog.lookbermuda/CahowCam

The government's Department of Conservation Services is one of the parties behind this webcam that gives a live look inside a man-made cahow burrow on protected Nonsuch Island. The once near-extinct seabirds have made a comeback through a carefully monitored conservation program that has received worldwide kudos.

Bermuda Weather Service
www.weather.bm/webcam.asp
With images updating every two minutes, this webcam located at the weather radar site at Cooper's Island, St. George's, gives you a real-time look at how the forecast is shaping up, with views of cloud formations, passing squalls, and the East End horizon.

Port Bermuda Webcam
www.portbermudawebcam.bm
A 24/7 live-streaming, HD-quality video broadcast from the lofty veranda of historic Commissioner's House at the westernmost point of the Royal Naval Dockyard. With a view over the ramparts, you can see the cruise ships make port, as well as boat traffic around Heritage and King's Wharves and in the Great Sound beyond.

Index

A

B

C

D

E

F

G

H

IJK

LM

N

O

P

QR

S

T

UV

WXYZ

List of Maps

Acknowledgments

I am perennially surprised by the pace of change in Bermuda between each book edition. Of course there are the constant, naturally shifting pieces of the island's tourism landscape—restaurants and retailers opening and closing, or moving down the block. But, beyond those predictable elements, there are always deeper underlying trends that reveal the morphing mood of this quirky little society and define its outreach and offerings to visitors.

Heading into the second half of the 2010s, positive change is picking up here after several recessionary years. Today, Bermuda is reinvesting in several hotel properties and a more strategically organized national approach to events, attractions, and activities. There is also a fresh grassroots optimism among islanders that has sparked the launch of many new retail, foodie, and tour treats.

A trusted sounding board of friends, relatives, and contacts has helped me keep my finger on the pulse of this recent buzz of activity. Bermuda folk are known for their very frank take on what's good and why, and I count myself lucky to be able to tap into such a reliable resources. I am grateful to everyone who weighed in when asked what they prefer in this parish or that, which vendor they lean towards for a weekend adventure, or where to source the standout fish sandwich or pair of sandals.

Special gratitude goes to my coterie of girlfriends who never let me down when polled at dinner parties, by phone, or even during marathon trail runs. Thank you, Christine Patton, Anne Feakins, Liz Stewart, Peggy Couper, Claire De Ste Croix, Ronda Grearson, Judy Lee, Bonnie McGlynn, and Deborah Sagurs. Your first-hand experiences and solid suggestions have informed much of my writing.

Thanks also to experts in the field whose fact-checks, tips, and insider knowledge were invaluable. Claire Hattie, maven behind the super-popular, must-see website, nothingtodoinbermuda.com, was a fountain of information, as was longtime tourism ambassador Alison Outerbridge, who now is in ultra-capable command of Hamilton's Visitor Information Centre.

I even enlisted my family as guinea pigs. Thanks, Paul, Gabriel, Robert, Kim, Brinley, and Lilly for generously allowing me to piggyback my research expeditions on our island itineraries or vacation outings.

I am proud to have worked with the highly talented Perseus Book Group team, including Grace Fujimoto, Erin Raber, Kat Bennett, Domini Dragoone, and Sierra Machado. Thanks especially for graciously granting me leeway on my deadlines when Hurricanes Fay and Gonzalo hit.

To my late parents, who fell in love with Bermuda and then each other, I remain grateful to you both for bringing me up as an islander. Thank you, Mum and Dad—your spirits live strong in the turquoise horizons and velvet fairways you always treasured.

MAP SYMBOLS

- Expressway
- Primary Road
- Secondary Road
- Unpaved Road
- Feature Trail
- Other Trail
- Ferry
- Pedestrian Walkway
- Stairs
- City/Town
- State Capital
- National Capital
- Point of Interest
- Accommodation
- Restaurant/Bar
- Other Location
- Campground
- Airport
- Airfield
- Mountain
- Unique Natural Feature
- Waterfall
- Park
- Trailhead
- Skiing Area
- Golf Course
- Parking Area
- Archaeological Site
- Church
- Gas Station
- Glacier
- Mangrove
- Reef
- Swamp

CONVERSION TABLES

°C = (°F - 32) / 1.8
°F = (°C x 1.8) + 32
1 inch = 2.54 centimeters (cm)
1 foot = 0.304 meters (m)
1 yard = 0.914 meters
1 mile = 1.6093 kilometers (km)
1 km = 0.6214 miles
1 fathom = 1.8288 m
1 chain = 20.1168 m
1 furlong = 201.168 m
1 acre = 0.4047 hectares
1 sq km = 100 hectares
1 sq mile = 2.59 square km
1 ounce = 28.35 grams
1 pound = 0.4536 kilograms
1 short ton = 0.90718 metric ton
1 short ton = 2,000 pounds
1 long ton = 1.016 metric tons
1 long ton = 2,240 pounds
1 metric ton = 1,000 kilograms
1 quart = 0.94635 liters
1 US gallon = 3.7854 liters
1 Imperial gallon = 4.5459 liters
1 nautical mile = 1.852 km

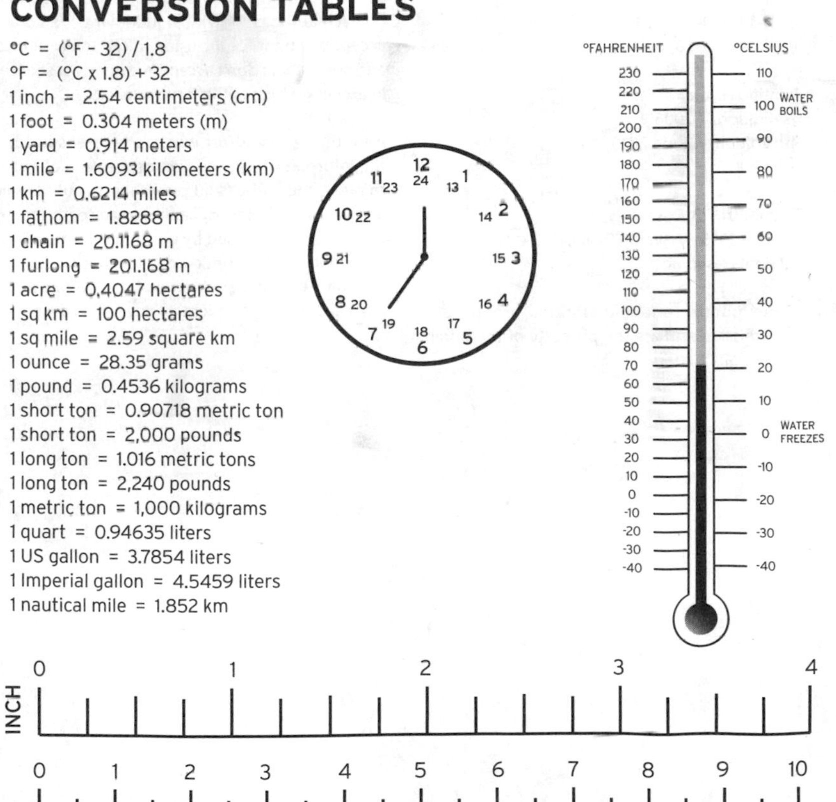

MOON BERMUDA

Avalon Travel
a member of the Perseus Books Group
1700 Fourth Street
Berkeley, CA 94710, USA
www.moon.com

Editor: Erin Raber
Series Manager: Kathryn Ettinger
Copy Editor: Brett Keener
Graphics Coordinator: Rue Flaherty
Production Coordinator: Rue Flaherty
Cover Design: Faceout Studios, Charles Brock
Moon Logo: Tim McGrath
Map Editor: Kat Bennett
Cartographers: Suzanne Service, Lohnes + Wright, Stephanie Poulain
Indexer: Greg Jewett

ISBN-13: 978-1-63121-043-3
ISSN: 1932-7870

Printing History
1st Edition — 2006
4th Edition — June 2015
5 4 3 2 1

Front cover photo: John Smith's Bay © Michael Turek/Getty Images

All interior photos © Rosemary Jones except pages 5, 8, 20, 246 © Paul Shapiro; 7, 249, 269 © Gabriel Jones

Printed in Canada by Friesens